AN ILLUSTRATED HISTORY OF BOXING

An Illustrated History of

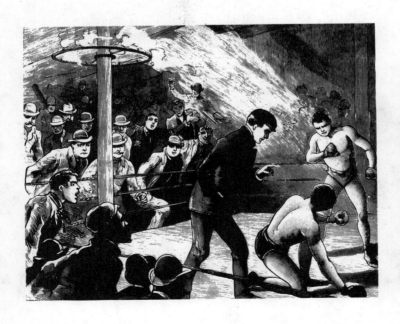

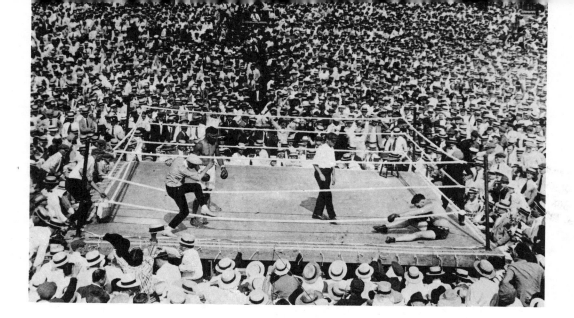

BOXING
Fifth Revised and Updated Edition
by Nat Fleischer and Sam Andre

A CITADEL PRESS BOOK
Published by Carol Publishing Group

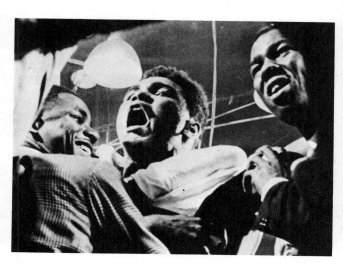

MARQUIS OF QUEENSBERRY

New Revised and Updated edition 1997

Copyright © 1959 by Sam E. Andre and Nat Fleischer
First revised edition copyright © 1975 by Sam E. Andre and Nat Loubet
Copyright © 1987 by the estate of Sam E. Andre and Nat Loubet
1987 edition revised and updated by Gilbert Odd
1993 edition revised and updated by Peter Arnold
1997 edition revised and updated by Nigel Collins

A Citadel Press Book
Published by Carol Publishing Group
Citadel Press is a registered trademark of Carol Communications, Inc.

Editorial, sales and distribution, and rights and permissions inquiries should be addressed to Carol
Publishing Group, 120 Enterprise Avenue, Secaucus, N.J. 07094.

In Canada: Canadian Manda Group, One Atlantic Avenue, Suite 105, Toronto, Ontario M6K 3E7

Carol Publishing Group books may be purchased in bulk at special discounts for sales promotion,
fundraising, or educational purposes. Special editions can be created to specifications. For details, contact
Special Sales Department, Carol Publishing Group, 120 Enterprise Avenue, Secaucus, N.J. 07094.

Manufactured in the United States of America
10 9 8 7 6 5 4 3 2 1

Library of Congress Cataloging-in-Publication Data

Fleischer, Nat, 1887-1972.
    An illustrated history of boxing / by Nat Fleischer and Sam Andre. —
1997 ed. / revised and updated by Nigel Collins.
        p.   cm.
    "A Citadel Press Book."
    Includes index.
    ISBN 0-8065-1900-2 (pb)
    1. Boxing—History.   2. Boxing—History—Pictorial works.
I. Andre, Sam, 1907-   . II. Collins, Nigel.   III. Title.
GV1121.F63   1997
796.83'09—dc21   97-33542
                                                              CIP

Photographs, etchings, drawings and other illustrations used in this book are from
private collections of the author, from *The Ring* magazine, and the United Press
International, with additional photographs from AllSport (UK) Ltd (Simon Bruty,
Chris Cole, Mike Powell), Allsport Inc., AP/Wide World, Christopher M. Farina (Las
Vegas, Nevada, USA), Focus on Sports (New York, USA), Frank Spooner/Gamma, John
Topham Picture Library, Popperfoto, Rex Features, Sport and General, Sporting
Pictures (UK), Syndication International, Yoo Chang Kem (Seoul, Korea).

CONTENTS

Introduction   7

THE HEAVYWEIGHTS   8

Pugilism's First Heroes   8

Period of Double-Crosses   13

First Jewish Champion   18

The Transition Period   23

The Negro Invasion   26

America Takes Up the Sport   39

Battles of Champions   43

England Loses Prestige   48

The End of an Era   52

John L.'s Entrance and Exit   57

Science Replaces Force   71

Lanky Bob Fitzsimmons   78

Jeffries, the Iron Man   82

Johnson, Ring Marvel   90

Dempsey and the Fabulous Twenties   95

The Crown Goes Overseas   115

Era of the Brown Bomber   127

Era of Big TV Money   157

Ali, Master Showman   160

Self-Destructing 'Iron Mike' Tyson   183

The Cruiserweights   185

THE LIGHT HEAVYWEIGHTS   188

The Super-Middleweights   212

THE MIDDLEWEIGHTS   215

The Light-Middleweights   256

THE WELTERWEIGHTS   261

The Light-Welterweights   286

THE LIGHTWEIGHTS   291

The Junior Lightweights   331

THE FEATHERWEIGHTS   336

The Light-Featherweights   363

THE BANTAMWEIGHTS   367

The Light-Bantamweights   388

THE FLYWEIGHTS   392

The Light-Flyweights   407

The Mini Flyweight or
Strawweight Champions   410

UPDATE FOR THE 1997 EDITION   412

Index   439

INTRODUCTION TO FIRST EDITION

Over the years, hundreds of books have been published about boxers, boxing champions, and boxing in general. The missing link among them, however, has been a complete pictorial history of the sport. It has long been our aim to complete the chain, and we believe we have accomplished it in the present volume.

A *Pictorial History of Boxing* is the product of more than five years of research and planning. It was made possible by pooling our vast personal collections of photographs and illustrations. We were especially fortunate, too, in having at our disposal the rich files of *The Ring* Magazine, without which no history of boxing can be written.

We believe that this book justifies the monumental task involved in preparing it for publication. We regard it lovingly as a valuable contribution to boxing history, with its pictures of all the great champions and thrilling scenes of their famous battles assembled in one volume. Many of the portraits and fight scenes are very rare and, in most instances, are being published for the first time.

We have begun the book with "the father of modern pugilism," James Figg of England, who in 1719 introduced the sport, defeated all opponents, and was recognized as first champion. Although the history of boxing stretches back into the mists of antiquity, it is with Figg that the art and science of modern boxing begins.

Emphasis has been laid on picturing as many of the champions and the top contenders as possible in every division.

Producing this volume has been a pleasure for us, and our greatest hope is that it will give sports fans throughout the world many hours of enjoyment.

NAT FLEISCHER
SAM E. ANDRE

THE HEAVYWEIGHTS

PUGILISM'S FIRST HEROES

It was not until the early part of the eighteenth century that boxing became popular as a sport in the British Isles. Though the start of fist fighting in England coincided with the arrival of the Romans, boxing as we know it really got under way with the acknowledgement of James Figg as first British heavyweight king in 1719. Through the pages of ring history, the story of the heavyweights is the story of boxing itself.

When James Figg announced the opening of his Amphitheatre, his name became the first on the long roll of British prize ring champions, and because he was the first to advertise openly the teaching of boxing and exhibitions of skill, he has become known as the Father of Boxing. He was more expert as a cudgeller than as a pugilist. A master with the sword and an expert fencer, he attracted the patronage of the English "bloods," the sports element of the country.

It was Figg who popularized sparring exhibitions, and his initiative was responsible for the opening of many other amphitheatres. In these, wooden rails instead of ropes formed the ring enclosure, which was elevated upon a stage, the referee officiating outside the ring.

Figg died in 1740 and George Taylor, one of his pupils, succeeded to the championship.

Taylor was followed by the father of boxing rules, Jack Broughton, who in 1734 formulated the first code and invented the boxing glove, which at the time was used only in sparring exhibitions.

Figg's card (left) was designed by his great friend Hogarth, and was distributed among the patrons at his Amphitheatre and booths at Southwark Fair and elsewhere. This was the first advertisement used to promote the new sport of boxing. Figg resigned his title in 1734 and died in 1740, leaving a wife and several children. George Taylor (above) opened a booth when Figg retired, and claimed the title. He defended it against all comers until 1740, when he was soundly beaten by Jack Broughton before a large crowd in Taylor's own booth.

This portrait of James Figg, boxing's first champion, was painted by William Hogarth, famous 18th-century English artist.

Southwark Fair, London, where Figg's booth was patronized by both aristocrats and the more lowly followers of pugilism. The spectators were entertained here with fencing, cudgelling, backsword, and well-organized and lively boxing exhibitions.

Broughton studied defense and attack and depended on the use of this style. Previously boxing was a toe-to-toe match, but Broughton introduced into the sport stopping and blocking, hitting and retreating. He was six feet tall, weighed 196 pounds and was quite intelligent.

The Duke of Cumberland took a deep interest in him, and obtained for Broughton a position with the Yeomen of the Guard which he held until his death at the age of eighty-five. Broughton's Rules governed boxing from August 18, 1743, until 1838, when a new code, "The London Prize Ring Rules," was adopted.

From Figg to Muhammad Ali is a long stretch—over 250 years—and in that period many famous heavyweights came to the fore. There were big men, small men, fat and lean ones; men of the rough-and-tumble school and men of science; fighters who were sluggers and those who were cool-headed boxers; men of culture, some of only an ordinary education, and others with none at all. But each was a champion —a heavyweight who had gained the top rung of the pugilistic ladder.

Eliminating the bare-knuckle and skin-tight gloves era, which covered a century and three-quarters of boxing, and coming down to the period governed by the Marquis of Queensberry Rules that called for glove contests, we find twenty-five heavyweights as kings of the division and one claimant, Marvin Hart. Many thrilling battles were fought in the reign of these Kings of Pugilism, and the majority are vividly portrayed in this volume.

10

Badly battered and with both eyes closed, Jack Broughton (*right*) protested bitterly when beaten by Jack Slack in 1750. Appealing to his patron, the Duke of Cumberland, who had wagered heavily on him, Broughton cried: "I'm blind, but I'm not beat!"

As champion, Broughton (*left*) won impressively in a gruelling 45-minute battle with George Stevenson, known as "the Coachman." This mezzotint by John Young (after John Henry Mortimer) was one of the first art representations of a boxing match.

Introducing many innovations to the prize ring, Broughton became known as the "Father of British Boxing." in 1743 he devised "mufflers" (gloves) to minimize the risks of facial damage to students at his private school, many of whom were of aristocratic families.

"Broughton's Rules" (*left*), the first ever written for boxing, were adopted on August 16, 1743. The rules barred gouging and hitting a fallen opponent, but wide latitude was left for wrestling and rough-and-tumble fighting. Despite his long, rugged career, Broughton lived to be 85 and was buried with Britain's great in Westminster Abbey. John Smith (*below*), an ugly, misshapen character called "Buckhorse," often appeared in Broughton's exhibitions.

RULES

TO BE OBSERVED IN ALL BATTLES ON THE STAGE

I. THAT a square of a Yard be chalked in the middle of the Stage; and on every fresh set-to after a fall, or being parted from the rails, each Second is to bring his Man to the side of the square, and place him opposite to the other, and till they are fairly set-to at the Lines, it shall not be lawful for one to strike at the other.

II. That, in order to prevent any Disputes, the time a Man lies after a fall, if the Second does not bring his Man to the side of the square, within the space of half a minute, he shall be deemed a beaten Man.

III. That in every main Battle, no person whatever shall be upon the Stage, except the Principals and their Seconds; the same rule to be observed in bye-battles, except that in the latter, Mr. Broughton is allowed to be upon the Stage to keep decorum, and to assist Gentlemen in getting to their places, provided always he does not interfere in the Battle; and whoever pretends to infringe these Rules to be turned immediately out of the house. Everybody is to quit the Stage as soon as the Champions are stripped, before the set-to.

IV. That no Champion be deemed beaten, unless he fails coming up to the line in the limited time, or that his own Second declares him beaten. No Second is to be allowed to ask his man's Adversary any questions, or advise him to give out.

V. That in bye-battles, the winning man to have two-thirds of the Money given, which shall be publicly divided upon the Stage, notwithstanding any private agreements to the contrary.

VI. That to prevent Disputes, in every main Battle the Principals shall, on coming on the Stage, choose from among the gentlemen present two Umpires, who shall absolutely decide all Disputes that may arise about the Battle; and if the two Umpires cannot agree, the said Umpires to choose a third, who is to determine it.

VII. That no person is to hit his Adversary when he is down, or seize him by the ham, the breeches, or any part below the waist: a man on his knees to be reckoned down.

As agreed by several Gentlemen at Broughton's Amphitheatre,
Tottenham Court Road, August 16, 1743.

PERIOD OF DOUBLE-CROSSES

When Broughton passed out of the picture, boxing suffered because it had lost the man who was recognized as the "Father of the English School of Boxing." His rules formed the groundwork of fair-play and his introduction of gloves, or "mufflers," added to the sport's popularity. His honesty made him beloved by his patrons. They expected emulation of his conduct by those who followed him.

But they were in for a shock. Shortly after Broughton's retirement, crookedness crept into the sport. It made its appearance during the reign of Broughton's successor, Jack Slack, the Norwich Butcher, the first "Knight of the Cleaver" to win an English title. Slack not only "tossed" fights but assisted in the arrangement of other "cross affairs of the knuckles."

Slack's early triumphs were gained more through fearlessness than ability. He introduced the "chopper," which was the equivalent of the modern rabbit punch.

Slack's reign extended from 1750 to 1760, and during that decade British boxing was almost at a standstill. The public lost interest and faith in it because of charges of crookedness made against outstanding fighters.

The Duke of Cumberland became Slack's backer in the fight for the crown with Bill Stevens, "The Nailer"; the Duke of York was the challenger's patron. That contest took place on June 17, 1760, and another surprise was furnished the Corinthians when "The Nailer" won the title. The victor was a notorious character whose double-crosses had brought pugilism to a low level.

After Slack had been shorn of his championship, he became the backer of George Meggs and arranged a battle for the crown with Stevens, whom Slack had bought off. The champion,

Jack Slack, a Norwich butcher and the conqueror of Broughton, was known as the "Knight of the Cleaver." Slack, the grandson of James Figg, held the title for ten years—1750 to 1760.

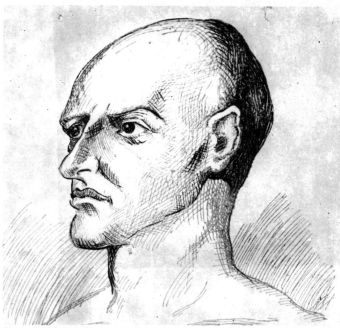

Bill Stevens, "the Nailer," beat Slack in 1760. Slack's patron was the Duke of Cumberland who again lost a large amount on the outcome. Convinced he was sold out by Slack, the Duke became an arch-enemy of boxing.

George Meggs, "the Collier," came from the pugilistic nursery of Bristol and won from Stevens in 1761. Meggs was trained for the fight by the canny Jack Slack, and Stevens boasted he was paid to lose to the inferior Meggs.

The battle between defending champion Bill Darts *(left)* and Tom Lyons, "the Waterman," in 1769. After dethroning Darts, Lyons gave up the title and retired.

Monsieur Petit, the giant, was the first Frenchman to take up boxing. Standing six feet, six inches, and weighing 220 pounds, he met British title-holder Jack Slack and was defeated in less than 25 minutes.

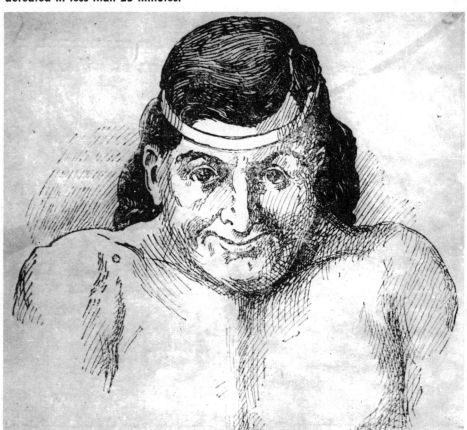

for a financial consideration, agreed to permit Meggs to win, and for arranging the "cross," Slack received fifty guineas from Meggs.

From 1761 to 1783, a period of twenty-two years, the championship was in an unsettled state. It was knocked about from one head to another.

Meggs, who bought the title from "The Nailer," soon saw it wrested from him by Baker Milsom, and the Baker in turn soon was dethroned by Tom Juchau. Then followed Bill Darts, who won the crown from Juchau. Darts held the title for nearly five years before losing it to "Waterman" Lyons in a desperate struggle.

Lyons thought so little of his exploit, or the fame thereby attained, that at the expiration of two weeks he retired and returned to the peaceful pursuit of ferrying passengers across the Thames. Darts regained the crown, only to lose it in the shortest bout for a heavyweight title in fistic annals to Peter Corcoran of Ireland, the first of his race to win a British championship. The contest lasted less than one minute.

After Tom Lyons retired, Bill Darts reclaimed the title, but didn't hold it long. In a meeting with Peter Corcoran in 1771, Darts *(left)* was knocked out with one punch in less than a minute. Corcoran was the first Irish-born pugilist to win a British championship.

Peter Corcoran of Ireland, who invaded England, fought his way to the championship, and reigned for five years, lost, in a questionable match, to Henry Sellers in 1776.

Corcoran's first important fight took place near Hyde Park on September 4, 1769, with Bill Turner, who previously had defeated Bill Stevens, a former champion of England. Corcoran gave Turner an unmerciful beating.

While in London, Corcoran was introduced to Colonel O'Kelly, a conspicuous character on the turf. He was the owner of Eclipse, the famous race horse, and became Corcoran's sponsor. Colonel O'Kelly arranged a bout for Corcoran for Derby Day, May 18, 1771, against Bill Darts, the English title holder, and the Colonel backed his countryman heavily and collected a handsome sum when Corcoran knocked out Darts in less than one minute of the opening round. The Colonel was accused of bribing Darts to "lay down" in order to make the wagering a "sure thing."

As Corcoran had whipped Bob Smiler, the brickmaker, Tom Dalton, and Joe Davis, and had challenged Lyons, who a few months before had won the title from Darts, Corcoran claimed the championship and was duly recognized.

In 1774 Corcoran fought Sam Peters at Birmingham, the battle taking place near Waltham Abbey. In that contest also there was considerable dissatisfaction, the spectators calling the affair a fake.

Then came the set-to with Harry Sellers, the West of England fighter who hailed from Jack Slack's Bristol School. They clashed at the Crown Inn, Staines, on October 10, 1776, and on this occasion, the flag of the Irishman was lowered, Sellers winning.

The English reported this fight as one sold by Corcoran and the report proved a sad blow to the former champion. Though he prospered out of the proceeds of the fight, he lost the friendship of his admirers and when he died he had to be buried by subscription.

Thus ended the career of the first Irishman to be crowned champion of England. Sellers, who took the crown from Corcoran, held it for four years and was deposed by another Irishman, Duggan Fearns by name. Fearns' victory, like that of Corcoran over Darts, was gained in quick time. The fight lasted only a minute and a half, Sellers falling after the first punch and declining to continue. Fearns was an Irish boatswain.

Following Sellers' dethronement, the championship of England fell into the hands of Tom Johnson, who put in his claim for the title and supported it with dignity and courage. Through him boxing regained public confidence. Johnson, christened Thomas Jackling, ruled from 1783 to 1791.

From the time he assumed the crown until 1789, Johnson waded through his opponents as if they were so many novices. A search was made at Bristol, the hotbed of pugilism, and there an opponent was found in Bill Warr, but he was polished off as easily as were others. Then came a battle with Isaac Perrins at Banbury, Oxfordshire, on November 22, 1789, and this likewise resulted in victory for Johnson.

In 1791, however, the Duke of Hamilton came forth with a challenge for Benjamin Brain (Big Ben), and in this fight Johnson was struck heavily on the nose in the second round. Bothered considerably by this damage and the breaking of the metacarpal bone of the middle finger of his right hand by striking it on a spike, he lost the crown. Thus was the renowned Tom Johnson deprived of the title he had so long held with honor.

With the victory of Big Ben and the defeat of Johnson ends the first period of heavyweight boxing. The second starts with the rise of the great Daniel Mendoza and ends with the reign of John Belcher.

A PARTICULAR and SCIENTIFIC ACCOUNT of the most tremendous BATTLE that ever occurred either in the *Broughtonian* or *Johnsonian* Schools, fought at WROTHAM, in *Kent*, between BIG BEN, alias BENJAMIN BRIAN, and THOMAS JOHNSON, on the 17th of *January*, 1791.

This portion of Lord Byron's screen depicts the tremendous battle for the championship between Tom Johnson and Big Ben Brain, on January 17, 1791. Johnson *(left)*, unable to avoid Big Ben's blows after breaking his hand on a ring post, lost in 21 minutes.

Tom Johnson *(left)* demolished the giant challenger Isaac Perrins in one hour and 15 minutes, on October 22, 1789. Perrins, six inches taller and 70 pounds heavier, was slowly weakened by body blows and finished with an attack to the head.

FIRST JEWISH CHAMPION

A large portion of the glory of the prize ring has been contributed by men whose forebears centuries ago fought against the Philistines, the Egyptians, the Arabians, the Babylonians, and the Romans. The Jews, like the Irishmen, took to boxing like a duck to water. They accepted the sport as an institution in which they could use the weapons God gave them —their fists—to settle their disputes, and in which they could face an enemy, man to man, in a test of individual skill and courage.

Daniel Mendoza, whose keen, flashing eyes and aquiline features are portrayed in old English prints, was the first Jew to gain a championship. He was much above the intellectual level of his contemporaries.

Prior to Mendoza's advent as a pugilist, brute strength and endurance, rather than scientific finesse, were the qualities most esteemed in the ring. However, after his first battle in which, though the victor, he sustained severe punishment, Dan set his active brains to work to study new means of defense. For three years he devoted himself assiduously to perfecting a system of guarding, sidestepping, and effective use of the straight left, before he again ventured on the test of actual battle.

The development of boxing as a really scientific proposition reached its first polished stage in the able hands of the extraordinary young Israelite. His new tactics were crowned with success. The men of the old-style school attempted in vain to stem the victorious march onward of scientific Daniel. By defeating Bill Warr on Bexley Common, November 12, 1794, Mendoza became champion.

Many boxing critics of his day wrote enthusiastically about the swiftness and grace of the Jewish lad. They praised his generalship and superb science. Others, though these were in the minority, complained that there was something cowardly about a fighter who frequently retreated and relied on superior agility and speed to win rather than standing up in true British bulldog style and hammering away doggedly until he or his opponent dropped.

Thus he revolutionized the Prize Ring. His advent ended the reign of

Daniel Mendoza, a Spanish-English Jew, was boxing's first prominent Jewish boxer and 16th champion of England, reigning from 1791 to 1795. Standing 5' 7" and weighing 160 pounds, Mendoza developed and cultivated ring science. After retiring he became a celebrated boxing instructor and died at the age of 73. Richard Humphries (*below*) known as "the Gentleman Fighter," whipped Mendoza twice, in 1787 and 1788, before the latter became champion. Humphries lost to Mendoza in 1789 and again on September 29, 1790, after which he retired.

Richard Humphries (*left*) and Daniel Mendoza meet in the center of the stage to start their second battle at Odiham, in Hampshire, on January 9, 1788. As in their first contest at Epping, the year before, Humphries again won, this time in 29 minutes.

William Wood, known as "the Coachman," claimed the crown in 1794, following the severe illness and sudden death of the champion, Big Ben Brain, with whom he had been matched.

William Hooper, "the Tinman," a skillfull boxer backed by Lord Barrymore, stopped Wood in 1795 and was recognized as champion. Hooper was one of many star pugilists from Bristol.

Another of the many scenes that decorated Lord Byron's screen shows the former champion, Tom Johnson, interfering with Mendoza (*right*) during the 1788 battle with Humphries. Rushing to aid Mendoza are his seconds, Jack Jacobs and Harry Isaacs.

Tom Owens is credited with the invention of the dumbbell. A native of Hampshire, he defeated William Hooper, on November 14, 1796, in Harrow, winning in 50 rounds. He claimed the title, but failed to get any recognition. On July 4, 1820, at the age of 52, Owens defeated Dan Mendoza, aged 56, in 12 rounds at Banstead Downs.

the crude slugger. Even the conservative critics who decried Mendoza's prowess were compelled to admit that his rapid thinking and fine strategy had never heretofore been exhibited in ring warfare.

Mendoza had wrought this miracle and convinced the younger generation that while a strong offensive sometimes makes for victory, careful attention to a proper means of defense was no means to be despised. He had introduced this new type of fighting—the scientific style—and it soon became the rage, particularly among the amateurs.

The Celtic race is proverbially a fighting race, yet, strange as it may seem, it was this Jewish boy, Daniel Mendoza, to whom the Irish owe much for popularizing the fistic sport in Ireland, where he established a school in which he taught the art after his defeat of Squire Fitzgerald, the pride of Erin, during a tour of the Emerald Isle. Following Fitzgerald's defeat, Ireland developed many great gladiators and much of their success may be traced directly to Mendoza's tour.

Like Mendoza, another heavy-weight pugilist, John Gully, who wore the championship crown in 1807, attracted considerable attention from the literary tribe, due to the fact that he became a Member of Parliament and was received in London society. Gully's whole life reads like a romance.

The son of a merchant, he embarked in business for himself, failed signally and landed in the King's Bench Prison as a debtor, with extremely poor prospects of ever being discharged. The law against debtors, as it then existed, could hold an unfortunate in jail for the rest of his natural life, unless some kind Samaritan paid the money and set him free.

Gully had a friend in Henry Pearce, known to the Fancy as the "Game Chicken." Pearce, born in Bristol, the town in which Gully first saw the light of day, was then champion and he visited his luckless pal in prison. As an amateur boxer, Gully could hold his own with the best, and to please some of his fellow prisoners, John consented to spar a few rounds with the title holder.

The mufflers were produced and, much to everyone's amazement, the youthful prisoner had no trouble in outpointing Pearce, whose fame, be it said, rested more on his strength than cleverness. The story of the remarkable amateur's feat became the talk of London town, with the result that Gully's debts were paid by a prominent sportsman on the condition that he fight Pearce for the title.

To a young athlete pining for his freedom and with a strong liking for the game, this way of escape was ideal. Accordingly, Gully and Pearce met in the ring, but the veteran was too much for Gully.

Gully's showing was so good, despite his defeat, that when ill health forced Pearce to retire, the "Game Chicken" declared that young John was the only man fit to succeed him. This election was approved by the Pugilistic Club, a sort of Boxing Commission of the time which regulated ring affairs. But neither the public nor Gully was entirely satisfied until the

John Gully, the son of a Bristol butcher, was released from debtors' prison, after his debts were paid by sportsman Colonel Harry Mellish, on condition that he fight the champion, Henry Pearce. He lost to Pearce in a fierce 64-round fight, but later became a great champion, wealthy bookmaker, and member of the British Parliament.

right to hold the championship crown had been duly established by a signal victory.

So it was not until Gully had thoroughly whipped Bob Gregson, the Lancashire Giant, that he really was accorded the plaudits of the Fancy as a genuine king. Gregson, not satisfied that Gully was the better man, challenged him again for the title, and in a mill lasting an hour and a quarter Gregson was unable to answer the call of time for the twenty-eighth round and Gully bowed his acknowledgements to a wildly cheering crowd.

Bob Gregson, "the Lancashire Giant," lost two slashing fights to Gully, which determined the successor to Hen Pearce's crown.

21

The excellent engraving of John Gully (left) and Henry Pearce was part of the lower section of Lord Byron's screen. The shortening of Pearce's given name to "Hen" prompted his followers to dub him "the Game Chicken," a name he lived up to throughout his career. Pearce, a product of the nursery of British boxers in Bristol, was invited to London by Jem Belcher in 1803 to qualify for the title. Belcher, the champion, when he was only 22 had an eye knocked out in an accident during a game of racquets. Believing his career at an end, Belcher gathered the top men in England for an elimination tournament, which Pearce won. The bruising fight (below) between Pearce and Gully, on October 8, 1805, ended after one hour and 17 minutes, when Pearce (right) landed a powerful blow on Gully's throat. Gully's breathing was affected and the fight was stopped.

A remarkable young man in several respects was Gully! Although he entered the prize ring through a prison gate and won the highest honors pugilism could accord him, it is probable that had not Fate forced him into the fistic game, he would never had turned professional. At heart, his ambition was to belong to the gentry. He had little use for the professional ring and its shady followers, who had once picked clean his financial bones. Immediately following his second victory over Gregson, he made a speech to the spectators in which he thanked them for their applause, but stated that he was absolutely through with fighting and would remain a private citizen in the future.

He kept his word. Vainly did sportsmen of wealth and influence try to coax Gully back for "just one more mill." It is said that even Royalty, in the person of the Duke of York, deigned personally to plead with the retired champion to break his pledge.

Gully remained obdurate. He would henceforth have nothing to do with fighting save as an observer. On the turf, the ex-champion accumulated a fortune. He had great success as a stable owner, winning the English Derby twice. He became a rich land proprietor, and, as before mentioned, a Member of Parliament.

Gully died in 1863 at the ripe age of eighty, leaving a large family in comfortable circumstances.

THE TRANSITION PERIOD

Among top pugilists who at various intervals wore the heavyweight crown, "Gentleman" Jackson and Jem Belcher are listed as two of the most popular. Each had a colorful background which had an appeal for fiction writers.

Jackson at the age of nineteen, despite parental objections, decided on a boxing career, and his initial contest was a victory over a renowned pugilist, Fewterell of Birmingham, a giant in stature and scaling 230 pounds. Jackson weighed only 195. The battle took place at Smitham Bottom on June 9, 1788, and was attended by a distinguished group including the Prince of Wales.

A year elapsed before young Jackson again appeared in a bout. He then fought George Ingleston, known as "The Brewer," and at Essex on May 12, 1789, on a floor made slippery by a heavy downpour, Jackson turned his ankle and was forced to quit. The defeat hurt his pride and he retired for six years, during which Mendoza ruled the roost as champion.

It was only after Mendoza's rise to fame and the praise he was receiving as a master of boxing that Jackson, now called "Gentleman" Jackson by the Fancy, decided to return to the ring. He fought Mendoza on April 15, 1795, at Hornchurch in Essex, in a swift and melodramatic combat in which his ring generalship electrified the spectators. Jackson was crowned new champion after eleven minutes of activity.

With that victory began a new era in British boxing. Jackson was the first to show that a hit was not effective unless distance had been properly judged. He also was the first to give

William Futrell (above) had an unbeaten string of victories until he was defeated by "Gentleman" John Jackson, in one hour and seven minutes, at Smitham Bottom, Croydon, on July 9, 1788. Futrell was publisher of the first boxing paper.

John Jackson (right), called "Gentleman" because of his polished demeanor and excellent reputation, was an all-around star in track and field as well as boxing. He possessed a finely-built body, standing 5' 11" and weighing 195 pounds. Jackson was only 18 years old when he slaughtered the huge Futrell before astonished spectators, among them the Prince of Wales, later George IV.

The Jackson-Futrell (sometimes spelled Fewterell) battle scene above shows how the seconds operated during a fight. Note, too, Jackson holding the wrist of Futrell while about to deliver a blow to his head. Two panels from the famous Lord Byron screen *(below)* give a general idea of what the screen consisted of. The panels were completely covered with scenes and clippings of the famous pugilists in the early era of boxing in England. Byron was a boxing enthusiast and attended many of the bouts during 1811 to 1816, when he was in England. His favorite was "Gentleman" Jackson, who had retired in 1795, and he titled him the "Emperor of Pugilism."

Jem Belcher, 20th champion of England, came from fighting stock. He was the grandson of Jack Slack. Belcher introduced the Ascot tie, which he is shown wearing.

Joe Berks, of Shropshire, had a violent temper. He was knocked out three times by Belcher in championship contests.

Jem Belcher, the "Napoleon of the Ring" (below), after losing an eye in 1803, retired in favor of Henry Pearce, who qualified for the crown. Belcher (above, left) returned to fight Pearce on December 6, 1805, and was soundly beaten in 13 rounds.

considerable attention to footwork.

Among his numerous admirers was Lord Byron, who paid him many tributes in his literary works. His was a warm friendship for the gentleman pugilist.

Jackson did more for the uplift of boxing in his era than any of his predecessors. He died on October 7, 1845, at the age of seventy-seven.

Jem Belcher, known as the "Napoleon of the Ring," was the grandson of Jack Slack, fourth boxer to hold the heavyweight crown. Like Jackson, he was a magnificent boxer, lithe and graceful. His brother Tom also was a pugilist. Jem was born April 25, 1781. He was eighteen when he made his boxing debut. His agility and speed in hitting were his best assets.

On December 6, 1805, at Blyth near Doncaster, Belcher, handicapped by an injured eye, lost the title to Henry Pearce, the "Game Chicken." Friends urged him to quit, but twice more he fought, each time against Tom Cribb. In the first bout at Mousley Hurst on April 8, 1807, Belcher was forced to retire at the end of forty-one rounds. He was whipped again in the second contest two years later at Epsom Downs when he broke his right hand. He was the originator of the use of "colors" attached to a post in the ring.

THE NEGRO INVASION

For many years after prize fighting flourished in England, the white man reigned supreme and it was seldom that a principal with black skin ventured to dare fortune in the ring. Here and there in the old records, we read of a Negro donning the mufflers, generally some servant of a spark of nobility who had taught his valet a little of the science which he himself had learned from a pugilistic star.

Bill Richmond, the son of a Georgia-born slave who drifted North as the property of Reverend John Charlton, was the first to cross the Atlantic Ocean and display in British rings the science he had absorbed while working on a plantation. He was born on August 5, 1763, on Staten Island, New York, and was the forerunner of a great array of Negro ringmen whose deeds have gained for them a niche in the Boxing Hall of Fame.

During 1777, while New York was held by British troops, Richmond, by whipping in quick succession three English soldiers who had set upon him in a tavern, attracted the attention of General Earl Percy, who afterwards became the Duke of Northumberland. The British General took Richmond into his household, and under his patronage the Negro, who was only a middleweight, defeated several top heavyweights. His first defeat was at the hands of George Maddox.

With several victories under his belt, Richmond looked for bigger prey and challenged Tom Cribb. Cribb accepted and knocked Richmond out.

That defeat was taken to heart by Richmond. He temporarily retired and didn't appear again in a public ring until he faced Jack Carter at Epsom Downs on April 25, 1809. Though he clashed with one of England's best heavyweights and was knocked down in the second round, Richmond quickly recovered and at the end of twenty-five minutes he battered his man into submission.

In his next contest, the American beat Atkinson of Bandbury in twenty minutes and followed that with a victory over Ike Wood, a waterman, on April 11, 1809, in twenty-three rounds.

On August 9, 1809 Richmond again faced his first conqueror, George Maddox, and the latter, then fifty-four years old, was stopped in the fifty-second round.

For four years Richmond remained idle, then at the age of fifty-two he

This magnificent etching, "Boxeurs," was done by the great French painter, Théodore Géricault. It represents the combat between British champion Tom Cribb (right) and the American, Tom Molineaux. Many great painters immortalized masters of the ring.

made a successful comeback by beating Tom Davis and Tom Shelton.

In 1818 Jack Carter, then aspiring to the championship, threw down the gauntlet to the American invader, who accepted the defi, and on November 12, the former slave, despite his fifty-six years, downed his man and emerged the victor. That fight was Richmond's last.

Richmond died on December 28, 1829, in London at the age of sixty-six. He was the first native-born American to acquire high honors in the ring. It was his success that induced another Negro warrior, also hailing from this side of the Atlantic, the celebrated Tom Molineaux, to invade the London field.

Tom came from a family of fighters. He was born in Virginia on March 23, 1784.

When he landed in England, he resolved to follow in Richmond's footsteps. With Richmond's help, he found a backer who matched him with Burrows, the "Bristol Unknown." The latter was a protégé of Tom Cribb, who won the championship in 1809 and then retired.

Much to Cribb's chagrin, Burrows was hopelessly outclassed and Cribb, determined on avenging this defeat, selected Tom Blake, a veteran of many battles, as the Negro's next opponent. Blake was also defeated. Cribb's choice proved a disappointment and it was this defeat and Molineaux's claim to the heavyweight title that caused Cribb to accept Molineaux's challenge.

This international title bout on December 18, 1810, at Copthall Common, was the first between a Negro and white man in which the crown was involved. Cribb was returned the victor in thirty-three rounds and he retired temporarily.

Unable to coerce Cribb into a return engagement, the American issued a challenge to any man in England, and this was accepted by Joe Rimmer. Molineaux once more claimed the heavyweight championship after defeating Rimmer, and Cribb came to his country's rescue by agreeing to fight Molineaux again.

Bill Richmond (above), called "the Black Terror," weighed between 165 and 170 pounds and stood 5' 6". Although born in America, all of his battles were fought in England. Tom Molineaux (left), who was two inches taller than Richmond, weighed 185 pounds. Both enjoyed great success in the British ring, but neither could whip Tom Cribb, the British champion. Richmond was knocked out by Cribb in 1805 and Molineaux, who was known as "the Moor," succumbed to him twice, in 1810 and 1811.

Tom Cribb was one of England's most celebrated champions, whose performances won national prominence for him. Cribb was born in Hanam, Gloucestershire, on July 8, 1781. Big and strong for his age, he went to London when only 13 years old and worked as a stevedore, then as a coal heaver. He was named "the Black Diamond" when he engaged in his first fight, in 1805, against George Maddox. He defeated Maddox in 76 rounds. He won from Jem Belcher in 41 rounds in 1807. When he again defeated Belcher in 31 rounds, in 1809, he was presented with a championship belt and a silver cup (below).

The fight took place at Thistleton Gap, Leicester, with a crowd computed at 25,000 in attendance, and lasted nineteen minutes and eleven seconds with Cribb the victor. Molineaux died on August 4, 1818, at the age of thirty-four.

Tom Cribb, still champion, had fought his last battle, and on May 18, 1822, he named Tom Spring as the successor to his throne.

Cribb, born at Hanham, Gloucestershire, July 8, 1781, engaged in eleven contests, then retired. He opened a public house, "The Union Arms," and was well patronized. He died in his sixty-eighth year.

28

In the first battle between Cribb and Molineaux, in a chilling rain and heavy wind, Molineaux, badly battered, had to be carried from the ring when the end came in the 33rd round. The bout was hard-fought throughout, with Molineaux suffering many hard knockdowns. In the last round he collapsed, raised his hand, and said to Bill Richmond, his second, "Me can fight no more." He then fell into a stupor, amid the frenzied cheers of Cribb's followers.

The engraving (below) by George Cruikshank illustrates the end of Molineaux in the second great battle, held on December 18, 1811. The contest was staged in a 25-foot ring, before a crowd of 25,000. Early in the fight Cribb's eye was closed tight by one of Molineaux' blows. Cribb had a difficult time, until his second, John Gully, lanced it. From then on, Cribb slowly wore down the American Negro, and with a vicious assault in the 11th round, ended the fight.

The memorable contest between Tom Spring and Jack Langan for the championship, on January 7, 1824, was the first in boxing for which a grandstand was erected. An enormous crowd of 30,000 came from all parts of England to witness the battle, which took place on the Worcester race course. Just before the contest started, one of the quickly-erected stands collapsed, sprawling hundreds of spectators among the wreckage. One person was killed and others were injured. The fight was viciously fought, both men taking severe punishment, but neither giving way. As Spring and Langan sparred for the lead in the ninth round, another section of the stand gave way. Both men fell back, dropped their hands and waited for the confusion to subside. The excitement among the spectators was so intense that they surged forward, giving the ring-keepers a terrible time driving them back. At times the fighters had but five or six feet to fight in. Despite the recurrent invasions of the ring, the fight went into the 77th round. With Langan severely cut and bleeding and barely able to stand, Spring's last blow crashed him to defeat.

The second Spring-Langan contest, on June 8, 1824, ended a round earlier. Langan was brutally beaten, and Spring's hands were so damaged that he never fought again.

Tom Hickman, "the Gasman," who appears in William Hazlitt's literary classic "The Fight," was a terrific whirlwind hitter. A challenger for Spring's crown in 1821, he met Bill Neate on December 10, and was knocked out of time in 18 rounds.

30

RING'S GREATEST RISE

With the passing of Molineaux and the rise of Cribb to fistic heights, boxing took an upward trend. Cribb took a fancy to a seventeen-year-old boxer whose name was Thomas Winters but who started boxing under the name of Tom Spring. So pleased was Cribb with Spring's first performance against "Hammer" Hollands, a fighter with great hitting power, that he became Tom's coach and teacher and imparted to him much of the ringcraft and generalship which had gained fame for Cribb.

Spring had defeated Jack Stringer in twenty-nine rounds, following which, through Cribb's influence, he was matched with Ned Painter and Cribb's protégé again triumphed. A return bout was arranged in which Spring injured his right eye and had to default in the forty-second round. This was the only time in a long and honorable career that Spring suffered defeat.

The youngster whipped in turn Jack Carter, Ben Burn, Bob Burn, Joshua Hudson, called the "John Bull Fighter," and Tom Oliver, all top pugilists. It was because of those victories that Cribb announced his retirement as champion and named Spring his successor. But Bill Neate of Bristol, whose battle with Tom Hickman, "The Gasman," gained international recognition through William Hazlitt's literary classic, *The Fight,* challenged the procedure.

Spring accepted Neat's challenge and the latter was forced to surrender after thirty-seven minutes of fighting on May 17, 1823, at Hinckley Downs. Following his successful title defense, Spring engaged Jack Langan in two bouts, winning each, and then retired.

The years between 1814 and 1824 saw the greatest rise in British pugilism, with the Spring-Langan contests the outstanding ones. The champion scaled 190 pounds to 176 for his challenger. Spring, with his fighting career ended, became an innkeeper and prospered. He died on August 20, 1851, at the age of fifty-six. Langan became a hotel proprietor in Liverpool. He died on St. Patrick's Day, 1846, at the age of forty-seven.

Bill Neate, "the Bristol Bull," was lacking in skill but could hit like a pile-driver and absorb punishment. In his championship fight with Tom Spring, Neate suffered a broken arm and was forced to quit.

Josh Hudson, known as "the John Bull Fighter," was one of the many tough contenders for the championship crown. He battled Tom Spring at Mousley Hurst in 1820 and was scientifically cut down within six rounds.

Champion Tom Spring (right) was almost six feet tall. He excelled in scientific boxing but was never a hard hitter. He did much towards eliminating the crude slugging methods of the ring. Starting his career in 1814, he retired after his second battle with Jack Langan in 1824.

31

Tom Cannon, "the Great Gun of Windsor" (above), gained recognition as champion after the retirement of Tom Spring. He was unknown until his first defeat of Josh Hudson, when he was over 30 years old. He met and was easily beaten by Jem Ward at Warwick, July 19, 1825. The intense heat of the sun exhausted Cannon and made him an easy target for Ward to pick up (left) and slam down on the boards. The fight ended in 10 minutes with Cannon hopelessly limp and bleeding profusely.

Spring's successor to the heavyweight crown was Tom Cannon, who was named champion after his defeat of Joshua Hudson in two contests. With Spring and Langan retired, Hudson's victory over Jem Ward gained him recognition by the Corinthians as leading contender for the throne. Cannon disputed the claim and their two bouts followed to settle the matter. Cannon won the first encounter in the seventeenth round and the return affair in one round less. Thus he was acknowledged Spring's successor.

Jem Ward relieved him of the crown the following year. Cannon entered the ring for the last time with Ned Neale as his opponent and won in thirty minutes. He retired and spent his last days in poverty. He died on July 11, 1858, by his own hand.

Ward was the twenty-sixth champion, an excellent fighter but a man of ill repute. Twice he was accused of

Jem Ward was 5' 10" tall and weighed 175 pounds. He accepted Peter Crawley's challenge, to clinch his title claim.

Peter Crawley, called "Young Rump Steak," was six feet tall and weighed 180 pounds. He held the crown only two days.

engaging in fake contests. Despite his skill, his reign brought disgrace to himself and undermined his profession. In each he wagered on himself to lose. He was the first pugilist to receive a championship belt.

He held his honors until Peter Crawley, the "Young Rump Steak," a butcher boy by trade, stopped him on January 2, 1827, in the eleventh round. Peter held the crown only two days, the shortest in ring history. He announced his retirement; Ward reclaimed the title and successfully met a challenge by Jack Carter on May 27, 1828, stopping Carter in the seventeenth round.

Simon Byrne also disputed Ward's claim and he and Jem fought for the right to wear the crown. Their battle at Warwick on July 12, 1831, ended with Byrne the loser after an hour and seventeen minutes of fighting. Ward was now for the second time proclaimed the heavyweight king, the only person to regain his throne in that division either in the bare-knuckle or gloves era. On June 25, 1832, Ward announced his retirement. He died at the age of eighty-one.

Peter Crawley and Jem Ward, after close exchanges of blows, often fell upon each other. Crawley, suffering from a hernia, tried to avoid such falls. In the 11th round, he knocked out the tiring Jem Ward with a solid blow to the mouth.

James Burke, "the Deaf 'Un," fought the longest championship bout on record, 99 rounds in three hours and 16 minutes, against Simon Byrne. Byrne was punished so badly that he died. Burke was exonerated and claimed the crown.

Simon Byrne, the Irish champion, who died as a result of the beating by Burke on May 30, 1833, was himself the cause of a ring death. On June 2, 1830, at Selcey Forest, Byrne gave a brutal beating to Sandy McKay in 47 rounds. When McKay died from injuries, Byrne was arrested, tried for manslaughter, and acquitted. Among the top men Byrne met in combat was Jem Ward, who won in 33 rounds.

The first globe trotter in ring history followed Ward as wearer of the crown. His name was James "Deaf" Burke. Although born in England, he had the Celtic tag pinned on him because his parents were Irish. He was the twenty-ninth champion of England and his bouts were more numerous than those of any who preceded him. He fought twenty times and lost only twice. He was a strong, well-built boxer with an abundance of stamina and a master in rough-and-tumble battling.

After Jem Ward, who had whipped Byrne for the heavyweight title of England, announced his retirement, Burke laid claim to the crown. His record entitled him to the laurels but Harry Macone challenged the claim and was accommodated and defeated in fifty rounds of tough milling. Thus Burke clinched the title.

Now Simon Byrne of Ireland came forth to contest Burke's right to such honors and in a struggle at St. Albans that lasted ninety-eight rounds for a total of three hours and sixteen minutes, the longest championship fight on record, Burke won. Unfortunately, however, his opponent died from a ring injury and thereafter Burke was hounded both in his own country and in America, where he went in disgust at the treatment he was receiving.

In America his arch enemy, Samuel O'Rourke, who had crossed the Atlantic to make his fortune, slandered Burke and took every opportunity to antagonize him. In this he succeeded and because of their feud, a fight was arranged for New Orleans where O'Rourke, a gambler and gangster, awaited his arrival, prepared with a mob to do Burke bodily harm.

Their rough battle went only three rounds when Burke was attacked by O'Rourke's gangsters, who cut the ropes and engaged Burke's followers in a free-for-all in which even firearms were used. Burke escaped and came to New York, where he had one more bout at Hart's Island with Paddy O'Connell. After winning that fight he returned to England, where he lost his championship to William Thompson, known as "Bendigo."

O'Rourke's end was written in blood. He drifted to a lumber camp in Canada, lost his money in gambling and turned to smuggling. He was found murdered by a fellow lumberjack. Thus came to an end the career of one of the most notorious characters in the early history of American fisticuffs.

William Thompson (*above*), called "Bold Bendigo," won the crown from Burke on a foul, but retired with a knee injury. Six years later, September 9, 1845, he returned to fight Ben Caunt, a 6'2" giant, weighing 196 pounds. Bendigo was 5'9" tall and weighed 164 pounds. The fight was bitter. Caunt often tried to raise Bendigo by the neck (*right*) and fall over him on the ropes, to break his back. In the 93rd round, Caunt was disqualified for falling without being hit.

"Bendigo" retired after an accident which injured his left kneecap, and Ben Caunt, better known as "Big Ben," claimed the title. Five years later "Bendigo" recovered from his injury sufficiently to re-enter the ring. Twice "Bendigo" and Caunt had fought, each scoring a victory on a foul.

In the third bout they fought seventy-five bitterly contested rounds, when "Bendigo" slipped to a fall and the referee awarded the decision to Caunt on the plea that "Bendigo" had violated the Prize Ring rule which disqualified any boxer who went down without being hit.

"Bendigo's" last fight resulted in a victory for him over Tom Paddock on a foul. Then he retired to become a clergyman. He was the first man in ring history to leave a championship for the pulpit. He died following internal injuries sustained by a fall

Upon his death in 1861, this death mask was made of the very popular Ben Caunt.

William Perry, "the Tipton Slasher," who became champion after the retirement of Bendigo by winning over Tom Paddock.

Harry Broome, a Birmingham pugilist whose triumph on a foul over William Perry enabled him to mount the throne.

Nick Ward, younger brother of Jem Ward, held the crown from 1835 to 1841. He died in 1850, after a successful career.

Charles Freeman, "the American Giant," who fought Perry in England and won on a foul, died shortly after of tuberculosis.

down a flight of stairs on August 23, 1880.

Ben Caunt, a giant in size, lost the championship to Nick Ward, a younger brother of the veteran ex-champion, Jem Ward, but recaptured the title from his conqueror in a return match. Caunt then adventured abroad, visiting America, where he scored a big financial success with exhibitions throughout the country.

Receiving a challenge from Charles Freeman of Michigan to fight for $10,000 and the world's championship, Caunt returned to New York. He declined the challenge when he learned that Freeman was six feet ten inches tall. Instead, he took Freeman on a tour of Europe.

When they reached England, William Perry, "The Tipton Slasher," decided to tackle the American. Seventy rounds were fought when the referee called a halt on account of the gathering shades of night and ordered the bout continued the following day. However, Perry, who had suffered severely, succeeded in having the continuation of the battle put off for two weeks.

The referee disqualified Perry in the thirty-seventh round in the second stage of the battle and Freeman was declared the victor.

Shortly after that, Freeman became seriously ill, a victim of tuberculosis, and died on October 18, 1845.

Perry, outside of his defeat by Freeman, decisively defeated the best men of his day in England, and when "Bendigo" retired in 1850 he was matched with Tom Paddock in a battle for the championship that terminated in a victory for the Slasher in the twenty-seventh round on a foul.

On September 29, 1851, Perry dropped the title, losing on a foul to Harry Broome.

Tom Paddock, who had three times contested for the championship, was the man to wrest the title from Broome on May 19, 1856, winning in fifty-one rounds of gruelling fighting. About two years later, on June 16, 1858, the greatest fighting man of his inches in England—Tom Sayers—defeated Paddock for the heavyweight crown in a battle lasting one hour and twenty minutes.

William Perry (*left*) batters the right eye of Harry Broome, whom he has brought to his knees. Perry was disqualified for foul tactics. The battle, which took place in 1851, ended in the 33rd round. Peter Crawley, former champion, refereed the contest. Perry had protested the choice of Crawley, fearing a "raw deal." The fight was rough from the beginning, not only in the ring but outside it, for each man had violently partisan fans.

Tom Sayers, only a middleweight by modern standards, was one of Great Britain's most prominent fighters. He reached the top rung of the ladder, after a long uphill climb, on June 15, 1858, when he beat Tom Paddock in 21 rounds for the championship. The illustration below shows Sayers delivering the knockout punch that won him the crown. As in all early fights, the spectators crowded around the ring and partisan feeling ran high.

Tom Hyer, America's first heavyweight champion, was born on January 1, 1819. He stood over six feet and weighed 185 pounds.

AMERICA TAKES UP THE SPORT

By a sort of traditional consent, the fight between Jacob Hyer and Tom Beasley in New York in 1816 is established as the first ring battle in America in which the public-at-large was represented and in which the rules that governed boxing in England were accepted by the principals. We accept Jacob Hyer of New York as the first American to fight professionally in public, and his son Tom as the first American heavyweight king.

After Tom Molineaux and Bill Richmond, each of whom had gained prominence as fighters in England though each was an American, there is a long hiatus in U. S. heavyweight history, the first advertised ring affair thereafter being the Hyer-Beasley mill. While pugilism was flowering in England, it was only budding in America, where the majority of those who took part in fights were sailors who had come to the Eastern ports in ships that crossed the Atlantic.

Their contests were usually staged in the back rooms of taverns, in stalls and out-of-the-way places where they could steer away from the police, since fights were prohibited by law.

Thirty-three years after the Hyer-Beasley battle, the first heavyweight championship bout took place in the United States with Tom Hyer, son of Jacob, facing "Yankee" Sullivan for a $5,000 side bet and the championship of America. It was fought at Still Pond Creek, near Baltimore, on

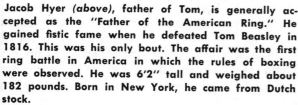

Jacob Hyer (above), father of Tom, is generally accepted as the "Father of the American Ring." He gained fistic fame when he defeated Tom Beasley in 1816. This was his only bout. The affair was the first ring battle in America in which the rules of boxing were observed. He was 6'2" tall and weighed about 182 pounds. Born in New York, he came from Dutch stock.

Yankee Sullivan (right) was born James Ambrose, in Ireland. He won over good men in England and came to America in 1841, becoming a power in politics and the ring. In a fight for the title, he lost to Tom Hyer.

The great fight between Tom Hyer *(right)* and Yankee Sullivan, for $10,000, took place on a cold day with a layer of snow on the ground. In this Currier and Ives print, referee Steve Van Ostrand is on the ropes at the left. The seconds kneel in their corners.

February 7, 1849, with Hyer the victor in sixteen rounds. Hyer decided to remain inactive thereafter due to the failure of Sullivan's backers to put up a side bet of $10,000 for a return bout.

Though William Fuller, a Britisher of mediocre talent, visited America to open a public gymnasium and academy for boxing and declared himself the champion, he had no basis for this since he was a citizen of England and had also been badly whipped by Tom Molineaux at a time when the Negro was well past his prime. Fuller returned to England and was followed in this country by Deaf Burke and O'Rourke, whose presence aroused interest in boxing. But still the game lagged until after Tom Hyer became the first acknowledged champion heavyweight of America.

Boxing and politics went hand-in-hand in those days, with the Native Americans pitted against the Irish every time a ring battle was staged. After Hyer's gruelling contest at Caldwell's Landing, New York, on

September 9, 1841, against George McChester, known as "Country Mc-Cluskey," Yankee Sullivan and his mobsters picked on Hyer and his supporters and frequent encounters followed. The bout with McCluskey took two hours and fifty-five minutes to decide, with Hyer winning in 101 rounds.

The bitterness between the Hyer and Sullivan ranks resulted in a bout for the title that took place at Rock Point, Maryland, February 7, 1849, and ended in sixteen rounds with Hyer retaining his crown. Hyer retired following his failure to entice William Perry, "The Tipton Slasher," to come to America to fight him for world honors. Tom Hyer died in New York on June 26, 1864.

From the time of the Hyer-Sullivan feud until well into the twentieth century, boxing in America could be dubbed the history of Irish supremacy. Hibernians from abroad, and some of those who lived in America, ruled the roost for many years. Shortly after Hyer whipped Sullivan, another good

heavyweight appeared in the person of John Morrissey, a son of Erin who came to this country at the age of three and with his parents settled in Troy, New York. He was born in Templemore, County Tipperary, February 5, 1831.

Morrissey was a leading politician, became a power in Irish-American affairs, was a top man in the strong political institution, Tammany Hall, and fought for his rights at the drop of a hat. In his later years after retirement, he opened a gambling house in Saratoga, New York, owned race horses, and was the first Congressman and Senator to be elected from among boxers in our country.

After Hyer retired as champion, he went to California, but upon his return, his sparring partner, who had accompanied Tom as a prospector, remained and to earn extra money fought a friend of Morrissey, John Willis. Morrissey, who was present, wagered heavily on his man and had many of his followers on hand to see that "justice" was done to his boy.

John Morrissey packed a remarkable amount of strength in his six-foot frame. He was not too good as a boxer, but his power and ability to take punishment wore his opponents down. His battles with Sullivan and John C. Heenan were ring classics.

Yankee Sullivan, here seen dressed for a Tammany Hall organization parade, was killed in California by the Vigilantes.

George Thompson, Hyer's pal, had all the better of the milling, but sighting danger ahead, he deliberately fouled to lose the fight, thus saving his neck. Morrissey cleaned up on the victory of Willis and on returning to New York, he made an unsuccessful attempt to match Willis with Hyer or with himself. He then accepted a defi from Sullivan to battle for Hyer's crown and on October 12, 1853, he whipped Sullivan at Boston Corners, New York, Sullivan quitting in the thirty-seventh round.

Upset by losing to his bitter Tammany Hall rival, Sullivan quit New York and went to California to try his luck as prospector. He got in difficulties there and was hounded by the Vigilante Committee. Following his arrest, he was found dead in his cell, apparently a victim of a Vigilante's deed.

The bitter rivalry between Sullivan and Morrissey found a counterpart in that between Morrissey and his fellow townsman, John C. Heenan, known as the "Benicia Boy." Their feud reached its culmination at Long Point, Canada, on October 20, 1858, when Morrissey gained the right to the American heavyweight championship by defeating his rival, who had lost the use of his right hand when it struck a stake in a neutral corner.

Morrissey then retired and operated his luxurious gambling houses both in New York City and Saratoga. He served two terms in the U. S. Congress and was also elected in the New York Senate but never served because of illness. He died on May 1, 1878, at the age of forty-seven.

With the retirement of Morrissey, Heenan had the field to himself. He was the outstanding heavyweight of his period in America and was generally recognized as title holder because Morrissey had refused to give him a return bout following the mishap he had suffered in their Canadian bout. With no suitable opponent in America, Heenan's friends urged him to issue a challenge to Tom Sayers, British title holder, for the highest honors in fistiana. Adah Isaacs Menken, who later became his wife, was instrumental in forcing the issue, and it was her influence, combined with that of George Wilkes, editor of the *Spirit of the Times* of New York, who challenged Sayers on behalf of Heenan, that resulted in the match being made. It was the first in which an American heavyweight title holder was pitted against a British champion.

Thus, with Heenan's trip overseas, ended the first phase of boxing in the United States.

An artist representing *Leslie's Weekly* drew these scenes of the John C. Heenan-John Morrissey fight for the American championship. Steamboats, filled with 2,000 thugs, thieves, gunmen and so-called sportsmen, sailed from Buffalo at midnight and arrived at Long Point, Canada, at daybreak, October 20, 1858. Sand bars prevented the steamers from landing close to shore, so small boats were used. The ring was pitched next to the lighthouse and a second ring was set up to keep the crowd 20 feet away. In this area 50 ringkeepers were on duty to keep order. Morrissey was in better physical condition than Heenan, who had been ill for a week before the fight, with a festering leg ulcer. They bashed each other for 11 rounds, and only the fifth round ended with a knockdown, by Heenan. The others ended with falls. Heenan collapsed in the 11th round and was carried to his corner. When he failed to come out for round 12, Morrissey was crowned the new champion.

BATTLE OF CHAMPIONS

Of all the names of champion heavyweights who upheld ring prestige, that of Tom Sayers stands out in bold relief. His great contest with John Camel Heenan of America at Farnborough, England, on the morning of April 17, 1860, was the first international ring combat that stirred public interest to fever heat on both sides of the Atlantic. His fighting weight was only 140 pounds, less than the welterweight limit in these days, yet he opposed the leading middleweights with success. Later he fought in the heavyweight division though he seldom scaled beyond 152 pounds.

His only setback was at the hands of Nat Langham on October 18, 1853, in which bout Sayers was blinded and was forced to retire. He tried to obtain a return bout but Langham retired rather than face Tom again. In British ring history, Sayers is rated among the greatest of all time. He was an amazingly clever pugilist. For his pounds and inches he was listed a marvel.

On June 16, 1857, Sayers clashed with William Perry, the celebrated "Tipton Slasher," in a match for the heavyweight crown. It took Sayers an hour and forty-five minutes of battling before he could down his man and win the championship. Perry's seconds tossed in the sponge.

The following year, Sayers added to his laurels by twice defeating Bill Bainge, known as "Benjamin," and whipping Tom Paddock and Bob Brettle, each of whom he knocked out.

The Sayers-Heenan match was a great international event in which both countries, aroused by what might be termed "wild patriotic enthusiasm," heavily supported the native son. Not only was the British press represented at the scene by special writers, but the New York *Spirit of the Times* and Frank Leslie's *Illustrated Weekly*, the leading sports journals, assigned their best reporters and artists to cover the event.

Never before had a prize fight drawn together such a huge and

England's champion, Tom Sayers (left), and America's title-holder, John C. Heenan, met in England, for the world's championship on April 17, 1860. This first international fight, for $1,000 a side and to a finish, was given wide coverage by the British and American press. British police had plans to prevent the fight but were unsuccessful—and probably reluctant.

Heenan's training in England was often interrupted by warnings that the police were on their way to arrest him. Because of this constant threat, he had to move from village to village. His final weeks of training were done in a barn (above) in Haram, Wiltshire, where he kept a pit-bull dog, to prevent any tampering with equipment and to scare off strangers. Heenan and his trainer, Jack Macdonald, are seen inspecting the punching bag, filled with 30 pounds of sand, one of the first bags used in training. When the day of the fight approached, Sayers, after nine weeks of training, left Newmarket secretly in a horsebox (below) to avoid police on arrival at London Bridge station, where a train was to leave for the scene of battle.

varied gathering. They flocked in thousands to the field near the town of Farnborough in which the ring was pitched.

If the records of the chroniclers of the early American ring history are to be taken at their face value, Heenan was the most terrific hitter of the bare-knuckle days, a fighter with indomitable courage, of great strength and endurance. No fight in the history of the sport ever received more comment, no fight has had so much written about it, than the famous Heenan-Sayers affair.

Heenan was a native son, born in America of Irish parentage. He first saw the light of day in Troy on May 2, 1833. When he left school, his father taught him the trade of machinist and at the age of seventeen he had mastered the profession and gained the rank of first-class mechanic.

Although his father had mapped out the plans for the boy's future, he filed no objection when young Heenan made known the fact that he would like to see life and had decided to

Sayers *(left)*, and Heenan, both in disguise, met for the first time at London Bridge station on the morning of the fight. The police could have prevented the bout, since all London was wild with excitement, and two long trains were filled with spectators waiting to leave for the battle scene. Instead, police were stationed within 15 miles of London, knowing full well the fight would not be held inside that area. Sayers was first to scale officially *(below)* for the bout.

visit the Pacific Coast to try his luck there. On his arrival in San Francisco he found immediate employment in the workshops at Benicia belonging to the Pacific Mail Steamship Company, and it was here that he gained the reputation as a pugilist of note and was called "The Benicia Boy."

When Heenan returned to New York he was hailed by the sporting fraternity. He reached New York City on December 4, 1857, with James Cusick, a friend, and on December 10, he gave an exhibition at the National Hall on Canal Street and was wildly received. Shortly after, he became the most talked of man in ring history.

Joe Coburn consented to put on the gloves with Heenan after the crowd had repeatedly called for a demonstration, and the sports were electrified by Heenan's style, his hitting and countering. Coburn, at that time the most scientific boxer in the world, praised Heenan by declaring he had everything a champion needs.

There are some tales which the fight fan is never tired of hearing and one of these is the great international fight at Farnborough. After bitter battling,

The Heenan-Sayers fight at Farnborough attracted celebrities from all parts of England and France and special correspondents from the *Police Gazette, Leslie's Weekly* and other American newspapers. There was a great difference in size when both men stripped for action. Heenan weighed 195 pounds and stood 6'2''. Sayers scaled only 152 pounds and was 5'8'' tall. Newbold, in his *Great Battle for the Championship,* writes: "The crowd was the most representative ever seen at a fight in our country. Compared to former mills, the present congregation must unhesitatingly be pronounced the most aristocratic ever assembled at a ringside. It included the bearers of names highly distinguished in British society, officers of the Army and Navy, of Parliament, justices of the peace and even brethren of the cloth. The muster of literati included William Thackeray and Charles Dickens."

the ropes were cut in the thirty-seventh round, the crowd surged into the ring and a free-for-all followed. The referee disappeared, but the fighters decided to continue and for five rounds they fought without an official.

The British were certain that Sayers had won the contest while the supporters of Heenan took the opposite side.

In America it was the universal opinion, based on reports that came from abroad, that had the ropes not been cut, Heenan would have carried off the honors. Thus, after two hours and twenty minutes of terrific battling, the first heavyweight championship bout for the world title ended in a draw and a championship belt was given to each man.

The American, a true sportsman, viewed the attacks on Sayers as unjust. He and Tom became friendly and went on an exhibition tour together. Heenan's contention was that Sayers was not to blame for the rowdyism of the mob.

Heenan, on Sayers' retirement, was universally acknowledged as champion of the world, and he decided to return to Europe. Once again the "Benicia Boy" crossed the Atlantic and entered the ring on December 8, 1863, with Tom King for his opponent and Tom Sayers as Heenan's second. This time the gods were unkind to the American, for he was beaten in the twenty-fourth round, after thirty-five minutes of milling. Heenan then retired.

He was thirty-eight when he died at Green River Station, Wyoming Territory, October 28, 1873, and his remains were brought to Albany where he was buried.

When Sayers showed signs of tiring in the 37th round, Heenan rushed him against the ropes, forced his neck across the top strand (above) and pressed down on his throat. The partisan gathering around ringside went wild. They stormed the ring and several thugs cut the ropes. Sayers' seconds interfered and Heenan had his hands full warding them off. The referee had abandoned the scene, but they fought on for five more rounds. Heenen demanded that a new site be found to continue the battle, as stated in the rules, but the fight was called a draw. Heenan, angry at the decision, ran to the train pursued by a mob (right). British and American writers differed as to who was leading when the fight ended.

ENGLAND LOSES PRESTIGE

Boxing was forced into the background in England for a time following the disorder in the Sayers-Heenan battle. The police became more belligerent, the clergy more alert, the attacks on the sport more prevalent. The sport had entered into a rough period. But two men's names stood out prominently: Tom King, who conquered Heenan; and the great Jem Mace, known as the "Swaffham Gypsy," one of the greatest ring men with the gloves that boxing has produced.

On Tom Sayers' retirement, Tom Paddock claimed the British title, and in a bout with Sam Hurst, his challenger, the latter, a 210-pound giant, clinched the championship by stopping Paddock in nine minutes and thirty seconds. But Hurst lacked color and ability and his reign failed to arouse enthusiasm among the British followers of boxing. It remained for Mace to bring new life into the sport.

A cabinet-maker by trade, he was born at Beeston in Norfolk, on April 8, 1831. He was one of four brothers, three of whom were blacksmiths. He was extremely fond of music and in his youth he frequently traveled the country as an itinerant fiddler. Though called a gypsy, he and his family denied he had any Romany blood.

Mace learned his boxing in the booths where he would offer his opponent the choice of gloves or bare-knuckles, but invariably he succeeded in having the former used. He discouraged bare-fist fighting and thus brought public attention to the use of the mitts, a procedure later followed by John L. Sullivan.

He won the British middleweight crown and after defeating Slasher Slack and Bill Thorpe, a clever middleweight, he lost to Bob Brettle, then whipped "Posh" Bill and Bob Travers. In a return bout with Brettle, he was returned the victor. By this time Mace had grown heavier and he resolved to try for heavyweight honors. He was matched with Sam Hurst for the British title and stopped Hurst in eight rounds lasting fifty minutes.

Thus Mace won the British crown on June 18, 1861. On January 28 of the following year he defended his crown successfully against Tom King, who outweighed him by thirty pounds. The bout went forty-three rounds.

In a second encounter on November 26, 1862, King, on the verge of exhaustion, landed a wild swing on Mace's temple, flooring him. Mace collapsed two rounds later and a new champion was crowned.

Tom King at once announced his retirement. But with Heenan clamoring for the world's championship by virtue of his memorable struggle with Sayers, British sportsmen insisted that King should fight the "Benicia Boy." Public opinion was too strong and King came out of retirement and beat Heenan, who was forced to quit.

Jem Mace (left), known as the "Swaffham Gypsy," was the greatest ringman with gloves England ever produced. He was called the father of scientific boxing. Sam Hurst (below), the "Stalybridge Infant," followed Sayers as champion, but lacked support.

The engraving above shows clearly every person who witnessed the battle between Tom King *(left)* and Jem Mace on November 26, 1862, at Medway. In the 19th round King landed a wild blow on Mace's temple. Mace weathered the storm of blows that followed, but in the 21st round he collapsed and King was awarded the championship of England. On December 3, 1863, King knocked out John C. Heenan for the world's title.

Having regained the world's championship for his country, Tom King declared he had fought for the last time. True to his word, he remained in retirement.

Later, he became a familiar figure on the English turf. Dame Fortune followed him, for when he died in his fifty-fourth year, October 3, 1888, his estate was estimated at $300,000, a very respectable fortune in those days.

With King definitely out of the fistic picture, Mace was again universally recognized as world's heavyweight champion. In a battle with Joe Goss on September 1, 1863, Mace won in one hour, forty-five minutes and thirty seconds, and proved that as a scientific artist, he stood head and shoulders over all contemporaries.

While Mace was enjoying his victories overseas, Joe Coburn clinched his claim to the American championship after Heenan's retirement, by defeating Mike McCoole at Charlestown, Maryland, on May 5, 1863.

A year later, Coburn went to England for the purpose of fighting Mace.

Tom King was a well-proportioned champion, 6'2" tall and weighing 175 pounds. He learned to box in the Royal Navy, where he engaged in many bare-knuckle and glove bouts. After retiring from the ring, he amassed a huge fortune.

49

After Tom King abdicated the throne, Jem Mace decided he was entitled to wear the crown, and received recognition as champion. Another Englishman, Joe Goss, challenged his right to the title. On September 1, 1863, they met at Thames in a bout that lasted almost two hours. Goss (left) was game, but he was outclassed and stopped by Mace in 19 rounds. Goss tried twice more, in 1866, to gain Mace's crown, but was held to a draw and was stopped again, in 21 rounds, on August 6.

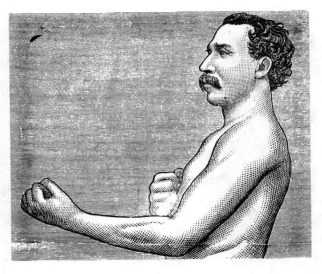

Ned O'Baldwin, born in Lismore, Ireland, in 1840, was called the "Irish Giant." He stood 6'5" and fought at 210 pounds. Upon arriving in America, he visited the durable John Morrissey, who was to test his ability. In a 20-minute sparring match with gloves, Morrissey was floored twice. Mike Donovan, the master, always insisted that O'Baldwin was the greatest fighter he ever saw. O'Baldwin was shot and killed in 1875 by his liquor store business partner in New York.

Mace accepted the challenge and a match was arranged to be fought in the vicinity of Dublin, Ireland, on October 4, 1864. The affair ended unpleasantly when Coburn refused to accept any referee but his personal friend, James Bowler, and the bout was called off. Coburn returned to America and Mace remained idle until May 24, 1866, when he again clashed with his former foeman, Joe Goss, in an unsatisfactory bout that ended in a draw.

Mace was accused of not trying; with his reputation at stake, he offered Goss another match. On August 6, 1866, Mace gave Joe a terrific beating, stopping him in twenty-one rounds.

At this time, public feeling in England was decidedly opposed to the activities of the brethren of the thudding fists. A reform wave swept the country. The clergy preached against the "ruffians of the ring" and staging fights became a perilous pastime.

Ned O'Baldwin was matched with Mace, but the bout had to be cancelled. He then went to America. Tom Allen, Joe Wormwald, Joe Goss and others did the same.

The fistic tide was now rising in the United States, where champions in all classes were developing.

With no opponents in sight at home, Mace departed on a tour of Australia, where he gave boxing exhibitions.

In the meantime, O'Baldwin and Joe Wormwald met in a battle at Lynnfield, Massachusetts, on October 20, 1868. The police interfered, and since Wormwald declined to "fight out matters" later, O'Baldwin was declared the winner. There was no title involved, since Mace still reigned as monarch.

By this time Mace decided that his proper base of operations was in the New World and he joined the exodus of pugilistic talent. On his arrival in America he was matched with Tom Allen. The latter, born in Birmingham, England, had beaten "Posh" Price, Parkinson, Illes, and fought a thirty-four rounds draw with Goss.

Before Allen took up his residence in the United States, Jim Dunn,

Joe Goss, born in England in 1838, started boxing in 1859. He lost to Jem Mace in 19 rounds in 1863, held Mace to a draw in 1866, and was again defeated by Mace in London in 21 rounds that same year.

The Jem Mace (right)-Tom Allen contest at Kennerville, Louisiana, on May 10, 1870, gave Mace a firm hold on the world heavyweight championship. Allen could not cope with Mace's scientific plan of battle and proved an easy victim in ten rounds.

Jimmy Elliott, and John Dwyer had each claimed and held the American championship at intervals.

Coburn had retired temporarily. Mike McCoole won from Allen on a foul, and since McCoole refused to meet Allen again, the latter was recognized as the best man to face Mace for the world's title.

The Mace-Allen battle took place at Kennerville, Louisiana, on May 10, 1870, and Mace won in ten rounds.

Coburn then challenged Mace and they met at Bay St. Louis, Mississippi, on November 30, 1871. It was a hard-fought combat and was declared a draw.

Mace retired immediately after the Coburn engagement. His name was held in great esteem by his countrymen. He did more to foster the pure science of boxing than any other man of his era.

Great as Mace was when fighting under London Rules, it was as a glove artist that he appeared at his best. Following his retirement, his friends in New York presented him with a huge, handsome silver belt which now rests in "The Ring" Museum in Madison Square Garden in New York City.

Mace passed away on November 30, 1910, in Liverpool, England, at the age of seventy-nine.

Joe Coburn fought Mace twice in 1871. Neither struck a blow in the first bout and the second was a 12-round draw.

Jem Mace, photographed in Liverpool, England, in 1909, was 79 years old and active until his death on Nov. 30, 1910.

51

THE END OF AN ERA

In the long history of boxing there have been many romantic figures, but few who gained such prominence as Ben Hogan, born in Wurtemburg, Germany, in 1844, the first German to lay claim to the American bare knuckle heavyweight crown, though he was never recognized as a champion. His fame rests on his battle with Tom Allen in 1872 for the championship, a contest that ended unsatisfactorily when Hogan refused to continue after he had been fouled in the third round.

He was one of the most picturesque characters in American ring history: a Union and Confederate spy during the Civil War, a gambling house operator, oil magnate, theatrical producer, and the inventor of the floating palace gambling house, in addition to being a professional pugilist. He was baptized Benediel Hagen, but following his arrival in New York he changed his name to Hogan.

The story of Hogan is vibrant with human interest. It is the tale of a man who sought adventure and got a bellyful before he settled down to the life of an evangelist. He married a Salvation Army worker, opened a flophouse in Chicago and there preached the Gospel to those who sought shelter.

Following the retirement of Heenan after his defeat by Tom King, there was speculation among Americans as to who would be Tom's successor. Opinion favored Jimmy Elliott, a powerful man with a pugnacious temperament, and Joe Coburn. They were the two best bare knuckles artists in America.

After a few side-bet contests, Elliott challenged Coburn to fight him for the championship and when the latter refused, following the procedure of those days, Elliott's friends claimed the crown. On May 10, 1867, he and Bill Davis clashed in a ring pitched at Point Pelee Island, Lake Erie, Canada, to decide the championship issue. Elliott won by a knockout and was proclaimed the new title holder.

The following year, on November 12, 1868, Elliott fought Charley Gallagher at Peach Island, near Detroit. Gallagher's backer withdrew his man at the end of the twenty-third round after several appeals to the referee for action on Elliott's foul work, and the latter retained his title.

On May 9, 1879, he and John Dwyer of Brooklyn fought at Long Point,

Jimmy Elliott (left), a mean, tough ring veteran, was sent to prison for assault and robbery. Released with a pardon, he was matched to fight Johnny Dwyer of Brooklyn, (below) for the American championship, May 8, 1879, at Long Point, Canada. Badly punished for nine rounds, Elliott wet his hands with turpentine and blinded Dwyer. Fresh water restored Dwyer's sight and from then on he beat Elliott unmercifully, finally knocking him out in the twelfth round. Dwyer never fought again.

Mike McCool *(left)* and Joe Coburn, both claiming the title, met for the championship and one thousand dollars a side on May 25, 1863. After 67 rounds of vicious fighting near Cumberland, Maryland, McCool's seconds were forced to throw in the sponge.

Mike McCool, born in Ireland, was a riverman in Cincinnati who developed a powerful body ad packed a terrific punch.

Joe Coburn, Irish-born and one of the cleverest men of his time, was fast, strong and could hit hard with both hands.

Canada, in a bout listed for the American championship. In a gruelling affair, Elliott was stopped in the twelfth round, following an injury to his ribs.

He was an able boatman, an adventurer, a handy man with fists and gun, and an able wrestler. In a tavern brawl he was shot and killed by Jere Dunn, a notorious character who had been the Chief of Police of Elmira.

Mike McCoole, known as the "Deck Hand Champion of America," born in Ireland, March 12, 1837, was another of the many sons of Erin who ruled the roost as U. S. title holders. He was the first heavyweight developed outside New York City to gain the top rung of the ladder. From Tom Hyer, who reigned in the Forties, to John L. Sullivan, the East held a monopoly of heavyweight stars, but McCoole changed that. He went to the Midwest at an early age because of difficulties with the police, and as a bargeman the six feet, two inches tall pugilist carried his battering ram wallops into the ring in impromptu battles quite often.

McCoole and Joe Coburn fought for the championship on May 5, 1863, in Maryland, Coburn winning. A return bout with Coburn was arranged for Cold Springs Station, Indiana, May 27, 1868, but Coburn was taken into custody by the police and McCoole, having put on his fighting togs and entered the ring, claimed the crown and was acclaimed champion. He then fought Tom Allen of Birmingham, England, for the championship at Foster Island near St. Louis, June 15, 1869. He was badly punished, but the referee awarded the decision to Mike. In their return engagement near St. Louis in 1873, Allen won decisively

53

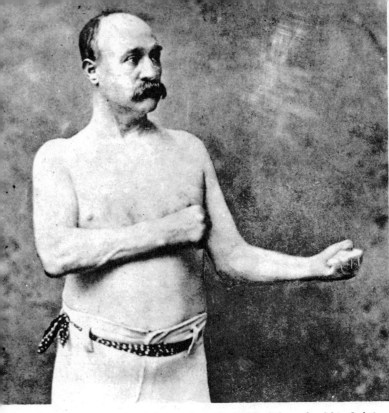

Tom Allen, an Englishman, born in 1840, did much of his fighting in American rings. Upon retiring in 1876, after his loss to Joe Goss, he settled in St. Louis and opened a saloon.

Joe Goss, born in England in 1838, had eleven fights in the Empire. In his only bouts in America, he won over Tom Allen in 1876 and was knocked out by Paddy Ryan in 87 rounds in 1880.

Paddy Ryan, a handsome gentleman, retired in 1886 and settled at Green Island, near Troy, N. Y., where he died in 1901.

in twenty-nine rounds and McCoole retired.

He died in the Charity Hospital of New Orleans on October 17, 1886. He was the last of the slugging bare knuckle pugilists, if we except John L. Sullivan, who later returned to boxing with gloves.

After Tom Allen had stopped Mike McCoole in their return engagement on September 23, 1873, and McCoole retired from pugilism, Allen claimed the heavyweight crown but found himself challenged by Joe Goss, rated next to Jem Mace. Goss defeated Allen on a foul and he became the undisputed king of the division. Now a new American menace had made his appearance in this country, a young giant from upper New York whose physical prowess was such as to make him the talk of the fistic circles.

His name was Paddy Ryan.

Like Morrissey, Paddy Ryan was a Tipperary man, and like Morrissey and John C. Heenan, Ryan brought fistic fame to Troy, which he made his home when he first came to America.

The Trojan Giant, as he was dubbed, was born in the town of Thurles, County Tipperary, Ireland, March 15, 1853. He was five feet, eleven inches tall and weighed far more than the majority of his predecessors among the champions, his normal weight being 200 pounds.

He had only two battles under the London Rules: in the first he captured the title from forty-two-year-old Joe Goss; and in the second, he lost the crown to John L. Sullivan, when Ryan refused to continue after he had been badly whipped in nine rounds. In his youth he had lost a bout to Joe McAuliffe with skin tight gloves.

Ryan's battle with Goss took place on May 30, 1880, at Colliers Station, West Virginia. In this bout, Ryan did what no other fighter in American ring history has ever accomplished—he won the championship in his first professional battle!

In the eighty-sixth round a severe right-hand cross counter felled Goss and his seconds claimed a foul, but this was disallowed. They carried Joe

Paddy Ryan's reign as champion was brief. Winning the title in his first bout (*below*), he lost it in his second, when John L. Sullivan knocked him out in the ninth round in 1882 (*above*). The match was held in a ring pitched in front of the Barnes Hotel in Mississippi City, Mississippi, and lasted only ten minutes and 30 seconds. The stakes were five thousand dollars and the title.

Crude, but extremely powerful, Paddy Ryan needed 87 rounds to dispose of lighter but more experienced Joe Goss in their championship meeting at Collier's Station, West Virginia, in 1880. The fight lasted one hour, 24 minutes. When Goss could not get up to toe the mark, his seconds conceded victory to Ryan. Collier's Station, situated on the Pennsylvania-West Virginia border, was the scene of many notable bare-knuckle bouts during the days when London Prize-Ring Rules governed boxing.

to his corner and when time arrived for the start of the eighty-seventh session, his seconds called a halt. Thus we have the remarkable feat of a heavyweight champion being crowned whose only fistic contests prior to the titular mill were encounters in ordinary bar-room fights!

Within two years after Ryan had defeated Goss, dark clouds began to gather on the Trojan's horizon. The clouds took the shape of John L. Sullivan, whose friends issued a challenge for the American title. Ryan accepted the Sullivan defi and at Mississippi City, Mississippi, on February 7, 1882, just thirty-three years to a day after Tom Hyer and Yankee Sullivan had engaged in the first recognized heavyweight championship of America, Ryan was stopped in the ninth round.

Later, on November 13, 1886, Sullivan knocked out the Trojan again, this time in the third round. Never before in the history of pugilism did a fighter win the title in his first contest and lose it in his next. With the crowning of John L. Sullivan as champion, a new era in boxing began.

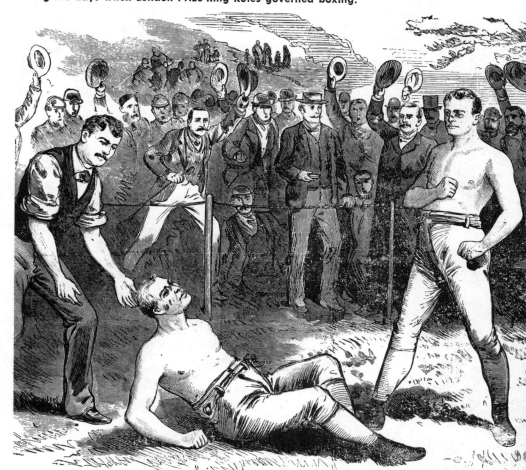

John L. Sullivan, photographed on left at the height of his career, was five feet, 10½ inches tall and weighed 190 pounds. He faced 35 opponents, won 16 by knockouts, was held to a draw three times, and was knocked out once, when he lost the crown to Jim Corbett. The late Arthur Brisbane, brilliant columnist for the Hearst newspapers and close friend of Sullivan, made the above comments in his column on the eve of the Dempsey-Tunney fight in Philadelphia in 1927.

JOHN L.'S ENTRANCE AND EXIT

Like the red planet Mars, shining emblem of war, the bright star of John L. Sullivan suddenly flared into flame on a fistic horizon hitherto dimly outlined in mists of mediocrity. For three years prior to his New York debut there had been considerable talk in metropolitan circles about this heavy-hitting Boston youth who scored victories over such men as Cockey Woods, Dan Dwyer, Mike Donovan and George Rooke within the precincts of the cultured Hub and had beaten Professor John Donaldson in Cincinnati, Ohio.

But it was not until New York saw him in action that the wise men of Gotham realized his standing as a combatant extraordinary. The speed and ferocity of his attack not only amazed the spectators, but led many of them to conclude that the likes of this savage young conqueror had never before been seen in a ring.

In or out of the ring, "John L." was quick to wrath and a bad hombre to cross at any time. Yet he won the whole-hearted devotion of fistic followers as no other pugilist before or after him succeeded in doing.

Not even those later day idols, Jack Dempsey and Joe Louis, exercised such a lasting spell of fascination on the public mind as did the picturesque, indomitable biffer from Boston. When the ring followers called him "The Champion of Champions" it was no idle phrase. They really meant it. In their eyes Sullivan had attained the status of a god, all-powerful, super-human, the world's greatest fighter with bare fists or the padded mitts.

John Lawrence Sullivan was born on October 15, 1858, in Concord Street, Roxbury, Massachusetts, in the Highlands of Boston. He came of hardy Irish stock, his father, Michael, hailing from Tralee, County Kerry, and his mother from Athlone, County Roscommon. His paternal grandfather was a noted Celtic wrestler and champion performer with a shillelagh. His dad was agile and pugnacious, of diminutive stature, but big of heart, as savage as a wild cat if aroused and kingpin with the fists among the hod carriers with whom he worked.

A victory over Cockey Woods, a husky Boston scrapper, launched Sullivan on the pugilistic ocean. That triumph brought him an exhibition tour and the following year a bout with Dan Dwyer in Revere Hall, Boston, where he easily won. As Dan was the recognized champion of Massachusetts, the fact that Sullivan slapped him around light-heartedly was a big feather in the youngster's cap. He followed this by decisively whipping Tommy Chandler, a well known and formidable heavyweight.

Fight fans now began to talk about the young New England sensation, and his big chance that opened the way to a dazzling future came when Professor Mike Donovan, then world middleweight champion, visited Bos-

In the engraving on the left, the artist portrayed the "Fighting John L." You can see alertness in his eyes, powerful arms, chest and shoulders, and almost feel the fierce mood and challenging attitude.

The fight that established Sullivan (*right*) as a potential champion was the one in which he scored over John Flood in 1881. It was Sullivan's first appearance in the New York area, and the fight was held on a barge anchored in the river off Hastings, near Yonkers. The Bostonian lived up to his exciting advance notices by winning decisively in eight rounds (16 minutes).

John Flood, known by the inspiring title of "Bull's Head Terror," wasn't so inspiring against John L. He was knocked down in every round until he finally quit.

ton to give an exhibition in the latter part of 1879. The professor, who later held the post of boxing instructor at the New York Athletic Club, was deservedly rated as one of the most scientific boxers of the day. Yet the young Boston "Strong Boy" battered him and all but knocked him out.

"You're the goods, young fellow, and I'm betting you'll go far in this game!" said Donovan after the set-to.

Besides William Muldoon, the latter's friend Billy Madden had seen Sullivan fight. The two were staging a variety show in Boston and they agreed to put "John L." on in an exhibition bout. Joe Goss, once claimant of the heavyweight title, was to appear in a benefit arranged for him at the Hub and Madden induced him to take on Sullivan for four rounds.

Goss was clever and tricky, but despite all his cleverness, he was clearly outclassed.

Following the Goss affair, Sullivan earned new prestige by giving George

Rooke a terrific beating. Rooke was knocked down seven times.

By now Sullivan's fame had spread to America's sporting centers and he was much in demand. Macon McCormick, America's ace sports reporter, then editor of the *Cincinnati Enquirer*, was an ardent fight-patron and made up his mind that this new knockout artist must show his wares in the Midwest, and he arranged to have Sullivan box John Donaldson. In the third round, Donaldson decided that he had had enough and quit. But the crowd grew hostile and Donaldson consented to resume sparring, but a moment later, he threw up his hands and quit again.

Two months after the Cincinnati affair, they again faced each other in a contest, without gloves, held in a back room of the Atlantic Garden in the same city, and in the tenth round Sullivan cornered his elusive opponent and knocked him out.

Sullivan's first important fight around

Fighting with the gloves was preferred by John L. Sullivan to battling with the bare knuckles. One of his earliest glove contests was with Professor John Donaldson (right) at Cincinnati in 1880. John L. won by a kayo.

(Above) The artist's conception of the bare-knuckle fight between Paddy Ryan (left) and John L. Sullivan, in 1882, included the huge camera perched high above ringside, a novelty in those days. Pictured in the foreground are many notables of the day, among them, Richard K. Fox (extreme right), Ryan's backer. Ryan (below) was badly outclassed and knocked out by Sullivan in nine rounds after absorbing a great amount of punishment. With this victory, Sullivan became American champion.

New York State took place on a barge anchored in the Hudson River off Yonkers. John Flood, known as the "Bull's Head Terror," was his opponent. Five hundred sports paid ten dollars each to see the battle. Sullivan and Flood fought with skin-tight gloves, under London Prize rules, for a stake of $1,000, of which $750 went to the winner and $250 to the loser.

The fight lasted sixteen minutes, with Flood down in every round. The latter's seconds threw in the sponge in the eighth, acknowledging defeat.

The Philadelphia fans saw him knock out Fred Crossley in less than a round, followed by John L. whipping two well known sluggers for the edification of Chicago ring patrons: Captain James Dalton, a tugboat skipper, in four rounds; and Jack Burns in two minutes of the first frame.

When Sullivan and Madden returned to the East, negotiations were well under way for John's title shot at Ryan's crown. These were concluded on October 5, 1881, when articles were signed for a fight to a finish with bare knuckles, to take place the following February, for $2,500 a side.

This battle for the heavyweight championship was held at Mississippi City on February 2, 1882, the "Boston Strong Boy" stopping his man in nine rounds.

For the first time in American journalistic history, the newspapers hired famous novelists, dramatists, and even members of the clergy to write their impressions of a prize fight, so deep an interest was there in this title bout. Among those so employed were Henry Ward Beecher and the Reverend Thomas De Witt Talmage. Nat Goodwin represented the dramatic brotherhood in that capacity, and Oscar Wilde, then on a lecture tour of the United States, accepted an assignment to write a story for a British publication.

The Sullivan-Ryan battle, as already told, was exciting and yet a rather one-sided affair. Sullivan, the more powerful of the two, had much the better of Ryan in the wrestling mixups permitted by London rules, and he threw Paddy frequently.

When time was called for the ninth round, Ryan could scarcely move. He staggered out gallantly and Sullivan wasted no time. He tore in like a human battering-ram and it was all over. A new champion had been crowned.

Thereafter, for ten long years, the

Charlie Mitchell, England's best pugilist, was a skillful boxer with a sharp punch. He came to America and spread the word that he was here for one purpose: "To knock out Mr. Sullivan."

Jake Kilrain (*right*) of Quincy, Massachusetts, was groomed and backed by Richard K. Fox, editor of the *Police Gazette*, to dethrone John L. Before meeting Sullivan, Kilrain had some tough battles.

Below is the scene in Mechanics Hall, Boston, where an overflow crowd saw Charlie Mitchell and Jake Kilrain engage in a 4-round draw on May 26, 1884. The contest followed the appearance of the Britisher in several New York bouts and served as a test for the rising young star, Kilrain. Mitchell was beaten by Sullivan in 1883, but Kilrain did not get his chance until 1889.

Charlie Mitchell finally got his chance to meet John L. Sullivan, May 14, 1883, at Madison Square Garden, but lasted only three rounds. After giving Sullivan a battle the first round, Mitchell was knocked out of the ring in the second (left) and floored in the third round, when Police Captain Williams (right) ordered the fight stopped to save Mitchell from any further punishment.

"Boston Strong Boy" met all comers in the heavyweight division except Negroes.

In 1883, Sullivan faced Charley Mitchell of England in a glove bout staged in New York City and stopped him in the third. The police intervened.

Herbert A. Slade, the Maori, was Sullivan's next opponent. Slade made his American debut before a New York gathering and early in the third round the man from the Antipodes was hurled across the ring by the impact of a clubbing right to his jaw and was unable to continue.

These successive victories over foreign invaders naturally added fresh lustre to Sullivan's laurels. But what finally established him on the pinnacle of public fame was a tour he made of the United States, during which he offered the sum of $1,000 to any man who could stand up to him for four rounds, with the gloves.

First Sullivan beat Slade on August 6, 1883, and the following month he began his trip, meeting all comers. Across the continent he went, never evading a challenger.

From January, 1884, to December, 1886, Sullivan reigned the undisputed monarch of all he surveyed in the fistic world, adding fourteen victories to his credit and fighting a four round draw with Duncan McDonald at Denver. In a battle with Patsy Cardiff at Minneapolis on January 18, 1887, Sullivan broke his left arm; nevertheless he succeeded in securing a draw in 6 rounds.

The most notable contests in his career, other than the Ryan mill, were his thirty-nine rounds draw with Mitchell at Chantilly, France, his seventy-five rounds kayo of Jake Kilrain, the last bare knuckle championship contest, and his defeat by Corbett.

The site selected for Sullivan's fight with Mitchell was Baron Rothschild's picturesque estate at Chantilly, France. Most of the spectators were British, and owing to the secrecy maintained in order to avoid interference and arrest by the authorities, the crowd was strictly limited in number. Only a handful of sports saw the contest and among these were Sullivan's chère amie, Ann Livingston, dressed as a boy, a role which that talented young lady had frequently filled on the American stage.

The ring was set up in the rear of a stable, on ground utilized as training quarters for the Baron's racing steeds. For thirty-six hours a heavy rain had been falling. It had stopped when the fighters were squared off, but it left the ground so soggy that the battlers were ankle-deep in mud. Intermittent showers after the combat got underway persisted, a fact which did not add to the gladiators' comfort.

The fight did not come up to expectations, but it was so important that the result was eagerly looked for in boxing circles all over the world. There was a wide difference of opin-

The first round of the international "passage at arms," in which John L. Sullivan and Charlie Mitchell faced each other on the estate of Baron Rothschild near Chantilly, France, on March 10, 1888. The contest was staged during a heavy rain, which made the footing precarious. After 39 rounds the seconds decided to call a halt, and the bout ended in a draw.

Sullivan, his head bandaged, sits in a jail cell, where he was temporarily held after the contest. Both boxers suffered injuries, but Mitchell's were more serious. He is seen here (right) awaiting an examination by a doctor.

ion regarding the showing of the men. The Sullivan cohorts insisted the champion had by far the better of the milling and based this assertion on the fact that the Englishman had often fouled by going down without being hit.

Mitchell's adherents declared that he had proved his superiority and that the decision to call off hostilities at the end of the thirty-ninth round and make the affair a draw was fortunate for Sullivan.

Back in America, Sullivan was hounded by Richard K. Fox, owner of the *Police Gazette,* who sought a match between "John L." and Jake Kilrain, to whom Fox had awarded the *Police Gazette* championship belt because Sullivan had refused to accept Kilrain's challenge. But now things were different. Riled by his poor display in France, Sullivan signed for a Kilrain bout.

He and Kilrain clashed under the London Prize Ring rules, bare knuckles, for a side bet of $10,000, at Richburg, Mississippi.

The twenty-four-foot ring was pitched on the turf. Kilrain was first to climb through the ropes and then John entered, accompanied by William Muldoon and Mike Cleary. A blazing sun beat down on the strange scene.

John Fitzpatrick, who later was elected Mayor of New Orleans, was the referee. Bat Masterson, once sheriff of Dodge City and in later years

Jake Kilrain's battle with England's champion, Jem Smith, at Isle des Souverains, France, on December 19, 1887, hastened the match with Sullivan. Kilrain dropped Smith in the 17th round (below), but both carried on for 106 gruelling rounds before the contest was stopped because of darkness and called a draw. As a result of this fight, Sullivan claimed the world title after beating Kilrain in 1889.

the boxing expert of the *Morning Telegraph* of New York, was the timekeeper for Jake while Tom Costello held the watch for John.

The fight lasted two hours and sixteen minutes, Kilrain's seconds throwing in the sponge in the seventy-fifth round. From the outset Sullivan

forced matters, but was met halfway by Kilrain in the early stages of the battle when Jake fought with great gallantry and spirit.

The Sullivan-Kilrain encounter was the last heavyweight championship fight held under London Prize Ring rules. Henceforth, the gloves were to

63

The Sullivan-Kilrain fight, last of the bare-knuckle era, was well represented by artists from the various sporting papers then in vogue. The artist from the *Police Gazette* depicted the fight in close-up form (*above*), showing Sullivan, on the left, poised to counter any move made by Kilrain. The scene shows Sullivan's corner in the background. The second man from the left is Dan Murphy, an important corner-man, whose duty is to guard against tampering with the water. Sullivan's other seconds were Mike Cleary, next to the ring post, holding a round fan, and William Muldoon, next to Cleary.

In this rare photograph (*below*), showing Sullivan and Kilrain clinched in the center of the ring in the seventh round, the camera recorded the actual details of the over-all scene. The day was reported as blistering hot, but note the men wearing coats.

The artist from the *Police News*, rival to the *Police Gazette*, injected much more detail in his version of the fight. In the center of the ring are Sullivan *(right)* and Kilrain. To the left are Kilrain's corner-men, Charlie Mitchell, Mike Donovan and bottle-holder Johnny Murphy. The timekeeper, holding a watch in the center, is Tom Costello. Around the ringside holding Winchesters, are Captain Tom Jamieson and his twenty Mississippi Rangers. Sullivan objected to their appearance, but was assured they were necessary "to keep the peace." Standing in the second ring, in the foreground, is referee John Fitzpatrick. The three illustrations below were the artist's version of crucial moments during the fight: Both go down *(left)* in the first round; Sullivan scores the first knockdown in round seven *(center)*; and Kilrain, very weak, is carried by his seconds in the 65th round.

 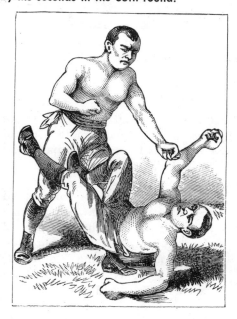 

John L.'s popularity on the stage, in plays or personal appearances, was tremendous. Wherever he appeared the theatre was sure to be sold out. Sullivan's theatre earnings, ending in 1915, were over $900,000.

decide the arguments of title-claimants. The fighter, discarding Nature's weapons, was translated into the boxer. The bare knuckle man had had his day.

During 1890 John L. Sullivan appeared on the stage as the hero of a melodrama entitled *Honest Hearts and Willing Hands*. On June 4, 1891, he boxed a four round exhibition bout at San Francisco with Jim Corbett, prior to sailing for a tour of Australia. On March 10, 1892, he signed articles to fight Jim Corbett with five ounce gloves before the Olympic Club of New Orleans for a $25,000 purse and $20,000 stake, the bout to take place on September 7th.

More than three years had elapsed since Sullivan beat Kilrain. During that period "John L." had not donned a glove except for exhibition purposes. Idleness, the enervating life of the stage, long nights of carousal with boon companions, had taken toll of his vitality, shortened his breath and increased his stomach's circumference.

Sullivan underestimated Corbett, believing firmly that, in or out of condition, he could defeat the Californian easily. He had reached that stage in a fighter's career where training is a thing of horror.

At his best, "The Boston Strong Boy" heartily disliked the task of conditioning himself. At his worst, with no William Muldoon, who trained him for the Kilrain fight, to drive him, he went through daily exercises in de-

While Sullivan was busy with his exhibition tours, a new heavyweight threat appeared in the person of Frank Slavin of Australia. Claiming the British Empire title, Slavin was eager to meet the American champion. To force the issue, the Australian's first match in the United States was with John L.'s old rival, Jake Kilrain. The bout, held in Hoboken, New Jersey, in 1891, resulted in a decisive victory for the Australian, who needed only nine rounds to dispose of Kilrain. The referee (bearded) was Jere Dunn, who shot and killed Champion Jim Elliott in 1883.

With the swashbuckling Sullivan as champion and the United States being invaded by challenging Britishers, interest in American boxing was increasing. Negro ringsters were becoming more numerous. The best of the lot was George Godfrey, of Chelsea, Massachusetts, who advertised himself as the "American colored champion." Godfrey's ambitions were dealt a crushing blow, however, when "Old Chocolate" faced Joe Choynski, young San Franciscan, at Coney Island in 1892 and was kayoed (below) in the 15th.

67

One of the most elaborate programs in boxing history was the three-day "Carnival of Champions" staged at the Pelican Athletic Club in New Orleans, Louisiana, on September 5, 6 and 7, 1892. The principals were heavyweights John L. Sullivan (1) and James J. Corbett (2), lightweights Jack McAuliffe (3) and Billy Myer (4), and featherweights George Dixon (5) and Jack Skelly (6). McAuliffe and Dixon were successful in defending their titles, but the "cycle of three" was shattered when Sullivan lost his laurels.

to Sullivan's face. The opening was there and Corbett saw it, made mental note of it and long afterward repeated the operation, though the second time he failed to withhold his fist and swung the blow flush to Sullivan's face, to the undoing of the Boston man.

The articles of agreement for the first championship battle under Queensberry rules were entered into without any of the quarreling and bickering that have marked the agreements of more recent years. Each man was anxious for the contest; neither desired an

He had his battle completely planned in his mind and it is a fact that he won the fight just as he had planned, forcing Sullivan to the final count one round earlier than he had expected.

Trained on the Cars.

In the baggage car attached to the train which took Corbett to New Orleans a gymnasium had been fitted up. There Corbett continued his training as he sped through the country, and just as the train entered New Orleans he authorized a friend who was with

had been making another effort to discourage opponent.

There was a hush through the building as the clanged, a little after nine o'clock, and brough two men together. Sullivan rushed, and as proached Corbett he swung his left, which C ducked under and hopped away just in time to e a vigorous right intended for the jaw. Sulliva carried almost off his balance, but he steadied self by catching the rope with his left hand

Again he plunged toward Corbett, swinging and left, while the crowd was inclined to jeer C for his evasive tactics. Rush after rush was by the champion. Again and again he swung h mendous right, followed by his no less 'remendou It seemed that Sullivan 'expected the jeers o

Aging, dissipated Sullivan (left) proved an easy victim for young, clever Jim Corbett, who cut him to shreds in 21 rounds. This newspaper illustration tells the complete story, with Sullivan making a futile attempt to rise after being counted out.

sultory fashion. The result? Corbett knocked the "Boston Strong Boy" out in the twenty-first round.

The title passed from America's most popular gladiator to the lithe, handsome youth, the "California Dandy" whose fistic prowess flowered to full bloom on the sun-kissed slopes of California. Coincident with the crashing of the premier pugilistic idol from his pedestal, the bout definitely set the seal of public approval on the use of gloves in heavyweight championship contests as opposed to the

bare knuckles and rough mauling tactics of the London Prize Ring.

The Queensberry era of boxing came triumphantly into its own with the successful staging of the Battle of New Orleans.

There isn't much to the story of that battle. Corbett, young, active, and brainy, stepped jauntily around the massive hulk of what had once been a great fighting man and evaded Sullivan's sweeping leads, hooked, countered on the retreat and cut and jarred "John L." incessantly. Sullivan rushed

in vain. His formidable right hand, which had won for him so often, was useless in this crisis and he was an easy victim for his young challenger.

It was a fight in which speed, youth, and scientific generalship were pitted against bulky muscular power slowed down by age and fast living, a gifted exponent of a new style of boxing against old traditional slugging methods and archaic milling tactics which were doomed to defeat. One hour and twenty minutes after the start, the cool, smiling youth from California

William Muldoon, noted wrestler, physical conditioner, trainer, and friend of Sullivan, later became a New York boxing commissioner.

Richard K. Fox, editor and publisher of the *Police Gazette*, was an enthusiastic sportsman but a bitter enemy of Sullivan. Fox, who popularized the custom of presenting championship belts, supported many of John L.'s foes.

John L. Sullivan as he appeared in later years, when he became a teetotaler and toured the United States giving lectures to the public on the "Evils of John Barleycorn."

was crowned the new world champion in the first battle staged for that title under the Marquis of Queensberry rules with gloves.

It was the herald of a new day in boxing. The game was destined henceforth to rise to recognized respectability as a means of entertainment for all classes of both sexes, and ultimately to attain the commercial rating which culminated in the establishment of the 20-million dollar gate!

The shock of the Sullivan idol crashing from its pedestal rocked the sporting kingdom to its uttermost confines. Men of "John L.'s" generation didn't regard his defeat as a mere misfortune—it was a catastrophe. The Battle of New Orleans was to Sullivan admirers what Waterloo was to the French!

The legend of invincibility woven around Sullivan persisted even after his signal defeat.

After his retirement, Sullivan went on the stage and later became a prohibition lecturer. He died at Abingdon, Massachusetts, on February 2, 1918.

SCIENCE REPLACES FORCE

James J. Corbett lifted boxing out of the barroom slough, the evil influences of its habitués, and started it towards its moral revolution. Prior to his rise to pugilistic heights, his predecessors for the most part were men who scorned the conventionalities of decent social life. Corbett changed that. He won the support of a better class of patrons for the sport.

At the zenith of his career there wasn't a man in the ring who could be compared favorably with him in cleverness and quick thinking. He was not of the slugging type as was Sullivan, but he was by no means a weak hitter, as Bob Fitzsimmons, who wrested the title from him, testified when interviewed on Gentleman Jim's punching powers.

Corbett was born in San Francisco, California, September 1, 1866, of Irish parents. He was one of twelve children.

After leaving school, Corbett entered a mercantile establishment where he became a clerk with a reputation for quick figuring. He quit that job for one as a teller in a bank and retained the latter position until he turned to professional boxing for a living.

His real boxing education began when he became a member of the famous Olympic Club, where Professor Watson tutored him.

After he started his professional career, his greatest rival was Joe Choynski, a clever, fast, hard hitting battler. On May 30, 1889, they engaged in their first mill at Fairfax, California, with two-ounce gloves, but the police interfered and the bout was halted in the fourth round. Hostilities were resumed on June 5 to settle the matter of supremacy, this time on a

James J. Corbett, ex-bank clerk who became champion of the world, was six feet, one inch tall and weighed about 185 pounds. His manager Bill Brady *(insert)* also handled all theatre bookings for "Gentleman Jim," who had a natural acting aptitude.

Peter Jackson, born in the West Indies in 1861, began his boxing career in Australia in 1882. A fine physical specimen, he was six feet, one inch tall, weighing 200 pounds.

Eager to meet Sullivan, Jim Corbett *(right)* took on the great Peter Jackson in 1891 and held him to a bruising 61-round draw. Corbett's followers saw it as a victory for Jim, since he conceded thirty pounds and less experience to Jackson.

barge anchored near Benicia. After twenty-seven furious rounds in which Choynski bled profusely from the mouth and nose, Joe quit. A third bout was arranged and this one went only four rounds, with Corbett the winner.

Corbett's defeat of Jake Kilrain in New Orleans on February 18, 1890, brought the young Californian into national prominence.

On May 21 of the following year, Gentleman Jim astonished the boxing world by holding the great Peter Jackson to a sixty-one rounds draw before the California Athletic Club. This bout stamped him as ready for a crack at Sullivan's crown, a bout already discussed.

Following the defeat of the "Boston Strong Boy," Corbett made his very successful stage debut. He appeared in a melodrama, *Gentleman Jack*, and thereafter did considerable theatrical work, his vocation after his retirement. After winning the heavyweight title, Corbett retired for more than a

CORBETT AND COURTNEY FOUGHT BEFORE THE KINETOSCOPE.

AND THEN LANDS ON COURTNEY'S STOMACH.   COURTNEY GROGGY   AND——OUT.

Heavyweight Champion Jim Corbett knocked out Peter Courtney, of Trenton, New Jersey, before Thomas Edison's Kinetoscope on September 8, 1894, marking the first use of a motion picture camera to film a fight. The event took place at the Edison Laboratory, in Orange, New Jersey, where a Kinetographic theatre, known as "Black Maria" *(above)* was built. Since the Kinetoscope required strong sunlight, the fighters arrived early that morning and were assigned dressing rooms. "Black Maria" was only 15 feet wide and its sides were heavily padded up to a height of six feet, making the use of ropes unnecessary except in the front and back of the improvised arena. Before the Kinetoscope was put into operation, the entire structure was moved, so that the direct sunlight was focused on the ring. This was done again occasionally between rounds. The rounds lasted about a minute and a half at most, before the film would run out. Time was called as soon as the whirring of the camera ceased. The rest period was about two minutes, the time required before the camera could go into action again. This was a legitimate fight and to a finish. Corbett flattened Courtney in the sixth round, as recorded by the *New York World* artist at the scene, and received $5,000 to Courtney's $1,000. The films have never been shown.

In his first title defense Corbett knocked out British veteran Charlie Mitchell (left) at Jacksonville, Florida, in 1894. (The artist who drew this sketch couldn't have seen the bout, which was fought with gloves, not bare knuckles.)

At the Olympic Club in New Orleans, on March 2, 1892, Bob Fitzsimmons and Peter Maher, both potential champions, fought a slashing 12-round bout, with Fitzsimmons the winner by a knockout. Note the second ring, built to prevent any mob interference.

year from ring affairs, but persistent abuse from the Britisher, Charley Mitchell, finally got Corbett back into harness. He handed Mitchell a shellacking in their bout at Jacksonville, Florida, on January 25, 1894, stopping him in the third round.

With that bout, the champion decided to quit and announced that he had turned over his crown to Peter Maher, the Irish heavyweight. It was a good gesture on his part, but futile, since the public didn't take it seriously. Nor did Bob Fitzsimmons, who was eager for a shot at the title. Fitzsimmons took on Maher and knocked him out in one round, thus forcing the hand of Corbett.

At Carson City, on March 17, 1897, in the first open-air arena built especially for boxing, Corbett was knocked out by Fitzsimmons in the fourteenth round. In that fatal round, "Freckled Bob" shot several lefts to the face, then feinted with a right for the jaw.

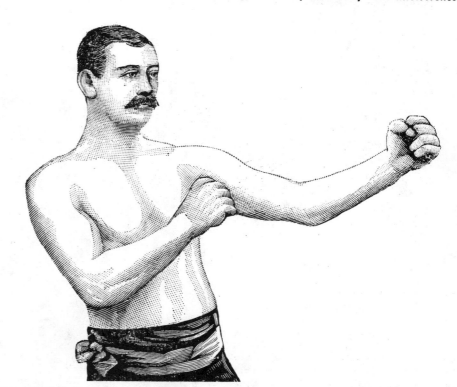

Peter Maher, born in Galway, Ireland, in 1869, came to America in 1891 with a good record. He was six feet tall, weighed about 190 pounds, and carried a powerful wallop in his right arm. He fought all of the best men in America from 1891 to 1907.

75

A champion five years, Corbett seemed destined to extend his reign when he dropped the spindly-legged Cornishman, Bob Fitzsimmons, in the sixth round at Carson City, Nevada, in 1897. Bleeding and battered, Fitz's chances appeared to be hopeless.

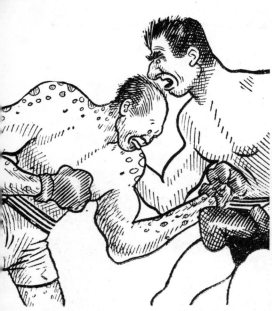

The crafty, hard-hitting Englishman survived the early drubbing and just kept waiting for the opening he knew was sure to come. Early in the fourteenth round, Fitz sidestepped one of Corbett's blows and, seeing an opening, came in with a left hand to the stomach and, without changing the position of his feet, shot the same hand to the jaw. The "solar plexus" blow (above) was born, and Fitzsimmons (right) watches Corbett take the count.

As Corbett raised his arm to protect himself, Fitzsimmons executed his famous shift, bringing his right foot forward. Then, like a bolt from the sky, he shot a right to the heart and a left that landed with paralyzing force into the pit of Corbett's stomach for the knockout. A new champion had been crowned and with that knockout was born the "Solar Plexus" blow.

On May 11, 1900, Corbett put up his greatest battle when he almost succeeded in regaining the crown from James J. Jeffries at the Seaside A.C. of Coney Island, New York. For twenty-two rounds Corbett had far the better of the fighting with his spectacular footwork and two-handed attack, but in the next frame Jeffries cut loose with the winning wallops. A right to the jaw then put Corbett on the canvas, his head resting on the lower rope. In this position he was counted out by Referee Charley White. It was one of the finest exhibitions of science versus brute strength that the ring had known.

The following August, Corbett and Kid McCoy fought in Madison Square Garden of New York in an unsatisfactory bout that ended in the fifth round and created considerable talk. An investigation was held and the unsavory taste left by the bout resulted in the repeal of the Horton Law, under which boxing was permitted in New York, and put a temporary end to public bouts. Corbett had won on a questionable knockout.

For three years Corbett eschewed the temptations of the roped square. Then on August 14, 1903, he again attempted a comeback, this time against Jeffries in San Francisco, and the "Grizzly Bear" of the West put Corbett away in the tenth round. With that bout Corbett quit. Henceforth his entire attention was devoted to the stage.

Corbett appeared in *The Naval Cadet* and *Byron Cashel's Profession*.

He died from cancer in his Bayside, Long Island, New York, home on February 18, 1933, in his sixty-seventh year.

His name shines as the Master Scientist of the Squared Circle.

JOHN KELLY. REFEREE

Towards the close of his ring career, Corbett's splendid record was tainted by a suspicious bout with Tom Sharkey at the Lenox Athletic Club in New York; on November 22, 1898. While Corbett and Sharkey were exchanging punches in the ninth round, Connie McVey, one of Corbett's seconds, crawled through the ropes (above). This action prompted referee "Honest John" Kelly to call all bets off and award the fight to Sharkey on a foul. There were cries of "fake," and newspapers rapped the event in the same tone. An investigation was started but soon forgotten. (Right) Corbett as he looked when appearing in a Broadway play.

LANKY BOB FITZSIMMONS

Robert Fitzsimmons was not as fortunate as his predecessor, who ruled his kingdom for five years. "Freckled Bob's" reign lasted only two and a quarter years. He was shorn of his crown by a comparative novice, James J. Jeffries, a twenty-four-year-old California boilermaker to whom Fitzsimmons spotted thirteen years.

Fitzsimmons was born on June 4, 1862, at Elston, Cornwall, England. When he was nine years old his family moved to Lyttleton, New Zealand, where Fitz went to school and distinguished himself in athletic lines, specializing in sprinting and football.

Below the waist Ruby Robert looked like a featherweight. One could scarcely believe that in bruising fights his sketchy legs could successfully bear the weight of his muscular upper frame.

His first ring battle was with a huge blacksmith named Tom Baines, better known as the "Timaru Terror." The youngster tamed the "Terror" by knocking him out in less than a round, after which Fitzsimmons was selected to represent Timaru in a boxing tourney promoted by Jem Mace, world's champion then touring the Antipodes. Bob weighed only 140 pounds, but

he was large of frame and loose-jointed, with sinewy arms and fine back muscles, and in that tournament the young blacksmith knocked out four men in a row.

A year later, Mace again made his appearance with a show of fistic stars. Mace at that time was grooming Slade, the Maori heavyweight who he fancied had the making of a champion, and he arranged for his charge to box Fitzsimmons, who pounded the Maori so fast and viciously that Mace stopped the battle in the second round. Fitzsimmons now proceeded to take up fighting professionally.

He made a fine beginning, knocking out Arthur Cooper in three rounds, Jack Murphy in four, and Jim Crawford in three.

There was little money to be made in Timaru and Fitzsimmons decided to go to New South Wales. On December 17, 1889, he whipped Dick Ellis in three rounds before a Sydney club and was matched with Jem Hall for February 10 of the following year, a bout in which Fitzsimmons was counted out in the fourth round.

In his first fight in America, Fitzsimmons met Billy McCarthy at the California Athletic Club for a $1,250 purse and stopped him in the ninth round.

On June 28, 1890, Fitzsimmons met Arthur Upham and stopped him in five rounds before the Audubon Club of New Orleans. "Freckled Bob's" fame as a new star was now sufficiently established to warrant a match with middleweight champion Jack Dempsey, the celebrated "Nonpareil." He stopped Dempsey at the Olympic Club in New Orleans, January 14, 1891, and won the world's middleweight crown. The end came in the thirteenth round of a vicious battle in which Dempsey was dropped several times.

Dempsey answered the call of time in the thirteenth, but was dazed after the severe punishment he had received in the previous sessions. Fitzsimmons sent the "Nonpareil" down with a right-hander to the mouth and then followed with a vicious dig to the

Bob Fitzsimmons had the legs of a lightweight, but above the waist he was a heavyweight, with powerful shoulder muscles developed during his days as a blacksmith.

Wyatt Earp, famed marshal of the Old West, gave a flagrantly unfair decision when he refereed the Fitzsimmons-Sharkey bout.

right side which hurled Dempsey panting to the ropes. Fitz landed on Dempsey's jaw and put him down again. Weak and exhausted, he tried to regain his feet but could not, and his seconds threw up the sponge.

During the next two years, Fitzsimmons, who had almost fought himself out of opponents in the middleweight division, stopped Peter Maher, Irish heavyweight champion, in twelve rounds. He also scored a signal revenge on his old rival and former conqueror, Jem Hall, by knocking the latter out in four rounds before the Crescent City Club of New Orleans.

A bout between Joe Choynski and Fitzsimmons at catchweights on June 17, 1894, was stopped by the Boston police in the fifth round, after Choynski, repeatedly floored, was about to be counted out. The following September, Fitz fought his last battle as a middleweight, knocking out his fellow countryman Dan Creedon in two rounds.

On February 21, 1896, Peter Maher, chosen as successor to the heavyweight title by Jim Corbett when the latter retired, was knocked out again by Fitzsimmons near Langtry, Texas.

In December of the same year, Tom Sharkey was declared winner on a foul over Ruby Robert in eight rounds at San Francisco. This was a flagrant

To avoid the ever-vigilant Rangers (prize fighting was illegal in Texas), the bout between Peter Maher (left) and Bob Fitzsimmons was moved from Langtry to Mexican territory across the Rio Grande. Fitz flattened Maher in one round.

example of ring robbery, the verdict being rendered by Wyatt Earp, a Western marshal, after Sharkey had been knocked out by a blow which landed fairly above the belt.

Fitzsimmons won the world's heavy-weight championship from Corbett, as already stated, in fourteen rounds on March 17, 1897, at Carson City, Nevada. Fitzsimmons' weight was officially given as 167 pounds, Corbett's 183.

TRYING TO HOIST FITZSIMMONS INTO THE RING.

CORBETT, McCOY, MAHER, RUHLIN AND SHARKEY ALL WANT A CRACK AT "THE CHAMPION WHO WON'T FIGHT." LANKY BOB THINKS HE WILL GO ON SHOWING AND FAKING FOREVER AND FOREVER, BUT THERE'LL COME A TIME SOME DAY.

Bob Fitzsimmons did no fighting for two years after winning the title from Corbett. Instead, he toured the country with a theatrical group and cashed in handsomely. For this he was widely criticized in print, as shown in the cartoon above.

For more than two years after winning the heavyweight championship, Fitzsimmons toured the country with a theatrical show. Then he put his title on the line in a bout with young James J. Jeffries at Coney Island. The unexpected result of the battle, a knockout of Fitzsimmons in the eleventh round, was a stunning surprise.

Knockouts of Jim Daly, Ed Dunkhorst, Gus Ruhlin and his oldtime enemy, Tom Sharkey, qualified him for a second chance with Jeffries.

They clashed on July 25, 1902, at San Francisco and for nearly eight rounds Fitzsimmons hammered the giant mercilessly with both hands, breaking his nose, cutting both cheeks to the bone and opening gashes over each eye, until it seemed as though the downpour of blood and consequent blindness must compel the big fellow to surrender.

But Jeffries, a mountain of a man, all solid bone and sinew, a miracle of endurance, kept pressing doggedly

forward and suddenly sank a terrific right to the stomach, followed with a crashing left hook to the jaw, and Fitz was counted out.

Fitzsimmons had seen his best days but obstinately refused to retire. In 1903, he defeated George Gardner in

twenty rounds at Mechanics Pavilion, San Francisco, winning the title of light heavyweight champion, a newly constituted class only recently recognized by sporting authorities. This was the third crown he had gained, the first fighter in ring history to gain such laurels.

On December 20, 1905, with the light heavyweight title at stake, Philadelphia Jack O'Brien, one of the fastest and most scientific fighters of his day, stopped Fitzsimmons in thirteen rounds at Mechanics Pavilion, San Francisco.

Two years later, Jack Johnson knocked out the sturdy old veteran in two rounds. Revisiting Australia, Bob engaged in a contest with Bill Lang, then champion of his country, and was defeated in twelve rounds at Sydney. His final ring appearance was at Williamsport, Pennsylvania, where Dan Sweeney and Fitzsimmons (now fifty-two) fought a no-decision six rounds bout.

Fitzsimmons retired and went into vaudeville. He died from influenza in Chicago on October 22, 1917, at the age of fifty-six.

JEFFRIES, THE IRON MAN

It was a great occasion in ring affairs when James J. Jeffries defeated Fitzsimmons to win the heavyweight title.

Jeffries was taken in hand by three wise ringmen, Billy Delaney, Bill Brady, and Tommy Ryan, and they developed him into one of the greatest pugilists of modern times. Born in Carroll, Ohio, April 15, 1875, he came from stock that traced its ancestry back to Normandy. His family moved to California in 1881, and Jeffries lived in that state until his death on March 3, 1953 at Burbank, California.

Jim was six feet, two inches tall and weighed 220 pounds stripped when he was only sixteen years old. He was a gruff, taciturn man whose ox-like strength gained for him the heavyweight crown. He lacked style, dash, boxing skill, and other assets of an excellent fighter when he made his climb, but by the time he reached the heights, he gained international acclaim.

In action he looked like a big bear, with his massive hairy chest, and he fought with the ferocity of one. Such giants as Gus Ruhlin, Bob Fitzsimmons, Jim Corbett, Tom Sharkey among others, tried to subdue him, but without success.

Jeffries was an iron worker, and while in that employ he learned how to box. He won a couple of contests and then Harry Corbett, a California sportsman, introduced him to Billy Delaney, who was looking for a sparring partner for Jim Corbett, then in training for his fight with Fitzsimmons.

He wanted one who was big and husky, one who could take Corbett's punches without wilting. Jeff accepted the post, and in camp he absorbed the knowledge that enabled him to climb to the top. Billy Delaney saw a find in him, took him in hand, and trained him. A couple of years later Jeffries surprised the world by trouncing Fitzsimmons to gain the world heavyweight championship.

He was called the Iron Man of the Roped Square. He could batter an opponent into submission with his TNT wallops but could easily be hit and often took severe punishment until he perfected his crouch as a means of defense. In his first battle with Corbett, and his twenty-five round bout with Tom Sharkey in which he broke two of Tom's ribs, Jeffries received as much as he gave, but his endurance surpassed his rivals' and he won.

The same happened in his fights with Bob Fitzsimmons. When Jeffries faced Ruby Robert for the first time, he scaled thirty-eight pounds more than his freckled opponent, who came in at only 167. Fitzsimmons was an old man as boxing ages go, thirty-seven years, when he faced Jeff, thirteen years his junior. Here is how their bout ended:

Jim Jeffries, who stood 6' 2" and scaled a solid 220 pounds of beef and brawn, was one of the most formidable fighting machines the prize ring ever produced.

Rated among the all-time classics was the meeting of champion Jim Jeffries *(right)* and challenger Tom Sharkey, on November 3, 1899, at Coney Island. This was the first fight in which motion pictures were made under artificial lights. Despite the heat of day and 400 arc lamps, the fight went 25 slashing rounds, with Jeffries the winner of a sensational battle. A rare photo *(below)* of ex-sailor Tom Sharkey, shows his cauliflower left ear and the famous star and ship tattoo on his chest.

Jeffries advanced carefully. Then his long left crashed to the jaw of the champion. A feint at the body was followed by a powerful left again to Fitzsimmons' jaw. His knees buckled, and his brain was benumbed.

Jeffries launched his right with 205 pounds behind the toss and it landed with a thud against "Freckled Bob's" jaw. He fell. Jeffries stood and looked down on his defeated opponent while Referee George Siler counted the doleful decimal.

Fitzsimmons lay on his back. His eyes were closed. His blood-stained shoulders quivered. The great arms that had wrenched the crown from Corbett, doubled up the powerful Tom Sharkey, and hammered Gus Ruhlin into submission, lay inert at his side. Over him swept the cheers that he had so often heard before, but this time they were not for him. They were for a new fistic hero from the Golden West.

Five months after winning the crown, Jeffries tackled Sharkey in a twenty-five rounds bout in Coney Island, New York, that developed into one of the most brutal seen during the early days of the gloves era. The former gob, who had previously lost a decision to Jeffries in twenty rounds,

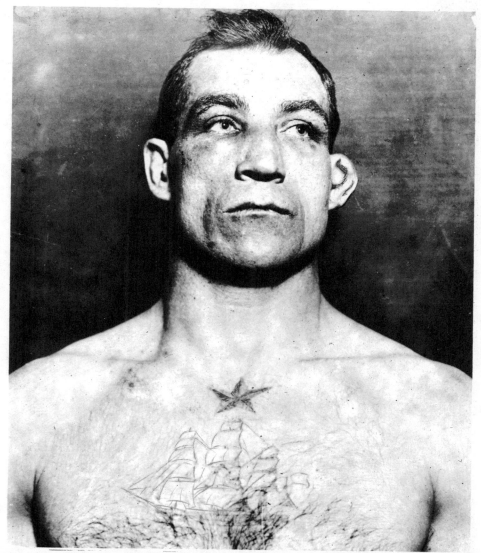

Jeffries *(left)* and Sharkey were showing the effects of the brawl and were "resting" in a clinch when referee George Siler pulled them apart as the bout ended.

Marvin Hart of Kentucky claimed the title when he knocked out Jack Root, on July 3, 1905, in Reno, Nevada. Jeffries, who chose both to fight for the title, refereed.

was a much improved battler this time. Though he failed to win, he made a desperate effort to do so.

Before the gong sounded for the last round, it was obvious that only a knockout could win for Sailor Tom, but he still was full of fight despite two broken ribs and severe lacerations brought on by Jeff's cutting, stinging blows. Jeffries charged from his corner and overwhelmed his opponent with a fusillade of lefts and rights that forced Tom to retreat. At the bell ending the fight, Sharkey was in a sorry state. Referee Siler held up the hand of Jeffries, the victor. Sharkey had to be removed to a hospital.

An exhibition tour followed and several minor contests were staged by Jeffries. In one, he faced a burly miner, inexperienced but powerful Jack Munro, who surprisingly dropped Jeffries with a blow to the jaw. Jack Curley, a promoter, took advantage of the situation and through ballyhoo aroused sufficient interest to rematch the pair. This time, Munro was knocked out in the second round. During World War One he joined the Princess Pat Regiment of Canada and was one of the outstanding heroes in the famous outfit.

It was after that bout on August 24, 1904, that Jeffries, unable to obtain suitable opponents, retired and selected Marvin Hart and Jack Root to fight for the vacated throne, with Jeffries to act as referee. When Hart knocked out Root in the twelfth round, he was proclaimed new champion.

But dissension arose. There were other excellent heavies in the field who protested Jeffries' act. One of these was Tommy Burns (Noah Brusso of Canada, born June 17, 1881). He challenged and cleaned up the field, taking on all comers in various parts of the world. Through his triumphs he received universal recognition as champion.

Jack Johnson, the Galveston Giant, was one of several top ringmen who contested the right of Burns to the crown. He followed Tommy all over the world to force him to accept a challenge to settle the matter of supremacy. Burns was finally cornered

Tommy Burns (left) was an overblown middleweight when he wrested the title from Marvin Hart. Burns won easily in 20 rounds at Los Angeles, on February 23; 1906. After following Burns to England and Australia, Jack Johnson proved too big and powerful for Tommy, when they met at Sydney in 1908. Shorter and 20 pounds lighter, the courageous Burns was far outclassed. With Burns helpless in the 14th round, the police stepped in and ordered the bout stopped.

in Australia, where Snowy Baker guaranteed Tommy $30,000 to fight the Negro at Rushcutter's Bay, Sydney, on Boxing Day, December 26, 1908.

That huge sum, the largest offered to any fighter up to that time, was the golden egg from which were hatched the millions Dempsey, Tunney, Joe Louis and others later drew. Tommy received a shellacking from his tormentor, who in an avenging spirit took pleasure in cutting up his opponent. The police stopped the bout in the fourteenth round.

When he beat Burns, Johnson had a record of sixty-seven ring battles. He was a cautious, tantalyzing performer. He stood six feet, one-quarter inch and at his best scaled 210 pounds. He possessed great ring science, was a master of the now lost art of feinting, and carrying punishing power with his stiff jabs, he could make things most uncomfortable for an op-

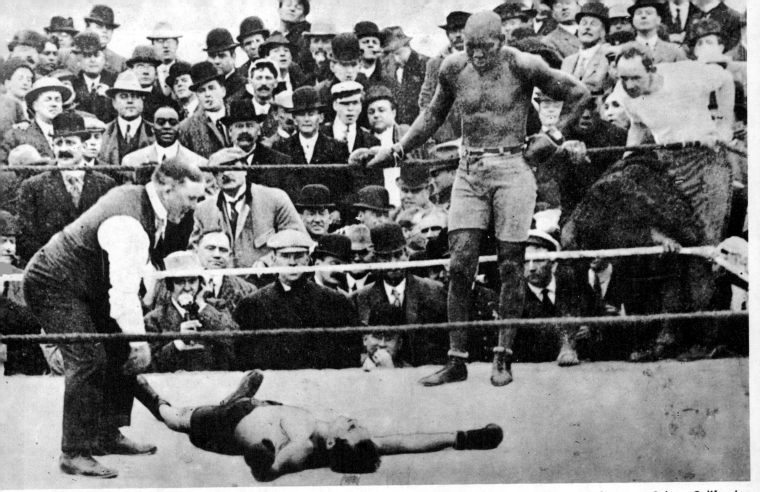

Despite great disadvantages in height, weight and reach, middleweight champ Stanley Ketchel met Johnson at Colma, California, on October 16, 1909. Ketchel had the satisfaction of flooring Johnson in the 12th, but was knocked out in the same round.

Joe Jeannette and Sam McVey, two great fighters who fought Johnson often, met in Paris in 1909. After a total of 38 knockdowns—Jeannette 27 and McVey 11—McVey quit in the 49th round. McVey is shown below, down for the 10th time.

ponent. He was a fighter with a perfect stance.

Following his triumph in Australia, he fought Victor McLaglen, the movie actor, Philadelphia Jack O'Brien, and Al Kaufman, and won from each handily. Then came his historic battle with Stanley Ketchel, middleweight champion, in which, though an agreement was reached whereby there would be no knockout, Ketchel, seeing an opening, lashed a powerful blow to Johnson's jaw in the twelfth round and dropped the big heavyweight king. So angered was Johnson that, quickly rising, he squared off, let go his left, and it was curtains for Ketchel. He was knocked flat on his back and was counted out.

The quest of a "White Hope" was now on. In every country, enterprising managers were scouting for a Caucasian to whip Johnson, whose escapades and marriages to white women

In trouble with the Federal authorities, Jack Johnson avoided arrest by skipping the United States in 1912. With him, in Paris, is Lucille Cameron, first of several white wives.

Sam Langford, (*above*) in action against Ian Hague in London, in 1909, gave Johnson such a rough time in their fight in 1906 that Johnson avoided any second meeting with Langford.

A momentous occasion in boxing history was the signing of Jack Johnson and Jim Jeffries (*second from right*), who came out of retirement after six years. The signing, in Hoboken, New Jersey, was attended by a gathering of newspapermen and sportsmen.

had turned public sentiment against him. Charged with violation of the Mann Act, for which he later served a year in Leavenworth Prison, Johnson left America for Europe and later South America, while promoters were kept busy digging up talent to obtain an outstanding Caucasian as an opponent for Galveston Jack.

Before going overseas, however, Johnson had one more important contest in the States. Jeffries, urged by his friends, particularly Jack London, the author, who had been present in Sydney and following the Burns slaughter had written to Jeffries pleading for him to come out of retirement and bring back the title to his race, signed for a fight with Johnson. Tex Rickard, who was both promoter and referee, staged it at Reno, Nevada, July 4, 1910.

Jeffries, a shell of his former self, proved easy for the Galveston Giant,

The once-mighty Jeffries, now only a hollow shell, reached the end of the trail when, battered, bleeding, and exhausted, he was stopped by Johnson in the 15th round *(above)*. Awaiting the opening bell *(below, left)* is a grinning, confident Johnson. In the audience *(below, right)* were former rivals James J. Corbett *(left)* and John L. Sullivan. Corbett was one of Jeffries' chief advisors and Sullivan was reporting his observations in a special series of articles for a Boston newspaper.

who handed the Boilermaker a severe beating, almost as terrible as he had given to Burns. In the middle of the fifteenth round, Sam Berger, Jeff's chief second, tossed in the sponge in token of defeat and Rickard, acknowledging the gesture, held up the hand of Johnson.

That victory redoubled the action of the promoters seeking someone who might take the crown from the Negro. The "White Hope" race was now on in earnest.

With Johnson's triumph ended another era in the heavyweight division —an era that boasted of the greatest array of talent since Tom Hyer's installation as America's first champion.

It seemed now that a White Race cult had suddenly come into existence that took the stand that only a Caucasian heavyweight could hold the championship—a ridiculous situation.

When on January 1, 1914, Gunboat Smith knocked out Arthur Pelkey in fifteen rounds in San Francisco, the New Yorker laid claim to the "White Heavyweight Title." The "White Hope" craze suddenly went into crescendo. Among the leading boxers were Luther McCarty, a giant cowboy, Carl Morris, Tom Cowler, Fred Fulton, Arthur Pelkey, Gunboat Smith,

Luther McCarty (above, right) was the No. 1 "white hope" when he posed before fatal bout with Arthur Pelkey on May 24, 1913.

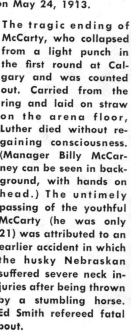

Frank Moran, Al Palzer and Jess Willard. They were the more prominent from among whom it was expected the man to beat Johnson would be found. And he was.

The "White Hopes" thrived between 1910 and 1915, and they were a mighty impressive lot, far better than the majority of the contenders in recent years. For a time it seemed that Frank Moran might be the successful candidate, and then the eyes of the boxing world became centered on a better all-around heavyweight, Luther McCarty. Unfortunately, in a bout for the championship of the Caucasian race, staged by Tommy Burns at Calgary, Canada, McCarty died a few minutes after his contest with Arthur Pelkey got under way, not from a blow he had received, but, as the autopsy showed, from a broken collarbone, an ailment not disclosed prior to the affair.

With him out of the way, all eyes became focused on another giant, Jess Willard of Pottowatomie, Kansas, who through a number of knockouts over pretty good heavyweights and a na-

The tragic ending of McCarty, who collapsed from a light punch in the first round at Calgary and was counted out. Carried from the ring and laid on straw on the arena floor, Luther died without regaining consciousness. (Manager Billy McCarney can be seen in background, with hands on head.) The untimely passing of the youthful McCarty (he was only 21) was attributed to an earlier accident in which the husky Nebraskan suffered severe neck injuries after being thrown by a stumbling horse. Ed Smith refereed fatal bout.

tional ballyhoo campaign by Billy McCarney, who was handling his affairs, gained national recognition.

He started his career in 1911, and by the time he was ready for the leap into the field of challengers he had taken into camp, among others, Sailor White, Soldier Kearns, Billy Young, who died following a knockout in the eleventh round, and Boer Rodel, with whom he previously had gone ten rounds in addition to fighting ten rounds no-decision contests with such stars as Pelkey, McCarty, and Carl Morris.

It was after his knockout of Rodel in Atlanta, Georgia, that Willard's preliminary work had been completed and he was ready for the shot at the crown.

JOHNSON, RING MARVEL

The reign of Jack Johnson lasted from 1908 until April 5, 1915, when he was deposed by Jess Willard at the Oriente Race Track of Cuba, in the outskirts of Havana. Johnson, rated by most experts as the best all-around heavyweight since the Corbett-Sullivan bout, was born on March 31, 1878, at Galveston, and was known as the Galveston Giant. He developed the art of feinting to a high degree, had a rapier-like left and superb defense.

When he fell into disfavor with the U. S. Government, due to his escapades, he exiled himself following his bout with Jim Flynn in 1912 in Las Vegas, which was stopped by the police in the ninth round, with Jack the winner. He went to Europe, where he lived a gay life, squandered his fortune and engaged in three title-defense bouts. He stopped Andre Sproul in two rounds, fought an unsatisfactory draw of ten rounds with Jim Johnson, and beat Frank Moran in twenty rounds. Then he went to Buenos Aires and disposed of Jack Murray in three rounds.

The champion, homesick, in poor physical condition at the age of thirty-seven, and in financial distress, was now ready to accept a bout with the outstanding Caucasian of the "White Hope" era. The Negro had the men who could stage the bout in Jack Curley and Harry Frazee, a theatrical producer. Big Jess Willard, the Pottowatomie Giant, was the choice of the promoters, and under a broiling sun Johnson was knocked out in the twenty-sixth round. The bout was the longest under modern rules.

"The Battle of the Camera Shot" is what the Willard-Johnson affair might be termed, since the photo of the knockout has received more prominence in sports than any ever snapped in the roped square. It is the picture showing the Negro resting on the canvas, flat on his back, shading his eyes from the terrific sun's rays, while Referee Jack Welsh is counting him out.

Had the arrangement been made for a twenty rounds bout instead of

At the age of 37, after years of careless living, Jack Johnson lost the title to Jess Willard in 26 rounds at Havana, Cuba. Johnson claimed that he threw the fight, offering this photo as proof that he used his gloves to "shield his eyes from the sun."

Regarded by many authorities as the best all-around mechanic in heavyweight history, ex-stevedore Jack Johnson stood slightly over six feet in height and at his peak *(right)* he scaled 195 pounds. He combined power with clever boxing skill, two-handed punching power and shrewd generalship. *(Above)* Johnson as he appeared around 1930.

forty-five, the last such in boxing, Willard would not have captured the title. Johnson had a good lead at the time the affair was terminated.

In the first twenty rounds, the Galveston Giant hit Big Jess with stinging blows frequently, but couldn't down him. He repeated to a great extent the tactics he had used to annoy Jeffries.

Jess was no boxer. He was an ungainly fighter who previously had lost a twenty rounds decision to Gunboat Smith and in 1914 was whipped by Bearcat McMahon in twelve. His size, more so than his fighting qualities, plus shrewd management, got him the shot at the title.

However, Jess worked hard to offset Johnson's superiority by employing a wearing-down system. He kept plodding and figured that with the extreme heat that lowered the vitality of the contestants, and with his weight

Jess Willard (left), the giant Kansan, stood six feet, six inches, and weighed 250 pounds. He had not proved himself the best of the "white hopes"—he lost several decisions to lighter rivals —but because of his tremendous size, strength, and durability, he was considered to have the best chance to beat Johnson in a 45-round bout and "restore the prestige of the white race." Johnson (above, right) did all the leading in the early rounds. In the final round (below) Johnson's knees begin to sag after Willard landed a right-hand blow to the jaw.

and height, he would tire the champion. That's just what happened as the affair progressed.

In the ninth round Willard had a deep cut on his right cheek and was bleeding from the mouth. From the tenth round through the twentieth, Johnson made every effort to end the fight by a knockout and his performance in those rounds clearly indicated the falsity of the charge that he had faked his knockout.

In the twenty-first round it became apparent that Johnson had worn himself out. He couldn't go much further.

He had shot his bolt, tossed away his Sunday punch without being able to stop his rival.

He was slow in answering the bell for the twenty-sixth round, before which, realizing his condition, he motioned to his wife at the ringside to leave the arena as he didn't want her to see him knocked out. Jess met Jim two-thirds across the ring and let go a powerful blow to the face. Johnson's head snapped back. The Kansas Giant smashed home a right to the stomach.

That proved Jack's undoing. Another left to the same place, and as

Johnson lowered his guard, a right to the jaw put him down. He was counted out by Referee Welch while Johnson was shading his eyes.

The detractors of Johnson point to the photo as proof that he "laid down" for Big Jess, and his "confession," purchased by *The Ring Magazine* tends to bear this out, though *The Ring* editor, who reported the fight and bought the "confession," is confident the affair was on the level and that Jack sold the "confession" because he was urgently in need of funds.

Johnson was far in the lead when he

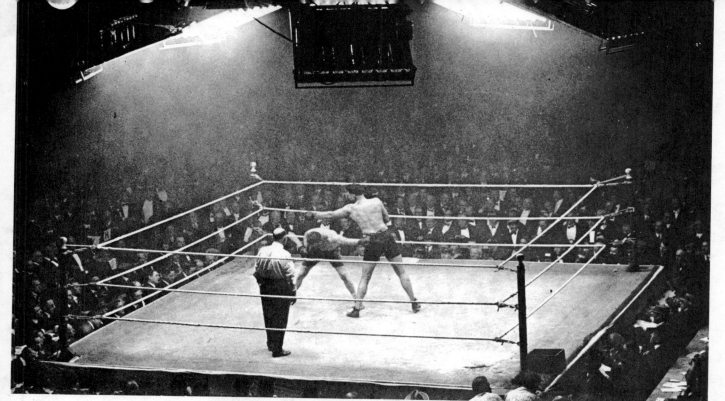

Nearly a year after winning the title, Willard made his first appearance in the ring as champion. In the spring of 1916 he outpointed hard-hitting but slow-moving Frank Moran of Pittsburgh in a ten-round no-decision bout in Madison Square Garden.

finally caved in from the heat, physical exhaustion, and the spurt of his rival in the fatal round.

Johnson was killed in an automobile accident at Raleigh, North Carolina, on June 10, 1946.

It is quite a paradox that Willard, one of the poorest of the heavyweight champions, should have taken the crown from one of the greatest. Big Jess was a slow-moving pugilist who disliked training as much as he disliked the sport itself. He went into boxing to obtain what he could out of it financially and the lackadaisical manner in which he tuned up for his contests, his disinterest in camp life, proved costly.

He quickly left Havana for the States after winning the crown, got into entanglements with his group of managers and trainers, joined a circus group, and the following year, March 25, 1916, he fought Frank Moran in the old Madison Square Garden in a no-decision ten-rounder in which he could not lose the crown unless he was knocked out.

When he placed the title on the

Willard didn't fight again until 1919, when he faced Jack Dempsey in Toledo, Ohio. At his training camp Big Jess (far right) is pictured with (left to right) sparring partner Jack Hemple, ex-champion Jim Jeffries, sports writer Bob Edgren, another ex-ring great, Kid McCoy, and sports enthusiast Army Major Cushman Rice.

block again on July 4, 1919 in Toledo, he collected his largest purse, $100,000 and took a terrific battering from Jack Dempsey, losing the title by quitting at the end of the third round. Willard's heart was never really in the fighting game, but he displayed an abundance of courage and fortitude while taking his shellacking from the Manassa Mauler.

With his downfall, Dempsey, the most popular boxer since Sullivan's rise to fistic fame, was crowned king of the heavyweights.

93

DEMPSEY AND THE FABULOUS TWENTIES

In every sport there emerges one person who stands out so prominently that he is referred to as "The Idol." Such a man was Jack Dempsey in boxing. While in there tossing punches, he was the most spectacular heavyweight since John L. Sullivan. He participated in the first million-dollar gate — $1,789,238 — when he fought Georges Carpentier and before he hung up his gloves, the receipts of four other contests in which he fought

Jack Dempsey (*above*) as he looked during his rugged early days in the ring, when fights were tough, purses small and discouragement frequent. Dempsey (*left*) at the peak of his career and bursting with power. Middle-aged Dempsey (*right*), the successful business man. Still a rover, with his varied and scattered activities keeping him constantly on the move, "Manassa Jack" remains a popular figure with the sports-loving public. To them, he is always "The Champ."

The most spectacular fighter-manager combination in ring history was dynamic Dempsey *(left)* and flamboyant Jack Kearns. Their partnership began with a casual meeting in a San Francisco bar in 1917. Dempsey, then 22, was a small-time slugger who, except for one brief and not too impressive visit to New York, had done his battling on the "tank-town" circuits of Colorado, Utah and Nevada. He had just drifted to California, looking for fights and a manager. Destiny steered him to Kearns, an experienced pilot, colorful showman, and ballyhoo artist. The tie-up was an immediate success. Within a year Dempsey became the outstanding contender for the championship. Promoter Tex Rickard entered the scene and the "Golden Triangle" of Rickard-Dempsey-Kearns introduced the million-dollar gate in boxing. Rickard promoted most of Dempsey's important bouts—the one in which Jack won the title from Jess Willard and his subsequent clashes with Bill Brennan, Georges Carpentier, Luis Angel Firpo, Jack Sharkey, and the two with Gene Tunney. Five of the bouts drew $1,000,000 or more in receipts, the second Tunney match setting an all-time record of $2,658,660.

exceeded those figures. His last fight with Gene Tunney grossed $2,658,660, for a grand total in five bouts of $8,453,319.

Every time Jack defended his crown an epic battle ensued. His sensational mixup with Luis Angel Firpo, the Wild Bull of the Pampas, was one of the most thrilling in pugilistic annals, and his joust with Tunney in Chicago, the "Battle of the Long Count," is the most controversial.

He scored the quickest knockout in a heavyweight bout of national importance when he flattened big Carl Morris in New Orleans in fourteen seconds on December 16, 1918, bettering by four seconds the time in which he disposed of Fred Fulton, the Sepulpa Plasterer, in Harrison, New Jersey, on July 27 of the same year. Both were non-championship affairs, since the Manassa Mauler had not yet won the title.

It was the start of his career as world champion that got the Golden Era of Boxing under way, with him as the ace pugilist; Jack Kearns, his manager, as the king of the ballyhoo artists who beat the publicity drum; and Tex Rickard, as the promoter.

It was in the fall of 1917 that Dempsey, born in Manassa, Colorado, June 24, 1895, six feet, one inch tall and scaling 180 pounds, met Kearns, the man who through extraordinary ballyhoo steered Dempsey into the million dollar class of fighters and a world crown. It was the turning point in young Dempsey's career and a lucky stroke for the kid from Colorado.

Up to the time that Jack Dempsey had stopped Willard, he had scored forty-two knockouts, but it wasn't until after he had put big Fred Fulton down for the count that he received sufficient recognition to be considered a proper challenger for the champion. The quick Fulton victory gained for him the bout with Jess Willard.

William Harrison Dempsey was a tough young hobo. He had fists of iron and a granite jaw.

The Manassa Mauler, who rode the rods on his way to fame and fortune, landed in New York broke and pleaded for a chance to display his

Dempsey held a deep affection for his family and kept in constant touch with them. Here he and Kearns are seen visiting Dempsey's brother, Bernard *(far left)* and Bernard's wife and three children. Unidentified man in center was hired farm hand.

George Lewis ("Tex") Rickard, erstwhile cowboy, town marshal, prospector, honky-tonk proprietor and gambler, who got into boxing by accident but went on to become the greatest promoter the rugged prize fighting business had yet known.

Most spectacular of Dempsey's triumphs on his march to the championship was the quick demolition job on Fred Fulton in 1918.

fighting qualities. He had many managers but only Kearns gets credit for Dempsey's fabulous career. Kearns' publicity campaign, following Dempsey's triumph over Fulton, succeeded in getting Rickard to stage the Dempsey-Willard match.

It was on July 4, 1919, that Dempsey reached the goal of his ambition —the world championship—when he battered big Jess Willard into submission in three rounds. Willard regarded Dempsey as easy prey, did little training, and paid for it with a merciless beating, one of the worst ever suffered by a heavyweight king. Not in the memory of the oldest fan could anyone recall when a title holder received

97

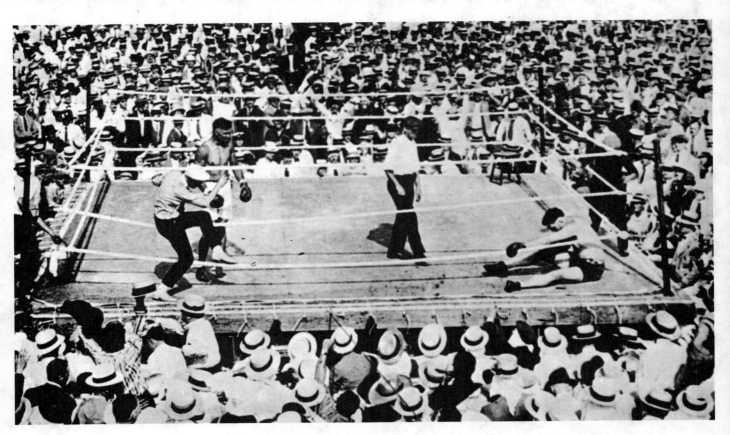

such murderous punishment as did Jess. Yet he responded after each knockdown by rising from the rosin canvas to absorb more punishment.

Willard, scaling 245 pounds to 187½ for his opponent, was dropped for counts seven times in the opening round and was reeling, dazed, in a stupor, when the gong came to his rescue as he was sitting on the canvas, mouth wide open, eyes glazed, blood streaming from the nostrils and gushing down his parched throat. He was staring wearily and aimlessly into space as his seconds dragged him to his corner. The broiling sun added to his discomfiture.

The referee, Ollie Pecord, hadn't heard the bell ending the round and held up Dempsey's hand in victory, but after Jack had left the ring and Pecord was apprised of his error by Warren Barbour, the official timer, he quickly recalled Dempsey and the bout continued.

Willard made a game attempt for a comeback in the second round but fared little better than in the opening frame.

Now the claret was flowing freely from mouth and nose, both cheeks were puffed, two front teeth had found their way to the canvas. His right eye was closed and the right side of his head was swelling rapidly. He looked as if he were struck by a blackjack. Yet he fought on.

In the third round he walked out of his corner a pitiful object. He faced another severe attack, but handed back a number of solid punches. Soon his left eye was tightly closed, his face looked as if it had passed through a threshing machine. The bell sounded and the fight was over for

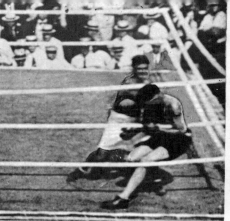

Conceding five inches in height, the same in reach and 58 pounds in weight, an irresistible Dempsey swarmed all over Willard and battered the aging giant to the canvas seven times in the thrilling first round of their championship battle on the sun-drenched holiday afternoon of July 4, 1919, in Toledo, Ohio. Willard was game, however. Surviving the cruel beating in these opening three minutes, Jess fought courageously for the next two rounds, and Dempsey was unable to drop him again. But Jess absorbed such a frightful lacing he was utterly exhausted when he stumbled back to his corner at the end of the third round. During the minute's rest he announced he was unable to continue. How badly the big Kansan was hurt is evidenced in photograph at right. After having his gloves removed, Jess needed the help of his handlers to lift himself to his feet and leave the ring. He had been champion four years and three months, and was 37 when he lost to the 24-year-old Dempsey.

In the excitement, nobody heard the bell ending the first round, with Willard down for seventh time, and Dempsey, thinking the fight was over, scrambled out of the ring. Notified the bout was still on, Manager Jack Kearns (arrow points to him) yelled for Dempsey to return.

In his first start as champion Dempsey met Billy Miske at Benton Harbor, Michigan, in 1920. Miske gave Dempsey two hard battles before Jack won the title, but he was now a sick man, recovering from serious illness, and Dempsey knocked him out in the third round.

The colorful combination of French idol Georges Carpentier and his manager, François Descamps. Although Carpentier actually was only a light heavyweight, the American public believed that his sharpshooting right gave him a chance against Dempsey.

In his second appearance as champion Dempsey encountered unexpected opposition when he faced Bill Brennan in Madison Square Garden in 1920. Brennan actually outpointed Dempsey for 10 rounds, but Manassa Jack rallied to knock durable Bill out in the 12th.

Big Jess. He called the referee to his corner, where he had been virtually dragged by Walter Monahan, his second, and announced his retirement.

The King had abdicated; a new King was crowned.

Prior to the Dempsey-Carpentier fight on July 2, 1921, Dempsey had stopped Billy Miske in a title defense in three rounds at Benton Harbor, Michigan, on September 6, 1920, and Bill Brennan in Madison Square Garden on December 14, 1920, in twelve rounds.

The Golden Era got under way when the champion faced the Orchid Kid from France, a popular boxer who had previously annexed the world light heavyweight championship.

The bout, called "The Battle of the Century," took place at Boyle's Thirty Acres in Jersey City, New Jersey, and ended with the dramatic knockout of

A view of the tremendous crowd that turned out for boxing's first million-dollar extravaganza, which pitted Dempsey against Carpentier on July 2, 1921, in a vast wooden bowl built especially on Boyle's Thirty Acres in Jersey City. The bout attracted an overflow attendance of more than 80,000 and gross receipts of $1,789,238. *(Below)* Referee Harry Ertle instructing the fighters before the start of bout.

Carpentier in the first million dollar gate in ring history.

Tex Rickard's enterprise at Toledo, on the shores of Maumee Bay, was a piker's gamble compared to what he faced when he undertook to stage the Dempsey-Carpentier mill. But he was amply rewarded with a record attendance and receipts. The colorfulness of the contestants brought out more persons, including the cream of the social set, than ever before in boxing. The success of the venture proved the crowning point in the career of Tex Rickard.

The Frenchman took the offensive at the clang of the gong in the second round after Jack had easily won the opening one, and for one complete round had the greatest boxer of recent years rocking and backing under the fury of the onslaught. A swooping overhand punch was responsible.

The end of a gallant challenger came in the fourth round when heavier, stronger Dempsey knocked Carpentier out, but not until after the "Orchid Kid" had supplied a real thrill for the onlookers by staggering the champion in the second round.

Following his victory over Carpentier, Dempsey didn't fight again for two years. Among his "outside" interests was a horse racing stable, and on a visit to New Orleans he posed with 16-year-old Ivan Parke, a riding sensation at the time.

Then came the turn of the battle. With 80,000 cheering the Orchid Kid as he came out for the third round, Jack leaped forth with an attack and shot in several hard right hand blows to the face and a solid right smash to the stomach that changed the tide. The Frenchman covered up, was cornered and bombarded with body blows. He looked like a weakling in the hands of his now vicious opponent. The bell was sweet music to his ears.

It took but little time in the fourth and final round to end the fray. The champion's deadly left hook found its mark to an unguarded body and the Frenchman slipped limply to the canvas. He took a count of nine. Through all this, scarcely a sound was heard as the huge gathering gasped in astonishment at what was happening.

Dempsey swung against the jaw of the challenger and again he went down, his body stretched across the floor. He didn't move until eight was counted and then attempted to get to his feet but couldn't make it. The fight was over and Dempsey became a national hero.

Dempsey returned to the ring in July, 1923, to meet aging but clever Tom Gibbons in Shelby, Montana. Dempsey had trouble with the light, speedy Gibbons, but strength eventually prevailed, and the champion retained his title on a 15-round decision.

Younger, heavier brother of "Phantom Mike," Tom Gibbons (seen here with son) was 34 when he was given the chance to wrest the heavyweight title from Dempsey.

New York State Athletic Commission chairman William Muldoon supervised the weighing-in of the crude but powerful South American, Luis Angel Firpo, for his championship meeting with Dempsey at the Polo Grounds on September 14, 1923.

Following two years of idleness, Dempsey tackled Tom Gibbons at Shelby, Montana, on July 4, 1923, and the best he could do was to win a decision in fifteen rounds before only 7,202 paid spectators, the lowest in Dempsey's championship career. The city went bankrupt through its guarantee of $300,000 to the Manassa Mauler, a sum that was far beyond what had been taken in at the gate.

The fight was a financial flop and four Shelby banks went broke.

The Shelby fiasco was followed by Dempsey's greatest battle—that in which he knocked out Luis Angel Firpo of Argentina in the second round at the Polo Grounds in New York on September 14, 1923.

The champion floored the Wild Bull of the Pampas seven times in the opening round and twice in the second before putting him away. A short right uppercut to the jaw ended the thriller.

But in those three minutes and fifty-seven seconds of fighting, there was crowded more action than ordinarily

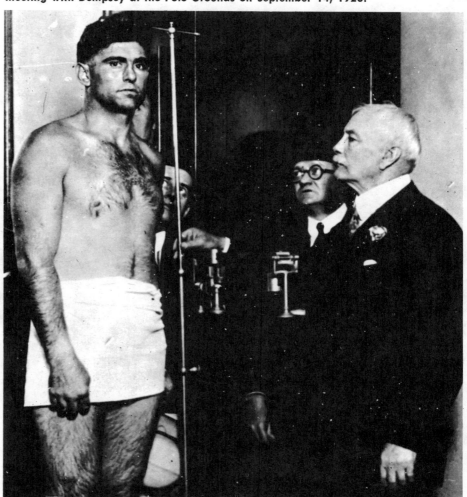

The big thrill of the Dempsey-Firpo bout occurred in the first round, when the "Wild Bull of the Pampas," knocked down seven times, became infuriated, rushed Jack across the ring and battered the champion through the ropes. (*Below*) Dempsey, assisted by occupants of the working press section, clambered back into the ring in time to avoid being counted out by Referee Johnny Gallagher.

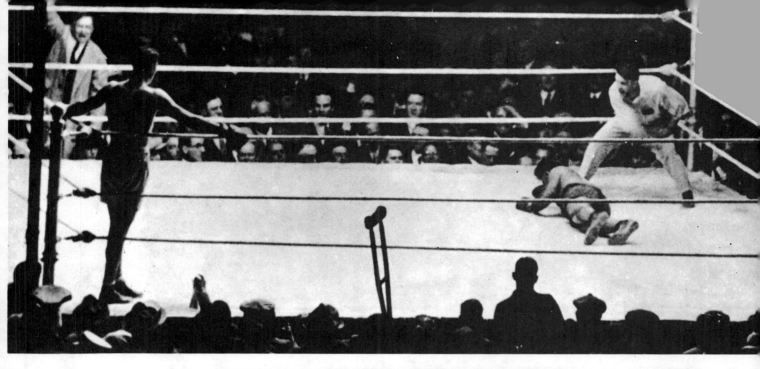

Dempsey's tumble out of the ring only delayed the inevitable. The champion resumed his savage assault in the second round and within 57 seconds Firpo was down twice, the second time for the full count. After his unfortunate experience in Shelby, Dempsey had returned to the promotional banners of Tex Rickard, and the Firpo bout drew a turnout of 82,000 and gross receipts of $1,188,603.

On a tour of Europe in 1925, Dempsey and his wife, motion picture star Estelle Taylor, were given an enthusiastic reception in Berlin. Introduced by American and British troops after World War I, boxing was becoming popular in Germany, and the visit of the colorful world heavyweight champion helped to establish the sport on a major scale there.

is witnessed in fifteen rounds of a championship match. In those minutes of thrilling, whirlwind, terrific battling. Dempsey was knocked through the ropes, out of the ring, and hadn't friendly hands pushed him back, he would have lost his title.

In that space of less than two rounds, Firpo gave a marvelous exhibition of gameness. Battered and bloody, groggy from the severe punishment, he showed a fighting heart by coming back following those crushing drives and almost relieving Jack of his crown.

It was the most dramatic fight in the history of modern pugilism. It was a gripping, nerve-shaking contest between lion-hearted, heavy-hitting ringmen.

Firpo had the world within his grasp, the richest title in pugilism almost in hand, yet failed to triumph because he lacked one great essential in boxing—a fighting brain. Twice he floored Dempsey in the first round but couldn't take advantage of the opportunity by following up his attack properly. The wild-eyed, excited, infuriated giant, who saw his opponent swaying groggily before him, was unequal in the emergency. Dempsey, fully recovered in the second round, made quick work of his task with speed, agility, and fighting fury.

When Dempsey decided to return

A public clamor for a match between Dempsey and Negro challenger Harry Wills resulted in several futile efforts to bring the pair together. Floyd Fitzsimmons (*above*) signed bout for Benton Harbor, Michigan, and (*below*) Rickard even had date set and tickets printed for Jersey City promotion.

Gene Tunney moved into a contender's role in 1925 by knocking out the veteran Tom Gibbons in 12th round in New York. His decisive victory over the man who had gone the 15-round route with Dempsey spurred Tunney to challenge for the championship.

to the ring in 1925, he was pressed by the New York State Athletic Commission to accept Harry Wills, a Negro of national prominence, as his challenger, but he refused. This was done after a previous agreement for such a match had fallen through. His decision resulted in Jack's being barred in the Empire State. Tex Rickard was appealed to by the Boxing Board and he decided against staging a mixed bout, declaring that he had received a hint from Governor Al Smith that such a contest was not desired in New York, but James A. Farley, Chairman of the New York Commission, emphatically denied the report.

When Rickard arranged to have Gene Tunney face Dempsey and selected the Yankee Stadium for the bout, the Commission put its foot

down and refused to sanction it. The Boxing Board drove the fight out of New York, and the Sesquicentennial Stadium of Philadelphia was awarded the promotion for September 23, 1926. In that bout Jack lost his title.

It was another million-dollar bout and drew an attendance of 120,757, the largest in boxing history. The gate was $1,895,733.

The fight took place in a driving rainstorm that made the canvas slippery and drenched spectators and participants alike. Tunney, far better physically, was master of the situation in all except two rounds, in one of which, the fourth, he was on the verge of a knockout.

In several rounds Tunney made the champion look foolish as Jack missed and floundered about the ring. He was far off his usual tearing-in, fast-

punching style. He seemed to have lost his punch, his vicious attack and all that in his heyday made him the "Man Killer."

The champion was awkward, slow, and couldn't follow through as he did in the famous battles with Willard, Carpentier, and Firpo. Some blamed it on the weather conditions; others on his difficulties with his manager with whom he broke following his marriage to Estelle Taylor, the movie actress.

Gene, on the other hand, exhibited cleverness and sharp hitting. He fought his greatest battle. He often beat Jack to the punch and several times rocked his head. He opened a gash over Jack's eye in the fifth round. In the sixth, Dempsey succeeded in checking his rival's attack, but Tunney came back with power in the last portion of that round and the next to

Rusty from three years of ring inactivity and beset by domestic and professional worries, Dempsey (*left, above; right, below*) was beaten decisively by younger, well-conditioned Tunney in 10 rainy rounds in Philadelphia on September 23, 1926.

toss punch after punch to the head and body without a return from the champ.

And that's how it went from then to the tenth and final session with Tunney always leading, striking effectively, and Jack missing. For the first time in his career, the Manassa Mauler found himself entirely on the receiving end.

His left eye was closed, his face puffed, and he was wobbly when the gong ended the affair. Tunney, the New York boy who had won the light heavyweight crown in the American Expeditionary Force in France, was now the world heavyweight champion.

Both Rickard and Dempsey were eager to obtain a return engagement, but Tex had to get Manassa Jack back into the top challenger's post before he could sell Dempsey to the public again.

The heavyweight chosen to give

A product of the sidewalks of New York, 28-year-old Gene Tunney (*above*) awaits the official decision that would crown him the new heavyweight champion of the world. The one regret in Tunney's triumph was that, because of political pressure, he was deprived of the chance of winning boxing's highest honors in his home town. (*Below*) Tunney, who had served with the United States Marines in World War I, and had won the American Expeditionary Forces light heavyweight title in France, stages a lively reunion with his former buddies. The Leathernecks, proud of Gene's accomplishment in defeating the mighty Dempsey, promptly commmissioned him an "honorary colonel."

Gene Tunney, shown as he looked at the height of his career, boxed from 1915 to 1928 and lost only one battle—to Harry Greb, whom he later defeated. In 77 bouts, he scored 40 kayoes, won 15, drew once, won on a foul, had one no-contest and 18 no-decisions.

One month after Tunney dethroned Dempsey, Jack Sharkey exploded the Harry Wills "bubble" by thrashing the Negro and winning on a foul in the 13th round in Brooklyn.

With Tunney signed to meet the winner, Dempsey and Sharkey clashed in New York on July 21, 1927. This shot shows Sharkey (*left*) grimacing from a low punch, just before Dempsey shifted to his chin and knocked him out in the seventh round.

Dempsey a tryout was Joseph Paul Zukauskas, otherwise known as "Jack Sharkey," who figured as the outstanding fighter among the big fellows plodding toward the championship goal. Sharkey had a good record, his most noteworthy performance being a victory over Harry Wills, the Negro gladiator who for years had vainly challenged Dempsey. It was this removal of what had come to be known as "The Black Menace" from the roster of title-contenders which boosted Sharkey's stock and gained for him the match with the ex-champion.

The bout took place at Yankee Stadium, New York, on July 21, 1927, Dempsey winning by a knockout in the seventh round before 75,000 fans who paid $1,083,530, the fourth million-dollar gate. In the contest's early stages, Sharkey elected to fight at long range. A fast boxer, he outpointed Dempsey, whose speed did not equal that of his antagonist.

But Sharkey, abandoning his cautious attitude, unwisely went in to mix matters, a style of milling which exactly suited the iron-fisted Dempsey. The latter pounded Sharkey's body savagely and in the seventh round landed a stomach punch at close quarters which seemed to some of the spectators to be a trifle low. Sharkey imprudently turned his head to protest to the referee and in the same instant, Dempsey smashed a hook to the jaw which sent the ex-gob down and out. He claimed a foul, but Referee Jack O'Sullivan disallowed it.

Opinions were about evenly divided among the spectators as to whether Sharkey had actually been fouled. With that victory, Rickard announced the Dempsey-Tunney rematch.

They met at Soldier's Field, Chicago, September 22, 1927 in a title match that has gone down in ring history as "The Battle of The Long Count," the fifth in the series of million-dollar-gate contests in which Dempsey took part, with 104,943 persons paying the all time record sum of $2,658,660.

It had been agreed before the fight that the neutral corner rule be observed and that in the event of a knockdown, the man scoring it should go to the farthest neutral corner. When Dempsey dropped Gene in the seventh round, he refused to obey that rule and Referee Dave Barry stopped the count until Jack did. Thus, Dempsey was penalized and Tunney received additional time to regain his senses.

As in Philadelphia, Dempsey was defeated. This time he came pretty close to winning by a knockout in the seventh round, but his failure to obey the rules and go to a neutral corner cost him the victory. Though Tunney has often declared he could have gotten to his feet at any time within the allotted ten seconds, the photo of the knockdown with Gene resting against the ropes, glassy-eyed, indicated otherwise.

Second Tunney-Dempsey bout, September 22, 1927, drew a crowd of 104,943 and all-time record receipts of $2,658,660 to Soldiers Field, Chicago. Tunney won again, but had a close escape from defeat in the "long count" episode in the seventh round.

How long Tunney actually was down was never determined, but estimates ranged from 12 to 16 seconds. Dempsey's hesitancy in going to a neutral corner when Tunney sank to the canvas was responsible for Referee Dave Barry's delay in starting the count. That one flash was the nearest Dempsey came to regaining the title. Tunney, arising at the official count of nine (*above*), recovered from the knockdown and resumed his systematic battering of the former champion. Dempsey was tiring rapidly in the eighth round and sagged to one knee (*below*) from a volley of Tunney punches. Dempsey was near exhaustion at the final bell in the 10th round.

Yet in the next round, Tunney, his brain cleared, danced around the ring, tossed jabs and then dropped Dempsey with a right to the jaw. He quickly got to his feet but was outpointed by a wide margin in that and the succeeding two rounds, with Gene getting a well deserved decision.

The long count knockdown has become one of the most talked about, controversial points in boxing. Some of the ringsiders said Gene received a fourteen count, as did the official timekeeper, while others, mostly newspapermen, said it was seventeen. The writer's stop watch caught it at fourteen. Here is what happened:

Gene opened the round with a right to Dempsey's head then delivered several effective jabs. Dempsey rushed him and smote two rights to the head that landed Gene against the ropes. The last punch was hard enough to drop him to the canvas, where he lay in an awkward position in Dempsey's corner with body half twisted and eyes glassy.

In interviews he declared that he knew what was going on, however. He watched Dave Barry closely and when Dempsey went to a neutral corner and Barry's count was started, Gene slowly worked his way upward. Dempsey rushed in, but Gene, his equilibrium regained, moved about the ring, making Jack miss, and the round ended with both hugging each other.

Thus ended the fighting career of one of the great ringmen of all time. Though Dempsey tried a comeback and gained a fortune in exhibitions after the second defeat, his real fighting terminated with the "Long Count" battle.

James Joseph Tunney, born May 25, 1898, the first New York-born ringman to win the crown under glove rules, had a proud record before winning the heavyweight title. Prior to joining the Marines and gaining the A.E.F. light heavyweight title in Europe, he had a few contests, but it was after his return from World War One that he took to the sport in earnest and set the championship as his goal.

He defeated Battling Levinsky for the American light heavyweight

In his last title defense, on July 23, 1928, Tunney gave a masterful exhibition in whittling Tom Heeney of New Zealand into defeat in 11 rounds at New York's Yankee Stadium. Heeney had won an elimination tourney to determine Tunney's opponent, but he proved no match for the champion. A few days later Gene announced his retirement.

crown, January 13, 1922. At that time he had won twenty-nine contests and didn't experience a single setback. He lost the title to Harry Greb in May of that year, regained it from Greb on February 23, 1923, and never again did he suffer a defeat.

In 1925 he threw down the gauntlet to the heavyweight class, scored knockouts over Tommy Gibbons and Bartley Madden, and defeated Johnny Risko in twelve rounds.

From a slender, though sinewy athlete, he had developed into a splendid specimen of muscular manhood, with massive shoulders, deep chest, and stalwart frame. His weight and punching power increased without sacrificing the agility and speedy footwork for which he was celebrated. Not the least surprising thing about the Philadelphia meeting with Dempsey when the heavyweight title passed to Tunney, was the unsuspected strength of the victor which enabled

him to tie up and control in the clinches a pugilist who had hitherto been deemed invincible in a test of roughing it at close quarters!

Nearly a year passed before Tunney again defended his title. This time Tom Heeney, known as the "Australian Hard Rock," was selected to oppose him. Out of a lot of rather mediocre heavies in an elimination tournament conducted by Tex Rickard at Madison Square Garden, Heeney and Sharkey had forged to the front. A meeting between the two pugilists resulted in a draw, but, as Sharkey had already been knocked out by Dempsey, the Australian was awarded the match for the championship.

Tunney and Heeney met on July 26, 1928, at the Polo Grounds in New York City. The fight was halted by Referee Eddie Forbes eight seconds before the conclusion of the eleventh round, when Heeney, game to the core, but literally cut to pieces by the

Man of many interests, Jack Dempsey, operating the Dempsey-Vanderbilt Hotel in Miami Beach in 1938, often took his daughters for a run on the sands. *(Right)* Dempsey's duties with the Coast Guard in World War II included athletic instruction.

(Left) Three months after retiring from the ring, Gene Tunney, followed by fiancée Polly Lauder, disembarked at Naples, Italy, en route to their marriage in Rome.

As a Navy Commander *(below)* in World War II, Tunney kept distinguished company. On a visit to the Mitchell Field Air Force base on Long Island in 1942, Tunney appeared *(second from left)* with Brigadier General Jimmy Doolittle; Colonel Douglas Johnston, commanding officer of the post, and Lieutenant Colonel John S. Allard, former vice-president of Curtiss-Wright.

champion's unerring punches, was blind and utterly helpless. From first to last Heeney never had a chance. The man who stood off the best of the heavyweight contenders was little better than a novice in the hands of the most scientific pugilist since the day of James J. Corbett.

Financially the bout was a dismal failure. It was the first non-profitable championship battle staged by Rickard. It resulted in a loss of $152,000. Gene was guaranteed $500,000.

The glamor and color of Dempsey's name was missing. Despite the most frantic efforts of the press agents, the public remained coldly indifferent as to what would happen to Tom Heeney. There was nothing spectacular about the man from the Antipodes. He was a persevering, dogged, plodding fighter and the fans guessed correctly in advance as to what his fate would be.

Speculation as to Tunney's next opponent ceased suddenly when the champion announced his retirement. There were no "if's" about Gene's statement. It was short, definite, to the point. He was through forever with the ring.

Tunney married an heiress, Miss Polly Lauder, and became a very successful businessman.

THE CROWN GOES OVERSEAS

After Tunney's retirement, Jack Sharkey, Young Stribling, Johnny Risko, and Germany's Max Schmeling were the leading contenders for Gene's vacated throne. An elimination was ordered by the National Boxing Association and the New York Commission.

Tex Rickard set about to get such a tourney under way. He went to Miami, Florida, with the intention of matching Sharkey and Stribling, but while there, Rickard died following an appendix operation. Jack Dempsey, who had been associated with the promoter in several ventures, accepted a call from the Madison Square Garden Corporation, and in association with that organization promoted the fight on February 27, 1929, with Sharkey gaining the decision.

In the meantime, Schmeling, who had knocked out Joe Monte in the Garden in eight rounds and followed that with a knockout of Risko in the same arena in nine rounds, was clamoring for a shot at the winner. This was temporarily denied him, and while waiting, he won a thrilling fifteen-rounds contest from Paulino Uzcudun, the Basque, while Sharkey put Tommy Loughran out in three rounds.

The heat was now on for a Schmeling-Sharkey fight, but the Garden officials decided to have the German,

William Lawrence (Young) Stribling, the pride of Dixie, became one of the leading contenders for the vacant title when Tunney retired from the ring wars. Stribling began boxing as a bantamweight and fought in every division up to heavyweight. He was only 28, but a veteran of nearly 300 bouts, when his life ended tragically in a motorcycle crash in 1933.

A newcomer flashed across the heavyweight scene in 1928 when a young German, Max Schmeling, scored a one-round knockout over the Italian Michele Bonaglia in Berlin.

Recovering from knockout by Dempsey, clever Jack Sharkey (*below*) went on to establish himself as one of the best of the American bidders for Tunney's vacated laurels.

As a preliminary to the championship bout with Schmeling, Jack Sharkey was awarded a knockout victory over Phil Scott of England, on February 28, 1930, in Miami. Scott, a boxer with fair skill, but fragile, refused to continue after three knockdowns in the third round, claiming that all of the blows were foul. Referee Lou Magnolia stopped the proceedings and declared Sharkey the winner.

The meeting between Jack Sharkey and Max Schmeling, to decide the successor to the heavyweight crown, ended in complete confusion. Schmeling, sitting on the canvas claiming foul, insisted Sharkey's left to the stomach landed below the belt.

a young, well built, scientific boxer who possessed a powerful right, wait it out while the Boston gob and Phil Scott of England engaged in an international elimination at Miami Beach in which the Britisher was halted in the third round. The stage was now set for the final in the elimination series, Schmeling representing Europe and Sharkey, America; this despite a British howl that Scott had been fouled and that Sharkey should have been disqualified.

In the Miami bout, Sharkey, outboxed in the opening round, dropped Phil in the second with a punch and a push, and in the third, put the Englishman on the canvas with a left hook to the stomach. Phil cried foul.

Twice again he was floored by similar blows and when he refused to get to his feet, declaring all punches were below the belt, Referee Lou Magnolia halted proceedings, insisted on Scott deciding whether he wanted to continue or quit. Phil chose the former, but when he went down from another punch in the mid-section, he remained squirming on the canvas and Magnolia gave the decision to Sharkey.

On June 11, 1930, Sharkey and

In the sequence above, the camera recorded the controversial blow. Referee Jim Crowley (*below, left*) not in position to see the blow, took the word of one of the judges who saw the foul and awarded the title to Schmeling. While Schmeling is carried to his corner, his manager, Joe Jacobs, protests to Crowley that the blow was foul.

Schmeling clashed in the Yankee Stadium before a gathering of 79,222 fans. The gross gate of $749,935 was the first during the Golden Era that failed to reach the million dollar mark.

Sharkey's stock had been given a scant boost because of the besmirched victory he had achieved. The fans were in no mood to wax enthusiastic over the ex-gob's triumph over "Phainting Phil" and gave Schmeling more than a fighting chance to win the crown. And that's what he did.

Max was proclaimed world champion following a blow to the stomach that had left him reposing on the canvas, writhing in pain. It was a powerful drive which he and Joe Jacobs, his mentor, insisted was low and in that they had the heavy support of Arthur Brisbane, editor of the Hearst publications, who demanded that Referee Jim Crowley disqualify Sharkey or Brisbane would have the Walker Law repealed. Neither Harold Barnes, a judge, nor the referee had seen the low punch, but Charles F. Mathison, the other judge, agreed with Schmeling, and for the first time a challenger gained the world heavyweight title while resting on his haunches.

Max Schmeling, in his first defense of the title, knocked out Young Stribling (*above*) in the 15th round. Referee George Blake stopped the bout with one minute to go. Schmeling (*below, left*), just over six feet tall and weighing 195 pounds, was a very good boxer and a methodical ringman. He carried dynamite in his right hand, and his record, from 1924 to 1948, is studded with knockouts.

Jack Sharkey, an ex-gob from Boston, was a good boxer, but his temperamental nature led to many erratic performances. In 55 bouts, from 1924 to 1936, he lost 13, and scored 15 knockouts.

Prior to the incident, Schmeling had been outpointed. It was the first time under modern rules that a Teuton had won the crown.

The New York Commission was hotly in favor of a return match, but Schmeling and his manager turned thumbs down. As a result, New York vacated his throne until such time as Sharkey was given an opportunity to fight for the championship again. In the meantime, Young Stribling, who had a huge knockout record and had stopped Otto Van Porat in one round and Phil Scott in two in London, was accepted by Schmeling as a suitable opponent. The German put his title on the line in the Cleveland Stadium on July 3, 1931, Herr Max winning by a knockout in the fifteenth round with only fifteen more seconds to go. Stribling had been outclassed and Referee George Blake halted the affair.

Only in the five opening rounds did Stribling look like he would carry off the honors. From then on it was all Schmeling's bout. He carried the battling to the challenger all the way and it was simply a romp after the sixth round.

Two years and nine days after their first engagement, Max and Sharkey clashed again, this time in the Garden's Long Island Bowl, and the title changed hands on what many thought was an unfair decision. Schmeling, as in the first bout, raised a cry, but to no avail. There was little over which to enthuse in that contest, most of the fighting being done after the affair.

Most of the effective work was accomplished by Schmeling, who carried the fight to Sharkey, maneuvered his opponent cleverly, and landed the best punches of the few that really meant something.

Max's next fight of importance was his best—other than his first contest with Joe Louis. The mill took place on September 26, 1932, with Mickey Walker, former welter and middleweight king, as his opponent. Mickey was knocked out in the eighth round of a thrilling affair, a hair-raiser, one of the best seen in New York in years. Sixty thousand persons saw the Ger-

On the night of June 21, 1932, Sharkey (*right, above*) and Schmeling met in a return championship bout, in which Sharkey won the decision and title, in 15 rounds. The fight was not exciting, both men depending on left hand jabs throughout. Most of the sportswriters decided in Schmeling's favor. However, the championship was back in America, at least for a whiile. The third man in the ring is former heavyweight Gunboat Smith, a good referee.

Schmeling's next fight, after losing the title to Sharkey, was a sensational battle with Mickey Walker, slated for 10 rounds. In the eighth round, Schmeling had Walker badly cut and bleeding. After flooring him with a powerful right, Schmeling pleaded (*right*) to referee Denning to stop the fight, which he did.

man vanquish his rival in Schmeling's greatest fight since coming to America.

The last round was one of three minutes of action. Floored in the opening frame, Mickey shaded Max in the second and at the end of the seventh was leading four rounds to three. Then came the turn. Max battered

Walker's body and face until Mickey was helpless. A powerful right dropped him. He was bleeding from mouth, nose, and cuts over his face, and one eye was closed. Referee Denning stopped the bout.

The following June, in another thriller, Max Baer halted Schmeling

Several times in his first fight with Schmeling, Louis, befuddled, struck his opponent low and after the bell. Here Referee Arthur Donovan warns the Brown Bomber. 39,878 persons saw the bout and the paid attendance was $547,531. Both fighters received the same amount, $125,535, which was 30 per cent of the net. Louis, a hot favorite, cost his backers heavily when he was knocked out.

in the tenth round in the Yankee Stadium and that was followed by a loss in twelve to Steve Hamas, former four-letter man at Penn State University. Max then went home, drew with Paulino in Barcelona in twelve rounds, stopped Walter Neusel in eight, Steve Hamas in a return bout in nine, and Paulino again in twelve, and now came back to America for another campaign.

Joe Louis was now coming along as

a threat to the heavyweights and Mike Jacobs was priming him for a title shot. Believing that Max was ready to be taken into camp by Joe, he arranged to have them meet in the Yankee Stadium on June 19, 1936. To the surprise of all, Schmeling gave his greatest performance in knocking out the Brown Bomber in the twelfth round, a triumph that put Max back into the championship picture as the outstanding challenger.

The left side of Louis' face was so swollen that it appeared he had a double cheek. He was staggered often and received severe punishment. His left eye was completely closed and his lips were bleeding.

Max scored his first knockdown in the fourth round and henceforth, a more determined Schmeling never faced an opponent. When the fight ended, Louis was resting in a praying position supported by the ropes.

The dramatic finish of the first Louis-Schmeling fight. Louis (*left*) stands groggy and helpless; a powerful right lands on his jaw; and he drops to a praying position. It was a stunning blow to the reputation of the Brown Bomber, who had been touted as invincible. (*Below*) Trainer Max Machon (*left*) and second escort Schmeling to his corner in glee. Manager Joe Jacobs is at right.

Now Schmeling pleaded for another chance at the championship, but complications arose that paved the way for Louis to obtain the lucrative bout.

After Schmeling had lost the title to Sharkey, the latter, in an unsatisfactory affair that created considerable discussion, dropped the championship to "Satchel Feet" Primo Carnera of Italy. The Italian, a crude heavyweight who lacked both science and hitting power, stopped the Boston Gob on June 29, 1933, in the Garden Bowl in the sixth round.

Following that victory he went back home and in Rome he outpointed Paulino Uzcudun in fifteen rounds, then trimmed Tommy Loughran in Miami in a bout of fifteen rounds in which he had a weight advantage of eighty-six pounds. But on June 14, 1934, he was shorn of his crown by Max Baer of Livermore, California. The bout was staged in the Garden Bowl.

The "Comedy Battle" it has been dubbed, because there were many knockdowns and tumbles. Baer dropped the Italian Goliath eleven times before the bout was halted.

Baer, known as the "Merry Madcap" for his eccentricities, was a playboy, like Harry Greb, who paid little attention to training, and his tenure as world title holder lasted only one year. He had an excellent record, but success doomed him and he fell prey in his first and only championship defense to the cleverness of James J. Braddock, who came off the relief rolls to gain a place in the Fistic Hall of Fame.

Baer continued to ply his trade for several years, during which he faced the cream of the division, among them Joe Louis, who stopped him; Tommy Farr, who beat him in London, Eng-

Primo Carnera (above), the Italian giant who was dubbed "Satchel Feet," was one of the poorest of all heavyweight title holders. He was a crude fighter with little skill. (Left) A knockdown in the Carnera-Sharkey fight, in which Sharkey lost his title by a knockout in the sixth round at Madison Square Garden's Bowl.

Clever, hard-hitting Ernie Schaaf, a young heavyweight title contender, was knocked out by Primo Carnera at Madison Square Garden, on February 10, 1933. Schaaf went down from a light blow in the 13th round and was rushed *(above)* to a hospital, where he lingered a few days, then died as the result of a brain injury. It was believed that Schaaf entered the ring concealing an injury sustained in an earlier bout with Max Baer. Ernie, 25 when tragedy struck, was born in Elizabeth, New Jersey.

Max Baer *(right)* over six feet tall and weighing 195 pounds, had the finest physical equipment a ringman could want. He had massive shoulders, long and supple muscular arms, slim waist, strong legs, and a deadly right hand. Unfortunately, he never took boxing seriously, always clowning and depending upon his right hand to end matters. In his fight with Carnera for the title Max swang the huge champion in the clinches and knocked him down 11 times, joining him on the canvas once *(below)*. Greatness might have been his, had he learned to box and set up a defense.

Max Baer fought Lou Nova twice and was stopped both times. On June 1, 1939, Nova cornered Max in the 11th round and when a straight left struck Max on the throat (left) he staggered back, gasping for air. A this point the referee stopped the fight. On April 4, 1941, Baer took another shellacking (below) from Nova and was halted in eight rounds. After this fight, Baer retired from the ring.

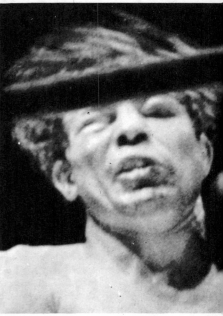

land; Lou Nova, by whom he was knocked out twice, and Two-Ton Galento, who was halted in eight. Each was a sensational affair, thanks to the showmanship of Max. He retired in 1942 when he enlisted in the U. S. Army.

Braddock, the "Cinderella Man," born in New York on December 6, 1905, fought as a light heavyweight for a number of years with ordinary success. His triumph over Baer was one of the biggest upsets in the history of the division. He fought Tommy Loughran for the light heavyweight title on July 18, 1929, and lost in fifteen rounds. Thereafter he dropped decisions to such top men as Leo Lomski, Maxie Rosenbloom, Yale Okun, Babe Hunt, Ernie Schaaf, Al Gainer, Tony Shucco, and Lou Scozza, who knocked him out.

But with talent scarce at the time the Garden was seeking an opponent for Baer, Braddock came out of retirement to stop Corn Griffin in three

Jimmy Braddock did the unexpected when he knocked out Tuffy Griffiths on November 30, 1928. He hit the downgrade afterwards, until he made his new start in a comeback.

Braddock, the "Cinderella Man," as he looked when he recorded the upset of the year, June 13, 1935, when he gained the decision over Max Baer at the Garden Bowl in a bout that went the limit of 15 rounds. Jimmy, in contrast to the man whom he dethroned, was a serious fighter that day as can be seen in the lower photograph, in which he is ready to crash his right into Baer's jaw. Throughout the fight Baer clowned, to the astonishment of a large crowd.

rounds on the Baer-Carnera card and then whipped Art Lasky in fifteen rounds. Those victories, especially the last named, since Art was being groomed for the title shot, put Braddock in line for the bout that gained him the world championship. The "Cinderella Man" he was called thereafter.

Now came an historic turn in boxing. The Garden Corporation had a contract with Schmeling to fight Braddock for the championship, but Mike Jacobs, who owned the Twentieth Century Club, a Garden rival, had the biggest attraction in America in Joe Louis, the young Detroit Bomber who, after an unsullied record studded with knockouts, had been stopped by Schmeling. It was Jacobs' intention to keep Louis in the headlines by matching him with Braddock. So good was the inducement that Braddock turned against the Garden and accepted Jacobs' offer. The agreement called for the champion to receive his percentage of the gate in

Jim Braddock, the guy who kept trying, who couldn't be discouraged, even against all odds, has his hands raised (above, left) in token of victory over Max Baer and is declared the new heavyweight champion of the world. In the press room of the Twentieth Century Boxing Club (left), in the old Hippodrome, Braddock is in discussion with (left to right) Walter Stewart, now sports editor of the Memphis Commercial Appeal, Lester Scott, trainer Doc Casey, Tommy Farr and a sports writer from Europe. (Above) Braddock, battered by Joe Louis, went out like a champ, in eight rounds, on June 22, 1937, in Chicago.

addition to ten percent of Jacobs' share of all Louis' championship fights should he gain the crown.

Despite protests by Schmeling and his country, he was shunted to the sidelines and the Braddock-Louis bout took place in Chicago on June 22, 1937, with Louis a winner by a knockout. Braddock dropped the Bomber in the opening round but Louis stopped him in the eighth and carried off the world championship.

Jimmy engaged in only one more bout after that, whipping Tommy Farr in ten rounds. He then retired and became a captain in the U. S. Army during World War Two.

In the Chicago contest, Braddock was on his feet until his brain was numbed by a right hand wallop, his eyes were dimmed and his body paralyzed from the vicious attack of the Brown Bomber. Jimmy went down a fighting champion.

Braddock won 51 of 85 career bouts, 26 by KO. Born December 6, 1905, Jimmy died of a heart attack on November 24, 1974, at North Bergen, N.J.

Battered and bruised, lips badly cut, a severed artery bringing forth the claret in spurts, face cut into crimson ribbons, one eye closed and the other puffed, but game to the very last, Braddock lay unconscious on the rosin-covered canvas, a champion shorn of his crown. He fell like a poled ox, while the spectators, intense with excitement, looked on in awe.

For Louis it was the kind of finish that adds to ring romance. The blasting right that landed with a thud against Braddock's chin in the fatal round, turned the trick for the newly crowned king. The end came in 1.10 of the eighth round.

ERA OF THE BROWN BOMBER

Joe Louis was one of the greatest and most colorful boxers in modern fisticuffs. Only Dempsey since the gloves era got under way and Sullivan in the bare knuckle and skin-tight gloves periods compared to him in popularity and ability. This Alabama-born boxer who first saw the light of day on May 13, 1914, and whose father, "Mun" Barrow, was a cotton picker, was a pugilistic symphony with a tempo geared to bring him across the ring with all the grace of a gazelle and the cold fury of an enraged mountain lion. He combined excellent harmony of movement with crushing power stored in each hand.

His career was one that won't be

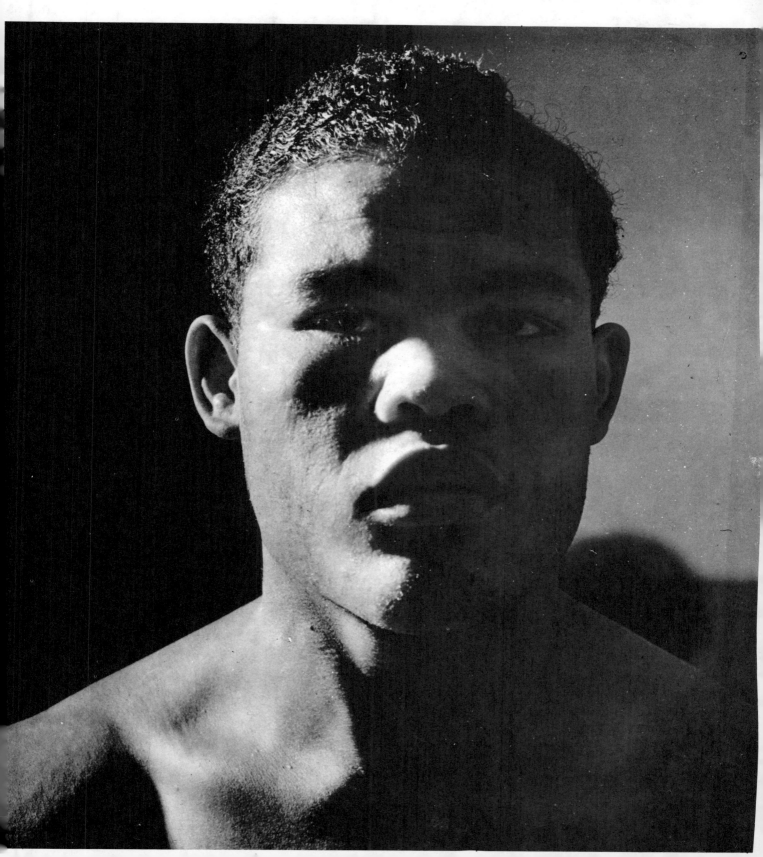

Mike Jacobs and Joe Louis leave Yankee Stadium after Joe's knockout of Schmeling. Jacobs promoted all of Joe's major fights after 1935. Louis' gross earnings in all fields, including his final bout with Rocky Marciano, amounted to $4,626,721.

forgotten in a hurry. The Brown Bomber did everything expected of a champion. He pulverized, paralyzed, or poked his way beyond a larger number of challengers than any heavyweight king who wore the Royal Robe before him.

He lacked the technique of the masterful Johnson, the powerful offense of Jeffries from a crouching position, the sinking body clouts of Freckled Bob Fitzsimmons, the beautiful ring science of Jim Corbett and the speed of Dempsey in carrying the fight to an opponent. But he combined a good portion of each of the assets of these great ringmen in addition to a mighty punch to roll up the largest string of successes ever attained by a heavyweight champion. Long before he retired, the Bomber's place among ring immortals had become a topic of world-wide discussion.

Louis brought back to boxing life and color that was sadly needed, and when he had no more worlds to conquer he retired.

In his rise to fame he faced the good and mediocre, and in his entire career he lost only three contests: his knockout by Schmeling before he became a title holder, and his loss to Ezzard Charles and knockout by Rocky Marciano after he made his comeback attempt.

Louis started his professional career following his defeat by Max Marek in the finals of the national amateur championships. Henceforth he was to make a steady rise until he gained the top rung of the ladder.

Prior to the knockout he had suffered at the hands of Schmeling, he had won twenty-seven consecutive bouts, all except four by knockouts. Among his victims were many of the better class heavyweights, including Stanley Poreda, Charley Massera, Patsy Perroni, Natie Brown, Roy Lazer, Roscoe Toles, and Hans Birkie.

Then those who had launched his professional career—John Roxborough and Julian Black—aided by Mike Jacobs, who promoted all of his major fights after March 28, 1935, when Joe had won the decision over Brown in

Joe Louis knocked out three former heavyweight champions before winning the title from Braddock. He knocked out game but ineffectual Jack Sharkey in three rounds on August 17, 1936.

Louis knocked out Max Baer in four rounds on September 24, 1935. Max made only token attempts at fighting back and, absorbed a great number of Louis' punches before succumbing.

Detroit, figured that the Bomber was ready for the top men of his division. In successive bouts, Joe knocked out Primo Carnera, in six rounds; King Levinsky in one; Max Baer in four; Paulino Uzcudun in four; and Charley Retzlaff in one. Then came the only setback he suffered during his pre-championship and championship day, the knockout by Schmeling.

So thorough and masterly a job did the Uhlan perform, that the thousands who had come in expectation of seeing the Brown Bomber put another opponent to sleep because of his supposed invincibility sat dumfounded watching the so-called Executioner executed. Not since the day when the great John L. Sullivan was dethroned by James J. Corbett had such a jolt been meted out to the fight public. The "Superman of Boxing" was a pathetic figure as he sat in his corner, first aid administered to him by his trainer Jack Blackburn and his man-

agers after the fatal ten had been counted over him. Face puffed, mouse under his eye, thumbs sprained, he looked nothing like the man who had been mowing down opponent after opponent.

When the fight was over, Joe's mind was set on only one thing—revenge. He quickly decided on plans to prepare himself for a return bout and Mike Jacobs arranged for his comeback with the aim of building him up for a title bout.

Jack Sharkey was his first victim. He went out in three rounds. The murderous fists of the Brown Bomber worked beautifully that night. Next came Al Ettore of Philadelphia. He lasted through part of the fifth session. Jorge Brescia went out in three, Eddie Simms in one, and Steve Ketchell in two.

The start was most satisfactory. Joe's handlers and Jacobs were delighted with his comeback. Uncle

Primo Carnera, completely outclassed, took an unmerciful beating, lasting six rounds with Joe Louis, on June 25, 1935.

Prior to winning the title, Louis won a 10-round decision over Bob Pastor (*right*), shown waiting for the verdict. Tommy Farr (*above*, *left*), a tough Welshman, lost a fifteen round decision to Louis, in Louis' first defense of his crown. Farr put up a game, tough fight, making his American debut before 32,000 fans in New York.

Trainer Jack Blackburn laces Louis' gloves, while the champ sits calmly in his corner before his second meeting with Schmeling.

Smiling Max Schmeling sits in the opposite corner, looking confident, as he waits to be introduced to a crowd of 70,000.

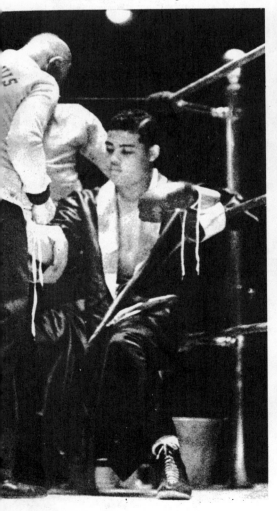

Mike then matched Joe with Bob Pastor of New York, who temporarily halted the steady stream of kayoes by lasting ten rounds of what the scribes termed a running match. Bob back-pedalled throughout the ten frames.

Another knockout of Natie Brown followed, and in the next session, Louis defeated Braddock to win the world crown. The goal of his ambition had been reached but what he wanted most, next to that, was to avenge his knockout by Schmeling. He sought a quick return bout and this he received after he had outpointed Tommy Farr of Wales in an international championship bout.

Tommy gave an excellent performance against the Bomber, and those among his countrymen who saw the affair both at the ringside and in the movies were strongly of the opinion that Farr had won. But the majority of the scribes and the judges thought otherwise and correctly so, for Louis, despite the aggressiveness of Tommy, tossed leather at a steady gait in the majority of the rounds. His effectiveness was far superior to that of the

A scared Schmeling faced Louis in their second bout. In this fight the Brown Bomber went all out from the start to avenge the knockout he had suffered previously. As Louis kept tossing rights, Max twisted his body and took the punches on his side. After the fight he declared he had been fouled.

Welshman. It was a stirring bout and an excellent final tuneup for Louis.

His triumph over Schmeling followed. He scored the second quickest knockout in the history of the heavyweight championship bouts, 2:04 of the opening round, and in accom-plishing this wonderful feat he handed Schmeling a terrible beating. Joe collected $349,288.40, an average of $2,832 per second, the record up to that time in any championship fight.

The fists of the Bomber crushed his former conqueror in a manner that left no doubt about his superiority. Though Schmeling complained bitterly about being struck foul kidney punches, every blow was a fair one. Any that struck Max in the kidneys were caused by the twisting of Schmeling's body as he held on to the

A right that landed with a thud caused Schmeling to reel, topple on his side, roll over and land on all fours, from which position Referee Donovan counted him out. Though Max Machen, who seconded Max, tossed in the towel, under New York rules this was not permitted and Referee Donovan hurled it out of the ring. It landed on the upper strand where it remained until the count on Schmeling had been completed.

upper strand and tried desperately to avoid the vicious attack of his opponent. The first two punches, powerful left hooks, started Schmeling on his downfall. Once Louis got the range, he kept up a steady bombardment until Max had been halted.

The first knockdown followed a right to the chin. The German fell on his shoulder and rolled over twice before coming to a rest with his feet in the air. Louis did most of his attack with his right. Nine such blows landed with accuracy in the first minute. Max was down twice more. The second time, after a count of two, he got to his feet, a powerful right crashed against his jaw and Max went down on all fours. He tried to straighten himself to rise, but while in the process, his chief second, Max Machon tossed in the towel. Since this is not permitted under New York rules, Arthur Donovan, the referee, hurled it back, took a good look at Schmeling, and as Timekeeper Eddie Joseph had reached eight, Donovan halted the bout.

The King had proved his right to the throne.

With that great victory, a series of contests was arranged for Louis before his enlistment in the Army, in which he tackled all comers in what became known as the "Bum of the Month" battles. Louis disposed of John Henry Lewis, Jack Roper, Tony Galento, and Bob Pastor in 1939, all by knockouts. Galento floored him but suffered a severe shellacking.

Louis started the next year with a discouraging affair with Arturo Godoy of Chile, who lasted the fifteen rounds as a result of unorthodox tactics, but later Joe got even with him by stopping him in a return engagement after first halting Johnny Paycheck. A kayo over Al McCoy ended that year's campaign.

His biggest successes were registered in 1941 when Red Burman, Gus Dorazio, Abe Simon, Tony Musto, Buddy Baer, Billy Conn, and Lou Nova were taken into camp. The Simon bout in Detroit, as well as that with Pastor two years previous, was scheduled for twenty rounds but

Four months after Joe Louis won a 15-round decision over Arturo Godoy of Chile, they met again and Louis won in eight rounds, when the bout was stopped. Godoy, angered at the referee, refused to go to his corner insisting he be allowed to continue. Louis got protection from trainer Jack Blackburn (left) and manager Julian Black.

Lou Nova is helped to his corner by manager Ray Carlin, Dr. William Walker and his second, Ray Arcel, after being knocked out by Joe Louis. Nova, who practiced Yoga for this fight, was an easy six-round victim for the champion.

133

"Did you ever see a ghost walking? I did." That's what one reporter wrote following the two-round knockout of an outclassed Johnny Paychek by Joe Louis.

Abe Simon (*left*) went thirteen rounds with Joe Louis before being stopped in 1941. Abe convinced his manager, Jimmy Johnston (*right*), that he would win the title in a re-match. Simons, a huge, 255-pound heavyweight, met the Brown Bomber—who was outweighed by 48 pounds—again, on March 27, 1942 and was knocked out in six rounds. Louis donated his purse to Army and Navy relief. Abe was a very successful actor on stage and television. He died of a heart attack on February 7, 1970, at New Paltz, N.Y., at the age of 56.

Buddy Baer knocked the Brown Bomber through the ropes in the first round of their bout on May 23, 1941. When Buddy refused to come out for the seventh round, the fight was awarded to Louis. Baer claimed he was hit after the bell sounded ending the sixth round and Louis should have been disqualified. They met again on January 9, 1942, and Louis knocked Buddy out in one round and donated his purse to the Naval Relief Fund.

neither went the distance. Simon was knocked out in the thirteenth round and Pastor in the eleventh.

The bout with Baer resulted in Buddy's disqualification when he refused to come out for the seventh round, claiming a foul. He had put Joe through the ropes in the opening round of that mill. Buddy asserted that Joe had struck him after the bell had sounded ending the sixth round.

Joe's victory over Baer marked the champion's sixth outing in as many months. It had been a busy and wearying campaign of continuous training and fighting, but Louis wasn't prepared as yet to call it quits. He wanted to keep going.

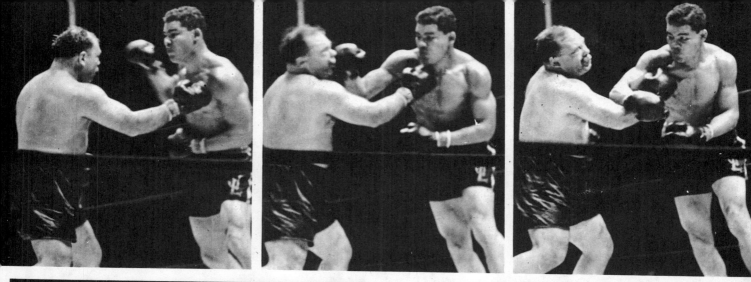

Tony Galento, a wild-swinging, rough and tumble ringman, possessed no talent other than hitting power. Though he took a severe shellacking from Louis in Yankee Stadium (top), where he was stopped in four rounds, Galento had the satisfaction of putting the Bomber on the canvas (above) with a round-house blow. Joe, surprised at finding himself on the deck, got to his feet and lambasted his rival, until referee Arthur Donovan stopped the fight. Galento's manager, Joe Jacobs and chief second Whitey Bimstein (right), after hauling the game, but badly beaten, challenger to his corner, worked feverishly to get Tony in condition so that he could leave the ring.

Billy Conn, a brilliant light heavyweight champion, had been clamoring for a crack at Louis. Billy, a flashy boxer, had been enjoying consistent success against the bigger fellows, and a thirteen round kayo of Bob Pastor had convinced him of his ability to cope with Louis.

Louis wanted a June fight, and since Conn shaped up as the only possible opponent in sight, the match was arranged for the Polo Grounds.

The battle was to prove one of the most tumultuous of Louis' career, for Conn, outweighed more than twenty-five pounds and at further disadvantages in height and reach, came within the proverbial eyelash of dethroning Louis.

In this contest, the bludgeon was too much for the rapier. For the greater part of thirteen rounds, the beautiful jabbing, clever maneuvering of Conn gave him the advantage.

If Billy Conn had been more cautious when he faced Joe Louis in a title fight in 1941, he might have won the heavyweight crown. He was ahead on points going into the 13th round, then decided to slug it out with Louis, and was knocked out.

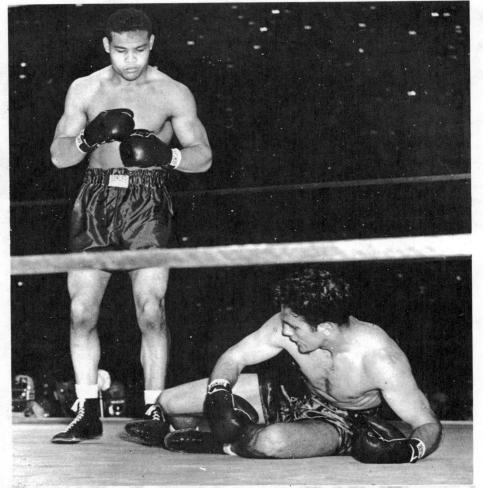

Then Billy, cocky, confident he was Louis' master, gambled a fortune on a knockout. He elected to trade punches with his heavy hitting rival and with only two seconds more to go before the bell would end the thirteenth frame, he was counted out by Referee Eddie Joseph.

A finishing right from the Bomber's TNT fist rang down the curtain on the dazzling show. The game Pittsburgher was within grasp of the crown yet tossed it away by attempting to outslug Joe at a time when the champion was a bewildered title holder and not too steady. From the eleventh through to the finish, Conn had suddenly turned aggressor and handed the champion a sound thrashing, much to the amazement of 54,487 fans who rocked the stands with their enthusiasm.

Overconfidence caused Billy's downfall. They were slugging it out, Billy with a grin on his face and Joe with a look of bewilderment, when Louis landed a powerful left hook to the jaw. He followed that with even a harder right and Conn was in a state of collapse. He had little left after that but courage as Louis battered his body with lefts and rights until the finishing right hand wallop came with only seconds more to go.

Billy Conn came nearest to defeating Louis. When he was halted by Joe, he was ahead on the cards of two of the officials. Judge Marty Monroe had the tally seven to four for Conn with one round even, Referee Eddie Joseph, seven to five for Billy. Judge Healy tabbed it six to six.

After enlisting in the U. S. Army, Louis went overseas on many exhibition tours. Before doing so he fought a return contest with Buddy Baer for the Naval Relief Fund and stopped Buddy in one round. He then tackled Simon in an Army Relief Fund bout and halted him in six.

When Louis and Conn were discharged from the Army, Mike Jacobs decided to match them in a repeater, figuring the public was ready, now that World War Two had ended, for a big time promotion in boxing. He was correct. With a ringside top of $100 for the first three rows, that bout, staged on June 18, 1946, at the Yankee Stadium, drew a paid attendance of 45,266 with a gross gate of $1,925,564, but the affair wasn't worth more than a $10 tops show.

From the standpoint of the fans, it was a flop, with little in it to arouse enthusiasm. It was one of the dullest in Joe's career, owing entirely to the tactics of Conn, who, fighting an entirely different battle from his first encounter with the Bomber, elected to back step. He took no chances.

Of the twenty-three minutes involved, more than three-quarters was packed with dullness and inaction. Conn offered the patrons nothing but flying feet and was knocked out in 2.19 of the eighth round. Louis couldn't catch up with Conn to make the bout interesting and Billy wouldn't mix it. It was inconceivable that these were the same two who had thrilled a vast gathering only five years before!

Up to seven rounds little had been

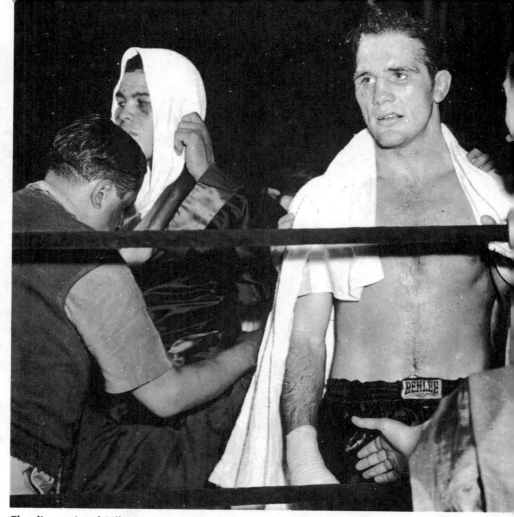

The disappointed Billy Conn (right) stands bewildered in his corner after being kayoed by Joe Louis, who nearly lost his title. After winning over Henry Cooper, J. T. Turner and Tony Zale in January and February of 1942, Conn entered the Army.

Joe Louis (center) and two buddies, in a U.S.O. canteen. Joe defended his title against Lou Nova in September of 1941, then joined Uncle Sam's Army. While in service, he twice defended his title and donated his purses to the Army and Navy Relief Funds.

Out of the Army after four years, Louis renewed his argument with Conn at Yankee Stadium on June 19, 1946. Conn also had put in four years of Army service, but hadn't retained as much of his former skill as had Louis. Joe had an easy time of it in the return bout; Conn offered feeble resistance and was knocked out in the eighth round of a slow, disappointing affair. The match attracted an attendance of 45,266 and the second highest gate of all time for boxing, $1,925,564.

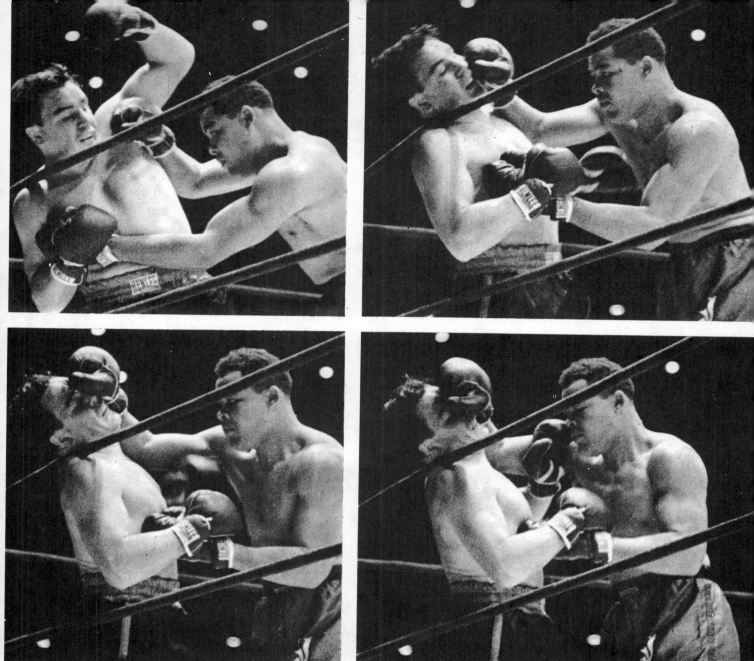

Louis' next title defense, also in Yankee Stadium, was on September 18, 1946, and it resulted in a quick victory over Tami Mauriello. At the opening bell Mauriello rushed out of his corner and nailed Louis with a right that staggered him and sent him reeling back into the ropes. An annoyed Louis smeared Tami's face, then cut loose with an attack that finished Tami in two minutes and nine seconds.

accomplished by either. Here and there a weak-hearted jab was tossed. Conn threw nothing that even looked like a punch. Louis tried, but his delivery was ineffective because of the roaming tactics employed by his opponent.

When Conn landed on the canvas he assumed exactly the same posture as did Jack Johnson in Havana—he shaded his eyes from the hot lights, as Johnson did from the sun, while being counted out.

The one round knockout of Tami Mauriello followed, a bout in which Tami came close to dropping the champion in the first half minute. But Louis, after being hurled almost across the ring with the blow, rushed into his opponent with a vicious attack and it soon was all over.

Then came a series of exhibitions before the Bomber accepted another title defense, this time against aged Joe Walcott of Camden, New Jersey. That historic battle in the Madison Square Garden Arena on December 5, 1947, almost saw the termination of Louis' long successes.

Louis retained his crown because

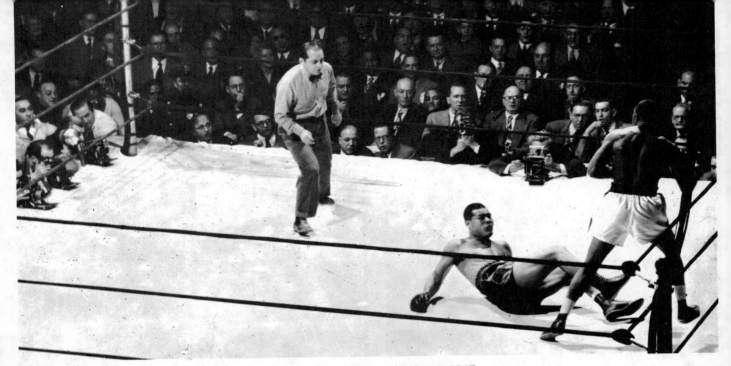

Despite easy victories over Conn and Mauriello it became evident on December 5, 1947, when Louis met Jersey Joe Walcott in Madison Square Garden, that advancing years and his long Army hitch had taken much of his former ring stuff away from the champion. Expected to be another easy victim, Walcott gave a surprising performance which included two knockdowns over Louis. A bruised, bleeding champion (below) received the decision in 15 rounds, but it aroused a storm of protest among many who felt Walcott had won.

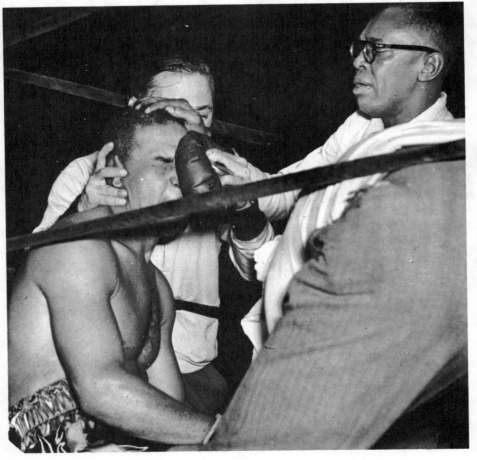

he received a split decision verdict, unpopular with the fans and scribes. Walcott lost his chance to take the crown through his back-pedalling. Never in the history of the division has a boxer won a championship running away without attempting a defensive counter-fire. Though Joe won the decision, he was nearer to dethronement than he ever had been through his ten years reign as world champion.

He was knocked down twice. The first occurred in the opening round for a count of two and the next in the fourth for a count of seven. The Brown Bomber was battered hard and bleeding. At times he looked foolish as he tried to catch up with his elusive target. His reflexes were bad and his defense poor. All that was revealed plainly to 18,194 persons who paid $216,477 to see the battle, which was considered so one-sided when it was arranged that the odds were 1 to 10.

Referee Ruby Goldstein saw the challenger the victor, crediting Walcott with seven rounds to six with two even. Marty Monroe, one of the judges, gave the decision to Louis, nine to six, and Judge Frank Forbes called Louis the winner, eight to six and one even.

Walcott's finish in the second bout. The unpopular verdict in the first meeting resulted in a Louis-Walcott rematch on June 25, 1948, at Yankee Stadium. Dropping Louis again, Jersey Joe was ahead on points when the champion rallied in the 11th round for a knockout victory.

Left jabs and several hooks baffled Louis in the opening round and a solid, short right to the jaw dropped him. The fourth was not a minute old when Walcott crashed his right to the jaw, again toppling Louis in his tracks.

Not until the ninth round did Louis catch up with his foe. Like a maniac he went after Jersey Joe. Though the blows carried jarring force, Jersey Joe withstood them. From then on Walcott missed many roundhouse rights and kept racing madly away from Louis, only occasionally halting momentarily to toss effective jabs to the head. It was the sprinting tactics of Jersey Joe which cost him the fight.

In a return bout six months later, June 25, 1948, at the Yankee Stadium, 42,657 persons saw Louis decisively whip his tormentor by knocking Wal-cott out in the eleventh round. It was Joe's twenty-fifth and last title defense. Louis came back a long way to overcome a crafty antagonist who had baffled him for ten rounds, then crumbled to the canvas when the Bomber caught up with him.

Two minutes of the eleventh round had slipped away in a contest that had been quite tame and had drawn the boos of the crowd. Louis kept pressing, Walcott kept slipping aside, but the champion was in no mood to go through a repetition of their first encounter. Walcott was leading during the first two minutes of the round when his antagonist suddenly attacked with fury. Lefts and rights landed on Walcott's head, but he made the error of coming off the ropes to swap blows with the Bomber. Jersey Joe thought he had the fight cinched and there's where he erred.

Louis nailed him with a right after three beautiful straight lefts to head and face had numbed Walcott's brain. His legs were now rubbery. A right to the body and he dropped his guard. As he began to sag, a fast and furious barrage followed.

Louis went after the kill, backed his man against the ropes, pounded away with both fists and while Louis set himself for the knockout punch, Nature beat him to it. Walcott collapsed, rolled over on his back, struggled to his knees, and began to crawl as the eight and nine counts were recorded by Referee Frank Fullam. Jersey Joe was still down when the fatal ten was reached.

With that victory, Joe Louis made

141

James D. Norris (*left*) took over the boxing empire of the ailing Mike Jacobs in 1949, formed the International Boxing Club, and ushered in boxing's TV era, backed by John Reed Kilpatrick (*right*) chairman of the board of Madison Square Garden.

Former light heavyweight champion Gus Lesnevich (*left*) congratulates Charles after Ezzard knocked him out in the 7th round of their Yankee Stadium bout in 1947.

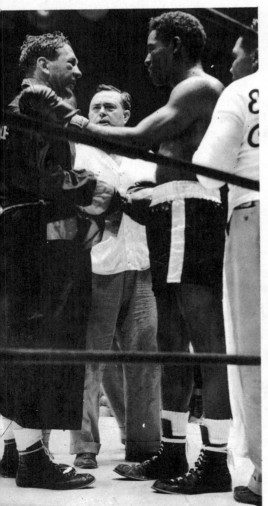

Louis (*right*) attempted a comeback on September 27, 1950, facing Charles in Yankee Stadium, but was badly beaten in his effort to regain the laurels. Charles was too young and too speedy for the faded veteran.

up his mind to quit. He went on another long exhibition tour and on March 1, 1949, he announced his retirement.

Louis requested that Ezzard Charles of Cincinnati, and Walcott, who hailed from Camden, New Jersey, fight for the right to succeed him, since they were the outstanding heavyweight contenders. In a contest in Chicago on June 22, 1949, Charles was returned the winner over his Jersey opponent in fifteen rounds.

The National Boxing Association accepted this as a world title match, but neither the European Federations nor the New York Commission acknowledged Charles as the new champion. To prove his right to the crown, he stopped Gus Lesnevich, former light heavyweight king and Pat Valentino of California, each in eight rounds. Then he added New York to his supporters by stopping Freddie Beshore in Buffalo in fourteen rounds.

Unlike Jack Dempsey, with whom Louis has frequently been compared, the Brown Bomber had a vulnerable chin. He couldn't take it as the Manassa Mauler could. That was evidenced by the number of times Louis was dropped to the canvas.

In addition to being floored twice by Jersey Joe Walcott, he was put down by Buddy Baer, Tony Galento, and Jimmy Braddock in championship contests, and by Max Schmeling twice before, and by Rocky Marciano after returning as champion.

He grossed $4,626,721.69 during his fighting career, yet following his retirement he owed more than a million dollars in taxes to the U. S. Government due to the loss of his fortune in poor investments and high living.

Louis was not the last of the champs in a million dollar gate promotion.

Louis' friends were now clamoring for him to return to the ring and attempt to regain the throne he had abdicated. He challenged Charles. The champ accepted and further clinched his claim to world laurels. He gained universal recognition as Joe's successor when he easily outpointed the Brown Bomber in fifteen rounds at Yankee Stadium.

142

The boxing writers estimated at least a million dollars in flesh was introduced to the fight fans, when former champion Ezzard Charles (left) and champion Jersey Joe Walcott, flanked Joe Louis, greatest of all champions since Dempsey. They were introduced to 61,370 fans, from the Polo Grounds ring on September 12, 1951, in ceremonies just before the start of the Ray Robinson-Randy Turpin title fight.

Knockouts of Nick Barrone in eleven rounds, Lee Oma in ten, a victory over Walcott in fifteen rounds in Detroit and one over Joey Maxim at the same distance, brought Charles into another engagement with Walcott. In that contest, staged in Pittsburgh, a new champion was crowned.

Jersey Joe surprisingly knocked out the defending title holder in the seventh round. In a return bout, Walcott, whose age at the time was officially listed at thirty-eight years, but who was reported to be close to forty-two, gained a points verdict in fifteen rounds, June 5, 1952, and three months later, September 23, the title changed hands to Rocky Marciano, the Brockton Blockbuster, who crashed a knockout blow to the chin of the champion.

Father Time caught up with Joe Walcott just as it seemed he would be acclaimed the "winner and still champion." One short, powerful right hand punch and age were sufficient to bring about his downfall. The manner in which Marciano ended the tough, brawling, furious battle in forty-three seconds of the thirteenth round was a reminder of the days

One of the big boxing surprises in the summer of 1951 was the knockout of Ezzard Charles by Jersey Joe Walcott, in Pittsburgh. This was their third in a series of title bouts and Charles, a 1 to 6 favorite, lost his crown in the seventh round.

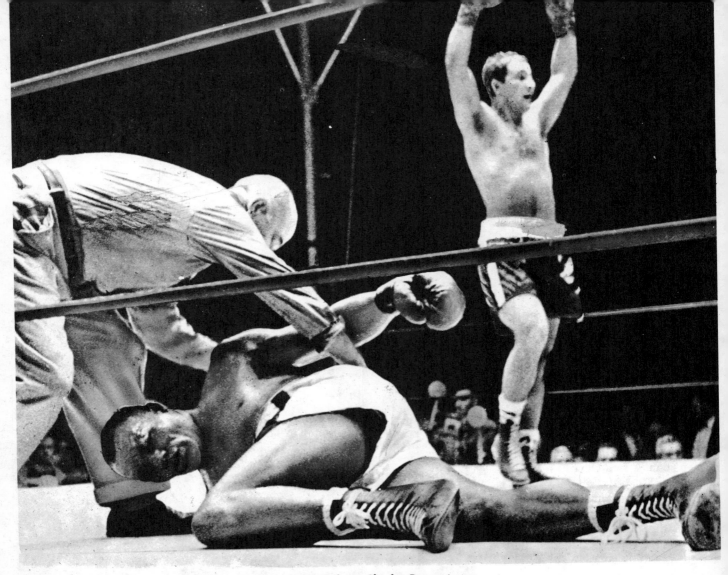

An elated Rocky Marciano lets out a whoop after seeing Referee Charles Daggert complete the count that gave the Brockton Blockbuster the championship. Daggert, with count completed, stoops to help the defeated title holder to his corner. But Jersey Joe was so helpless that his seconds and the medical advisor rushed to his aid. The kayo wallop was one of the hardest punches ever landed by Marciano.

when another New Englander, John L. Sullivan, ruled the roost by virtue of his mighty fists.

At the time of the knockout, according to the official tallies of the judges, there was only one way in which Rocky could win—via the knockout route. And he did it with one solid crash.

The ending was as unexpected as was the knockout of Ezzard Charles by the man whom Marciano had dethroned. The clout struck its mark with such suddenness and swiftness that many in the vast Municipal Stadium of Philadelphia didn't see it. But what they did see was old Jersey Joe sprawled against the ropes in a grotesque position, an inert mass.

Charley Goldman (above), a crack bantamweight in the early days, is the alert teacher and trainer who developed Rocky's technique. He changed Marciano's awkward stance and taught him proper balance, to get the most out of his punching power. Rocky's greatest disadvantage, was his 67-inch reach, shortest of all heavyweight champions. He often had to leap at his opponents to score (right).

Under the impact of the punch that made him helpless, Jersey Joe's body began to sink as he was resting against the ropes, then he slid down on his left side. Walcott's left hand grabbed instinctively at the middle strand as he went down on one knee. He slumped slowly forward and he landed on his head. His face was on the canvas as Referee Charley Daggert counted him out.

The new champion, a product of the Army and amateur ranks, born on September 1, 1923, takes his place like Louis and Dempsey, among the world's top clouters, a fighter with iron fists. He was the only heavyweight who went through a career without a loss. Starting as a profes-

When Joe Louis tried a comeback in 1951, he felt confident that he could put Rocky Marciano away as he had done so often with other opponents. Rocky surprised him by landing a haymaker in the eighth round. This bout set Marciano up for a title shot.

sional in 1947, he scored forty-nine victories, forty-two by knockouts, and retired undefeated.

It was not until he fought Roland LaStarza in 1950 and gained a disputed decision that he became a headliner. He continued his rise by shunting to the sidelines mediocre talent until the mid-summer of 1951, when his knockouts of Rex Layne in six rounds and Freddie Beshore in four brought him into the championship spotlight. He continued his rise by handing Louis a terrific beating, stopping the erstwhile Bomber in the eighth round, after which Lee Savold, Gino Buonvino, Bernie Reynolds, and Harry Matthews were put out of the picture. With those triumphs he was now ready for a shot at the world crown, which he won when he defeated Walcott.

Marciano defended his title six times. In his initial defense, a return

End of the trail for the Brown Bomber. After being knocked through the ropes, Louis made an attempt to fight back his rushing opponent, but Marciano, with the stakes high, didn't let Louis get away from him. He pounced on the former champ and soon had him helpless. Referee Ruby Goldstein stopped the fight. Note Joe's look as he is attended by Dr. Nardiello.

Harry Matthews came out of the West with an idea that he could check Marciano's rise toward a title shot. But Rocky knocked him out in the second round and his next bout was with Walcott for the championship. Matthews is resting comfortably in his corner.

Marciano found Walcott a much easier victim when they met again in Chicago on May 15, 1953. With Rocky's first offensive outburst, Jersey Joe was knocked to the canvas and counted out in two minutes, 25 seconds.

(*Below*) Outboxed for six rounds, Marciano's heavy guns eventually began to reach the target and clever Roland LaStarza (*right*) was battered into defeat in 11 rounds at the Polo Grounds, New York, on September 24, 1953.

First clash (*above*) of Marciano and Charles at Yankee Stadium on June 17, 1954, was one of history's most gruelling battles for the heavyweight championship. It was a savage give-and-take brawl with Marciano's youth and stamina deciding the issue. With blood streaming out of a gash above his left eye, Rocky staged a roaring finish to edge out a close decision. (*Below*) Charles was a disappointment in a return match in the same ring three months later. He seemed too scared to fight. Although he ripped Marciano's nose early in the bout, he devoted his time mainly to skittering around the ring, trying to avoid Marciano's punches. He was finally knocked out in the eighth round

bout, he knocked out Walcott in the opening round of a disappointing fight in Chicago. Four months later in New York he disposed of Roland LaStarza in the eleventh round.

The following year he fought two thrillers with Ezzard Charles. In the first, on June 16, 1954, at the Yankee Stadium, Rocky retained the throne, gaining the decision in fifteen rounds; and in the second, on September 17, in the same arena, Ezzard was knocked out in the eighth round. Each bout was replete with action and drama. The knockout was a stunner The power behind Rocky's punches was in evidence.

Then came the international championship mill in San Francisco where he easily stopped Don Cockell, British

After causing a sensation by knocking Marciano down early in bout, light heavyweight champion Archie Moore found Rocky's youth, strength and stamina too much for him, and he collapsed in his own corner in ninth round of a furious battle in Yankee Stadium on September 21, 1955. (*Below*) Marciano heads for opposite corner as the referee, Harry Kessler, begins the final count over Moore.

The first international heavyweight title fight since Louis defeated Farr found Don Cockell, British Empire champion, an easy mark for Rocky Marciano, who stopped him in the ninth round at San Francisco (1955). The Britisher walked into a buzz saw and was battered into helplessness. A Cockell handler is seen entering the ring to save Don, but the referee halted the one-sided bout.

Empire champion, in the ninth round and followed that with his farewell fight, a contest in New York in which he stopped Archie Moore, holder of the light heavyweight crown, in the same number of rounds. With that knockout ended the brilliant career of the Brockton Blockbuster. Only one other heavyweight king retired undefeated and made it stick, Gene Tunney.

His six title defenses netted Marciano purses totaling $1,462,961. With his pre-championship income and his side income following his rise to the top, his earnings were well beyond the $2,000,000 mark.

John L. Sullivan popularized boxing in the United States; James J. Corbett set the model for scientific boxing; Jack Dempsey set the record for the million dollar gate; Gene Tunney was the first to retire undefeated and remain so; Joe Louis established an all-time record for title defenses; and Rocky Marciano is hailed as the only heavyweight king who not only won every bout in which he engaged as a professional but hung up his gloves with that clean slate and stuck to his decision.

Marciano's retirement brought about a world elimination in which Archie Moore received a bye and Floyd Patterson and Tommy (Hurricane) Jackson entered the final elimination, with Floyd winning a twelve rounder on a split decision. He then tackled Moore in the Chi-

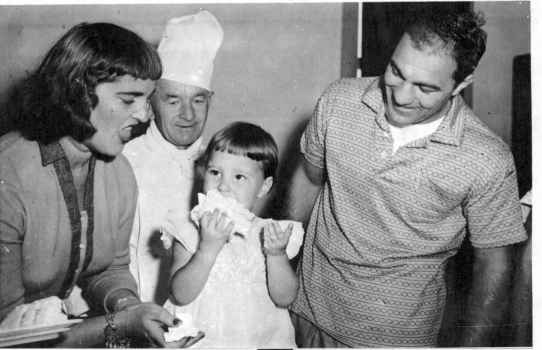

Under manager Al Weill's (*above*) piloting, Rocky rose to the top of the heavyweight division and divided a fortune with Weill. From 1947, when he began as an unknown preliminary boy, until he retired in 1955 as champion, Marciano's ring purses grossed $1,462,291. Undefeated in his career of 49 bouts, Rocky scored 43 knockouts, while six opponents went the route. Marciano, shown with wife Barbara and daughter Mary Ann, died in an airplane crash in Newton, Iowa, August 31, 1969, the day before his 46th birthday.

Floyd Patterson holding bouquet awarded him when he beat Vita of Roumania to win the Olympic middleweight championship.

Floyd Patterson, who on August 30, 1956, became the youngest world heavyweight champion, successor to the throne left vacant by Marciano, had his ups and downs as an amateur. In the Eastern Golden Gloves tourney he won a decision over Mike Zecca of the U. S. Marines in the eliminations. The next night he lay flat on his back (above) after being put to sleep in the quarter-finals by Charley Williams of Buffalo. In the picture below Patterson annexes the world title by halting Archie Moore in the fifth round.

cago Stadium on November 30, 1956, and in a surprising upset put Moore, the favorite, away in the fifth round to become Marciano's successor.

Born in Waco, North Carolina, on January 4, 1935, the former Olympic middleweight king who won his crown at the Helsinki Games in 1952, became the youngest professional ever to gain the top rung of the ladder. He is a fast moving, clever heavyweight with a snappy punch, though his blows lack the steam of those Louis, Marciano, and Dempsey could deliver.

He made his professional start after returning from his successful trip to Helsinki. His most important bouts prior to winning from Moore were those with Joey Maxim, in which the latter won an unpopular decision—

In his first title defense, Patterson *(above, left)* knocked out Hurricane Jackson. The eccentric Jackson lacked ability, but could absorb an enormous amount of punishment. Referee Ruby Goldstein stopped the bout when Jackson, dazed and helpless, was floored in the 10th round *(below)*. The New York boxing commission suspended Jackson's license to protect his future well-being.

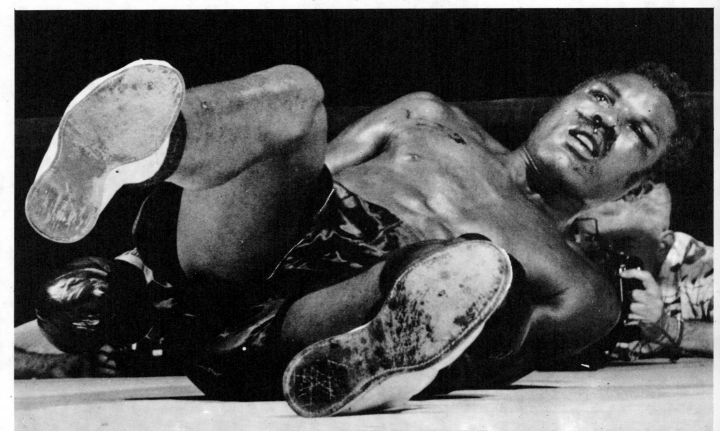

the lone loss suffered by Patterson; his knockouts of Jimmy Slade and Willie Troy; and his twelve rounds victory over Jackson.

In the fight with Moore, the panther-like son of a Brooklyn sanitation truck driver disposed of his opponent in 2.27 of the fifth round before a roaring gathering in the Chicago Stadium.

Patterson was piling up a lead on the official score cards against a wildly-missing Moore when he crashed home a terrific left hook to the jaw. The blow had a delayed action effect on the old warrior. He started to step forward then he spun and fell on his face. Moore barely beat the count of Referee Frank Sikora.

As Archie wobbled, Patterson finished him off with another powerful left, sinking him to his haunches. Moore started to pull himself up, and just as he was getting to his feet, Sikora had completed the count.

The attendance was 14,000, with gross receipts of only $228,145—far from the figures Joe Louis' bouts registered.

On July 29, 1957, at the New York Polo Grounds, Patterson engaged in his first championship defense. He defeated Tommy (Hurricane) Jackson.

In that contest, Patterson accomplished what had been expected. The 14,458 persons who paid $156,936 to see the affair witnessed a bout in which the defending title holder was never in danger. Referee Ruby Goldstein halted it in one minute and fifty-two seconds of the tenth round after a smashing left and right to the jaw had placed Jackson at the mercy of his opponent. Many protested the referee's action, but he was justified. Jackson was dropped in the first round as the bell sounded; went down for a count of two in the second, though the knockdown timer continued to toll off six; and was floored again in the ninth for a count of four.

It was the first independently promoted heavyweight championship bout in many years, with Emil Lence, a New York dress manufacturer, in-

Peter Rademacher, Olympic heavyweight king, the first amateur to challenge for the world professional crown, dropped Floyd Patterson in the second round at Seattle but thereafter took a shellacking. Patterson retained the title by a kayo in the sixth round.

stead of the International Boxing Club, in charge. Jackson received $61,929.81 for the lacing he took, and the champion, after agreeing to cut $50,000 off his guarantee to save Lence from losing heavily on the promotion, got $123,859.62.

Jackson started off well, but as the fight progressed, he couldn't defend himself. He absorbed terrific body clouts and many to the jaw. Though floored three times, he continued to display raw courage in his attempt to go the route.

Three days following that fight, Patterson went into training again, this time to face the world amateur champion, Peter Rademacher, Olympic title holder in the latter's debut as a professional, an unheard of procedure. Boxing commissions throughout the world appealed to both Gov-

ernor Rosselini of Washington and his commission to prevent the staging of the bout, but the appeal was vetoed. The fight took place on August 22, 1957 at Seattle and the amateur title holder was knocked out. Tommy Loughran, the referee, counted off the doleful decimal. The time was two minutes and fifty-seven seconds of the sixth round. Rademacher had been sent to the canvas seven times.

The Olympic champion surprised by not only remaining in action so long following the pre-fight predictions that he would be lucky to last two rounds, but winning the opening round and decking Patterson for a count of four in the second frame. Thereafter, however, he was never in the running.

Rademacher was down for nine in the third round, four times for nine

Pete Rademacher *(above, left)* won the 1956 Olympic heavyweight title on December 4, when he clobbered Russian L. Moukhine so fiercely in the first round that the referee stopped the bout. Rademacher was the first amateur champ to fight for the professional heavyweight title in his first bout. In the fifth round of his bout with Floyd Patterson, Pete *(above, right)* heard referee Tommy Loughran toll the count of nine for the fourth time, as Patterson stood in a neutral corner.

Roy Harris, dead game but badly outclassed in his title bout with champion Floyd Patterson, gasped for air as he took the count of nine on one knee *(below)* in the 12th round. Harris returned to his corner with his face a bloody mess from cuts and his legs on the verge of buckling from Floyd's body blows. The fight ended when Roy's seconds would not let him come out for the 13th round.

in the fifth and once prior to the final count in the sixth round. Four times Referee Loughran faltered at the count of nine when he could have counted Peter out.

The history-making fight, the first time an amateur fought a professional heavyweight champion for the crown, brought out a gathering of 16,961 persons for a record Northwest gate of $243,030 and a net of $209,556. Youth Unlimited which backed Rademacher, lost close to $120,000 on the promotion. Peter received nothing for his services while Patterson, guaranteed by his backer $250,000, received that amount.

Floyd Patterson made his second title defense in Los Angeles on August 18, 1958, against Roy Harris of Cut and Shoot, Texas. After being decked in the second round, he battered the Texan into submission. Referee Mushy Callahan halted the bout when Harris' trainer, Bill Gore, told him that Roy could not come out for the twelfth. Attendance was 21,680 and the gate amounted to $234,183. Another 196,-762 fans paid $763,437 to see the bout on closed-circuit TV. Harris, though game, was outclassed.

On the rainy evening of June 26, 1959, 18,215 fans at Yankee Stadium in New York watched 196-pound, 4-to-1 underdog Ingemar Johansson of Gothenburg, Sweden, win a knockout victory over 182-pound Floyd Patterson. Referee Ruby Goldstein halted the bout in 2:03 of the third round.

After two rounds of minor action, Johansson let loose a stunning right, his much vaunted "hammer of Thor,"

Floyd Patterson, an easy target, rubs his nose as Johannson's left is on its way to Patterson's head. Floyd, on all fours, suffered seven knockdowns before the end.

which sent Patterson reeling and flat on his back.

Six more times Patterson went down. When he staggered up after the seventh knockdown, Goldstein stopped the fight. By scoring seven knockdowns in one round, Johansson had equaled a heavyweight-title-fight record set by Jack Dempsey against Luis Firpo in 1923.

In terms of the live gate, the fight was a financial failure for promoter William Rosensohn, but it grossed more than $1 million in closed-circuit telecasts. This was the dawning of an age when money was to be made, not from the live audience, but from TV.

Johansson, born September 22, 1932, was lively, handsome, and gregarious, with a lust for life that he shared with his lovely fiancée, Birgit Lundgren.

A many-sided man, Johansson showed ability not only as a sportsman, but also as a singer, actor, and businessman who made a sizable fortune outside the ring.

Having won the International Golden Gloves in 1951, and eighty of his eighty-nine amateur matches, he went on to participate in the 1952 Olympic finals in Helsinki, but was disqualified for "not trying" in his fight with Ed Sanders of the United States.

From the time he turned professional until his ascension to the heavyweight throne, Johansson scored

Ingemar Johannson stands over badly battered Floyd Patterson who is trying to regain feet as referee Ruby Goldstein rushes in. Johannson's victory was a stunning upset.

Floyd Patterson became the first man in ring history to regain the heavyweight title when he knocked out Ingemar Johansson in the fifth round of their return match. Arthur Mercante counts the Swede out. Floyd, humiliated in their first bout, was never better.

Referee Bill Regan signals that it's all ove for Ingemar in the rubber match with Floy at Miami Beach in 1961. Not too much wa heard from Johansson after this knockou

twenty-two straight victories, fourteen by kayos. Included in the string was the defeat of Franco Cavicchi, of Italy, in 1956, for the European heavyweight title.

When he fought Patterson the second time, at New York's Polo Grounds, on June 22, 1960, Johansson faced a man who was looking, not for revenge, but rather for personal redemption from the humiliation he had suffered in losing his title. A bigger, stronger, and restyled Patterson knocked out Johansson in 1:51 of the fifth round.

From the beginning, Patterson, weighing 190 pounds, was the aggressor, keeping the 194-pound defending champion off balance with left jabs and two-handed flurries. By the fourth round Johansson was standing off balance, with his feet wide apart, but he kept boxing himself out of serious trouble.

Forty-nine seconds into the fifth round Patterson landed a blazing left hook to the jaw that sent Johansson down for a count of nine. On his feet again, Johansson tried to keep going, but a barrage of lefts and rights and a final left hook caught Johansson's chin and knocked him cold.

A crowd of 31,892 who paid $824,-814 and a closed-circuit-TV audience of 500,000 who paid $2 million were witnesses while Patterson, by reclaiming the heavyweight crown, accomplished what other heavyweight champions had attempted and failed to do. *The Ring Boxing Encyclopedia* lists unsuccessful attempts by James J. Corbett, Bob Fitzsimmons, James J. Jeffries, Jack Dempsey, Max Schmeling, Joe Louis, Ezzard Charles, Jersey Joe Walcott, Ingemar Johansson, Sonny Liston.

A third Patterson-Johansson bout took place in Miami Beach on March 13, 1961. Patterson and Johansson were the heaviest in their careers at $194\frac{3}{4}$ and $206\frac{1}{2}$ respectively.

Patterson retained his title by knocking out Johansson in 2:25 of the sixth round with a sharp left, then an overhand chopping right that struck Johansson high on the side of his head. Johansson started to get to his feet, then pitched forward. He got up a split second after referee Bill Regan reached the count of ten. Films confirmed the referee's decision.

The fight was clumsily sporadic. What the crowd of 13,984 spectators saw was the bloody pounding of tw fighters out to annihilate each other

The scorecards of referee Bill Rega and judges Carl Gardner and Gu Jacobson all showed Patterson ahea in four of the five rounds before th knockout.

Johansson's boxing career wasn quite over. He won back the Euro pean heavyweight title on June 1 1962, by knocking out Dick Richard son. Then he retired in mid-1963 devote his full time to business.

Patterson's last successful defens of his crown was against the stron game, but woefully inexperience Tom McNeeley, December 4, 196 at Toronto. A crowd of 7,813 watche McNeeley hit the canvas ten time A left to the jaw ended the fiasco round four.

After two years of waiting in the number-one contender's spot, Charles (Sonny) Liston got his chance against Patterson September 25, 1962, in Chicago. At 212, he outweighed Patterson by 25 pounds and outreached him thirteen inches.

Sonny was in control from the beginning, pounding both hands to Patterson's body and jabbing accurately. The end came when the second of two powerful lefts decked Patterson in 2:06 of the first round. The 18,894 fans were stunned at the speed with which the bout ended. Liston had the honor of landing the third-fastest knockout in heavyweight history. The fastest was 1:28 credited to Tommy Burns in his match with Bill Squires, while Joe Louis scored the second-fastest when he dispatched Max Schmeling in 2:04 in their return bout.

Liston was born May 8, 1932, on a marginal farm in Arkansas, to a field hand. He was probably the most disliked heavyweight the United States had spawned since Jack Johnson won the title in 1919 and had the newspapers calling for a "white hope."

Reputedly one of twenty-five children, Liston ran away to St. Louis, where at the age of thirteen he joined a bad crowd that, in his words was "just always lookin' for trouble." After serving time in prison, he became associated with unsavory underworld characters. His 6-foot-1½-inch height, 220-pound weight, 17½-inch neck, 14-inch fists, an often sullen expression, and his checkered past all contributed to his being cast in the role of bad guy.

When Liston was eighteen, the Missouri penitentiary athletic director, Father Alous Stevens, encouraged Liston to take up boxing. Five years later, in 1953, he won the Golden Gloves. He turned pro shortly afterward.

On the way up, Liston fought thirty-four fights, knocking out twenty-

three opponents and losing only to Marty Marshall in an eight-round decision in 1954.

Patterson was given a rematch on July 22, 1963, at Convention Hall in Las Vegas, with the odds 5 to 1 against him. Again Liston outweighed his opponent 215½ to 194½, and again Patterson could do little to retaliate for the torrent of powerful blows Liston delivered. Counted out in 2:10

of the first round by referee Harry Krause, Patterson had landed only one substantial punch, a hard right to the jaw following his own first knockdown. Patterson was decked once more before the knockout, preceded by a flurry of rights and lefts to his head. Liston's left hook and crushing right to the ribs set Patterson up for a right and left that crumpled the ex-champ.

Charles (Sonny) Liston waited a long time for his shot at the title but it was well worth it as he dispatched Patterson in the first round at Chicago in 1962 (above), then repeated the act in Las Vegas the following June (below). The "Ugly Bear" as he was referred to by Cassius Clay, was thought to be practically invincible by most experts.

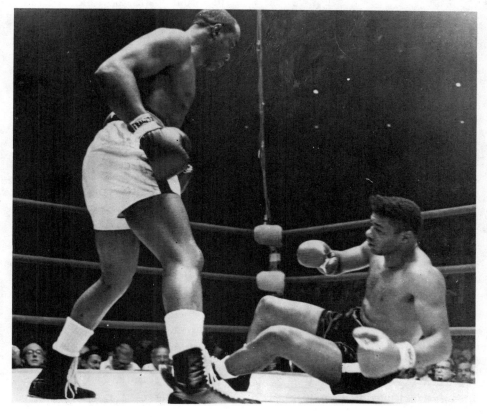

ALI, MASTER SHOWMAN

When loquacious Cassius Clay signed for a match with Liston, only three of the forty-six "experts" polled failed to pick Liston to be an easy winner over the "Louisville Lip," or "Mighty Mouth, as Clay was dubbed. His bravado made people overlook the fact that the Louisville, Kentucky, youth had fought his way up, starting boxing at the age of twelve. When he won the light-heavyweight championship at the 1960 Olympics in Rome, eighteen-year-old Clay had won 108 amateur bouts, including 6 Kentucky Golden Gloves titles and the 1969 International Golden Gloves heavyweight crown, while losing only 8 fights.

After Clay returned to Louisville, a syndicate of businessmen managed his pro career, and Angelo Dundee managed his training. Clay's gibes, poems, predictions, and antics mounted along with his pro victories, which numbered twenty by the time he entered the ring against Liston.

Clay had a genius for getting attention, and mass media made instant copy of his clowning and physical appeal. Color and excitement, which had been missing in boxing since the time of Jack Dempsey, returned.

Surprisingly, the Clay-Liston bout, on February 25, 1964, in Miami, was a financial fiasco for promoter Bill MacDonald, with a turnout of only 8,297. Even more surprisingly, Clay won the fight when Liston failed to answer the bell for the seventh round.

Clay charged out in the first round and failed to land any telling blows, although he demonstrated his speed in delivering quick jabs to Liston's head while dancing and moving away from Liston's vaunted left hook. Early in the third round, Clay opened a nasty gash under Liston's left eye, but the champion retaliated well enough in that round and the following one to keep the score fairly even.

The fifth round brought a dramatic turn as Clay stopped punching and kept moving away from Liston, claiming he couldn't see because of some foreign substance on Liston's gloves.

Clay balked at coming out for the sixth round because of blurred vision, but with the prodding of his second, Angelo Dundee, Clay answered the bell, recovered his vision, and fought a furious round that tired Liston badly.

As the seventh round was about to get underway, referee Barney Felix announced that Liston refused to continue, owing to eye cuts and an injury to his left shoulder. When the fight was stopped, the officials, Felix, and judges Bill Lovitt, and Gus Jacobsen, had scored the bout a draw.

Cassius Marcellus Clay, son of a sign painter, was born January 17, 1942, in Louisville, Kentucky. He decided early in life that he wanted to be both rich and heavyweight champion of the world.

At the age of twenty-one, Clay had obtained half of his dream, the heavyweight crown, as well as a new religion, Islamism, and a new name, Muhammad Ali. Shortly after his bout with Liston, Ali entered into the first round of what was to be a long-drawn-out battle with the United States armed forces after flunking two intelligence tests for the draft and being classified 1Y.

No title fight in any class ever stirred up so many questions, charges, suspicions, or angry reverberations as did Ali's 1:42 knockout of Liston in Lewiston, Maine, on May 25, 1965. Ali leaped out of his corner and

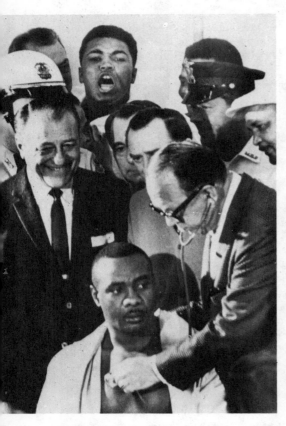

While Liston is being checked at the weigh-in for their bout in Miami Beach in 1964, Clay (rear) heckled the proceedings and continuously shouted at the champion.

Cassius Clay, later to become Muhammad Ali, becomes the new champion as referee Barney Felix declares the bout ended with Liston sitting on his stool claiming an injury

Clay seemingly taunts Liston as the latter sprawls on the canvas in the first round of a return match at Lewiston, Maine. In a most confusing ending, Liston was finally declared to have been stopped at 1:42, though referee Jersey Joe Walcott did not halt it until 2:12 upon hearing shouts from *Ring* editor Nat Fleischer that Liston was out.

immediately connected with a right and a left to Liston's head. Suddenly he landed a corkscrew right to the left side of the head, and Liston sagged to his knees, then rolled over onto his back. Liston struggled to get up but again fell on his back. Ali danced over to the fallen man, calling him names and telling him to get up and fight, ignoring the exhortations of referee Jersey Joe Walcott to go to a neutral corner.

The rules say that there can be no legal count over a fallen boxer, so long as the standing fighter refuses to go to a neutral corner; nevertheless, knockdown timekeeper Frank McDonough started counting when Liston hit the canvas. He eventually got as far as twenty-two before Liston lurched to his feet. Both fighters began to throw punches, and then referee Jersey Joe Walcott heard Nat Fleischer shout, "Joe, the fight is over!" Although Ali had not gone to a neutral corner, Walcott accepted the timekeeper's count, separated the men, and declared Ali the winner.

Aside from the controversial issue of whether the knockdown timekeeper calling a fight, experts argued whether the knockdown blow had really been hard enough to knock down the massive Liston. When films of the fight were examined, with watches synchronized to TV film frames, the velocity of Ali's punch remained unresolved. All that was proved was that Liston had hit the mat in 1:42 and that the referee had stopped the bout at 2:12.

Although Liston continued to fight, he was never again considered a major contender. Five years later, on January 5, 1971, his wife found him

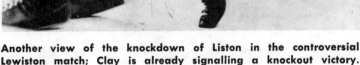
Another view of the knockdown of Liston in the controversial Lewiston match; Clay is already signalling a knockout victory.

Former champ Patterson takes a mandatory eight-count in the 6th round against Clay, who administered a frightful beating.

dead in his Las Vegas home. The circumstances surrounding his death remained mysterious, even sinister—a balloon of heroin was discovered in his kitchen at the time he was found.

On November 22, 1965, Patterson stepped into the ring with Ali in Las Vegas, hoping to win back the heavyweight title for a third time. Instead, the ex-champion received a merciless beating from a younger, taller, heavier, and sharper opponent. Ali, at 210 pounds, bewildered the 194-pound contender with left jabs and jolting rights to the body. The one-sided affair was halted at 2:18 of the twelfth round by referee Harry Krause.

Although 1966 was a successful year for Ali pugilistically, it opened by taking an emotional toll. Since becoming a Muslim he had become increasingly involved in his adopted religion. In January he divorced his wife, the former Sonji Roi, a model, because, he said, "she would not abide by the Muslim standards" by giving up her flashy dressing and makeup.

Then, in February, a reporter showed up at Ali's home to tell him that his local draft board had reclassified him 1A and that he could expect to be called up shortly. With what turned out to be unfortunate timing, the media picked up Ali's "I got no quarrel with them Vietcong," and a brushfire of "patriotic" reaction raced across the country, causing the cancellation of a proposed fight with Ernie Terrell.

Public sentiment drove Ali out of the country to seek matches on foreign soil for almost a year while he waited for a decision on his appeal for draft deferment as a conscientious objector and then as a Muslim minister.

Prior to his bout with Henry Cooper in London, Ali fought unpolished but lion-hearted George Chuvalo in Toronto on March 29, 1966. Chuvalo managed to stand up for the full fifteen rounds but the game Canadian took a terrible beating.

England welcomed Ali with open

George Chuvalo, the hard rock from Canada, went 15 rounds with Clay in 1966. He was never knocked down in his career.

arms since he offered Britain the possibility of regaining the heavyweight title lost back in 1898 by Bob Fitzsimmons. Accordingly, a sellout crowd paid $450,000 to watch 188-pound Cooper try to flatten 201¼-pound Ali with his powerful left hook. In June 1963, the Englishman had come close when he knocked Ali off his feet at the end of the fourth round, the bell just barely rescuing Ali. However, Cooper was stopped in round five when facial cuts made it too dangerous for him to continue.

On May 21, 1966, Cooper got a second chance, but his hope was quenched suddenly in the sixth round when Ali landed two swift punches to the head, opening up a deep, jagged wound over Cooper's left eye and sending cascades of blood down his face. Referee George Smith halted the fight.

Three months later, badly outclassed Brian London, at 200½ pounds, landed only two punches of minimal potency before Ali hit him with a right to the jaw in the third round, sending London down on his face. At the count of seven he raised himself partially, looked at referee Harry Gibbs, and went down again to be counted out as 11,000 fans booed their countryman.

Ali defended his title for the fourth time in five months when he met the 194½-pound champion of Europe, Karl Mildenberger, on September 10, 1966, in Frankfurt, Germany, before an audience of 45,000.

Ali toyed with the German until late in the fourth round, when the champion became angered after Mildenberger landed two jolting lefts to the liver and launched a two-fisted attack that drove Ali across the ring. Ali recovered and delivered a left-right combination that opened a gash over Mildenberger's right eye.

From the sixth round on, Ali battered Mildenberger, then stepped back occasionally to survey his handiwork.

Englishman Henry Cooper, who had put Clay on the deck in their first meeting in 1963, became a bloody mess during their second bout in 1966, stopped in the 5th round.

Another Englishman, lantern-jawed Brian London, soon became Clay's next victim, going out in three rounds. In an earlier title bout against Patterson, London was also stopped.

In what turned out to be one of the tougher fights of his career, Clay, by now known as Muhammad Ali, finally halted German southpaw Karl Mildenberger in the 12th round.

Tired and bloody, Mildenberger managed to come out for the twelfth round. After Ali backed the German into the ropes and belted him with a flurry of lefts and rights, referee Teddy Waltham stopped the bout.

"The Big Cat," Cleveland Williams, received a similar beating from Ali on November 14 that year, in Houston, Texas. Ali decked the 210½-pound challenger three times in the second round and once in the third before referee Harry Kessler stopped the fight.

Three months later, Ernie Terrell, weighing 212½, suffered the slow punishment and humiliation Ali had promised him for refusing to acknowledge the champion's adopted Muslim name. The fight went the full fifteen rounds, but Ali's superiority was obvious, and referee Kessler and judges Jimmy Webb and Ernie Taylor unanimously awarded thirteen rounds to the champion.

New York's Madison Square Garden drew a gate of $244,471 on March 22, 1967, as 13,780 fans watched thirty-four-year-old Zora Foley succumb to an extremely fast Ali in the seventh round.

Ali gave the first three rounds to his opponent as he danced around the ring. At the opening of the fourth round, chief second Angelo Dundee told Ali to "get going," at which point Ali showed what a breathtaking fighter he really was. Every punch he delivered was sharp and on target.

At the start of the seventh round, Ali maneuvered Foley into position. A short downward right, similar to the "phantom" punch that had decked Liston at Lewiston, downed Foley, and the fight was over.

While Ali was busy piling up victories, the U.S. government was reviewing and turning down Ali's request for a ministerial deferment.

On April 28, 1967, Ali was ordered to report to the Houston induction

In what was to be his final bout as champion before being stripped of his title by various boxing bodies, Clay administered the quietus to Zora Folley, counted out in 7th.

Many thought Cleveland Williams, the Big Cat, would give Clay a tough battle, but Cassius took care of him in three rounds, knocking down the challenger four times.

6'-6" Ernie Terrell, his left eye bandaged due to what he claimed was thumb-gouging by Clay, went 15 rounds with the champ in a one-sided bout, Clay winning 13 rounds.

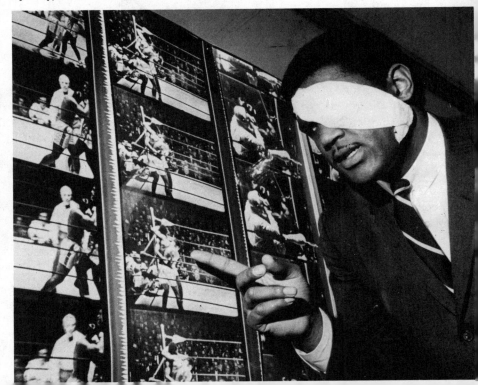

center. He reported but refused induction. On May 9, a federal grand jury indicted him on the charge of failing to submit to the draft. Within a few hours both the New York Boxing Commission and the World Boxing Association stripped Ali of his title and banned him from fighting anywhere in the United States.

Ali was tried on June 19 and 20 in the United States District Court for the Southern District of Texas, in Houston, presided over by Judge Joe Ingraham. With the judge's emphatic statement that the court was to consider only whether Ali had refused induction, not the fairness of the 1A classification or Ali's status as a Muslim, there was little surprise at the guilty verdict. What caused surprise was the maximum penalty of a five-year sentence and a $10,000 fine. Ali was released on bail, and his lawyer, Hayden C. Covington, of New York, filed an appeal. Meanwhile, Covington had also initiated a civil case questioning the legitimacy of the Louisville, Kentucky, and Houston draft boards because there were no blacks on either board.

Shortly thereafter, the Fifth Circuit Court of Appeals in New Orleans upheld the district court's verdict of guilty, and a further appeal was filed with the U.S. Supreme Court. On August 3 Judge Ingraham refused Ali's request for permission to travel to foreign countries to honor fight contracts. Ali was ordered to turn in his passport.

One bright light appeared for Ali. On August 17, he married seventeen-year-old Muslim Belinda Boyd.

While the case was pending in Supreme Court, the federal government disclosed that five telephone conversations involving Ali had been tapped by the F.B.I. The Supreme Court ordered the district court to reconsider the case, and on July 24, 1969, Judge Ingraham ruled that all five conversations were irrelevant to

Ali, his title taken away, was soon found guilty of refusing to be inducted. In photo above, Ali leaving court with attorney Hayden Covington (*center*) and Lt. Col. Edwin Mc-Kee, commanding officer at U.S. Army induction center. *Below*, Ali, holding pack of records, is interviewed at Houston Army center.

Obtaining a license in Georgia to return to ring action, Clay (*left*) stopped Jerry Quarry in three in Atlanta.

the conviction.

A year elapsed before the Fifth District Court of Appeals upheld the lower court's decision. During that time Ali had held a press conference —on February 3, 1970—to say emphatically that he would not enter the ring as a professional. He called Nat Loubet, editor of *Ring*, to inform him that he had quit boxing. At this time *The Ring* magazine acknowledged the vacancy the New York and World boxing associations had declared two years earlier.

Two years after Ali's match with Foley, he managed to get a license in Georgia to fight an eight-round exhibition against three minor heavyweights in September, and then to fight Jerry Quarry, whom he kayoed in three, on October 25 at Atlanta, Georgia.

A breakthrough occurred when Federal Court Judge Walter E. Mansfield nullified the New York Commission's refusal to give Ali a license, calling it "arbitrary and unreasonable action." Despite his insistence that he

Returning to a New York ring for the first time since stopping Folley, Ali scored a KO in the 15th round over Argentina's Oscar (Ringo) Bonavena, who was a tough hombre.

George Chuvalo's face was pounded into a bloody pulp by the up-and-coming Joe Frazier, 1964 Olympic gold medal winner, in July 1967, as Joe marched onward.

was through with professional boxing and no longer the title holder, on December 7, 1970, Ali met and kayoed Oscar Bonavena of Argentina in the fifteenth round in New York.

Finally, on June 28, 1971, the Supreme Court handed down its long-awaited ruling. The decision was eight to nothing in Ali's favor, with Justice Thurgood Marshall abstaining. Ali was back in the boxing game.

Nothing caused so great a muddle around the heavyweight title as had Ali's draft case. The W.B.A. had taken the title from him, and now it had to find a replacement. Three months later it sanctioned the organization of an eight-man elimination tourney headed by Mike Malitz's Sports Action, Inc., a New York-based firm, to determine who would take over Ali's "vacated" title.

The intent of the tourney was somewhat thwarted when officials of New York's Madison Square Garden arranged a bout between George Chuvalo, of Canada, and Joe Frazier, of Philadelphia, for July 19, 1967. Frazier knocked out Chuvalo in the fourth round, then refused to join the elimination group. The group consisted of Frazier, Thad Spencer, Ernie Terrell, Oscar Bonavena, Karl Mildenberger, Jimmy Ellis, Floyd Patterson, and Jerry Quarry.

In retaliation, the W.B.A. dropped Frazier from number one to number nine in its ratings, to enable Leotis Martin to get into the number-eight spot as Frazier's substitute.

The New York Boxing Commission further complicated matters by declaring that the winner of the W.B.A tourney would not be recognized unless that champion defeated Frazier

The round-robin began on August 5, 1967, with Spencer pitted against Terrell, and Ellis against Martin, in Houston, Texas. Spencer, from Portland, Oregon, won a twelve-round decision over Terrell, of Atlantic City New Jersey. On the same day and in the same arena, Ellis, from Louisville, kayoed the Philadelphian, Martin, in the ninth.

In Frankfurt, Germany, Bonavena beat Mildenberger in twelve rounds on September 16, 1967.

The final match in the first round was fought between Patterson and Quarry on October 28 in Quarry's home state, California. Quarry won a split decision in which referee Vern Bybee voted a draw while judges Lee

Grossman and Joey Lomas gave the fight to Quarry.

Now Mexico and Britain entered the picture. Mexico's governing body for boxing tried but failed to get Manuel Ramos placed in the W.B.A. listings. Ramos had stopped Terrell on October 14. Likewise, the British couldn't get Eduardo Corletti, victor over Johnny Prescott on October 17, into the tourney.

In the final round, on December 2,

1967, Ellis and Bonavena met in Louisville, Kentucky, where Ellis decked Bonavena twice and went on to win a unanimous decision in twelve rounds.

In Oakland, California, Quarry stopped 6-foot, 4-inch Spencer in the second semifinal, three seconds before the bell ended the twelve-round fight on February 3, 1968.

The final bout of the tournament took place on April 27, 1968, in Oak-

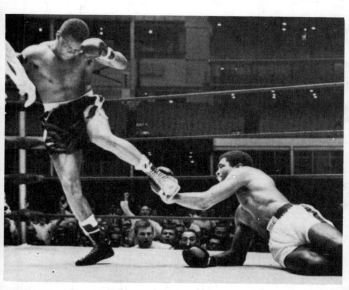

In a W.B.A.-staged tournament for the vacant crown held in 1967, Thad Spencer (*above, left*) easily defeated Ernie Terrell (*on floor*) at Houston. A bit later on, Floyd Patterson (*on canvas, above right*) dropped a split decision to Jerry Quarry in 12 rounds.

Quarry (*below, left*) gained the tournament final by halting Spencer in the 12th round at Oakland in early 1968. (*Below, right*), Jimmy Ellis, who was to go on to the final, disposes of Leotis Martin via a nine-round stoppage at Houston's Astrodome.

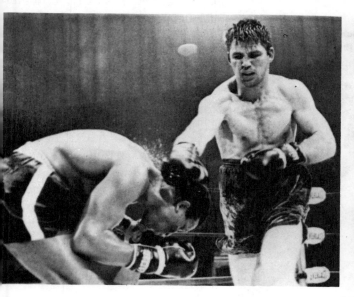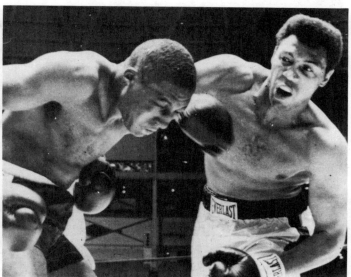

167

Quarry and Ellis met in the final of the W.B.A. tourney at Oakland. Jimmy (*above, right*) was given a split nod and lifted by handlers (*below*) after being awarded the partial title.

Joe Frazier's face is contorted after absorbing a blow from Oscar Bonavena during their first meeting in 1966. This was the first of Frazier's big wins on the road to the title.

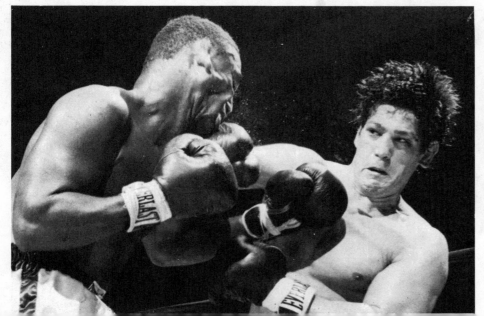

land, where the 197-pound Ellis won over the 195-pound Quarry in a fifteen-round split decision. The referee, Elmer Costa, and judge Fred Apostoli, the former middleweight champ, awarded the fight to Ellis, while judge Rudy Ortega scored the match a draw. The 11,356 fans brought a gate of $186,700.

Ellis was the W.B.A. champion, but the New York Boxing Commission announced that it would recognize the winner of the Joe Frazier–Buster Mathis bout as the new champion. Five state commissions, as well as those of Mexico and South America, followed New York's decision. Thus, when Frazier stopped Mathis in the eleventh round, New York, Maine, Pennsylvania, Texas, Massachusetts, and Illinois recognized Frazier as the champion while the others recognized Ellis.

The opposing powers were reconciled when Frazier stopped Ellis in the fifth round on February 16, 1970, at New York. The title, stripped from Ali, had finally been filled.

Joe Frazier, born in Laurel Bay, South Carolina, on January 12, 1944, was the youngest of thirteen children. He started his fistic career at age nine, when he rigged up a homemade punching bag of moss and leaves.

Twelve years later, after having married at sixteen, he moved to Philadelphia, where he won the Golden Gloves in 1962, 1963, and 1964 and won America's only gold medal in boxing at the Tokyo Olympics.

With a group of businessmen from Philadelphia, Cloverlay, Inc., as his sponsor, Frazier launched his professional career on August 16, 1965, with a one-round knockout over Woody Goss. He piled up ten straight kayos before meeting Oscar Bonavena on September 21, 1966.

Bonavena floored Frazier twice in the second round, but Frazier rallied to win a ten-round decision. After four more victories, three of which were kayos, Frazier was pitted against George Chuvalo on July 19, 1967. In the fourth round, the tough Canadian was knocked out for the first time in his fifteen-year career.

When Frazier fought Buster Mathis on March 4, 1968, he was determined to clear any hint of tarnish from his Olympic medal. (Before Frazier went to Tokyo, he had won thirty-eight of forty fights. His two losses had been to Mathis in the Olympic trials. When Mathis had broken a knuckle, Frazier had substituted.)

"Smokin' Joe" flattened Mathis with a left hook in 2:33 of the eleventh round.

Frazier became undisputed world champion on February 16, 1970, when the gong rang for the opening of the fifth round and the W.B.A.'s champion, Jimmy Ellis, couldn't come out.

After the first round, in which Ellis held a margin, Frazier dominated the match with a steady and relentless style of strong, heavy pressure. As the end of the fourth round approached, Frazier bombarded Ellis's body and head until the Kentuckian sank to the mat for a count of nine,

Frazier won recognition as champion in six states after halting hulking Buster Mathis on the opening card at the newly-built Madison Square Garden in March of 1968.

Frazier eyes Ellis after flooring him in the fourth round of their contest to determine an undisputed titleholder in February, 1970. Ellis was unable to answer fifth-round bell.

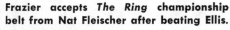

Frazier accepts *The Ring* championship belt from Nat Fleischer after beating Ellis.

169

In the most electrifying moment of their so-called "Fight of the Century" in 1971, Frazier sends Ali to the canvas in 15th round.

during which the bell rang. Raising himself at nine, Ellis managed to get to his corner. When the fifth-round gong sounded, manager Angelo Dundee motioned to referee Tony Perez that Ellis could not continue.

The first of three encounters with Ali took place on March 8, 1971, at Madison Square Garden before 20,445 fans plus 1.3 million watching closed-circuit theater TV. Ali, who described his own fighting style as "Float like a butterfly, sting like a bee," was slowed down by Frazier's constant pounding.

Ali's strategy was to let Frazier become arm weary while flicking tiring jabs at his opponent, but despite a 6½-inch disadvantage in reach, Frazier managed to get in under Ali's jab to land countless left hooks to the Muslim's body.

Frazier suffered a swollen jaw and lumps around both eyes, while Ali merely sported a hematoma on the

It happend in Chicago, but not as a result of the famous fire. Fans wrecked the Coliseum when closed-circuit showing of Ali-Frazier was cancelled due to projector failure.

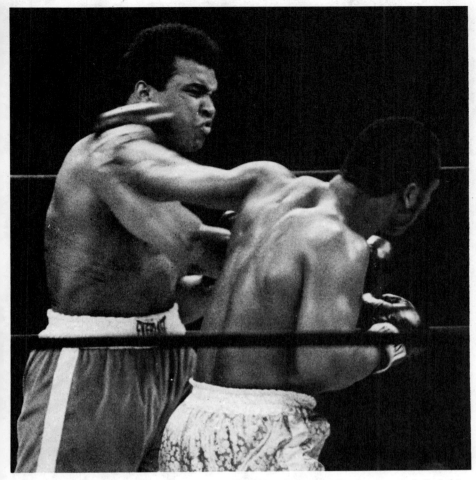

The ubiquitous Ali upstages television sports personality Howard Cosell, who has interviewed Muhammad on numerous occasions, sometimes with rather bizarre but entertaining results.

Good shot of famed Frazier left hook as it landed on Ali's jaw and felled him.

right side of his jaw. Frazier won unanimously, with referee Arthur Mercante giving him eight rounds, six to Ali, with one even. Judge Artie Aidala awarded nine to Frazier and six to Ali, and judge Bill Recht awarded eleven to Frazier and four to Ali.

The only knockdown occurred in the fifteenth round, when Ali was dropped for the third time in his career but bounced back after the mandatory eight count.

Before facing George Foreman, Frazier fought Terry Daniels in New Orleans on January 15, 1972, then Ron Stander, in Omaha, on May 25, 1972. The odds against his two opponents were 15 to 1 and 20 to 1 respectively. Daniels lasted four rounds; Stander, five.

On January 22, 1973, at Kingston, Jamaica, Frazier, a 3-1 favorite, was

Manager Yank Durham raises Frazier's arm in victory after decision over Ali was announced. It was unquestionably the high point of Joe's professional fistic career.

171

floored six times by Foreman before referee Arthur Mercante stopped the action at 1:35 of the second round before 36,000 fans.

Frazier pressed the attack, but was met by a challenger who moved not a step backward. A right to the jaw by Foreman achieved the first knockdown midway into the first round. Frazier got up, exchanged a few punches, and was down again from a series of rights to the head.

Again Frazier rose quickly, but obviously dazed, and was decked a third time as the bell ended the round. As set down by the rules, counting did not end with the bell, but was continued until Frazier struggled up at the count of three.

Frazier opened round two with a rushing attack and a left hook to the head, but it was a short rally. Foreman, who weighed 217 to Frazier's 214, sent the champion to the mat for the fourth time with a left-right to the jaw. Up at the count of two, Frazier was dropped by two left hooks. Again Frazier struggled up but then went down for the last time from a series of punches.

Frazier gamely got to his feet, but referee Arthur Mercante looked at his glazed eyes and reeling figure and signaled that there was a new champion.

Foreman had come a long way since his first bout January 26, 1967, in the Parks Diamond Belt Tournament, which was fought during the period in which he was being trained by the Job Corps.

"Doc" Broadus, Parks Job Corps Center vocational-guidance director, noticed Foreman's size and speed playing football and persuaded him to try his hand at boxing.

Born in Marshall, Texas, January 22, 1948, to a railroad construction worker, Foreman, fifth of seven children, spent most of his early youth in trouble. In his words, "You name it, I'd done it." He credits the Job Corps,

In a shocking development Frazier, the 1964 Olympic hero, was floored six times by the 1968 Olympic champion, George Foreman, in two rounds, being virtually demolished.

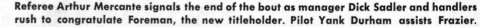

Referee Arthur Mercante signals the end of the bout as manager Dick Sadler and handlers rush to congratulate Foreman, the new titleholder. Pilot Yank Durham assists Frazier.

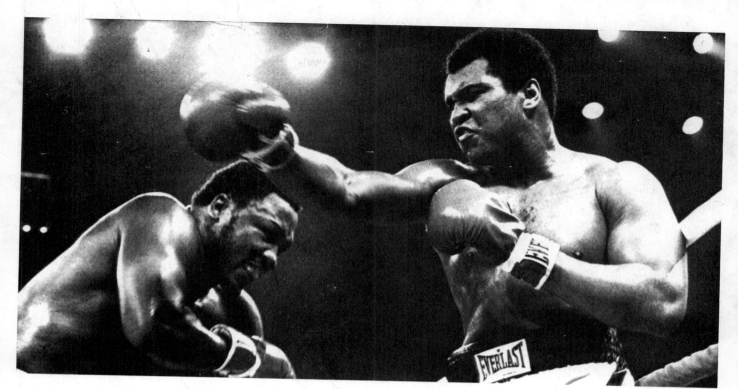

The seventh round of the third Ali-Frazier fight in Manila, and Ali glances a right off Joe Frazier's head *(above)*. **Ali, starting strongly, puts his full force from the shoulder in a right to Frazier's face** *(right)*.

to death—the closest thing to dying he knew of.

Ali rested for only four months before resuming the defence of his title. He beat four challengers in 1976; on February 20, Jean-Pierre Coopman, the Belgian heavyweight champion, by a knock-out in the fifth round at San Juan; U.S. contender Jimmy Young on points over fifteen rounds at Landover on April 30; Richard Dunn, the British, European and Commonwealth champion, who was stopped in five rounds at Munich, and the man who broke his jaw three years earlier, fellow-countryman Ken Norton, who was outpointed over fifteen rounds on September 28 at Madison Square Garden, New York. Two challengers were satisfactorily dealt with in 1977. On May 16 at Landover, Alfred Evangelista, the European champion, who was beaten on points, and on September 29, Earnie Shavers from Ohio, who was also outpointed in New York.

In his first defence in 1978, however, at Las Vegas on February 15, Ali was surprisingly outpointed by twenty-four-year-old Leon Spinks, from St. Louis, Missouri, who had won

The 24-year-old Leon Spinks connects with a right hook while taking the title off Ali in February 1978.

Larry Holmes (left) emphatically beat the ageing Ali to retain his W.B.C. title in October 1980.

the Olympic Games light-heavyweight gold medal in 1976, had turned pro the following year and was unbeaten in his seven paid bouts. His points victory over Ali was on a split decision, Referee Art Lurie, voting for the champion and the two judges for the challenger. The World Boxing Council, however, declared the title as vacant because Spinks refused to meet Ken Norton and the latter was announced champion on March 18, 1978, but on June 10 Norton lost this claim when outpointed by Larry Holmes, from Philadelphia, who was thereupon recognised as world titleholder by the W.B.C., but not by the majority of boxing followers. This claim was made even more absurd when on September 15 at New Orleans, Ali regained the title from Spinks by a unanimous points verdict.

Thus Ali became the first man in Boxing history to win the Heavyweight Championship three times and he had taken part in no less than twenty-four world title bouts. Afterwards he indicated that having achieved this objective he would retire from the ring thus leaving Holmes as the outstanding contender. On November 10, 1978, he strengthened his claim to titular recognition by knocking out Alfredo Evangelista (Italy) in seven rounds at Las Vegas. Ali received five million dollars in his

return fight with Spinks and he will go into the records as having earned in eighteen years of ring warfare, millions of dollars more than any other boxer.

Holmes then disposed of three challengers in 1979, stopping Osvaldo Ocasio (Puerto Rica) in seven rounds; Mike Weaver (Los Angeles) in twelve and Ernie Shavers (Ohio) in eleven, all three contests taking place at Las Vegas, and all were in defence of his W.B.C. title. In 1980 Holmes continued his slaughter of championship contenders by knocking out the European heavyweight champion, Lorenzo Zanon (Italy) in six rounds at Los Angeles on February 3; halting Leroy Jones (Denver) in eight rounds at Los Angeles on March 31. At Bloomington, Minn. on July 7, he stopped Scott Le Doux (Minneapolis) in seven rounds.

On October 2, however, he made himself the undisputed world champion when he forced Muhammad Ali to retire at the end of the tenth round at Caesars Palace, Las Vegas, after a pathetic display by the former triple titleholder, who had not fought for two years and had undergone a drastic weight reduction that left him a mere shadow of 'his former greatness'

In 1981 Holmes disposed of three more challengers. On April 11 at Las Vegas he outpointed Trevor Berbick (Canadian holder of the British Com-

monwealth heavyweight title), then on June 12, Leon Spinks (former world heavyweight champion) was forced to retire after three rounds at Detroit, whilst Renaldo Snipes was stopped in 11 rounds at Pittsburgh on November 6. There were two defences in 1982, first on June 12 against Gerry Cooney, a large-size challenger from Huntington, N.Y., who at 225½ pounds outweighed the champion by 13 pounds. The fight created enormous interest and Cooney put up a brave show until the 13th round when his position was hopeless and he was saved from further punishment by the referee.

On November 26 Holmes outboxed Randall (Tex) Cobb at Houston to win a clear-cut decision over 15 rounds. His 14th defence of the title saw him outpoint the European Boxing Union's heavyweight champion, Lucien Rodriguez (France) over the new W.B.C. distance of 12 rounds on March 27, 1983 at Scranton, Nevada. On May 20, at Las Vegas, he was given a hard fight by Tim Witherspoon before gaining a points verdict and on September 10 he stopped Scott Frank in five rounds at Atlantic City. It was then proposed that Larry should defend his crown against Marvis Frazier, son of the former world heavyweight champion, but both the W.B.C. and the W.B.A. rejected the

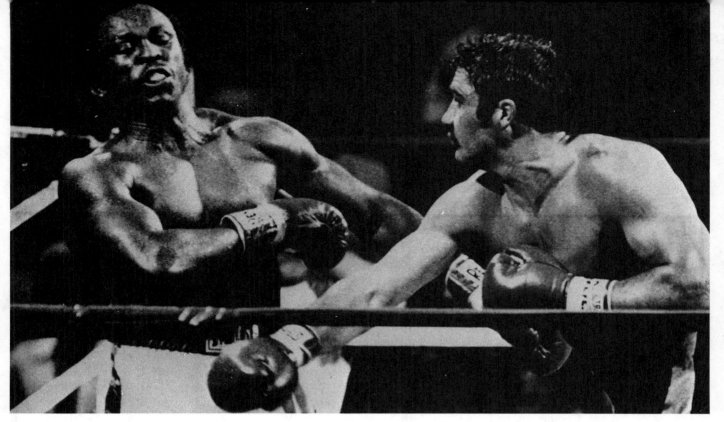

(Above) Gerrie Coetzee knocks Michael Dokes to the ropes at Richfield in 1983. Coetzee took the W.B.A. title with a tenth round knock-out.

(Below) Greg Page in trouble on the ropes as Tim Witherspoon fires in the punches in the first round at Las Vegas in 1984. Witherspoon took the vacant W.B.C. title.

idea and declared that if Holmes decided to go ahead with the match, he was in danger of forfeiting his claim to the Championship. The contest, if such it could be called, duly took place at Las Vegas on November 25 under the auspices of the newly-formed International Boxing Federation, and Frazier was beaten into helplessness in 2 minutes 57 seconds of round one.

The W.B.C. deposed Holmes and appointed Tim Witherspoon (Philadelphia) to meet Greg Page (Louisville) for its vacant heavyweight throne at Las Vegas on March 9, 1984. Witherspoon scored a points win over 12 rounds and remained champion for just over five months, losing on points to Pinklon Thomas (Pontiac, Michigan) on August 31, again at Las Vegas. Irrespective of this move, Holmes won on a cut-eye verdict over James (Bonecrusher) Smith in the 12th round at Las Vegas on November 9 in another I.B.F. bout. There were therefore two claimants to the Richest Prize in Sport, plus the W.B.A. candidate of whom more anon.

Plenty of activity was seen in 1985. On March 15 Holmes preserved his title by stopping David Bey in ten rounds at Las Vegas, and on May 20 he outpointed Carl Williams over 15 rounds at Reno. But ringside observers could see that the champion, now well past his 35th birthday, had slowed down considerably and was finding it harder each time to deal with his younger challengers. The day had come to consider retirement, but there were one or two records that he would like to make before he peeled off his gloves for good. Rocky Marciano had retired undefeated as champion with 49 wins to his credit and six successful defences. So far Holmes was unbeaten in 48 bouts. He aimed at one more win to equal the Brockton Blockbuster's record or two more to beat it. So far he has surpassed Marciano by winning eighteen championship bouts and drawing one.

He could have met the two pretenders to his throne, Pinklon Thomas (W.B.C.) or Tony Tubbs (W.B.A.) to try and achieve his purpose. Instead he chose Michael Spinks, brother to Leon, whom he had already beaten. The reigning world light-heavyweight champion was unbeaten in 27 bouts, 19 of which had been won inside the distance. He was the younger man by seven years and he also had a goal to reach. Over the years a number of light-heavyweight champions had tried to win the heavyweight crown without success – he hoped to make a new entry in the record books.

This Match of the Champions took place at Las Vegas on September 22, 1985 and after a tense struggle Holmes was judged a points loser. Spinks had built himself up to full heavyweight

without losing speed or resilience and although he used the outer perimeter of the ring for the best part of the contest, he made colourful bursts, while the champion plodded after him, striving to land a pay-off punch. So Spinks gained his objective and Holmes failed. He had been a great champion. Meanwhile Pinklon Thomas had knocked out former W.B.A. Champion, Mike Weaver, to keep a hold on his W.B.C. crown.

While all this was going on, the W.B.A. had been confusing the heavyweight championship situation still further. Upon Ali's retirement in 1978, the W.B.A. had refused to recognize the W.B.C. champion, Holmes, and had declared the title vacant. On October 20, 1979 the W.B.A. recognized John Tate, of Knoxville, Tennessee, as world champion when he outpointed Gerrie Coetzee of South Africa over 15 rounds at Pretoria. Tate did not reign long, being knocked out in the 15th round by Mike Weaver, who already styled himself heavyweight champion of America. They met at Knoxville on March 31, 1980, and on October 25 Weaver made

his first defence by knocking out Coetzee in the 13th round of a hard fight in South Africa.

On October 13, 1981, Weaver outpointed James Tillis (Chicago) over 15 rounds at Rosemount, Illinois, but on December 10 he was sensationally stopped in 63 seconds by Michael Dokes (Akron, Ohio) at Las Vegas, although some spectators thought the referee's action was premature. Weaver clamoured for a chance to regain the title and they met again on May 20, 1983 at Las Vegas, when, after a hard-fought battle they were judged to have drawn, a verdict that left Dokes still holding the W.B.A. crown. On September 23 he took it to Richfield, Ohio, for a defence against Gerrie Coetzee, the South African champion, who scored a surprising kayo win in round ten. However, on defending his title for the first time on December 1, 1984 at Sun City, Bophuthatswana, against Greg Page, he lost it in a most unsatisfactory manner. Put down in round eight, the bell sounded to end the session, but the referee continued to count and declared Page the winner by a knockout. Actually the last round occupied 3 minutes 50 seconds. Coetzee lost his title at a time when he should have been in his corner attended by his seconds. Whether they would have been able to get him fit for another round is debatable – but they did not get the opportunity. However, on April 29, 1985 Page was beaten on points over 15 rounds by Tony Tubbs (Cincinnati) after an unexciting bout at Buffalo, New York.

In 1986 a flamboyant American promoter, Don King, with the US Home Box Office cable television channel, set up an ambitious series of matches designed to unify the World Championship. The three title-holders plus the leading contenders were to take part in eliminating contests to produce an undisputed champion by the end of 1987.

On March 22, 1986, Pinklon Thomas lost the W.B.C. title to Trevor Berbick on points over 12 rounds at Las Vegas,

Light-heavyweight champion Michael Spinks became the first to add the heavyweight crown when he decisioned Larry Holmes for the I.B.F. title in 1985.

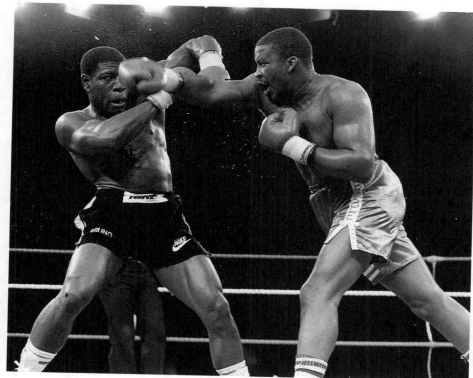

Frank Bruno's (left) gallant challenge ended when the WBA heavyweight title holder Tim Witherspoon stopped him in the eleventh round.

while on January 17 Tony Tubbs lost the W.B.A. title over 15 gruelling rounds at Atlanta to Tim Witherspoon, the former W.B.C. champion. At Wembley, London, on Sunday, July 20, at 1 o'clock in the morning (a time designed for American TV) Witherspoon disposed of the British candidate, Frank Bruno, who had relinquished the European title, with a knock-out in the 11th round.

Meanwhile, Mike Tyson from Brooklyn, had been demolishing heavyweights in a whirlwind career which saw hime beat his first 27 opponents, 25 of them inside the distance, including 15 first-round knockouts. He was incorporated into the unification series, and on November 22, 1986 at the Las Vegas Hilton he stopped Trevor Berbick in 2 minutes 35 seconds of the second round, to win the W.B.C. title. At 20 years and 5 months old he was the youngest man to claim a version of the heavyweight title.

Only a month later, on December 12, Tim Witherspoon took on James "Bonecrusher" Smith, who was boxing

as a substitute in New York for Tony Tubbs, who claimed to have been injured. Smith was not expected to win, but he surprised the world by flooring the champion three times in the opening round, obliging the referee to stop the unequal fight.

Efforts were immediately made to match Mike Tyson with Smith for Las Vegas, with both the W.B.A. and W.B.C. titles at stake. The hard-punching "Bonecrusher" promised much but produced little when the pair met on March 7, 1987. A rather dull contest travelled the full 12 rounds, with Tyson always ahead but continually frustrated in every attempt to catch up with Smith and knock him out.

No time was lost in the further promotion of the unification series. Michael Spinks had been deprived of his I.B.F. title because of his refusal to defend it against Tony Tucker, preferring to negotiate for a more lucrative bout in opposition to the gigantic Gerry Cooney. So Tucker was matched with James Douglas for the vacant championship, and their meeting took place at Las Vegas on May 30. In the 10th round the fight was stopped in Tucker's favour, but he was none too impressive, and had to play second fiddle to Tyson on the same programme, who looked much stronger when he demolished the former champion, Pinklon Thomas, in 6 rounds.

The climax of the unification series took place on August 1, predictably at the popular Las Vegas location. Since it involved three versions of the championship, the contest was originally scheduled for 15 rounds, the I.B.F. distance, but the W.B.C. insisted on a

'Iron' Mike Tyson (right), who was already W.B.A. and W.B.C. champion, stopped challenger Pinklon Thomas in 1987 while waiting for the new I.B.F. champion to emerge.

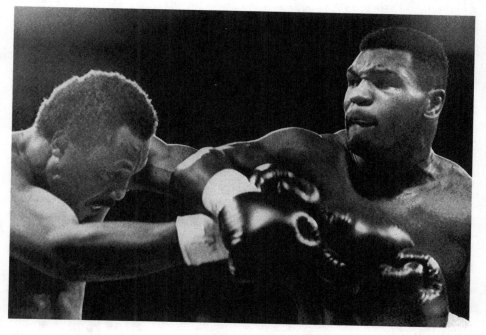

Ex-champion Larry Holmes claimed he could beat Tyson, but the veteran was knocked out in the fourth round.

Michael Spinks called himself the 'people's champion' but his unbeaten record lasted only 91 seconds against Tyson in 1988.

veteran Larry Holmes had come out of retirement, insisting that he knew the way to beat the all-conquering champion. A lucrative promotion ensued, at Atlantic City, on January 22, 1988, but the former champion stood no chance at all with "Iron" Mike. The younger man forced the action, while Holmes boxed on the retreat. But in the fourth round Tyson unleashed a lightning-like combination which deposited Holmes heavily on to his back. Although he rose, the damage was done, and when he fell spreadeagled from another ferocious attack the one-sided fight was brought to a speedy conclusion.

Tyson had now disposed of every high-ranking contender, with the exception of Michael Spinks, who had reduced the enormous Gerry Cooney to pugilistic impotence, and the skilful but latterly inactive Tony Tubbs. A fight versus Spinks was held over for the time being, and a match was made for Tyson to face the bulky Tubbs in Tokyo, on March 21, 1988.

The incredible champion boxed a cagey opening round and then began to unload some of his best shots in the second. Tubbs weathered a few early exchanges, but a terrific left hook to the temple sent him staggering on rubbery legs. He fell flat on his back, utterly defeated.

The only other claimant to the title of the world's best heavyweight was the still unbeaten Michael Spinks, who was still recognised in some quarters as the champion because of his line of succession through Holmes and Ali. The two

limit of 12, and got its way. The bout was interesting, but it lacked the thrills that had now come to be associated with Tyson. Tony Tucker did well to last the fight on his feet, and without stalling, but Tyson won comfortably on points, thus becoming the undisputed champion of the world. No too long afterwards he accepted the challenge of the clever and hard-punching Tyrell Biggs.

Although Biggs was courageous enough and made a good fight of it, he was completely outclassed when he faced Mike Tyson on October 16. By the 7th round the young champion had so far established his supremacy that the fight was stopped after Biggs had been pitched helpless and beaten to the canvas near his own corner.

This contest completed activity for Tyson during 1987, but he lost no time in returning to action in the new year. The

met on June 27, 1988 in a lucrative bonanza at Atlantic City. After all the hype the match was slow to begin as both men stayed in their dressing rooms as long as possible. Each regarded himself as champion with the consequent right to enter the ring second. Eventually Spinks made his way to the ring. The delay appeared to have affected him more, and he looked apprehensive during the announcements and boxed without conviction. Tyson attacked immediately and Spinks seemed shocked and hurt by Tyson's power. Tyson soon rushed Spinks to the ropes, where a terrific blow to the body sent Spinks to his knees on the canvas. Back on his feet, Spinks tried to repel the onrushing Tyson with a wild right. Tyson had no difficulty in avoiding it and leapt in with his own murderous punch which caught Spinks clean on the jaw and knocked him to the floor on his back, with his head below the ropes. There was no chance he could rise, and the great extravaganza was over in 91 seconds. It was three days before Tyson's 22nd birthday, and he had beaten all the best heavyweights in the world.

Mike Tyson takes a rest from the action in Jimmy Tocco's windowless gym in downtown Las Vegas, and makes sure his most valuable assets, his hands, are protected. Tyson spared nobody in training – neither himself nor his sparring partners.

SELF-DESTRUCTING 'IRON MIKE' TYSON

Mike Tyson's rise to undisputed heavyweight champion was quicker and more impressive than that of any heavyweight before or since. He was born on June 30, 1966 and brought up in the tough Brooklyn area of Brownsville. Even as a child he was extremely strong for his age. Mixing with street gangs, he was an experienced mugger by the age of 13, when he was confined in a reformatory for troubled juveniles. He was introduced to the trainer Cus d'Amato, who became his guardian and mentor, developing his boxing potential. As an amateur, he failed to make the 1984 U.S. Olympic team and turned professional in 1985. At 5ft 11in he was short for a modern heavyweight, his most notable physical characteristic being a 19¾in neck. At 218lb he was very fast for his weight and combined extraordinary handspeed with devastating punching power. He always entered the ring without a robe, wearing black trunks and black shoes, cultivating a no-frills executioner image. At the time be beat Michael Spinks he looked unbeatable and seemed assured of a long reign as champion.

But the seeds of his downfall were already present. Cus d'Amato had died in 1985, and Tyson's management team became Bill Cayton and Jim Jacobs, d'Amato's friends and sponsors in the development of Tyson as a boxer. In February 1988 Tyson married actress Robin Givens, who was allegedly pregnant by him. Givens, with her mother supporting her, had a difference of opinion with Cayton about Tyson's contract. Jacobs died of leukaemia. Tyson and Givens began to row publicly. The promoter Don King, with the intention of controlling the heavyweight division, persuaded Tyson to try to ditch Cayton and align himself with King. Soon Tyson's private life became as newsworthy as his boxing. He crashed cars and was involved in skirmishes with men and women, including a former opponent. After beating Spinks he drove into a tree in what some papers construed as a suicide attempt. He had fights with Givens who humiliated him on television, describing him as 'scary'.

The marriage lasted eight months before Givens filed for divorce.

Tyson sacked his cornerman Kevin Rooney, but won his next defence, on February 25, 1989, stopping Frank Bruno in the fifth round in Las Vegas, but was less impressive than usual. In July he looked back to normal in destroying Carl Williams in one round in Atlantic City. But he withdrew from a fight with Razor Ruddock to take on James Buster Douglas in Tokyo. The contest took place on February 11, 1990 with Douglas, the biggest outsider possible, being on offer at 42–1.

Douglas fought two weeks after the death of his mother, and with the mother of his own son seriously ill. Nevertheless he produced easily his best-ever performance. Tyson was sluggish and under-trained and, when his initial onslaught was easily resisted by Douglas, he ran out of ideas. Douglas's hooks and uppercuts began to shake Tyson and close his eye. In the eighth Douglas staggered Tyson with a right to the mouth but, as he followed up, he was dropped with an uppercut. Douglas rose at eight, more angry than hurt, survived the round, and resumed his supremacy, culminating in a tenth-round knockout of Tyson.

The W.B.A. and W.B.C., prompted by Don King, whose close associations with the sanctioning bodies, in particular the W.B.C., was the cause of much criticism in boxing circles in the 1980s and 1990s, 'suspended the result', on the ludicrous grounds that the referee, Octavio Meyran, had been slow in tak-

Tyson in the Marion County Court, Indianapolis, during his trial in February, 1992, when he was sentenced to six years imprisonment.

ing up the count in the eighth round, and that Douglas had received longer than ten seconds to recover. This manoeuvre was so laughed to scorn by the boxing press and public that it was unsustainable.

Tyson made a good recovery in the ring, with wins over Henry Tillman, Alex Stewart and Razor Ruddock (twice) and a title challenge was arranged with the new champion, Evander Holyfield, for October, then November, 1991. However, in September, Tyson, whose cavalier treatment of women acquaintances, and even strangers, had attracted attention before, was indicted on a rape charge. In February, 1992, he was convicted and sentenced to six years imprisonment.

The biggest upset in boxing history. Tyson being counted out to lose his title to Buster Douglas in Tokyo in 1990.

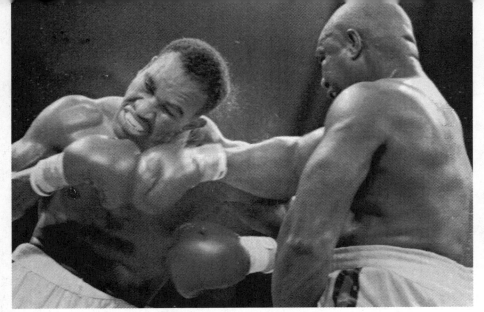

Buster Douglas's reign as champion did not survive his first defence. On October 25, 1990 Evander Holyfield, the former cruiserweight champion, knocked him out in the third round in Las Vegas. Holyfield had campaigned as a heavyweight since 1988, and was still unbeaten, having accounted for former heavyweight champions Pinklon Thomas and Michael Dokes. He had scientifically increased his weight from 190lb to 208lb.

Holyfield's first defence was against another former champion, George Foreman. Foreman had retired in 1976 and his weight had ballooned to over 300lb. But in March 1987, at 260lb, he began a comeback. With his head shaven, the huge Foreman beat 24 opponents, 23 by the quick route, before tackling Holyfield on April 19, 1991 at Atlantic City. Eighteen years had passed since the 43-year-old had first won the title, but he put up a good show and took Holyfield the distance.

After the cancellation of his defence against Tyson, Holyfield faced a substitute in Bert Cooper on May 15, 1992 in Atlanta. Cooper was stopped in the seventh, but not before he had floored Holyfield for the first time in his career. On June 19, 1992 Holyfield faced another comebacking ex-champ in Larry Holmes, who was in his 43rd year. Holmes was easily outpointed, but went the distance. He became the third heavyweight, after Louis and Ali, to contest the title in three separate decades.

With Riddick Bowe, Lennox Lewis and Razor Ruddock far worthier opponents than those he had faced so far, the Holyfield camp was party to an agreement in which he would face Bowe and Lewis would face Ruddock, the two winners to meet. Lewis knocked out Ruddock in the second round in London on October 31, 1992 and Bowe outpointed Holyfield on November 13, 1992 in Las Vegas. The size and power of Bowe, who was 30lb heavier than the champion at 235lb to 205lb, was too much for Holyfield, and only Holyfield's superb conditioning allowed him to remain standing and fight back. Bowe won a unanimous decision in an outstanding fight.

Having become champion, Bowe now declined to meet Lewis in his first defence and on December 14 was stripped by the W.B.C. Bowe retaliating by dropping the W.B.C. belt into a trash can. Lewis was proclaimed the W.B.C. champion.

Bowe made his first defence of the W.B.A. and I.B.F. titles on February 6, 1993 at Madison Square Garden, New York. Bowe came into the ring at 243lb, but was still a pound lighter than the flabby Michael Dokes, the 1982 W.B.A. champion, who was stopped in the first round. Lewis's first defence of the W.B.C. title was a much sterner task. He faced the 1987 I.B.F. champion Tony Tucker, whose only defeat was by Tyson on a decision. Lewis was a clear points winner on May 8, 1993 at Las Vegas.

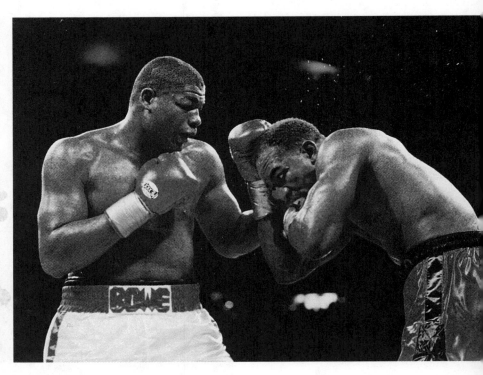

In the 1980s the World Boxing Organisation was formed and gained minor credibility with recognition by the British Boxing Board of Control. In 1989 this body decided not to recognise Mike Tyson as world champion and granted recognition to Francesco Damiani, of Italy, when he knocked out Johnny du Plooy, of South Africa, at Syracuse on May 6, 1989. Damiani stopped Daniel Netto of Argentina in the second in December, 1989 but was knocked out in the ninth round by Ray Mercer (U.S.A.) at Atlantic City on January 11, 1991. Mercer stopped Tommy Morrison (U.S.A.) at Atlantic City nine months later, but forfeited the title when refusing to defend against the unbeaten Michael Moorer (U.S.A.), the W.B.O. light-heavyweight champion. On May 15, 1992 Moorer won the W.B.O. heavyweight title when recovering from a knockdown to stop Bert Cooper in the fifth round in Atlantic City. However Moorer thought so little of this title that he gave it up in 1993 to challenge for the other versions of the crown.

Lennox Lewis (right) was named WBC champion when Bowe refused to meet him. Lewis outpointed Tony Tucker in his first defence in Las Vegas.

THE CRUISERWEIGHT CHAMPIONS

In 1979 the World Boxing Council took upon itself the inauguration of an entirely new weight division between the existing light-heavyweight class and the heavyweights. They named it cruiserweight, borrowing the former British title for light-heavies, and on December 8, Mate Parlov (Yugoslavia) was paired with Marvin Camel (U.S.A.), both former light-heavyweight champions, to fight 15 rounds for the new title at Split in Yugoslavia. The result was a "draw". The weight had been set at 190 pounds, but in October the following year it was raised to 195 pounds.

There had to be a return bout and at Las Vegas on March 31, 1980, Camel won on points. He defended his title only once, losing a points verdict to Carlos De Leon (Puerto Rico) at New Orleans on November 28, 1981, and in a return bout at Atlantic City, De Leon stopped his rival in the seventh round. S. T. Gordon, who preferred to be billed by his initials in this way, then caused a surprise by halting the champion in two rounds at Cleveland, Ohio, on June 27, 1982. He defended against Jesse Burnett (Los Angeles) at East Rutherford, N.J. on February 16, 1983, the referee stopping the contest in the eighth round, but in a second meeting with De Leon on July 17, lost the title on a 12 rounds points decision at Las Vegas.

Back in the saddle, Carlos remained champion for nearly a year, in which time he made three winning defences, beating Alvaro Lopez (Mexico) in four rounds at San Jose, California on September 21; Anthony Davis (Las Vegas) on points in his home town on March 9, 1984, and Bash Ali (Nigeria) on points at Oakland, California on June 2. Alfonso Ratliff (Chicago) gained the title on June 6, 1985, beating De Leon on points at Las Vegas, but he lasted only three months, being decisioned on September 21, also at Las Vegas, by Bernard Benton (Toledo).

In 1986 Benton was beaten on points by Carlos de Leon, winning the title for the third time, at Las Vegas on March 22. In August Carlos retained the title at Giardini Naxos, Italy, by stopping Michael Greer (U.S.A.) in the 8th round.

The World Boxing Association did not

launch its version of the Cruiserweight Class until February 13, 1982 in South Africa, when Osvaldo Ocasio (Puerto Rico) won on points over 15 rounds against Robbie Williams at Johannesburg, for the vacant title. He defended against Young Joe Louis (Chicago) on December 16 at Chicago, winning a points verdict. On May 20, 1983 at Las Vegas he outpointed Randy Stephens (Dallas) in a 15-rounder, and on May 5, 1984 stopped John Odhiambo (Kenya) in the 15th and last round at San Juan.

Returning to South Africa, Ocasio lost his crown on a points verdict to Piet Crous at Sun City, Bophuthatswana, on December 1, 1984. Crous stopped Randy Stephens in two rounds in the same ring on March 29, 1985 in a title defence, but crashed before Dwight Muhammad Qawi, former world light-heavyweight champion, at Sun City, on July 27, being knocked out in round eleven.

Qawi successfully defended on March 23, 1986, the referee stopping the challenge of former heavyweight champion Leon Spinks in the sixth round at Reno.

Ossie Ocasio, right, of Puerto Rico, lands a blow on Randy Stephens to retain his W.B.A. cruiser-weight championship.

The International Boxing Federation's first nominee as champion of the new division was the former W.B.C. title-holder, Marvin Camel, who defeated Rick Sekorski on May 21, 1983, in 9 rounds. Camel went on to stop Rod MacDonald that same year, but after a spell of inactivity he lost his share of the honours to Lee Roy Murphy on October 6, 1984, at Billings, Montana. Murphy made successful defences versus Young Joe Louis and Chisanda Mutti, and on April 19, 1986 he knocked out Dorcey Gaymon in 9 rounds at San Remo, Italy.

However, at Marsala, also in Italy, Murphy's reign came to an end when he was stopped in 10 rounds by Rickey Parkey on October 10. Chisanda Mutti got another chance at the title when he met Parkey at Camaiore, on March 28, 1987, but the challenger was halted in 12 rounds. Parkey's triumph was short-lived.

Meanwhile, with the W.B.A. belt at stake, Dwight Muhammad Qawi received a shock at Atlanta when Evander Holyfield outpointed him over 15 rounds on July 12, 1986, and showed promise of becoming a great champion. He looked to be the best cruiserweight of the lot, once he could get the other

claimants into a ring with him, and he did much to prove his point when he stopped the Olympic star, Henry Tillman, in 7 rounds at Reno on February 14, 1987. Holyfield seemed intent upon "doing a Tyson" and clearing up the confusion in his own division, for on May 15, before a Las Vegas crowd, he humbled the I.B.F. title-holder, Rickey Parkey, rather easily in 3 rounds.

On August 15, Holyfield took on the former claimant to the crown, Ossie Ocasio, placing both of his titles at stake at St. Tropez. Holyfield was far too good and strong for his man and the fight was stopped in 11 rounds.

The close of the year found Dwight Muhammad Qawi making a gallant attempt to win back the belt. He boxed Holyfield on December 5, but only the I.B.F. title was in jeopardy, since the bout was contracted for 15 rounds and the W.B.A. would not give its blessing to such an extended meeting. But as it happened, 4 rounds were quite sufficient for Holyfield to establish complete supremacy and knock his opponent out.

During this time Carlos de Leon, the Puerto Rican W.B.C. champion, was not inactive. On August 10, 1986, at Giardini Naxos, in Italy, he beat Michael Greer in 8 rounds. Also in Italy, this time at Bergamo, on February 21, 1987 de Leon defeated Angelo Rottoli rather easily in 4 rounds. Then, in a supporting bout on the Tyson-Holmes bill at Atlantic City on January 22, 1988, Carlos de Leon boxed José Maria Flores in defence of the W.B.C. championship. The kingpin outboxed his opponent rather easily, but he was unimpressive. The consensus of opinion was that he would give Evander Holyfield no trouble in a unification contest.

This proved to be the fact. When the pair faced each other at Las Vegas on April 9, Holyfield punched the Puerto Rican into submission in eight rounds. The referee stepped in and stopped the fight after de Leon sustained a bad cut over his left eye.

No sooner had Holyfield unified the division than he relinquished the title to campaign as a heavyweight. By the end of 1989 there were four claimants to the crown. The W.B.A. version was decided first, when Taoufik Belbouli of

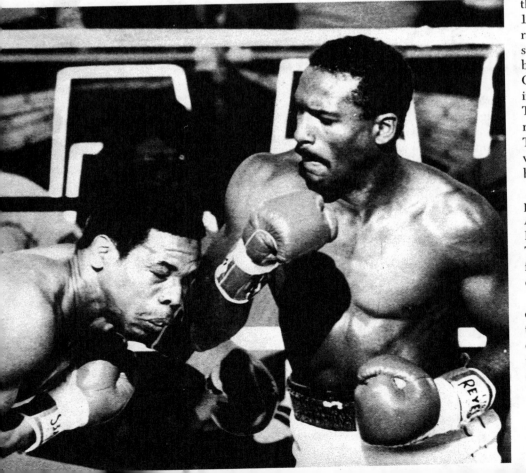

France stopped Michael Greer (U.S.A.) in the eighth round in Casablanca, on March 5, 1989, but he relinquished the title without defending. On November 28, Robert Daniels (U.S.A.) became W.B.A. champion by outpointing veteran ex-champ Dwight Muhammad Qawi at Noget sur Marne. He defended with a points win over Craig Bodzianowski (U.S.A.) and a draw with Taoufik Belbouli before losing the title on points to former light-heavyweight champion Bobby Czyz (U.S.A.) at Atlantic City on March 9, 1991. Czyz retained the crown with decisions over Bash Ali (Nigeria) and Donny Lalonde (Canada).

The W.B.C. version of the title was won by veteran Carlos de Leon, who stopped Sam Reeson (G.B.) in the ninth round in London on May 17, 1989. He drew with Johnny Nelson (G.B.) in Sheffield and then lost the title on a disqualification to Massimilliano Duran (Italy) at Capo d'Orlando on July 27, 1990. Referee Bob Logist ruled that de Leon deliberately hit Duran after the bell to end the eleventh round and made his decision after a crowd riot in which spaghetti was thrown into the ring. Duran, with only 16 bouts before becoming champion, retained the crown with another disqualification decision against Anaclet Wamba of France in Terrara. Referee Larry O'Connell threw out the challenger for butting nine seconds from the end of the fight, having previously deducted five points for the same offence. The fight was nevertheless still in the balance on all cards before the last round.

Wamba stopped Duran in the eleventh round in Palermo on July 20, 1991 to become champion, beat Duran again, and defended successfully against Andrei Rudenko (Russia), Andrew Maynard (U.S.A.) and David Vedder (U.S.A.).

The I.B.F. crown was won by Glenn McCrory (G.B.) who outpointed Patrick Lumumba (Kenya) at Stanley on June 3, 1989. He defended against Siza Makhatini (South Africa) before losing the title to Jeff Lampkin (U.S.A.) on a third round knockout at Gateshead on March 22, 1990. Lampkin defended against Makhatini, then relinquished the title. James Warring (U.S.A.) won it with a first-round knockout of James Pritchard (U.S.A.) at Salemi on September 6, 1991. Warring defended successfully against Donnell Wingfield (U.S.A.) and Johnny Nelson (G.B.) before being outpointed by Al 'Ice' Cole (U.S.A.) in Stanhope on July 30, 1992. Cole outpointed the veteran Uriah Grant, who challenged on February 28, 1993.

The first W.B.O. cruiserweight champion was Boone Pultz (U.S.A.) who outpointed Magne Havnaa (Norway) at Copenhagen on December 3, 1989, but Havnaa stopped Pultz in the fifth round in the return at Aars on May 17, 1990. Havnaa then outpointed Daniel Netto and Tyrone Booze (U.S.A.) before giving up the title. Tyrone Booze won the vacant crown by knocking out Derek Angol (G.B.) in the seventh round in Manchester on July 25, 1992. He then outpointed Ralf Rocchigiani (Germany) before losing the title to another German, Marcos Bott, on points in Hamburg on February 13, 1993.

THE LIGHT HEAVYWEIGHTS

Each division in boxing except the light heavyweight got its start in England. This division, known in Europe as the cruiserweight, was instituted in America in 1903. It was fathered by Lou Houseman, a Chicago newspaperman, promoter, and manager at the time of Jack Root, who after scoring many victories as a middleweight had outgrown the division.

Houseman conceived the idea that there should be a grade established to include boxers between the middleweight and heavyweight sections, since there was a large weight difference in many contests. After receiving the green light from America's leading middleweights and the press, Houseman arranged to have Root fight Kid McCoy. The bout took place in Detroit on April 22, 1903, with Root the winner and champion of the new division.

George Gardner contested the right of Root to the honors and succeeded in proving his point by knocking Jack out on July 4, 1903, in twelve rounds in Buffalo, New York. The British accepted the new class and thereafter it became one of the most popular in Great Britain.

The division has never been too popular in our country, however, because the men who scaled between 160 and 175, the official top weight for a championship match, learned that only occasionally has the group been a good money-making class. Most of the top men have aimed for the heavyweight crown. After reaching the top or getting close to it, they invariably leaped into the heavyweight ranks, where the financial returns were best.

Some of the world's greatest ringmen have fought in the division, among them such stars as Kid McCoy, Harry Greb, Tom Gibbons, Jack Delaney, Young Stribling, Paul Berlenbach, Billy Conn, Gene Tunney, Jack Dillon, Battling Levinsky, Georges Carpentier, Philadelphia Jack O'Brien, Jimmy Slattery, Tommy Loughran, and Bob Fitzsimmons. Fitzsimmons won the crown after losing the heavyweight title. He gained it when he beat Gardner via the decision route at the end of twenty rounds in San Francisco on November 25, 1903, and he in turn lost it to Jack O'Brien, who knocked him out in the thirteenth round in the same city on December 20, 1905. Thus the title during its first year changed hands three times—unusual in boxing.

Like most of the light heavyweights of later years, Philadelphia Jack O'Brien preferred to confine his ring battles to the higher division and

Kid McCoy (left) boxed Jim Corbett before movie cameras in an early attempt to weave a plot around a boxing match. McCoy was past his prime when matched with Jack Root for the first light heavyweight championship in 1903, in which he lost in 10 rounds.

Bob Fitzsimmons (*right*) at the age of 41 gave Gardner a 20-round boxing lesson in San Francisco, thus adding a third crown to his spectacular career. A veteran of 13 years, Fitzsimmons lacked the punching power he once possessed, but his boxing skill and ring-craft befuddled the younger Gardner. The new championship, in its first year, 1903, changed hands three times.

Philadelphia Jack O'Brien, knocked Fitzsimmons out after 13 hard-fought rounds, to become the fourth light heavyweight champion. O'Brien fought 185 battles in his career (1896-1912).

Jack Root easily whipped McCoy to become the first light heavy-weight king. In a 54-fight career (1897-1906) Root scored 24 knockouts and was stopped three times, his only losses.

George Gardner dethroned Root via a knockout in 12 rounds at Fort Erie, Canada. Gardner, born in Lisdoonvarna, County Clare, Ireland, started boxing in 1897 and retired in 1908.

Battling Levinsky whipped Dillon at Boston in 12 rounds and fought many no-decision bouts while defending his title, which could only be won by a knockout. From 1910 to 1929 Levinsky met the the best men around.

Jack Dillon, the "Giant Killer" (left), claimed the title in 1908 when O'Brien failed to accept his challenge. Dillon held the title for eight years, until beaten by Battling Levinsky in 1916. In 14 years of boxing (1908-1923) Dillon engaged in over 240 contests, fighting anyone, anywhere.

made no attempt to defend his championship up to the time of his retirement in 1912. Then Jack Dillon, known as the Giant Killer, born February 2, 1891, in Frankfort, Indiana, claimed it, but like O'Brien he immediately started facing heavyweights until Battling Levinsky, a clever performer, challenged him. Levinsky, born June 10, 1891, in Philadelphia, signed with Dillon for twelve rounds in Boston. In this contest the Battler, avoiding the heavy blows of his opponent through the employment of ring science, emerged the victor on points and the newly crowned king.

It is noteworthy that while many boxers won more than one championship and a number regained the crown after having lost it, no light heavyweight king other than Bob Fitzsimmons ever held more than one title and no light heavyweight ever rewon the championship, though Mike McTigue reclaimed it.

Levinsky laid claim to the world title and was generally recognized in our country, but Georges Carpentier, Champion of Europe, had his share

Georges Carpentier (left) of France, European light heavyweight champ, kayoed Levinsky in Jersey City, New Jersey, and was acknowledged world champion. With him is famed boxing promoter Jack Curley (center) and his manager Francois Descamps.

(Above) Gene Tunney and Bob Martin (right) were AEF champs in 1919. Tunney defeated 20 opponents in an elimination series to win the light heavyweight title. He then beat champ Martin in a special four-round bout. After his discharge Gene won 22 bouts, 15 by kayo, and won the American light heavyweight title from Battling Levinsky in 1922. (Above, left) The only loss on Tunney's record came at the hands of the great Harry Greb (left), who beat Gene for the title that same year. The referee is Kid McPartland. (Below) Tunney regained the title from Greb in 1923 in 15 rounds.

Battling Siki, a Senegalese who did some boxing in a territorial regiment of the French Army, sprang a fistic surprise in 1922, in Paris, when he knocked out Georges Carpentier. The gallant Frenchman held his own the first three rounds, even dropping Siki for a short count. But from that point on, he was badly punished. In the sixth round, Siki ended the slaughter with a round-house blow.

Gene Tunney made a step in his climb towards the heavyweight crown when he stopped Carpentier in the 15th round, July 24, 1924, at Yankee Stadium. A solid blow to the mid-section dropped Carpentier for the full count. The victim's manager, François Descamps, claimed foul, but it was disallowed. Carpentier did no fighting in 1925, had four bouts in 1926, then retired.

of supporters. To settle the dispute, Carpentier and Levinsky fought for world supremacy in Jersey City, on October 12, 1920, with Carpentier clinching the laurels. It was that victory that gained for him the heavyweight championship contest with Jack Dempsey the following year.

Levinsky retained the U. S. title despite his defeat by the Orchid Kid, and on January 13, 1922, he lost it to Gene Tunney in the old Madison Square Garden in twelve rounds.

With his defeat by Dempsey in the higher division, Carpentier returned to France and there defended his world light heavyweight crown against Battling Siki, the Singular Senegalese, who surprised everyone by halting Georges in the sixth round.

Gene Tunney, his mind set on the heavyweight title possessed by Dempsey, once more put his U. S. light heavyweight title on the line against Harry Greb—he had previously lost it to Harry and had then rewon it after defeating him in fifteen rounds. Gene now decided to work towards a heavyweight title bout.

Mike McTigue battered Battling Siki around for 20 rounds (above) to win the title on St. Patrick's day, 1923, in Dublin. It was a day of celebration for the Irish, who were enjoying the battle in the indoor arena while Irish rebels were using gunfire against the British outside the stadium. Siki, greeted by "Bold Mike" upon arrival in New York in 1924 (below) engaged in 23 bouts before his death.

With Gene's retirement, Mike Mc-Tigue, one of the top Americans in the division, went to Dublin, where on St. Patrick's Day, 1923, in the midst of the Sinn Fein insurrection, he whipped Battling Siki in twenty rounds and came back to America with the world crown.

Of those who up to this stage held top honors, Greb and Siki were the most colorful. The Greb-Tunney battles in the light heavyweight class were sensational ring encounters. They faced each other five times, with Greb winning only once. Twice he was defeated in American championship matches with Tunney and twice they engaged in no decision bouts.

Greb was a most unusual fighter. He wasn't a hard hitter but a tantalizing one. Seldom more than a middleweight, he fought the best of the heavyweights with considerable success. He punched with accuracy and rapidity, tossing punches from all angles.

He was blind in one eye, yet fought without others knowing it for the better part of his great career.

In Siki, the sport had a unique, queer character, a fun-making, fight-loving figure whose escapades eventually cost him his life by murder. His real name was Louis Phal, a boy of the jungle who lived his life as a simple lad, with a savage's brain, an uncontrollable temper, and a steady thirst for drink.

When McTigue returned to America he was offered a fight with Young Stribling, the pride of Georgia. He accepted, handed the Georgian a shellacking but received no better than a draw from Referee Harry Ertle, who was threatened by the Southern supporters of Stribling and, fearing violence, figured such a decision would pacify the mob. Despite the verdict, he, McTigue, and the latter's manager Joe Jacobs, had to make a hasty exit from the state when the fans rushed the ring to get at the fighter and official. Stribling faced Mike again in Newark a year later. Though it was a twelve rounder no-decision affair, Mike was on the loser's end.

Paul Berlenbach, who possessed a deadly clout, succeeded McTigue as title holder when he gained a 15-round decision in 1925, in Yankee Stadium. Paul was the 1920 Olympic wrestling champion.

After losing the crown to Jack Delaney, Berlenbach faced Mike McTigue in a return contest in Madison Square Garden, January 28, 1927. The battle was a slam-bang affair until the fourth-round, when McTigue staggered and floored Paul for the full count.

In later years, Stribling, who fought both as a light heavyweight and heavy against the cream of both divisions, was killed in a motorcycle accident. His leading battles were against Jack Sharkey, Jimmy Slattery, Paul Berlenbach in a title match which he lost in fifteen rounds in New York on June 10, 1926, and his fight for the heavyweight crown with Max Schmeling in Cleveland in which he was stopped with only fifteen seconds to go in the fifteenth and final round. He, like Siki and Greb, was a colorful figure.

McTigue held on to his throne for two years. On May 30, 1925, he faced a terrific puncher in Paul Berlenbach, an amateur wrestler turned boxer, and Mike was outpointed in New York in fifteen rounds to lose his laurels. He was a clever boxer, one of the smart men of the ring of his era, but couldn't overcome the hitting power of his opponent.

Two years later, after Paul had lost the title, these two former champions engaged in another encounter, a thriller, in which McTigue, now an old man as fighter's ages go, suddenly became a tiger in an effort to avenge the loss of his championship and battered Berlenbach into submission in four rounds, one of the ring's major surprises.

McTigue engaged in a number of additional contests, finally retiring at the age of thirty-eight. In his latter years he fought such stars as Leo Lomski, Tony Maurullo, Armand Emanuel, Tuffy Griffiths, George Hoffman, Bob Godwin and Patsy Perroni, each of whom whipped him. Griffiths stopped him in a round. When he retired, the 1929 crash and depression that followed cost Mike his mind and

Jack Delaney was dropped (*above*) for a short count in his losing battle in 1926 with Berlenbach. But a year later he stopped Paul in six rounds. After entering the heavyweight picture, Delaney was knocked out in one round by Jack Sharkey (*below*) on April 30, 1928, in a controversial bout that was discussed long after the result. Photo shows referee Jack Purdy ordering Sharkey to a neutral corner.

On July 16, 1926, Berlenbach retained his title in a great 15-round fight with Jack Delaney (*right*), a masterful boxer and powerful hitter.

fortune. Confined to a mental institution, he died August 12, 1966.

Berlenbach, unlike many others who have held world championships, didn't place his crown in moth balls for an unlimited time. He defended his title twice during the year in which he won it.

In the first bout he knocked out Jimmy Slattery, a very clever boxer from Buffalo, in eleven rounds, then he and Jack Delaney fought a masterpiece in which Oom Paul retained his laurels via the decision route in fifteen rounds in Madison Square Garden.

The following year, after outpointing Stribling in fifteen rounds in New York, he again tackled Delaney for the Italian Hospital Fund at Ebbets Field, Brooklyn, and in another thriller in which 49,186 persons paid the record sum of $461,789. Delaney gained the crown.

Delaney, a boxer of extraordinary cleverness, with a rapier-like jab, decided there was more to be made in the heavyweight division than his own, and retired to fight in the top class. He fought Berlenbach again in Chicago and stopped him in the sixth round and lost to Jimmy Maloney and Johnny Risko prior to dropping a fifteen round bout to Tom Heeney of New Zealand. Then he was knocked

out by Jack Sharkey in the first round of a much-discussed, controversial affair, and a year later he retired to enter business.

Delaney was born in St. Francis, Canada, March 18, 1900, lived most of his life in Connecticut, and died at Katonah, New York, November 27, 1948.

After Delaney's retirement as light heavyweight boss, McTigue reclaimed the title and on October 7, 1927, Tommy Loughran, another clever boxer who hailed from Philadelphia, relieved him of it by outpointing him in New York in fifteen rounds. Tommy had lots of class.

Jack Delaney's fourth fight as a heavyweight, August 11, 1927, ended in confusion. While Jack is being attended to in his corner, Paolino Uzcudun, the Basque, stands bewildered and angry after being disqualified in the seventh round for hitting low. Pete Reilly, Jack's manager, stoops along ringside, displaying dented cup in an effort to convince skeptical boxing writers, of the foul.

On March 1, 1934, Tommy Loughran, four years a heavyweight, tried unsuccessfully to wrest the heavyweight crown from Primo Carnera. Carnera scaled 270 pounds to Loughran's 186, an 84-pound handicap that created a record for a championship bout.

He put his title on the line against Jimmy Slattery, Leo Lomski, Pete Latzo (twice), Mickey Walker, and Jimmy Braddock, winning each and displaying in those contests the ring cleverness that brought world prominence to Jim Corbett.

After defeating Braddock in fifteen rounds, Loughran retired undefeated to enter the higher division.

He was knocked out by Jack Sharkey in the third round in his first heavyweight attempt but was quite successful thereafter and succeeded in getting a crack at the heavyweight title held by Primo Carnera. In that he gave away considerable weight, eighty-six pounds, yet managed to go the distance, losing the verdict at the end of fifteen rounds in Miami.

In his contest with Leo Lomski, he fought for a time in a stupor due to punishment; in his first contest with Ray Impellettiere, the bout was halted because of a bad cut over his eye, but Commissioner William Brown ordered the bout resumed. Yet Lough-

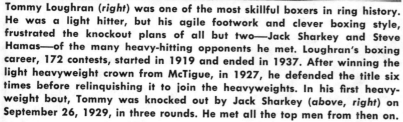

Tommy Loughran (*right*) was one of the most skillful boxers in ring history. He was a light hitter, but his agile footwork and clever boxing style, frustrated the knockout plans of all but two—Jack Sharkey and Steve Hamas—of the many heavy-hitting opponents he met. Loughran's boxing career, 172 contests, started in 1919 and ended in 1937. After winning the light heavyweight crown from McTigue, in 1927, he defended the title six times before relinquishing it to join the heavyweights. In his first heavyweight bout, Tommy was knocked out by Jack Sharkey (*above, right*) on September 26, 1929, in three rounds. He met all the top men from then on.

In Loughran's second defense of his title, he was floored in the first round by Leo Lomski, a dangerous hitter. Tommy took the count of nine and managed to hold off the onrushing Lomski until the last minute of the round, when a looping right floored him again for another nine count before the bell rang, ending the round. From the second to the 15th round the fight was all Loughran's.

Jimmy Slattery (left) defeated Lou Scozza in 15 rounds on February 10, 1930, in the eliminations final staged by the New York Commission. Slattery's victory made him the new champ.

Maxie Rosenbloom (left) clinched his title claim on June 25, 1930, when he beat Slattery in 15 rounds in Buffalo. In a return match in 1931, Slattery was again defeated in 15 rounds.

Bob Olin, standing over Rosenbloom who slipped during title bout on November 16, 1934, gained the crown in 15 rounds before a slim crowd in Madison Square Garden. Rosenbloom, a real veteran of the ring, engaged in 285 bouts from 1925 to 1939.

ran managed to win both bouts. He gave up his title in August, 1929, and in a tourney to choose his successor, Maxie Rosenbloom succeeded in clinching the honors by decisively outpointing Jimmy Slattery, who on February 10, 1930, in Buffalo, had outpointed Lou Scozza in fifteen rounds in the final of an elimination staged by the New York Commission. Rosenbloom received world recognition when he beat Slattery in Buffalo on June 25, 1930.

Slapsie-Maxie, as Rosenbloom was called, was a clever boxer but an exceedingly weak hitter. The New Yorker, born September 6, 1904, was a most active battler. He lost only a few of the several hundred bouts he fought. He defended his crown often, his best championship battles being a fifteen rounder with Mickey Walker in New York and one with Lou Scozza in Buffalo.

"Slapsie Maxie" Rosenbloom has enjoyed great success in movies, nightclubs, and TV.

Maxie lost his title to Bob Olin in Madison Square Garden in a dull fifteen round affair and thereafter continued campaigning throughout the country. When he retired in 1939, he became an actor and entertainer in night clubs and appeared in many movies and television shows.

It was on November 16, 1934, that Olin gained the crown. He was an ordinary boxer who lacked color. On October 31, 1935 he dropped the championship to John Henry Lewis, a Negro who gained the decision in fifteen rounds in St. Louis.

John Henry, like many of his predecessors, was a clever boxer, but he could also punch. He defended his title twice—against Emilio Martinez, whom he stopped in the fourth round in Minneapolis, and Al Gainer, whom he whipped in New Haven in fifteen. Each was a mediocre affair that lacked interest.

Three months after the last fight, he gave up his title at the request of the New York Commission to enter the heavyweight class and fight Joe Louis. The bout lasted less than one round, with John Henry knocked out. He retired shortly after that dismal contest.

Melio Bettina and Tiger Jack Fox were the survivors in an elimination to decide his successor, and on February 3, 1939, Bettina stopped Fox in the Garden in the ninth round.

John Henry Lewis, after beating Olin in 15 rounds, gave up the title for a crack at the heavyweight crown and was kayoed by Joe Louis in one round on January 5, 1929.

Melio Bettina (right) of Beacon, New York, scored a nine-round knockout over Tiger Jack Fox in Madison Square Garden and mounted the vacated light heavyweight throne.

Billy Conn, a clever Pittsburgher, came along to depose the southpaw Bettina in Madison Square Garden by outpointing him in fifteen rounds to win world support. Billy, born October 8, 1917, was one of the ring's classiest light heavyweight performers. In that respect he followed the trend of the division.

Billy outpointed Gus Lesnevich of Cliffside Park, New Jersey twice in title contests, once in New York and again in Detroit, then vacated the throne to seek a match with Joe Louis for the heavyweight title. He was stopped by the Bomber in the thirteenth round on June 18, 1941; again on June 19, 1945, in eight.

With Conn's retirement another elimination was started, New York naming its men and the National Boxing Association selecting a field of its own. After each had obtained its top performer, Anton Christoforidis of Messina, Greece, and Melio Bettina faced each other in Cleveland, with the Greek winning. Then he met Lesnevich in Madison Square Garden to decide U. S. supremacy and Gus won.

Since the war was on and European boxers were inactive, it was generally agreed that Lesnevich was the world's best in his division, but to clinch the top honors he accepted a challenge from the leading contender, Tami Mauriello of New York, whom he defeated twice to clinch his place in the sun.

Gus entered the Coast Guard during the war, was inactive until 1946, then on his discharge began to campaign in the States. He knocked out Joe Kahut in Seattle, in one round; was stopped by Lee Oma in four; then went to England to fight the British Empire champion, Freddie Mills, whom he stopped in the tenth round.

Back in the States he kayoed Billy Fox in ten, and again in one in title bouts; defeated Tami Mauriello, then stopped Tami in seven and Melio Bettina in one, in non-title affairs. He then returned to England to give Mills another chance. In this bout the Britisher took the crown from Gus

HE WON'T GET AWAY
FROM ME WHEN HE'S HURT

DRAWN BY
Billy Conn

Billy Conn, shown on opposite page, was the most handsome of all ringmen. He was an excellent boxer with a fair punch and beat many of the national favorites. Billy outpointed Melio Bettina for the crown on July 13, 1939, and after three title defenses, gave it up to go after Joe Louis. Billy had Louis beaten for 13 rounds in the first fight, got careless and was kayoed. Training for the second Louis fight Conn *(above)* drew a prediction *(right)* that came true in reverse.

Gus Lesnevich *(above, right)* gained National Boxing Association recognition as champion by defeating Anton Christoforidis on May 22, 1941, then clinched the American title by beating Tami Mauriello *(below, left)* on August 26, in 15 rounds.

By knocking out Freddie Mills in 10 rounds on May 14, 1946, Lesnevich was declared undisputed world champion. The fight, held in London, was vicious, with Gus handicapped by a closed left eye.

Freddie Mills, declared victor over Lesnevich by referee Ted Waltham on July 26, 1948, gained the world title for England.

Joey Maxim, a veteran campaigner from Cleveland, Ohio, won the title on January 24, 1950, by battering Freddie Mills into submission in the 10th round of a 15-round match. Maxim outclassed Mills throughout the fight, which took place at Earl's Court in London. Maxim, still available, started in 1941.

Archie Moore (left), another veteran, outpointed Maxim in St. Louis on December 17, 1952, in 15 rounds and is yet to be beaten for the light heavyweight crown. Moore has engaged in over 195 fights since the start of his career in 1936.

by winning the decision at the end of fifteen rounds.

Gus entered the heavyweight class after losing to Joey Maxim in a contest for the vacant American light heavyweight title. He faced Ezzard Charles for the N.B.A. heavyweight championship following Joe Louis's retirement and was stopped in the seventh round. That ended his career.

After Maxim had annexed the U. S. championship, his manager, Jack Kearns, took him to England to challenge Mills, who accepted. That match, staged in London on January 24, 1950, brought the world title back to America, Joey stopping the Britisher in the tenth round of a thrilling engagement.

Maxim, born March 28, 1922, in Cleveland, Ohio, on returning to America engaged in many contests.

He tackled Ezzard Charles in a heavy-weight championship mill in Chicago and lost in fifteen rounds, then successfully defended his crown against Bob Murphy in New York and stopped Ray Robinson in fourteen rounds after being well behind on points. Ray, the middleweight king, trying to annex another crown, collapsed from the excessive heat in the Yankee Stadium.

In his next defense on December 17, 1952 in St. Louis, Maxim lost his title to the veteran Archie Moore.

After Moore gained the crown, he and Maxim met twice in championship battles. The first, in Ogden, Utah, on June 24, 1953, resulted in Moore's winning a close decision to retain his laurels. In the second, at Miami, on January 27, 1954, Archie won by a wide margin in fifteen rounds.

Light heavyweight champion Joey Maxim (above, left) retained his crown on June 25, 1952, by outlasting middleweight champion Ray Robinson, who collapsed suddenly from exhaustion. Despite the excessive heat at Yankee Stadium that night, Robinson was well ahead on points until he began to wilt in the 13th round, falling face down at Maxim's feet before the round ended. When Robinson was unable to answer the bell for the 14th round, referee Ray Miller signified the fight was over and declared the jubilant Maxim (right) winner by a knockout.

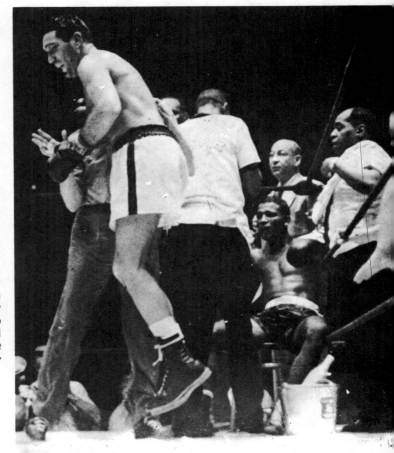

Moore knocked out Harold Johnson in New York on August 11, 1954, in the fourteenth round in defense of his crown; then he stopped Bobo Olson, the middleweight king, in the third round on June 22, 1955, in another title bout.

On September 21, 1955, Moore decided to try for the heavyweight championship and was knocked out by Rocky Marciano in the ninth round. Archie then went to England and on June 5, 1956, halted Yolande Pompey in London in the tenth round of a title mill.

When Rocky Marciano retired undefeated, Moore and Floyd Patterson fought for the vacant heavyweight throne and Floyd stopped Archie in the fifth round on November 30, 1956, to become Rocky's successor.

On July 8, 1957, both the New York Commission and the National Boxing Association declared the light heavyweight throne vacant due to Moore's failure to defend it and ordered Tony Anthony of New York and Harold Johnson to decide supremacy, they being the top contenders. But a day later they rescinded the order and Moore and Anthony were matched for the crown, Los Angeles being·chosen as the battleground on September 20.

Though Moore virtually slaughtered Anthony, he actually *talked* him out of the title. All through the early rounds he kept saying to the youngster, "You're looking great. Keep up what you're doing. You're the next champion!"

In the sixth and seventh rounds Anthony took a terrible battering, and the referee stopped the fight in the latter round.

In one of the most sensational fights seen in years, Archie Moore knocked out Yvon Durelle of Baie Ste. Anne, New Brunswick, Canada, in the 11th round (below), to retain his crown. The battle, held in the Forum in Montreal, on December 10, 1958, was packed with thrills. Floored four times, three times in the first round (above), Moore staggered back to knock Durelle down four times, twice in the final round. Ancient Archie now holds the record for career knockouts, with 127.

A schism arose in the light-heavyweight ranks when, on October 25, 1960, the National Boxing Association lifted Archie Moore's title for inactivity and then named thirty-three-year-old Harold Johnson, of Philadelphia, as their champion after he kayoed Jess Bowdry, of St. Louis, forty-five seconds into the ninth round on February 7, 1961. "Old Man" Moore, recognized as world champion by every other boxing board, had beaten Johnson in four out of five encounters between 1949 and 1954, and he still holds the record for longest-held title in his division.

In February 1962, the New York Commission withdrew its recognition of Moore, and when Johnson, a clever pugilist with a classic style, was awarded a unanimous decision over Doug Jones on May 12, 1962, in Philadelphia, he received international recognition.

The champion's superior punching power brought him another victory when he defeated Gustav Scholz, of Germany, in fifteen rounds on June 23, 1967, in Berlin.

A rare event occurred in the Johnson family. On June 22, 1936, Johnson's father, Phil, was kayoed by Jersey Joe Walcott in three rounds

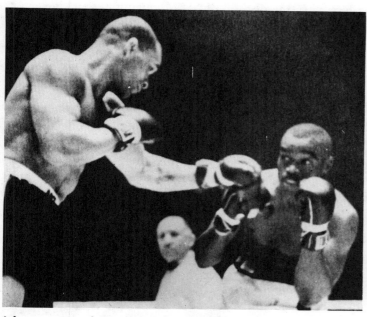

Johnson received international recognition as king of the division after defeating Doug Jones on May 12, 1962.

After scoring a technical kayo over Jesse Bowdry on February 7, 1961, Harold Johnson won N.B.A. recognition.

One of Johnson's best triumphs was the 15-round verdict he pounded out over Germany's Gustav Scholz in 1967.

Harold Johnson (left) spars with his father, Phil. Oddly, both were kayoed by Jersey Joe Walcott 14 years apart.

in Philadelphia. Fourteen years later, Feburary 8, 1950, Harold also was kayoed by Walcott in three rounds at Philadelphia.

Willie Pastrano, at 173½ pounds, unexpectedly found himself first Johnson's challenger, then his conqueror, when he outboxed the 174-pound Johnson in fifteen rounds in a split decision on June 1, 1963, in Las Vegas.

With blood flowing from a cut over Gregorio Peralta's eye, Pastrano retained the title with a six-round knockout on April 10, 1964, in New Orleans, after having lost a ten-round decision to the Argentinian in 1963.

The referee and most writers had the champion leading when he knocked out Terry Downes in 1:17 of the eleventh round, in Manchester, England, on November 30, 1964, to retain his title.

Always a fast-moving, wily, and defensive boxer but never known for his punching power, Pastrano met his match in Puerto Rico's idol José "Chegui" Torres, a recent graduate from the middleweight ranks. On March 30, 1965, Torres decked Pastrano for the first time in Pastrano's career, then kayoed him when the defender was too weary to answer the bell for the tenth round.

An extroverted yet gentle man and a lover of the arts, Torres learned his peek-a-boo stance from his manager, Cus D'Amato. The stance served him well when he was a member of the 1956 Olympic team and then won the Golden Gloves in 1968, and he continued to use it in his next two title bouts against Wayne Thornton, of California, and Chic Calderwood, the British Empire title holder. Torres beat Thornton in fifteen rounds on May 21, 1966, and kayoed Calderwood in the second round on October 15, 1966.

Richard Ihetu, former middleweight champ and better known as Dick Tiger, ascended the light-heavyweight throne on December 6, 1966, in New York, when officials decided that he had been more aggressive and faster on recoveries over the fiteen rounds than the surprisingly lethargic Torres. Torres's loss was even more surprising considering his seven-year, nine-pound, and two-inch advantages over the thirty-seven-year-old, 167-pound, five-foot-eight-inch Tiger.

Willie Pastrano (*right*) became the new 175-pound champion by scoring an upset 15-round decision over Johnson at Las Vegas on June 1, 1963, outboxing his heavier foe.

It was on November 30, 1964, that Pastrano traveled to Manchester, England, where he halted Terry Downs in the 11th.

Pastrano, retained his title by knocking out Gregorio Peralta (*below, left*) of Argentina in sixth round on April 10, 1964.

Tiger, who grew up in the Ibo tribe of eastern Nigeria, and was trained to box by British army officers, was one of boxing's best-liked heroes. Sincere, modest, affable, and gentlemanly, Tiger was also a man of conscience. When civil war broke out in his native Nigeria, he became a lieutenant in the morale corps of the Biafran army.

Already old for a boxer when he won the title, Tiger was past his peak when he entered the ring against 173¼-pound Bob Foster on May 24, 1968. The 168-pound champ started off well, landing a good left hook early in the first round, but the second and third rounds were Foster's as he eluded Tiger's shots while peppering his opponent with left jabs. A left

hook toppled Tiger onto his back and the champ was counted out by referee Mark Conn. This was the only time in Tiger's fifteen-year career that he was knocked out.

Tiger continued to fight until 1971, when he retired. Shortly afterward, on December 14, the Nigerian died of cancer in his homeland.

Foster went on to defend his title fourteen times, the record number for his class. From 1969 to 1973 he kayoed Frank DePaula, Andy Kendall, Roger Rouse, Mark Tessman, and Hal Carroll. He beat Ray Anderson, then kayoed Tommy Hicks, Brian Kelly, Vincent Rondon, Mike Quarry, and Chris Finnegan and ended the string with two decisions over Pierre Fourie of Johannesburg, South Africa.

Stepping up to the heavyweight class, he was knocked out by Joe Frazier in two rounds on November 18, 1970. On November 21, 1972, Ali kayoed him in eight rounds.

On June 17, 1974, Foster met a tartar in Jorge Ahumada, of Argentina. In the University of New Mexico Arena in Albuquerque 13,000 fans watched their "hometown son" fight a fifteen-round draw with Ahumada.

At 174 pounds, Foster was one-half pound heavier than his rival, but his thirty-two-year-old body almost spelled his doom. Nat Loubet, editor of *Ring*, scored the fight thirteen rounds for Ahumada to two for Foster. The draw decision was considered dubious, to say the least, by most of the fans and experts alike.

Foster was the favorite at 8 to 5,

Dick Tiger, who had taken the crown from Torres in December, 1966, successfully defended it against Jose on May 17, 1967.

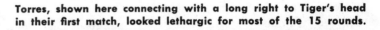

Torres, shown here connecting with a long right to Tiger's head in their first match, looked lethargic for most of the 15 rounds.

and although he had height and reach on his challenger, he never "got off." As the contest progressed, Ahumada gained confidence and finished strongly.

It was the fourteenth title defense for Foster and the least convincing of his career.

On September 17, 1974, Foster, who was 34, announced his retirement. The World Boxing Council then recognized the fight at Wembley on October 1, 1974, between Jorge Ahumada and John Conteh of Great Britain as being for the vacant title. Conteh, 23, from Liverpool, proved too strong and skillful for the Argentine and won a decision to become the first Briton to hold the title since Freddie Mills in 1950.

Meanwhile the W.B.A. recognized the battle between Ahumada's countryman Victor Galindez and Len Hutchins of the U.S.A. Galindez stopped Hutchins in the twelfth to become W.B.A. champion. In 1975 Galindez defended three times, gaining decisions against Pierre Fourie, of South Africa, in Johannesburg, against Jorge Ahumada, and against Fourie again in a Johannesburg return on September 13, 1975.

Conteh defended his W.B.C. title against Lonnie Bennett, of the U.S.A., at Wembley on March 11, 1975, and stopped his challenger, who was led back to his corner with blood pouring from a cut eye after one minute and ten seconds of the fifth round.

Conteh made one defence of his W.B.C. crown in 1976, outpointing Alvaro "Vaqui" Lopez in Copenhagen on October 9, but was stripped of his laurels in May 1977 through his failure to defend it and on May 21 Miguel Angel Cuello, from the Argentine, won the vacant championship by knocking out Jesse Burnett in nine rounds at Monte Carlo. On January 7, 1978, Cuello surprisingly lost his title to Mate Parlov, of Yugoslavia, by a knockout in nine rounds at Milan, who kept his crown by outpointing John Conteh at Belgrade on June 17, but it was not a popular verdict as the Englishman appeared to have done enough to get the decision. Parlov did not keep his title for long, being forced

Bob Foster jumps for joy after winning the light heavyweight title by knocking out Tiger in the fourth round on May 24, 1968. It was the only knockout ever suffered by Tiger.

to retire to Marvin Johnson, from Indianapolis, in ten rounds at Marsala on December 2, 1978.

Meanwhile, Victor Galindez maintained his hold on the W.B.A. version of the championship. In 1976 he made three successful defences against Harald Skog who retired in three rounds at Oslo on March 28; Richie Kates, who was knocked out in the final round at Johannesburg on May 22, and Kosie Smith, who was out-

pointed over fifteen rounds at Johannesburg on October 5. In 1976 he made three more successful defences, outpointing Richie Kates in Rome on June 18, outpointing Alvaro "Yaqui" Lopez in the same city on September 17 and outpointing Eddie Gregory over fifteen rounds at Turin on November 19. In 1978 Galindez defeated Lopez again, this time at Camaiore on May 6, but on September 15 he lost his title to Mike Ross

A right from John Conteh smacks home on the side of Jorge Ahumada's face (above) in their battle for the light-heavyweight crown on October 1, 1975 at Wembley.

man, from New Jersey, at New Orleans the bout being stopped in round thirteen. On December 5 Rossman made a successful first defence of his W.B.A. crown by stopping Aldo Traversaro in six rounds at Philadelphia.

He remained W.B.A. champion until April 14, 1979 when in a return match with Galindez he was stopped in ten rounds.

Eight days later, Marvin Johnson lost his W.B.A. title to Matt Franklin from Philadelphia, who knocked him out in eight rounds at Indianapolis. The new champion promptly changed his name to Matthew Saad Muhammad and his first defence, on August 18, 1979 at Atlantic City, was against John Conteh (Great Britain), who was endeavouring to regain the title he had lost to Mate Parlov in 1978. The champion sustained a badly gashed eyebrow and his seconds used an illegal substance to heal the wound. Conteh gave him a hard fight throughout, but was adjudged a narrow points loser at the end of 15 exciting rounds. A return bout was ordered and they met at Atlantic City on March 29, 1980, but this time Conteh boxed badly and was put down five times before the bout was stopped in round four.

Matthew Saad Muhammad made three more successful defences in 1980. On May 11 he stopped Louis Pergaud, from the Cameroons, in five rounds at Halifax, N.S. On July 13 he beat Alvaro Lopez (Stockton, Cal.) in 14 rounds at Great Gorge, N.J., and on November 28 he ruined the hopes of Lotte Mwale from Zambia, by knocking him out in three rounds at San Diego.

His winning way continuing, Saad Muhammad made three successful title defences in 1981, all at Atlantic City. On February 25 he stopped Vonzell Johnson in 11 rounds; on April 25 Murray Sutherland was knocked out in nine, while Jerry Martin was rescued by the referee in the 11th on September 26. In the same ring, however, Dwight Braxton (Baltimore) took over by stopping the champion in ten rounds on December 19. Jerry Martin had another try at

the title on March 21, 1982 at Las Vegas, but was stopped in six rounds, then Braxton gave Saad Muhammad a return bout at Philadelphia on August 7, this time halting him in six rounds. In celebration, the winner changed his name to Dwight Muhammad Qawi and was billed thus when he stopped Eddie Davis (U.S.A.) in 11 rounds at Atlantic City on November 20, 1982.

Qawi's reign came to an end on March 18 the following year when he lost to the W.B.A. champion, an event that unified the 175 pound title. It is worth recording, however, that on April 21, 1985 at Atlantic City, Marvin Johnson stopped Eddie Davis in six rounds in a contest which the W.B.C. labelled as a final eliminator for its light-heavyweight title.

Back to the W.B.A. championships. On November 30, 1979, Marvin Johnson changed sides and won the W.B.A. title by stopping Galindez in eleven rounds at New Orleans, but on March 31, 1980, he was himself stopped in eleven rounds by Eddie Gregory (New York) who got into the fashion by changing his name to Eddie Mustapha Muhammad. Under this guise he beat off challengers: Jerry Martin (Philadelphia) stopped in ten rounds at Mcaffe, N.J., and Dutchman Rudi Koopman, the European champion, stopped at the end of the third round at Los Angeles, to enter 1981 still as champion.

Enter Michael Spinks (brother to

Leon, one time heavyweight king) who was to make boxing history in more ways than one. An Olympic Games gold medallist at middleweight in 1976, he turned pro the following year and up to his first fight for the world light-heavyweight title, was unbeaten in sixteen bouts, eleven inside-the-distance. On July 18, 1981 he outpointed Eddie Mustapha Muhammad at Atlantic City to take the World Boxing Association's version of the 175-pound title and in the next ten months accounted for five challengers, all at Atlantic City and none going beyond nine rounds: on November 7 Vonzell Johnson (seven rounds); on February 13, 1982, Mustapha Wasajja (six); on April 11 Murray Sutherland (eight); on June 11 Jerry Celestine (eight); on September 18 Johnny Davis (nine).

Anxious to prove himself the very best in the world, Spinks challenged Dwight Muhammad Qawi, the W.B.C. champion, and outpointed him over 15 rounds on March 18, 1983, again at Atlantic City, to become undisputed world light-heavyweight champion. His first defence on November 25 saw him halt Oscar Rivadeneyra (Peru) in eight rounds at Vancouver. On February 25, 1984 Spinks outpointed Eddie Davis (U.S.A.) over 12 rounds at Atlantic City, and in the same ring on February 23, 1985 demolished David Sears (U.S.A.) in three rounds. Jim McDonald was stopped in eight rounds at Las Vegas on

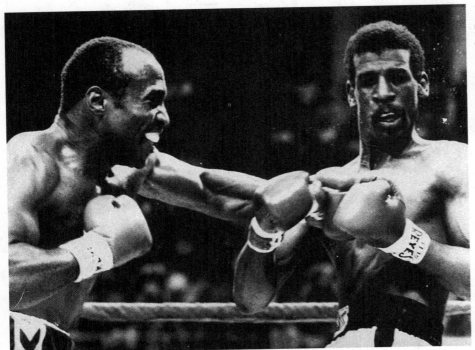

Dwight Muhammad Qawi (formerly Dwight Braxton), the W.B.C. champion, lands a left on Michael Spinks, the W.B.A. champion, in 1983, but Spinks took the unified championship.

June 6, this being his tenth title defence and, as it turned out, his last.

He and brother Leon were the second pair of brothers to win world titles and Michael was the first light-heavyweight champion to win the world heavyweight crown. Up to that feat he was undefeated in 27 bouts, 19 of which had been won inside the scheduled distance. When he beat Larry Holmes he had built up his weight to 204 pounds. When it was announced that he would not defend the light-heavyweight title again, both the W.B.C. and the W.B.A. declared it vacant and Spinks went into the record books among the very few who have been unbeaten when relinquishing a world title.

The W.B.C. proclaimed J. B. Williamson, an ex-marine from Los Angeles, as their champion when he outpointed Prince Mohammed (Ghana) over 12 rounds at Los Angeles on December 10, 1985, while the W.B.A. named Marvin Johnson, who beat Leslie Stewart (Trinidad), the referee stopping the contest at Indianapolis on February 9, 1986.

On April 30, 1986, Dennis Andries (Great Britain) outpointed J.B. Williamson in London to take the W.B.C. title.

There now arose a new star in the division. He was a white-skinned hitter, named Bobby Czyz. He had a great following with his all-action non-compromising style, and on September 6 he completely defeated Slobodan Kacar at Las Vegas to annex the I.B.F. crown. Before the year was out he easily beat David Sears on December 26 in the

very opening round. Not content to place his title in cold storage he soon took on Willie Edwards at Atlantic City on February 21, 1987, and he knocked his man out in a couple of rounds. By May he was at it again, and on the 3rd of that month he found that he had little to beat in his challenger Jim MacDonald, who stalled his way into the 6th round, in the same city, when the referee halted a somewhat ridiculous encounter.

Meanwhile, on September 10, 1986, in London, Dennis Andries faced a rather surprising challenge from the British war-horse, middleweight Tony Sibson, who, despite having failed in a world championship bid against Marvin Hagler some years earlier, felt sure that he could lick Andries for the light-heavyweight crown. He made a gallant effort, but Andries was too big and strong for him, and the bout was halted in the 9th round to give Dennis his first successful defence of the W.B.C. belt.

Ten days later, at Indianapolis, the

Tony Sibson, veteran British middleweight, on the floor and about to be stopped when challenging Dennis Andries for the W.B.C. title in London in 1986.

veteran Marvin Johnson stopped Jean-Marie Emebe in 13 rounds to retain his hold on the W.B.A. honours. Although there was some talk of an attempt at unification, a bombshell of a challenge emerged from Detroit. Thomas Hearns, that incredible combination of boxer and fighter, announced his intention of going for the light-heavyweight title, versus Dennis Andries, and a match was made for March 7, 1987 at his home town. An exciting contest ensued, with numerous knockdowns and much wild swinging, culminating in a 10th round intervention by the referee when Andries was still game but absolutely helpless.

At Port of Spain, Trinidad, Marvin Johnson, who had stopped the West Indian Leslie Stewart the previous year, faced the same man again on the challenger's home ground. This time Stewart reversed matters and forced the W.B.A. champion into retirement in 8 rounds, on May 23.

It was September 5 before the new W.B.A. title-holder risked his laurels, and the first Trinidadian to claim a major championship lost it at his very first defence. Although he made a courageous battle, he was defeated in 4 rounds by Virgil Hill.

The following month, on October 29, the very active Bobby Czyz put his honours on the line in opposition to "Prince" Charles Williams at Las Vegas, and it looked to be merely a matter of time when the champion dumped his challenger to the boards early in the contest. But thereafter Williams boxed a cagey contest and also closed Bobby's right eye completely. He was giving the champion a good going over when, after 9 rounds, the medicos inspected Czyz's condition and his corner-men reluctantly surrendered.

In Paris, on November 21, Virgil Hill made his initial defence of the W.B.A. belt and he came through with flying colours. He won every one of the 12 rounds when outpointing Rufino Angulo. A week later, on November 27, Port of Spain was selected as the venue to decide a successor to Thomas Hearns, who had summarily relinquished his W.B.C. belt after stopping Andries and proving a point he had wanted to make.

The two contenders chosen to battle it out for the vacant throne were Canada's "Golden Boy", the good-looking Don Lalonde, and the veteran New Yorker, Eddie Davis.

Davis was making his third attempt at a title, but Lalonde proved that youth will be served and, after almost winning by a knockout in the opening round, his first attack in the 2nd caused the referee to stop the uneven contest immediately.

Lalonde stopped challenger Leslie Stewart, and then ran into Sugar Ray Leonard. Leonard, who had retired, saw a chance of increasing the number of weights at which he had won a world title from three to five and was allowed to return straight into a title fight. Lalonde, moreover, was persuaded to defend against Leonard at 168lb, thereby allowing the W.B.C. to inaugurate its super-middleweight title, both championships being at stake. Although he floored Leonard at Las Vegas on November 7, 1988, Lalonde was stopped in the ninth round. He thus lost his light-heavyweight title despite having to come in at seven pounds below the limit. However the purse was his biggest. Leonard, his object achieved, immediately relinquished the title.

In the meantime W.B.A. champion Virgil Hill built up a long list of victories, successfully defending against Ramzi Hassan (U.S.A.), Willie Featherstone (Canada), previous champion Bobby Czyz, Joe Lasisi (Nigeria), James Kinchen (U.S.A.), David Vedder (U.S.A.), Tyrone Frazier (U.S.A.) and Mike Peak (U.S.A.), before he was surprisingly outpointed by former W.B.C. champion Thomas Hearns at Las Vegas on June 3, 1991. Hearns lost the crown on his first defence, being himself surprisingly outpointed by the super-middleweight champion Iran Barkley on March 20, 1992 in Las Vegas. Barkley chose to concentrate on the super-middleweight title and Virgil Hill regained the W.B.A. light-heavyweight crown in Bismarck by outpointing Frank Tate, the former middleweight champion, on September 29, 1992.

Hill retained the title in bizarre fashion on February 26, 1993 when he won a technical decision against Adolpho Washington in Fargo, North Dakota. Before the 12th and last round, the ringside physician examined Washington's eye. With the cornerman and manager also hovering, a TV cameraman attempted to get a close-up and banged Washington's eye with the camera. The eye began bleeding badly, and Washington could not continue. Hill again defended the W.B.A. crown successfully in Paris on March 12, 1993 against Fabrice Tiozzo, winning a split decision.

Prince Charles Williams had an even longer run than Hill. He successfully defended his I.B.F. title against Richard

Dennis Andries (right) three times held the W.B.C. light-heavyweight title, losing it for the final time in a return match with Australia's Jeff Harding in 1991.

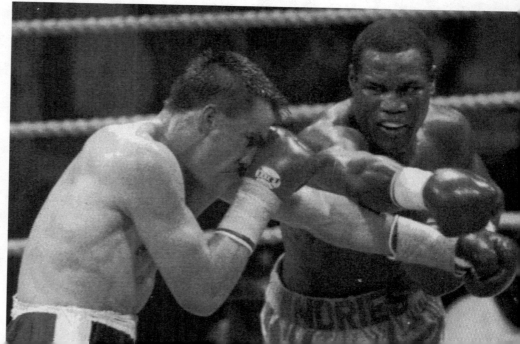

Caramanolis (France), Rufino Angulo (France), Bobby Czyz, Frankie Swindell (U.S.A.), Mwehu Beya (Italy), James Kinchen (U.S.A.), Vince Boulware (U.S.A.), and Freddie Delgado (Puerto Rico). Only Beya took him the distance, and Williams often fought on his opponent's territory. This fine run came to an end on March 20, 1993 when he was outpointed by Henry Maske of Germany in Dusseldorf. His reign lasted for nearly 5½ years.

After Leonard relinquished the W.B.C. title, it was regained by Dennis Andries, with a fifth-round stoppage of Tony Willis (U.S.A.) in Tucson on February 21, 1989. Andries had three tremendous fights with Jeff Harding (Australia). On June 24, 1989 in Atlantic City, Harding took the title with a 12th round stoppage after Andries had built up a big lead. Harding stopped Tom Collins (G.B.) and Nestor Giovanni

(Argentina) and then lost the crown back to Andries on July 28, 1990 in Melbourne. After being behind, Andries staged an all-or-nothing rally in the seventh round and knocked out the previously unbeaten Harding.

Andries successfully defended twice, against Sergio Merani (Argentina) and Guy Waters (Australia), and then accepted a rubber match with Harding on September 11, 1991 at the Hammersmith Odeon, London. Harding won a close decision after another hard battle. He subsequently defended successfully against Christophe Tiozzo (France) in Marseille and David Vedder (U.S.A.) in St Jean de Luz.

The first W.B.O. champion was another long-reigning titlist, making it regrettable that there was never an attempt to unify the division in the late 1980s. Michael Moorer won the inaugural championship with a fifth-round

stoppage of Ramzi Hassan at Cleveland on December 3, 1988. He defended successfully against Victor Claudio (Puerto Rico), Frankie Swindell, Freddie Delgado, Leslie Stewart (Trinidad), Jeff Thompson (U.S.A.), Marcellus Allen (U.S.A.), Mario Melo (Argentina) and Danny Lindstrom (Canada) before relinquishing the title in 1991 to campaign as a heavyweight. Leonzer Barber (U.S.A.) won the vacant title by forcing Tom Collins to retire in the fifth at Leeds on May 9, 1991, and defended successfully against Anthony Hembrick (U.S.A.) and Mike Sedillo. Barber's points win over fellow-American Sedillo took place in Beijing on February 27, 1993, and was erroneously claimed to be the first boxing promotion in China for 44 years. Nevertheless a crowd of 18,000 was present at the Capital Gymnasium and 400 million watched the bout live on television.

THE SUPER-MIDDLEWEIGHT CHAMPIONS

Yet another weight division was incorporated in professional boxing in 1984, when the I.B.F. inaugurated the super-middleweights, a division set at 168 lb. The first title bout at this poundage was contested at Atlantic City, on March 28, 1984, when Murray Sutherland, a Scotsman, was paired with Ernie Singletary over 15 rounds.

Sutherland won on points and thus became the first super-middleweight king.

His reign, however, was short-lived. He travelled to Seoul, South Korea, and on July 22 he was knocked out in 11 rounds by Chong-Pal Park.

Park proved to be a very active champion, and throughout 1985, 1986, and 1987 he faced all-comers. He visited Los Angeles to outpoint Vinnie Curto, but he was a great attraction in Seoul and district, and he boxed frequently on his home territory. He knocked out Roy Gumbs in a couple of rounds, outpointed Curto before giving him the return fight in the States, and then boxed a technical draw with Lindell Holmes, when both men clashed heads accidentally and the bout was halted. Park then won on points against Marvin Mack, and stopped Doug Sam in the last round. He also defeated Lindell Holmes over 15 rounds in a return match.

(left and right) Scotsman Murray Sutherland, wearing tartan shorts, lost his title in Seoul in 1984 to Chong-Pal Park, a South Korean who proved successful, becoming a dual champion in 1987.

It was inevitable that the other governing bodies would fall in line with the I.B.F. and in 1987, after Chong-Pal Park had easily beaten Emanuel Otti in 4 rounds, he was matched with Jesus Gallardo for the W.B.A. title. Park took this title with a second-round stoppage and relinquished the I.B.F. crown. Park made only one successful W.B.A. defence, a knockout of Polly Pasieron, before losing a decision to the veteran Fully Obelmejias of Venezuela in Suanbao on May 23, 1988. Obelmejias had twice lost to Hagler as a middleweight and was a surprise but emphatic winner. Obelmejias returned the title to South Korea on his first defence, being stopped in the 11th round by In-Chul Baek in Seoul on May 27, 1989. Baek made two successful defences in the East, against Ronnie Essett (U.S.A.) and Yoshiaki Yajima, before facing Frenchman Christophe Tiozzo in Lyon and being stopped in the sixth round on March 30, 1990.

Christophe stopped two U.S. challengers, Paul Whittaker and Danny Morgan, in 1990 before a Panamanian, Victor Cordoba, stopped him in the ninth round in Marseille on April 5, 1991. Cordoba made his first defence in Paris, stopping an Italian, Vincenzo Nardiello, but on September 12, 1992, he ran up against the flamboyant Michael Nunn, the former middleweight champion, and lost a very controversial split decision in Las Vegas. A return fight at the New Pyramid Arena, in Memphis, Tennessee on January 30, 1993 was marked with persistent fouling, particularly by Cordoba, who decked Nunn four times but had four points deducted for low blows. The fight might have been stopped in Nunn's favour in the second round, in which Cordoba took a beating which included two blows struck while he was down. In the end the brilliant Nunn won a comfortable points verdict. On February 20, the W.B.A. manipulated their ratings so that Nunn could knock out the outclassed Danny Morgan in the first round in Mexico City. The busy Nunn was in action again on April 23

when he stopped Crawford Ashley, a British challenger, in the sixth round at Memphis.

Meanwhile the vacant I.B.F. title was won by the unbeaten Graciano Rocchigiani, from a West German boxing family. He stopped Vince Boulware (U.S.A.) in Dusseldorf on March 12, 1988. The busy Rocchigiani saw off three challengers, Nicky Walker, Chris Reid and Thulani Malinga before relinquishing the title. Lindell Holmes (U.S.A.), a previous unsuccessful challenger, took the crown by outpointing Frank Tate, a former middleweight champion, on January 27, 1990 in New Orleans. He beat Carl Sullivan, Thulani Malinga and Antoine Byrd before becoming the first I.B.F. champion in this division to lose his title in the ring, being knocked out in the 11th round by Darrin Von Horn (U.S.A.), in Verbania on May 18, 1991. Van Horn made one successful defence, against John Jarvis, but was then stopped in the second

round in the inaugural fight card at the Paramount, the new Madison Square Garden arena. This was January 10, 1993 and the new champion was the veteran ex-middleweight champ Iran Barkley.

Barkley lost the title when he could not concede eight years to 24-year-old James Toney, the I.B.F. middleweight champion. The ringside physician halted the bout between the 9th and 10th rounds at Caesars Palace on February 13, 1993 because of a cut eye. Toney expressed himself happier at 168lb than at the middleweight limit.

One of the most eagerly anticipated contests in Great Britain was a return between Michael Watson (left) and Chris Eubank for the vacant W.B.O. super-middleweight championship. Watson was winning the fight until he scored a knockdown in the 11th round. Eubank rose to catch him with an uppercut and Watson was badly injured after catching his neck on the bottom rope.

The W.B.C. introduced its championship in this division when Sugar Ray Leonard challenged Donny Lalonde for the light-heavyweight title. By agreeing to the match at 168lb, the winner would also be recognised as super-middleweight champion. Leonard won, as reported in the previous section, and the way was open for a lucrative return contest with Tommy Hearns, the new W.B.O. champion, and also a world 'champion' at five weights. Leonard had beaten Hearns in a terrific battle to unify the welterweight title in 1981. Hearns had sought revenge ever since, and many thought he had achieved it on June 12, 1989 at Caesars Palace, when he had Leonard down in the 3rd and 11th rounds. But with one judge voting for each and the third unable to split them, the result was a draw. Leonard then easily beat veteran Roberto Duran on points to win the private series between those two by 2–1, and then, as he had done before at

other weights, relinquished his interest in the division.

The new W.B.C. champion was Mauro Galvano of Italy, who outpointed Dario Matteoni (Argentina) at Monaco on December 15, 1990. Galvano then beat Ronnie Essett and Carlos Giminez before Nigel Benn, the former W.B.O. middleweight champion, forced him to retire after the third round in Marino on October 3, 1992. Benn stopped Nicky Piper of Wales, and outpointed Galvano in a return in Glasgow.

The first W.B.O. champion in the division was Tommy Hearns, who outpointed James Kinchen (U.S.A.) for the title in Las Vegas on November 14, 1988. After his draw with Leonard, Hearns outpointed Michael Olajide and gave up the title. The W.B.O. then cynically introduced Britons Chris Eubank and Michael Watson into their ratings at numbers 1 and 2. The two had fought a W.B.O. middleweight title fight three months earlier, when the

result had been controversial, and the W.B.O. ploy meant that their return fight could be for the vacant title. The bout, at Spurs' football ground at White Hart Lane, London, on September 21, 1991, proved to be a tragic one. Watson appeared to have the contest well won, especially when he dropped Eubank in the 11th round. But Eubank got up to fell Watson with an uppercut. As he fell Watson's head caught the lowest rope. Although he beat the count and began the 12th, the referee was forced to intervene when Watson was clearly in trouble. He sank into a coma, and although his life was saved, he began a period of rehabilitation confined to a wheelchair with partial paralysis.

Eubank proved to be a busy champion but his opponents were not always genuine world class, and he beat Thulani Malinga, John Jarvis, Ronnie Essett, Tony Thornton, Carlos Gimenez and Lindell Holmes in just over a year.

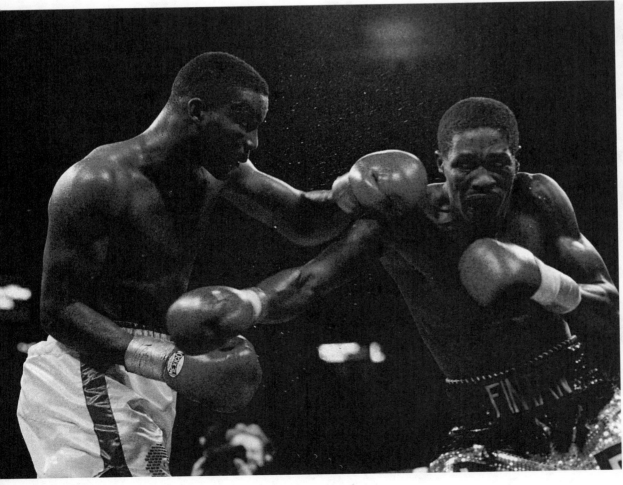

Michael Nunn (left) seemed destined to become one of the outstanding middleweight champions of the 1990s until he was surprisingly stopped by James Toney. However he moved up a division to take the W.B.A. super-middleweight crown from Victor Cordoba in 1991, and proved a busy and impressive champion.

THE MIDDLEWEIGHTS

When one discusses great fighters, the stars of both the middleweights and welterweights come in for their share of praise. The middleweight class in particular has been the most colorful and most intriguing. It stands out as the toughest over the years. It is a class in which every asset of greatness must be displayed by those who seek to gain the top rung.

Its stars have been many and their performances occupy a special niche in the Fistic Hall of Fame. Its battles have been thrillers, in number far superior to those of any other class. Boxing ability, speed, stamina, heavy hitting—these have all been on display in the majority of the championship fights in this division.

The list of outstanding boxers in the class comprises names of men whose ring battles are historic. Often listed as tops are Stanley Ketchel, most frequently named as the king of the class for all time; Bob Fitzsimmons, who won the title from Nonpareil Jack Dempsey in a stirring encounter, the first of his three title triumphs; and Sugar Ray Robinson, a ring marvel, whose defeat of Carmen Basilio enabled him to establish a world record. Robinson is the first to win the championship in the middleweight sector five times, regaining it four.

Kid McCoy, the wily corkscrew artist, a cagey, clever battler; Tony Zale, a powerful hitter; Rocky Graziano, a colorful, two-fisted fighter whose championship contests with Zale—the

Jack Martin, born in 1796, was a baker by trade and was dubbed "Master of the Rolls." He had fast hands and won his first fight when he was only 17 years old. Martin, 5'9" tall and weighing 150 pounds, always met heavier men.

Nat Langham (right), born in Leicestershire in 1820, was middleweight king from 1843 to 1857. He weighed only 157 pounds, but he was so good that ring patrons favored him as a candidate for the heavyweight crown. Harry Orme, a 200-pound giant, was the only man to defeat him, but it took 117 rounds and three hours. Langham beat the celebrated Tom Sayers (his only loss) in 61 rounds in 1853.

Jack Randall, the original "Nonpareil," also called the "Prime Irish Lad," was born in London in 1794. Randall was the most accomplished middleweight ever developed in England. During his career (1815-1821) he won all of his 15 bouts by knockouts.

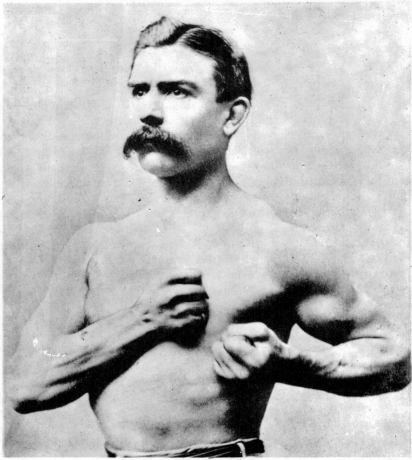

Mike Donovan *(left)* and George Rooke *(above)* were twice matched for a middleweight title bout, but police prevented both meetings. When Donovan decided to join the heavyweights, Rooke declared himself middleweight champion. In later years, Donovan was boxing instructor at the New York Athletic Club.

first of which he lost and the second of which was a sensational victory for him—made ring history; Jake LaMotta, who lost the crown to Ray Robinson; Randy Turpin, who relieved Robinson of the title, then lost a thriller to him before a record-breaking paying gate of $767,626 and attendance of 61,370 at the Polo Grounds on September 12, 1951; Marcel Cerdan, French ace who was killed in an airplane accident; Vince Dundee and Billy Soose—these are only a few of the stalwarts who kept the class in the spotlight.

It is a division that set many records in marks for attendance, receipts, and exciting contests: bouts in which Billy Papke and Ketchel engaged; the clever artistry of Mike Gibbons and Jeff Smith; the short but marvelous career of Les Darcy, Australian champion; the ring science of Tommy Ryan

and the all-around ability of Jimmy Clabby, Eddie McGoorty, George Chip, Harry Greb, Jack Dillon, and Frank Klaus. They all left their mark for future stars to shoot at.

The trio whose names are mentioned most frequently, however, when ring greatness comes up for discussion, are Ketchel, Robinson, and Darcy, whose untimely death deprived the game of one of its luminaries.

Long before middleweights as such were listed as a separate class in the United States, the British had such a division. In our country the middleweights—and even the welterweights—were too busy engaging pugilists who scaled from 160 up to 200 pounds. Fighting heavier men was a steady diet for middleweights.

The first American to obtain recognition as middleweight champion was

Tom Chandler, who defeated Dooney Harris in San Francisco by a knockout in the twenty third round on April 13, 1867. Chandler held on to the crown until 1872 with little fighting, and when challenged by George Rooke he refused to defend the crown and retired. On July 17, 1872, Rooke, was acclaimed title holder.

On March 10, 1881, Rooke tackled Prof. Mike Donovan in the Terrace Garden of New York in a championship match, and so badly was Rooke beaten that the police stopped the affair in the second round, Donovan gaining the crown.

Donovan didn't remain at the head long. He retired the following year to box exhibitions with heavyweights. This left the middleweight throne vacant for two years. Then George Fulljames of Toronto, Canadian title holder, announced that he was pre-

RING Nº 1
FIGHTING IN THE RISING
TIDE WATER

RING Nº 2
THE FINISH

Jack Dempsey and Johnny Reagan, after two postponements due to police vigilance and fog, finally met for their title fight, at Huntington, Long Island, on December 18, 1887. After eight rounds, the rising tide from the nearby Sound flooded the ring and the fight was halted. Reagan refused to fight on sand, so the 25 spectators, led by Dempsey and Reagan, boarded their tug and found a turf spot, 25 miles away. Resuming (above), Reagan was badly outclassed, but gamely went 45 rounds before he was forced to quit.

Dempsey was ambitious to reach the top. In his third fight (left) he met Harry Force, an experienced battler, for $100 a side, at Coney Island, New York. At that time the resort was a dumping ground for derelicts and criminals escaping police. The ring was a circle formed by the fans, who witnessed a rousing battle, until the 11th round, when police raided the scene. The referee set a new date—September 17—for the fight, but Force failed to appear.

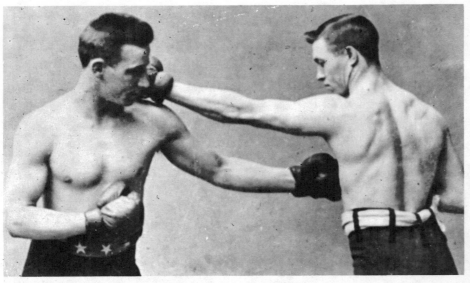

Tommy Ryan *(left)*, shown sparring with Jim Dineen, was recognized as middleweight champ when Bob Fitzsimmons abandoned the class to aim for the heavyweight crown. Ryan had defeated all challengers for the middleweight title.

POISONED GLOVES USED IN

Deadly Oil of Mustard Was Smeare Bonner's Fighting Mits, Nearly Blinding His Opponent.

BLINDED BY A BLOW FROM A POISONED GLOVE:

Tommy West *(above)* gave Ryan a rough time before being kayoed in the 14th round in 1898. In 1899 West won on a foul over Jack Bonner in the eighth round, when he was blinded *(left)* by the oil of mustard which had been smeared on Bonner's gloves. In 1900 West forced Joe Walcott to quit in 11 rounds, but the following year he was again knocked out by Ryan at Louisville, Kentucky. This 17-rounder was the bloodiest battle ever seen in the South.

t to a clinch. to the body the right on started to

o a straight p early. He trying with gave him a wing to the tried at the West's left He bled a urriedly got ey dove into nt an awful

ind. Bonner left for the at the head. the left a od. Toward ried with a West clinch- he body, but e time.

ing.

inual efforts gan to tell. n. Then he d West was t from gong wed a bit. isposition to lloping. grind, Bon- and landing. calling for few straight and one real close, had a

uneventful. th the left, the right- got to Bon-

there was something on the gloves. He staggered back, half blinded, and caught one of the arms, which had blocked Bonner's blow, as if burned. The referee said: "I smell it," and turning to Bonner sent him to the corner.

The police flooded Bonner's corner and took charge of the seconds, while the crowd stood up. West, in the meantime was in agony from the burns he had received, and White was nearly blinded. Bonner finally admitted he had oil of mustard in his corner for his legs. The fight was given to West.

Every circumstance of the fight between West and Bonner points to a job. The betting, which, on the past performance of the men, should have been no better than 6 to 5, was 2 to 1, with Bonner a favorite. Some were offering 100 to 40, and it is said one man offered to bet 50 to 15 he could name the winner. The betting was all o' of keeping with honesty, and those wao had thought of betting on West got fright- ened and refused to bet at all.

Bob Fitzsimmons knocked out Dempsey for the title and defended it only once.

Stanley Ketchel, 5' 9" and 154 pounds of fury, was christened Stanislaus Kiecal on September 14, 1887, in Grand Rapids, Michigan. He left farm life at 15 and "rode the rods," wandering through the West where he fought his way out of hobo jungles into the ring. From 1903, when he started, to 1910, when he was murdered, Ketchel fought 63 battles. He scored 46 knockouts, 14 in rapid succession in 1905.

pared to meet any middleweight in the world, to decide the ownership of the vacant throne. Nonpareil Jack Dempsey, accepted the defi.

The men met at Great Kills, Staten Island, on July 30, 1884. They fought with heavy driving gloves and Full-james was battered into submission in the twenty-second round. From then on Dempsey successfully defended his crown until he was knocked out by Robert Fitzsimmons on January 14, 1891, in a vicious encounter at New Orleans, in which Dempsey was halted in the thirteenth round.

Previously—in 1886—Dempsey stopped the great George LaBlanche, "The Marine," in the thirteenth round; but in 1889 LaBlanche, with the aid of the pivot punch, knocked out Dempsey in the thirty-second round. Since LaBlanche was overweight, Dempsey retained his crown.

Prior to that, in 1888, public opinion had forced Donovan out of retirement

Exciting battles lay ahead, when Stanley Ketchel, named "the Michigan Assassin," claimed the middleweight crown. On June 4, 1908, he whipped Billy Papke in 10 rounds. They met again on September 7, at Los Angeles, and in a surprise finish, Papke (right), known as the "Illinois Thunderbolt," knocked Ketchel out in 12 rounds. Ignoring the preliminary handshake, Papke floored Ketchel with a terrific right. Down four times in the first round, one eye shut tight, and fighting in a daze, Ketchel took a horrible beating for 12 rounds.

Willus Britt (below, right), who handled Stanley Ketchel's ring affairs, also managed lightweight Jimmy Britt, his brother.

Jack (Twin) Sullivan was knocked out after going 20 rounds with Ketchel. His twin brother, Mike, lasted one round.

to fight Dempsey for the world championship. "The Nonpareil" agreed. They fought on November 15, in Brooklyn, and the contest ended in a six-round draw, with Dempsey retaining his throne.

What Robinson is to the present day school of middleweights, Ketchel was to the old. Stanley, born of Polish parents, September 14, 1887, in Grand Rapids, Michigan, engaged in many scintillating contests, the best of which were those with Joe Thomas and Billy Papke.

He knocked out Mike Twin Sullivan on February 22, 1908 in one round to win the crown and three months later, stopped his brother Jack Twin, in twenty. Then, in successive months, he defeated Billy Papke in ten rounds in a championship match; stopped Hugh Kelly in three; knocked out Joe Thomas in two; and lost his title in the twelfth round of his battle

Two months after being slaughtered by Billy Papke, Ketchel regained his crown, before a packed arena in San Francisco. Ketchel sailed into Papke from the first bell and never let up until he caught him with a clean shot on the jaw in the 11th round.

When Ketchel met Jack Johnson on October 16, 1909, he weighed 160 pounds to Johnson's 209. In rounds 8, 9, 10 and 11, Ketchel pressed the attack. Ketchel's first blow in round 12 put Johnson down (left). But Johnson got up and kayoed him.

with Billy Papke in Los Angeles, September 7, 1908. Two months later, November 26, he rewon his throne, halting Papke in the eleventh round in San Francisco.

The following year Ketchel and Jack O'Brien engaged in a hair-raising affair in New York in which the final gong found Philadelphia Jack's head resting in the sawdust pail. It was a vicious encounter, a no-decision bout, with O'Brien saved from a knockout by the bell. He then stopped O'Brien in Philadelphia in three rounds. Then came his fourth affair with Billy Papke in Colma, California, the most thrill-

Ketchel's next fight after regaining his crown from Papke was with the clever warrior, Philadelphia Jack O'Brien. They met on March 26, 1909, at the Pioneer Athletic Club in New York, which was once a horse market. O'Brien's defensive skill and ring craft warded off many of the boring-in attacks by Ketchel. Most of Jack's blows landed, but they were not good enough to slow Ketchel down. Going into the 10th round, O'Brien seemed to be ahead, though the bout was a no-decision affair. With only eight seconds to go in the 10th and final round, Ketchel unleashed a furious attack *(right)* and landed a deadly right on O'Brien's jaw. Jack toppled over backwards, completely out, with his head resting in the resin box *(below)* in his own corner. The referee tolled off the count, but only reached eight when the final bell rang.

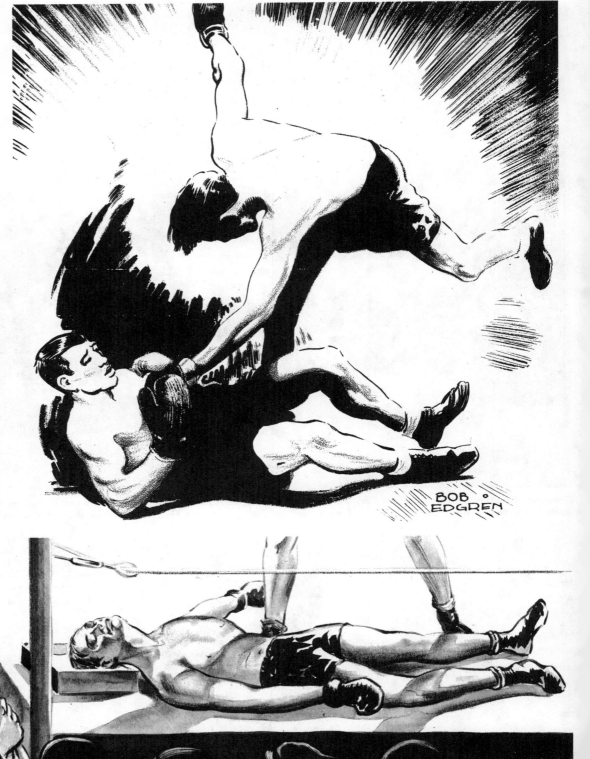

ing of all his engagements. It was fought in a raging storm, and Stanley, now dubbed the "Michigan Assassin," won on points after twenty rounds and held on to his throne.

Three months later he tried to wrest the heavyweight title from Jack Johnson, and though he put the giant Negro down in a surprise maneuver, he was knocked out with the next punch by Johnson after Jack quickly regained his feet in the twelfth round.

On October 15, 1910, Ketchel was killed by a jealous farmhand, Walter A. Dipley.

Kid McCoy could have won the middleweight crown without much trouble, but he put on weight to go after the heavyweight title.

Les Darcy, middleweight champion of Australia, was 5' 6" tall and scaled 158 pounds. He had skill and stamina.

Les Darcy was never seen in an American ring. Judged from his wonderful performances in Australia against the cream of the American talent, had he not died from a combination of a broken heart and pneumonia in Memphis, Tennessee, after he was hounded by U. S. sports writers as a "slacker," there is no telling how far he would have gone in his chosen profession. He might have been greater than Ketchel.

He came to New York on an oil tanker, after leaving his native land without permission. He was signed to fight Jack Dillon in the old Madison Square Garden, but Governor Whit-man of New York, following concerted attacks, not only refused permission for Darcy to perform in the Empire State, but induced other Governors to do likewise in their domains. He issued a statement declaring that Les had run away from his native land to avoid induction into the Army for World War One service, and wherever Darcy went this stigma followed him.

He enlisted in the National Guard Air Corps in Tennessee but died from what most people thought was a broken heart. Thus, while termed a slacker in our country, this nineteen year old fistic phenom from Australia passed away as a member of our armed forces.

In Australia, he knocked out Eddie McGoorty twice, George Chip, beat Jimmy Clabby, George K.O. Brown, and Fritz Holland; lost to Jeff Smith in five rounds and beat him on a foul in two. He had an excellent record.

Kid McCoy was another who stood out in the class. He was a clever, sharpshooting boxer with a bunch of tricks up his sleeves. He and Tommy Ryan set the pace for their division in the early days. McCoy killed himself, as did Papke.

With the death of Ketchel, there was a wild scramble for the vacated

Frank Mantell, who came from Pawtucket, Rhode Island, bolstered his title claim when he beat Papke in 1912. Mantell, a 12-year veteran, retired in 1917, after being knocked out by Harry Greb in one round and Mike Gibbons in three rounds.

Billy Papke, shown weaving under Jim Sullivan's left (above), scored a knockout over Sullivan in London on June 8, 1911, in nine rounds, and reclaimed the crown when Cyclone Thompson could no longer make the weight.

Cyclone Johnny Thompson, of Sycamore, Illinois, won handily over Papke in 20 rounds and clinched his claim for the crown. Thompson's ring career started in 1892, when he was 16 years old.

throne. Billy Papke claimed the title. Previous to the death of Ketchel, he fought no decisions with Willie Lewis and Frank Klaus and kayoed Lewis in three rounds in Paris, stopped Joe Thomas in sixteen rounds in San Francisco and won from Jack Twin Sullivan in Boston. He was in Australia at the time of Ketchel's demise and as the former champion and number one contender declared himself champion.

On February 11, 1911, he was out-pointed in twenty rounds in Sydney by Cyclone Johnny Thompson. But Thompson couldn't hold on to his newly won laurels because he became overweight and Papke reclaimed the championship.

Frank Mantell disputed the claim and on February 22, 1912, at Sacramento, California, he whipped Papke in twenty rounds and received considerable support as world champion.

Others who were in the field and

In 1913 Jeff Smith had five bouts in Paris. He drew with Frank Mantell in 20 rounds and later lost a 20-round decision to Georges Carpentier *(right)*.

Mike Gibbons, a boxing marvel, fought 132 bouts in a career from 1908 to 1922.

Jimmy Clabby, another tough ring veteran, battled the best from 1906 to 1923.

Jeff Smith, who had been fighting only two years, was beginning to meet the best men when he put in a claim for the title. Born in New York on April 23, 1891, Jeff boxed all over the United States and Europe for 17 years.

Eddie McGoorty won the Wisconsin State Amateur title when only 15. A pro for 11 years, he was kayoed in Australia by Les Darcy in 15 rounds on July 31, 1915.

contested the right of Papke and Mantell to hold the crown were Eddie McGoorty, Jimmy Clabby, Les Darcy, Jack Dillon, Jeff Smith, Mike Gibbons, and Frank Klaus.

For two years the title was in dispute, but after Papke had lost on a foul to Klaus in fifteen rounds on March 5, 1913, in Paris, Klaus received general recognition as world champion. He was knocked out by George Chip at Pittsburgh, on De-

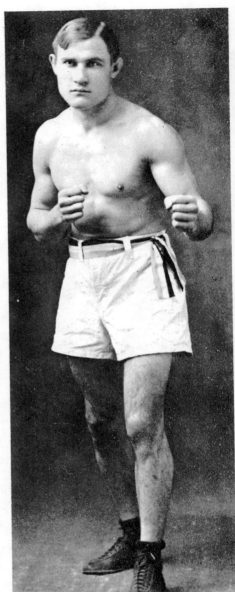

George Chip (above), born in Scranton, Pennsylvania, in 1888, gained the middleweight crown in 1913 by knocking out Frank Klaus in Pittsburgh. Chip's career started in 1909.

Al McCoy (left), after six years of boxing, scored a big upset with a one-round knockout over Chip in 1914. Since the title could be won only by a knockout, McCoy held it three years, before Mike O'Dowd turned the trick on November 14, 1917.

Frank Klaus, after nine years of campaigning, won the crown from Billy Papke in March 1913, lost it to George Chip in October, then retired. Klaus, born in Pittsburgh in 1887, died there in 1948.

Johnny Wilson (left) lifted the crown from Mike O'Dowd in 12 rounds, but the decision was protested. They met again in 1921, and Wilson clinched the title with a 15-round decision. The famous announcer, Joe Humphries, holds the championship belt.

cember 23, 1913, in five rounds and Chip ascended the throne.

George didn't last long. In a surprise that astounded the boxing world on April 6, 1914, Al McCoy, a southpaw, knocked Chip out in Brooklyn in the opening round. He held the title for three years, losing it to Mike O'Dowd in the sixth round in Brooklyn, on November 14, 1917.

Although Mike protested the decision at the end of twelve rounds

Harry Greb (right) loved "night-life" and cared little for training. In the ring, he was a dynamo, throwing punches from all angles. Because of the fast pace he set in his bouts, he was called "the Human Windmill." His unorthodox style frustrated nearly all of his opponents. In a span of 14 years, he fought over 500 battles, lost 7 and was knocked out once, by Joe Chip, in 1913, his first year in boxing. Greb (below, left) won the crown in 1923 by drubbing Johnny Wilson in 15 rounds. He fought many of his last battles with one eye sightless, and died October 22, 1926, following an eye operation.

Challenger Tiger Flowers (below, right) got a crack at the title and won it from Greb in 15 rounds on February 26, 1926. In a return title bout on August 19, Flowers again won a 15-round decision.

of his contest with Johnny Wilson in Boston on May 6, 1920, Wilson succeeded O'Dowd as crown wearer. Slightly over a year later, July 21, Wilson gained a decision over Bryan Downey in Cleveland on a foul, and despite the refusal of the Cleveland Commission to recognize Wilson as winner, he retained the throne but lost it to Harry Greb on August 31, 1923, in fifteen rounds at the Polo Grounds of New York.

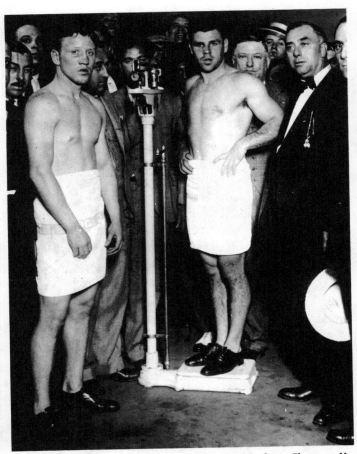

Jim Farley *(right)*, the New York State Boxing Commissioner in 1926, weighs in Harry Greb and Tiger Flowers for their last meeting. Boxing Secretary Bert Stand is next to Farley.

Mickey Walker, shown on scales, won the title from Flowers. He defended it successfully in 10 rounds against challenger Ace Hudkins *(left)* on October 29, 1929, at Chicago.

On February 24, 1925, in Los Angeles, Mickey Walker knocked Bert Colima out cold in his own corner. Dutch Meyers, Colima's manager, is seen about to administer smelling salts to his boy, while Walker protests the action. The referee disqualified Colima, in spite of the fact that he was kayoed.

Greb held the crown for nearly three years, when he was deposed on February 26, 1926, by Tiger Flowers, another southpaw, in fifteen rounds at New York City. Flowers was the first Negro to hold the crown.

Mickey Walker, of New Jersey, who held both the welter and middle-weight crowns, succeeded Flowers as banner bearer in the latter division. He rated close to the top. A terrific hitter with an abundance of courage, he fought in every division from welterweight through heavyweight. Though far outweighed, he always gave a thrilling performance.

Walker won the middleweight crown from Tiger Flowers in Chicago, December 3, 1926, in a ten round bout after having dropped the decision to Harry Greb in fifteen rounds in a scintillating, hair-raising mill in New York on July 2, 1925, an affair in which

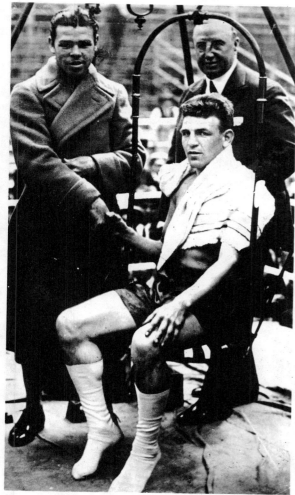

Having relieved Tiger Flowers of the crown, Mickey Walker defended his title against Tommy Milligan, in London. Milligan *(on scales)* and Walker weighed in for the fight, and eight hours later Walker knocked out the European champion in the 10th round *(right)*.

he attempted to annex the middle-weight championship while still holding the welter title.

As a middleweight he knocked out Tommy Milligan in London in the tenth round, June 30, 1927; won from Ace Hudkins in ten in Chicago, June 21, 1928; and beat Hudkins in Los Angeles in ten in a second bout for the title. He relinquished his crown on June 19, 1931, to compete against heavyweights.

He drew with Jack Sharkey in fifteen rounds of an interesting contest; knocked out Jimmy Maloney in two; won from King Levinsky and Paulino Uzcudun in ten rounds each; lost to Johnny Risko; knocked out Salvatore

Walker, the undisputed middleweight champion, is bade farewell by British promoter C. B. Cochran and Eugene Corri *(right)*, the sportsman who refereed the fight.

229

The day after the exceedingly popular "Toy Bulldog" fought a 15-round draw with heavyweight Jack Sharkey, he was on the golf links with tavern owner, Billy LaHiffe *(left)*; Jack Kearns, his manager; his young son; and Senator "Wild Bill" Lyons *(right)*. Since his retirement in 1935, Walker has earned great prominence as a painter *(below)* in the primitive art field.

Ruggirello; was stopped by Max Schmeling in eight vicious rounds of fighting in a campaign that kept him pretty busy during 1932. The following year, unsuccessful in his quest for heavyweight honors, he fought Maxie Rosenbloom for the latter's light heavyweight title and lost a close bout in fifteen rounds.

Mickey wound up his great ring career in 1935, winning six of eight bouts that year, four by knockouts. In his final contest, with Eric Seelig as his opponent, he was stopped in the seventh round and hung up his gloves.

He was a fabulous character, colorful, a powerful puncher; and while for a good portion of his career he was only an overstuffed welterweight, he made the grade in the three top divisions. After retiring, he turned to painting and had several successful exhibitions. He also owned a colorful and popular bar on 49th St. opposite Madison Square Garden. He is currently hospitalized in New Jersey.

The retirement of Mickey Walker brought to the class confusion even more complicated than that following Ketchel's death. Differences of opinion between the National Boxing Association and the New York Commission resulted in two claimants for a num-

230

Marcel Thil, after winning the middleweight championship of Europe in 1939, was married (lower right) to his manager's daughter, Georgette Taitard. With the middleweight class in complete confusion in America, Gorilla Jones, the NBA champ met Thil on June 11, 1932, in Paris and lost on a foul in the 11th round (right).

Lou Brouillard of St. Eugene, Canada, won the New York middleweight title over Ben Jeby in 1933 and lost it the same year to Vince Dundee. Three years later, Lou went to Paris to meet Thil in a title bout and lost on a foul in four rounds. In 1937 they met in Paris for the second time and Brouillard (below, left) was again disqualified for fouling in the sixth round.

ber of years before the ascendancy of Tony Zale.

Gorilla Jones came out on top in a National Boxing Association elimination and Ben Jeby was the New York Commission's choice. Marcel Thil, French champion, beat Jones on a foul in Paris, but New York refused to concur. Thil clinched his claim by defeating both the British and German title holders, Len Harvey and Eric Seelig.

The confusion continued with Lou Brouillard knocking out Ben Jeby, Vince Dundee outpointing Brouillard,

Ben Jeby, who lost the middleweight title to Brouillard in 1933 and retired in 1936, is shown giving advice in 1938 to a promising young lightweight named Jackie Savino.

Teddy Yarosz (below, left) of Pittsburgh won the American middleweight title when he decisioned Vince Dundee in 15 rounds on September 11, 1934, in the smoky city. Yarosz boxed from 1929 to 1942. Dundee, who was born in Italy, fought from 1925 to 1937. He died in 1949.

Babe Risko, born in Syracuse, New York, in 1911, won the crown from Teddy Yarosz on September 19, 1935, and lost it to Freddie Steele in 1936. He died in 1957.

Fred Apostoli (below, left) stopped Marcel Thil in the 10th round on September 23, 1937, and should have been declared champion. The New York Boxing Commission did not recognize Thil as champion and insisted the bout be fought as a non-title affair.

Dundee losing to Teddy Yarosz, the last named dropping a verdict to Babe Risko. All of these battles were really for the American crown only.

On February 15, 1937, Brouillard had lost to Thil on a foul in Paris, and when Thil came to America to fight Fred Apostoli on Mike Jacobs' Tournament of Champions program, the New York Commission insisted that the bout be listed as a non-title affair though both men were under the class limit. When Thil was defeated, Apostoli failed to gain the support of the New York Board as world champion, recognition he definitely should have received.

The confusion continued after Apostoli stopped Freddy Steele, who had

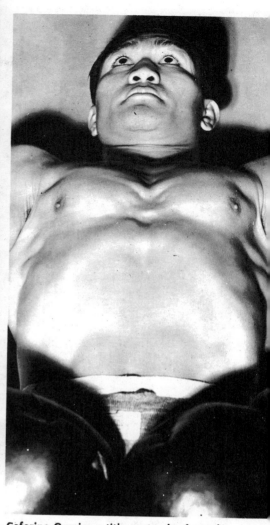

Freddie Steele from Tacoma, Washington, annexed the American middleweight crown from Babe Risko on July 11, 1936, in Seattle. Freddie battered Risko into the ropes *(above)* and floored him in the first round, then went on to an easy victory in 15 rounds. Steele defended the title in five bouts, then lost it to Al Hostak.

Ceferino Garcia, a title contender from the Philippine Islands, knocked out the New York Commission champion, Fred Apostoli, in seven rounds on October 2, 1939.

Solly Krieger, born in New York City, outpointed Al Hostak in 15 rounds on November 1, 1938, for the NBA title.

Al Hostak regained the middleweight crown in Seattle, when he knocked out Krieger in four rounds on June 27, 1939.

lifted the title from Risko in an overweight match; and when Steele refused to face Apostoli in a bout for the crown, the New York Commission ruled the latter world champion.

In the meantime Steele was knocked out in a round by Al Hostak in Seattle; Solly Krieger of New York gained a decision over Hostak in fifteen rounds, then was knocked out in four by Hostak, both for the N.B.A. crown. When Apostoli was halted by Ceferino Garcia in seven rounds in Madison Square Garden, the situation became still more confused.

Then Tony Zale knocked out Hostak; Garcia was defeated by Ken Overlin; and Overlin lost to Billy Soose. The N.B.A. declared Zale its

The first circular ring in the United States (a round ring was used in England in 1912) was built in a San Francisco shipyard and demonstrated before workmen on May 26, 1944. Former middleweight champ Fred Apostoli, who went into the Navy in 1942, is shown on the left, in an exhibition bout with Vic Grupico of San Francisco. Frank Carter was referee. The ring was made of aluminum tubing covered with heavy velvet cloth.

Tony Zale ended the NBA championship confusion, by knocking out Al Hostak, in 10 rounds on July 19, 1940, at Seattle. In a return title bout in Chicago on May 28, 1941, Zale again knocked out Hostak, this time in two rounds. Tony was a popular ringman and anxiously attempted to get a shot at the New York title-holder.

Ken Overlin shellacked Ceferino Garcia on May 23, 1940. On May 9, 1941, he met Billy Soose and lost the New York title in 15 rounds. Overlin, a ring-cutie (left, above), tried some tricks with Soose, but Billy waltzed away with the verdict.

Billy Soose, unable to make weight, vacated the New York middleweight title for the heavier class. Born in Farrell, Pennsylvania, in 1917, Billy attained ring prominence after attending Penn State College.

The middleweight muddle was finally cleared up in 1941, when Tony Zale was matched to meet Georgie Abrams, an outstanding contender. Zale, shown about to land a right to Abrams' head, won a 15-round decision and the world middleweight crown.

world title holder and the New York Board placed Soose on top.

Before a match could be arranged, Soose outgrew the class, and Georgie Abrams, who had thrice defeated Soose, was named to face Zale. When Tony won a fifteen round decision in Madison Square Garden on November 28, 1941, a universal title holder ruled the middleweight class for the first time in a decade.

Following four years service in World War Two, Zale won a victory over Rocky Graziano on September 27, 1946, that set aside all doubt as to his right to the throne. Rocky knocked out Zale in a return bout in Chicago a year later, and in a third encounter Zale regained the crown by halting Graziano in Newark in three rounds.

Rocky Graziano, the most colorful prize fighter to step into a ring since Stanley Ketchell, was born on the lower East Side of New York on June 7, 1922. Rocco Barbella (his real name) was 5' 7" tall and threw a right hand that was loaded with pure dynamite. He started fighting in 1942. When his career ended in 1952, he had fought 83 battles, winning 52 by knockout, 14 by decision and one by a foul. He drew in six bouts, lost seven decisions and was knocked out three times. Two stages in Rocky's amazing life are shown above. In his early zoot-suit period, Rocky, in the foreground, is leaving Stillman's Gym after a workout in 1943, munching on a Danish bun. The final stage was set in 1953, when Rocky, invited to appear on Martha Raye's television show, delighted audiences for weeks with his humorous speech and antics, as in the scene above with Miss Ray and Cesar Romero.

Thus the middleweight class returned to a normal status after years in which no world champion was recognized.

Graziano, a product of New York's slum districts, made the grade despite his ups-and-downs in a most controversial career. He turned to television and the movies after retirement and made a success of his new venture. The movie *Somebody Up There Likes Me*, the story of his rise to fistic fame, a Horatio Alger tale, earned him more than a quarter of a million dollars.

The Graziano-Zale fights in New York and Chicago went down in boxing history as epic ring battles. They were thrillers.

In the New York affair at the Yankee Stadium, Zale, on the verge of defeat, ready to collapse, suddenly dropped Rocky for the count. The gate for that bout was 39,827 with the gross receipts $342,497, but when

Rocky unleashed a sudden burst of power in the 10th round (above) and Charley Fusari was finished. For nine rounds, Fusari held the lead and had Rocky whipped, but he was unable to stop Rocky's do-or-die spirit in the last round. Graziano had lost the title to Zale the year before and was making a comeback on September 14, 1949, against Fusari, who was a fast-coming prospect from Irvington, New Jersey.

Marty Servo, the welterweight champ, lasted two rounds when he faced Graziano in an overweight match on March 29, 1946. A sudden switch in the odds, making Servo a 10-1 favorite, created rumors of a fix that almost canceled out the fight. Rocky insisted upon going through with the bout, and in less than six minutes, he smashed Servo to the canvas (right) with a broken nose and a face beaten to a pulp.

Rocky Graziano was at the height of his career on September 27, 1946. He had flattened 32 opponents and was ready to do the same to the champ, Tony Zale. Instead, Rocky was knocked out for the first time. He hit Tony with some solid bombs early in the fight and he missed some too, as the sequence above shows. Others had crumbled under Rocky's blockbusters, but Tony fought back with body punches, and Rocky was feeling the effects. By the end of the fifth round they were both getting tired and were both hurt. In the sixth round Zale whipped a solid blow to Rocky's stomach. Rocky went down, got up, and was floored again with a left. He struggled to rise (left) but referee Ruby Goldstein counted him out before he was half off the canvas. Once on his feet, Rocky wanted to continue, but the referee and trainer Whitey Bimstein prevented it (below), while Zale, tired but still middleweight champion, was led to his corner.

In an oven-like atmosphere at the Chicago Stadium in 1947, Zale and Graziano ripped each other apart until the sixth round, when Rocky let loose a barrage of lefts and rights and Tony went down against the ropes, forcing the referee to stop the slaughter. Rocky Graziano, with his left eye slashed open and the right one almost closed, was the new champion. As Rocky explains in his book: "This was no boxing match. It was a war, and if there wasn't a referee, one of the two of us would have wound up dead."

Less than a year later, Tony Zale made Graziano an ex-champion with a long left hook on the jaw. Rocky was counted out flat on his back in the third round.

Zale and Graziano resumed their warfare at the Chicago Stadium, the receipts from 18,547 paid admissions reached a new high for an indoor fight, $422,918.

The spectators in the Windy City were treated to one of the greatest middleweight championship fights on record. In a temperature that seemed to have reached the boiling point, Rocky won the crown July 16, 1947. It was a terrific encounter, and every minute was packed with drama.

Their third bout in Newark on June 10, 1948, lacked the fire of the previous pair as Tony won the title back hands-down.

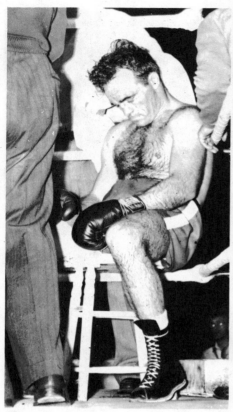

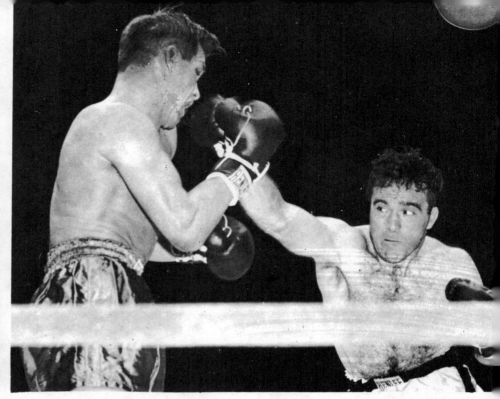

The middleweight crown went overseas on September 21, 1948, when Marcel Cerdan, of France (above, right) defeated Tony Zale so badly that Tony was unable to answer the bell for the 12th round. After this fight, Zale decided to retire from the ring.

Jake LaMotta (right) stands over Marcel Cerdan in their title bout, after Marcel went down from a half push. Cerdan (above) could not come out for the 10th round and Jake was declared champion. A return bout was delayed when LaMotta was injured, and Cerdan returned to his home in Casablanca. Returning to the States for the championship match, he was killed when his plane crashed on October 27, 1949. Cerdan had an excellent record. In 111 fights from 1934 to 1949, he won 64 by knockouts and 43 by decision. He lost four—one decision, two fouls and one kayo. LaMotta defended the title twice, then lost it to Ray Robinson.

Three months after Zale had knocked out Rocky, a Frenchman, Marcel Cerdan, dethroned Tony in the Roosevelt Stadium of Jersey City, the champion being unable to come out for the twelfth round. Marcel, after dropping the championship to Jake LaMotta, the "Bronx Bull," in Briggs Stadium of Detroit, June 16, 1949, was killed in an airplane accident in the Azores, while on his way back to the United States to train for a return bout with Jake. He had been halted by LaMotta in their title contest in the tenth round.

240

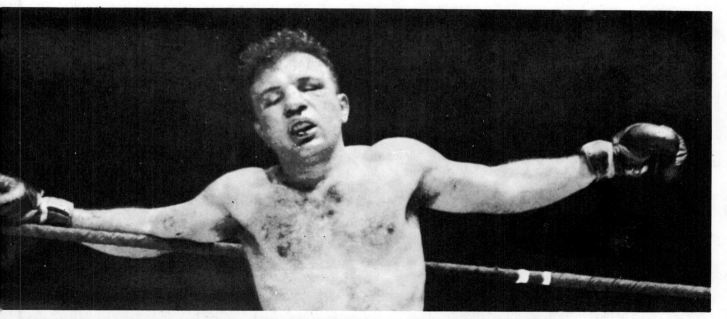

Jake LaMotta leans on the ropes, a courageous but beaten champion, after his bout with Sugar Ray Robinson was halted by the referee in the 13th round. This was Jake's sixth meeting with Robinson. He beat Sugar Ray once and lost four, all by decision. From 1941 to 1952, the "Bronx Bull" had 106 bouts, with 30 knockouts and 53 decisions. He lost 15 and was stopped four times.

Randy Turpin, the British and European middleweight champion, gave the boxing world a big surprise when he outpointed Ray Robinson in 15 rounds and annexed the world title. Turpin is seen lunging with a left past Sugar Ray's head in the action photo on the left, but it was the last round and Randy was all but wearing the crown.

Ray Robinson won the middleweight title for the first time when he halted LaMotta in the thirteenth round in Chicago, February 14, 1951. He then went on a long tour of Europe, neglected to keep physically fit, and in a surprise defeat lost the championship to Randy Turpin in London by a decision in fifteen rounds. That bout took place July 10, 1951. The return contest was staged at the Polo Grounds in New York, September 12, 1951, and a record gate for a non-heavyweight fight was set with a gross of $767,626.17. Ray rewon the crown,

Sugar Ray was in trouble in the 10th round of his return title match with Turpin. His left eye was sliced open and bleeding profusely. If he could go one more round, the bout might possibly be stopped. In desperation, he went all out with a barrage of blows, until Turpin lay flat on his back. Randy got up and, with his back to the ropes *(below)*, swayed helplessly as punches crashed against his jaw. Referee Ruby Goldstein halted the bout and Ray was champ again.

Ray Robinson came out of retirement in 1955 and for the third time recaptured the middleweight crown, when he stopped Bobo Olson in two rounds *(above)*. Five months later, he stopped him again in four rounds. After Ray quit on December 18, 1952, for a career as a night club entertainer, Olson and Randy Turpin met on October 21, 1953 for the vacant throne, which Olson won.

stopping the Britisher in the tenth round at a time when it appeared that Robinson, with a bad cut and on the verge of having the bout halted, landed a barrage that ended the affair in his favor via the knockout route.

As middleweight champion, he tried to wrest the world light heavyweight title from Joey Maxim at the Yankee Stadium, June 25, 1952, but after rolling up a good lead, exhaustion in the terrific heat caused him to collapse in

the fourteenth round. He announced his retirement six months later to become an actor in his own stage show.

The various commissions decided on an elimination to obtain his successor. In Europe, Randy Turpin, the British Empire champion, and Charley Humez, French and European title holder, were matched for a bout in London on June 9, 1953, and Turpin won the decision.

In America, Carl "Bobo" Olson of Hawaii and Paddy Young of New

York, the leading contenders, were billed for an American championship bout in Madison Square Garden June 19, 1953, and Olson won. Then Olson and Turpin were matched to decide who would succeed Robinson as world champion and Olson outpointed Randy to win the crown.

When Robinson's venture into the theatrical field ended in a failure, Sugar Ray decided on a comeback. He knocked out Olson in the second round in the Chicago Stadium, De-

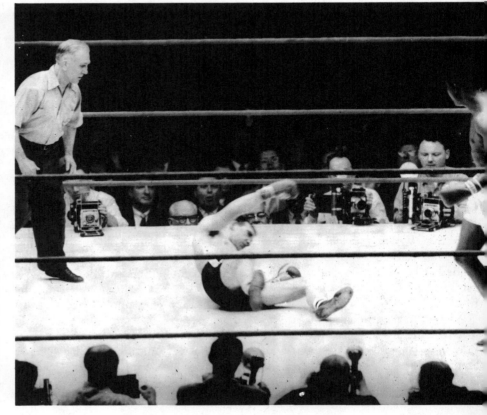

Gene Fullmer, a worthy challenger from Utah, knocked Robinson out of the ring in the seventh round *(above)* in 1957, and went on to win a unanimous 15-round decision and the middleweight title. Since 1951, Gene had engaged in 40 bouts. He won 37, 20 by knockouts, and lost three. On May 1, 1957, in a return bout, Ray stopped Fullmer in five rounds *(right)* and won the crown for the fourth time.

cember 9, 1955, to seat himself back on the throne which he had abdicated.

Gene Fullmer, a young Mormon from West Jordan, Utah, challenged and relieved Ray of the crown at Madison Square Garden on January 2, 1957, gaining the decision at the end of fifteen rounds. But three months later, Sugar Ray gained the plaudits of the world's boxing fans when in the Chicago Stadium on May 1, he knocked out Fullmer in a return contest in the fifth round to become the first in the history of the middleweight division to win the crown four times.

Carmen Basilio, the welterweight champion, connects with a smashing right to Robinson's jaw in the 10th round of their middle-weight championship bout. In the 13th round *(below)* Carmen acted as a leaning post for the tired Sugar Ray.

Carmen Basilio, blood-spattered but determined, won the world middleweight championship from 37-year-old Ray Robinson on a split decision at New York's Yankee Stadium on September 23, 1957, but surrendered it again to Sugar Ray in Chicago Stadium on March 26, 1958. In their New York contest the dogged body-puncher from Canastota, New York, lost referee Al Berl's vote, but received the verdict from judges Artie Aidala and Bill Recht.

It was a gruelling battle all the way. Both men were stunned and bewildered at different stages of the fight,

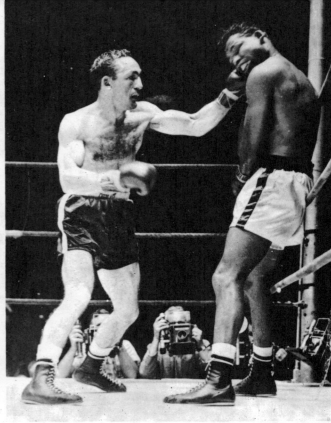

Basilio, a good little man, traded punches, skill, and determination with Sugar Ray, a good big man, and at the end of 15 rounds, Carmen was the new middleweight champion. In the sequence above, Basilio traps Ray on the ropes and lands with a left hook.

but neither gave an inch. Blood streaked Carmen's left cheek as Ray tried desperately near the wind-up to put across a killer. But the final round saw Basilio still battering away. All three officials agreed that he had won that frame and many of the thousands of spectators guessed that Basilio's final-round performance had won him the decision.

It was Basilio's fifty-second victory and his greatest triumph in 71 professional fights. He had won the welter title twice, and now with the middleweight crown in his possession, he was forced to vacate the 147-pound class throne.

The fight grossed $556,467, and the paid attendance was 38,072.

Their return engagement was fought with the same viciousness. Ray made ring history by regaining the crown for the fourth time and winning it for the fifth. Less than two months short of his thirty-eighth birthday the great ring warrior conquered an almost overwhelming weariness and stuck it out to the finish, even though at times

The story of the return match in which Carmen Basilio was dethroned by Robinson is graphically told (above) in Carmen's tightly-closed left eye. From the sixth round on, Basilio was at a disadvantage. Only his courage made the bout close.

246

Ray Robinson *(above, right)* came from behind after the fifth round to roll up a margin too great for Basilio to overcome. After 15 rounds of battle, Sugar Ray's hands were raised in victory, by announcer Ben Bentley *(right)* and co-manager Harold Johnson. Robinson showed why he is called a ring marvel by succeeding in doing what never before had been accomplished—winning the middleweight crown five times. His record performance is not ever likely to be repeated.

it appeared that his aging body could stand the punishment no longer. The turning point of the battle came in the fifth round, when a left hook to the head by Ray puffed up Carmen's eye, starting the downfall of the champ. Again there was a split decision, the two judges giving it to Robinson by big margins and referee Frank Sikora seeing it as a victory for the battered Basilio.

Neither man had much fight left as the bout neared its finish, so heavy was the bombardment and so fast the pace. There were no knockdowns, although each was staggered often. 17,976 spectators paid $351,955 to see the battle, which was as thrilling a contest as anyone had seen in years. No opponent ever whipped Robinson twice.

Never has there been a boxer in any division to boast of a record like Ray's. He's a standout not only in the middleweight class but in all boxing as one of the ring's stellar performers of all time. He was born in Detroit, May 3, 1920, and made his start in the amateur field.

The N.B.A. again moved in to vacate a title for inactivity, this time Sugar Ray Robinson's. Fullmer and Basilio met at San Francisco on August 28, 1959, for the N.B.A.'s middleweight crown. Fullmer kayoed a dazed and weary Basilio in the fourteenth round, when referee Jack Downey stepped between the two battlers.

New York, Massachusetts, Europe, and the Oriental Federation recognized Robinson as champion until a twenty-nine-year-old ex-fireman from Brookline, Massachusetts, Paul Pender, won a fifteen-round split decision over the almost legendary ring marvel on January 22, 1960. It was a fast and grueling battle in which Pender let the forty-year-old Robinson take the offensive and wear himself out, while the challenger fought a defensive battle, blocking punches, then moving away.

Having knocked out Terry Downes of England in seven rounds and won a decision over Basilio, Pender fought a rematch with Downes in London on July 11, 1961. This time Pender quit at the end of the ninth round,

After the N.B.A. vacated Robinson's crown for inactivity, Fullmer met Basilio at San Francisco on August 28, 1959 and KOd him in the 14th to receive N.B.A. recognition.

Meanwhile, Robinson (left) recognized by New York, Massachusetts, Europe and Oriental Federation, lost a 15-round split decision to Paul Pender in early 1960 at Boston.

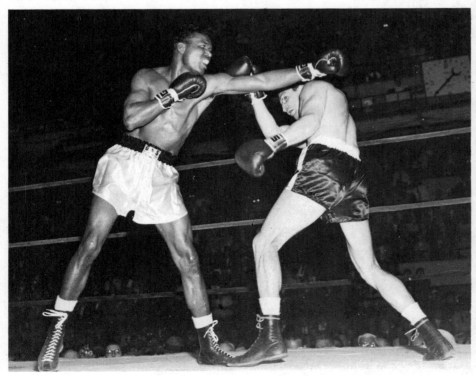

On January 14, 1961, at Boston, Pender scored a knockout in the seventh round over British challenger Terry Downes. This photo shows the bloody-faced Downes ducking under a long left thrown by Pender in the fifth round.

In return match in London on July 11, 1961, Pender (*right*) quits at the end of the ninth round, Downes thus winning a portion of the world middleweight championship.

Meanwhile, Dick Tiger of Nigeria was recognized as the titleholder by the World Boxing Association after defeating Fullmer in 15 rounds. (*Above*) Fullmer slips. (*Below*) Tiger and pilot Jersey Jones after Tiger clinched title via KO of Fullmer in Nigeria.

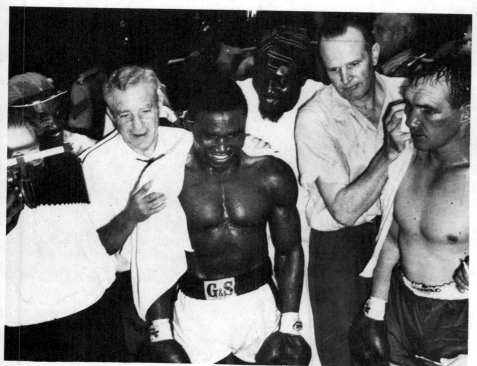

after savage warfare, and gave the champion of British Isles that portion of the world title which Pender had captured from Robinson.

Downes's reign was short-lived; Pender recaptured the title on April 7, 1962, in a fifteen-round decision in Boston.

In the meantime, the World Boxing Association title was awarded to thirty-three-year-old Dick Tiger when he won a unanimous decision over thirty-one-year-old Fullmer, on October 23, 1962, in San Francisco.

Tiger's boxing skill had overcome Fullmer's aggressive style in 1962, but it brought only a draw when the two met again on February 23 of the next year.

Tiger was finally recognized as world middleweight champion when Pender retired on May 7, 1963, but he clinched the title when he kayoed Fullmer in the seventh round on August 10, 1963, on Tiger's home soil.

Four months later, Joey Giardello's style of moving, jabbing, and sharpshooting befuddled Tiger, and the

Joey Giardello and beaming wife are shown after Giardello captured title on 15-round decision over Tiger in 1963.

challenger won the fifteen-round decision in Atlantic City, N.J., on December 7, 1963. Both men scaled 159¾ pounds.

In a return bout Tiger landed heavier blows and sapped Giardello's strength, and he regained his title by a unanimous decision in fifteen rounds on October 21, 1965.

Flashy, happy-go-lucky Emile Griffith, born on February 3, 1938, in the Virgin Islands, became the world's next champion on April 25, 1966, when he won a fifteen-round decision over Tiger in New York. He was the

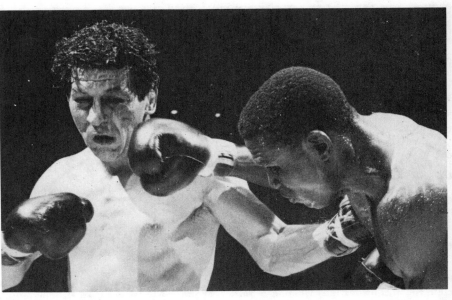

In a return bout on October 21, 1965, Tiger regained the 160-lb. title from Giardello on a unanimous 15-round decision. (*Above*) Tiger lands a right to the jaw. (*Below*) Joey connects with a left.

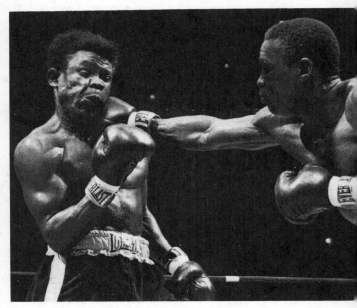

On April 25, 1966, Emile Griffith, the welterweight champion, captured the title by decisioning Tiger in 15 rounds. (*Above*) Tiger is sent to the canvas in the ninth. (*Right*) Griffith takes a hard right from Tiger which contorts his features.

third man in the history of boxing to win the middleweight title after holding the welterweight crown, the others being Robinson and Basilio.

Just one year later Griffith was defeated by Italy's Nino Benvenuti, a romantic and handsome figure. The fifteen-round match on April 17, 1967, in New York, was a fast-paced affair in which Benvenuti used his 3½-inch height and 5½-pound weight advantages to keep Griffith at bay while weakening his opponent with jabs.

In the 1960 Olympics, the same Olympics in which Muhammad Ali participated, Benvenuti had been named the most proficient boxer in the games over his more colorful and extroverted fellow pugilist.

Benvenuti and Griffith fought two more duels. In the first, on September 29, 1967, Griffith defeated the Italian in fifteen rounds, and the second bout, on March 4, 1968, saw Benvenuti beat Griffith by a unanimous decision.

Benvenuti's love of "the sweet life"

was his undoing, on November 7, 1970. Evenly matched at 159¾ pounds, Benvenuti and Carlos Monzon, of Argentina, met in Italy. The strong, aggressive Monzon knocked out the Italian in a stunning upset in the twelfth round with a crushing right flush on the chin.

The powerful Argentinian went on to score nine successive kayos over Emile Griffith, Frasier Scott, Jean-Claude Bouttier, Benvenuti, Denny Moyers, Tom Bogs, and Roy Dale and to win three bouts by decisions.

On February 9, 1974, he knocked out welterweight champ José Napoles in seven rounds at Paris. The 159-pound champ overpowered his game 153-pound opponent who was making a bid for the middleweight crown.

In April, 1974, however, Monzon was deprived of his title by the World Boxing Council for failing to defend same against its official challenger, Rodrigo Valdes, of Colombia, who they recognised as champion on May 25 when he knocked out Bennie Briscoe in seven rounds at Monte

Carlo. Monzon ignored this ruling and defended his title against Tony Mundine (Australia) at Buenos Aires on October 5, winning by a knockout in seven rounds. In 1975 he made two more successful defences, stopping Tony Licata in ten rounds in New York on June 30 and Gratien Tonna, of France, by a fifth round kayo in Paris on December 13.

On June 26, 1976, Monzon once again made himself undisputed world middleweight champion by outpointing the pretender to the throne, Rodrigo Valdes at Monte Carlo. This performance was repeated on July 30, 1977, again at Monte Carlo, after which Monzon announced his retirement from the ring after a reign of nearly seven years, undefeated in fourteen title defences.

Back to Valdes, who had made four successful W.B.C. title defences; against Gratien Tonna by a kayo in eleven rounds at Paris on November 30, 1974; Ramon Mendez, who was stopped in eight rounds at Cali, Colombia, on May 31, 1975; Rudy Robles, outpointed at Cartagena on August 16, and Max Cohen, who re-

Marvin Hagler jolts Minter with a right in taking the middleweight title at Wembley in September 1980.

Alan Minter celebrating after stopping Vito Antuofermo at Wembley in June 1980 to retain his title.

251

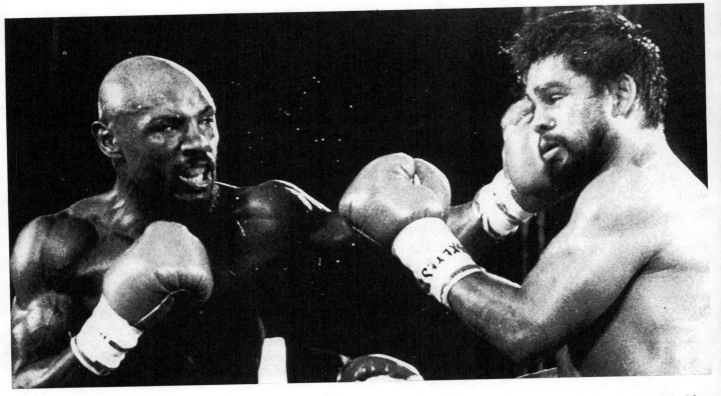

Marvin Hagler outpointed the ageing Roberto Duran in defence of his title at Las Vegas in 1983.

tired in the fourth round at Paris on March 28, 1976. Immediately after Monzon's retirement, Valdes came back into the world title picture by outpointing Bennie Briscoe at Campione D'Italia on November 5, 1977, and was then recognised as undisputed champion by both the W.B.C. and W.B.A. He lost this distinction on April 22, 1978, being outpointed by Hugo Corro, from the Argentine, at San Remo. On August 5 Corro outpointed Ronnie Harris (USA) at Buenos Aires, and on November 11 he again won the decision over Valdes in the same city to remain champion.

On June 30, 1979, Corro was outpointed over 15 rounds by Vito Antuofermo (New York) and lost his title. The new champion kept his crown against Marvin Hagler (Brockton), but was held to a draw. Alan Minter gave up his British title to concentrate on winning the world crown and he did this handsomely at Las Vegas on March 16, 1980, when he outpointed the champion after a thrilling 15 rounds contest.

On June 28 at Wembley Arena, London, Minter enhanced his position as undisputed world middleweight champion by stopping Antuofermo,

who retired after eight rounds, but on September 27 in the same ring, he lost his title to Marvin Hagler, the bout being stopped in round three because the Englishman had sustained a badly gashed right eyebrow. There were ugly scenes at the conclusion of the contest when some of the disappointed spectators stormed the ring and tried to assault the winner and the referee. It was a bad night for British boxing in every respect.

Everyone was soon made to realize that Hagler was a world-beater in every sense of the term. He was well versed in boxing skill, was hard as iron and punched with devastating effect. He was the best all-round fighter the middleweight division had seen since the illustrious Carlos Monzon and the more he fought the more destructive he became. Born at Newark, New Jersey, on May 23, 1954, he won as an amateur the 1973 National A.A.U. middleweight championship, and in seven years as a pro had risen to the top with 45 wins, two points losses, and a drawn bout over 15 rounds by the time he made his first attempt to win the world title.

His mastery of Minter saw him acknowledged universally as world king, this being one of the rare occasions when both the W.B.C and the W.B.A.

have recognized the same titleholder. Hagler's first defence was against Fulgencio Obelmejias (Venezuela), who had earned the role of challenger with an impressive record, having won all his 30 contests, 28 of them inside the scheduled distance. He stayed the best part of eight rounds with Hagler at Boston on January 17, 1981 before the referee saved him from complete annihilation. Vito Antuofermo was given a second chance to regain the title he had lost to Alan Minter, but on June 13, again at Boston, was forced to retire in the fourth round to Marvin's pounding fists. On October 3 Hagler put his crown at stake against Mustafa Hamsho from New York, who had just taken a points verdict off Minter at Las Vegas, but at Rosemount, Illinois, although he made a brave showing, he had to be saved by the referee in the 11th round.

Now for Hagler every fight was a championship affair. On March 7, 1982 he stopped William "Caveman" Lee (Philadelphia) in 67 seconds at Atlantic City and on October 31 gave Obelmejias another opportunity to become world champion. They met at San Remo and this time Marvin gained a kayo victory in the fifth round. Next came a challenge from Tony Sibson, the British and Euro-

252

Sugar Ray Leonard made an amazing comeback after nearly three years out of the ring to beat Marvelous Marvin Hagler on points in 1987.

pean champion, a tough hard puncher with seven years and 51 fights behind him, of which he had won all but four. On February 21, 1982 at Birmingham, he had outpointed Dwight Davison (Detroit) over 12 rounds in a W.B.C. eliminator, so was entitled to have a shot at the major crown. He met Hagler for the title at Worcester, Mass. on February 11, 1983 and put up a valiant display, but the referee was forced to intervene 20 seconds before the end of the sixth round.

Hagler agreed to defend against Wilford Scypion (New York), who had never been stopped, and on February 13, 1983 had won the U.S.B.A. (United States Boxing Association) middleweight title by outpointing Frank "The Animal" Fletcher at Atlantic City. The W.B.C. objected to this piece of matchmaking and authorized a contest between Mustafa Hamsho and Wilfred Benitez (former triple world champion) as a final

Frank Tate gets a right to the chin of Michael Olajide on his way to the vacant I.B.F. title.

eliminator, the winner being the official challenger for the middleweight crown. Hamsho gained a 12 rounds points win at Las Vegas on July 16, 1983, but had to wait nearly a year before he got the promised title bout with Hagler.

Hagler, meanwhile, having ignored this W.B.C. edict, had gone ahead with his defence against Scypion and they duly met at Providence, R.I. on May 27, the challenger being stopped in round four. Marvin continued to ignore the W.B.C. ruling. Instead he agreed to meet that amazing warrior, Roberto Duran (Panama) in a title defence at Las Vegas on November 10. What a fight the pair put up, thrilling the millions of television spectators from start to finish, when the verdict wént to Hagler on a unanimous points margin. At once the W.B.C. stated it would not recognize the bout as for the championship as it had been fought over 15 rounds and not its new stipulated distance of 12 rounds. They took away Marvin's title.

It was a stupid move and achieved nothing as everyone else in the boxing world recognized Hagler as undisputed champion. On March 30, 1984 he met Juan Roldan (Argentina) at Las Vegas and forced him to retire in the 10th round, and on October 19 finally took on a clamouring Hamsho and knocked him out in three rounds at Madison Square Garden, New York. It was the champion's tenth successful defence and he promptly had his name re-registered as "Marvelous Marvin Hagler".

For some time Thomas "Hit Man"

Hearns, former welter king and now the W.B.C. light-middleweight champion, had been throwing challenges at Hagler and eventually they were brought together at Las Vegas on April 13, 1985. It was a multi-million dollar staging, but lasted only three rounds with the challenger helpless on the canvas and the referee calling an immediate halt. It was a shock verdict for Hearns' fans who could not believe that their idol had been destroyed so quickly and completely.

Hagler continued his winning ways in 1986, knocking out John Mugabi, of Uganda, in Las Vegas on 10 March.

Although this great champion had shown slight signs of deterioration in opposition to Mugabi, he was still favoured to win when it was announced that Sugar Ray Leonard, who was returning to the ring after a virtual five-year layoff, had challenged Hagler for his undisputed titles. It proved to be the richest promotion in the history of the sport, and an epic encounter ensued.

While there were no knockdowns and very little to alarm the more squeamish, the battle at Las Vegas which took place on April 6, 1987 was a classic between master boxer and master fighter. And for every hundred who witnessed the contest via TV and thought Leonard had won, there were ninety who felt convinced that Hagler had done enough to snatch the decision. Two judges disagreed, but the third scored overwhelmingly for the challenger.

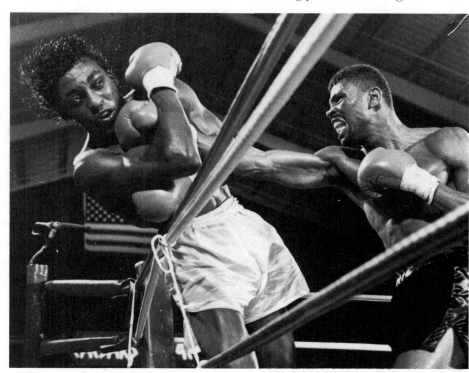

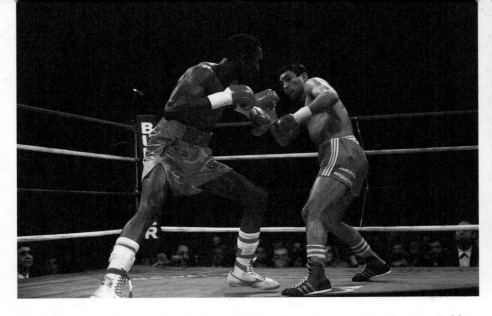

Thomas Hearns (*left*) winning his fourth world title with a victory over Juan Domingo Roldan for the W.B.C. middleweight crown in October 1987.

Sumbu Kalambay (*left*) took the vacant W.B.A. title with a win over Iran Barkley.

Leonard did not capitalise on his success, and appeared to turn a deaf ear to all propositions that he should continue his career. Inevitably, the title was thrown wide open, and the unification of this division became a thing of the past.

The I.B.F. named Frank Tate and Michael Olajide as the foremost contenders, and on October 10 they boxed at Las Vegas. Tate rather surprisingly beat his opponent, but despite knockdowns he was unable to stop his man.

Tate went on to beat Tony Sibson at Stafford on February 7, 1988, ending the veteran Briton's career, but was then stopped in the ninth round by the flashy unbeaten Michael Nunn, who found some terrific punching to go with his outstanding skills.

The new W.B.A. champion was Sumbu Kalambay, a veteran who was born in Zaire, but who fought out of Italy. Kalambay easily outpointed Iran Barkley, from New York, in Livorno on October 23, 1987. Kalambay then surprisingly inflicted a first defeat on the former light-middleweight champion, Mike McCallum, outpointing him in Pesaro. He then outpointed Robbie Sims, Marvin Hagler's half-brother, and stopped Doug de Witt, but forfeited W.B.A. recognition for failing to meet the obligatory challenger, Herol Graham (G.B.).

Thomas Hearns picked up his fourth

world title on October 29, 1987 when coming back from light-heavyweight to knock out the tough Argentinian Juan Domingo Roldan for the W.B.C. belt vacated by Leonard. Thus there were new champions of all three authorising bodies within 19 days of each other. Hearns then showed the first signs that his great career was winding down by being surprisingly knocked out in the third round by Iran Barkley. However Barkley was himself surprised when the veteran Roberto Duran, long past his great days as a lightweight, put on possibly his last great performance in outpointing Barkley at Atlantic City on February 24, 1989. Duran forfeited the title by refusing to make a written undertaking to defend it.

So less than 18 months after the division had three new champions all was in the melting pot again. Michael Nunn, the I.B.F. champion, beat Roldan and then astonished everybody by knocking out Sambu Kalambay in the first round in Las Vegas. He outpointed the persistent Iran Barkley and then Marlon Starling, the W.B.C. welterweight champion. He stopped Don Curry, a former great welterweight champion, in Paris, and having proved easily the best of the middleweight champions, was surprisingly stopped on May 10, 1991 by James Toney. Toney, from Ann Arbor, Michigan, came from

way behind to flatten Nunn in the 11th round in Nunn's home town of Davenport, Iowa. Having suffered his first defeat, Nunn moved up a division.

Meanwhile the W.B.A., having ditched Kalambay, matched Mike McCallum with Herol Graham, McCallum winning a hard decision at the Albert Hall, London, on May 10, 1989. McCallum outpointed Steve Collins, Michael Watson and gained revenge on Sumbu Kalambay. On December 13, 1991, McCallum fought the I.B.F. champion, James Toney who, since taking the title from Nunn, had defended against Reggie Johnson and Francisco dell'Aquila. The idea was to unify the two titles, but the W.B.A. stripped McCallum in advance for taking the fight. With only the I.B.F. title at stake, the two fought a draw, so McCallum lost his crown without being beaten.

With the middleweight division in flux in 1989, the W.B.O. added to the number of claimants by making Doug de Witt their first champion for his decision over Robbie Sims at Atlantic City on April 18, 1989. De Witt then stopped Matthew Hilton, but was himself stopped after a slugging war with Britain's Nigel Benn in Atlantic City on April 29, 1990. Benn stopped Iran Barkley in the first round in a brutal display in Las Vegas but lost the title in a much-hyped fight with his British rival Chris

Eubank at the Exhibition Centre, Birmingham on November 18, 1990. Benn succumbed in the ninth round after another good battle.

Eubank won his first defence with a technical decision over Canada's Don Sherry at Brighton. Eubank executed a backward butt on Sherry in the tenth, catching him with the back of his head while the two were tied up on the ropes. With Sherry unable to continue, Eubank was docked two points by the referee, but still took a controversial decision. After beating fellow-Briton Gary Stretch, Eubank, whose statuesque bodybuilder-type posing in the ring between rounds was not to everybody's liking, won another controversial verdict when he was given the decision over another Briton, Michael Watson, in June 1991. Eubank then relinquished the title as both boxers moved up a weight.

Meanwhile, the W.B.C. title remained vacant for a long time after Duran had forfeited it. Eventually Julian Jackson, the W.B.A. light-middleweight champion, fought Herol Gra-

ham for it in Benalmadena on November 24, 1990. Jackson was not allowed to fight in Britain because of a damaged retina. Graham was outclassing Jackson with his outstanding skills and was pressing for a quick win in the fourth round when Jackson knocked him out with one punch – Jackson's own particular specialty. Jackson then added to his victims Dennis Milton (first round), Ismael Negron (first) and Ron Collins (fifth), before he was forced to go the distance with Thomas Tate in August 1992. Jackson's reign came to an end on May 8, 1993 when he was stopped in the fifth round by Gerald McClellan of Detroit, the W.B.O. champion, shortly after McClellan had been given 20 seconds to recover from a low blow from Jackson.

After I.B.F. champion James Toney had drawn with McCallum, he took a very controversial decision over Dave Tiberi (U.S.A.) at Atlantic City on February 8, 1992. There were ugly crowd scenes after two judges had scored 115–112 and 115–111 for Toney. The third scored 117–111 for Tiberi.

Senator William Roth of Delaware, Tiberi's home state, was so incensed that he chaired a Senate Investigating Committee which began looking into corruption in boxing. Toney continued with a decision over Glenn Wolfe and then outpointed Mike McCallum in Reno. In February Toney won the I.B.F. super-middleweight title and faced a decision as to which division to campaign in.

The title taken from McCallum by the W.B.A. was dormant for a year and was eventually won by Reggie Johnson (U.S.A.) who outpointed Steve Collins (Ireland) at East Rutherford on April 22, 1992. He successfully defended against Lamar Parks, Ki-Yung Song and, in 1993, Wayne Morris.

Gerald McClennan won the W.B.O. title vacated by Eubank with a first-round stoppage, on November 20, 1991,

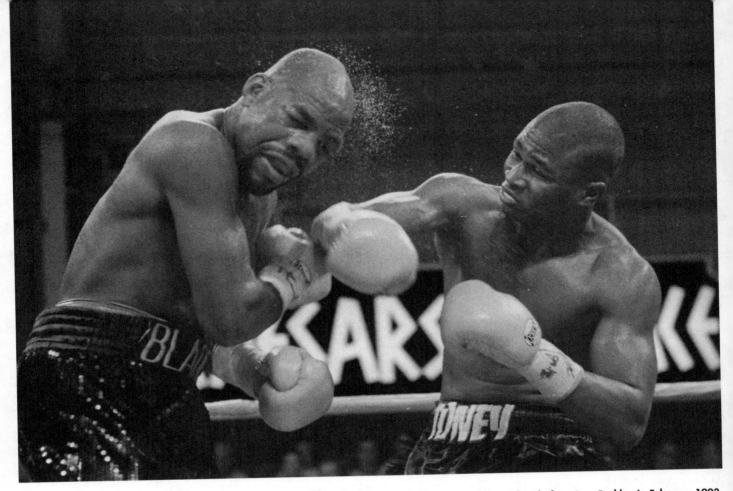

of John Mugabi, who had fought Hagler for the undisputed title back in 1986. But McClennan relinquished the title to go after the W.B.C. title, which he won.

James Toney (right) taking the I.B.F. super-middleweight title from Iran Barkley in February 1993. He was already middleweight champion after a shock knockout of Michael Nunn and a controversial decision over Dave Tiberi which inspired a senate investigation into corruption in boxing. Nevertheless Toney proved in two contests with Mike McCallum to be one of the most durable and hard-hitting of the champions of the 1990s.

THE LIGHT-MIDDLEWEIGHT CHAMPIONS

In 1962 it was generally agreed that a new weight division, between welter and middleweight was desirable, and on October 20 of that year Denny Moyer was matched to fight Joey Giambra (Buffalo, N.Y.) for the world junior-middleweight title. They met in Moyer's home-town of Portland, Oregon and he won a popular points verdict over 15 rounds. A defence was made on February 19, 1963, Stan Harrington being outpointed at Honolulu, but on April 29 Ralph Dupas gained a points verdict at New Orleans and successfully defended the title in a return contest on June 17 at Baltimore with a points decision.

Sandro Mazzinghi knocked out Dupas in Milan on September 7 and stopped him in 13 rounds in a return bout staged in Sydney, Australia on December 3. Tony Montano (kayoed in 12) and Fortunato Manca (points) were beaten in 1964, then Mazzinghi was knocked out in six rounds by fellow-Italian Nino Benvenuti on June 18, 1965 at Milan. In a return title bout at Rome on December 17, Nino won a points verdict. Surprisingly he was outpointed himself by Ki-Soo Kim at Seoul on June 25, 1966, who himself defended successfully against Stan Harrington (points) on December 17, and Freddie Little (points) on October 3, 1967. On May 15

the following year the Korean lost his crown back to Mazzinghi, who kept it when his defence against Little on October 25 was declared "no contest" in round six. Following this the Italian was stripped of his title for failing to meet an approved challenger.

Fred Little then outpointed Stan Hayward for the vacant throne on March 17, 1969, then retained it against Hisao Minami (knockout, second round) on September 9 and on March 20, 1970 against Gerhard Piaskpwy (points) in Berlin. Carmelio Bossi outpointed Little at Monza on July 9 to take the crown. Jose Hernandez held him to a draw at Madrid on April 29, 1971, on his first defence and, six months later, on October 31 at Tokyo, the Italian lost his crown to Koichi Wajima on a points decision. The Japanese fighter defended against Domenico Tiberia, whom he knocked out in the first round on May 7, 1972, and Matt Dobovan who was knocked out in the third on October 3. In 1973 he met three contenders: April 20 Ryu Sorimachi (points); June 9 Miguel De Oliveira (drew 15); and August 14 Silvano Bertini (knocked out in the thirteenth).

Wajima outpointed De Oliveira in a return fight in Tokyo on February 5, 1974, but on June 3 at Tokyo was knocked out in the 15th and final round by Oscar "Shotgun" Albarado (Pecos, Texas). As there had been only 66 seconds to go to the finish, the Japanese boxer thought he was entitled to a re-match and on January 21, 1975 in the same ring, he regained his title with a fine points victory. Prior to that Alvarado had made a successful defence by knocking out Ryu Sorimachi in seven rounds at Tokyo on October 8, 1974. The W.B.C. called upon Wajima to meet De Oliveira for a third time and when Wajima refused, his title was said to have been forfeited. On May 7, 1975 Miguel De Oliveira outpointed Jose Duran (Spain) at Monte Carlo to win the vacant W.B.C. title. From this time onwards there were two light-middleweight champions of the world, the W.B.A. deciding to uphold Wajima's hold on the championship. It was also mutually decided to rename the division this way.

Elisha Obed (Bahamas) defeated De Oliveira by the kayo route in 11 rounds at Paris on November 13, 1975, but after keeping his crown against Tony Gardner, by a second-round knockout at Nassau on February 28, 1976, and Sea Robinson on points at Abidjan on April 25, he lost by a knockout in ten rounds to Germany's Eckhard Dagge on June 18. In his first defence Dagge outpointed veteran Emile Griffith, former welter and middleweight champ, over 15 rounds at Berlin on September 18. British champion Maurice Hope then held him to a draw on March 15, 1977, and on August 6 he was knocked out in five rounds by Rocky Mattioli.

The Australian made a good start by disposing of two former champions – Elisha Obed, by a seventh round knockout at Melbourne on March 11, 1978, and Jose Duran by a fifth round knockout on May 14. On March 4 the following year, however, he was forced to retire to Maurice Hope in 8 rounds at San Remo. The Britisher defended successfully against Mike Baker, the ref stopping it in the seventh on September 25, and in a return with Mattioli at Wembley on July 12, 1980, he won by a stoppage in 11 rounds. On November 25 Hope outpointed Carlos Herrera over 15 rounds, but on May 23, 1981 he was knocked out in the 12th round by Wilfred Benitez (New York). The new champion, who had previously held two world titles, kept his latest one against Carlos Santos on points at Las Vegas on November 13, made another successful defence on January 30, 1982 by outpointing Roberto Duran over 15 rounds, also at Las Vegas, but at New Orleans, he had to give way to Thomas Hearns on a points decision on December 3.

Hearns did not defend the W.B.C. title in 1983, but did so three times the following year, beating Luiji Minchillo on points over 12 rounds on February 11, Roberto Duran by a second round knockout on June 18 and Fred Hutchins when the referee stopped the fight in the third on September 15. In 1985 Hearns turned his attention to Marvin Hagler's middleweight crown, but failing to take it defended his light-middleweight title with an easy win against Mark Medal (U.S.A.), the referee stopping the fight in the eighth round at Las Vegas on June 23, 1986.

Meanwhile, when the W.B.C. deprived Koichi Wajima of his light-middle title in 1975, the W.B.A. matched him with Jae-Do Yuh on June 7 at Kitakyushu. The Korean won by a kayo in round seven and on November 11 knocked out Masahiro Misako at Shizuoka in six rounds. When he gave Wajima an opportunity to win back his crown on February 17, 1976, he was stopped in the final round at Tokyo, the Japanese thus winning the title for the third time. It was a short-lived triumph, however, Wajima being knocked out by Jose Duran in 14 rounds on May 18. The Spaniard lasted less than five months, losing on points to Miguel Angel Castellini (Argentina) who scored a points victory in Madrid on October 8. He, too, remained champion for a bare five months, being decisioned by Eddie Gazo (Nicaragua) at Managua on March 5, 1977.

Koichi Wajima popped up again, but his attempt to become champion once more was foiled on June 7 when he was knocked out in the 11th at Tokyo. Kenji Shibata was beaten on points on September 13 and a similar fate befell Chae-Keun Lim on December 18.

Wilfred Benitez covers up on the way to losing his light-middleweight championship to Thomas Hearns at New Orleans in December 1982.

The indestructible Roberto Duran pounds Davey Moore into submission at Madison Square Garden in 1983 to win his third world title.

Gazo remained champion until August 9, 1978 at Akita where he dropped a decision to Masashi Kudo (Japan). Kudo seemed likely to stay awhile as he outpointed Joo-Ho at Osaka on December 13; Manuel R. Gonzalez at Tokyo on March 13, 1979, and the same man by a knockout in 12 rounds at Yokaichi on June 20. A new star arose on October 24, 1979 when Ayub Kalule (Uganda) gained the decision over the Japanese and then in Copenhagen on December 6 outpointed Steve Gregory (Columbus, Ohio). Kalule thwarted the ambitions of three challengers in 1980: Emiliano Villa (twelfth round knockout) on April 16; Marijan Benes (points) on June 12 and Bush Bester (points) on September 6 – all in Denmark.

On June 25, 1981 he came up against fabulous Sugar Ray Leonard at Houston and suffered a 9th round kayo defeat to lose the championship. Setting his sights on more profitable things, Leonard was content to relinquish the light-middle crown and on November 7, Tadishi Mihara (Japan) outpointed Rocky Fratto (U.S.A.) to win the vacant W.B.A. title. His reign lasted only to February 2, 1982 when he was stopped in six rounds at Tokyo by Davey Moore (New York). Here was a colourful crowd-pleasing fighter with a pay-off punch. At Johannesburg, South Africa on April 26, he knocked out Charlie Weir in five rounds. At Atlantic City on July 17 he disposed of former champion, Ayub Kalule in ten rounds, while on January 29, 1983, also at Atlantic City, Gary Guiden was knocked out in four rounds. His next defence was disastrous, that amazing warrior, Roberto Duran gaining his third world title by stopping Moore in eight rounds on June 16 at New York. Duran immediately went after the middleweight crown and on October 19, 1984, Mike McCallum (Jamaica) outpointed Sean Mannion, former U.S.B.A. champion, at Madison Square Garden, New York, to take the vacant W.B.A. crown. He successfully defended it on December 1 by stopping Luiji Minchillo in 13 rounds at Milan, then, on July 28, 1985 stopped David Braxton (Detroit) in eight rounds to keep the title.

The I.B.F. had made its presence felt, in 1984, when it recognised Mark Medal as the champion of this division when he beat Earl Hargrave at Atlantic City. Carlos Santos had subsequently outpointed Medal, and had gone on to serve Louis Acaries the same way the following year. But the title was taken from him by the I.B.F. after his refusal to meet Davey Moore. On June 4, 1986, Buster Drayton established his right to the belt by beating Santos over 15 rounds at East Rutherford. Very soon afterwards, on August 24, Drayton stopped Davey Moore in 10 rounds at Juan-les-Pins, and he carried his honours to nearby Cannes. Here, on March 27, 1987, the challenger was halted in 10 rounds after a game battle.

But on June 27 the old war-horse, Drayton, went into action once too often, when he faced the brilliant young Canadian, Matthew Hilton. Drayton lost on points, at Montreal. Hilton made his first defence of his portion of the title when, on October 16, at Atlantic City, he crossed gloves with Jack Callahan, who had won 24 contests in a row. But the challenger stood no chance at all with Hilton. He was badly beaten during the first 2 rounds and was not allowed to continue for a third.

Mike McCallum continued on his winning way with his W.B.A. belt at stake. August 23, 1986 found him easily beating Julian Jackson in a couple of rounds at Miami. He then went to France, and knocked out Said Skouma in 9 rounds in Paris, on October 25. It was not until April 19, 1987 that the Jamaican boxed seriously again, but he showed his complete superiority over the former welterweight king, Milton McCrory, retaining his W.B.A. belt at Phoenix. But the shock of the year in this division took place when McCallum boxed the Texas Cobra, Donald Curry, at Las Vegas. It was a keen and evenly contested bout until the Jamaican launched a perfect left hook in the 5th round and literally flattened his challenger.

McCallum now decided to mix matters with the full middleweights, and Julian Jackson, the Virgin Islander, was matched with South Korean In-Chul Baek for the W.B.A. crown. Jackson proved to be far superior, and the bout

Mike McCallum caused a surprise when he knocked out the former welterweight champion Donald Curry in 1987 to retain his unbeaten record.

was stopped halfway through the 2nd round, in a fight held on October 21 at Las Vegas.

Jackson proved a good champion with a devastating punch and defended successfully against Buster Drayton (stopped in third), Francisco de Jesus (kayo in eighth) and Terry Norris (stopped in second) before he gave up the title to challenge for (and win) the W.B.C. middleweight crown.

Meanwhile, on the W.B.C. front, the champion Thomas Hearns had also moved up to full middleweight and on December 5, 1986 at Las Vegas Duane Thomas beat John Mugabi for the vacant title, the bout being surprisingly stopped in the third round with Mugabi in distress, claiming that he had been thumbed in the eye. Thomas was outpointed in Bordeaux in his first defence on July 12, 1987 by a Mexican, Lupe Aquino. Aquino, having won the title in France, defended it in his opponent's home town of Perugia, Italy, on October 2, 1987, and was well beaten by Gianfranco Rosi, who then disposed of Thomas but was stopped by Don Curry, the former welterweight champion. Curry reigned for seven months, until February 11, 1989 when he was

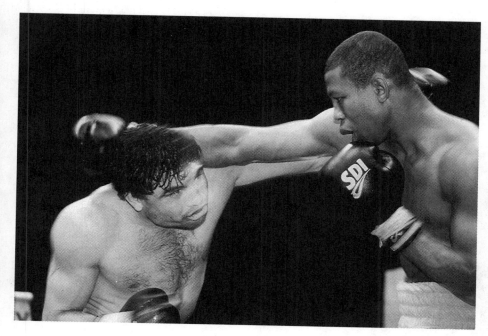

Above: Argentina's Julio Cesar Vasquez (left) became W.B.A. champion in 1992. Tyron Trice (right) was a frequent challenger in the light-middleweight class.

Below: Terry Norris (right), the W.B.C. light-middleweight champion, has W.B.A. champion Meldrick Taylor in trouble before the referee stopped the contest in the fourth round.

drick Taylor, in four rounds in Las Vegas on May 9, 1992. On February 20, 1993 Norris fought on the Mexico City championship bill which drew a world record attendance of 136,000 to the Azteca Stadium. Norris was chillingly efficient in stopping Maurice Blocker, the reigning I.B.F. welterweight champion, in the second round.

The I.B.F. light-middleweight title, meanwhile, was lost by the Canadian Matthew Hilton on his first defence, when he was outpointed by Robert Hines (U.S.A.) at Las Vegas on November 4, 1988. His reign lasted three months and was ended when he was outpointed by Darrin van Horn, who was himself outpointed on July 15, 1989 at Atlantic City by the former W.B.C. champion, Gianfranco Rosi. This time round Rosi proved to be another durable champ. Rosi made successful defences against Troy Waters (1989), Kevin Daigle, Darrin van Horn and Rene Jacquot (all 1990), Ron

outpointed by Rene Jacquot of France at Grenoble. The division's game of musical chairs continued when John Mugabi challenged again and stopped Jacquot in the first round in Paris on July 8, 1989. Mugabi, too, failed to make a successful defence, and like Jacquot he was beaten in the first round; Terry Norris, one of boxing brothers from Lubbock, Texas, applying a clean knockout at Tampa on March 31, 1990.

Norris proved to be a real champion and brought some continuity to the W.B.C. branch of the division. He outpointed Jacquot and then earned a big payday and grabbed international notice by taking on Sugar Ray Leonard, who saw a chance to regain a version of the title he'd relinquished ten years earlier. Leonard's ambition was to fight in Madison Square Garden, but the occasion, on February 9, 1991 was not an auspicious one for him. The younger Norris beat him comprehensively and Leonard finally retired for good. Norris subsequently beat Don Curry, Brett Lally, Jorge Castro and Carl Daniels before putting up his most impressive performance to date in stopping the W.B.A. welterweight champion, Mel-

Amundsen, Glenn Wolfe and Gilbert Baptiste (1991), Angel Hernandez and the deposed W.B.A. champion, Frenchman Gilbert Dele (1992). This last was a hotly disputed split decision at Monte Carlo, and there was a return in Avoriaz, France, on January 20, 1993. This time the veteran Rosi won more clearly, although it was another split decision.

Gilbert Dele had won the W.B.A. title on February 23, 1991, stopping Carlos Elliott at Point a Pitre when the two met for the title vacated by Julian Jackson. Dele beat Jun-Suk Hwang but lost it on his second defence, in Providence on October 3, 1991, when he was stopped in the last round by Vinnie Pazienza (U.S.A.). After a great battle, Pazienza, a former lightweight champion who was making a 14lb jump up to light-middleweight, won when Dele turned his back on him having received a thumb in the eye. Pazienza was ahead on points and would have anyway inflicted his first defeat on Dele.

Pazienza's world crashed in November, when his neck was broken in an automobile accident. With a metal halo screwed into his head he vowed he would box again, but in the meantime was forced in October 1992 to relinquish the title through his inability to meet the deadline for a defence. On December 21, 1992 Julio Cesar Vasquez of Argentina stopped Hitoshi Kamiyama of Japan in the first round of a match in Buenos Aires to take the vacant title. He did even better on his first defence, a 45-second knockout of Panama's Aquilino Asprilla at Mar del Plata on February 22, 1993. Vasquez put his title on the line again on April 25 in Madrid against the Spaniard Francisco Javier Castillejos and this time was given a tough fight before taking a close, but unanimous, decision.

The W.B.O. inaugurated its version of the title on December 8, 1988 when John David Jackson (U.S.A) stopped Lupe Aquino in the seventh round at Detroit. He made a bid to become the division's longest running champion by defending successfully against Steve Little (1989), Martin Camara and Chris Pyatt (1990), Tyron Trice (1991), and Pat Lawlor and Michele Mastrodonato (1992).

Terry Norris won the W.B.C. light-middleweight title with a first-round knockout of John Mugabi, then ended Sugar Ray Leonard's career. In the photograph he is celebrating after a demolition of W.B.A. welterweight champion Maurice Blocker in front of 136,000 fans at Mexico City in February, 1993. Norris's brother, Orlin, was a contender in the cruiserweight class.

THE WELTERWEIGHTS

It was not until about the middle of the nineteenth century that the gap between the lightweight and heavyweight classes (10 stone or 140 pounds and up) was somewhat closed by the adoption of both the welterweight and middleweight groups. A medium of 142 pounds was set for the former and Paddy Duffy emerged the victor and first champion. That was in 1878.

But the class soon became dormant and it was not until December 14, 1892, that we find it again active with Danny Needham and Mysterious Billy Smith fighting for the crown, which was won by the latter. Prior to that, Nonpareil Jack Dempsey and George Fulljames, each scaling well within the welterweight limit, engaged in a championship fight, but Dempsey, who carried off the honors in twenty-two rounds of heavy milling, preferred to call himself the middleweight champion and went on to defend that crown until he was shorn of it by Bob Fitzsimmons.

When Mysterious Billy Smith whipped Needham in fourteen rounds in San Francisco, he was acknowledged king of the division. There were

Harry Jones (above), known as "the Sailor Boy," was an aggressive welterweight with a bruising style. With the possible exception of Paddington Jones, he fought more battles than any fighter of his time. The recorded number of bouts is 36, but he is known to have fought many more.

Young Dutch Sam (left) was the greatest welterweight ever produced in England. He was the son of Dutch Sam, probably the hardest hitter in pugilistic history. Young Sam was born on January 30, 1808. At 15, in his first battle, he knocked out Bill Dean. His weight was never more than 145 pounds, and he stood a little over 5' 9". He was an extraordinary phenomenon, graceful of foot, and most accurate with his blows, which were brutal. He could whip any man with only his left hand, as demonstrated in his bout with Gypsy Cooper, whom he cut to pieces with a left jab. His backer, Mr. Hughes Ball, a young man of wealth prominent in society, never lost a wager on Sam, who won all of the 16 fights he engaged in from 1823 to 1834. Young Sam died at 35.

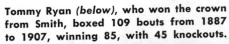

SMITH GETS INSIDE WITH A HARD LEFT

Mysterious Billy Smith *(below)*, born in Eastport, Maine, knocked out Danny Needham for the title in 1892. He ended the bout with a left to the jaw, as illustrated above in the *New York Journal*. Smith lost to Tommy Ryan, who lost to Kid McCoy. When McCoy and Ryan vacated the class, Smith reclaimed the crown.

Tommy Ryan *(below)*, who won the crown from Smith, boxed 109 bouts from 1887 to 1907, winning 85, with 45 knockouts.

many good ringmen at his weight in the East, the best of whom was clever, speedy, sharp-shooting Tommy Ryan of Redwood, New York. After stopping Mike Shaugnessey of Detroit in twenty-three rounds, Danny Needham in seventy-six, and engaging in a draw of six with Smith, all while scaling less than 150 pounds, he challenged Billy for the championship. In a thrilling encounter that went twenty rounds, Ryan gained the crown in Minneapolis on July 26, 1894.

Ryan was one of the cleverest men in the division. Smith protested the verdict, but public sentiment favored Ryan and he was generally accepted as the titleholder. It was a bout loaded with action. The police interceded, with Ryan leading at the time.

The class, like the one above it, has been brightened with the names of boxers who will never be forgotten. Many made their mark in more than one division, while others, after losing the title, regained it.

Boxing enthusiasts were thrilled by the stirring performances of such stars as Mickey Walker, Henry Armstrong, Barney Ross, Sugar Ray Robinson, Tommy Ryan, Kid McCoy, Joe Walcott, Jimmy McLarnin, Mike Gibbons, Packey McFarland, Kid Gavilan, Ted Kid Lewis and Jack Britton among many others who made the division famous.

In Armstrong it boasted of the only boxer in ring history who held three titles simultaneously—feather, welter, and lightweight.

In Walker it had a fighter who won both welter and middleweight crowns, a two-fisted champion who was as good as a light heavyweight and heavyweight as he was in the lower sectors.

In Ray Robinson it boasts of the only titleholder to win the crown five times in the middleweight class after he had retired from the lower group.

In Ted Kid Lewis of England we find one of the few ringmen who fought with success in all divisions from bantam through heavyweight.

Sam Langford was one of the world's greatest, not only in the welter class but in each of the next higher

Rube Ferns, born in Pittsburgh, Kansas, in 1874, was known as "the Kansas Rube." After winning the crown from Smith in January, 1900, he won seven bouts, five by knockouts, and lost the title to Matty Matthews in October. He knocked out Matthews the following year in 10 rounds, and regained the welterweight title.

Matty Matthews (left) held the title six months. He was born in Brooklyn on July 13, 1873, and began boxing in 1891, scoring a knockout, but did not fight again until 1894, when he engaged in only one bout. He fought twice in 1895 and became active from 1896 to 1904, engaging in 79 bouts. Matthews, a good boxer, met and defeated, or held to a draw, most of the top men.

Joe Walcott, who started boxing in 1890, lost two title chances in 1898 to Mysterious Billy Smith and finally won the crown in 1901, when he stopped Rube Ferns in Canada.

groups. His bout with Jack Johnson at Chelsea, Massachusetts, in which he was outpointed, gained for Sambo recognition as one of the greats in the top division.

Kid McCoy, a pupil of Ryan, relieved Tommy of the championship at Maspeth, Long Island, March 2, 1896, in fifteen rounds, after which both retired from the division to enter the middleweight class. Mysterious

Billy Smith then reclaimed the crown. In a battle with Rube Ferns in Buffalo on January 15, 1900, Smith lost the championship to Rube on a foul in the twenty-first round. On October 16 of that year, Ferns was outpointed by Matty Matthews in fifteen rounds at Detroit, but regained the crown on May 24 of the following year when he knocked out Matty at Toronto, Canada, in the tenth round.

Then came the rise of Joe Walcott, the Barbados Demon. A short, thick-necked, furious fighting man, he knocked out Ferns at Fort Erie, Canada, in the fifth round to be acclaimed champion. When Dixie Kid won on a foul from Walcott in the twentieth round of a hectic battle in San Francisco, the decision was disputed. The winner left shortly after for England and announced his retirement from

Billy (Honey) Mellody beat Walcott for the crown and a month later won again over Joe. Mellody scored 33 knockouts since 1901, when he started, but was stopped three times. His career ended in 1913.

Mike (Twin) Sullivan won the title from Mellody on April 23, 1907, then grew out of the class. Mike and his twin brother Jack hailed from Cambridge, Massachusetts. In 67 bouts, from 1901 to 1913, Mike lost one decision, was stopped once by Stanley Ketchell and twice by Joe Gans.

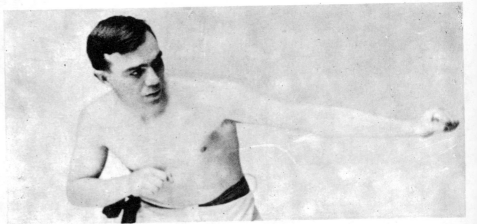

Jimmy Gardner also claimed the title. Born in County Clare, Ireland, in 1885, he started in Boston in 1902 and retired in 1913 after 100 bouts, with only six losses.

Mike Glover, of Lawrence, Mississippi, was one of many who claimed the vacated title. Glover boxed from 1908 to 1916. In his last bout he lost to Ted Lewis.

the division due to weight difficulties, and Walcott reclaimed the crown.

Honey Mellody outpointed Joe in Chelsea, Massachusetts, on October 16, 1906, and he in turn was outpointed by Mike Twin Sullivan on April 23, 1907, in Los Angeles in twenty rounds, after which he gave up the crown to enter the higher division.

Now the championship was variously claimed by a group consisting of Jimmy Clabby, Ray Bronson, Jimmy Gardner, Clarence Kid Ferns, Mike Gibbons, Kid Graves, Mike Glover, Ted Kid Lewis, and Jack Britton; for several years there was no universally recognized titleholder. It was not until Lewis, a Britisher, outpointed Britton on August 31, 1915, in Boston in twelve rounds, the first of twenty bouts between the pair, that a semblance of order came out of the chaotic state.

For four years they kept fighting with varying results until on March 17, 1919, Britton knocked out Ted in Canton, Ohio, in the ninth round. Then the public conceded top laurels to Britton.

Ted Kid Lewis, who often fought Jack Britton, had a career that extended from 1910 to 1929. In 1925 Lewis lost on a foul (above) to Marcel Thuru of France, who is seen being dragged to his corner.

World War One was now on. Many of our stars of the fistic world enlisted or were drafted. The cream of the U. S. pugilists, among them Mike Gibbons and Packey McFarland, donned uniforms as boxing and physical training directors. These two were master technicians. They and Sam Langford never held a title, though Mike claimed one, but they came no better than this trio in boxing history. Though McFarland masqueraded as a lightweight, he found it difficult to make the class limit and fought mostly in the welter division with great success. The fighting qualities of the three were unexcelled.

When after the war many of the top boxers returned to normal life, Packey and Mike among them, the welter class again became the most active. The most conspicuous boxers in the class following World War One were Mickey Walker, Britton, and Lewis. Walker and Britton were matched for a Madison Square Garden bout on November 1, 1922, and Mickey, the "Toy Bulldog" from Elizabeth, New Jersey, walked off with the championship via a decision. It was

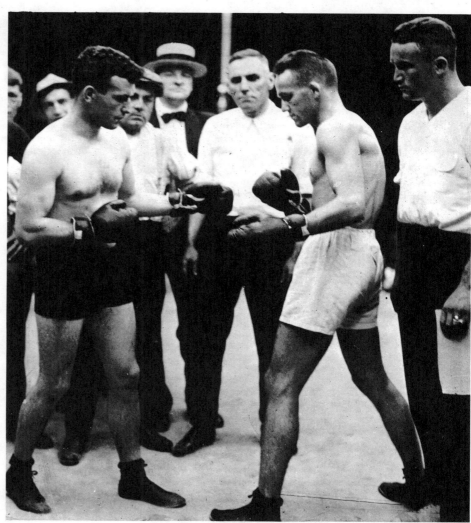

The two best ringmen in the welterweight class were Packy McFarland (left) of Chicago and Mike Gibbons, of St. Paul, who met in a no-decision battle in 1915. On the right is young heavyweight Tom Gibbons, standing behind brother Mike.

Mickey Walker *(left)* in his fourth year of boxing, beat Jack Britton for the crown on November 1, 1922. Britton's amazing career totaled 300 bouts from 1905 to 1930. He was knocked out once, in 1905.

The new welterweight champ visited Washington in 1922 and met Congressman Fred A. Britten *(left)* of Illinois, a former amateur lightweight champion of the world.

Pete Latzo, born in Coloraine, Pennsylvania, had been boxing since 1919 when he met and defeated Walker in 1926. Pete defended his crown twice, then lost it to Joe Dundee in 1927. He retired in 1934 after a knockout by Teddy Yarosz.

an excellent match in which the fans were treated to fifteen rounds of fine boxing and heavy hitting.

The Elizabeth battler held on to the title about four years before he was dethroned by Pete Latzo on May 20, 1926, in ten rounds at Scranton, Pennsylvania.

Latzo wasn't as fortunate as Walker. He held on to the crown only a little more than a year, losing it to Joe Dundee of Baltimore on June 3, 1927, in fifteen rounds at the Polo Grounds. Joe, a brother of Vince, who later was a middleweight champion, dropped the title to Jackie Fields of Chicago on July 25, 1929, at Detroit, when the referee awarded the decision to Fields on a foul in the second round.

The welter class went into a tailspin after Dundee had gained the crown, and for a time it passed back and forth among a group consisting of Fields, Young Jack Thompson, Tom-

Pete Latzo (above, right), pride of the Scranton, Pennsylvania, coal miners, lands a left on Mickey Walker's jaw. By keeping on top of Mickey through the 10 rounds, he became champion.

Joe Dundee (above, right), born in Italy in 1902, won the welterweight crown from Latzo in a 15-round bout. Dundee, whose real name was Sam Lazzaro, boxed from 1921 to 1930.

Manager Max Waxman (left) and Dundee appeared in a Los Angeles court in 1927 on a false advertisement charge. Dundee failed to go through with a title bout with Ace Hudkins.

Jackie Fields (right) won the championship from Dundee on a foul in two rounds in 1929, then lost it to Young Jack Thompson (left) on a decision in 15 rounds the following year.

267

Tommy Freeman (above) won a 15-round decision and the crown from Jack Thompson on September 5, 1930. Freeman defended the title successfully five times in 1931, then lost the crown to Thompson again at Cleveland on April 14, when he could not come out for the 13th round.

On October 23, 1931, Lou Brouillard outpointed Young Jack Thompson for the title, then lost it to Jackie Fields on January 28, 1932. Young Corbett III (real name, Ralph Giordana), shown at left missing a left hook to Jackie Fields' head, won six of 10 rounds from Fields at San Francisco in 1933 and was crowned welterweight champion.

Jimmy McLarnin, a perfect ringman and a lethal puncher who moved up from the lightweight class, met Young Corbett III for the welterweight championship in 1933 and knocked him out (above) in one round. This was McLarnin's only bout that year.

my Freeman, Lou Brouillard, and Young Corbett III.

The change for the better came with the rise of Jimmy McLarnin, who on May 29, 1933, knocked out Young Corbett in the opening round in Los Angeles to gain the top rung of the ladder. With his appearance in the field, the division received a lift. It began to thrive again, with huge gates and large attendances once more making the class an outstanding one in popularity.

McLarnin was one of the brightest stars of the era. He was a clever, sharp-shooting youngster who had come out of the amateurs in the Northwest. He was managed by shrewd Pop Foster, who brought him up from the ranks to become a star first in the fly-weight class, in which he put an end to the career of the great little Fili-pino, Pancho Villa, whose death fol-lowed the loss of a ten rounder to

The new welterweight champ, Barney Ross, vacated the lightweight throne and gave McLarnin a return crack at the title. In a hard-fought 15-round bout on September 17, 1934, McLarnin regained the crown. Ross won three bouts after losing the title and on May 28, 1935, met McLarnin for the third time. The contest was a remarkable boxing exhibition, loaded with action. At the end of 15 rounds Ross (*above, right*) and McLarnin embraced. Ross was declared the winner and re-won the crown.

Jimmy at Oakland, California on July 4, 1925. McLarnin went on to fame and fortune as a lightweight and welterweight.

McLarnin lost the welterweight crown to Barney Ross on May 28, 1934, in the Madison Square Garden Bowl of Long Island City, in fifteen rounds, but rewon his laurels a few months later, September 17, in the same bowl in fifteen frames. They engaged in a third bout, again a thrilling exhibition of ring cleverness combined with sharp hits, on May 28, 1935, at the Polo Grounds. Ross once more came out on top at the end of fifteen sessions.

McLarnin, a boy of wealth, engaged in only three more contests before hanging up his gloves. He lost to Tony Canzoneri, beat him and Lou Ambers in ten rounds, then quit never again to box in professional competition.

The best of all training camps were Barney Ross's at Grossinger's, a summer resort in New York's Catskill Mountains. Besides the serious training routine, there was always time for fun, as above. Officials and friends from Chicago attended all of Ross's camp sessions, and later cheered him on at ringside.

After enlisting in the United States Marines in 1942, Barney received a sharpshooter's medal (above) at the Marine Corps Base in San Diego, California. Later that year Ross was awarded the Congressional Medal of Honor, for saving 10 Marine buddies by wiping out 20 Japs from a Guadalcanal foxhole.

After McLarnin's defeat by Ross, who previously had won the lightweight championship, Barney kept the welterweight class in the spotlight with his scintillating performances. He was a very popular champion who possessed all the assets of greatness in ring warfare. He ruled three years, during which he defended his title successfully against Ceferino Garcia and Izzy Jannazzo, before losing the decision to Henry Armstrong on May 31, 1938. In addition to defeating Garcia in a championship match, he twice whipped him in ten rounders.

In 1942, Ross, who was born in New York, December 23, 1909, enlisted with the U. S. Marines. He served with distinction. For extreme bravery at the battle of Guadalcanal, he was awarded the Congressional Medal of Honor.

In Armstrong, boxing had equally

Henry "Hurricane Hank" Armstrong, battled 175 opponents from 1931 to 1945. He won 144, scoring 97 knockouts, and lost 19. He lost one on a foul, one was no-decision. He drew in eight and was knocked out twice. Hank held three titles simultaneously.

General John Phelan (left) New York boxing commissioner and Dr. William Walker *(center)* officiated at the weighing-in of welterweight champ Barney Ross and challenger Henry Armstrong, who held the featherweight title. Hank won the welterweight crown and later annexed his third title when he defeated Lou Ambers for the lightweight crown. There was no rule, as there is now, requiring a champion to give up a title if he wins one in a heavier class. It was put into the books because of Armstrong.

The night of May 31, 1938, saw the end of a great champion and the rise of another, when Ross *(below, left)* took a terrific beating for 15 rounds from Armstrong, the new champion.

Editor Nat Fleischer *(left)* presents *The Ring* Magazine feather- and welterweight championship belts to Armstrong and a medal to Joe Louis, for being the outstanding fighter of 1938.

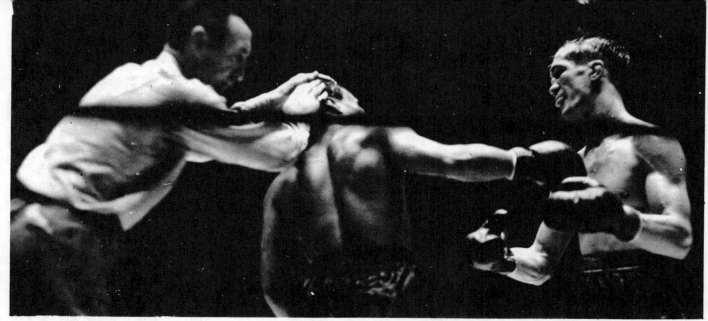

Armstrong defended the title 19 times, scoring 16 knockouts. He lost the crown to Fritzie Zivic on October 4, 1940, and was stopped by Zivic on January 17, 1941. Referee Arthur Donovan stepped in *(above)* and halted the contest in the 12th round.

The fighting Zivics, left to right, were: Joe, middleweight, 1918-1922; Fritzie, welterweight, 1931-1949; Eddie, lightweight, 1932-1940; Jack, lightweight, 1919-1929; Pete, bantamweight, 1919-1929. Fritz was the only title-holder.

Fritzie Zivic *(below)* of Pittsburgh boxed from 1931 to 1949, during which he fought in 230 battles. He won 155, including 80 knockouts, lost 61, drew in 10 and was kayoed four times. Fritzie, the youngest of the five Zivic brothers, held the welterweight title for six months before losing it to Freddie "Red" Cochrane, on July 29, 1941, in 15 rounds.

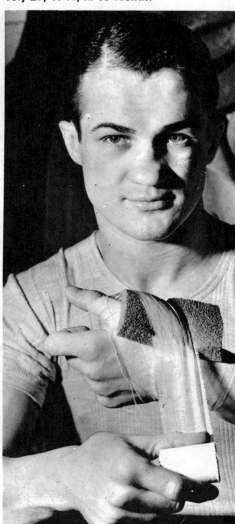

as great a titleholder as in Ross. He was born December 12, 1912, in St. Louis, Missouri, and started his professional career in 1931, following a crack at the amateur game.

He first won the featherweight championship from Petey Sarron in Madison Square Garden in October, 1936, then the welterweight championship on May 31, 1938, and in his next contest on August 22 he defeated Lou Ambers to win the lightweight crown. He wound up the year 1938 successfully defending the welterweight title against Ceferino Garcia in fifteen rounds via a decision and halting Al Manfredo in three, after which he vacated the featherweight throne.

In 1939, besides his lightweight championship contest which he lost to Ambers, he engaged in eleven defenses of his welterweight crown. In one, he took Ernie Roderick, British Empire champion, into camp, gaining the verdict in London in fifteen rounds.

In his final contest, in 1940, he was shorn of his crown by Fritzie Zivic, who won the verdict on October 4

272

Except for two years in the Navy, Freddie Cochrane boxed from 1933 to 1946. Freddie lost the crown to Marty Servo on February 1, and retired. Referee Eddie Josephs helps Cochrane to his feet (above) after the knockout in the fourth round.

Marty Servo was forced to give up the crown in 1946, because of a nose that was badly injured when he was knocked out by Rocky Graziano. Servo (below, right) is explaining his decision to sport writers Lewis Burton and Bill Heinz in the boxing commission office. Promoter Mike Jacobs, wearing hat, waits for the official ruling.

in New York in fifteen rounds after Henry had engaged in six title matches besides one with Garcia in which the latter's New York version of the middleweight title was at stake. They fought a draw in Los Angeles.

Zivic held the welter championship until July 29, 1941. The Pittsburgher, born on May 8, 1913, lost it in Newark to Freddie (Red) Cochrane of Elizabeth, New Jersey. Freddie marched off to the Navy with his new crown and when World War Two was over and he was discharged, he fought Marty Servo of Schenectady, New York in Madison Square Garden on February 1, 1946, and was knocked out in the fourth round. Cochrane, born May 6, 1915, prior to losing to Servo, had been knocked out by Rocky Graziano twice in the tenth round in non-title contests after Freddie led all the way.

Servo, because of a nose ailment, was forced to retire and the New York commission named Ray Robinson as his successor following attempts to get some of the leading welters to face Sugar Ray in an elimination. The only one who would agree to such a contest was Tommy Bell, who was an easy victim on December 20, 1946, in Madison Square Garden, losing in fifteen rounds in which he was outclassed. With that victory, Ray gained the support of all other commissions as world champion.

Then Robinson vacated the throne after winning the middleweight title five years later. In a National Boxing Association elimination, Johnny Bratton of Little Rock, Arkansas, born September 9, 1927, decisioned Charlie Fusari of New Jersey on March 14, 1951, in Chicago, and this victory led to a fight with Kid Gavilan of Cuba in New York City on May 18, 1951, in which Gavilan whipped Bratton and gained the support of the N.B.A. and New York, but not that of Europe as Robinson's successor.

In Europe, Charley Humez was the top man, and it was not until after he announced his retirement from the welter class to fight as a middleweight, and after Gavilan's defeat of Billy Graham of New York, that the Cuban

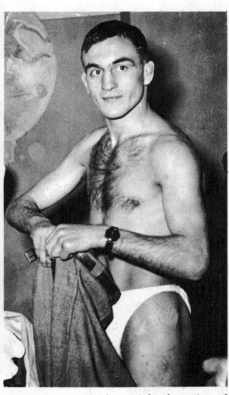

Ray Robinson was named successor to the welterweight throne and the only boxer who would meet Ray was Tommy Bell (above, left) of Youngstown, Ohio, who lost in 15 rounds. Ray defended the title eight times before winning the middleweight crown.

Charles Humez, welterweight champion of Europe, had European backing and held the key to the world championship.

Kid Gavilan (below, right), spectacular fighting machine from Camagüey, Cuba, outfought Johnny Bratton (left) on May 18, 1951, for the welterweight throne vacated by Robinson. Europe recognized the bout only as for the American title.

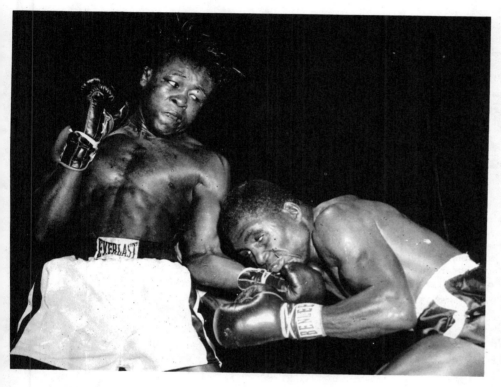

Kid Gavilan was given a hotly-disputed decision over Billy Graham in New York on August 29, 1951. With Humez out of the welterweight class, Gavilan was recognized as world champ. Graham (above, right) met Gavilan for the world title in Havana, Cuba, on October 5, 1952 and was again defeated in 15 rounds. Gavilan is shown in the seventh round, about to deliver the flashy "bolo punch" which he made famous.

Johnny Saxton is met with an uppercut to the jaw by Gavilan (left) during their title bout in Philadelphia on October 20, 1954. Saxton lifted the welterweight crown from the Kid in a dull 15-round bout. Gavilan, born Gerardo Gonzalez on January 6, 1926, had his first bout in 1943. Up to 1958, he had engaged in 140 fights, won 105, drew in 6, had one no-contest, and lost 28. He was never knocked out. Johnny Saxton, born in Newark, New Jersey, on July 4, 1930, won 54 out of 63 bouts from 1949 to 1957. He drew twice, lost three times, and was knocked out four times, twice by Carmen Basilio.

received world recognition as new champion. The Gavilan triumph was hotly disputed, the majority of the reporters and the public favoring Graham.

Another disputed decision, that in which Johnny Saxton of Brooklyn defeated Gavilan in Philadelphia, October 20, 1954, brought about a change in the ownership of the welter crown. Gavilan, a colorful fighter, an excellent drawing card, contested the loss, but to no avail. That same year, on April 2, he tried to win the world middleweight title in Chicago, but

was turned back by the titleholder, Bobo Olson, in fifteen rounds.

Johnny Saxton was knocked out by Tony DeMarco on April 1, 1955, in Boston in the fourteenth round to lose his crown. The loser tried for a return bout, but Carmen Basilio of Canastota, New York, beat him to it, and on June 10, 1955, Basilio stopped DeMarco in the twelfth round to gain top honors.

Saxton had been promised an engagement with Carmen if he would relinquish his rights to a contract he held for a return bout with DeMarco, but consented to let Basilio fulfill the

agreement with Tony. This fight was staged in Boston and Basilio again knocked out DeMarco in the twelfth round. Then he gave Saxton his chance.

They met in the Chicago Stadium on March 14, 1956, and in a contest in which it was almost unanimously agreed that Basilio had easily defeated his rival, the decision was against the champion.

Saxton was induced to lay his crown on the line against Carmen in a return bout at Syracuse on September 12, 1956, for which he received a

Tony DeMarco *(above, right)* became the new welterweight champion when he knocked out Saxton on April 1, 1955. Referee Mal Manning stepped in to save the glassy-eyed Saxton from further punishment. DeMarco, whose real name is Leonardo Liotta, was born in Boston on January 14, 1932. In 64 bouts, from 1948 to 1957, Tony won 54 with 31 knockouts, lost 5, drew once, and was kayoed 4 times. Less than three months after winning the crown, DeMarco was dethroned by Carmen Basilio *(below, right)* in 12 rounds. Carmen repeated the kayo in November. He lost the crown to Saxton in 1956 on a disputed decision, but regained it the same year, when he knocked him out. Carmen relinquished the crown in September, after winning the middleweight title.

handsome fee, and this time, Basilio made certain that no decision would be given against him by halting Johnny in the ninth round. It was a battle in which Basilio went all out from the tap of the opening gong and continued until the championship was in his hands again.

Then in a third engagement, February 22, 1957, in Cleveland, Ohio, Saxton was completely outclassed. Basilio knocked him out in the second round. Following that triumph, Carmen decided to go after Ray Robinson's middleweight crown, a bout which from the standpoint of interest was the outstanding of the year.

On September 6, 1957, Saxton was stopped by Joe Miceli of New York in the third round of a ten round contest in Washington, District of Columbia, and announced his retirement.

Vince Martinez and Virgil Akins, weigh in *(above)* under the supervision of Charles Pian *(right)* of the Missouri commission for the title bout, which ended in four rounds.

Unheralded Don Jordan *(left)* of Los Angeles scored a stunning upset on December 5, 1958, when he gave Virgil Akins a sound beating in 15 rounds and became the new welterweight champion. Jordan, 24, a 3-1 underdog, won a unanimous decision over the 30-year-old Akins, who was defending his crown for the first time. The nationally-televised contest was held in Los Angeles' Olympic Auditorium.

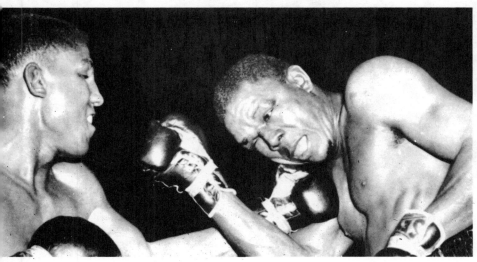

When Basilio defeated Robinson to become the middleweight champion, his welterweight crown became vacant, so the New York Commission and the National Boxing Association, assisted by the World Championship Committee, decided to find a successor through an elimination. Named by the group were: George Barnes of Australia, Tony DeMarco of Boston, Isaac Logart of Cuba, Vince Martinez of Paterson, New Jersey, Gaspar Ortega of Mexico, and Gil Turner of Philadelphia.

However, on the day this was announced Virgil Akins of St. Louis kayoed DeMarco in a Boston contest, and took over his place.

Logart outpointed Ortega in Cleveland, and Martinez decisioned Turner in Philadelphia. Barnes refused to come to America to compete, so the final group consisted of Logart, Turner, and Akins.

A drawing from a hat was held in the offices of *The Ring* Magazine under the direction of the author and Commissioner Helfand. Martinez drew the bye. Akins then kayoed Logart in six rounds in New York and was matched with Martinez in St. Louis on June 6, 1958.

In a one-sided contest in which Vince was floored nine times Akins became the new champion.

On December 5, 1958, Virgil Akins lost his crown to Don Jordan, who held the title for a year and a half before he succumbed to a terrific body beating dealt out by Benny (Kid) Paret. The twenty-three-year-old Paret, an ex sugar-cane cutter from Cuba, won a unanimous decision over the twenty-five-year-old champion on May 27, 1960, in Las Vegas.

Paret and Griffith fought the first of a three-bout series that would ultimately result in the Cuban's death on April 1, 1961, in Miami. Control of the match swayed back and forth, until unexpectedly, at 1:11 of the thirteenth round, Griffith landed a left hook to the chin, followed by a solid right that put the champion away and transferred the crown to his own head.

Paret regained the title when he won a split decision over Griffith in a return bout on September 30, 1961. The New York audience, jeering at the officials' decision, indicated that the match had been very close and controversial enough to merit a return bout.

The tragically final third bout, on March 24, 1963, left a comatose Paret on the canvas in the twelfth round,

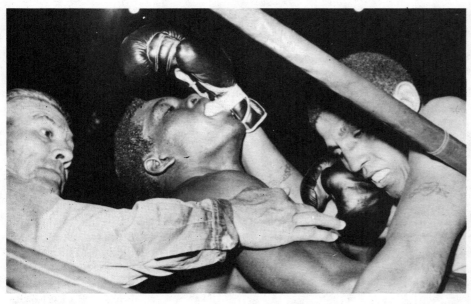

Benny (Kid) Paret, pulled away by referee Charlie Randolph, won the welterweight title from Don Jordan at Las Vegas, Nevada, May 27, 1960. Paret won a 15-round verdict.

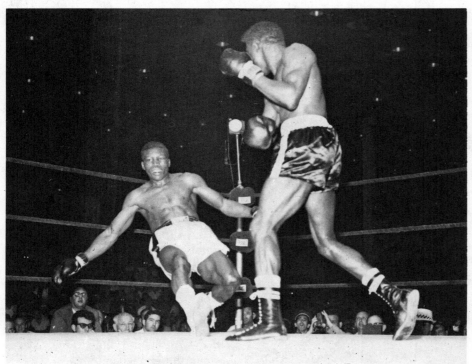

(Left) Emile Griffith administers the *coup de grace* to Paret in the 13th round of their Miami Beach bout on April 1, 1961, Emile thus capturing the 147-pound crown. Griffith (*above*) does a headstand while Paret still lies on the ring floor, dazed and beaten.

after an infuriated Griffith, insulted by Paret's calling him a homosexual, meted out a vicious and merciless beating while the Cuban hung on the ropes, partly out of the ring. The official count had Griffith delivering twenty-one blows before referee Ruby Goldstein halted the fight. Before the defending champion's collapse, there had been no evidence of severe injury, and Griffith had been substantially ahead on all score cards. Paret remained unconscious until he died on April 3.

Another Cuban refugee, Luis Rodriguez, briefly held the title for nearly three months after winning a close but unanimous fifteen-round decision over Griffith on March 21, 1963. He lost it again in a rematch on June 8. Awarded a close split-decision over fifteen rounds, Griffith became the first man to gain the world welterweight crown three times.

The strong, hard-hitting champion went on to win another fifteen-round split decision over Rodriguez on June 12, 1964, then three unanimous decisions over José Stable of Cuba, Brian Curvis of England, and Manuel Gonzales of the U.S., before relinquishing his title on May 18, 1966, and stepping up to the middleweight ranks, to win that crown.

In what was accepted as a bout to decide the successor to Griffith, Curtis Cokes, with an advantage of twelve inches in reach, defeated Jean Josselin of France in Dallas on November 28, 1966, by jarring his game opponent with stinging left jabs over fifteen rounds.

This match was the result of an elimination in which Cokes had gained the W.B.A. title by defeating Gonzales and Rodriguez.

Other American contenders, Ernie Lopez of Las Vegas, Nev., and Ted Whitfield of Amherst, Mass., were defeated in bouts previous to the elimination.

José Napoles, of Mexico, hammered Cokes into submission after thirteen rounds and captured the welter-

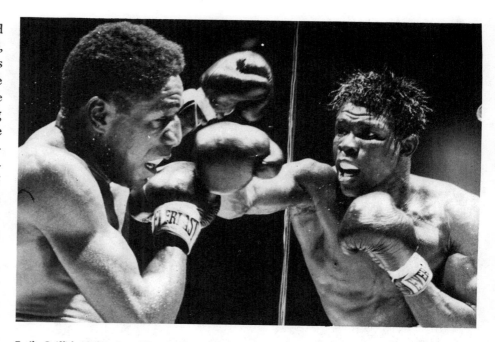

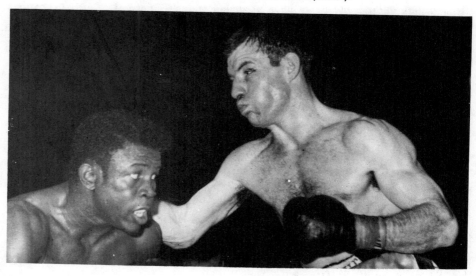

Emile Griffith *(right, above)* lost the title to Luis Rodriguez, but regained it on a split decision in 1963. In 1964 he pounded out a decision against Britiain's Brian Curvis *(below)*.

weight title on April 18, 1969. Napoles, at 143 pounds, scored his forty-first knockout in sixty-one professional fights when he kayoed Cokes in ten rounds in a return bout on June 29 in Mexico City.

Billy Backus of Syracuse, who had quit boxing in 1965 because he couldn't win, returned in 1967 and in four years scored twenty-one wins out of twenty-five bouts. On December 3, 1970, he scored a stunning upset over Napoles when the bout was halted in the fourth round, the result of a gash above Napoles' left eye.

Backus, a southpaw with a plodding

style, was no match for the smooth, sharpshooting Napoles when the two met in a rematch in Los Angeles on June 4, 1971. The bout was halted in the eighth round after the ring physician examined Backus's badly battered face.

On February 9, 1974 Napoles, one of the better world champions, attempted to add the middleweight title to his welterweight crown, but found conceding 6 pounds to Carlos Monzon, himself one of the best champions, too much and was knocked out in the seventh round.

Napoles was not up to form in his

After Griffith vacated the crown upon becoming middleweight boss, Curtis Cokes took over the title by defeating Jean Josselin in 1966. *Above*, the action; *below*, adulation.

successful defense against the American challenger, Hedgemon Lewis, on August 3, 1974. However, the champion outboxed and outpunched Lewis to win a knockout over his challenger when referee Ramon Berumen halted the contest in the seventh round.

Even though he won, he was not the Napoles of times past. He was not as sharp or as speedy. Lewis had a bad night, and that proved the difference.

On December 14, 1974 Napoles kept on the winning trail by knocking out challenger Horacio Saldanho, of

Argentina, in the third round, and made two successful defenses in 1975 against Armando Muniz of the United States, stopping him in the twelfth round in the first encounter and gaining a decision in the second. On December 6, 1975 Napoles was challenged by John H. Stracey the British and European champion. The fight took place at Mexico City, but not before Stracey had threatened to pull out when he learned that all the officials were to be Mexican. The main doubts among Stracey's supporters concerned the unaccustomed high altitude at which their champion was fighting and his notorious slow start, a doubt which seemed justified when Napoles put Stracey down in the first round. Stracey weathered the storm and in the succeeding rounds seemed to get stronger as Napoles wilted. After putting Napoles down and battering him till his left eye was badly swollen and his right cut, Stracey's continuous pressure finally told in the sixth round, when Napoles was punched to a standstill and the referee was forced to stop the fight. Stracey's first defense, fifteen weeks later, on March 20, 1976, at Wembley, against Hedgemon Lewis, took a similar

John H. Stracey, the British and European champion, after being knocked down in the first, gets a left to Napoles' battered face and adds the world title to his collection in Mexico City on December 6, 1975.

course. Lewis began very fast, and the fight was even for five or six rounds, but Stracey's skill, strength and aggression told, and Lewis was battered and helpless when stopped in the tenth.

Stracey's wins, however, made him world champion only in the eyes of the W.B.C. as in 1975 the W.B.A. set up its own titleholder by recognising a match between Angel Espada (Puerto Rico) and Clyde Gray (Canada) as being for the vacant title. Stracey was beaten on June 22, 1976, at Wembley Arena by Carlos Palomino (Mexico), the bout being stopped in the twelfth round and the new champion made four successful title defences the following year, beating Armando Muniz, stopped fifteenth round at Los Angeles on January 22; Dave Green (Great Britain) who was knocked out in eleven rounds, also at Wembley Arena, on June 14; Everaldo Costa, who was outpointed at Los Angeles on September 13 and Jose Palacios, who was knocked out in thirteen rounds, on December 10, also at Los Angeles. In 1978 Palomino disposed of three more challengers, beating Ryu Sormachi at Las Vegas on February 11 by the knockout route in round seven; Mimoun Mohatar, stopped in nine rounds at Las Vegas on March 18, and Armando Muniz, outpointed over fifteen rounds at Las Vegas on July 27. On January 14, 1979, however, he lost his W.B.C. title to Wilfredo Benitez (Puerto Rico) on a points decision at San Juan.

W.B.A. welter king, Angel Espada, kept his crown against Johnny Gant (USA) with a fifteen rounds points verdict at Ponce on October 11, 1975, but lost the title to Jose "Pipino" Cuevas (Mexico) in two rounds at Mexicali on July 18, 1976. The new champion successfully defended against Shoji Tsujimoto in six rounds at Kanazawa on October 27 and in 1977 overcame challenges from: Miguel Angel Campanino, ref stopped fight, second, at Mexico City, March 12; Clyde Gray, knocked out in the second at Los Angeles August 6, and Angel Espada, ref stopped fight, eleventh, at San Juan on November 19. In 1978 Cuevas remained W.B.A. champion, defeating Harold Weston (USA), the ref stopping the fight in the ninth at Los Angeles on March 4; Billy Backus, stopped in the first at

Boxing found a new star attraction to replace the fading Ali when Sugar Ray Leonard won the welterweight crown, and although losing it to Duran, regained it in November 1980.

Los Angeles May 20, and Pete Ranzany, stopped in the second at Sacramento on September 9. On January 30, 1979, when beating Scott Clark in two rounds at Los Angeles, Cuevas was making the eighth defence of his W.B.A. title.

A new star emerged in the W.B.C. version of the welterweight title when, after twice successfully defending the championship by outpointing Carlos Palomino (Mexico) and Harold Weston (U.S.A.), Benitez was knocked out in the 15th round by Sugar Ray Leonard, from Maryland, a gold medallist in the 1976 Olympic Games. He possessed a flamboyant style and punching power reminiscent of the young Cassius Clay, and on March 31, 1980 made an impressive first defence of his crown by knocking out Dave Green (Great Britain) in four rounds at Landover. On June 20 he suffered a shock defeat at the hands of Roberto Duran, former brilliant lightweight champion, being narrowly outpointed at Montreal. In a return fight at New Orleans on November 26, Leonard won back his title by forcing Duran to quit of his own accord in the eighth round.

The W.B.A. champion, Pipino Cuevas, continued to defeat his challengers, beating three in 1979 and Harold Volbrecht, the South African

champion, in five rounds at Houston on April 6, 1980. At his 13th defence, on August 2 at Detroit, he was sensationally stopped in two rounds by unbeaten 21-year-old Thomas Hearns, known as The Motor City Cobra, because of his phenomenal height and reach. At Detroit on December 6 Hearns retained his title by knocking out Luis Primera (Venezuela) in six rounds.

Randy Shields (U.S.A.) was stopped in 12 rounds on April 25, 1981 and Pablo Baez (Dominica) suffered a similar fate in four rounds on June 25. It seemed that Hearns was likely to be another long-reigning champion, but when he was matched with the W.B.C. titleholder, Sugar Ray Leonard, to fight for the undisputed welterweight championship of the world at Las Vegas on September 16, he was halted in 14 rounds and thereafter boxed as a light-middle. Everyone expected even more great things from the winner, but suddenly it was discovered that he had a detached retina of the eye which necessitated an operation and although this was successful, it was doubtful if he would ever box again. Out of the ring for five months, he decided to give himself a tryout and defended his title against fellow-countryman Bruce Finch at Reno

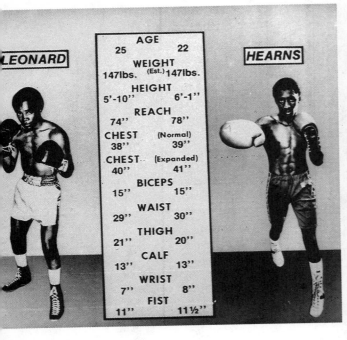

	LEONARD	HEARNS
AGE	25	22
WEIGHT	147lbs. (Est.)	147lbs.
HEIGHT	5'-10"	6'-1"
REACH	74"	78"
CHEST (Normal)	38"	39"
CHEST (Expanded)	40"	41"
BICEPS	15"	15"
WAIST	29"	30"
THIGH	21"	20"
CALF	13"	13"
WRIST	7"	8"
FIST	11"	11½"

(Left) The statistics of the two contestants for the undisputed welterweight championship bout at Las Vegas in September 1981. *(Right)* The winner, Leonard, gets in a left late in the fight.

on February 15, 1982 and although winning in three rounds, was so dissatisfied with his showing that his retirement from the ring was announced on November 9.

With the welter title vacant, both controlling bodies leapt into action to set up a new champion. First in the field was the W.B.A., who matched Don Curry (U.S.A.) with Jun-Suk Hwang (Korea) at Fort Worth on February 13, 1983, the American winning on points. Curry maintained his grip on the title by

The undisputed champion in 1985, Don Curry, after he had knocked out W.B.C. champion Milton McCrory in a unifying title bout.

stopping Roger Stafford (U.S.A.) in 1 minute 42 seconds of the opening round at Marsala in Sicily, on September 3. He next defeated Marlon Starling (U.S.A.) on points over 15 rounds at Atlantic City on February 4, 1984; Elio Diaz (Venezuela) was forced to retire in round seven on April 21 at Fort Worth; and Nino La Rocca (Italy) was stopped in six rounds at Monte Carlo on September 22. Curry next stopped British Champion Colin Jones on a cut eye in the fourth round at Birmingham on January 19, 1985, and at this point was unbeaten in 22 contests, with five successful defences of his title.

Meanwhile the W.B.C. had appointed Milton McCrory (U.S.A.) and Colin Jones (G.B.) to fight for its version of the welter title at Reno on March 19, 1983. The pair put up such a close contest that many thought the British Champion had won, but the officials decided it was a draw. A return bout was ordered and they met at Las Vegas on August 13 when McCrory outpointed the Welshman over 12 rounds after another great effort by the challenger. The American kept his title

against Milton "Mad Dog" Guest (U.S.A.) by stopping him in six rounds at Detroit on January 14, 1984; he then halted Gilles Elvilea (France), also in six rounds, at Detroit on April 15. On March 9, 1985 Pedro Vidella (U.S.A.) was outpointed over 12 rounds in Paris, while his fourth successful defence was made at Monte Carlo on July 14, when he stopped Carlos Trujillo (Panama) in three rounds.

On December 6, 1985 there occurred one of those rare occasions in world boxing when Curry and McCrory (the W.B.A. and W.B.C. champions) clashed at Las Vegas in a unified title bout. Don Curry won by a clean-cut knockout in round two to become indisputed world champion. He retained the title with another second round knockout, of Eduardo Rodriguez of Panama, at Fort Worth on March 10, 1986.

Lloyd Honeyghan (Great Britain), the British, Commonwealth and European champion, unbeaten in 27 contests, took on Curry at Atlantic City on September 27, 1986 and caused one of boxing's biggest surprises by completely overpowering the champion, causing Curry to retire at the end of the sixth round with a badly cut eye.

With the British fighter viewed by the world as the undisputed ruler of the

ped on March 22, but he had a harder task on April 18 when he faced Maurice Blocker. He was taken the full 12 rounds to a close decision.

Mark Breland, who was thought to be Honeyghan's master by many if they could be brought together in a unification bout, placed his newly won W.B.A. title at stake on August 22 against Marlon Starling at Columbia, South Carolina, but he was completely outclassed before being knocked out in the 11th round. A few days later, on August 30, before a Spanish crowd at Marbella, Honeyghan disposed of Gene Hatcher very easily with a flurry of punches which floored the challenger in a matter of seconds.

The British boxer next elected to defend his W.B.C. title, over 12 rounds only, at Wembley versus the Mexican Jorge Vaca, on October 28. The champion was having a hard struggle when the pair clashed heads in the 8th round. Vaca was the worse injured, with a badly cut eye, and since the officials ruled that whichever man was ahead on points up to the end of the previous round

division, it came as something of a surprise when Honeyghan made a political gesture in returning the W.B.A. belt to its officials on the grounds that he would not have anything to do with their foremost contender, Harold Volbrecht, of South Africa. His action was somewhat premature, since Volbrecht had not yet been named as Honeyghan's logical opponent. When the South African was matched with Mark Breland at Atlantic City on March 6, 1987, he was shown to be definitely second best and was knocked out in 7 rounds, in a match for the vacant championship.

Retaining his other two belts, Honeyghan first of all made short work of Johnny Bumphus in a couple of rounds at Wembley, when the fight was stop-

Mark Breland, a former Olympic champion, was expected to have a long reign as W.B.A. champion, but found Marlon Starling his master in 1987.

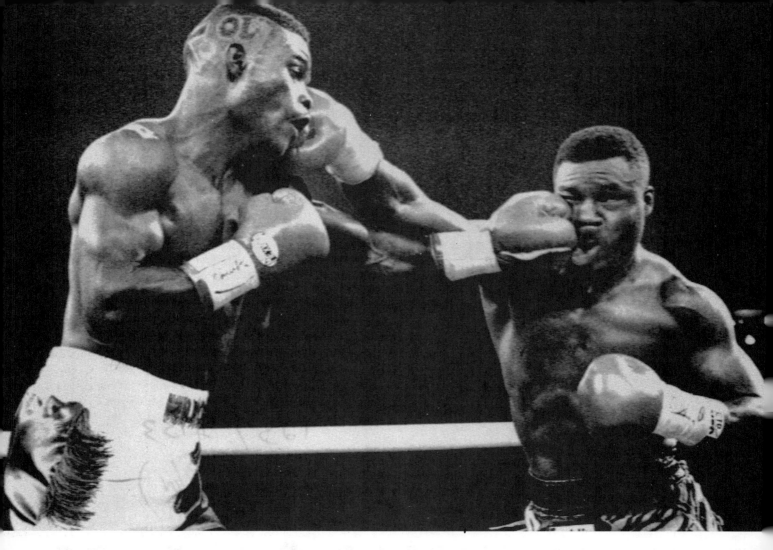

should be declared the victor, Lloyd Honeyghan lost his W.B.C. title on a matter of a single point. Although his I.B.F. championship had not been at stake, the contest being only a scheduled 12-rounder, the officials of that ruling body now declared its welterweight title vacant.

On February 5, 1988, Marlon Starling, who had looked so good against Mark Breland, won a very dull and disappointing points verdict, over 12 rounds at Atlantic City, against an inferior opponent, Fujio Ozaki, of Japan. The challenger did his best, but Starling merely foiled his efforts and coasted to an easy victory.

Starling's next defence was a return with Mark Breland, at the Las Vegas Hilton on April 16, 1988. The harder-punching Starling built an early lead but was then outboxed by the lanky Breland. Nevertheless most observers thought Breland was lucky to scrape a

draw. Starling was robbed of his title on his next defence, at Atlantic City on July 29. He was comfortably on top of his Colombian challenger, Tomas Molinares, as the sixth round ended but, as the bell rang to end the round, and Starling relaxed, so Molinares caught him with a right to the jaw which completely laid him out. The referee decided that Molinares was in the process of throwing a combination when the bell sounded, and that therefore the punch was not a foul, and he was given the title. It was doubly unsatisfactory in that Molinares subsequently found it difficult to make the weight and did not defend.

Meanwhile Lloyd Honeyghan had regained the W.B.C. title by knocking out Jorge Vaca in the third round at Wembley, and he defended on the same bill as the Molinares-Starling contest. This, too, ended in controversy, with Honeyghan, well ahead in the

fifth, uppercutting his opponent, Yung-Kil Chung, in the groin. Chung was given the statutory five minutes to recover, but his seconds withdrew him.

There was another double-welterweight championship bill at Las Vegas on February 5, 1989, when Marlon Starling took the W.B.C. crown by stopping Honeyghan in the ninth, and Mark Breland took the vacant W.B.A. title with a first-minute stoppage of Seung-Soon Lee. The veteran Starling was the best welterweight around at the time, but after outpointing Yung-Kil Chung he lost his title on points to Maurice Blocker, from Washington, known as the 'Thin Man', at Reno on August 19, 1990. Breland's reign was also short, but he stopped Rafael Pineda, Mauro Martelli, Fujio Ozaki and former champion

284

Lloyd Honeyghan before he was surprisingly knocked out in the ninth round by New Yorker Aaron Davis at Reno on July 8, 1990.

Meanwhile the I.B.F. title, which had been declared vacant in 1987, was picked up by Jamaican-born Simon Brown, who stopped Tyrone Trice in the 14th round at Berck-sur-Mer, France, on April 3, 1988. In a tremendous battle, Brown recovered from a near knockout himself in the second round to gradually get on top. Brown enjoyed a long reign, beating challengers Jorge Vaca (stopped, third), Mauro Martelli (points), Jorge Maysonet (stopped, third, in the unusual fight town of Budapest, Hungary), Al Long (knockout, seventh), Bobby Jo Brown (stopped, second), Luis Santana (points), Tyrone Trice (stopped, tenth), and Maurice Blocker, the newly crowned W.B.C. champion. Brown stopped Blocker in the tenth round at Las Vegas on March 18, 1991 and relinquished the I.B.F. title to concentrate on the W.B.C. version.

Unfortunately for Brown, his first challenger for that title was former light-welterweight champion James Buddy McGirt, whose career had survived a ruptured left bicep tendon in 1990. In a classy fight McGirt won a clear decision at Las Vegas on November 29, 1991. McGirt outpointed Patrizio Oliva and Genaro Leon but lost his title to the outstanding Pernell Whitaker, who had proved himself the world's best lightweight and was stepping up a division. McGirt seemed to have trouble with his left arm from halfway, and Whitaker was awarded a close but unanimous points decision at New York on March 6, 1993.

Meanwhile another outstanding champion was gracing the division in Meldrick Taylor, a former light-welterweight champion. Taylor relieved Aaron Davis of the W.B.A. crown when he outpointed him on Davis's first defence at Atlantic City on January 19, 1991. Taylor, whose only defeat had been a controversial one by Julio Cesar Chavez, outpointed Luis Garcia and Glenwood Brown in challenges but, in May 1992, took on the light-middleweight champion, Terry Norris, and

Crisanto Espana (right) staggers champion Meldrick Taylor on his way to taking the W.B.A. welterweight title in London in October, 1992. Espana was a Venezuelan from a boxing family and a member of Barney Eastwood's Belfast gym.

suffered his second defeat when stopped in the fourth round. Taylor was well below his best when stopped again on 31 October 1992 by Crisanto Espana on the undercard of the Lennox Lewis–Razor Ruddock fight at Earls Court, London. The unbeaten Espana, a Venezuelan boxing out of Belfast, and a marathon runner whose family of 15 includes older brother Ernesto, a former lightweight champion, stopped the declining Taylor with an eighth-round stoppage. In 1993 he outpointed Rodolfo Aguilar in his first defence.

The I.B.F. title which Simon Brown relinquished in 1991 was won by former W.B.C. champ Maurice Blocker on October 4, 1991 when he outpointed Glenwood Brown. He outpointed Luis Garcia on his first defence. Blocker lost in a challenge for Terry Norris's W.B.C. light-middleweight title in February 1993, but his welter title was not at stake.

The W.B.O. title was inaugurated on May 8, 1989 when the Mexican Genaro Leon knocked out Danny Garcia in Santa Ana. Leon relinquished the title without defending and Manning Galloway outpointed Al Hamza for the title at Yabucoa on December 15, 1989. Galloway's elusive and tricky southpaw style did not make for attractive contests, but was sufficient to overcome a number of challengers: Nika Khumalo (points), Gert Bo Jacobsen (retired, eighth), Racheed Lawal (retired, seventh), Jeff Malcolm (points), Nika Khumalo again (points) and Pat Barrett (points). A second fight with Gert Bo Jacobsen ended freakishly in the first round in Randers, Denmark, on November 27, 1992 when a small cut on Jacobsen's temple caused by a clash of heads spurted blood which could not be contained. The 'result' was a no-decision. A third meeting between them at Randers on February 13, 1993 saw Jacobsen win the title by unanimous decision, although the press described the verdict as a robbery. However, as the judges were from the U.S.A. (two) and the Dominican Republic, the decision could hardly be described as a home-town favour for the Dane.

THE LIGHT-WELTERWEIGHT CHAMPIONS

In 1922 Mike Collins, who was publishing a weekly entitled *The Boxing Blade*, was also managing a few fighters, one in particular being Myron "Pinkie" Mitchell, younger brother to Richie, a leading contender for the lightweight title. Unfortunately, Pinkie was at an in-between poundage, so Collins invented a light-welterweight division at 140 pounds and organized a competition among his readers to vote who should be the first champion. Strange to behold it was Mitchell who tallied the most votes and he was duly proclaimed titleholder on November 15. He kept his crown for nearly four years by the simple process of not defending it, but when he did, on September 21, 1926, he lost on a ten rounds verdict to Mushy Callahan (U.S.A.). Callahan defended it successfully three times, but lost to Jack "Kid" Berg (G.B.) in London on February 18, 1930, the bout being stopped in the 10th round. This was the famous occasion when Lord Lonsdale at the ringside stood up and protested that there was no such weight when the fighters were being introduced.

The Whitechapel Whirlwind proved a great champion, defending his title nine times in fifteen months in American rings, but when he made a bid to win the lightweight crown from Tony Canzoneri, he was beaten in three rounds and was considered to have lost his "Junior" title in the process. Canzoneri lost the title to Johnny Jadick at Philadelphia on January 18, 1932, on points over 10 rounds and failed to regain it in the same ring on July 18. Battling Shaw took over with a ten-rounds points win on February 20, 1933, but on May 21, was outboxed by Canzoneri, who regained the crown at New Orleans. Making a bid to win back his lightweight crown, Tony was outpointed by Barney Ross and forfeited his light-welter crown as well. This was over 10 rounds at Chicago on June 23 and on September 12 in New York, Ross outpointed him again, this time over 15 rounds. Ross, who was to prove a fine champion at three weights, made ten successful defences of his junior-welter title, eventually giving it up on May 28, 1935.

The division was left without a champion until April 29, 1946 when Tippy Larkin outpointed Willie Joyce over 12 rounds at Boston, and repeated this feat in New York on September 13. He made no further defences and it was not until June 12, 1959 that Carlos Ortiz knocked out Kenny Lane in two rounds at New York to win the vacant crown. Ortiz defeated challenger Battling Torres by a knockout in the tenth on February 4, 1960, retained his title against Duilio Loi on points on June 15, then lost the title in a return match with the Italian at Milan on September 1. Loi proved himself a fantastic champion. He fought from 1948 to 1963, having 126 bouts of which he lost only three. He reigned as world light-welter champion for two years and defended twice successfully, finally losing his crown to Eddie Perkins (U.S.A.) on September 14, 1962. In a return bout at Milan on December 15, he outpointed the American over 15 rounds. By now he was well past 33 and it was no surprise when he announced his retirement in January 1963.

This event brought about the formation of the World Boxing Association (formerly the National Boxing Association) who matched Roberto Cruz (Philippines) with Battling Torres for the vacant crown. On March 21, 1963 at Los Angeles Cruz won sensationally in 2 minutes 7 seconds of round one, but he remained champion only until June 15 when he lost over 15 rounds at Manila to Eddie Perkins, who thus gained the title for the second time. Perkins retained it against Yoshinori Takahashi (Japan) with a seventh round knockout and Bunny Grant on points, then was outpointed by Carlos Hernandez (Venezuela) at Caracas on January 18, 1965. Two quick defences followed: on May 15, against Mario Rossito, who was knocked out in the fourth, and on July 10, against Percy Hayles, who went the same way in the third, then Hernandez lost the title to Sandro Lopopolo at Rome on a points decision on April 29, 1966. The Italian knocked out Vicente Rivas in eight rounds on October 21, but on April 30, 1967 was knocked out in two rounds by Paul Takeshi Fujii (Hawaii) in Tokyo. Challenger Willi Quatour was stopped in four rounds on November 16, also in Tokyo.

The World Boxing Council had gone along with its rival body until now but when the W.B.A. endorsed a bout between Fujii and Nicolino Loche (Argentina) the W.B.C. objected on the grounds that the champion had forfeited the title by ignoring a challenge from Pedro Adigue (Philippines), whom they paired with Adolph Pruitt (U.S.A.). Loche won with a ten rounds kayo at Tokyo on December 12, 1968 and two days later at Manila, Adigue outpointed Pruitt. From then onwards the division had two title claimants.

Loche (W.B.A.) proved the busier champion of the two, defending his crown twice in 1969, once in 1970 and twice in 1971, all points wins. On March 10, 1972 he lost a decision to Alfonso "Peppermint" Frazier (Panama), who staved off a challenge from Al Ford on June 17 with a fifth round knockout, but was beaten by Antonio Cervantes (Colombia) by a knockout in the 10th round on October 28. The new champion proved to be a good one, defending his

286

title successfully on ten occasions (1973-1976). He lost it for a while to Wilfredo Benitez (Puerto Rico) on points on March 6, 1976 but came into it again under the W.B.A. banner when it became vacant later on. Benitez beat challenger Emiliano Villa on points on May 31 and Tony Petronelli, who was stopped in the third on October 16. In December, however, he was stripped of his title for not defending against Cervantes, but was granted a reprieve, and on April 3, 1977 defended successfully against Guerrero Chavez, who was knocked out in the 15th and last round. Benitez then went after the welter title and Cervantes came back into the picture, winning the vacant championship by knocking out Carlos Giminez in six rounds on June 25. He proved he had not lost his touch by outpointing Adriano Marrero on November 5, and in 1978 he knocked out Tomgta Kiatvayupak in six rounds on April 28 and Norman Sekgapane in nine on August 26.

Cervantes was proving as good a champion in his second spell as he had been in his first. On January 18, 1979 he outpointed Miguel Montilla in New York and on August 25 scored similarly over Kwang-Min Kim at Seoul. On May 29, 1980 he beat Montilla with a knockout in the seventh round of a return bout, but his reign came to an end on August 2, when he was himself knocked out in four rounds by Aaron Pryor at Cincinnati. Pryor, another outstanding boxer in this class, made eight successful defences in the next three years and retired undefeated in December 1983 with 34 bouts, all but two of which had been won inside the distance. Johnny Bumphus (U.S.A.) won the vacant W.B.A. title on January 22, 1984 by outpointing Lorenzo Garcia (Argentine) over 15 rounds at Atlantic City, but his reign lasted less than six months. He was stopped in 11 rounds by Gene Hatcher (U.S.A.) at Buffalo, N.Y. on June 1 and Hatcher then gained a points verdict when defending against Ubaldo Sacco (Argentine) on December 15. It had been a close thing however, and in a return title bout at Campione de Italia on July 21, 1985, Sacco caused a surprise by stopping Hatcher in nine rounds.

"Mad Dog" Gene Hatcher *(left)* outpointing challenger Ubaldo Sacco of Argentina in 1984, but Ubaldo stopped Hatcher in nine rounds to take his title in 1985.

On March 15, 1986, Sacco defended at Monte Carlo, and lost his title to Patrizio Oliva (Italy), who gained a 15-round decision.

The winner strengthened his claim to the W.B.A. laurels. He beat Brian Brunette rather easily at Naples, on September 6, and on January 10, 1987 he outpointed Rodolfo Gonzalez at Agrigento. Oliva then made a third defence when he faced the challenge of Juan Martin Coggi at Riberia, on July 4. Coggi upset all the odds by flattening Oliva for the full count in the 3rd round.

Meanwhile, champions and contenders were being kept busy under the auspices of the W.B.C. Pedro Adigue did not reign long, being outpointed by Italy's Bruno Arcari at Rome on January 31, 1970. Here was another superb champion who kept his title against nine challengers over the next four years, six times within the scheduled limit. He retired unbeaten in August 1974 and Perico Fernandez (Spain) outpointed Lion Furuyama (Japan) on September 24 for the vacant title. After knocking out Joao Henrique (Brazil) in nine rounds at Barcelona on April 19, 1975, Fernandez was forced to retire to Saesak Muangsurin (Thailand) at Bangkok on July 15. If the record books are correct the new champion, who was 25, achieved success in only his third pro fight; prior to that he had been a kickbox champion. In his first defence he outpointed Lion Furuyama in Tokyo on

Janaury 25, 1976, but lost on a fourth round disqualification to Miguel Valasquez (Spain) on June 30 at Madrid. In a return title bout on October 29, the Thailander regained the championship by knocking out Valasquez in two rounds. He remained titleholder for more than two years, checking seven contenders and finally falling to Sang-Hyun Kim by a knockout in the 13th round at Seoul on December 30, 1978.

The Korean outpointed Fitzroy Guiseppe on June 1, 1979 and knocked out Masahiro Yokai in the eleventh on September 29, but his reign came to an end on February 23, 1980 when he was stopped by Saoul Mamby (U.S.A.) at Seoul. The new champion reigned until June 26, 1982 when he lost to Leroy Haley (U.S.A.) on a points verdict. In between he had turned back five challengers, mostly on points. Haley kept his title with a points win against Juan Jose Ciminez on October 20 and with another points win in a return bout with Mamby on February 13, 1983. Next time out, however, on May 18, Bruce Curry (U.S.A.) joined his brother Don as a world champion by outpointing Leroy over 12 rounds at Las Vegas. He lasted only eight months, but he got in two successful defences, defeating

Hidekazu Akai with a seventh round knockout on July 7 and Haley on points on October 19, before being stopped in ten rounds by Bill Costello (U.S.A.) on January 29, 1984. Ronnie Shields on July 15, Saoul Mamby on November 3 and Leroy Haley on February 16, 1985, all tried in vain to take the title from Costello, being beaten on points over 12 rounds, then Lonnie Smith (U.S.A.) caused a distinct upset by knocking him out in eight rounds on August 21. Staged at Madison Square Garden, New York, the fight was a thriller with Smith on the canvas in the first round and Costello down four times before the final kayo that made Lonnie the new titleholder.

Smith did not keep the title long, being knocked out in the fifth round when he defended against Rene Arredondo (Mexico) at Los Angeles on May 5, 1986.

Arrendondo did not remain a champion for long, either, at that time. On July 24, in Tokyo, Tsuyoshi Hamada delighted the Japanese fans by knocking the Mexican cold in the opening round. And on December 2, Hamada strengthened his claim to the W.B.C. belt by outpointing Ronnie Shields over 12 rounds in the same city, but almost a year after winning the title so dramatically, on July 22, 1987 Hamada was stopped by cuts in the 6th round, again before a Tokyo crowd, by René Arrendondo, who thus regained the belt. But in defending it at Los Angeles on November 12, 1987, Arredondo once again lost his hold on the title, when he was halted in 6 rounds by Roger Mayweather.

When Aaron Pryor had retired in 1983, few people imagined that he would be back in action in less than a year. But on June 22, 1984 he outpointed Nicky Furlano at Toronto in a bout which was recognised by the recently formed I.B.F. He made only one defence of the championship, being returned the victor over Gary Hinton at Atlantic City the following March 2, and he forfeited the belt due to inactivity. Gary Hinton, his most recent victim, became recognised by the I.B.F. after outpointing Antonio Reyes Cruz in Lucca, Italy, on April 26, 1986. But on October 30 of the same year, at Hart-

ford, Conn., Hinton was knocked out by Joe Manley in 10 rounds.

Manley travelled to Basildon, home town of British Terry Marsh, and placed his belt at stake in an enormous circus tent, which was jammed with Marsh's supporters. It was a great night for Basildon when the challenger completely demolished Manley in 10 rounds on March 7, 1987. But the Englishman boxed only one more contest. He had little difficulty in halting the Japanese Akio Kameda on July 1 at the Royal Albert Hall, but he incurred a badly-cut brow in the process.

Terry Marsh then dropped something

Terry Marsh (left) took the I.B.F. title with a win over Joe Manley at Basildon, but after his defence Marsh declared he was epileptic and retired unbeaten.

of a bombshell when he announced that he suffered from epilepsy, almost immediately after signing a new contract with his manager. He retired from active boxing, and his foremost challenger, Frankie Warren, was paired, in his home-town of Corpus Christi, with James McGirt, of New York, for the I.B.F. championship. While Warren was a strong favourite to win, he was stopped in 12 rounds by his opponent, on February 14, 1988.

McGirt registered a first-round knockout of Howard Davis in his first defence, but on September 3, 1988 was stopped in the 12th round by Meldrick Taylor at Atlantic City. McGirt was favourite to beat the unbeaten Taylor, the 1984 Olympic featherweight champion, but Taylor was ahead all through and finished with an assault that forced the referee to step in. Taylor stopped John Meekins and outpointed Courtney Hooper in his first two defences.

Roger Mayweather, the W.B.A. champion, knocked out Maurice Aceves, outpointed Harold Brazier, stopped Rodolfo Gonzalez in the last round and outpointed Vinny Pazienza before losing his title to another of the decade's best fighters in Julio Cesar Chavez, who had stepped up from lightweight. Mayweather was forced to retire after ten rounds. Chavez stopped Sammy Fuentes and knocked out Alberto Cortes before taking on I.B.F. champion Meldrick Taylor in the Las Vegas Hilton on March 17, 1990. This proved to be one of the best and most controversial contests of recent times. Both boxers were unbeaten. Taylor's plan was to use his speed to outscore the heavier punching Chavez, but the plan was discarded after the first round when a blow to his left eye, causing a blow-out fracture, upset Taylor's judgement of distance and forced him to keep in close to Chavez. However Taylor boxed so well he was well ahead into the last round. But halfway through the last he ran out of steam and Chavez put him down. Taylor rose, but referee Richard Steele stopped the contest with two seconds left, thus depriving Taylor of victory.

Juan Martin Coggi meanwhile held on to the W.B.A. title without meeting opponents of the calibre of Taylor or Chavez. He beat Sang-Ho Lee (knockout, second round), Harold Brazier (points), Akinobu Hiranaka (points) and Jose Luis Ramirez (points) before he lost the title on points in Nice on August 17, 1990 to Loreto Garza (U.S.A.). Garza, virtually unknown outside Sacramento, won his defence against former lightweight champion Vinny Pazienza on a foul in the 11th round, having demoralised the challenger into

constant holding, but he lost the title on his second defence when stopped in the third round by another ex-lightweight champion, Edwin Rosario, on June 14, 1991. Both Garza's defences were in Sacramento. Rosario was stopped in the first round in his first defence, in Mexico City on April 10, 1992, by Akinobu Hiranaka, from Tokyo. The two boxers waded into each other from the bell, but the blows of the heavily bearded and moustached Japanese were the more effective, and although Rosario refused to go down he was reeling round the ring when the referee stepped in at 1 minute 32 seconds.

Former lightweight champion Pernell Whitaker at the weigh-in before his successful challenge to Rafael Pineda for the I.B.F. light-welterweight crown.

Hiranaka also lost on his first defence. Morris East of the Philippines went to Tokyo and stopped the champion in his own city in the 11th round on September 9, 1992. East, however, could do no better than the previous W.B.A. title-holders, and back in Mar del Plata, Argentina, he was stopped in the eighth by Juan Martin Coggi on January 12, 1993. Coggi resumed where he had left off in 1990 by stopping Joe Rivera on his first defence.

The W.B.O. had their first champion at the weight when Hector Camacho, a former lightweight champion, outpointed another in Ray Mancini in Reno on March 6, 1989. He outpointed yet another in Vinny Pazienza and then outpointed Terry Baltazar before dropping a decision to Greg Haugen, yet another ex-lightweight champ, in Las Vegas on February 23, 1991. However Haugen failed the post-fight drug test, and the title was restored to Camacho who, three months later, outpointed Haugen in Reno. Camacho then relinquished the W.B.O. title, and it was picked up by the Mexican, Carlos Gonzalez, who stopped Jimmy Paul (U.S.A.) in the second round at Los Angeles on June 30, 1992. Carlos 'Bolillo' Gonzalez brought some dash to the W.B.O. crown, going one better in his first defence by knocking out Rafael Ortiz of Dominica in 93 seconds. Matched with Tony Baltazar, who came out throwing big punches at Inglewood on March 22, 1993, Gonzalez, who hardly seemed a fighter at a puny-looking 5ft 9in, fought back with patient but mercilessly accur-

ate uppercuts and combinations and won on the three knockdown rule, again in the first round. At that stage, the 20-year-old high school graduate Gonzalez, who began boxing aged nine, was unbeaten in 37 contests, 19 of his 34 stoppages coming in the first round.

Julio Cesar Chavez, meanwhile, continued his long unbeaten run by defending his W.B.C. and I.B.F. titles and stopping Kyung-Duk Ahn and John Duplessis, whereupon he relinquished the I.B.F. version of the title. He defended the W.B.C. title with wins over Lonny Smith (points), Angel Hernandez (stopped, fifth), Frankie Mitchell (stopped, fourth), Hector Camacho (points) and Greg Haugen (stopped, fifth). This last fight was on a four-championship fight card at the Estadio Azteca, Mexico City, on February 20, 1993. The programme drew a world record boxing crowd of 136,000, with popular idol Chavez, unbeaten in 85 contests, the main draw. Chavez set a record in achieving 13 years unbeaten, the previous best being Jack McAuliffe's 12 years 11 months (with

Carlos Monzon and Joe Louis close behind). It was Chavez's 23rd title fight at three different weights. Chavez was soon in action again, however, on the undercard of the Lewis-Tucker fight at Las Vegas on May 8. His all-action affair with Terrence Alli of Guyana was promising to become one of the battles of the year before the relentless punching of Chavez proved irresistible and the fight was stopped in the sixth.

The I.B.F. title which Chavez relinquished was won by Rafael Pineda of Columbia, who stopped former champ Roger Mayweather in the ninth at Reno on December 7, 1991. Pineda subsequently stopped Clarence Coleman but Pernell Whitaker, the former lightweight champion, took his title with a points win at Las Vegas on July 18 1992. Whitaker later moved up to welterweight to win the W.B.C. title in that division.

Mexican idol Julio Cesar Chavez (left) drew 136,000 fans to the Estadio Azteca to see him stop Greg Haugen and set a 13-year unbeaten record.

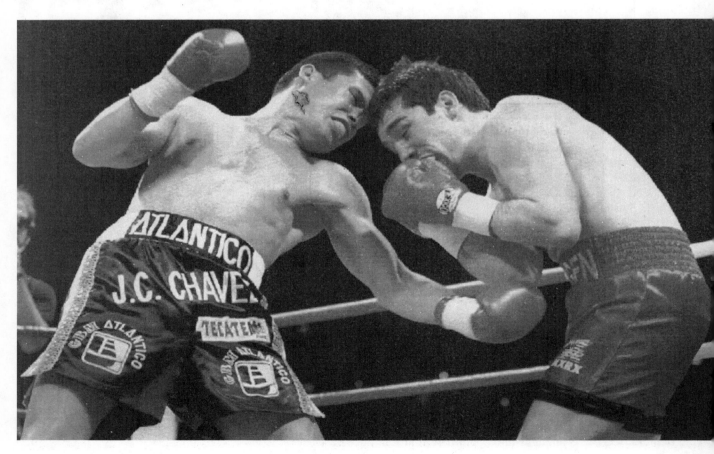

THE LIGHTWEIGHTS

Excepting, perhaps, the heavyweight class, no division in boxing has produced more colorful, exciting, and dramatic history than the lightweight. From the Victorian eighties when Jack McAuliffe ruled the roost, the light ranks have fairly teemed with outstanding ringmen, brilliant boxers, rugged sluggers, robust punchers, and quaint characters who, despite their strange antics in the ring and out, could really fight.

A list of the greats, champions and non-champions, those who contributed their bits to the glory of the division, shows such historic ring figures as Dick Burge, Jim Carney, Billy Myer, Young Griffo, Jack McAuliffe, Harry Gilmore, Frank Erne, George Elbows McFadden, Kid McPartland, Patsy Haley, Freddie Welsh, Joe Gans, Ad Wolgast, Benny Leonard, Joe Rivers, Battling Nelson, Matt Wells, Johnny Dundee, Willie Jac: on, Matty Bald-

win, Lew Tendler, Al Singer, Sammy Mandell, Billy Petrolle, Tony Canzoneri, Lou Ambers, Jackie Kid Berg, Harry Mason, Barney Ross, Beau Jack, Henry Armstrong, Bob Montgomery, Ike Williams, Rocky Kansas, Charley White, Phil Bloom, Richie Mitchell, Pal Moran, Joe Benjamin, Joe Azevedo, Frankie Callahan, George Kid Lavigne, Joe Mandot, among many others.

It was the first episode in the classic

Dutch Sam (above), inventor of the upper-cut, was feared as the deadliest puncher of the London Prize Ring. He was born in Whitechapel, London, on April 4, 1775, of Jewish parents. He attracted wide attention in 1801, after he had knocked out some good lightweights and repeatedly knocked out heavier men. Sam was 5' 6½" tall and weighed only 133 pounds, but he was deep-chested and muscular. He died in 1816. His son, Young Dutch Sam, became welterweight champion in 1825.

Dick Curtis (right), lightweight champion from 1820 to 1828 and popular with fast noblemen, was called "the Pet of the Fancy." After beating Barney Aaron in a fierce 55-minute battle on February 27, 1827, he remained in the ring and seconded his pal, Young Dutch Sam, who was to fight Gypsy Cooper a half hour later.

Goldfield, Nevada, gained world-wide attention when Tex Rickard, a daring young gambler, promoted the Battling Nelson-Joe Gans title fight there. The top photo is a scene of Main Street in 1905. The bottom photo is the same Main Street, one year later. Rickard put up an astoundingly large purse of $34,000. The gate receipts of $69,715 were also astounding for that era.

Battling Nelson-Joe Gans series that introduced to boxing a young gambler destined to become the world's top promoter—George Lewis 'Tex' Rickard. Goldfield, Nevada, was at the height of its boom in 1906 and a committee of local citizens, with Rickard as chairman, was appointed to promote an event that would attract outside attention to the town. Someone suggested a prize fight.

It met with favor in the eyes of Rickard, who put up $30,000 for Nelson and Gans to split, with the Battler guaranteed $20,000 and $2,000 for signing and $500 for expenses. The purse, $34,000 all told, was the biggest ever offered for a lightweight title bout up to that time, yet in the days of Jimmy McLarnin, Barney Ross,

Beau Jack, Benny Leonard, Lou Ambers, Ike Williams, Tony Canzoneri, Sammy Mandell, Al Singer, among others of their era, it was not unusual for lightweight contests to register $200,000 gates, with the fighters reaping $50,000 or more as their share. The Nelson-Gans fight ushered in the era of big gates and super-promotion in the division.

The lightweights were always in the public eye because of the speed and decisive action usually on view. Three fighters especially hold the spotlight in this class since Jack McAuliffe, born in Cork, Ireland March 24, 1866, retired undefeated after holding the crown during the bareknuckle days and part of the gloves era. They are Gans, Nelson, and

Benny Leonard. These are considered the greatest of all lightweights, the supermen of the group.

Whether Gans was Leonard's master or vice-versa has been a topic for discussion since Benny gained world prominence. There can be no doubt that Gans was the master of the boxers in his class when he was in his prime, and that Benny was tops among the later day lightweights.

In the earlier days, Jack McAuliffe, who defended his crown for the last time in New Orleans during the Carnival of Champions, September 5, 1892, reigned supreme from 1885 to 1896. His last defense was against Billy Myer whom he knocked out in the fifteenth round.

The title bouts in the lightweight

Arthur Chambers, born in Salford, England, started boxing at 17. He weighed 125 pounds for the Edwards fight and was taking a shellacking, until he tricked the referee into awarding him the title on a foul. Chambers lived in Philadelphia after retirement and died May 5, 1923. He was 75.

Billy Edwards, born in Birmingham, England, stood 5' 5" and weighed 126 pounds. He came to America in 1865 and beat the best lightweights around. Sneak tactics by Chambers' second cost him the title. After retirement Edwards wrote a treatise on how to box.

Edwards and Chambers met for the title on September 4, 1872, at Squirrel Island, Canada. Chambers rushed out for the 26th round, clinched, and screamed that he was bitten. Referee Bill Tracy, noting the teeth marks, declared Chambers the winner on a foul. Actually, Chambers' second, Tom Allen, did the biting between rounds.

class in America were tussles confined mostly to foreigners until McAuliffe retired and gave an opportunity to George Kid Lavigne, a native American, to claim and successfully defend the championship for three years.

The first recorded king of the division had been Abe Hicken, whose reign extended from 1867 to 1872, when he retired. Elimination matches among Johnny Clark, Billy Edwards, and Arthur Chambers resulted in the last named taking the crown. Chambers retired in 1879 and Nonpareil Jack Dempsey forged to the front, but never claimed the laurels since he quickly outgrew the class. His pal McAuliffe asserted himself as head of the group, his claim based on the refusal of Jimmy Mitchen, top ranking lightweight to meet him in a fight for the American title.

293

Yours Truly
Jack McAuliffe
Lightweight
Champion of
the World

294

Jack Dempsey, the Nonpareil (above), claimed the lightweight crown, but by 1885 he outgrew the class, and Jack McAuliffe ascended the throne, reigning until 1896, when he retired. Dempsey was McAuliffe's chief second in the Carney battle.

Jem Carney, shown wearing his British championship belt, was a first class fighting man. He stood 5' 4" and his best fighting weight was 133 pounds. His battle to a draw with McAuliffe prevented Jack from winning the world crown.

Around a twenty-four-foot ring in a Revere, Massachusetts, stable on the night of November 5, 1887, sat a gathering of guests especially invited to watch a match for the world lightweight championship. Jack McAuliffe of the United States and Jem Carney, British title-holder, were the opponents. After seventy-four bloody rounds, the spectators broke into the ring, and the referee called off the proceedings.

For four hours before the affair the invited guests, because of fear of po-

lice interference, arrived in pairs at a designated hotel, and after each had passed muster, he was permitted to remain until the march to the stable under the guidance of the hotel proprietor, who led the way with a lantern.

At the barn the spectators found a Salvation Army group practicing hymns, and their presence helped throw the police off the trail.

Carney tipped the scales at 129 and McAuliffe at 126. Throughout the early rounds the men hooked and

jabbed, landing few blows of any consequence. McAuliffe was dropped in the seventh round, but came back strong.

When the sixtieth round arrived, McAuliffe showed signs of fatigue. His backers, fearing the loss of their wagers, became unruly. The break came in the seventieth frame, when Carney scored a clean knockdown that looked like a finisher. Only interference by McAuliffe's friends saved him. Order was restored, and the bout went on until the seventy-fourth round,

when Carney again put McAuliffe down and it seemed the American could not continue. The spectators rushed the ring again. Tom McKay, the hotel proprietor, appealed to referee Stevenson to call a halt before the police arrived on the scene. Stevenson agreed and declared the contest a draw, although Carney was in the lead.

One of the most incredible figures the ring has ever known was Young Griffo, an Australian, who though actually a featherweight fought and whipped the top lightweights of his era. Griffo never was one to take his professional career seriously. Training was a nuisance to him, and he preferred hanging around barrooms and guzzling his liquor. Seldom, indeed, was Griffo sober for a fight, yet so amazingly clever was he that regardless of the state of his physical and mental condition at the moment, he invariably held his own or could and did whip his opponent.

The longest fight on record was a lightweight meeting between Andy Bowen and Jack Burke in New Or-

Carney and McAuliffe re-enacted their historic skin-tight glove battle 27 years later in London. The affair, in 1914, was refereed by Charley Mitchell, the former British heavyweight champion, who is shown walking to the center of the ring (above, left) while McAuliffe waits in the right corner and Carney in the left. The battlers got in their pet blows wearing big gloves. Carney, shown facing the camera (above, right) watches McAuliffe wind up a roundhouse right.

Young Griffo (right) born in Sydney, Australia, in 1871, started there with bare-knuckle fights and came to America in 1894. Never a title-holder, Griffo was considered one of the most skillful boxers that the ring ever produced.

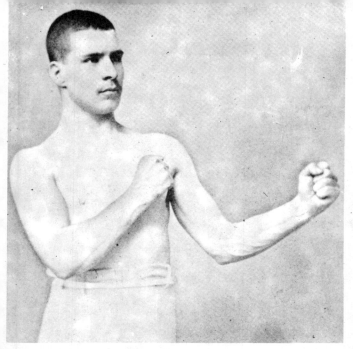

Jack Burke (above) and Andy Bowen (right) on April 6, 1893, fought the longest battle on record: seven hours, 19 minutes. They started at 9:15 P.M. and ended at 4:19 A.M. When the 110th round ended, they were exhausted, their eyes puffed, their arms swollen from stopping each other's blows, and their faces looking like raw beef. Referee Duffy, who refused to let the fight go to a finish as originally agreed upon, stopped it and called it a draw. The battlers split the $2,500 purse.

After George Kid Lavigne (left) claimed the crown, his manager, Sam Fitzpatrick (right), took him to England, where Lavigne kayoed Dick Burge for the world title.

leans, April 6, 1893, a contest that waded through 110 rounds, spread across seven hours and nineteen minutes, when, exhausted, they couldn't continue and the referee halted the affair and called it a draw.

On June 1, 1896, George Kid Lavigne, born in Bay City, Michigan, December 6, 1869, succeeded to the throne left vacant by McAuliffe's retirement. Lavigne knocked out Dick Burge, British champion, in London in seventeen rounds to gain universal recognition. Burge was a scientific boxer; Lavigne, an aggressive, savage fighter. In that battle, Lavigne's mouth and nose were cut and badly bleeding while the body of his British opponent was full of blotches from the terrific pounding it had received. In the final round, heavy barrages weakened Burge. Then followed a left and right to the stomach that brought down Burge's guard and the finisher, a right to the jaw followed, giving the world crown to America.

Lavigne on July 3, 1899, at Buffalo, lost the championship to Frank Erne,

"KID" McPARTLAND

Kid McPartland, a title threat, lost a 25-round disputed decision to Lavigne on February 8, 1897. He later became a referee in New York.

George Kid Lavigne (right) a durable punishing fighter, was called "the Saginaw Kid." He started in 1895 and was unbeaten until 1899, when he lost a bout to Billy Smith and the title to Frank Erne. Among the top men Lavigne met were Young Griffo, whom he held to a draw, and Andy Bowen, who died from injuries following a knockout blow.

Dick Burge, England's lightweight champion (left), gave Kid Lavigne a stiff battle for 17 rounds on June 1, 1896, but Dick's ambition to become world champion was halted by Lavigne's cruel body punishment.

The contemporary sketches below depict the slashing battle between Lavigne and Joe Walcott, at Maspeth, Long Island, December 2, 1895. Walcott lost the decision, as had been agreed, when he failed to knock out the lightweight champion.

Almost a Finishing Touch.

T BATTLE WITH KID LAVIGNE AT BUFFALO LAST N

RANK ERNE THE WORLD'S C

AFTER TWENTY HARD ROUNDS, WITH BOTH READY

ERNE LANDING A HARD LEFT ON HIS FOE.

ship were read from Joe Gans, Kid Mc-Partland, George McFadden, Jim Popp and Tim Kearns. and rushed. Uppercuts straightened him up and he remarked as a left-hander caught him flush on the stomach. "That was a blocked. Frank puts hard right on head. Toward the last the Kid landed on face and body, while Erne jabbed him in the

Frank Erne *(left)* born in Zurich, Switzerland, on January 8, 1875, was raised in Buffalo, New York, and started boxing in 1894. His first two losses were to Martin Flaherty and George Dixon in 1897. He won over Dixon the year before in 20 rounds. Erne lifted the crown from Kid Lavigne on September 28, 1898, in a cleverly-fought 20-round bout, as illustrated in the *New York Journal* the following day.

The great Joe Gans quit to Erne in 1900. In 1902, Gans stopped Erne in one round and won the lightweight championship.

Jimmy Britt *(below)* tried to claim the title from Gans, but when they met in 1904, Britt fouled Joe in the fifth round.

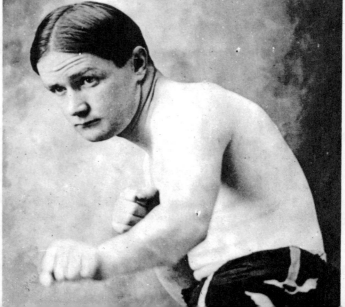

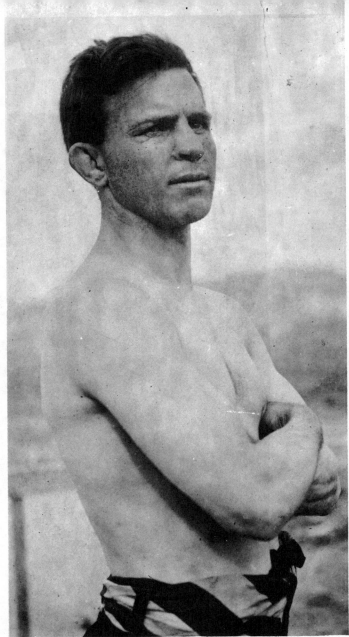

Battling Nelson (*above*), "the Durable Dane," was born in Copenhagen, Denmark, on June 5, 1882. In 132 battles, from 1896 to 1923, he won 37 of 57 by knockouts, won one, lost two on fouls, had 15 no-decisions, drew in 19, lost 15 and was kayoed twice. Nelson knocked out Gans twice in title bouts.

Joe Gans (*right*), the "Old Master," was born November 25, 1874, in Philadelphia. He had 156 fights from 1891 to 1909 and won 54 of 114 by knockouts. He won five on fouls, drew 10, 18 were no-decision, lost three, and was kayoed five times. Gans was one of the all-time great ringmen.

who outpointed him in twenty rounds. The following March, Gans was stopped by Erne in the twelfth round, the Baltimore Negro quitting. But in their second engagement, at Fort Erie, May 12, 1902, an upset that aroused considerable talk enabled Gans to win the title by a knockout in the opening round. The first punch did the trick, the first time in history that a champion was disposed of with the only blow delivered.

Jimmy Britt of California set up a plea that Gans had declined to make the weight and therefore had forfeited his title. Gans proved how baseless this claim was when on October 31, 1904, he handed Britt a terrific beating, Britt striking low when nearly out in the twentieth round. By way of good measure, Gans knocked out

Nelson and Gans touch gloves *(above)* before their battle in Goldfield, Nevada, in which Tex Rickard made a successful debut as a boxing promoter. Gans displayed too much skill for Nelson during the bout. In the 42nd round Gans crumbled to the canvas from a low blow and Nelson was disqualified. The bout was profitable to Rickard despite what was then considered a fantastic purse of $34,000. When they met in 1908, Nelson's boring-in style was too much for Gans who was down five times. Nelson knocked out Joe in the 17th round *(below)* and became champion.

Britt in the sixth round on September 9, 1907.

The Goldfield battle on September 3, 1906, in which Gans won from Battling Nelson in the forty-second round on a foul, and their second bout on July 4, 1908, in San Francisco, in which the Baltimore Negro lost the championship by a knockout in the seventeenth round, were among the most spectacular battles in the lightweight class. Gans also was stopped in their next bout in Colma, California, September 9, 1908, in the twenty-first round.

The following year Gans died from pneumonia in Baltimore.

Melodramatic also was the encounter in which Nelson met defeat at the hands of Ad Wolgast, the Michigan Wildcat. Bloody, battered, desperate, game to the last, the Dane struggled on only to hear Referee Eddie Smith proclaim Wolgast, born in Cadillac, Michigan, February 8, 1888, the winner in the fortieth round of a truly Homeric engagement. That affair took place February 22, 1910, at Point Richmond, California.

One of the most extraordinary windups that ever terminated a lightweight championship contest occurred when

Bat Nelson met Ad Wolgast in a 45-round title grudge-affair in 1910. Foul rules were out except if, in the opinion of the referee, fighter was completely incapacitated. Nelson, on the left in both photos above, and Wolgast posed before the bout, which turned out to be bloody and brutal. Nelson was in a helpless state in the 40th round and referee Ed Smith stopped the slaughter.

Packey McFarland was a rising star in 1908 when he kayoed Jimmy Britt *(below)* in six rounds. Britt's seconds are shown vainly coaxing Jimmy to get up. In 48 bouts Packey scored 33 knockouts and was never given a chance at the title.

Ad Wolgast had 14 bouts after winning the crown from Nelson. On July 4, 1912, Ad met Mexican Joe Rivers in a title match that had a weird ending, referred to as the double knock-out. In the 13th round, Ad drove a low blow to River's body. At the same time, Rivers landed a left hook on Wolgast's jaw. Both fighters dropped (left), with the champion on top. Then referee Jack Welch did an extraordinary thing. With his left hand he helped Wolgast to his feet (below) and with his right went through the motions of counting Rivers out. Ad staggered to his corner while Joe managed to get to his feet unaided. Welch was still counting when the bell ended the round, and spectators said he had only reached the count of eight, at most. While both fighters were in their corners being handled, Welch pointed to Wolgast as the winner, and a small riot ensued. Welch escaped harm and the decision still stands.

Wolgast and Joe Rivers fought at Vernon, California, July 4, 1912. In the thirteenth round Wolgast hooked a left to the stomach that dropped Rivers. Wolgast, unable to check his momentum, crashed on top of the Mexican. Joe got to one knee as the referee, Jack Welsh, started the count. Both fighters were helpless at the time, but Welsh, contrary to the rules, extended a helping hand to Wolgast, raised him to his feet while counting out Rivers to the amazement of the fans.

Willie Ritchie of San Francisco,

On July 4, 1911, Wolgast belted Owen Moran with a right to the stomach that had Owen gasping for breath as he was counted out in the 13th round by referee Jack Welch. Moran, a tough British lightweight, had kayoed Bat Nelson in 1910.

Willie Ritchie, covered with blankets *(right)*, had to wait for Wolgast to appear for their title bout in 1912. Ritchie held his own until the 16th round, when he was awarded the title on a foul.

born February 13, 1891, took the championship from Wolgast on a foul at Daly City, California in the sixteenth round, November 28, 1912, and lost it in turn in London to Freddie Welsh of England in twenty rounds, July 7, 1914. Ritchie, when he won the crown, had raised the limit for the class from 133 to 135 pounds. In his title defenses, he knocked out Joe Rivers in the eleventh round and fought a stirring battle of twenty rounds with Harlem Tommy Murphy and won the verdict.

304

In Ritchie's first title defense he knocked out Mexican Joe Rivers (left) on July 4, 1913. The following year, on July 7, he lost the crown to Freddie Welsh in 20 rounds in London.

Two of England's greatest, Freddie Welsh and Jem Driscoll, met (below) in Cardiff, Wales for the British lightweight crown. Driscoll, on his knee from a slip, lost to Welsh on a foul in the 10th round.

Freddie Welsh (below) boxed from 1905 to 1922. He engaged in 166 bouts, lost only three, and was kayoed once, by Benny Leonard. Winning the title from Willie Ritchie cost Welsh $500 of his own money to meet the $26,500 guaranteed to Ritchie.

Welsh reigned nearly three years before he was dethroned by Benny Leonard in a surprise knockout in the ninth round of a no-decision bout in New York at the Manhattan Casino, May 28, 1917. There was never anything sensational about Welsh's performances, other than that he was a very clever boxer. He was a light puncher, but one of the finest defensive boxers in this division's history. He was born in Pontypridd, Wales, March 5, 1886. It required a combination boxer and hitter like Leonard to penetrate his seemingly impenetrable guard and acquire the crown.

During his eight years as a champion, Leonard outclassed a field of the greatest lightweights that ever

305

While Benny Leonard was lightweight champion, he met Jack Britton (above, right) for the welter crown on June 26, 1922. In the 13th round, Jack dropped to one knee from a body blow and protested to referee Patsy Haley that the punch had been low. When Haley continued to count over Britton, Benny struck Jack while he was down, and was disqualified. It was said Benny had no desire to win the crown and was only trying for a draw decision.

Leonard met Johnny Dundee eight times in no-decision bouts from 1914 through 1920. Dundee (below, right) was a nine-year ring veteran when he posed with Benny before their eight-rounder on June 16, 1919, in Philadelphia.

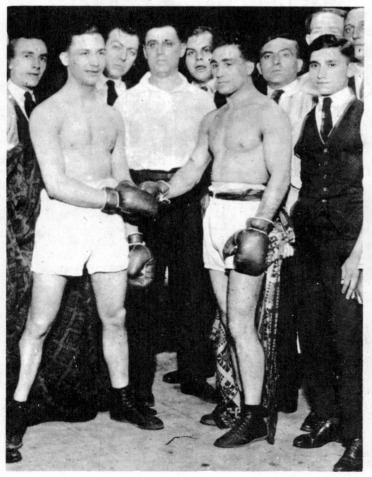

Benny Leonard, born Benjamin Leiner in New York on April 17, 1896, boxed from 1911 to 1924 and made a comeback in 1931. He was knocked out in his first and last bout. He had a total of 209 fights, won 88, with 68 kayoes, won once and lost once on a foul, was kayoed four times, and had 115 no-decisions. He retired undefeated in 1925.

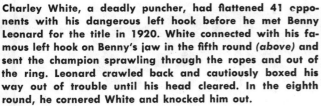

Charley White, a deadly puncher, had flattened 41 opponents with his dangerous left hook before he met Benny Leonard for the title in 1920. White connected with his famous left hook on Benny's jaw in the fifth round *(above)* and sent the champion sprawling through the ropes and out of the ring. Leonard crawled back and cautiously boxed his way out of trouble until his head cleared. In the eighth round, he cornered White and knocked him out.

The "Milwaukee Marvel," Richie Mitchell *(below, left)* gave Leonard a scare in 1921. Arising from a knockdown, Richie floored the champ, who got up dazed and dared Richie to come in and mix it. Richie became wary and was kayoed in round six.

appeared at one time in the division. Leonard could punch with sluggers and outbox the best scientific pugilists. Three times in his scintillating career as champion, one of the best the division boasted, he was on the verge of a knockout.

Charley White almost turned the trick on July 5, 1920, in Benton Harbor, Michigan; Richie Mitchell came close in Madison Square Garden, January 14, 1921, on the card for Ann Morgan's Fund for Devastated France; and Lew Tendler was talked out of a possible kayo in Jersey City, in a twelve round no-decision contest on July 27, 1922.

In the fight with White, Benny was sent over the ropes and out of the ring with a deadly left hook. White was the best left hook artist in the game. Leonard was dazed when he climbed back, but his wily generalship staved off the impending disaster. He stalled off White as he did Mitchell, until his brain cleared, then went on to give Charley a lacing and halt him.

When he fought Mitchell, Benny

Ever Hammer cut Leonard's eye early in their bout on October 18, 1916. Ben, a master of every trick in boxing, tied him up continuously (above) preventing any further damage to the eye until the 12th round, when he knocked Hammer out.

Rocky Kansas lost a 15-round decision to Leonard in a title bout in New York on February 10, 1922. Kansas met the champion again on July 4 in Michigan City, Michigan, and was stopped (right) in eight rounds.

In the eighth round on July 23, 1922, Lew Tendler (below, left) drove a vicious left to Leonard's stomach, paralyzing his legs. Leonard told Lew to "keep them up." Lew stopped to argue about the blow, long enough for life to return to Ben's legs.

Lew Tendler, a Philadelphia southpaw, posed (below) with his two-year-old son Phil in 1922. Lew was talked out of a possible kayo victory by Leonard in 1922. In the second bout on July 23, 1923, Lew lost to the champ in 15 rounds.

was dropped in the opening round, was dazed and very unsteady, yet talked his way into scaring Richie, then came back like a fighting wildcat to stop the Westerner after putting Richie on the canvas three times.

Johnny Dundee was another great fighter in both this class and the feather. He gave Leonard a lot of trouble both before and after Benny mounted the lightweight throne.

From 1914 through 1920, they fought nine times in no-decision contests.

Dundee was a fast, clever, aggressive fighter and a miracle of endurance. His trickery with the ropes baffled his opponents. He was a master at fighting off the strands. Only once did he go down for the full count when Willie Jackson, a terrific puncher, knocked him out in the first round in Philadelphia.

When Leonard retired in 1925, after a reign of seven and a half years, he claimed he did so to please his mother.

Nathan Straus, a noted New York merchant and philanthropist, was an enthusiastic follower of Leonard's ring career.

In 1931 Leonard made a comeback as a welterweight and knocked out Pal Silvers *(left)* in two rounds on October 6. Except for one draw, he won 18 bouts through 1932 and met Jimmy McLarnin in New York, on October 7. Paunchy and 36 years old, Leonard was an easy mark for the youthful fists of McLarnin and was counted out by referee Arthur Donovan *(below, left)* in the sixth round. Thus ended the extended boxing career of one of the finest ring mechanics of all time. In 1943 Benny became a popular licensed referee *(below)* on the staff of the New York State commission. While refereeing a bout at the St. Nicholas Arena in New York on April 17, 1947, he suddenly collapsed and died.

Jimmy McLarnin became the idol of New York with his knockouts over top lightweights, among them Ruby Goldstein, whom he kayoed *(above)* in two rounds on December 13, 1929. In spite of the great Depression, he drew sell-out crowds.

Billy Petrolle and manager Jack Hurley *(below)* from Fargo, North Dakota, were a perfect team. Hurley arranged exciting matches and Billy executed them. From 1910 to 1934 Petrolle had 157 fights and won 85, scoring 63 knockouts.

Coming down to later times, one vividly recalls the thrills that Jimmy McLarnin gave to New Yorkers when he was campaigning as a lightweight and scoring one and two round knockouts with such persistency over likely lads of the calibre of Sid Terris and Ruby Goldstein, New York's ace performers; Phil McGraw, Stanislaus Loayza, Joe Glick, and Sgt. Sammy Baker, among other top fighters. But his most thrilling bout took place when he faced Billy Petrolle, the Fargo Express, and took a licking that might have spelled finis to the career of a less courageous, stouthearted battler.

No one who saw that mill in the Garden in 1930 can ever forget it. Dropped in the opening round with a jaw-smash that hit him with the force of a club, Jimmy got to his feet and from then to the finish absorbed terrific punishment, yet refused to quit even when asked to do so by Referee Patsy Haley. Twice afterwards they fought and McLarnin won each in ten rounds.

Petrolle, though never a title holder,

Billy Petrolle floored Jimmy McLarnin twice with smashing rights to the jaw, in their first meeting, on November 21, 1930. The "Fargo Express" unleashed his vicious blows in the first round, but Jimmy weathered the storm and put up a sensational battle for 10 rounds. Billy was awarded the decision, but lost the verdict both times when they met on May 27 and August 20, 1931.

Jimmy Goodrich (left) and Stanislaus Loayza (above) of Iquique, Chile, met in the final match of a tournament to determine the successor for the vacant throne. Goodrich stopped Loayza in two rounds and was generally recognized as the lightweight king by boxing writers all over the country. In 110 bouts from 1923 to 1930, Jimmy won 44 and lost 33, drew 15 times, and had 18 no-decisions.

was one of the outstanding fighters of the division. His battle with Justo Suarez of Chile was another long-to-be-remembered contest which Billy won.

When Leonard retired undefeated in 1925, the New York Commission set up an elimination to decide his successor.

Jimmy Goodrich, born July 30, 1900, in Scranton, emerged the winner when he knocked out Stanislaus Loayza on July 13, 1925, at Long Island City in the second round. But he didn't retain the title long, for on December 7 of the same year, Rocky Kansas of Buffalo gained the verdict over Goodrich in fifteen rounds to relieve him of his laurels.

Then half a year later came Sammy Mandell, born February 5, 1904, in Rockford, Illinois, who on July 3, 1926, outpointed Kansas in Chicago in ten rounds and became the sceptre bearer. But on July 17, 1930, at the Yankee

Defending the lightweight crown on May 21, 1928, Sammy Mandell uncovered one of the finest exhibitions ever seen in New York, and completely outclassed Jimmy McLarnin in 15 rounds. Veteran announcer, Joe Humphries raises Mandell's arm in token of victory *(left)*, as McLarnin acknowledges defeat.

Al Singer *(below)* created a sensation on July 17, 1930, when he won the title by knocking Mandell out cold in 1.46 of the first round. Singer, a protégé of Benny Leonard, boxed from 1927 to 1935. In 70 bouts, he scored 24 kayoes while winning 60, drew twice and lost 8, four of them by knockout.

Stadium, the fans were treated to one of the biggest surprises in the division in years, when Al Singer of New York flattened clever Sammy in one round to win the championship.

Singer, born September 6, 1907, like several of his predecessors, went out in a jiffy. He lasted only a few months, for on November 14, 1930, Tony Canzoneri, born November 6, 1908, at Slidell, Louisiana, a lad with an enviable record, put Singer away in a round in Madison Square Garden.

Less than four months after winning the crown, Singer was overpowered by Tony Canzoneri on November 14, 1930, and knocked out in 1.06 of the first round. Tony forced Singer into his corner and in a flurry of blows, sent him through the ropes onto the ring apron *(right)*, where he was counted out by referee McAvoy. Still dazed and limp, Singer was helped to his feet by Tony's manager, Sam Goldman, as Canzoneri was declared winner *(below)* in the fourth fastest knockout in championship history. The others were: Jackie Paterson over Peter Kane, 1943, 1.01; Emil Pladner over Frankie Genaro, 1929, 0.58; and Al McCoy over George Chip, 1914, 0.45.

Singer is the only champion in boxing annals to have won and lost the crown by one round knockouts.

Canzoneri was a real fighting champion, a colorful pugilist and a good crowd-pleaser. He had come up from the flyweight class as an amateur and held eight titles during his career as a simon pure. He beat Benny Bass for the pro feather crown following an elimination after Dundee retired, then went on to greater heights.

He could box well and could hit.

He lost the lightweight title to Barney Ross in Chicago, June 23, 1933, and failed to regain it from Barney a short time later, Ross winning it by a very slight margin. Both affairs furnished fistic fireworks.

When Barney outgrew the division to enter the welter class, the New York Commission decided on an elimination in which Canzoneri and Lou Ambers were named to fight it out for the vacated crown. Tony won May 10, 1935, and again wore the

purple robe. He gained the verdict in fifteen rounds at the Yankee Stadium.

When he lost the championship to Ambers, September 4, 1936, in Madison Square Garden by a fifteen round decision, he gave his usual excellent performance. Tony successfully defended the title against Al Roth in fifteen rounds and on May 7, 1937, he tried to wrest the laurels from Ambers in their third match but again failed, the bout going the distance with Lou the victor. This contest was

Canzoneri risked his crown against Barney Ross, a fast coming lightweight from Chicago, who had lost only one of 48 bouts. After 10 sizzling rounds on June 23, 1933, Barney (on right) walked off with the title. In a return match on September 12, Ross repeated the victory in 15 rounds, but increasing weight later forced Barney to vacate the title. Tony was a great and busy ringman. From 1925 to 1939 he had 178 battles, winning 140 with 44 knockouts. He drew 11, had three no-decisions, was kayoed once.

Lou Ambers and Canzoneri, the top contenders for the vacated title, met on May 10, 1935. After 15 rounds Tony was again the champion. In a re-match on September 3, 1936, Lou outpointed Canzoneri in 15 rounds and became the new champion. The smiling winner (right) is flanked by his manager, Al Weill, left, and trainer Whitey Bimstein. In the "Carnival of Champions," September 23, 1937, Ambers successfully and brilliantly defended the crown against Pedro Montanez (below, left).

also fought in the Madison Square Garden arena.

On the Tournament of Champions card staged by Mike Jacobs in New York's Polo Grounds, Lou defeated Pedro Montanez of Puerto Rico in a stirring contest of fifteen rounds to retain his throne.

Then came his bout with Henry Armstrong, one of the best fought in the division in years. Before a gathering of 18,340 fans in Madison Square Garden, Homicide Hank added his

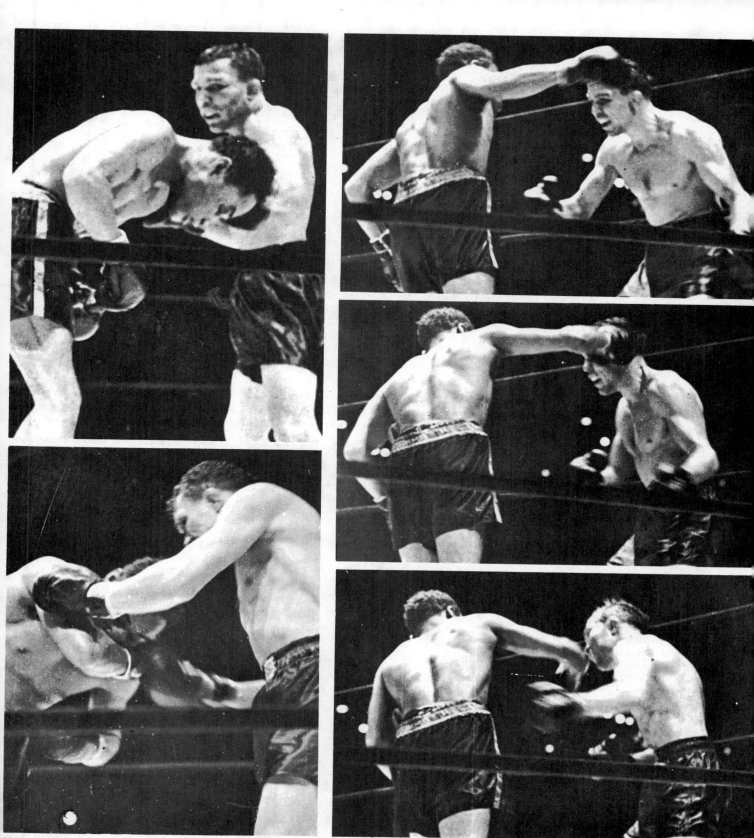

Not satisfied with two titles, Henry Armstrong, who ruled the featherweight and welterweights, dropped back into the lightweight division on August 17, 1938, and in a blood-spattered battle with Lou Ambers, won his third title. "Hammerin' Hank" was busy every second of the bout, swinging from all angles and taking advantage of split-second openings *(three photos at right)* to put over a crushing blow. The last few rounds were furious. When it seemed like Ambers was weakening, Lou would lash back with solid smashes that rocked Henry *(two photos at left)*. There wasn't a second's rest for either man throughout the battle and, at the end of 15 rounds, Armstrong, stubbornly holding his early lead in the final rounds, was the decisive winner of the lightweight crown.

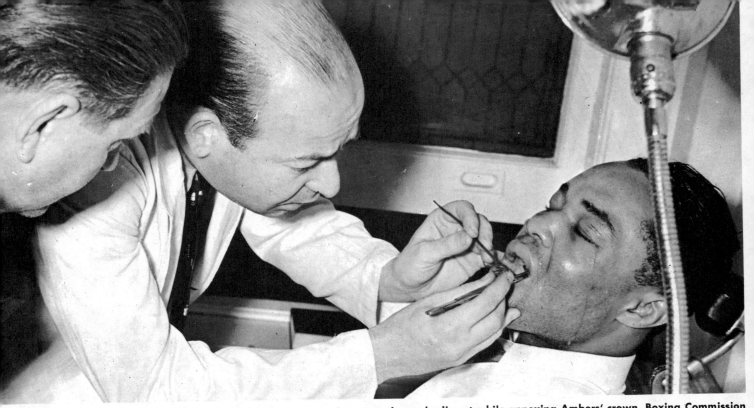

A tear trickles down the cheek of Henry Armstrong, whose mouth was badly cut while annexing Ambers' crown. Boxing Commission physician Dr. Alexander Schiff probes inside Henry's mouth the following morning, as manager Eddie Mead (left) looks on.

Ambers regained the crown from Armstrong in 1939. Immediately after hearing the official verdict, Lou's manager, Al Weill, leaped into the air (left) with joy. Low blows cost Armstrong five rounds.

third championship to his list by outpointing Ambers in fifteen rounds after having dropped the defending titleholder twice. The Herkimer boy didn't give up easily. He came back strong in the finishing rounds to have his conqueror wobbly and gory at the close of a vicious encounter.

Great was the confusion and loud the squawks when in their return engagement at the Yankee Stadium on August 22, 1939, Ambers regained the championship from Armstrong. The Herkimer Hustler, a gallant, shrewd little fighter, had Henry's right eye almost closed and his left damaged before the final bell clanged. Referee Arthur Donovan had taken five rounds away from Armstrong for what he termed low hitting, an unusual procedure in any contest, especially a title bout, and that's what brought about the howl of discontent from Henry's supporters.

Nine months later, May 10, 1940, Lou, born in Herkimer, New York, November 8, 1913, again lost the crown when he was knocked out by Lew Jenkins, born December 4, 1916, in Milburn, Texas. Jenkins turned the trick in the third round in Madison Square Garden.

Striking with deadly accuracy and the precision of a rattlesnake, the boy from the desert trails hammered the defending champ to the canvas four times and had him reeling helplessly when Referee Billy Cavanagh halted the affair. They fought again in a non-title bout on February 28, 1941, and this time Ambers was stopped in the seventh round in the same arena. It was Ambers' farewell bout. He was lying on his face when Referee Donovan intervened to save him from more punishment.

Jenkins was a colorful, hard socking ringman, whose career was highlighted by thrilling bouts in the ring and high jinx outside the ring. He first turned to boxing while in the Army, and when World War Two got under

Lew Jenkins knocked the crown from Lou Ambers' head in 1940, with whip-like jolts that almost put an end to Lou's career. Jenkins sent Lou spinning to the canvas (above) for the first of four knockdowns that rendered Ambers helpless within three rounds. When Ambers retired in 1941, he had battled 102 opponents since 1932. He won 59, with 25 knockouts. He lost six, drew in six, and was kayoed twice, by Jenkins.

When Mike Belloise was stopped by Lew Jenkins on November 21, 1939, he was the fourth victim of eight consecutive knockouts that led Lew to the title. Jenkins and manager Hymie Kaplan visit Belloise' corner after the seventh-round knockout.

317

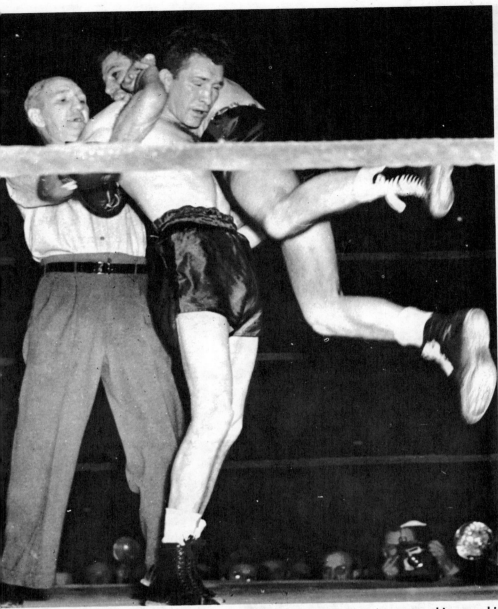

Sammy Angott's clutching tactics provoked Lew Jenkins into trying to toss him over his head during their title bout in 1941. Angott went on to win a unanimous decision and the lightweight crown. Lew Jenkins had 97 bouts from 1934 to 1950. He scored 38 kayoes while winning 55. He was stopped 13 times.

Beau Jack was recognized as champion only in New York in 1942. He was sponsored by a Georgia syndicate and drew huge gates during the flush war years.

way, Lew enlisted in the Coast Guard. He served with honor and was among the crew of the first LST to hit the beach at Normandy.

After hanging up his gloves in 1948, Lew rejoined the Army and was honored for his heroic actions during the fighting in Korea. He has made a career of serving his country.

When Sammy Angott dethroned Jenkins in Madison Square Garden on December 19, 1941, the first unpopular king of the class was crowned.

Angott, born January 17, 1915 in Washington, Pennsylvania, was a clever boxer but persisted in clutching after almost every blow he delivered. It was his style, while effective, that failed to impress the fans. Sammy was the first to hang a defeat on the record of Willie Pep.

In his only defense of the crown against Allie Stolz in Madison Square Garden on May 15, 1942, he won a disputed split decision after being floored. Referee Frank Fullum, who

voted for Stolz, took two rounds away from the challenger for low hitting, and that saved Angott's crown.

He retired soon afterwards, November 13, 1942, then the following January announced a comeback as challenger for the crown he had vacated, which by now the New York Commission had awarded to Beau Jack, born in Augusta, Georgia, April 1, 1921.

The "Georgia Shoe Shine Boy," as he was dubbed, was one of the most

When Ike Williams *(above, right)* became undisputed lightweight champ, he gave Beau Jack a chance to regain the title on July 12, 1948. Jack was a wide-open target and was knocked out in six rounds. In a 112-bout career Jack won 83, in which he scored 40 knockouts. He lost 20, drew in five and was stopped four times.

Juan Zurita of Guadalajara, Mexico, won Angott's NBA title in 1944, scored five successive kayoes, lost the crown to Ike Williams in 1945, and retired.

Almost one year after vacating the world title, undefeated, Sammy Angott won over Slugger White and became the NBA lightweight champion. The title changed hands again on March 8, 1944, when Juan Zurita, a southpaw *(blow, left)*, outpointed Angott.

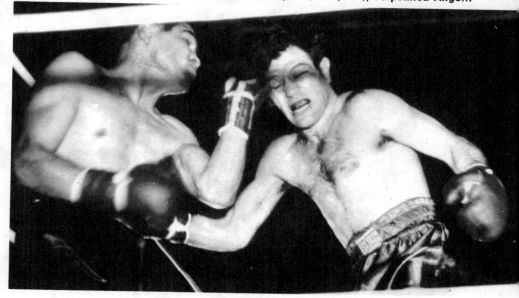

colorful lads the division had in many years. Win or lose, he drew in the throngs to Madison Square Garden. Beau Jack's popularity is attested to by the fact that in bouts in which he participated in the Garden, the total receipts were $1,578,069.

It was on May 21, 1943, that the New York Commission had Beau Jack and Bob Montgomery, the world's leading contenders, fight it out in Madison Square Garden, and Montgomery emerged the winner in fifteen rounds. But he wasn't generally accepted as the new champion, no more than was Beau Jack before him. On November 19 of that year, another match was arranged for Madison Square Garden, and Beau Jack regained the New York version of the championship.

They met for a third engagement on March 3, 1944, all bouts fought in the House that Tex Built, and Bob beat the champ in fifteen rounds, the title again changing hands. Immediately following that contest, Beau Jack joined the U. S. Army and five months later, his conqueror, born in Sumter, South Carolina, February 10, 1919, also became a member of the armed forces.

In all their contests, both had only the support of New York as world champions. The National Boxing Association refused to go along and sanctioned a bout between Sammy Angott and Luther Slugger White for its version of the world championship; Angott won in fifteen rounds. Then Juan Zurita, a Mexican southpaw, defeated Angott in Hollywood and he was recognized by the N.B.A.

Ike Williams became the undisputed lightweight champion of the world when he knocked out Bob Montgomery (left) on August 4, 1947, in six rounds. Ike had 42 battles from 1947 to 1951, and defended the title successfully five times. In his sixth defense of the crown, against Jimmy Carter on May 25, 1951, Ike was sent hurtling through the ropes (below) by a left hook in the 10th round, for the third knockdown of the bout. When Williams appeared hopelessly beaten in the 14th round, referee Pete Scalzo stopped the slaughter and Carter was hailed as the new lightweight champion. Ike Williams crowded 154 bouts into his career from 1940 to 1955, winning 125.

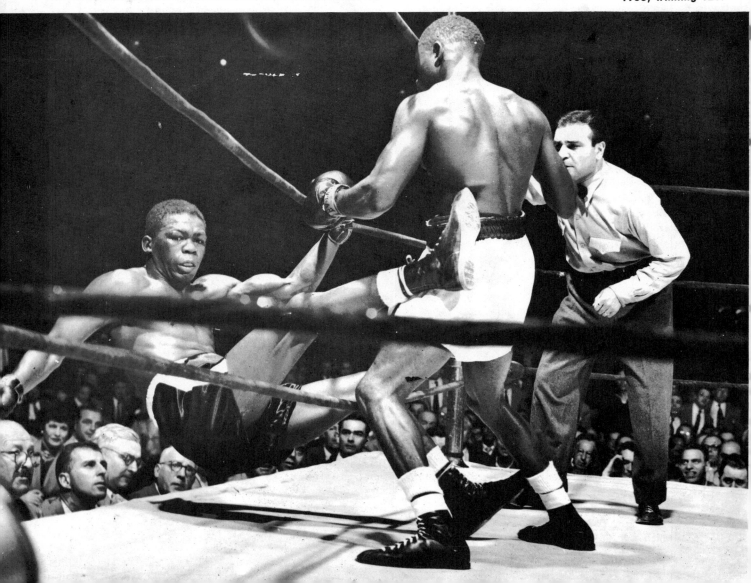

Jimmy Carter beat Lauro Salas in a title clash on April 1, 1952. In a return title bout on May 14th, Salas (right) won the crown in 15 rounds. Carter came back on October 1 and regained the title from Salas. From 1947 to 1958, Salas won 72 of 125 fights, half of them by knockout. He had nine draws, lost 42, and was knocked out four times. Carter lost the title to Paddy DeMarco (below, right) on March 5, 1954, and on November 17 he knocked Paddy out in 15 rounds and regained the crown. Carter lost the title to Wallace Bud Smith on June 29, 1955, and lost again, on October 19.

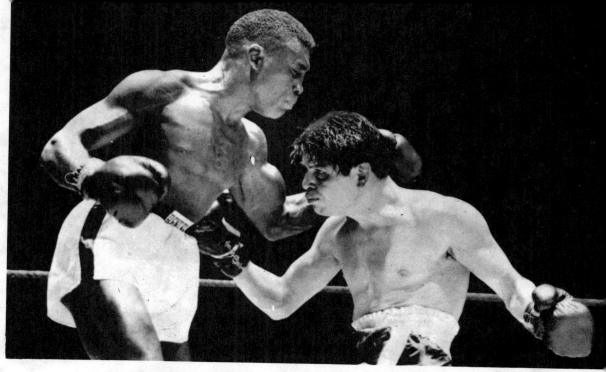

Paddy DeMarco (right) had 93 bouts from 1945 to 1957, winning 73, seven by kayo. He drew three, lost 17, and was stopped four times. Carter boxed from 1946 to 1957. He won 75 of 108 bouts, 28 by kayo, drew nine, lost 22, kayoed twice.

Ike Williams, born August 2, 1923, in Brunswick, Georgia, was pitted against Zurita in Mexico, April 18, 1945, and knocked out Juan in the second round. He went to Europe to fight British Empire champion, Ronnie James, in Cardiff, and by stopping him in the ninth round, September 4, 1946, Williams strengthened his claim on the crown. But it was not until he knocked out Montgomery in Philadelphia on August 4, 1947, that the confusion was ended, with Williams receiving international support as world champion.

James Carter, born in Aiken, South Carolina, December 15, 1923, but a resident of New York City, was next to ascend the throne. He ended Ike's reign when he put Williams away in the fourteenth round to win the title.

A year later, in Los Angeles, Lauro Salas, a Mexican born boy from Monterey, who first saw the light of day in 1927, deposed Carter by a decision in fifteen rounds. From that point on, as was the case in the mid-

dleweight division some years ago after Mickey Walker's retirement, the title kept changing hands among a group consisting of Carter, Paddy DeMarco, Wallace Bud Smith, and Joe Brown.

Carter rewon the title by decisioning Salas in Chicago, October 15, 1952, then lost it to Paddy DeMarco of

Brooklyn, born February 10, 1928, in fifteen rounds in Madison Square Garden on March 5, 1954. In the fall of that year, November 17, they engaged in a return bout in San Francisco and DeMarco, badly whipped, was stopped in the fifteenth round, Carter gaining the crown for the third time.

Then came a surprise loss, Carter

Wallace Bud Smith *(above, left)* lost the lightweight crown to Joe Brown on August 24, 1956, at Municipal Stadium in New Orleans. Smith boxed from 1948 to 1958. He had 59 bouts, won 32 of them, drew in six, lost 21, and was knocked out eight times.

Lightweight champion Joe Brown successfully defended his crown 10 times. Joe had 130 fights between 1946 and 1970, when he retired. He won 104, 48 by knockout. He lost 12 times, nine by knockout, one by Sandy Saddler, fought 12 draws and engaged in two no-contest.

Kenny Lane, a southpaw contender from Muskegon, Michigan, started boxing in 1953. He gave Brown his toughest fight and came close to dethroning the champ.

dropping the championship to Wallace Bud Smith in Boston in fifteen rounds on June 29, 1955. But Smith held it for only a year. After turning back Carter again in Cincinnati on October 19 of the same year, he was defeated by Joe Brown, a veteran, born in Baton Rouge, Louisiana, May 18, 1926, who on several occasions had retired and then made comebacks. Brown won in fifteen rounds by a decision at New Orleans on August 24, 1956, in a close bout.

They fought a return bout in Miami Beach on February 13, 1957, and this time Brown left no doubt of his superiority as he disposed of Smith in the eleventh round to retain the throne. On June 19 he again successfully put his title on the line by knocking out Orlando Zulueta of Cuba in the fifteenth round in Denver.

In 1958 Brown defended his crown successfully twice and had three non-title fights, one as part of the inauguration program of the spacious and beautiful new Sports Stadium in Havana. The champion of Cuba, Orlando Echevarria, opposed him. Echevarria lasted less than a round in this contest on February 26. Brown had previously kayoed Ernie Williams in five rounds in Washington.

His title bouts were against Ralph Dupas in Houston on May 7, in which he stopped the New Orleans battler in the eighth round, and against Kenny Lane, whom he defeated by a slight margin in the same city on July 23. Brown had a close call in this bout, but a rally in the last rounds enabled him to pull the chestnuts out of the fire.

On November 5, in a bout in which his crown was not at stake, he lost in ten rounds to Johnny Busso in the new auditorium at Miami Beach.

When thirty-five-year-old Joe Brown lost his title to the twenty-five-year-old world junior welterweight champion, Carlos Ortiz, on April 21, 1962, in Las Vegas, "Old Bones" had established a record of eleven successful lightweight title defenses in succession, a record no one has come close to matching.

In this fight, Brown just couldn't maneuver the volatile, outspoken, Puerto Rican–born New Yorker into position to throw his well-known combination, while Ortiz kept flashing left jabs. All three officials awarded Ortiz seventy-four of a possible seventy-five points.

Ortiz underestimated Panamanian Ismael Laguna and failed to train rigorously enough for their April 10, 1965 bout in Panama City. As a result, the defending champion lost the fifteen-round decision. Laguna, rel-

Carlos Ortiz (*left*) won the lightweight title from Joe Brown by taking a 15-round verdict on April 21, 1962, at Las Vegas, Nevada. Brown had made 11 successful defenses.

Ismael Laguna of Panama pokes a left to Ortiz' face on his way to winning the crown on a 15-round decision in Panama on April 10, 1965. Ortiz had failed to train seriously.

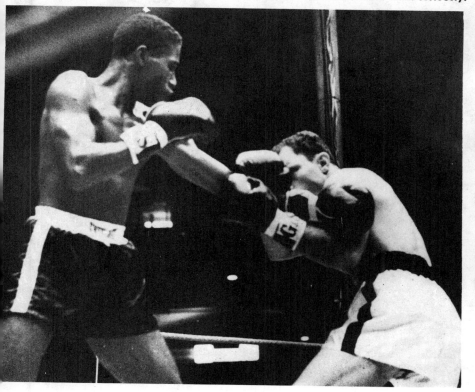

Ortiz regained his title on November 13, 1965, outpointing Laguna in 15 rounds in San Juan, Puerto Rico, and Ortiz, above, is shown successfully defending the crown against Laguna in 15 rounds at New York's Shea Stadium on August 16, 1967.

atively unknown internationally and fighting for the first time in the lightweight class, was reputed to be the fastest boxer ever seen in Panama—he had the ability to land a variety of punches with bewildering rapidity.

The ex-champion had learned his lesson. On November 13, 1965, a strong, well-conditioned Ortiz, at 135½ pounds, stepped into the ring, in Puerto Rico, for his rematch with the 133-pound Laguna.

The defending champion tried to keep up a steady jab, but he couldn't maintain the pace against the forceful attack of a stronger Ortiz, who gained a unanimous decision in fifteen rounds.

Teo Cruz, of the Dominican Republic, won a split decision over Ortiz in a grueling, consistently hard-fought bout on June 29, 1968. The decisive factor may well have been the decking of Ortiz in the first round from a

On June 29, 1968, Ortiz traveled to Santo Domingo, only to lose his precious crown to Carlos (Teo) Cruz on a split 15-round decision. Referee Zack Clayton voted for Ortiz, the two judges for Cruz. (Top) Cruz knocks Ortiz into the ropes. (Left) The foes approach each other very warily during the early going. (Right) Cruz being carried off by admirers after triumph.

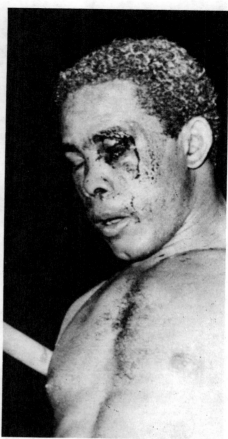

Cruz met 20-year-old Mando Ramos at Los Angeles on February 19, 1969, and was shorn of the lightweight title when the bout was halted in the 11th round because of a deep cut over Cruz' left eye, (*right*). *Left:* Cruz cuffs Ramos with both hands in first.

right cross to the jaw.

Cruz's reign was short-lived. On February 19, 1969, Mando Ramos, of California, opened a savage gash over Cruz's left eye with a looping right in the eighth round and went on to win by a knockout in the eleventh when the ring physician examined Cruz's eye for the third time and advised referee John Thomas to halt the bout.

Twenty-year-old Ramos, the youngest man to win the lightweight crown, had been befuddled in the early rounds by the Dominican's flatfooted, crouching tactics, but gaining confidence he used his 3½-inch advantage in reach to score effectively.

Laguna recaptured the crown on March 3, 1970, in Los Angeles, when Ramos's manager decided that his fighter, with both eyes bleeding profusely, had absorbed enough punish-

ment after the ninth round. Laguna and Ramos scaled 135 and 134½ pounds, respectively.

Gentleman boxer Ken Buchanan became Scotland's first lightweight champion when he won a split decision over the 5-to-2-favored Laguna on September 26, 1970, in Puerto Rico.

The fight was filled with action as Laguna, at 134½ pounds, bobbed and weaved, scoring with chopping right leads and short blows on the inside, while the 134-pound Buchanan moved in behind to deliver vigorous left jabs.

In a rematch a year later, on September 13, Buchanan retained his title in a unanimous fifteen-round decision.

When Buchanan met Roberto Duran, it was a battle between a clever, graceful "boxer" and a powerful

"fighter." Duran, with a telling right cross, a left hook, and a jab as his assets, scored a knockout in the thirteenth round on June 26, 1972, in New York.

Upon meeting Esteban DeJesus of Puerto Rico on March 16, 1974, at Panama, Duran was out to avenge the only defeat in' his record, a ten-round loss on November 17, 1972.

To even the score now, Duran knocked DeJesus out in the eleventh with a left hook to the head, a left hook to the jaw, and a right to the head. More exhausted than hurt, DeJesus sat on his haunches as he was counted out by referee Isaac Herrera.

On December 21, 1974, Duran KO'd Japan's contender, Masataka Takayama, in one round in Costa Rica.

He knocked out Ray Lampkin of the United States in the fourteenth at Panama in 1975 to record his thirty-fifth knockout in forty-four bouts, and

Laguna lost the crown to Scotland's Ken Buchanan in 15 rounds in 1970 and in a return match a year later, Buchanan won easily in 15. Buchanan misses with a right.

the same year knocked out Leoncio Ortiz in the final round at San Juan on December 20. 1976 saw two title defences in which he beat Lou Bizzaro by a knockout in fourteen rounds at Erie on May 23 and five months later disposed of Alvaro Rojas in a single round at Hollywood on October 15. The following year Vilomar Fernandez was knocked out in thirteen rounds at Miami Beach on January 29 and Edwin Viruet was outpointed in Philadelphia over fifteen rounds on September 17. On January 21, 1978, Duran beat off a challenge from Estaban De Jesus who was knocked out in twelve rounds at Las Vegas. At the end of the year, however, at the age of only 27, Duran announced that he was giving up the lightweight title to compete as a welterweight. He had successfully defended the crown twelve times.

Duran was disciplined by the W.B.C. for failing to meet Ken

Buchanan in a return title contest. Mando Ramos then outpointed Pedro Carrasco of Spain to win the vacant W.B.C. title on June 28, 1972. Chango Carmona then stopped Ramos in eight rounds at Los Angeles on September 15 and two months later Rodolfo Gonzalez took over by forcing Carmona to retire in twelve rounds at Los Angeles. On April 11, 1974, Guts Ishimatsu defeated Gonzalez by a kayo in eight rounds at Tokyo and the Japanese fighter enhanced his claim by outpointing Ken Buchanan in Tokyo on February 21, 1975. Estaban De Jesus came back into the title picture by outpointing Ishimatsu at Bayamon on May 8, 1976, and on September 11 knocked out Hector Medina in seven rounds at Bayamon. In 1977 De Jesus disposed of Buzzsaw Yamabe in six rounds on February 12 and on June 25 he knocked .out Vicente Saldivar in eleven rounds, both these defences taking place at

Bayamon. Then came his decisive defeat by Roberto Duran which made his W.B.C. title worthless.

When Duran relinquished the title in 1979, both the World Boxing Council and the World Boxing Association set up their own champions. On April 17, 1979, Jim Watt of Scotland, knocked out Alfredo Pitalua (Colombia) in twelve rounds at Glasgow to win the W.B.C. crown, the second Scotsman to become world lightweight champion. He made a successful first defence by knocking out Robert Vasquez (U.S.A.) in nine rounds on November 3, then on March 14, 1980, he beat Irishman Charlie Nash, who was stopped in four rounds, again in Glasgow. On June 7, at Ibrox Park, Glasgow, he outpointed Howard Davis (U.S.A.) and defeated his third American challenger on November 1 at Glasgow, his opponent, Sean O'Grady, being stopped in the 12th round because of a badly gashed forehead.

Jim Watt's reign came to an end on June 20, 1981 when Alexis Arguello (Nicaragua), who had held the W.B.C. super-featherweight title from 1978 to 1980, outpointed him over 15 rounds at Wembley, England. An outstanding performer, Arguello made four winning title defences: stopping Ray Mancini in 14 rounds at Atlantic City on October 3; knocking out Roberto Elizondo (U.S.A.) in seven at Las Vegas on November 21; stopping James "Bubba" Busceme (U.S.A.) in six rounds at Beaumont, Texas, on February 13, 1982; and disposing of Andy Ganigan (Hawaii) in five rounds at Las Vegas on May 22. After an abortive attempt to take the W.B.A. light-welter title from Aaron Pryor, he relinquished the lightweight championship in February 1983.

Edwin Rosario (Puerto Rico) won the vacant W.B.C. crown on May 1 by outpointing Jose Luis Raminez (Mexico) over the newly-introduced limit of 12 rounds at San Juan. He successfully defended it against Roberto Elizondo with a stoppage in 1 minute 56 seconds of the first round on March 17, 1984 at San Juan, and in the same ring on June 23, outpointed Howard Davis (U.S.A.). Raminez gained revenge over Rosario with a four rounds stoppage on November 3 also at San Juan, but on August 10, 1985 at Las Vegas was outpointed by

(Above) Jim Watt successfully defended his lightweight title three times in 1980, despite suffering bad cuts against Sean O'Grady (U.S.A.).

Roberto Duran avoided a flurry of wild blows by Esteban DeJesus in eleventh round, then knocked out DeJesus who is shown taking count in Panama City title bout.

Hector Comacho (Puerto Rico) to lose the W.B.C. title. Camacho kept the title by taking the decision against former champion Edwin Rosario on June 13, 1986, in New York, and former junior lightweight champion Cornelius Boza-Edwards on September 26, at Miami Beach.

Hector Camacho found it too difficult to make the weight, so he relinquished his W.B.C. belt and moved up to light-welterweight. With the vacant title now at stake, José Luis Ramirez, of Mexico, defeated Terrence Alli on points after a hard contest at St. Tropez, on July 19, 1987. On October 8 the new champion gave the veteran, Cornelius Boza-Edwards, a chance at the championship, and knocked him out in 5 rounds in Paris, to end "Boza's" career.

There was a controversial decision on Ramirez's next defence, against the unbeaten 1984 Olympic featherweight champion, Pernell Whitaker. In Paris on March 12, 1988, in a clever battle of southpaws, Ramirez was given a split decision which was not well received by the boxing press. On October 29 he fought Julio Cesar Chavez, the W.B.A. champion, to unify two of the versions of the title, and this time was unlucky to suffer a nasty vertical gash in his forehead after a clash of heads, which prompted the doctor to stop the fight. Ramirez was behind on all three cards and so lost on a technical decision, Chavez becoming champion of both W.B.A. and W.B.C.

On June 16, 1979, Ernesto Espana (Venezuela) won the vacant W.B.A. title by knocking out Claude Noel (Trinidad) in 13 rounds at San Juan. He successfully defended against Johnny Lira (U.S.A.) by a knockout in ten rounds at Chicago on August 4. On March 2, 1980 he was stopped in nine rounds by Hilmer Kenty (U.S.A.) at Detroit. The new W.B.A. champion made three defences in 1980, stopping Yong Oh Ho (Korea) in nine rounds at Detroit on August 2; beating former champion, Ernesto Espana in four rounds at San Juan, on September 20 and outpointing Vilomar Fernandez at Detroit on November 8.

Sean O'Grady (U.S.A.) took the W.B.A. title from Hilmer Kenty over 15 rounds at Atlantic City on April 12, 1981,

Hector "Macho" Camacho of Puerto Rico lands a solid left to Jose Luis Ramirez of Mexico, in taking the W.B.C. lightweight title in 1985.

Ray "Boom Boom" Mancini (*left*) losing his W.B.A. lightweight title to Livingstone Bramble at Buffalo in 1984.

but forfeited his crown in August for failing to meet his official challenger. On September 12 Claude Noel (Trinidad) defeated Ranolfo Gonzalez (Mexico) on points at Atlantic City to pick up the vacant crown, but in less than three months lost it on an eighth round knock-out to Arturo Frias (U.S.A.) at Los Angeles on December 5. On January 30, 1982, Frias retained the championship in unusual circumstances. Defending against Ernesto Espana (Venezuala) at Los Angeles, he sustained a badly cut eye in the ninth round, causing the referee to call a halt. However, the official ruling was that Espana had committed a foul and the fight was awarded to the champion. On May 8 a new lightweight star arrived in Ray "Boom-Boom" Mancini (U.S.A.), an aggressive, hard-punching fighter, who demolished Frias in 2 minutes 54 seconds at Las Vegas; halted Espana in six rounds on July 4, at Warren, Ohio, then knocked out Duk-Koo Kim in 14 rounds at Las Vegas on November 13. The Korean fighter never regained consciousness and died.

Mancini's next defence was on September 15, 1983 when he blasted out

Orlando Romero (Peru) in nine rounds in New York. On January 14, 1984 he halted Bobby Chacon (U.S.A.) in three rounds at Reno. Mancini met more than his match on June 1 at Buffalo, when in a tempestuous fight he was stopped in the 14th round by Livingstone Bramble (U.S.A.). In a return title bout at Reno on February 16, 1985, Mancini was outpointed over 15 rounds.

Bramble retained the title on February 16, 1986, the referee coming to the assistance of Tyrone Crawley (U.S.A.) in the 13th round at Reno. Former W.B.C. champion Edwin Rosario caused an upset, however, by knocking out Bramble in the second round at Miami Beach on September 26, 1986 to take the W.B.A. crown.

Rosario met his fellow Puerto Rican, Juan Nazario, on August 11, 1987 in Chicago, and knocked him out in 8 rounds. But on November 21, at Las Vegas, he was not so fortunate, for Julio Cesar Chavez, rapidly proving that he was among the greatest of all time, stopped Rosario in 11 rounds.

Chavez stopped Rodolfo Aguilar in Las Vegas, and then won a technical decision over Jose Luis Ramirez to unite the W.B.A. and W.B.C. titles, as described above. However, Chavez then relinquished both titles to campaign as a light-welterweight.

The I.B.F. did not become strongly established among the lightweights until Jimmy Paul scored a number of

Julio Cesar Chavez (*left*) gets a left to the head of Edwin Rosario in taking the W.B.A. crown in 1987. Chavez had been a brilliant junior welterweight.

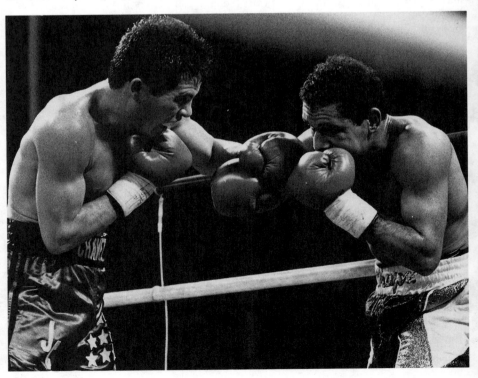

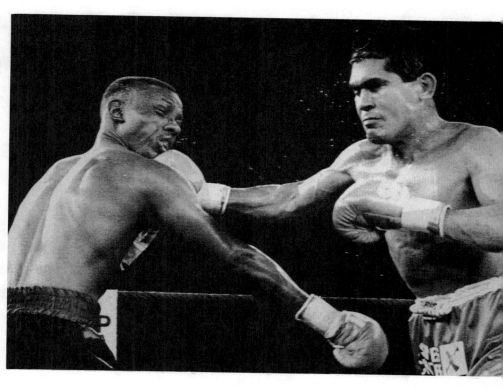

impressive victories in 1985 and the following year. The first nominated I.B.F. champion was Charlie Brown, who had outpointed Melvin Paul at Atlantic City, but his tenure was brief, for he was licked by Harry Arroyo in 14 rounds, three months later, on April 15, 1984. Arroyo made a couple of defences successfully, but at Atlantic City, on April 6, 1985, Jimmy Paul won a 15-rounder at his expense. Thereafter, Paul was successful against Robin Blake, Irleis Perez, and Darryl Tyson, but his reign came to an end when he was outpointed over 15 rounds by Greg Haugen at Las Vegas on December 6, 1986.

Haugen's immediate reign lasted six months, for at Providence, on June 7, 1987, he was defeated by local boy Vinny Pazienza, again over the full course. A return match was arranged for February 6, 1988, and in a bruising and exciting battle Haugen turned the tables and won back the belt with a unanimous verdict over 15 rounds.

Haugen's next defence was against a Puerto Rican, Miguel Santana, on April 11, 1988. This proved to be the first of two 11th-round technical decisions rendered in this division this year. It was a dull bout, and when the fighters clashed heads Haugen acquired a gash above the right eye, bad enough for the doctor to halt the bout. The challenger was announced from the ring as the winner, despite the fact that, at the time, Haugen was ahead on two of the three cards, Santana on the other. The fighters were in the dressing rooms when the result was reversed and Haugen was told he had kept the title. He then beat Gert Bo Jacobsen, who retired in a Copenhagen bout, but on February 18, 1989, in Hampton, he was outpointed by Pernell Whitaker, who thus took a version of the title some thought he deserved a year earlier.

Whitaker, a very fast and skilful boxer who could also punch, proved to be one of the outstanding champions of the early 1990s. He stopped Louie Someli in the third round, outpointed Jose Luis Ramirez in their return bout, which the W.B.C. decided would be for their title too, outpointed Freddie Pendleton and the outstanding super-featherweight champion Azumah Nelson, and then scored a first-round knockout of the new W.B.A. champion Juan Nazario to unify the W.B.A. version of the title with the W.B.C. and I.B.F. He defended all with points wins over Anthony Jones, Policarpo Diaz and the flamboyant Jorge Paez. He then relinquished the titles to campaign equally successfully in the heavier divisions in 1992.

After Chavez relinquished the W.B.A. and W.B.C. titles in 1988, the W.B.A. recognised Edwin Rosario as champion after his sixth-round stoppage of Anthony Jones at Atlantic City on July 9, 1989. Rosario lost his first defence on an eighth-round stoppage to Juan Nazario (Puerto Rico) on April 4, 1990 in New York City, and Nazario in turn lost to Whitaker, as recorded above.

The first W.B.O. champion was Mauricio Aceves of Mexico, who drew with Amancio Castro of Colombio at Monteria on January 21, 1989, but won the return on points at Santa Ana on March 8. He defended successfully with an eighth-round stoppage of Oscar Bejines but lost the title in Brownsville to a South African, Dingaan Thobela, on September 22, 1990. Thobela outpointed Mario Martinez and Antonio Rivera before vacating the title in 1992. Giovanni Parisi of Italy won it with a tenth-round knockout of Mexico's Javier Altamarino in Vighera on September 24, 1992.

When Whitaker vacated the division in 1992, the W.B.A., W.B.C. and I.B.F. went their separate ways again. The W.B.A. was first to acquire a new champion when Joey Gamache (U.S.A.) forced Chil-Sung Chun to retire after eight rounds on June 12, 1992. Tony Lopez (U.S.A.) stopped Gamache in his first defence in Portland on October 24, then outpointed Dingaan Thobele, the former W.B.O. champion, in Sacramento. At least, that was the official verdict, as Lopez, who comes from Sacramento, had a two-point margin on the scorecard of all three judges, but ringside opinion among the scribes was that robbery of old wild west proportions had taken place.

On August 24, 1992 Miguel Angel Gonzales of Mexico won the vacant W.B.C. title when Wilfredo Rocha of

Colombia was forced to retire after ten rounds, and he defended it by outpointing Darryl Tyson. At Aguascalientes on April 26, 1993 he outpointed his compatriot, Hector Lopez, to remain champion.

Tracy Spann and Freddie Pendleton were matched for the vacant I.B.F. title at Reno on August 29, 1992, but an accidental butt in the second round caused a bad cut on Pendleton's head and the fight was declared a technical draw.

Mexico's Miguel Angel Gonzalez gets a left to the face of Wilfredo Rocha of Columbia on his way to taking the W.B.C. lightweight title on a ninth-round stoppage.

Pernell 'Sweet Pea' Whitaker scores with a left uppercut to the chin of Poli Diaz of Spain in a 1991 W.B.C. defence.

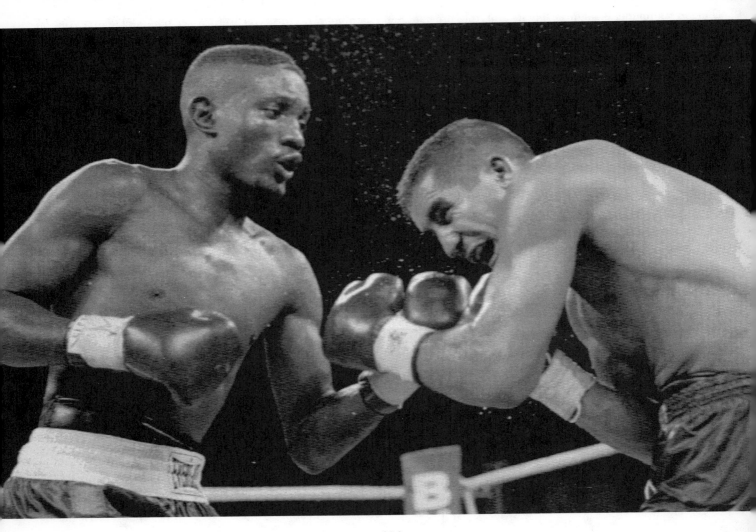

THE JUNIOR-LIGHTWEIGHT CHAMPIONS

This division started life as early as November 18, 1921 when Johnny Dundee, known as The Scotch Wop, won on a foul in the fifth round against George "K.O." Chaney at New York in a bout advertised as for the junior-lightweight championship of the world, the stipulated poundage being set at 130 pounds. Dundee defended the new title successfully with points wins against Jack Sharkey, Vincent "Pepper" Martin and Elino Flores, but on May 30, 1923 he was himself outpointed by Jack Bernstein. Seven months later, however, he regained the title in a return fight with a points win on December 17. On June 20, 1924 Steve "Kid" Sullivan decisioned him to take the title and on August 18 staved off a challenge from Martin with a points win. Sullivan next knocked out Mike Ballarino in five rounds on October 15, but in a second meeting on April 1, 1925 he lost the championship to Ballarino on a ten rounds points verdict. The new champion made two defences. On July 6 he decisioned Pepper Martin over 15 rounds, then was knocked out in the tenth round by Tod Morgan at Los Angeles on December 2.

Morgan was a phenomenal fighter. Born at Washington, he started boxing when he was 17, and kept active for 22 years, during which he participated in 205 bouts, winning 129 and drawing 28, spending the last ten years of his career in Australia. He made four defences in 1926, two in 1927, three in 1928 and three in 1929. On December 20 of that year, however, he came unstuck against Benny Bass who knocked him out in two rounds in New York. Bass retained the title by outpointing Lew Massey on January 5, 1931 but on July 15 was kayoed by stylish Kid Chocolate (Cuba) who kept his crown against seven challengers before losing to Frankie Klick on a seventh round knockout on Boxing Day, 1933. Klick never defended the title and it remained dormant until 1949, when on December 6 the renowned Sandy Saddler won the vacant championship by outpointing Orlando Zulueta at Cleveland, Ohio.

Saddler made two successful defences, knocking out Lauro Salas in nine rounds on April 18, 1950 and disposing of Diego Sosa in two rounds in Cuba on February 28, 1951. After that he ignored the title and it remained without a champion until July 20, 1959 when Harold Gomez ascended the vacant throne after outpointing Phil Jorgensen over 15 rounds at Providence, Rhode Island. Gomez remained champion until March 16, 1960 when he was knocked out by Gabriel "Flash" Elorde at Manila. In a return title bout on August 17, the Philippino took only 1 minute 50 seconds of round one to keep his crown.

Elorde proved another fantastic champion. He started his fighting career at the age of 16 and in all defended his world title 19 times in the next six years, finally losing it to Yoshiaki Numata (Japan) on a points verdict in Tokyo on June 15, 1967, when he was 37. On December 14 fellow-countryman Hiroshi Kobayashi took the title from Numata via a 12 rounds knockout. On his first defence on March 30, 1968 Kobayashi was held to a draw by Ireneo "Rene" Barrientos, a Philippino southpaw, but on October 6 he outpointed Jaime Valladares at Tokyo.

The title was split apart in 1969. The newly-formed W.B.C. ordered Kobayashi to meet Barrientos in a return match, but the Japanese boxer refused to comply and was promptly stipped of his title, which was declared vacant. As was to be expected, the W.B.A. backed Kobayashi and he enjoyed four more winning defences under their ruling: on April 6, 1969, against Antonio Amaya; on November 9 against Carlos Canete; on August 23, 1970, against Antonio Amaya again; and on May 3, 1971, against Ricardo Arredondo. All the bouts took place in Tokyo, and all were won on points.

Going to Aomori, Kobayashi's luck ran out as he was stopped in ten rounds by Alfredo Marcano (Venezuela) on July 29. The new champion then halted Kenji Iwata in four rounds at Caracas on November 7, but on April 25, 1972 he was outpointed by Ben Villaflor (Philippines) at Honolulu. After being held to a draw by Victor Echegaray (Argentina) on September 5, Ben was outpointed on March 12, 1973 by Kuniaki Shibata, former world featherweight champion, also at Honolulu. The Japanese champion outpointed Echegaray at Tokyo on June 19, then, on October 17 Villaflor won back the title with a sensational one round win (1 minute 56 seconds) over Shibata to become world junior-lightweight champion for the second time, and he was still only 21. In the next three years he made five successful defences against all comers until, on October 16, 1976, he was outpointed by Samuel Serrano (Puerto Rico) at San Juan.

Serrano proved to be another great fighting champ, holding the W.B.A. title from 1976 to 1983 and making ten defences in that time. This included losing by a sixth round knockout to Yasutsune Uehara (Japan) at Detroit on August 2, 1980 and regaining the crown on points in a return bout on April 9, 1981. Uehara had successfully defended against Leonel Hernandez on November 20, 1980, and now Serrano outpointed the same fighter on June 29, and ended the year by stopping Hikaru Tomonari at San Juan on December 10. The W.B.A. made a surprise decision on June 5, 1982 at Santiago when Serrano met challenger Benedicto Villablanca (Chile). The bout was halted in round 11, the champion being unable to continue because of a badly cut eye. As he was ahead on points at the time, the W.B.A. declared the decision null and void, which meant that Lucky Sam had kept his crown. However, he had to relinquish it on January 19, 1983 when he was knocked out by Roger Mayweather in the eighth round at San Juan.

A class boxer, the American forced Jorge Alvarado to retire in eight rounds on April 20 at San Jose, then on August 17 at Las Vegas he knocked out Benedicto Villablanca at the end of round one, the official time being 3 minutes 4 seconds. It was Mayweather's turn to suffer a one round knockout when he was beaten in 1 minute 31 seconds by Rocky Lockridge (U.S.A) at Beaumont, Texas, on February 26, 1984. The new champ stopped Tae-Jin Moon (Korea) in 11 rounds at Anchorage, Alaska, on June 12 and forced Kamel Boru Ali (Tunis) to retire at Rivadel-Garda, Italy, on January 27, 1985. Four months later, on May 19 at San Juan, Wilfredo Gomez, long-reigning champion of the W.B.C. light-featherweight title, outpointed Lockridge over 12 rounds. The veteran lost this title on May 24, 1986, however, the referee coming to his rescue in the ninth round as Alfredo Layne (Panama) became the new champion at San Juan. Layne, too, had a short reign, being knocked out in the 10th round by Brian Mitchell (South Africa) at Sun City on September 27, 1986.

Meanwhile, back to Ireneo "Rene" Barrientos. He became the first W.B.C. junior-lightweight champion by outpointing Ruben Navarro at Manila on February 15, 1969, but remained title-holder for less than two months, losing his title to Japanese star, Yoshiaki Numata, on a points verdict at Tokyo on April 5, 1970. Numata defended against Raul Rojas with a fifth round knockout on September 27, former champ Barrientos on January 3, 1971, and Lionel Rose (Australia) at Hiroshima on May 30, both beaten on points. His reign came to an end on October 10 at Sendai when Ricardo Arredondo (Mexico) knocked him out in the tenth round. The Mexican kept his title until February 28, 1974, making five successful defences until being outpointed by Kuniaki Shibata. Shibata kept his crown by outpointing three challengers, then on July 5, 1975 was knocked out by Alfredo Escalera (Puerto Rico) in five rounds at Tokyo.

Now followed a reign that lasted over two years and included ten title defences. It seemed that Escalera would go on for ever, then the renowned Alexis Arguello (Nicaragua) stopped him in 13 rounds at San Juan on February 4, 1979. Once again the division had found a fighter worthy of entry in boxing's Hall of Fame. Alexis, who had started pro fighting at 16, had been featherweight champion for four years. Now he was to reign as W.B.C. junior-lightweight king for another 2½ years, and then go on to become a triple world champion by capturing the lightweight crown. He was never defeated for either of these titles, his retirement coming after twice trying to gain a fourth crown. Arguello made ten successful defences as a junior-lightweight, only one of which went the scheduled distance. He relinquished this particular title in September 1980 and on December 11 Rafael "Bazooka" Limon (Mexico) took over the vacant throne by stopping Idelfonso Bethelmi (Venezuela) in the 15th and final round at los Angeles.

Limon lasted three months, being outpointed by Cornelius Boza-Edwards (Uganda) on March 8, 1981. Contender Bobby Chacon (U.S.A.) was knocked out by Boza-Edwards in the 14th at Las Vegas on May 30, then Rolando Navarrete (Philippines) won the championship with a knockout in five rounds at Viareggio, Italy, on August 29. His first challenger, Chung-Ill Choi was stopped in 11 rounds at Manila on January 16, 1982, but on May 29 Limon came back as ruler of the W.B.C. title by scoring a 12th round win over Navarrete at Las Vegas. Bobby Chacon was successful in his second attempt to win the crown by outpointing Limon at Sacramento on December 11, then on June 27, 1983 he was deprived of his title for failing to defend it.

Hector Camacho (Puerto Rico) came into the picture by stopping Limon in five rounds for the vacant throne at San Juan on August 8, and he knocked out fellow-countryman Rafael Solis, also in five rounds, in the same ring on November 18. Camacho relinquished the title in June 1984, and the vacancy was filled by a 23-year-old Mexican, Cesar Chavez, who stopped Mario Martinez in eight rounds at Los Angeles. The winner proved a crowd-pleaser. On April 20, 1985 he stopped Ruben Castillo (U.S.A.) in eight rounds; on July 7 he beat Roger Mayweather in

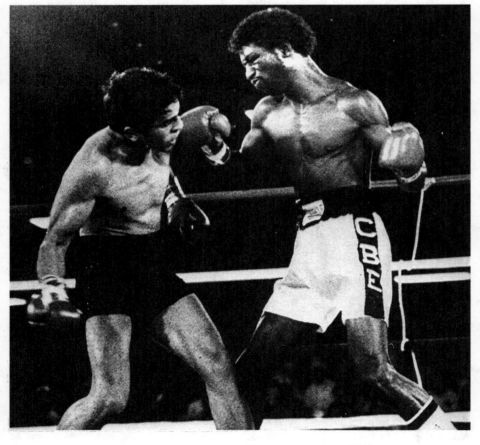

Cornelius Boza-Edwards of Uganda *(right)* **lands a right on the face of challenger Bobby Chacon (U.S.A.) in retaining his W.B.C. title in 1981.**

six, and he twice outpointed Dwight
Pratchett (U.S.A.) over 12 rounds at Las
Vegas, on May 21 and September 21.

Chavez continued his destructive
ways in 1986, going to Paris on May 15 to
dispose of Faustino Barrios (Argentina)
in the fifth, and to New York four weeks
later to halt Refugio Rojas (Mexico) in
the seventh, the referee having to stop
both contests.

The brilliant little Mexican remained
superbly active as he established himself. At Monte Carlo, on August 3, he
took a 12-rounds points verdict at the
expense of Rocky Lockridge, and then
travelled to New York, where he served
Juan Laporte the same way on December 12. Chavez opened the year 1987 in
the amphitheatre at Nîmes, France,
with a decisive victory over Franscisco
Tomas de la Cruz, when the bout was
hastily halted in round 3 on April 18.
There seemed to be no stopping this
accomplished fighter, for on August 21
he had very little trouble at Tijuana with
the Dominican, Danilo Cabrera, who
lasted the full 12 rounds but failed to win
a single one.

After nine successful defences,
Chavez put on a little weight and relinquished his title. With the junior-
lightweight or super-featherweight
crown now up for grabs, Azumah Nelson
crossed gloves with Mario Martinez, of
Mexico, at Los Angeles on February 29,
1988. The fight ended with a disputed
decision in Nelson's favour.

The I.B.F. had stepped into the
picture when on April 22, 1984, at
Seoul, the South Korean Hwan-Kil Yuh
outpointed Red Sequenan over 15
rounds, and this victory was followed on
September 16 with a win over Sak
Galexi in the 6th round at Pohang. But
when the champion travelled to Melbourne to face Lester Ellis on February
15, 1985, Hwan-Kil Yuh lost his title
after 15 rounds.

The new champion, an Australian,
knocked out Red Sequenan in 13 rounds
in his first defence, but when he faced
the Australian-based Englishman, Barry
Michael, on July 12, also at Melbourne,
he was outpointed. Michael chalked up
three impressive victories, at the expense of Jin-Shik Choi, Mark Fernando,
and Najib Daho, and then took on the
American, Rocky Lockridge, at Wind-

Champion Julio Cesar Chavez takes one on
the chin from Brazilian challenger Francisco
Tomas de la Cruz, but the referee stopped
the contest in his favour in the third round in
Nîmes, France, in 1987.

sor on August 9, 1987. It was a gruelling
battle, with Michael being obliged to
retire after 8 rounds. Lockridge placed
his title at stake on October 25, at
Tucson, Arizona, versus Johnny de la
Rosa, and stopped his man in 10 after
another hard fight.

Lockridge outpointed Harold Knight
but lost a decision to Tony Lopez in
Sacramento on July 27, 1988. Although
the I.B.F. were still insisting on 15-
round championship fights, they bowed
to the Californian authorities and confined this one to 12, in line with the
other ruling bodies. Lopez defended
twice in Sacramento, outpointing Juan
Molina and Rocky Lockridge, then
knocked out Tyrone Jackson in
Stateline.

On April 29, 1989 the Puerto Rican
Juan Molina outpointed his fellow-
countryman Juan Laporte at San Juan to
become the first W.B.O. champion, but

South Africa's Brian Mitchell (left) slips a punch from challenger Jim McDonnell in London in 1988. Mitchell won a hard points win and continued a championship career spanning five years.

he immediately relinquished this when matched with Lopez for the I.B.F. crown, and this time he stopped Lopez in the tenth round. This was at Sacramento on October 7, but having stopped Lupe Suarez, Molina lost the title back to Lopez when outpointed on May 20, 1990 at Reno.

Lopez was challenged by another colourful all-action boxer in Mexican Jorge Paez, who had enjoyed a long run as featherweight champion, but won a decision at Sacramento and then met the W.B.A. champion, Brian Mitchell, at Sacramento on March 15, 1991. It was a brilliant contest of both attack and defence before nearly 10,000 spectators, which swayed from one man to the other and ended in a draw, each fighter narrowly getting the nod from one judge while the third had it level. Lopez stopped Lupe Gutierrez in his next defence, but was then outpointed by Mitchell when the two met in a return at Sacramento on September 13, 1991. This time Lopez disappointed his home-town fans and Mitchell was a clear points winner. Mitchell had relinquished the W.B.A. title to win the I.B.F. version, but after beating Lopez he relinquished the I.B.F. title as well, announcing in January 1992 his retirement.

Brian Mitchell was one of two great junior lightweights who spanned the 1980s and 1990s. After taking the W.B.A. belt from Alfredo Layne on September 27, 1986, as described above, he kept the title on his first defence only by virtue of a draw with Jose Rivera of Puerto Rico at San Juan. Mitchell frequently defended in his challenger's home territory, and he did so again when he stopped Rocky Fernandez at Panama City. Frenchman Daniel Londas was outpointed at Gravelines, France, and Salvatore Curcetti of Italy was stopped at Capo d'Orlando. Jose Rivera was outpointed in a return, this time in Madrid, and Jim McDonnell of Great Britain suffered the same

fate at the Elephant and Castle, London. A return to Capo d'Orlando saw Mitchell stop Italy's Salvatore Bottiglieri, and then four American challenges were disposed of: Jackie Beard at Crotone, Irving Mitchell at Lewiston, Jackie Beard again at Grossetto and Frankie Mitchell at Aosta. After this came the two meetings with Tony Lopez already described, and Mitchell's retirement while still champion.

The other outstanding champion of the time was Azumah Nelson, the former featherweight champion who won the W.B.C. crown in February, 1988 as described. Few of Nelson's opponents went the distance as the muscled frame of the little man from

Ghana packed a punch to go with his boxing skills. He beat Lupe Suarez (stopped, ninth), Sidnei dal Rovere (knockout, third), Mario Martinez (stopped, 12th), Jim McDonnell (knockout, 12th) and Juan Laporte (points).

Nelson then met Jeff Fenech, the tough little battler from Sydney, Australia, who had already won world titles at the three weights below junior lightweight and was unbeaten. The bout took place at Las Vegas on June 28, 1991 and was a classic, with Nelson on top early and Fenech finishing better. The verdict was a draw, with one judge supporting each boxer and the third making it level. Press opinion favoured Fenech, but Nelson was not afraid to

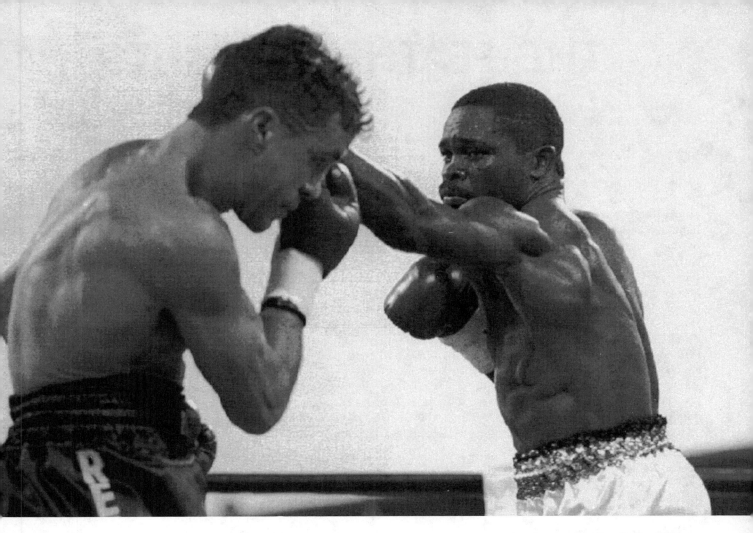

give his challenger another chance. It came in Melbourne on March 1, 1992 before 38,000 of the challenger's fellow Australians. Fenech, at 27, was six years younger than Nelson (at least – Nelson's age was uncertain) and was favourite to win, but Nelson produced one of his greatest displays and stopped Fenech in the eighth. It was his 17th world title fight and the first defeat for the Australian.

Nelson went on to outpoint Calvin Grove and, on the champions bill at Mexico City on February 20, 1993, before a record 136,000 spectators, he narrowly outpointed Gabriel Ruelas of Mexico.

The vacant W.B.O. title was won on December 9, 1989 by Kamel Bou Ali, of Tunisia, who at Terano scored an eighth-round knockout over Antonio Rivera of Puerto Rico. He fought a no-contest which ended in the second with Pedro Villegas and knocked out Joey Jacobs of Great Britain before losing the

title on a majority decision to the veteran Daniel Londas of France after a dull contest at San Rufo on March 21, 1992. Londas lost the title on September 4, 1992 at Copenhagen, on a bill in which two brothers made history by winning world titles on the same night at the same venue. The 25-year-old Jimmi Bredahl, a Danish southpaw and 13 years younger than Londas, won a clear points verdict on the same night that his younger brother Johnny won the W.B.O. light-bantamweight crown.

Meanwhile, the W.B.A. title vacated by Brian Mitchell was won first by Joey Gamache (U.S.A.) with a tenth-round stoppage of Jerry N'Gobeni of South Africa at Lewiston on June 28, 1991, but Gamache relinquished the title and Genaro Hernandez took it when forcing Daniel Londas to retire after nine rounds at Epernay on November 22, 1991. Hernandez's first defence was a points win over Omar Catari of Venezuela at Los Angeles, and he followed

Azumah Nelson (right) inflicted a first defeat on three-times champion Jeff Fenech in Melbourne.

this with two successful defences in Tokyo, against Masuaki Takeda and Yuji Watanabe, both of Japan. On April 26, 1993 at Inglewood, unbeaten Hernandez faced a challenge from Raul 'Jibaro' Perez, the former bantam and light-featherweight champion, who was trying to emulate his countryman Chavez and take a title at a third weight. Unfortunately a terrible clash of heads after only 28 seconds opened a gash on Perez's head and the fight had to be stopped as a technical draw.

Brian Mitchell's second discarded title, the I.B.F. version, was won by former champion Juan (or John-John) Molina, who stopped South African Jackie Gunguluza at Sun City on February 22, 1992. Two inside-the-distance wins followed against challengers Fernando Caicedo and Francisco 'Pancho' Segura.

THE FEATHERWEIGHTS

The activity in the three lower divisions—featherweight, bantam and flyweight—has dwindled considerably in the past few years owing to the scarcity of talent. Most of the boxers in the three bottom classes are from the Pacific Coast or from Mexico and other foreign countries, particularly bantams and flyweights. Good little battlers were plentiful in boxing's early days when the ring's greatest stars performed. Abe Attell, Terry McGovern, Casper Leon, George Dixon, Dave Sullivan, Jimmy Barry, Jimmy Wilde, Joe Lynch, Johnny Buff, Frankie Burns, Johnny Coulon, Kid Williams, Al Brown, Benny Lynch, Pancho Villa, Pete Herman among the old timers, and the marvelous Willie Pep among the more recent, have standout records.

In Australia the fans thought the world of Australian Billy Murphy in the feather class. In America in the early days of boxing, shortly after the gloves era got under way, George Dixon was considered tops. So evenly matched were many of the best men in the feather class that it is difficult to pick one as the greatest. Young Griffo of Australia was never defeated as a featherweight. He, like Attell and Pep, was a ring marvel. Abe Attell was so good, he had great difficulty in obtaining matches with men his weight. He had to face lightweights and often even went beyond that scale. Johnny Kilbane as a feather also often had to go out of his class to keep in action.

Two ounce gloves were just beginning to replace bare-knuckle fighting when during the late eighties Dal Hawkins and Freddy Bogan fought seventy-five rounds in San Francisco for the American featherweight crown. The fight, held indoors in 1889, was halted at five A.M. and was resumed the following day when Hawkins won by a knockout in the fifteenth round to assume the top spot in the division.

Hawkins outgrew the class, the weight of which at the time was 118 to 122 pounds, and Harry Gilmore claimed the crown. But Gilmore never went into a title defense. He offered to make 122 pounds for Ike Weir, the clever "Belfast Spider," who refused to accept the terms. Gilmore then entered the next higher division, leaving it to Weir and Frank Murphy of England to fight it out for the vacant throne. They fought a draw of eighty rounds at Kouts, Indiana, on March 31, 1889.

Murphy met Australian Billy Mur-

Dal Hawkins (left) was born in San Francisco, in 1871. He won the featherweight crown after battling Fred Bogan a total of 90 rounds. Ike Weir (right) born near Belfast, Ireland, in 1867, claimed the title when Hawkins outgrew the class.

Dick Hollywood (*above*) of New York, was a pioneer bare-knuckles champion, who claimed the feather-weight crown in 1867 after defeating Johnny Keating of Cincinnati.

Owen Swift (*left*) was probably England's greatest little man, but his courage was not enough to handle the powerfully heavier Hammer Lane, who terminated their battle (*above*) with crushing body slams to the turf. Swift carried the bruising battle on May 5, 1836, to 100 rounds, lasting over two hours. Born in 1814, Owen made his ring debut at the age of 15 and won 11 major battles before he was 20. He never weighed more than 128 pounds and lost only two battles in a 10-year career, the first as a youngster, the other when he met Lane. Swift gained two tragic ring victories. The results of his blows killed Anthony Noon (*right*) in 1834, for which he served six months in prison, and Brighton Bill, in 1838. He was acquitted of Bill's death and quit fighting.

Frank Murphy (*above, left*) and Ike Weir battled for the featherweight title in 1889. They fought to an 80-round draw with skin-tight gloves for a purse of $1,500. The contest was broken up by the police.

"Torpedo" Billy Murphy of Australia knocked out Weir in 14 rounds. The Americans insisted that the bout was for the British crown and not the world title.

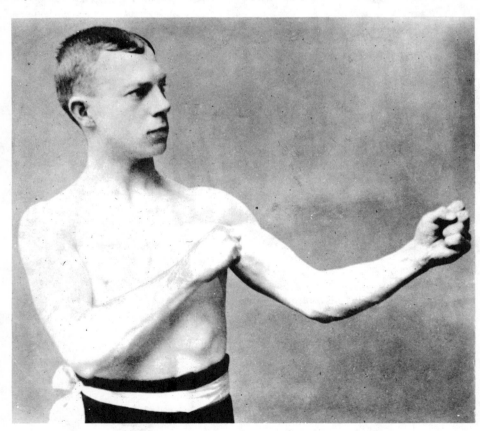

Cal McCarthy (*left*) of Troy, New York, held George Dixon to a 70-round draw in 1890, but was kayoed by Dixon in 1891.

phy at San Francisco two months later and they fought twenty-seven rounds to a draw. On January 13, 1890, Weir and Billy Murphy met in San Francisco and Murphy was acclaimed

champion when he knocked out Ike in the fourteenth round.

The American sports scribes refused to accept this as a championship bout, declaring that the battle settled only

the British Empire title and since Cal McCarthy and George Dixon, born July 29, 1870, were America's leading feathers who had graduated from the bantam division, they were matched for the American championship. "Little Chocolate" stopped McCarthy in the twenty-second round in Troy, New York, and was proclaimed titleholder. Through his manager, the weight was set at 115 pounds limit.

Australian Billy Murphy in the meantime had gone back to Australia and Johnny Griffin claimed his crown. After Weir and Griffin had fought a draw of four rounds, a bout stopped by the police, Tom O'Rourke, manager of Dixon, decided on a ruse. He took George to San Francisco to box Abe Willis, the British champion, and when on July 28, 1891, Dixon halted his opponent in five rounds, Dixon became the acknowledged world champion and for the first time a universal titleholder headed the division.

Because of his light weight, Dixon, really a bantam—a 115 pound boxer—took the best in the field into camp.

338

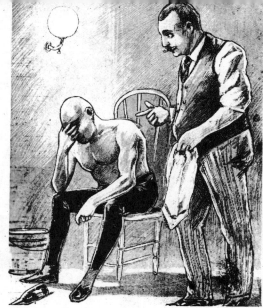

Solly Smith, a clever 19-year-old boxer from Los Angeles, gained the featherweight championship when he clearly outpointed the veteran George Dixon *(left)* in 1897, before an overflow crowd in San Francisco. Smith had been knocked out by Dixon in 1893 in his eighth pro bout, when he was only 15 years old. Dixon felt the 20-round loss of his title deeply and broke down in his dressing room *(above)* with only his manager, Tom O'Rourke, to console him.

Dave Sullivan *(below, right)* made sport-page headlines when he won the title from Solly Smith *(below, left)*. Sullivan was born in Cork, Ireland, in May, 1887.

OLLY SMITH'S ARM WAS BROKEN.

| en Then He Went hrough a Whole Round Before Giving Up. | The Bout Unsatisfactory, but Dave Sullivan Got the Purse. |

Dave Sullivan and Solly Smith he Greater New York Athletic night there was a chance to put on argument as to which was featherweight by saying, "Well, ou." Now the chance to argue still remains with no chance of

It was announced that the men were to break clear at the word, and they backed to corners. Then every one took a long breath and the bell clanged.

For full thirty seconds they feinted. Dave acted very nicely, he smiled, moved in and out gracefully, and finally brought a lead. Solly turned loose one of his far-famed, over-hand, left swings. Dave was not there. After a feint or two the younger of the Sullivan brothers tried a left to the body. It reached, but was very gentle and Solly blinked his beady eyes (that answers for a loud laugh for Smith). Then they feinted a bit, and both tried th eleft for the head and came together. They broke and Dave again began prodding at the body gently with the left. Solly blinked and again brought his left down from aloft. It missed a mile. Dave worked in, feinting Smith into some funny positions. Then away went the left at the head and the right hard after it. Both landed, but with no speed. Again they mixed and on the break Solly tried to sneak in a left and was hissed by some thousands of hissers and duly cautioned by the referee.

Dave Grows Bold.

In the second Dave grew bolder and jabbed his left into the body fairly good before Solly understood. Then Mr. Smith retaliated with his overhand left. Dave was inside of it. Again Dave jabbed his left fair to the works and still again. Then he smiled what is known as the Johnny Wise smile and tried at the head. Smith blocked and again tried the left like a south-paw cricket bowler. Dave was away and then in with his jab to the body. Then "bang" went the right to the slats and Solly, after a couple of hur-

half round. Dave pushed him off, jabbed at the body and again came the swing. Again it missed and Dave got to the head with left and the body with right. Dave had done no damage so far, but he looked to have Smith guessing hard.

In the third Dave began his body jab-

He was on the three days carnival card that was featured by the Sullivan-Corbett battle and on September 6, 1892, he knocked out Jack Skelly, a very good boxer from New York with a fine amateur record, at the Olympic Club of New Orleans, in the eighth round. That was Jack's initial bout as a professional.

Quite a complication existed in the early days of the class because of the many title claimants. After the Skelly fight, O'Rourke again raised the weight, this time to 126 pounds, when he found Dixon's foes were making it tough for him. At that weight he matched "Little Chocolate" with Solly Smith at San Francisco, October 4, 1897, Smith getting the verdict at the end of twenty rounds. Smith then made a match with Dave Sullivan for Coney Island, September 26, 1898. Handicapped by a broken arm, Smith quit in the fifth round.

Dixon then challenged Sullivan and at the Lenox A. C. of New York, on November 11, 1898, "Little Chocolate" stopped his opponent in the tenth

AROUND THE RINGSIDE

DIXON RUSHING SULLIVAN
TO THE ROPES

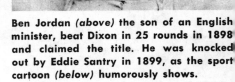

Ben Jordan (*above*) the son of an English minister, beat Dixon in 25 rounds in 1898 and claimed the title. He was knocked out by Eddie Santry in 1899, as the sport cartoon (*below*) humorously shows.

JORDAN GIVES HIMSELF UP TO ASTRONOMY IN THE 16TH ROUND

George Dixon regained the crown when Dave Sullivan was disqualified after his seconds entered the ring in the 10th round, to prevent a knockout. The newspaper cartoon (*above*) depicts the action and some of the characters at ringside.

Eddie Santry claimed the title after his knockout of Jordan. On July 14, 1899, Dixon won a six-round decision over Santry, and one month later they fought a 20-round draw, as illustrated (*below*) in the *New York Journal*.

round. Each scaled 118 pounds.

Meanwhile Ben Jordan of England, who laid claim to the championship after he had outpointed Dixon in twenty-five rounds in New York on July 1, 1898, had in turn been knocked out by Eddie Santry of Chicago on October 10, 1899, in sixteen rounds. Hence Santry, though he previously had lost to Dixon, asserted himself king of the division. Dixon then cleared the path for international recognition by whipping Santry in six rounds, then boxing a draw of twenty with him.

By now Dixon was on the down-grade and Terry McGovern, "The Brooklyn Terror," had come to the fore. He had beaten all comers, many by knockouts, and on January 9, 1900, at the Broadway A. C., "Little Chocolate" lost his crown to him. Dixon was knocked out in the eighth round.

McGovern, born in Jamestown, Pennsylvania, March 9, 1880, and Dixon were two of the top ringmen in the division. Dixon battled fearlessly against great odds until, in the eighth

DIXON'S AND SANTRY'S CONTRASTING STYLES

DIXON-SANTRY BATTLE

"Terrible Terry" McGovern (above, right) started in 1897 and ended in 1908. In 77 bouts, he won 59, 34 by knockout, lost two, boxed four draws and 10 no-decision bouts, and was kayoed twice. His brother Hugh (left) boxed from 1902 to 1905.

When McGovern knocked out Dixon, he was absolutely invincible. He had scored eight consecutive knockouts and went on to make it 12. On July 16, 1900, he met Frank Erne, the lightweight champion, who agreed to come in at 128 pounds and knock out Terry in 10 rounds, or take the loser's end of the purse. Although no championship was involved under those terms, Terry disposed of Erne in just three rounds at Madison Square Garden. The illustration (above) which appeared in the New York Herald, shows Erne down for the second time and his second (left) is about to throw in the towel, to save him from further punishment.

Terry is shown on the left, displaying his favorite blow, a right hand to the stomach, after slipping under his opponent's right-hand lead. Terry's vicious body blows, in rapid succession, set his victims up for the knockout.

The sporting world was content to agree that Terry McGovern would rule the feather-weight roost for years to come. But a stunning upset occurred on Thanksgiving Day in 1901, when Young Corbett (above, right) knocked Terry out in two rounds. In a return bout at San Francisco Corbett again kayoed McGovern, this time in 11 rounds.

Young Corbett (William H. Rothwell) was born in Denver, Colorado, in 1880. He fought only in the West, where he scored 22 knockouts from 1897 to 1901, before he invaded the East to fight McGovern.

Abe Attell (below, right) posed with his brother, Monte, claimed the throne when Corbett could no longer make weight.

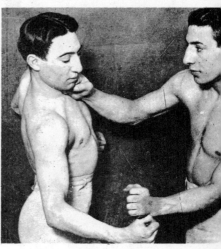

round, Referee Johnny White stepped in and halted the affair to save "Little Chocolate."

The following year, on Thanksgiving Day, November 28, a confident Mc-Govern faced Young Corbett, born in Denver, Colorado, October 4, 1880, in a battle for the feather crown. Mc-Govern set the weight limit at 126 pounds though he had won the title at 122. The contest at Hartford, Connecticut, lasted less than two rounds. It was a terrific battle despite its shortness, with "Terrible Terry" dropping the title.

Terry, who was discovered and developed by Sam H. Harris, the theatrical producer, got his start at the Greenwood Sporting Club of South Brooklyn, New York. He was a much harder hitter than was Dixon. He was a cruel puncher, fast and accurate.

Before his defeat by Corbett, he went all out putting his rivals out of the way. Among others he whipped were Jack Ward, Eddie Santry, Oscar Gardner, Tommy White, Pedlar Palmer, Frank Erne, and Joe Bernstein. He halted Joe Gans in Chicago in the

second round, a bout that was termed a "fake" and resulted in the killing of boxing in the Windy City.

One of his best performances was against Palmer, the British champion, on September 12, 1899, at Tuckahoe, New York. In that contest Terry won the world bantam crown by knocking the Britisher out in less than one round. Terry vacated the bantam class at the end of the year when he became overweight.

Corbett, McGovern's successor as feather king, put Terry down in the first round with an uppercut to the chin and put him away for keeps with several body punches followed by a hook to the jaw. Corbett defeated Kid Broad and Joe Bernstein, besides fighting no decision contests with Eddie Lenny, Young Erne and Crockey Boyle, then vacated the throne.

When Young Corbett found that he was putting on weight, he decided to retire from the class and enter the lightweight division. Then with the championship vacant, Abe Attell, a rising young clever featherweight from San Francisco, California, where

Abe Attell *(above, right)* and "Harlem" Tommy Murphy engaged in one of the bloodiest fights ever seen. They met on March 9, 1912, in Daly City, California, two weeks after Attell had lost his title to Johnny Kilbane. Both fighters were covered with blood during the entire 20 rounds of fighting. Murphy won the referee's decision.

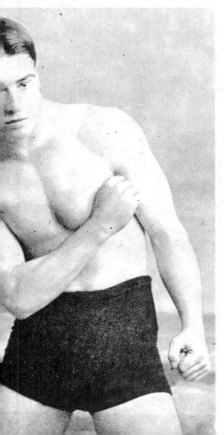

"Brooklyn" Tommy Sullivan, a seven-year veteran, knocked out Attell in 1904, but was deprived of the title for being over the featherweight limit for the fight.

he was born on Washington's birthday, 1884, laid claim to the throne. On October 20, 1901, Dixon, in an attempt to regain the championship, drew with Attell in twenty rounds, then faced him again a week later, October 28, and lost to Attell in fifteen rounds. Now Abe declared himself the successor to Corbett and announced his willingness to defend against all comers.

The "Little Hebrew," as he was called, engaged in many fifteen and twenty rounds contests with success but there were others, like Tommy Sullivan, who disputed Attell's right to top honors. After Abe had stopped Harry Forbes in five rounds in what was advertised as a championship match, he tackled Sullivan in St. Louis, October 13, 1904, in defense of his laurels and was knocked out in the fifth round. Attell insisted that Sullivan had not made the class weight and continued to assert his rights to

the crown. He was backed by the press in his claim and on April 30, 1908, Abe cleared up the confusion by knocking Sullivan out in the fourth round.

Now Attell received universal recognition, though for many months before this he kept successfully defending his claim against the cream of the division. During that period his greatest bouts were with Owen Moran of England, with whom he drew in twenty-five rounds and again in twenty-three.

Attell held the title for almost eleven years, including the disputed period, before he was dethroned by Johnny Kilbane, born in Cleveland, Ohio, April 18, 1889. During that long reign he faced the world's best in three divisions with considerable success. Among the many stars whom he met were Frankie Neil, Kid Herman, Jimmy Walsh, Brooklyn Tommy Sullivan, Battling Nelson, Matty Baldwin,

Jem Driscoll (above), the British feather-weight champion, met Attell on February 19, 1909, in a 10-round no-decision contest. Driscoll completely outboxed and out-fought Attell, but could not gain the crown unless he scored a knockout.

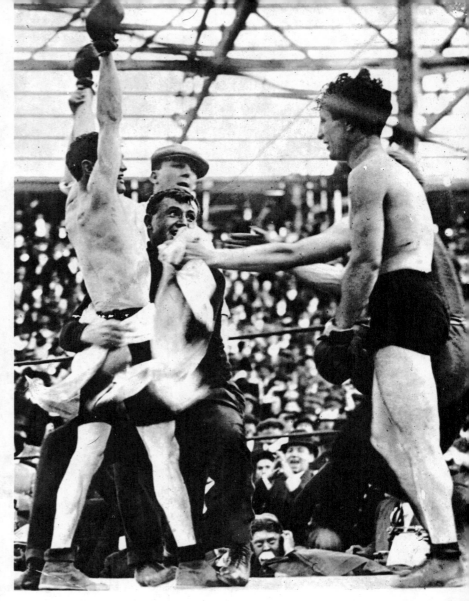

Big Mackay, Harry Forbes, Harlem Tommy Murphy, Pal Moore, Matt Wells, Patsy Kline, K.O. Brown, and Jem Driscoll, the British champion. His bouts with Tommy Murphy, like that with Driscoll, hold a special place in the history of the class as outstanding thrillers.

The fight with Driscoll was a masterpiece of ring cleverness in which the Britisher got the better of his opponent. Driscoll was so clever on that occasion that Attell often found his punches, usually most effective, hitting the ozone. Driscoll came to America heralded as a wizard and he lived up to his reputation. The throng that witnessed the bout at the National A. C. of New York saw wily Attell miss more often than ever before. It was a battle of ring cleverness.

Kilbane stunned the boxing world when he outclassed Attell in twenty rounds on February 22, 1912, in Vernon, California, to relieve Abe of

Johnny Kilbane raises his arms in joy (above) after receiving a popular 20-round decision in 1912 that ended Abe Attell's almost 11-year reign on the featherweight throne. Kilbane had been credited with a four-round knockout over Attell at Cleveland in 1911, when Attell quit, claiming his shoulder was broken.

Kilbane (right) started boxing in 1907 and retired in 1923. He engaged in 141 contests, of which he lost only four.

his laurels. Kilbane, though not as clever as Abe, was a scientific boxer with a fairly good punch. Most of his ring battles were no-decision affairs.

Eugene Criqui of France was the next title holder. He knocked out Kilbane in six rounds at the Polo Grounds on June 2, 1923, but held on to his championship for only one month and twenty-four days when he was dethroned by Johnny Dundee in the same arena in fifteen rounds.

In 1925 Dundee outgrew the featherweight class. Following an elimination, Louis Kid Kaplan of Meriden, Connecticut, replaced Dundee. The latter, called the "Scotch Wop," born in Shaikai, Italy, November 22, 1893, was one of the ring marvels of his era. Equally good as a lightweight and as a feather, he fought the best in each class. On April 29, 1913, Dundee fought a draw with Kilbane. The bout went twenty rounds and Kilbane was lucky to retain his featherweight crown.

Kaplan, one of the best pugilists ever developed in Connecticut, surrendered his title in 1927, because like

Johnny Dundee *(left)* was a 21-year ring veteran. He started in 1910 and hung up his gloves in 1932. In that time, he battled 320 opponents, losing to 31. After winning the featherweight crown, he went to Rome with manager Jimmy Johnston, where during a visit to the Vatican, they posed *(above)* before a bust of Pope Leo X.

Louis "Kid" Kaplan, born in Russia in 1902, succeeded Dundee to the throne when he knocked out Danny Kramer in an elimination tournament in 1925. In training for the January bout, Kaplan posed with his sisters *(below)* outside his work-gym.

345

When Kaplan vacated the title, the logical contenders, Red Chapman *(left)* and Benny Bass, on the scales, met in a 10-round contest. Bass was an easy winner. Earlier in 1927, Bass won from Chapman when he was fouled in the first round.

Young Tony Canzoneri, who had been boxing three years, me Bass in February of 1928. Tony *(above, left)* walked off with th decision and the featherweight crown, only to lose it eigh months later to André Routis, in 15 rounds.

André Routis, born in Bordeaux, France, in 1900, gained the title from Canzoneri in a fast 15-round bout. Routis, who started in 1919, won the bantamweight title of France in 1924 and had a fair record before coming to America in 1926. After campaigning here for two years, Routis won the title, then lost it one year later.

many other champions he no longe could make 126 pounds. Benny Bas and Red Chapman of Boston, th leading contenders, fought for th right to succeed him. Bass, born D cember 4, 1902, in Kiev, Russia, ou pointed his rival and was crowne king, September 12, 1927. He wa beaten on a decision in fifteen roun February 10, 1928, by Tony Canzone who hailed from New York, thoug born in Louisiana.

Another Frenchman soon took ov when Andre Routis outpointed Ca zoneri in the Garden on Septemb 28, 1928, in fifteen rounds. A few da short of a year later, the Frenchma lost the championship to Battling B talino in the latter's native city, Ha ford, Connecticut, via a decision

Routis found Bat Battalino too strong and tough. At the end of 15 rounds on September 23, 1929, Battalino's hand was raised as the new featherweight champion, in Hartford, Connecticut.

Bat Battalino was a rugged ringman who started boxing in 1927 and after 22 bouts won the featherweight title. He defended the crown successfully five times and met the best men in the class. Vacated the title in 1932, and retired in 1940.

Kid Chocolate, the Cuban bonbon, was a truly finished ringman. He was an excellent boxer, with an abundance of ring skill and a good puncher. In 161 bouts from 1928 to 1938, he won 145, 64 by knockouts. When he knocked out Lew Feldman (below) on October 13, 1932, he won New York recognition as featherweight champion.

he end of fifteen rounds. Routis, born uly 16, 1900 in Bordeaux, found Bat-alino, born February 10, 1908, far too trong and sturdy for him. The latter's ushing tactics and inside work be-ildered the foreigner.

When Battalino outgrew the class, elimination was staged both by ew York and the National Boxing ssociation, with Tommy Paul gain-g N.B.A. support through his victory er Johnny Pena in Detroit, May 26, 32, and Kid Chocolate of Havana, uba, receiving New York's blessing hen he knocked out Lew Feldman the twelfth round. But when Fred-e Miller on January 13, 1933, out-inted Paul to win the N.B.A. crown, ocolate relinquished his claim to ter the junior lightweight class.

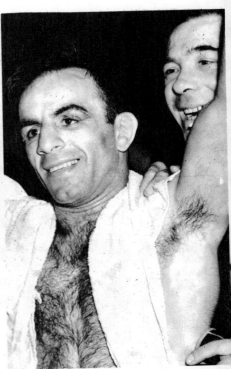

Petey Sarron, who won the title from Miller, boxed from 1928 to 1939. In 97 bouts he won 71, with only 17 knockouts.

Freddie Miller, born on April 3, 1911, in Cincinnati, Ohio, was one of the ring's busiest boxers. From 1928 to 1940 he engaged in 237 fights, winning 199. After losing a title bout to Bat Battalino in 1931, he gained the crown by defeating Tommy Paul in 1933. Freddie is shown above reading a cable from America in his Liverpool, England, hotel room, following his victory over Nel Tarleton in 1934.

Henry Armstrong (below, right) knocked out Petey Sarron for the first of three titles. Armstrong, kayoed in his first pro bout in 1931, had an indifferent record until 1937 when he scored 26 knockouts in 27 bouts, including that with Sarron and won one decision. He then went after the light and welterweight titles.

Freddie went abroad and proceeded to clean up the cream of foreign contenders in travels about Europe. There he lost only two out of thirty battles and received universal recognition as champion. His campaign was very similar to that of Tommy Burns in the heavyweight division many years before him.

On May 11, 1936, in Washington, D. C., Miller was defeated by Petey Sarron, born in Birmingham, Alabama, and Petey became the wearer of the crown. Sarron, like Miller, was a world traveller. He was a very active boxer who took part in more than 100 contests in many parts of America, England, and South Africa.

It was in Johannesburg, after he had won a twelve rounds decision from Miller in what was designated a world championship bout, that "The Ring Editor," following the rise of Henry Armstrong to fistic heights, arranged with Mike Jacobs to bring Sarron back to the States and pit Armstrong against him in a title bout. Sarron received a guarantee of $37,500.

The bout was fought in Madison

Mike Belloise, New York's featherweight champion, fought from 1932 to 1947.

Harry Jeffra, former bantam champ, lost the featherweight crown to Archibald.

Joey Archibald defeated Belloise for the title in 1938, lost it to Jeffra in 1940, and regained it in 1941. Joey entered the ring in 1932 and quit in 1943.

Chalky Wright became champion when he knocked out Archibald. Wright's career extended from 1928 to 1948. He had 124 battles, won 36, and stopped 52 men.

Square Garden, October 29, 1937, with Armstrong winning by a knockout in the sixth round. It was Mike Jacobs' first affair as promoter in Madison Square Garden.

Armstrong didn't defend his crown. He decided to go for higher laurels. He had his eyes on the welterweight and lightweight titles. These he won, as already stated, and after gaining the lightweight championship he gave up the title he had won from Sarron.

Following Armstrong's abdication of the throne, the New York State Commission put its stamp of approval on a contest between Mike Belloise, New York featherweight champion, and Joey Archibald, born December 5, 1915, of Providence, Rhode Island. This was to decide Henry's successor. Archibald, recognized by the N.B.A. as its outstanding challenger, defeated Belloise in fifteen rounds in the St. Nicholas Club of New York and gained international recognition.

Then came a bout between him and Harry Jeffra of Baltimore. Jeffra, born November 30, 1914, won in fifteen rounds on May 20, 1940. He lost the title back to Archibald in Washington, via a decision on May 12, 1941, after which, on September 11 of that year, Chalky Wright knocked out Archibald in the eleventh round in the Capitol City to gain top honors. Wright, who saw the light of day on February 10, 1912, at Durango, Mexico, had his crown vacated by the N.B.A. when he refused to meet Petey Scalzo of New York, born August 1, 1917, and the National Boxing Association declared him the title holder. But in the eyes of the fight enthusiasts, there was no doubt Archibald was the rightful owner when he regained it from Jeffra and that the crown then passed on to Wright.

As a result of this dispute, when Scalzo was knocked out in five rounds by Richie Lemos, a Los Angeles boy, born February 6, 1920, the N.B.A. recognized him as new champion. That bout took place on July 1, 1941. The following November, Lemos lost his title to Jackie Wilson, born in 1909 in Arkansas. Wilson was heralded as king of the division by his backers, but Wright still was generally recog-

349

The NBA featherweight champs, who defeated one another in succession, are *(above, left to right)* Pete Scalzo, of New York; Richie Lemos, of California; Jackie Wilson, of Pittsburgh. *(Below)* Jackie Callura of Canada and Phil Terranova of New York. They all claimed the crown, but Chalky Wright was the rightful champion.

Sal Bartolo *(above)* was the last of the NBA champs, after whipping Terranova. Sal was beaten by Willie Pep in 1943.

Willie Pep *(below, right)* defeated Chalky Wright for the crown on November 20, 1942, and again in 1944. Pep, who started his pro career in 1940, is still active in the ring and is rated among the world's greatest featherweights of all time.

nized as champion and when on November 20, 1942, Willie Pep defeated Chalky in Madison Square Garden, one of the greatest feathers of all time was acknowledged head of the division by the New York Commission and soon received popular approval.

On January 18, 1943, Jackie Wilson lost his N.B.A. crown to Jackie Callura of Canada and from him the N.B.A. title passed on to Phil Terranova of New York by a knockout in eight rounds. Then followed Sal Bartolo, of Boston, Massachusetts, who on March 10, 1944, whipped Phil in fifteen rounds. These bouts were all for N.B.A. laurels only.

Through all this confusion, the one who received the greatest world support was Pep. Willie, born in Middletown, Connecticut, September 19, 1922, takes his place among the greatest feathers of all time.

Clever, sharp, a beautiful boxer, a good hitter, exceedingly expert in countering, side-stepping, blocking and feinting, Pep for many years remained unexcelled. He started his career as an amateur, winning several titles, then turned pro and won sixty-two fights in a row before losing his first fight to lightweight Sammy Angott. After that loss he won all his

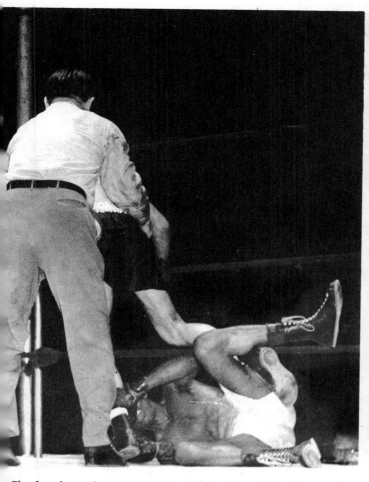

The fourth Sandy Saddler-Willie Pep featherweight title match on September 26, 1951, turned into a wild boxing-wrestling contest. Both were guilty of thumbing and fouling. In the sixth and eighth rounds *(above)* they wrestled to the mat, with Pep winning both falls. Sandy opened a deep cut over Pep's right eye in the second round and floored Willie with a left. Pep squatted in the corner *(below)* as referee Ray Miller tolled off a count of eight.

bouts except a draw with Jimmy McAllister, until he was stopped by Sandy Saddler in 1948, a total of 134 victories out of 136 bouts. With the second knockout by Saddler, Pep had engaged in a total of 156 fights, of which he lost one, drew in one, and was stopped twice.

To clinch his claim to world honors, Pep whipped the N.B.A. champion, Sal Bartolo; beat Wright in a return match; and took the measure of Terranova, Jock Leslie, and Humberto Sierra, each of whom questioned his right to top honors.

Pep gave many scintillating performances as champion. His record stands out among the members of his division. To add to his unique career, he served in the U. S. Army and then in the Navy during the Second World War. Though he was badly injured in an airplane accident and was refused a renewal of his license by the New York Commission, as late as 1957

Saddler retained his title, when Pep (left) failed to come out for the 10th round. As confusion reigned in Pep's corner as to whether he could continue or not, one of the judges, Arthur Aidala (above), listens to boisterous accusations by Saddler's manager, Charley Johnston, of being influenced in judging by Dr. Vincent Nardiello, the boxing commission physician. At the left of Aidala is George Bannon, the official timekeeper, who has served in that capacity for more than 50 years.

he was still engaged in boxing in N.B.A. states.

Saddler, born in Boston, Massachusetts, June 25, 1926, started his career as a flyweight. He won twenty-eight out of thirty-eight of his first fights as a pro by knockouts. He defeated the champions of seven countries before winning the world crown by a knockout in the fourth round. He was not a clever boxer, but a strong, sturdy, two-fisted, rough battler who was accused by his opponents and the public of engaging in unfair tactics to win his bouts. Like Saron and Miller, he fought in many parts of the world.

In a return contest with Pep on February 11, 1949, in Madison Square Garden, he lost his crown by a decision in fifteen rounds, but regained it in a third bout on September 26, 1951, at the Yankee Stadium, stopping Willie in the eighth round of a rough affair in which Pep, with a shoulder injury, couldn't continue.

After Willie Pep's eye was cut open in the second round, he staggered Sandy with a right to the jaw (above) and then landed 13 straight blows without a return.

Hogan (Kid) Bassey, born in 1932 in Nigeria, is the new featherweight champion. He started his boxing career in 1949.

Cherif Hamia, the European featherweight champion, was driven into the ropes (above) and knocked out by Kid Bassey, who then became the undisputed featherweight champion. Bassey's most important win in America was over Willie Pep.

Miguel Berrios, who was defeated by Kid Bassey for the crown, has since retired from the ring because of an eye injury.

Carmelo Costa, lost to Berrios in the elimination tournament in 1957. Costa, born in 1934, started boxing in 1952.

Board of the Boxing Commission, he abdicated his throne. Named for an elimination were Miguel Berrios of Puerto Rico; Hogan Kid Bassey of Calabar, Nigeria, British Empire Champion; Carmelo Costa of Brooklyn; and Cherif Hamia of France, champion of Europe. Berrios beat Costa, and Bassey defeated Berrios. Then Hamia, who had drawn a bye, faced Bassey in Paris, France, on June 24, 1957, and was knocked out in the tenth round. With that victory, Bassey, born June 3, 1932, became Saddler's successor.

After a three-round kayo of Ricardo Moreno on April 1, 1958, Bassey had two important non-title bouts in the United States—against Willie Pep in Boston on September 20 and Carmelo Costa in New York on October 31. Out-maneuvered by Willie Pep in the early going, Bassey's heavy fists took their toll on Pep's aging body, and Willie was knocked out in the ninth round. Costa was floored twice in the third round, but was saved by the bell. From then on it was a pursuit, and Bassey chased his man the rest of the way to win a unanimous decision.

When Sandy was inducted in the Army in 1952, Percy Bassett of Philadelphia was named the "Interim Champion" by the N.B.A. But the action of the N.B.A. was not taken seriously by other supervising organizations since Bassett's record was ordinary.

Saddler was badly injured in an automobile accident in the latter part of 1956 and after consultations with members of the Medical Advisory

The United States regained the featherweight title when Davy Moore kayoed Hogan K. Bassey in thirteen rounds on March 18, 1959, in an unusually vicious and bloody battle. The Nigerian was outclassed by the more aggressive, sharper-hitting challenger, who had never before fought more than ten rounds and seemed able to absorb all of Bassey's punches.

Moore lost his title and, two days later, his life, when he met Cuban-born Mexican Sugar Ramos on March 21, 1963, for the sixth defense of his title.

The bout was close through nine rounds. In the tenth, Moore landed a left hook that sent Ramos into the

After losing the featherweight title to Davey Moore in March, 1959, on a 13-round knockout, Hogan (Kid) Bassey attempted to regain his laurels five months later only to suffer the same fate, this time in the 11th round. Moore (*right*) connects with elbow to Bassey's brow and below, Bassey lands on seat of his pants in fourth. Bassey's closed eye and deep cut shows why bout was halted, while Moore has arm raised.

ropes. The Cuban came back with a rush, and after dropping Moore twice, Ramos let loose a furious two-fisted attack that sent the dazed and hurt Moore through the ropes as the bell rang. At this point referee George Latte halted the fight. An hour after the fight was over, Moore collapsed into a coma. He never regained consciousness.

After three successful defenses, Ramos was worn down and beaten to a pulp in the tenth and eleventh rounds of a bout on September 26, 1964, against fellow Mexican Vicente Saldivar. When the 124-pound Ramos was unable to answer the twelfth-round bell, twenty-one-year-old Saldivar, at 125 pounds, became the featherweight champion of the world.

Saldivar, a southpaw who had been

Moore had been champion for four years when he took on Ultiminio (Sugar) Ramos, in a bout which would end in tragedy. Above is a scene from the video tape showing Moore's head striking the lower rope after he was knocked down by Ramos in the 10th. Below we see Moore slumped over the middle strand as referee George Latka stops the bout. Moore, who went into a coma, never regained consciousness, died two days later.

called a pocket-version Rocky Marciano, successfully defended his title six times over the ensuing three years before retiring from the ring in 1967.

In 1964 he kayoed Fino Rosales of Mexico in eleven rounds. The following year he kayoed Raul Rojas in fifteen rounds at Los Angeles and won a fifteen-round decision over Howard Winstone of Wales. During 1966 he defended the title twice, knocking out Floyd Robertson in two rounds and beating Mitsunori Seki of Japan in fifteen.

Johnny Famechon, a twenty-three-

Ramos more than met his match in the person of Vincente Saldivar, a southpaw, who administered a terrible beating to the Cuban.

(*Right*) Saldivar is on the attack against Japan's Mitsunori Seki, whom he defeated twice, once by knockout, in championship bouts.

Floyd Robertson of Ghana was another Saldivar victim, along with Fino Rosales, Raul Rojas and Howard Winstone, beaten thrice.

year-old Australian, was awarded a disputed decision over Spain's José Legra in a fifteen-round bout in London on January 21, 1969, for the vacant world title. He lost it again four months later, when the stronger and more aggressive Saldivar returned to the ring and regained the crown on May 9 by a unanimous decision. The following day, Famechon announced his retirement.

In a stunning upset, the 125-pound Saldivar was knocked out by Japan's 126-pound Kuniaki Shibata on December 11, 1970, when the bloodied defending champion failed to come out for the fourteenth round.

Mexico's Clemente Sanchez, in one of the best showings of his career and his only fight in a year, battered Shibata out of action at 2:26 of the third round on May 19, 1972, in

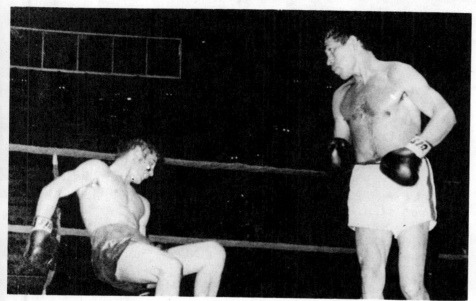

After his third victory over Winstone, Saldivar retired. Johnny Famechon (*above*) won vacant title, beating José Legra.

Saldivar launched a comeback in 1969, which culminated in his regaining his old title on a 15-round win over Famechon.

The Mexican's second reign was shortlived, however, for in his very first defense, Saldivar (*below*) was halted in 13 rounds by Kuniaki Shibata of Japan (*below, left*) at Tijuana, Mexico. Saldiver, quit in 1973.

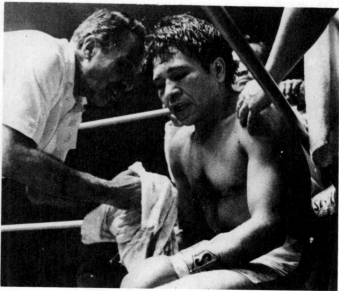

357

The 126-pound title again changed hands, once more via the knockout route, when Clemente Sanchez KO'd Shibata in three.

Tokyo. Both men scaled 126.

On the day of the Sanchez-Legra match at Monterey, December 16, 1972, Sanchez appeared at the weigh-in to announce that he could not make the weight and was vacating the title. It was decided that the bout would go on, but as a nontitle fight.

When Legra kayoed Sanchez in the tenth round, the World Boxing Council recognized him as champion, while the W.B.A. awarded its portion of the

Hard-hitting Ruben Olivares (bottom right), the ex-bantam champion, stopped Zensuke Utagawa (below) for the vacant W.B.A. crown after the retirement of Ernesto Marcel.

world title to Ernesto Marcel, of Panama, who had defeated Antonio Gomez on August 19, 1972, for the W.B.A. title.

Marcel retired in June 1974, having defended his title four times. At this point the W.B.A. named Ruben Olivares, former bantamweight champion, and Zensuke Utagawa, of Japan, to meet for the title. On July 9, 1974, Olivares kayoed Utagawa in the seventh round at Los Angeles.

Olivares lost his title to Alexis Arguello, of Nicaragua, who knocked him out in the thirteenth round in 1975, and Arguello successfully defended three times in 1975, getting a decision against Leonel Hernandez of Venezuela, stopping Roberto Riasco of Panama in the second, and knocking out Royal Kobayashi of Japan in

the fifth in Tokyo. At the end of 1976, however, Arguello gave up his W.B.A. title to compete in the Junior-Lightweight class.

Meanwhile, Eder Jofre, of Brazil, another former bantam champ, had won a fifteen-round split decision over Legra on May 5, 1973, in Brasilia, to win the W.B.C. version of the crown.

Jofre went on to defend his W.B.C. title with a four-round kayo over Saldivar on October 20, 1973, in Sao Paulo, Brazil.

When Jofre refused to fight Venezuela's Alfredo Marcano, the W.B.C. took away Jofre's title in June 1974 and named Marcano and U.S. champion Bobby Chacon as the contenders.

Three months later, on September 7, Chacon knocked out Marcano in

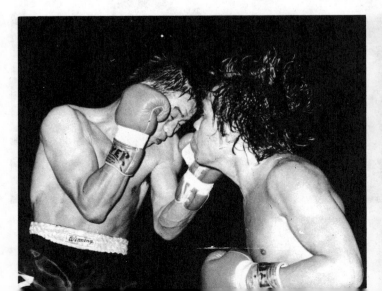

nine torrid rounds at Caracas and became the W.B.C. featherweight champion.

After defeating Jesus Estrada of Mexico with a second-round knockout in 1975, Chacon lost his title to the former W.B.A. champion, Ruben Olivares who stopped him in the second. Olivares' reign as W.B.C. champion lasted only three months, and in September 1975 he lost a decision to British Commonwealth champion David Kotei of Ghana.

Kotei kept his W.B.C. title until November 6, 1976, when he was outpointed by Danny Lopez (USA) before his own people in Accra. Lopez successfully defended his crown by stopping Jose Torres in seven rounds at Los Angeles on September 13, 1977, and on February 15, 1978, again beat Kotei, this time stopping him in six rounds at Las Vegas. On April 23 he disposed of Brazilian challenger, Jose De Paula in six rounds at Los Angeles. On September 15, at New Orleans, he kept his crown by knocking out Juam Malvarez in two rounds and on October 21 he won over Fel Clemente, who was disqualified in round four at Pessaro.

Meanwhile, the W.B.A. filled its vacant featherweight throne when Rafael Ortega outpointed Francisco Coronado at Panama City on January 15, 1977, but on December 12 he lost the title to Cecilio Lastra on a points verdict at Torrelavega. On April 16, 1978, Eusebio Pedroza became champion by stopping Lastra in thirteen rounds at Panama and he kept the title throughout the year by first stopping Ernesto Herrera in twelve rounds at Panama on July 2 and outpointing Enrique Solis, of Puerto Rico, at San Juan on November 27. Pedro made his third successful W.B.A. title defence on January 9, 1979, when he forced Royal Kobayashi (Japan) to retire in the thirteenth round at Tokyo.

He made three further defences in 1979, knocking out Hector Carrasquilla (Panama) in the eleventh; Ruben Olivares (Mexico) in the twelfth; and Johnny Aba (Papua) in the eleventh. In 1980 he continued his demolition of W.B.A. challengers by defeating Shig Nemoto (Japan) on points in 15 rounds; Kim Sa Wang (S. Korea), knocked out in the ninth; and Rocky Lockridge (U.S.A.) on points over 15 rounds.

Danny Lopez kept his W.B.C. title throughout 1979, knocking out Roberto Castanon (U.S.A.) in the second; Mike Ayala (U.S.A.) in the fifteenth; and Jose Caba (Dominica) in the third. On February 2, 1980 he was beaten by 21-year-old Salvador Sanchez (Mexico) who stopped him in 13 rounds at Phoenix, Arizona. Then, after outpointing Ruben Castillo (U.S.A.) over 15 rounds, at Tucson, Arizona on April 12, Sanchez gave Lopez a chance to recover the W.B.C. crown, but stopped him in 14 rounds at Las Vegas on June 21. On September 13 he made his third defence by outpointing Patrick Ford (Guyana) over 15 rounds at San Antonio. On December 13 at El Paso, Sanchez kept his crown by outpointing Juan Laporte (Brooklyn).

Sanchez was proving a truly great champion. On March 22, 1981 he made his fifth successful defence, stopping Roberto Castanon (Spain) in ten rounds at Las Vegas. On August 1, in the same ring, he disposed of Wilfredo Gomez (Puerto Rico), the reigning W.B.C. super-bantam (or light-feather) champion, in eight rounds. On December 12 at Houston, Pat Cowdell, the British champion, gave him a very close fight before losing on a split points decision. On May 8, 1982 the talented Mexican outpointed Jorge Garcia (U.S.A.) at Dallas and on July 21 stopped British Commonwealth champion, Azumah Nelson (Ghana) in the 15th and final round at New York. Twenty-two days later the fistic world was shocked to learn that Sanchez had been killed in a car crash near Queretaro, north of Mexico City. In 46 pro bouts he had scored 44 wins (32 inside the distance) with one draw and one points loss. He was only 23.

The tragedy left vacant the W.B.C. version of the world featherweight title and on September 15, 1982 Juan La Porte (Puerto Rico) became the new champion by stopping Mario Miranda (Colombia) in ten rounds at New York. He twice put his title at stake in 1983, outpointing Ruben Castillo (U.S.A.) over the new stipulated distance of 12 rounds on February 20 at San Juan, and Johnny de la Rosa (Dominica) in the same ring on June 25. His reign came to an end on March 31, 1984 when Wilfredo Gomez (Puerto Rico), former undefeated W.B.C. light-featherweight champion, made a comeback

Ghana's Azumah Nelson *(left)* exploding a left on the head of Irving Mitchell. Nelson won the W.B.C title in 1984.

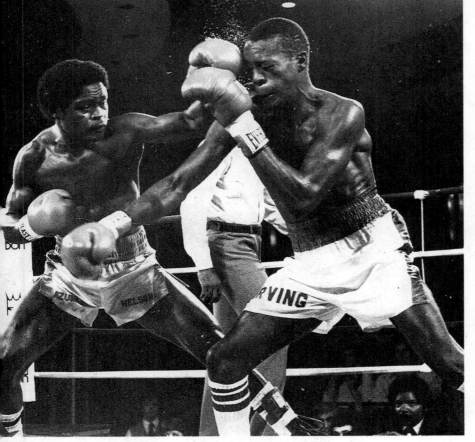

with a second bid for the heavier title and won on points at San Juan. Nine months later, on December 8, the 28-year-old Gomez had to give way under the hammering fists of Azumah Nelson, who stopped him in 11 rounds, also at San Juan. In his first title defence the Ghana boy knocked out Juvenal Ordonez (Chile) in five rounds at Miami, then he scored a lightning victory over Pat Cowdell (G.B.) who was knocked spark out in 2 minutes 24 seconds at Birmingham on October 12, 1985. In 1986 he continued his winning ways with a rare points win against Marcos Villasana (Mexico) at Los Angeles on February 25, and stopping Danilo Cabrera (Dominican Republic) at San Juan on June 22, the referee halting the proceedings.

Meanwhile Eusebio Pedroza continued his merry W.B.A. way during 1981, disposing of three challengers inside the scheduled distance. His 11th successful defence was at Panama City on February 14 when he knocked out Patrick Ford (Guyana) in 13 rounds. On August 1 he did the same to Carlos Pinango (Venezuela) in the seventh round at Caracas and on December 5 defeated Bashew Sibaca (South Africa) in five rounds at Panama City. Juan La Porte suffered a points reverse at Atlantic City on January 24, 1982, but Bernard Taylor (U.S.A.) held the champion to a 15 rounds draw at Charlotte, Carolina, on October 16. The following year, on April 24, Rocky Lockridge (U.S.A.) was outpointed at San Remo (Italy), while on October 22, at St. Vincent, Jose Caba (Dominica) also suffered a points defeat.

It seemed that the clever Pedroza would go on for ever, but there were signs that he was slowing down as there was only one title defence in 1984, Angel Mayor (Venezuela) staying the distance but losing on points before his home supporters at Maracarbo on May 27. Jorge Lujan, W.B.A. champion at bantamweight 1977-79, was the next challenger and he too stayed the scheduled course and lost on points on February 2, 1985 at Panama City. For his 20th title defence – a remarkable record – Eusebio was tempted to London to meet Barry McGuigan, the British and Euro-

pean featherweight champion.

At 24 the Irishman was unbeaten in four years of pro fighting, except for an eight rounds points set-back in his third paid bout. He had won the British title at the beginning of 1983 and the E.B.U. crown near the end of the year. Of his 27 bouts, 24 had been won on knockouts or stoppages, his devastating punching, especially left hooks to the body and rights to the jaw giving him many early victories. When it seemed that he was in world class, his mentors selected progressive rated opponents and in 1984 he saw off Jose Caba (who had gone 15 rounds with the reigning champion) at Belfast on April 4 in an official eliminator for the world title; Esteban Egula (Spain) for the European crown, knocked out in the third at the Albert Hall, London, on June 5; Paul De Vorse (U.S.A.), stopped in five rounds on June 30; Felipe Orozco (Colombia) stopped in two rounds on October 13; and Slough challenger Clyde Ruan, knocked out in the fourth in a dual title defence on December 19, the last three contests taking place in Belfast.

McGuigan really came into his own in 1985. On February 23 he outpointed

former W.B.C. featherweight champion Juan La Porte at Belfast after a hard bout, but a win which clinched a title contest on June 8 with Pedroza for the W.B.A. crown. This produced a mammoth crowd in the open air at Shepherd's Bush, London, which was thrilled with delight as the forceful Irishman carved his way to victory in an exciting 15-rounder to win an indisputable points decision. He proved himself a fighting champion by defending his title against Bernard Taylor (U.S.A.) on September 28 at Belfast. For three rounds the American outboxed the Irishman, but thereafter he was forced to take a systematic hammering that caused him to retire in his corner after the eighth round. McGuigan promptly relinquished his two minor titles to concentrate on defending his world throne.

He achieved this successfully on February 15, 1986 at Dublin, the referee coming to the aid of Danilo Cabrera (Dominican Republic) in the 14th round, but travelling to Las Vegas on June 23, he was outpointed over 15 rounds in great heat by Steve Cruz (Texas).

Eusebio Pedroza *(left)*, a great champion for seven years, lost his W.B.A. title to a worthy challenger in Barry McGuigan in London in 1985.

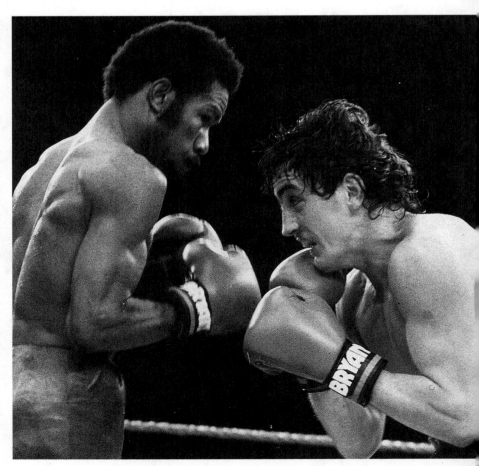

Azumah Nelson of Ghana won the W.B.C. championship in 1984 and beat all challengers until 1987.

The new W.B.A. champion did not wear his laurels for very long. On his home ground of Fort Worth, on March 6, 1987, he took on the Venezuelan, Antonio Esparragoza, and was beaten in 12 rounds, when the referee stopped the fight. That summer, on July 26, the title-holder returned to Texas and faced the challenge of Pascual Aranada, at Houston, and completely demolished his man when he scored a knockout in the 10th round.

Esparragoza's next defence was not easy, however. After an exciting battle which swayed from one to the other he was given a draw with Mexico's Marcos Villasana, one judge voting for each, the third unable to split them. But Villasana had had a point deducted in the fifth round for a low blow, and this made the difference between victory and a draw for him. Esparragoza went on to record five more successful defences with wins against Jose Marmolejo (knockout, eighth), Mitsuru Sugiya (knockout, tenth), Jean-Marc Reynard (knockout, sixth), Eduardo Montoya (knockout, fifth) and Chan-Mok Park (points) before he was outpointed in Kwangju, South Korea, on March 30, 1991 by the local Yung-Kyun Park.

The very day after Esparragoza had won the W.B.A. championship, Azu-mah Nelson, the hard-punching W.B.C. king, continued his winning ways when he knocked out Mauro Gutierrez in 6 rounds at Las Vegas on March 7, and on August 29 he took on Marcos Villasana for a second time. The bout again took place at Los Angeles, and once again the dangerous little man from Ghana was unable to put his man away. He was awarded a unanimous points decision, but the crowd voiced its displeasure at the verdict. Nelson now felt that he would be stronger and more comfortable in the super-featherweight division, and he reluctantly relinquished his W.B.C. title.

The I.B.F. had come on to the featherweight scene in 1984, when the third ruling body gave its blessing to a bout at Seoul, South Korea, when the local Min-Keun Oh was matched with Joko Arter, for March 4. Two rounds sufficed for the Korean to dispose of his opponent, and he then went on to outpoint Kelvin Lampkin and Irving Mitchell, to the delight of Oriental crowds, before he crossed gloves with fellow-countryman Ki-Yung Chung and was stopped in the very last session of a 15-rounder, on November 29, 1985. The new kingpin made two successful defences, versus Tyrone Jackson and Richard Savage before Antonio Rivera of Puerto Rico forced him to retire in the 10th round of a bout at Osan, South Korea, on August 30, 1986. Gamaches was the scene of Rivera's first defence, and he received a shock on January 23, 1988, taking an unexpected beating at the hands of Pennsylvania's Calvin Grove and being halted in the 4th round after having his challenger on the boards and the verge of a knockout defeat.

Grove outpointed Myron Taylor but lost the title to Jorge Paez of Mexico, who outpointed him on August 4, 1988 at Mexicali. The local challenger floored Grove three times in the 15th round to edge the decision – two judges being narrowly for him while one had it level. Paez proved a good champion, although given to histrionics in the ring as well as wild costumes and exotic haircuts. He knocked out Grove in the 11th round in the Mexicali return and then kept his title with a draw with Louie Espinosa in Phoenix. He outpointed former cham-pion Steve Cruz, knocked out Jose Mario Lopez and stopped Lupe Gutier-rez. He then won a points verdict after a terrific battle with Troy Dorsey.

Meanwhile the W.B.O. had insti-tuted their version of the title and it had been won on January 28, 1989 by Italy's Maurizio Stecca, the 1984 Olympic ban-tameweight champion, who stopped Pedro Nolasco in Milan. But after stop-ping Angel Mayor, Stecca was deposed by Louie Espinosa who stopped him in the seventh in Rimini on November 11, 1989. Having already drawn with Paez, Espinosa now met him with both I.B.F. and W.B.O. titles at stake. On April 7, 1990 at Las Vegas Paez won on points. Dorsey was a natural challenger for these titles and the pair had another terrific battle on July 8, this time the judges being unable to separate them. Paez remained the champion, but relin-quished the I.B.F. and W.B.O. crowns to campaign at a higher weight.

Meanwhile, after Azumah Nelson had given up the W.B.C. title, the new champion was Jeff Fenech, the unbea-ten Australian, who won his third world title by stopping Victor Callejas of Puerto Rico in his native Sydney on March 7, 1988. Fenech made three defences. Tyrone Downes and George Navarro were both stopped in the fifth round and Marcos Villasana was out-pointed, all these contests being in Melbourne. Fenech, still unbeaten, then followed Nelson up into the junior lightweights.

On June 2, 1990 Marcos Villasana was matched with Paul Hodkinson of Great Britain for the vacant title, and, after leading early, Hodkinson suffered cuts around the eyes and was stopped in the eighth round. Villasana then stopped fellow-Mexican Javier Marquez and Colombian Rafael Zuniga, and out-pointed Ricardo Cepeda of Puerto Rico before meeting Hodkinson again in Bel-fast on November 13, 1991. This time Hodkinson's eyes stood the test and he emerged a clear points winner after a punishing battle. Hodkinson had an easy first defence in stopping ex-cham-pion Steve Cruz, and a harder one with Frenchman Fabrice Benichou, who was eventually stopped in the tenth. Richardo Cepeda lasted four rounds in

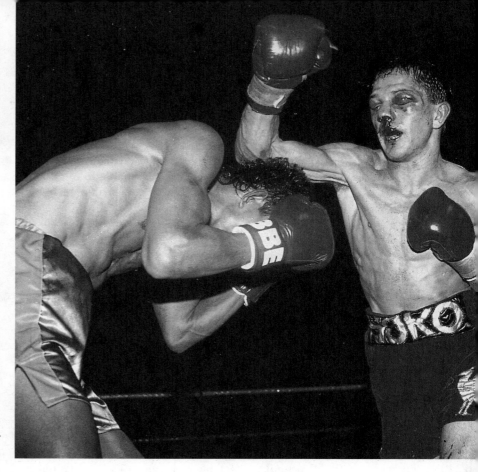

London on February 3, 1993. Hodkinson lost his title on April 28, 1993, in Dublin, when he encountered a brilliant Mexican champion, Gregorio 'Goyo' Vargas, the son of a former pro boxer. Hodkinson built up a lead and was ahead on all cards at the finish, but it was the cool boxing of Vargas which turned the fight with an assault in the sixth round and a stoppage in the seventh.

Yung-Kyun Park, the South Korean who won the W.B.A. title in 1991, proved a long-lasting champion. Fighting mostly in Korea he built up a list of beaten challengers: in 1991, Masuaki Takeda (Japan, stopped sixth) and Eloy Rojas (Venezuela, points); in 1992, Seiji Asakawa (Japan, knockout ninth), Koji Matsumoto (Japan, stopped 11th), Giovanni Nieves (Venezuela, points) and Ever Beleno (Venezuela, points); in 1993, Thanomjit Kiatkriengkrai (Thailand, stopped fourth).

The new I.B.F. champion after Jorge Paez relinquished the title was Troy Dorsey (U.S.A.), who had given Paez two hard fights. He scored a first-round knockout of Alfred Rangel at Las Vegas on June 3, 1991 but was then outpointed by a Mexican, Manuel Medina, at Los Angeles on August 12. Medina was only 20 but had turned pro at 13 and had already had 40 fights, with only three defeats. Medina was the underdog on his first defence, against Tom 'Boom Boom' Johnson of Detroit, on November 18 at Inglewood. An accidental clash of heads in the ninth round caused severe damage to Medina's left eye and the doctor stopped the fight. Medina was ahead on all cards and was awarded a technical decision. Medina outpointed Fabrice Benichou of France on his next defence, stopped Fabrizio Cappai of Italy in Capo d'Orlando and

outpointed Moussa Sangaree of France in Gravelines but lost the title when meeting Tom Johnson again in Melun, France, on February 26, 1993. Johnson won by a split decision, two judges giving it to him, one to Medina.

After Paez gave up the W.B.O. title, it was regained on January 26, 1991 by Maurizio Stecca, who stopped Armando Reyes in the fifth round at Sassari. Stecca outpointed Fernando Ramos of Mexico and Tim Driscoll of Great Britain but on May 16, 1992 was outpointed by Britain's Colin McMillan at Alexandra Palace, London. McMillan was a brilliant boxer who was expected to have a long reign, but on his first defence, against Ruben Palacio of Colombia in London he was stopped in the eighth round. Controversy surrounded the finish because, although McMillan was boxing poorly by his standards, he was ahead on all three cards when he dislocated his left shoulder. His corner argued afterwards that the dislocation was caused by a foul and that the decision should have rested with the judges' scorecards at the time of the stoppage, but the referee's decision to

award Palacio the fight stood.

Palacio's first defence was to have been against another Briton, John Davison, at Washington, Tyne and Wear, but injuries to Palacio twice postponed it. Then, 48 hours before the contest, Palacio failed the HIV test which the British Boxing Board of Control insist upon. As Palacio flew home (his career over, but not knowing at the time the seriousness of his health) the W.B.O. sanctioned Steve Robinson of Wales as a substitute challenger for the now vacant title, despite his poor career record of 13 wins, 9 defeats and a draw. But the fight proved to be an excellent all-action encounter, with a sustained attack by Robinson throughout the last minute of the last round possibly winning him the title: two judges had him a point ahead, while the third gave it to Davison by the same margin. It was an emotional night for Robinson, the first Welsh world champion since Howard Winstone in 1968, and for his manager Dai Gardiner, who left boxing for several years after his boxer Johnny Owen, another Welshman, had died after a world title challenge in 1980.

THE LIGHT-FEATHERWEIGHT CHAMPIONS

On September 22, 1922 at Madison Square Garden, New York, Jack "Kid" Wolfe (Cleveland, Ohio), outpointed former world bantamweight champion, Joe Lynch (New York) in a 15-round contest at 122 pounds (four pounds below the recognized featherweight limit) and advertised as for the junior featherweight championship of the world. Wolfe lost his crown to Carl Duane (U.S.A.) at Long Island on August 29 the following year, but the new champion never defended the title and it passed into obscurity.

It was re-introduced by the World Boxing Council as the super-bantam division on April 3, 1976 when Rigoberto Riasco (Panama) forced Waruinge Nakayama (Japan) to retire at the end of the eighth round at Panama City. Riasco successfully defended his title against Livio Nolasco with a 10th round knockout on June 12 in the same ring, and Dong-Kyun Yun (Korea) on points at Pusan on August 1. He met more than his match on October

10, however, when Kazuo "Royal" Kobayashi (Japan) stopped him in eight rounds at Tokyo. Alas, Kobayashi's hold on the new championship was restricted to 45 days, Dong-Kyun Yun beating him on points at Seoul on November 24. The Korean bested Jose Cervantes (U.S.A.) at Seoul on February 13, 1977, but on May 21 was knocked out in 12 rounds at San Juan by Wilfredo Gomez (Puerto Rico), who was destined to remain titleholder for a very long time.

In the next six years Gomez proved a most destructive fighter, disposing of his 17 challengers, all inside the distance; the one who stayed longest being Leonardo Cruz (Dominica) who lasted into the 13th round at San Juan on September 9, 1978. On May 22, 1983 Gomez reluctantly gave up the title owing to weight-making difficulties, but came back a year later as a featherweight. On June 15, 1983 Jaime Garza (Santa Cruz) knocked out Bobby Berna (Philipinnes) in two rounds at Los Angeles to win the vacant crown. He

defended it on May 26, 1984, knocking out Felipe Orozco (Colombia) in three rounds at Miami. In New York on November 3, 1984 Juan "Kid" Meza (Mexico) scored a 2 minutes 54 seconds win over Garza, after being on the canvas himself in the first 30 seconds of the fight. Meza won his first title defence by stopping Mike Ayala (U.S.A.) in six rounds at Los Angeles on April 19, 1985, but was outpointed by Lupe Pintor, former great bantam champion, over 12 rounds at Mexico City on August 18.

Pintor was champion for only five months, losing on 18 January, 1986, to Samart Payakarun (Thailand), who knocked him out in the fifth round at Bangkok.

Payakarun knocked out Juan Meza in the 10th round in a bout also held at Bangkok, on December 10, but was obliged to concede defeat to Australia's Jeff Fenech, the former holder of the I.B.F.'s bantam belt, when their fight was stopped in 4 rounds at Sydney, on

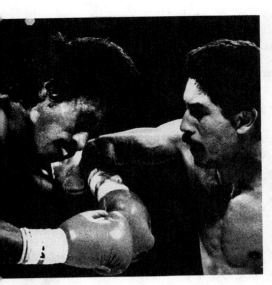

April 8. Again, before his local crowd, Fenech had no trouble with America's Greg Richardson, whom he stopped in 5 rounds. His next defence, against Mexican Carlos Zarate was brought to a close when the boxers clashed heads in the 4th round. Fenech had been ahead on points up to the accident, and he was awarded the decision. Fenech then relinquished the W.B.C. title to campaign as a featherweight.

It was not until November 26, 1977 that the W.B.A. elected to recognize a super-bantamweight class, Soo-Hwan Hong (Korea) knocking out Hector Carrasquilla (Panama) in three rounds at the loser's home town. Hong, who had been world bantam champion in 1974-75, made a successful title defence on February 1, 1978 by outpointing Yu Kassahara (Japan) over 15 rounds at Tokyo, but he was stopped in 12 rounds at Seoul by Ricardo Cardona (Colombia), who proved a long-lasting champion. Cardona outpointed five challengers in the next nineteen months, beating Reuben Valdes (Colombia), Soon-Hyun Chung (South Korea), twice, Yukio Segawa (Japan) and Sergio Palma (Argentina), but on May 4, 1980 he was knocked out by Leo Randolph (U.S.A.) at Seattle.

Randolph's reign lasted only three months, Sergio Palma taking full advantage of a second chance by scoring a knockout win in five rounds at Spokane on August 9. The Argentine boxer left his mark on the division by defending his title successfully against fellow-countryman Ulises Morales with a sixth round knockout on November 8; Leonardo Cruz on points on April 4, 1981; Ricardo Cardona, twelfth round knockout on August 15; Vichit Muangroi-Et on points on October 3; all these fights being staged at Buenos Aires, and Jorge Lujan on points at Cordoba on January 15, 1982. Leonardo Cruz, who had already made two abortive attempts to win the title, made it third time lucky when he outpointed Palma at Miami on June 12, 1982. He defended against Benito Badilla (Chile) with an eight rounds kayo victory on November 13; a points win over Soon-Hyun Chung (Korea) at San Juan on March 16, 1983 and a points win over Cleo Garcia (Nicaragua) at Santa Domingo on August 26.

Going to Italy on February 22, 1984 Cruz was surprisingly forced to retire to Loris Stecca in the 12th round at Milan. The Italian did not reign for long, being knocked out in eight rounds at San Juan by Victor Callejas (Puerto Rico) on May 26. The new champion made a winning first defence by outpointing Seung-Hoon Lee (South Korea) at San Juan on February 2, 1985, while on November 8 he retired Loris Stecca, former champion, in six rounds at Rimini, the Italian's jaw being broken.

Callejas refused to defend his honours against Louie Espinosa, of Arizona, and forfeited his claim to the belt. On January 16, 1987, Espinosa stopped Tommy Valoy in 4 rounds at Phoenix, his home town, and became the new champion. His next contest, July 15, versus Manuel Vilchez, was stopped in the title-holder's favour in the 15th and last round. He also knocked out Mike Ayala in 9 rounds at San Antonio on August 15. By now, Espinosa entered his bouts as a strong favourite, so it came as something of a surprise when he lost his honours on points, this time over 12 rounds, to Juan Gervacio, at San Juan.

Gervacio, a Dominican, found his tenure at the top a fairly brief one.

February 29, 1988 saw his defeat at San Juan against the Venezuelan, Bernardo Pinango. It was a very close contest, and only a knockdown in the 12th and final round clinched the verdict for the challenger.

Pinango also lost on his first defence, Juan J. Estrada of Mexico outpointing him at Tijuana. Estrada strung together some defences, stopping Takuya Muguruma and Jesus Poll, and outpointing Luis Mendoza, before he was disqualified in the ninth round against Jesus Salud (U.S.A.) at Los Angeles on December 11, 1989. Salud then forfeited W.B.A. recognition for failing to defend against Luis Mendoza.

The I.B.F. recognised this intermediate division when Bobby Berna was matched with Seung-In Suh for December 4, 1983, at Seoul. Berna forced his man to retire in 11 rounds, but in a return engagement at the same venue on April 15 of the following year, the South Korean reversed matters by knocking out his opponent in 10 rounds.

Seung-In Suh put Cleo Garcia down for the count in 4 rounds, again at Seoul, on July 8, before succumbing himself in the 10th to fellow-South Korean Ji-Won Kim on January 3, 1985. The new champion had a good run of title defences, defeating Ruben Palacios, Bobby Berna, Seung-In Suh again, and Rudy Casicas, all in South Korean rings, before he went into retirement and relinquished his belt.

Seung-Hoon Lee, another South Korean, knocked out Prayoonsak Muangsurin, of Thailand, in 9 rounds at Pohang on January 18, 1987, and won the vacant championship. The winner established his position soon afterwards, on April 5, when he delighted the Seoul crowd by flattening Jorge Urbina Diaz for the count in 10 rounds. His next victim was Lion Collins, the Filipino, who was stopped in 5 rounds at Pohang on July 19. Also at Pohang, on December 27, Lee won a popular 15-round decision over José Sanabria, of Venezuela.

Lee relinquished the I.B.F. crown to challenge for the W.B.C. crown and, on May 21, 1988 Sanabria won the vacant title by knocking out Moises Fuentes in the fifth round at Bucaramanga. Sanabria was very busy, accepting four challenges in less than a year. He outpointed Vincenzo Belcastro in Italy, and stopped Fabrice Benichou and Thierry Jacob in France, but then was outpointed on March 10, 1989 by Benichou at Limoges.

Benichou defended against two South Africans, beating Franie Badenhorst at Frasnone but losing the title when outpointed by Welcome Ncita in Tel Aviv on March 10, 1990. Ncita made six successful defences; against Ramon

Cruz (stopped, seventh, Rome), Gerardo Lopez (stopped, eighth, Aosta), Jesus Rojas (points, St Vincent), Hurley Snead (points, San Antonio), Jesus Rojas again (points, Sun City) and Jesus Salud (points, Trevilio). Ncita lost the title, however, when Kennedy McKinney, the 1988 Olympic bantamweight champion, knocked him out in the 11th round of an exceptional contest at Tortoli, Sardinia, on 2 December 1992. Ncita was ahead on all three cards when he had McKinney in trouble in the 11th round. McKinney turned his back on the champion and sank to one knee for a mandatory eight count. However when Ncita moved in to finish it off McKinney landed a right flush to the jaw which knocked Ncita flat on his back for the count. McKinney came from behind on his first challenge when he outpointed fellow-American Richard Duran at Sacramento on April 17, 1993. Duran nursed a grievance over a bad decision he claimed to have received against McKinney six years earlier as an amateur and out-fought the champion for the first few rounds. However, he faded badly in the later stages and McKinney took a unanimous decision.

Meanwhile, after Jeff Fenech gave up the W.B.C. title two former bantamweight champions from Mexico fought for it in Los Angeles on February 29, 1988, and Daniel Zaragoza had too much speed and energy for the 36-year-old veteran Carlos Zarate, whom the referee had to rescue in the tenth round. Zaragoza's first challenge was from the popular and talented I.B.F. champion, Seung-Hoon Lee, and Zaragoza held on to his crown with a draw in Youchan, both men having one judge voting for them. Zaragoza found things easier for a while after this, knocking out Valerio Nati, outpointing Paul Banke, stopping Frankie Duarte and outpointing Chan-Yung Park, but he lost the title on April 23, 1990 at Los Angeles when he was stopped after a savage battle in the ninth round in a return with Paul Banke (U.S.A.).

The title now changed hands rapidly. Banke stopped Ki-Jun Lee, but was himself stopped in the fourth round by

Welcome Ncita (right) of South Africa took the I.B.F. light-featherweight crown from Fabrice Benichou in 1990. He defended successfully six times.

March 13, 1993, gaining a unanimous decision over the former W.B.O. champion Jesse Benavides.

When Jesus Salud was stripped of the W.B.A. title in 1990, two Colombians, Luis Mendoza and Ruben Palacio, fought a draw for it at Cartagena, but Mendoza made no mistake in the return and became champion on September 11, 1990 in Miami. Mendoza had a good run, outpointing Fabrice Benichou, stopping Thailand's Noree Jockgym, and knocking out Brazil's Joao Cardosa de Oliveira, before he was outpointed in Los Angeles on October 7, 1991 by Paul Perez of Mexico. Perez's reign was short, as he was stopped in the third by the Puerto Rican Wilfredo Vasquez on March 27, 1992 in Mexico City. Vasquez outpointed Freddy Cruz, and beat off old campaigners and ex-champions in Thierry Jacob (stopped, eighth) and Luis Mendoza (points), both defences being in France.

The W.B.O. title was inaugurated when U.S.A.'s Kenny Mitchell outpointed former W.B.A. champion Julio Gervacio at San Juan on April 29, 1989. He then outpointed a South African challenger, Simon Skosana, but lost the title on a disqualification in Teramo to Italy's Valerio Nati on December 9, 1989. Nati was soon deposed by a Puerto Rican, Orlando Fernandez, who stopped him in the tenth round at Sassari on May 12, 1990. Fernandez was outpointed in turn by Texan Jesse Benavides on May 24, 1991 at Corpus Christi, where Benavides later stopped Fernando Ramos. He put the title on the line in London on October 15, 1992 against Duke McKenzie and was unanimously outpointed by reasonable margins, but nevertheless had some supporters in his claims to have been robbed. McKenzie, however, became the first British boxer in modern times to win world titles at three different weights.

cagey Thierry Jacob, who had been slugged over the head by an assailant a few weeks earlier.

Jacob confidently faced his first challenger in Albany, New York, on June 23, 1992 but was stopped in the second round by Tracy Harris Patterson, the adopted son of former world heavyweight champion Floyd Patterson, who trained him. Patterson went to Berck-sur-Mer for his first defence, and the challenger was the evergreen Daniel Zaragoza again. Patterson appeared fortunate to get a draw in a match where the judges differed wildly, each boxer getting the approval of one judge by a wide margin. Patterson made no mis-

an Argentinian, Pedro Decima, in Los Angeles on November 5, 1990. Four months later Decima took the belt to Nagoya, Japan, and left it with Kiyoshi Hatanaka, who stopped him in the eighth round on February 3. On June 14 the belt was back with Daniel Zaragoza again, as he travelled to Tokyo and won a points verdict. He won another in Seoul over Huh Chun and, back in Los Angeles, had a satisfying points win over old adversary Paul Banke, gaining a unanimous decision. But the 32-year-old southpaw went to Calais for his next defence on March 20, 1992 and was outpointed by another southpaw, the take in Poughkeepsie, however, on

THE BANTAMWEIGHTS

Times have changed in the rugged sock market.

Bantamweights and flyweights, once so popular and prosperous in the American boxing scene, today are a dime a dozen, if that many can be found in America. While throughout the rest of the world, particularly Mexico, the Philippines, Japan among other places in the Orient, and in Great Britain, France and Italy, they constitute the greatest portion of those who make professional boxing their vocation, in the United States they have become practically extinct.

Many of boxing's most illustrious performers were our little men, those who scaled from 100 to 115 pounds. Such ring immortals as George Dixon, Jimmy Barry, Casper Leon, and Tommy Kelly ("The Harlem Spider") reached headline status when they scaled 110 pounds, the bantam limit at the time. Then there were such master mechanics as Harry Harris, "The Bean Stalk champion"; Clarence and Harry Forbes, Johnny Coulon, Frankie Burns, Johnny Buff, Eddie Campi, and Kid Williams. Among others who quickly graduated into the higher divisions but started as bantams were Johnny Dundee, Jimmy McLarnin, Willie Jackson, Lew Tendler, Tony Canzoneri, and the hardest hitter, in the divisions from bantam through lightweight, George K.O. Chaney of Baltimore.

The bantam and flyweight classes hit their peaks of popularity during the lush, flamboyant, post-World War One era of the early twenties, when Tex Rickard, then holding forth in Madison Square Garden, was the kingpin of world promoters and the sport was flourishing all over the land. That was the era when such mighty mites as Joe Lynch, Pete Herman, Memphis Pal Moore, Little Jack Sharkey, Joe Burman, Midget Smith, Earl Puryea, Carl Tremaine, Frankie Jerome, Abe Goldstein, Young Montreal, Bud Taylor, Frankie Genaro, Pancho Villa, Cannonball Eddie Mar-

tin, Charley Phil Rosenberg and Fidel LaBarba, to list only a few of the many, packed the arenas. There was hardly a city, town, or hamlet in the nation in that era that didn't boast of at least one good little fighter.

Gradually the tiny tikes began to fade in both quality and quantity. During the thirties, following the depression, the flyweight class practically disappeared in America though the bantams held out for another decade. Then the decline took place at a rapid rate. When Manuel Ortiz of El Centro, California, born in 1917, went to Johannesburg and on May 31, 1950, lost his world title to Vic Toweel in fifteen rounds, that just about finished the 118 pounders as major factors in the American boxing curriculum.

It is unfortunate indeed that boxing finds the little fellows extinct as major attractions in the United States, since there were few more active divisions in the general international scene than the bantams and flyweights. Three of the greatest fighting men in the classes generally referred to as the gamecock groups were Jimmy Wilde, the "Mighty Atom" from Wales; George Dixon, "Little Chocolate," from Halifax, Nova Scotia; and Pancho Villa, the little "Yellow Man." Born at Iloilo, Philippines, August 1, 1901, Villa was brought from Manila to America by Frank Churchill. Villa put an end to the long and meritorious career of Wilde, then on the down grade. Jimmy was stopped in a hair-raising fight at the Polo Grounds. The Wilde-Villa-Dixon trio furnished the fans with many thrillers that made ring history.

There is no authentic record of the bantamweight division during the London Prize Ring days, but it is generally conceded that Charley Lynch was the American titleholder in 1856 when he went to England and laid

Tommy Kelly, the "Harlem Spider," claimed the bantam title and boxed a nine-round draw with George Dixon, in 1888.

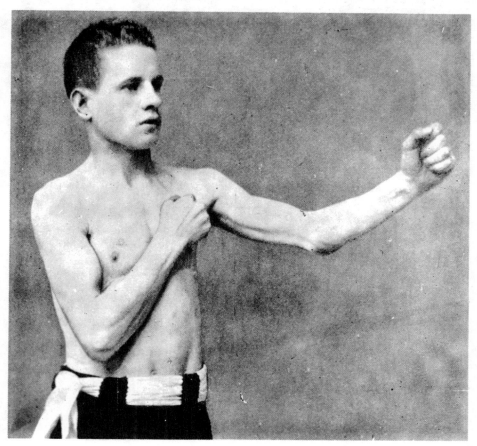

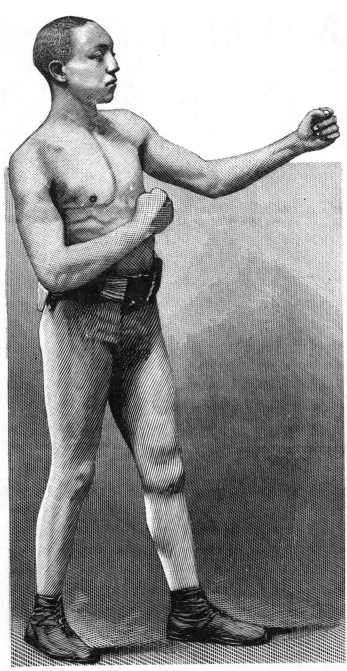

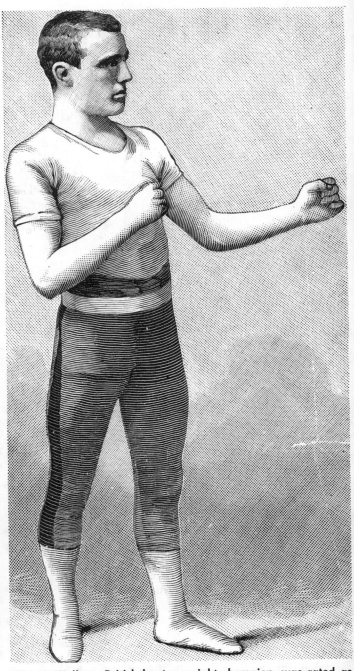

George Dixon, called "Little Chocolate," declared he would meet any challenger for the bantamweight crown, at 112 pounds.

"Nunc" Wallace, British bantamweight champion, was rated as unbeatable. Dixon knocked him out on June 27, 1890, in London.

claim to the world title when he defeated Simon Finighty in forty-three rounds. He then returned to America and retired. The New Yorker weighed 112 pounds.

We next hear of a title bout in the division when Tommy "Harlem Spider" Kelly, a New Yorker, drew with George Dixon in Boston in nine rounds with the weight limit set at 105 pounds. Manager O'Rourke, han-

dling Dixon, claimed the championship for his boy and issued a defi to all comers who contested Dixon's right to the honors to face him at 112 pound limit. The increase in weight was brought on by the inability of Dixon to fight at his best at the lower figures.

In 1890, Dixon engaged Cal McCarthy of New York in a draw of seventy rounds, fighting with two

ounce gloves. Then, with Tom O'Rourke, he sailed for England four months later to box Nunc Wallace, British bantam champion. Dixon in that bout won universal support as bantam king when he halted Wallace in the eighteenth round. He then added Jimmy Murphy to his list of victims, stopping him in the fortieth round in Providence, Rhode Island. With that triumph he vacated the

Jimmy Barry (left) born in Chicago, on March 7, 1870, was an outstanding ringman. In 68 contests, from 1891 to 1899, when he retired, he was never defeated. His meeting in 1897 with the British champion, Walter Croot, in London, ended tragically. Barry's right dropped Croot, whose skull struck the ring floor with such force he died from a brain injury. Barry was exonerated, fought a few more battles, and retired.

Casper Leon (above) was knocked out by Barry for the American title. He was born December 8, 1872, in Palermo, Sicily.

They called him "Terrible Terry" McGovern and the character cartoon (right), by the famous "Tad," most certainly makes him appear so. Terry was compactly built, fast, and packed a middleweight punch. He was born in Johnstown, Pennsylvania, of Irish stock and raised in Brooklyn. As a bantam, from 1897 to 1899, McGovern had 45 battles, winning 22 by knockout. He won the featherweight crown in his first bout in 1900.

bantam throne and set sail for the feather crown.

With Dixon's retirement, Jimmy Barry of Chicago claimed the crown. He and Casper Leon of New York, the best boy in the East, fought at Lamont, Illinois, September 15, 1894, and Barry won by a knockout in the twenty-eighth round and was accepted as new champion in the 112 pound class, then listed as the bantam division.

With the ownership of the title in dispute so far as the British were concerned, Barry accepted a challenge from Walter Croot, British titleholder, fought him in London, December 6,

1897, and knocked him out in the sixteenth round to win the international crown. Croot died the following day from a brain injury.

Barry, upset by the mishap, fought several more times, including a bout with Leon on December 29, 1898, a draw of twenty rounds, and a draw of six with Harry Harris of Chicago the following September, then retired undefeated.

Terry McGovern now claimed the crown based on his fine record, studded with knockouts and decision victories. To gain universal recognition, he agreed to fight Pedlar Palmer of Great Britain and at Tuckahoe,

369

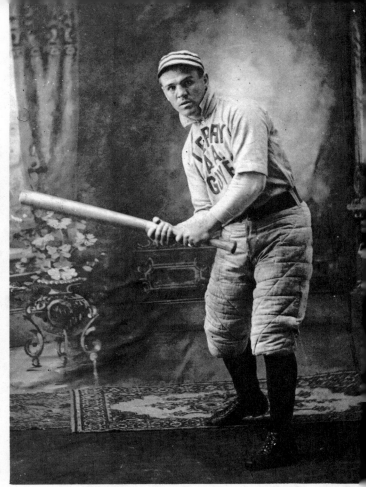

Manager Sam Harris and boxer Terry McGovern were typical fashion plates of their day. After piloting McGovern to two world titles, Harris became a noted producer in the theatrical field.

A great fighter, Terry McGovern was almost as adept at baseball and turned down several offers to play professionally. He often practiced with major league New York and Brooklyn teams.

One of the briefest title bouts in ring history was the international meeting of Pedlar Palmer (left), the British champion, and McGovern, the American representative. With the disputed world bantamweight laurels at stake, Palmer and McGovern met at Tuckahoe, New York, September 12, 1899. The clever Palmer was given no opportunity to display his vaunted skill. Overwhelmed by the rushing, hard-hitting McGovern, he was kayoed in one minute, 15 seconds.

370

How a contemporary artist portrayed the McGovern-Palmer finish. They had started boxing when the timekeeper accidentally hit the bell and referee Siler sent the boxers to their corners for a new start, which ended disastrously for Palmer.

New York, as already told, he knocked out Palmer in the first round. For that fight McGovern raised the weight from 112 to 116 pounds, but since the bout was postponed a day because of rain, they did not weigh in again. McGovern had set a new poundage for the bantam class.

In 1900 McGovern vacated the class to go into the higher sector, and Harry Harris, born in Chicago, Illinois, November 18, 1880, asserted his rights to top honors. Of course his claim was disputed, and to clinch international support he went abroad, won a decision in fifteen rounds from Pedlar Palmer, who was still British champion, and became the recognized king of the class. Like most of his predecessors, he soon became overweight and quit to fight as a feather.

Then Harry Forbes, born in Rockford, Illinois, May 13, 1879, came into

Harry Harris, born in Chicago in 1800, started boxing at 16. He beat Palmer in 1901 and claimed the open bantam title.

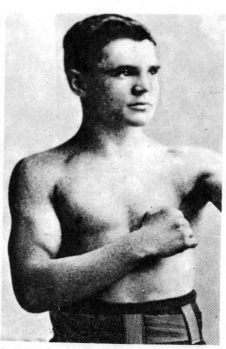

Harry Forbes nominated himself champion when Harris entered the featherweight ranks. Forbes boxed from 1897 to 1912.

371

Jimmy Walsh (left) a scrappy little bantamweight champion, was 5' 2" in height. He was 15 years old for his first bout in 1901 and met all of the top bantams until 1913, when he retired. He was recognized as world champion in 1905, when he defeated the British champ, Digger Stanley.

Frankie Neil (above) stopped Harry Forbes for the title in 1903. He invaded England the following year and lost his laurels to Joe Bowker. During Neil's first five years of boxing, he scored 20 knockouts in 30 bouts. In 1907 he was kayoed by Owen Moran, his only fight of that year. He returned in 1908 and quit late in 1909.

Joe Bowker (left) clearly outpointed Frankie Neil for the world bantamweight crown, before a capacity crowd at the National Sporting Club, in London. Unable to maintain the weight, he relinquished the title shortly after. An extremely clever boxer, Bowker enjoyed a long career—from 1901 to 1919.

the picture. He declared himself the champion and carried on for almost three years when Frankie Neil, of San Francisco, born July 25, 1883, stopped him in the second round in California, August 13, 1903, and became champion.

Neil defended his crown successfully against Billy DeCoursey, whom he halted in fifteen rounds, fought a draw of twenty with Johnny Reagan, knocked out Forbes in three rounds, and headed for London to fight Joe Bowker, then British king. Joe beat him in twenty rounds at 118 pounds, the British weight limit, on October 17, 1904, to become the crown wearer.

With Bowker's retirement, both Digger Stanley of London and Jimmy Walsh of Newton, Massachusetts, claimed the vacated throne. Walsh, born in 1886, fought Stanley in Chelsea, Massachusetts, October 20, 1905,

372

Johnny Coulon (above, left) Canadian-born Chicagoan, rightfully claimed the crown when he twice whipped Kid Murphy in 1908 and twice defeated the British champ, Jim Kendrick, in 1910. Coulon boxed from 1905 to 1917 and 1921.

Kid Williams (above, right) was born in Denmark and reared in Baltimore, Maryland. An aggressive puncher, he met all challengers after knocking out Coulon. Williams' career started in 1910, when he was 27 years old, and ended in 1925.

Johnny "Kewpie" Ertle (right) claimed the title when he won from Williams on a foul in 1915. Most of the boxing authorities ignored his claim and continued to recognize Williams as the champion.

and settled the matter of supremacy by winning in fifteen rounds. By 1907 both had outgrown the class.

In 1908 Kid Murphy of New Jersey claimed the crown as U. S. Champion. He was defeated twice that year in U. S. title bouts at Peoria, Illinois, by Johnny Coulon of Chicago, who was born February 12, 1889 in Toronto, Canada. In 1910 Coulon clinched international support when he defeated British champion Jim Kendrick at New Orleans twice: on February 19 in ten rounds, then on March 6 in the nineteenth round.

Kid Williams, a stocky lad from Baltimore, born December 5, 1893, in Denmark, succeeded Coulon, whom he knocked out in the third round on June 9, 1914, at Vernon, California. He fought a draw of twenty rounds with Frankie Burns of Jersey City in New Orleans in a title bout; drew in twenty with Pete Herman, February

7 of the following year in the same city; then lost the crown to Herman in twenty rounds in New Orleans, January 9, 1917, on a decision by Billy

Rocap, the referee. Williams had lost on a foul to Johnny Ertle of St. Paul on September 10, 1915, but the consensus among the scribes failed to

373

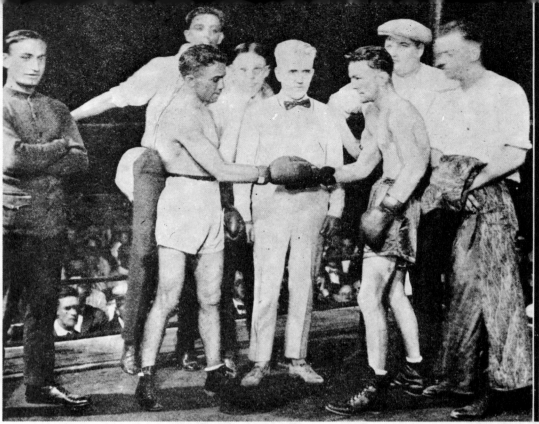

Pete Herman, a fine little ringman out of New Orleans, who fought from 1913 to 1922, gained a 20-round decision and the title from Kid Williams in 1917. Herman held the crown until 1920, dropping it to Joe Lynch in 15 rounds. Posing with Lynch before their return title match in 1921, Herman (above, left) regained the title. In photo on right, Pete waves to cheering fans

Johnny Buff, a 33-year-old New Jersey veteran, won the American flyweight title from Frankie Mason, on February 11, 1921, and on September 23 garnered the bantamweight laurels in a surprise victory over Pete Herman. Buff lost both titles in his only bouts in 1922. He was knocked out by Joe Lynch for the bantam crown and by Pancho Villa for the flyweight title.

sustain Ertle's claim and Johnny never received the honors accorded a champion.

A New Yorker, Joe Lynch, succeeded Herman. He gained the laurels when, after a number of successful title defenses by Herman, the latter lost in fifteen rounds via decision in the old Madison Square Garden. Herman had an excellent record. One of his best bouts was a victory over Frankie Burns in New Orleans, November 5, 1917.

Following World War One, while in England, Herman stopped Jimmy Wilde in seventeen rounds and on July 25 of that year, 1921, he regained the title that he had lost to Lynch on December 22, 1920, by defeating him in Brooklyn, in fifteen rounds. He lost the championship to Johnny Buff, born June 12, 1888 in Perth Amboy, New Jersey, in the old Madison Square Garden on September 23, 1921.

Herman retired, became blind, and in later years was a night club opera-

tor and a member of the Louisiana Boxing Commission.

As in the case of Herman, Joe Lynch regained the title when he knocked out Buff at the New York Velodrome, July 10, 1922, in fourteen rounds. The following year he was matched with Joe Burman. When he refused to go through with the bout, the New York Commission declared the championship vacant and designated Burman and Abe Goldstein to fight for the vacant throne.

Goldstein won but didn't receive the support of world bodies as newly crowned king. A bout was then arranged between Goldstein and Lynch, and the former won the championship by outpointing Joe in fifteen rounds in Madison Square Garden, March 21, 1924. Nine months later, December 19, in the same arena, Cannonball Eddie Martin dethroned Goldstein in fifteen rounds. Goldstein was born in New York in 1900; Martin was born March 3, 1903, in Brooklyn.

On March 20, 1925, Charley Phil

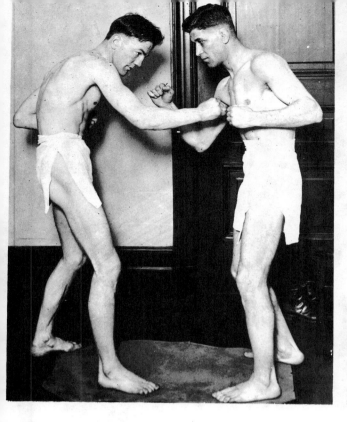

Joe Lynch (*far left*) spars with Abe Goldstein at weighing-in ceremonies for their championship fight in 1924. Goldstein (*above, right*) won the crown in a hard-fought battle. Neighborhood rivalries stimulated excitement in those days. Lynch's followers, from the Irish section of New York's West Side and Goldstein's, from the Jewish section of Harlem, filled Madison Square Garden with constant cheering during the thrilling bout.

Charley Phil Rosenberg, of New York (*below, right*) decisioned Eddie Martin, who held the crown only three months. Although Rosenberg beat Bushy Graham of Utica (*left*), he failed to make the weight and the bantamweight title was declared vacant.

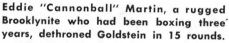

Eddie "Cannonball" Martin, a rugged Brooklynite who had been boxing three years, dethroned Goldstein in 15 rounds.

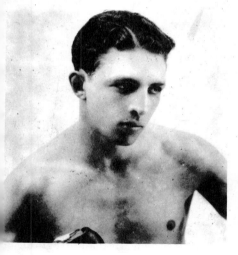

Rosenberg, another New Yorker, born August 15, 1902, relieved Martin of the crown, beating him in fifteen rounds in the Garden. Then on February 4, 1927, Rosenberg was deprived of his laurels when he was unable to make the weight for a championship bout with Bushy Graham, born in Italy, June 8, 1903.

Now came the usual confusion following an abdication or when a

Tragedy marked the rapid climb of Bud Taylor, of Terre Haute, Indiana, to the bantam-weight championship. On January 11, 1924, Taylor *(left, above)* punished Frankie Jerome, of the Bronx, so severely that Jerome, knocked out in the 12th round, died in a hospital. On February 9, 1928, Taylor, then claiming the disputed bantam title, was floored *(below)* by Joey Sangor, in a non-title match in Chicago. Bud protested that he had been fouled, but Sangor was credited with a seven-round knockout.

Panama Al Brown, was proclaimed cham pion in 1929, but campaigned in Europe where he lost the crown to Baltazar Sang chili, in Valencia, Spain, on June 1, 1935

champion was shorn of his title. Th N.B.A. and New York started elimina tions. Bud Taylor, born July 5, 190 in Terra Haute, Indiana, defeate Tony Canzoneri to win the N.B.A recognition, and Al Brown of Panama born July 5, 1902, after defeating Vide Gregorio, was proclaimed king in Ne York on June 18, 1929. Since Taylo had retired from the division o August 21, 1928, Brown had the fiel clear to himself. Instead of fighting i the United States, he decided to cam paign abroad, an act that caused th New York Commission to withdraw its support. But Brown's record wa so good that he was universally recog nized as champion.

Like some of the other fighters who when the title was in dispute, wen overseas to take on all comers, Brow whipped Eugene Huat, French cham pion, in fifteen rounds; Pete Sansto Scandinavian title holder, in Montrea in fifteen; Huat again in fifteen i

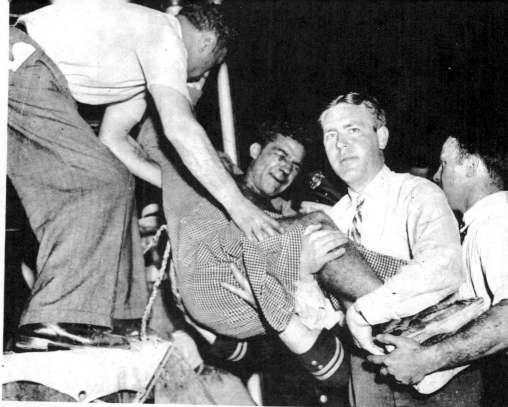

Baltazar Sangchili *(left, above)*, who had been boxing six years, mostly in Spain, when he deposed Brown as world champion, lost the crown to Tony Marino *(left, below)* of Pittsburgh. Sangchili had dropped Tony in the first round and was giving him a lacing, when in a dramatic finish in the 14th round, Marino rallied and knocked out Sangchili, who had to be carried *(above)* from the ring. On January 30, 1937, Marino battled Indian Quintana and died the next day from a brain injury.

Canada; Kid Francis in Marseilles in fifteen; stopped Emile Pladner in one round in Paris; won in twelve from Dom Bernasconi in Italy; defeated Young Perez in fifteen in Paris. Then, on June 1, 1935, he dropped the crown to Baltazar Sangchilli of Spain in Valencia, in fifteen rounds.

Sangchilli, born October 15, 1911, in Valencia, came to America to press his claim when New York refused to recognize him as champion. He tackled Tony Marino, New York's title holder, on June 26, 1936, and was stopped in the fourteenth round. Marino, born in Pittsburgh in 1912, then fought Sixto Escobar, born March 23, 1913, in Barcelona, Puerto Rico, and was kayoed in the thirteenth round. Now, the field clear again, the commissions throughout the world accepted Sixto as the new world title-holder.

On September 23, 1937, on the Tournament of Champions card

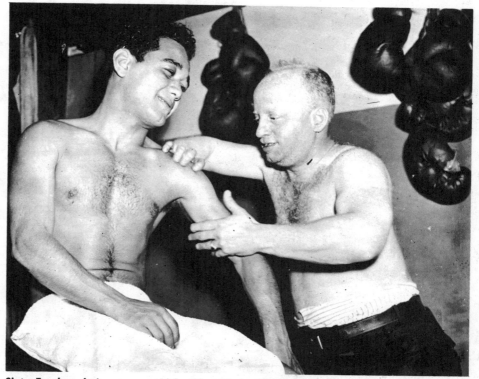

Sixto Escobar, being massaged by his trainer, Whitey Bimstein, was Puerto Rico's first world champion. After knocking out Tony Marino in 1936, Escobar lost and regained the title, but in 1939 increasing weight forced him to abandon his laurels.

377

Escobar and his main rival, Harry Jeffra, of Baltimore (right), who staged a give-and-take series for the crown, pose before their final bout in Puerto Rico in 1938.

Lou Salica, who won and lost the title to Escobar, became champion again by winning an elimination tournament in 1941.

Manuel Ortiz, a popular California boxer, outpointed Salica in 1942 and became the Pacific Coast's first bantam champion.

Harold Dade was champion for a brief period in 1947. Ten weeks after beating Ortiz, he lost to Manuel in a return bout.

The bantam title went to South Africa in 1950, when Vic Toweel outpointed Ortiz. Toweel's reign ended in 1952 when he was knocked out (below) by Jimmy Carruthers.

staged by Mike Jacobs, Harry Jeffra of Baltimore took the crown from Escobar, winning the decision at the end of fifteen rounds. A few months later, in San Juan, Puerto Rico, Escobar regained his laurels, beating Jeffra in fifteen rounds. Escobar gave up his crown on October 4, 1939, to fight as a featherweight, and another series of eliminations took place.

George Pace, born in Cleveland, February 2, 1916, and Lou Salica, born in New York City, July 26, 1913, were the leading contenders, the former with N.B.A. support, and Salica the New York champion. They fought a fifteen round draw at Toronto, on March 4, 1940. Then, on September 24, 1940 at New York, Salica won a fifteen round decision and support of both commissions.

Salica was outpointed by Manuel Ortiz, born in El Centro, California, August 7, 1942, in twelve rounds, and thereafter Ortiz defended his title eight times in 1943, four times in 1944, joined the U. S. Army in 1945, then defended successfully three more times in 1946. On January 6, 1947, he lost the championship to Harold Dade in San Francisco, but two months later, on March 11 in Los Angeles, Ortiz regained the crown. He defended the title successfully in Honolulu, Manila, Mexico, and Honolulu again, then decided to take a trip to South Africa, and on May 31, 1950,

Southpaw Jimmy Carruthers of Australia is declared victor over Chamrern Songkitrat by referee Bill Henneberry in 1954's "Battle of the Typhoon." Carruthers then retired, undefeated. He had won the bantam crown in his 15th bout.

he dropped the crown to Vic Toweel, who earned the decision in fifteen rounds.

Vic held it two years, defending it three times, then lost it to Jimmy Carruthers, of Paddington, New South Wales, Australia, born July 5, 1929. Jimmy knocked out Toweel in the first round on November 15, 1952, stopped him again on March 21 the following year in ten rounds, successfully defended the crown against Henry Pappy Gault of America in fifteen rounds in Sydney, Australia, on November 13, 1953, then wound up his career by gaining a decision in a championship bout in Bangkok, Thailand in what has been called the "Battle of the Typhoon" in twelve rounds.

It was one of the most weird affairs ever staged, with a terrific downpour drenching fighters and spectators, the ring flooded, the lights shattered every few minutes, and the boys boxing barefooted to avoid slipping. A record gathering of 59,760 persons paid $227,304 to see the battle.

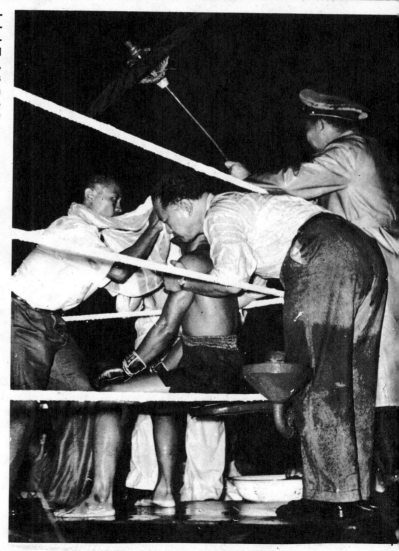

Tremendous excitement prevailed during the match between Carruthers and Songkitrat (above, right). Boxing was comparatively new in Thailand, and Songkitrat was the first native to fight for a world title. Barefoot to avoid slipping, they battled through a tropical rainstorm. The fight was halted twice to clear the canvas of debris, including shattered ring lightbulbs. Between rounds an umbrella was held over Chamrern (right) while his corner men worked over him. The closely-fought battle, held in Bangkok on May 2, 1954, set new bantamweight attendance records. A crowd of 59,760 jammed the National Stadium and braved a fierce storm to see their idol make a gallant but futile bid for the title.

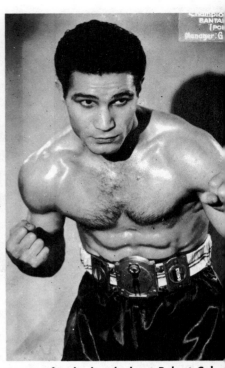

Deaf-mute Marion D'Agata (above, left) of Italy, was raised aloft by enthusiastic fans in Rome, after he knocked out Robert Cohen (right) for the title in 1956. Cohen announced his retirement. D'Agata lost the crown in 15 rounds to Alphonse Halimi in 195

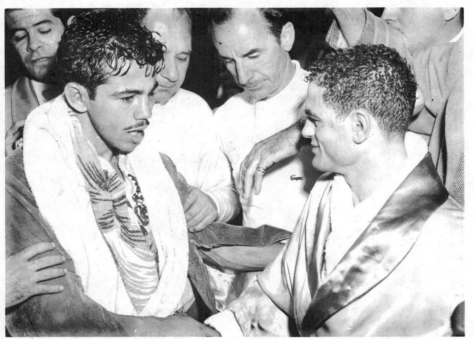

Alphonse Halimi (right) settled a dispute over the rightful owner of the bantamweight crown, by outpointing the NBA champion, Raul Raton Macias (left), a stiff puncher from Mexico. Champion Halimi, starting in 1955, has scored 12 knockouts in 23 bouts.

With Carruthers' retirement, the New York Commission, the World Championship Committee, and all supervising boxing bodies except the N.B.A. accepted a bout between Robert Cohen, European champion, and Chamrern Songkitrat, champion of the Orient and the boy who lost so gallantly to Carruthers in the above mentioned "Battle of the Typhoon" in Bangkok, to decide the new world sceptre wearer. Cohen, born in Bone,

Algeria, November 15, 1930, defeated Songkitrat, but when he failed to accept a match with the N.B.A. challenger, Raul Raton Macias of Mexico, the N.B.A. named Macias its champion. He and Songkitrat, already beaten by Cohen, fought in San Francisco on March 9, 1955, and Macias stopped the Thailander in the eleventh round. Only the N.B.A. regarded this as a title match. The contract stipulated it was a non-championship bout.

When on June 29, 1956, Mario D'Agata of Arezzo, Italy, European champion, knocked out Cohen in the sixth round in Rome, Italy, he was recognized as logical successor to the crown by all except the N.B.A., and when D'Agata, the deaf-mute, was outpointed in Paris in fifteen rounds by Alphonse Halimi, born in Constantine, Algeria, February 18, 1932, Halimi reached the top rung of the ladder as world title holder.

Halimi's first defense of his crown was in Los Angeles against champion (so-called by the NBA) Raul (Raton) Macias of Mexico. Alphonse gave his challenger a bad beating over the closing rounds, to retain his title easily

The bruising, crowding tactics of Joe Becerra, of Mexico, gave him a slight edge over defending champion Alphonse Halimi through seven brutal rounds on July 8, 1959. A crushing right to the body and a left hook to the jaw dropped the Frenchman for good in the eighth round, giving Becerra the bantamweight crown.

When Becerra was kayoed in the eighth round in a nontitle fight against Elroy Sanchez on August 30, 1960, he announced his retirement.

The N.B.A. and the European Boxing Union arranged eliminations to determine Becerra's successor. The European title was awarded to Alphonse Halimi, over the booing and stamping of the crowd, in a narrow fifteen-round decision over Freddy Gilroy, of Ireland, on October 15,

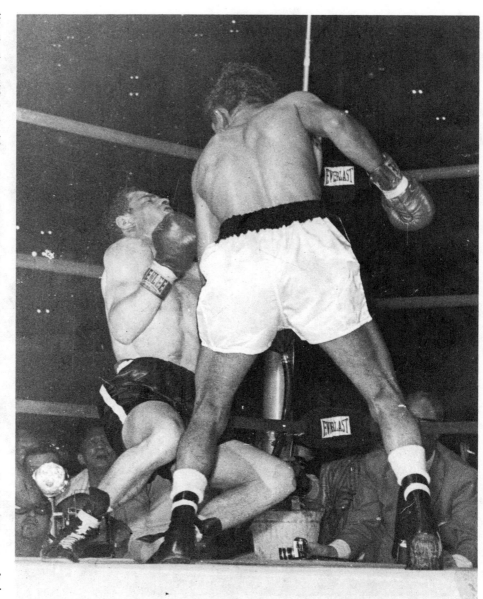

Halimi got much more than he bargained for in the person of Joe Becerra, who won the title by knocking out Alphonse in 8th.

After being halted by Eloy Sanchez in a non-title bout in 1960, Becerra (below, center) retired. Eder Jofre (left) stopped Sanchez (right) in sixth round for the American championship, in bout held in L.A.

In London, meanwhile, Jack Solomons (far right, center) promoted a Freddie Gilroy–Halimi bout, latter winning in 15 rounds.

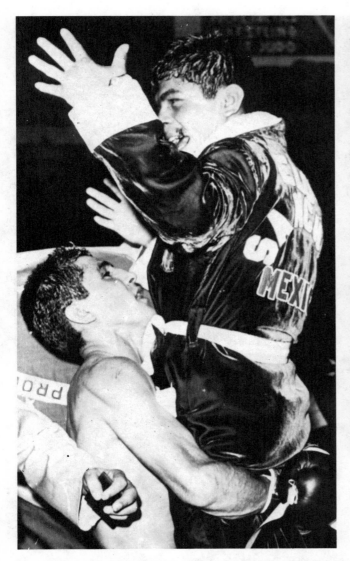

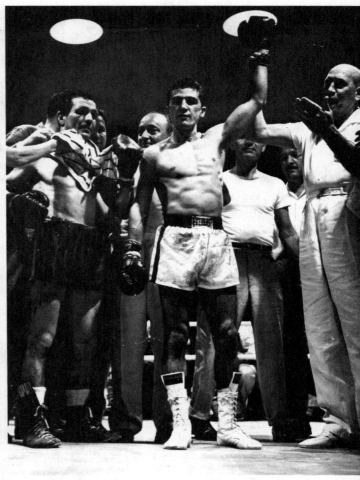

Jofre, shown at left lifting Sanchez in the air after stopping him, met Italy's Piero Rollo four months later after Halimi refused to box him. Jofre won universal recognition after knocking out Rollo in the 10th (*above*). Eder was to reign four years.

1960, in London. Shortly afterward on November 18, in Los Angeles Eder Jofre won the American title when he caught Eloy Sanchez flush on the jaw with a powerful right for a knockout victory in the sixth round.

Although the winners were supposed to battle for the international title, Halimi refused to accept Jofre. As a result, a match was arranged for Jofre with Italy's Piero Rollo, who was kayoed upon failing to answer the bell for the tenth round on March 21, 1961. With this victory, Jofre was recognized champion by *The Ring* magazine, the N.B.A., and the South American Boxing Federation.

Meanwhile, Johnny Caldwell beat Halimi with a blistering attack over fifteen rounds on May 30, 1961, in

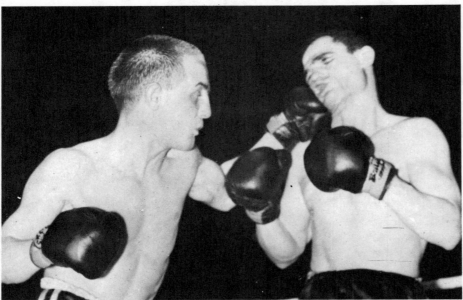

The European Boxing Union refused to go along with the other bodies, however, preferring to recognize winner of a Johnny Caldwell–Halimi bout. Caldwell (*left*) won in 15.

382

Lionel Rose an Australian Aborigine, took Harada's measure and his title on a 15-round decision in Tokyo in February, 1968. Rose was so overjoyed he bowls over one of his aides.

Ruben Olivares, who had KO'd Rose, was beaten in turn by Chucho Castillo in a 14-round stoppage.

Olivares, who regained the crown from Castillo in 1971, lost the title to Rafael Herrera (below).

(Above) Masahiko "Fighting" Harada being lifted in victory after taking the title from Eder Jofre in 1961.

(Below) Romeo Anaya knocked out Enrique Pinder in the third to take the title in 1973.

London, to become the European Boxing Union champion.

An international bantamweight champion was finally crowned on January 18, 1962, when Jofre stalked and pummeled Caldwell until the helpless Irishman's manager threw in the towel in the tenth round.

Having defended his title successfully seven times since beating Sanchez in 1961, the 118-pound Jofre succumbed to the windmill style of the 117-pound Fighting Harada of Japan in a fifteen-round decision on May 17, 1965, at Tokyo.

Lionel Rose, of Australia, stepping in as a last-minute substitute for Mexican Jesus Pimental on February 26, 1968, went on to win a unanimous fifteen-round decision over Harada with faster punching and harder hitting.

In Rose's third defense he was knocked out by Ruben Olivares, of Mexico, in the fifth round on August 22, 1969. Olivares had consistently been the aggressor, displaying a furious and constantly moving left hook.

Olivares, a flashy fellow who liked high living, lost his title to Chucho Castillo in the fourteenth, when the ring physician decided cuts around Olivares' left eye were too severe for him to continue. The bout took place in Los Angeles on October 16, 1970, with both men weighing 118 pounds.

In a return bout, April 3, 1971, Olivares regained the crown from Castillo, who was badly outclassed in fifteen rounds.

Rafael Herrera, a fellow Mexican, kayoed Olivares for the title at 1:28 of the eighth round on March 19, 1973, but lost it four months later, on July 30, to Panamanian Enrique Pinder in a fifteen-round decision.

Pinder held the title slightly longer than his predecessor, losing it to Mexico's Romeo Anaya on January 20, 1973, in Panama, in a three-round kayo.

South Africa's 114-pound Arnold Taylor, survived four knockdowns, landed a right cross to the 117¾-pound Anaya's jaw and scored a fourteenth-

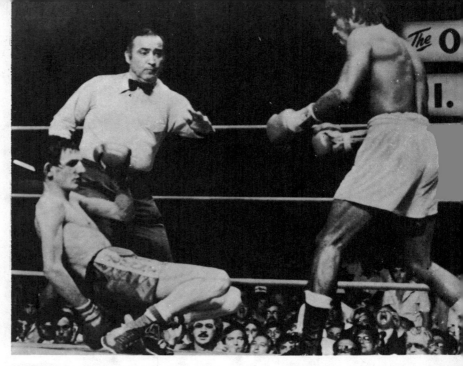

Lupe Pintor knocks out Welshman Johnny Owen in the twelfth round in Los Angeles, September 1980. Owen later died in hospital.

round knockout for the title, on November 3, 1973.

On July 3, 1974, Soo Hwan Hong of Korea put Taylor down four times in gaining a decision in Durban, but after a successful defense against Fernando Cabanela of the Philippines, he lost his title to Alfonso Zamora of Mexico, who knocked him out in the fourth. Zamora retained his crown when stopping Thanoujit Sukhotai of Thailand in the fourth round on March 14, 1975, and Socrates Batoto, kayo second, at Mexico City on December 6.

In 1976 Zamaro successfully defended his W.B.A. crown three times as follows: April 3, Eusebio Pedroza, kayo second, at Mexicali; July 10, Gilberto Illueca, kayo third, at Juarez; October 16, Soo Hwan Hong, stopped twelfth, at Inchon. But in 1977 he met only one challenger and was knocked out in ten rounds by Jorge Lujan (Panama) at Los Angeles, on November 19. In 1978 Lujan retained his title by stopping Roberto Rubaldino (Mexico) in eleven rounds at San Antonio on March 18, and Alberto Davila, who was outpointed over fifteen rounds' at New Orleans on September 15.

Back to the W.B.C. who stripped Enrique Pinder of his title in 1972

and on April 14, 1973, Rafael Herrera was installed as their champion when he stopped Rodolfo Martinez in twelve rounds at Monterrey. He kept his crown by outpointing Venice Borkorsor at Inglewood on October 13, 1973, and on May 25, 1974, he knocked out Romeo Anaya in six rounds at Mexico City. The following December 7, however, he dropped the title to his old rival Rodolfo Martinez, who stopped him in four rounds at Merida.

Martinez made two winning defences in 1975, stopping Nestor Jiminez in seven rounds at Bogota on May 31, and outpointing Hisami Numata over fifteen rounds at Sendai on October 8. On January 30, 1976, he again outpointed Venice Borkorsor over fifteen rounds, this time at Bangkok, but on May 8 lost his title to Carlos Zarate, who knocked him out in nine rounds at Inglewood.

The new Mexican champion soon showed he was in star class as a fighter and hard puncher. He had won forty-one consecutive contests since turning professional, forty of them inside the scheduled distance and was unbeaten. At once he set off to meet and beat all comers and on August 28, 1976, made the first defence of his W.B.C. title, stopping Paul Ferreri in twelve rounds at Inglewood. On November 13 he knocked out Philip

Waruinge in four rounds at Culiacan. In 1977 he made four more successful defences as follows: February 5 Fernando Cabanela, stopped third, at Mexico City; April 23, Alfonso Zamora, kayo fourth, at Inglewood; October 29, Danito Batista, stopped sixth, at Los Angeles; December 2, Juan Rodriguez, stopped fifth, at Madrid.

Zarate began 1978 in the same devastating fashion, on February 25 stopping Alberto Davila in eight rounds at Los Angeles. On June 10 he knocked out Emilio Hernandez in four rounds at Las Vegas. At this time he had defended his title eight times, none of his challengers being able to stay the course against his dynamic punching. But on October 27, 1978, his great winning run came to an end. In attempting to become a dual champion, he took on the Super-Bantam W.B.C. titleholder, Wlfredo Gomez, but was stopped in five rounds at San Juan. This Champion versus Champion fight brought 11,000 fans into the Roberto Clemente Stadium while a further 28,000 watched the contest on video in an adjoining open-air arena. Gomez received 175,000 dollars and Zarate 70,000 dollars. He was down for the third time when British referee Harry Gibbs called a halt. Zarate retained his W.B.C. bantamweight title.

He defended this successfully on March 10, 1979 by knocking out Mensah Kpalogo (Togo, W. Africa) in three rounds at Los Angeles, but lost his title on June 3, being outpointed over 15 rounds by Lupe Pintor (Mexico) at Las Vegas. On February 9, 1980 Pintor kept his crown by stopping Alberto Sandoval (U.S.A.) in 12 rounds at Los Angeles, but was held to a draw by Eijiro Murata (Japan) at Tokyo on June 11. On September 19 came his tragic defence against Johnny Owen of Wales at Los Angeles. Owen, holder of the British, Commonwealth and European titles, was knocked out in round 12 and never regained consciousness, dying in Los Angeles hospital 46 days later.

On December 19, 1980 Lupe Pintor retained his title, beating Alberto Davilla (Los Angeles) on points over 15 rounds at Las Vegas.

On April 8, 1979, Jorge Lujan kept his W.B.A. version of the championship by knocking out Cleo Garcia (Nicara-

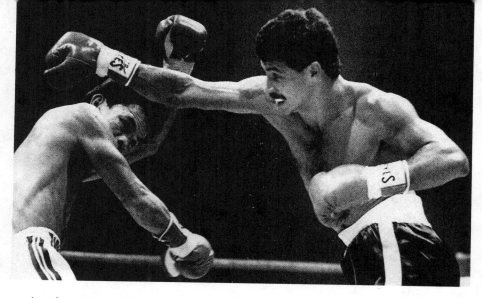

gua) in the 15th round at Las Vegas, and he performed an identical feat by disposing of Roberto Rubaldino (Mexico) at McAllen on October 6. On April 2, 1980 at Tokyo, he stopped Shuichi Isogami (Japan) in nine rounds, but on August 29 he lost his title to Julian Solis (Puerto Rico) on a 15 rounds points defeat at Miami. In the same ring on November 14, Solis was stopped in 14 rounds, losing his championship to Jeff Chandler (U.S.A.).

Chandler had an astonishing run of nine successful title defences that covered three full years, starting on January 31, 1981 when he outpointed Jorge Lujan (Panama) at Philadelphia. On April 5 he was held to a 15-rounds draw by Eijiro Murata at Tokyo. He then defeated Julian Solis with a seventh round knockout on July 25; Eijiro Murata was stopped in the 13th round on December 10; Johnny Carter was stopped in the sixth on March 21, 1982; Miguel Iriarte in the ninth on October 27; Gaby Canizales was beaten on points on March 13, 1983; Eijiro Murata stopped in the tenth on September 11; and Oscar Muniz stopped in the seventh on December 17. Chandler's reign came to an end on April 7, 1984 when he was battered into defeat by Ricardo Sandoval (U.S.A.) in the 15th and final round at Atlantic City. The new champion retained the title on September 22 by outpointing Edgar Roman (Venezuela) at Monte Carlo and on December 15 he stopped Cardenio Ulloa (Chile) in 8 rounds at Miami Beach.

The title changed hands in 1986, however, when Gaby Canizales (U.S.A.)

beat Sandoval, the referee intervening in the seventh at Las Vegas on March 10, 1986, and again when Canizales was outpointed by Bernardo Pinango (Venezuela) at New Jersey on June 4.

Pinango made three successful defences of his W.B.A. title before announcing his retirement from the ring. At Turin he stopped Ciro de Leva in 10 on October 4, served Simon Skosana the same way at Johannesburg on November 11, and then outpointed Frankie Duarte over 15 rounds at Los Angeles, on February 3, 1987.

The belt was contested on March 29 at Moriguchi, Japan, when native-son Takuya Mugurama knocked out Azael Moran in 5 rounds, but only two months later, on May 24, also at Moriguchi, the Japanese fighter was halted by South Korea's Chan-Yung Park in the 11th round. Once again the title changed hands quickly, when Wilfredo Vasquez, of Puerto Rico, so far outclassed Park that the bout was stopped when the South Korean turned his back on his challenger. Vasquez chose to make his first defence before a Japanese crowd at Osaka, when he faced Takuya Muguruma on January 17, 1988. It was a closely contested battle, and Vasquez retained the title only through a draw being declared.

Vasquez went to Bangkok for his next defence and on May 9, 1988 he was outpointed by Thailand's Kaokor

Migual Lora (*left*) had a long run after winning the W.B.C. title in 1985. This defence against Antonio Avelar in Miami in 1987 lasted less then four rounds.

Galaxy, the twin brother of the long-time light-bantamweight champion Kaosai Galaxy. It was a split decision disputed by Vasquez, who scored the only knockdown, but Kaokor's victory meant that he and his brother were the first identical twins to hold world titles. Kaokor's first reign lasted only three months and he lost the title on a technical decision. Defending against Sung-Il Moon in Rusan, he accidentally clashed heads in the sixth round with the South Korean, who was unable to continue. As Moon was in front in all cards he was given the decision.

Moon knocked out Edgar Monserrat and stopped Chaiki Kobayashi, but on defending in Bangkok on July 8, 1989 against Kaokor Galaxy he was outpointed by his old opponent. Galaxy's second reign was as short as his first, as he was stopped in the first round in Bangkok on October 18, 1989 by Luisito Espinosa of the Philippines. Espinosa kept the title for two years, but a car accident in which his brother escaped injury ended Kaokor Galaxy's career.

Back to the W.B.C. and Gwadalupe (Lupe) Pintor, who was establishing himself as another great bantam king, by beating off eight challengers in a reign that lasted three years. He made three winning defences in 1981, beating Jose Uziga on points on February 22; Jovito Rengifo, knocked out in the eighth on July 26; and Hurricane Teru, knocked out in the 15th on September 22. He then had a lay-off for nine months, coming back on June 3, 1982 to halt Seung-Hoon Lee (South Korea) in 11 rounds at Los Angeles. After a non-title bout in which he outpointed Jorge Lujan over 10 rounds, Pintor crashed against Wilfredo Gomez (Puerto Rico) on December 3, 1982 being saved by the referee in round 13 in a bout advertised as for the world super-bantamweight title at Houston.

In July of the following year Pintor was deprived of his bantam title for failure to meet an approved challenger, and on September 1, 1983, at Los Angeles, Albert Davila (U.S.A.), who had already had three stabs at the bantam championship, at last became title-holder by knocking out Francisco Bejines in 12 rounds for the vacant crown. It proved a tragic night as the unfortunate Mexican fighter never regained consciousness. Davila made one successful title defence in 1984, stopping Enrique Sanchez (Dominica) in 11 rounds at Miami on May 26 and then vacated the championship. It was won by Daniel Zaragoza (Mexico) at Aruba in the Dutch East Indies on May 4, 1985, when Freddie Jackson (U.S.A.) was ruled out for butting in round seven.

The winner's reign was restricted to only three months as on August 9 he was outpointed by Miguel Lora (Colombia) over 12 rounds at Miami. Lora retained the title on February 8, 1986, when he outpointed Wilfredo Vasquez (Puerto Rico) at Miami Beach.

Lora defended the W.B.C. version of the championship twice more in 1986, when he stopped Enrique Sanchez in 6 rounds at Miami on August 23, and outpointed Albert Davila over 12 rounds at Barranquilla, Colombia, on November 15. He had no trouble with Mexico's Antonio Avelar, again at Miami, on July 25, the following year, but Lora just managed to squeeze home to victory versus Ray Minus, the Bahaman Commonwealth champion, on November 27.

Lora continued by outpointing Lucio Lopez and Albert Davila, but his reign ended when he met Raul Perez of Mexico at Las Vegas on October 29, 1988. The lean and lanky Perez surprised the champion by overcoming slow start to take control by the en inflicting a first defeat on Lora.

The I.B.F.'s involvement in th championship dated from April 16, 198 when the Japanese Satoshi Shinga stopped Elmer Magallano in 8 rounds Kashiwara. Shingaki made a success defence of the title when outpointi Loves de la Puz at Naha City on Augu 4 of the same year, but he proved to no match for Jeff Fenech, of Australia, a Sydney ring, on April 26, 1985, wh the referee halted the match in the 9 round. August 23 found the champion having another go at th Australian, again at Sydney, but th time Fenech knocked him out in rounds.

The popular little Aussie made tv further successful defences of the I.B crown before his own fans in Sydne outpointing Jerome Coffee over rounds and halting Steve McCrory in before he announced his intention mixing with the heavier lig featherweights. Contesting the vacat championship, Kelvin Seabrooks, t American, was paired with Migu Maturana on May 15, 1987, at Ca tagena, but the crowd who turned out see their fellow-countryman were d appointed when the visitor knocked hi cold in the 5th round. On July 4, Calais, Seabrooks met the French cha lenger, Thierry Jacob, and the bo ended in confusion when a clash heads brought the fight to a close. Th opposing corners differed in their inte pretation of the rules, each claiming tl ght, and in the end the bout was declared a no contest. On February 6, 1988, Seabrooks returned to France, where he stopped Fernando Beltran rather easily in a couple of rounds before a Parisian crowd.

However Seabrooks met his match in the Texan Orlando Canizales at Atlantic City on July 9, 1988. Dropped in the first round, Seabrooks fought back gallantly in an exciting battle but, when he was dropped again in the 15th round, the referee was forced to intervene. This was the last 15-rounder in the division, and Canizales joined his brother Gaby, who had been the W.B.A. champion in 1986, among the sets of world champion brothers.

The W.B.O. instituted its championship on February 3, 1989 when Israel Contreras of Venezuela knocked out Italy's Maurizio Lupino in the first round at Caracas, and for a period of two years there was stability in the division with the champions of all four bodies, Perez, Espinosa, Canizales and Contreras holding on to their titles.

Contreras was first to go. He stopped Ray Minus in Nassau on September 2, 1990 but subsequently relinquished the title. Gaby Canizales, the former

W.B.A. champion, won it on March 12, 1991 when he knocked out Miguel Lora in the second round in Detroit, so for a while both Canizales brothers were champions together. Gaby lost the crown on his first defence, however, being outpointed in London on June 30, 1991 by Britain's Duke McKenzie, the former flyweight champion. McKenzie outpointed a Mexican, Cesar Soto, and a Puerto Rican, Wilfredo Vargas, but was surprisingly beaten on March 13, 1992 by another Puerto Rican, Rafael del Valle. At London's Albert Hall, McKenzie, who had never been knocked down before, was caught cold by almost the first punch del Valle threw and was counted out in the second minute. Del Valle kept the title when stopping Wilfredo Vargas in Conado, Puerto Rico in April 1993.

Meanwhile Luisito Espinosa, the W.B.A. champion, made three defences in 1990, forcing Hurley Snead to retire in the eighth at Bangkok, knocking out Yong-Man Chun in the first in Manila and, six weeks later, outpointing Thalerngsak Sitbobay in Bangkok again. However in October 1991 he was knocked out in the fifth round when defending back home in Manila against

the former W.B.O. champion, Israel Contreras. Contreras was then surprised by American southpaw Eddie Cook, who won the title by a knockout in the fifth round in Las Vegas on March 15, 1992. Unfortunately Cook could not maintain the momentum and on his first defence on October 10 he was outpointed by Colombia's Jorge Eliecer Julio at Cartagena. Julio beat another Colombian, Francisco Alvarez, on his first defence in April 1993.

Raul Perez, the W.B.C. champion, made three successful defences in 1989: against Lucio Lopez (points), Cardenio Ulloa (retired, seventh) and Diego Avila (points). He did even better in 1990 with four: former champion Gaby Canizales (points), Gerardo Martinez (stopped, ninth), Jose Valdez (drew) and Chanquito Carmona (knockout, eighth). However 1991 saw Perez's downfall at last when, on February 25, he was outpointed in Los Angeles by Greg Richardson (U.S.A.). Perez moved up a division and Richardson made one suc-

Raul Perez (left) had a good run as W.B.C. bantamweight champion, outpointing Lucio Lopez (right) in his first defence in 1989, the first of seven winning defences.

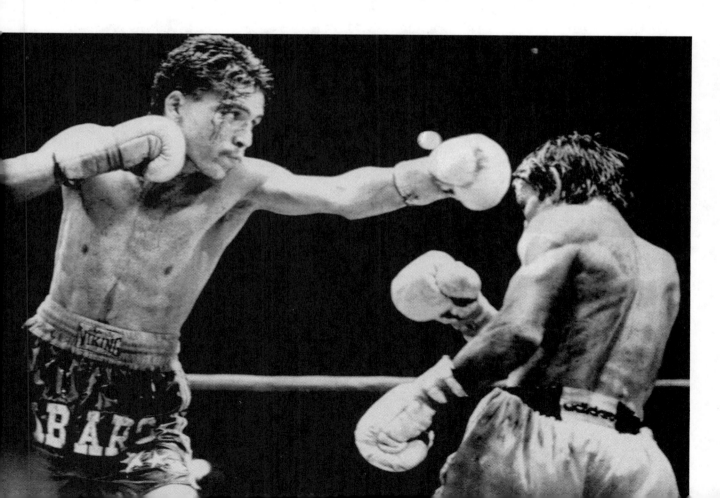

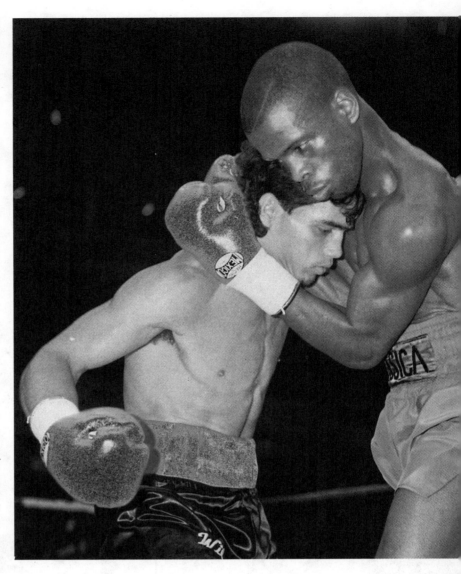

cessful defence, outpointing Victor Rabanales, but Richardson was forced to retire in the tenth against Joichiro Tatsuyoshi of Japan when they met at Tokyo on September 19, 1991. Tatsuyoshi, however, needed surgery for a detached retina immediately after the contest, and the W.B.C. declared the title vacant. Victor Rabanales won it on a technical decision over Yong-Hoon Lee of South Korea when, on March 30, 1992 at Los Angeles, Rabanales sustained a badly cut eye in the ninth round, but took the title as he was ahead on two score cards, having achieved an early knockdown. However there was a strange situation when Tatsuyoshi resumed training and claimed he was still champion. The W.B.C. solved it by deciding that Rabanales was the 'interim' champion. Rabanales defended his title with a stoppage of Luis Alberto Campo and a points win over Chang-Kyun Oh. On September 17, 1992 he met Tatsuyoshi in Osaka for the 'undisputed' W.B.C. crown and inflicted a first defeat on the Japanese fighter, who was stopped in the ninth round. The veteran Rabanales continued his run into 1993 with a points win over Dio Andujar of the Philippines, but lost on a decision to Jong-Il Byon of South Korea at Kyungju on March 27, 1993.

The outstanding bantamweight of the early 1990s was the I.B.F. champion Orlando Canizales. Making his first defence in November 1988, he scored a first-round knockout of Jimmy Navarro.

In 1989 he stopped ex-champ Kelvin Seabrooks in the 11th round in their return. Three defences in 1990 were against Britain's Billy Hardy (points), the 1984 Olympic champion Paul Gonzales (stopped, second) and Eddie Rangel (stopped, fifth). There were three more in 1991: Billy Hardy again (stopped, eighth), Fernie Morales (points) and Ray Minus (stopped, 11th).

In 1992 there were two points victori over Francisco Alvarez and Sam Duran. He won again, but only afte tough battle, on March 27, 1993 Evian, France, when challenged by unbeaten 18-year-old, Clarence 'Bon Adams, from Carmine, Illinois. Ada father threw in the towel in the 11 but the challenger had worried Ca zales in the middle rounds.

THE LIGHT-BANTAMWEIGHT CHAMPIONS

On February 1, 1980 the World Boxing Council introduced a new in-between weight division at 115 pounds or three pounds above the standing flyweight poundage. It was originally known as the junior-bantamweight class, al-

though later it became called the super-flyweight division. The first champion was Rafael Orono (Venezuela) who outpointed Seung-Hoon Lee (Korea) over 15 rounds at Caracas. Orono made three defences that year: on April 12

he beat Ramon Soria on points; on J 28 Willie Jensen earned a draw; a on September 15 Jovito Rengifo v knocked out in the third. On January 1981 however, at San Cristobal, he v put away in nine rounds by Chul-1 im (Korea), who made five defences: on April 22 Jiro Watanabe was beaten on points; on July 29 Willie Jensen was stopped in the thirteenth; on November 8 Jackai Maruyama was knocked out in the ninth; on February 10, 1982 Koki Ishii was knocked out in the eighth; and on July 4 Raul Valdez drew. On November 28 he gave Orono a chance to win back his lost laurels and was halted in six rounds at Seoul. The Venezuelan defended against Pedro Romero (Panama) kayoed in the fourth at Caracas on January 31, 1983 and Orlando Maldonado (Puerto Rico) who lasted only five rounds, on October 30. Thailander Payao Poontarat then took the title on a points verdict on November 27 at Bangkok and stopped Gustave Espadas (Mexico) in ten rounds on March 28, 1984.

Jiro Watanabe (Japan), the W.B.A. champion, made his second attempt to win the W.B.C. title on July 5 and outpointed the champion at Osaka, and in a return on November 29 he stopped Poontarat in 11 rounds at Kumamoto, Japan. On May 9, 1985 Watanabe outpointed Julio Soto Soleno (Dominica) over 12 rounds at Tokyo, and on September 17 halted Katsuo Katsuma (Japan) in seven rounds at Osaka. On December 13 the busy champion knocked out Yun Sok Hwan (Korea) in five rounds at Taegu, South Korea, but he lost his crown on March 30, 1986 when outpointed by Gilberto Roman (Mexico) Osaka. Roman retained the title with points win over Edgar Monserrat (Panama) at Paris on May 15.

The little Mexican proved to be a busy and formidable champion. Most of his contests travelled the full distance, but in a fairly short space of time he licked Ruben Condori, Kongtorance Payakarun, Antoine Montero, and Frank Cedeno, as well as getting a draw with Santos Laciar. Then, on May 16, 1987, in return battle with Laciar, Roman was humbled in 11 rounds at Reims, in France. The experienced little Argentinian, who had done so well as champion in the flyweight division, lost his new title at Miami on August 8, when Jesus Rojas, the Colombian, won a points verdict to become the new W.B.C. kingpin. In his first defence, which was again at Miami, on October 24, Rojas

scored an impressive victory over Gustavo Ballas, stopping him in 4 rounds.

The W.B.A. did not respond with its own version of the class until 18 months after the W.B.C. and started off by calling it the light-bantamweight championship. On September 12, 1981 at Buenos Aires, Gustavo Ballas (Argentina) knocked out Sok-Chul Bae (Korea) in eight rounds to take the vacant title, but he lost it first time out on December 5 to Rafael Pedroza (Panama), being outpointed over 15 rounds. Pedroza, too, had a short stay, on April 8, 1982 losing on points to Jiro Watanabe (Japan) at Osaka. It was Watanabe's second attempt to win the championship and now he was determined to keep it. There were two defences in 1982: Gustavo Ballas was knocked out in the ninth on July 29 and Shoji Oguma in the twelfth on November 11. On February 24, 1983 Luis Ibanez (Peru) was knocked out in eight rounds; Roberto Ramirez (Mexico) was outpointed in a 12-rounder on June 23. The Japanese southpaw defended against Soon-Chun Kwan (South Korea) on October 6 and sustained an eye injury that caused a stoppage in the 11th round. However the verdict went to the champion. On March 15 he stopped Celso Chavez (Panama) in the 15th and final round.

Whether Watanabe (W.B.A. champion) challenged Payao Poontarat (W.B.C. champion) or if it was the other way about, they met at Osaka on July 5 1984 when Watanabe won a 12-rounds points decision. This did not make him a dual titleholder as the W.B.A. deprived him of its championship because the fight had not been over their stipulated distance of 15 rounds, which demonstrates the futility of having more than one controlling body. On November 21, 1984 Koasai Galaxy (Thailand) knocked out Eusebio Espinal (Dominica) in six rounds at Bangkok to win the vacant W.B.A. title and there were two champions again in the division. Dong-Hoon Lee (South Korea) challenged for the crown on March 7, 1985, but was stopped in seven rounds, then on July 17, Rafael Orono, the former W.B.C. champion, tried to get back into the limelight, but was stopped in five rounds. In the third defence of his title,

Galaxy knocked out Edgar Monserrat (Panama) in three rounds at Bangkok.

Galaxy went on to prove his worth. On November 1, 1986, he flattened Israel Contreras at Curaçao in 5 rounds before tackling the formidable Elly Pical at Jakarta. Galaxy won by a knockout in 14 rounds on February 28, 1987. He then scored a fairly easy victory in 3 rounds at Bangkok, when Chung-Byong Kwan was counted out on October 12.

It soon became clear that Galaxy was one of the outstanding champions this division had seen. He made two defences in 1988, outpointing Kongtorance Payakarun in Bangkok and knocking out Chang-Ho Choi in Seoul, and there were four challengers in 1989, only one of whom went the distance. He knocked out in the second round South Korean Tae-Il Chang, was held to a draw by a Japanese, Kenji Matsumura, stopped in the tenth Alberto Castro of Colombia and ended the year by knocking out Kenji Matsumura in the last round of their return. Four more challengers all failed to make the final bell in 1990: Ari Blanca of the Philippines (knockout, fifth), Schunichi Nakajima of Japan (stopped, eighth), Yong-Kang Kim of South Korea (knockout, sixth) and Ernesto Ford of Panama (knockout, sixth). In 1991 Galaxy stopped Jae-Suk Park of South Korea in the fifth round, and then announced that he would retire after two more defences – time for the Thai authorities and his fans to stage a great farewell. In July he stopped Venezuelan David Griman in the fifth round in Bangkok. Before his final televised appearance on December 22, 1991, naturally in Bangkok, Galaxy was presented to the king, and there were 35 minutes of preliminaries in which he was given gifts and cheered by the 11,000 spectators. The challenger, Armando Castro of Mexico, nearly spoiled the party with a first-round knockdown of the champion, who was in trouble at the bell, but Galaxy recovered to take a points verdict. He had made 19 successful defences and his only defeat in 50 contests came when he first challenged for the Thai crown in his seventh bout, a defeat he subsequently avenged.

The vacant W.B.A. title was won by

Katsuya Onizuka of Japan, who outpointed Thalerngsak Sitbobay in Tokyo on April 10, 1992. He defended twice during the year, stopping fellow-Japanese Kenji Matsumura and outpointing Armando Castro.

The first contest involving light-bantamweight title-claimants held under the auspices of the newly-formed I.B.F. took place on December 10, 1984, at Osaka, Japan, when Joo-Do Chun, of Korea, knocked out Ken Kasugai in 5 rounds. The winner went on to defeat a number of challengers in Prayoonsak Muangsurin, Diego de Villa, Felix Marques, William Develos, and Kwang-Gu Park, all contests being held in his own country, before Elly Pical stopped Chun in 8 rounds at Jakarta, Indonesia, on May 3, 1985.

Pical was outpointed by Cesar Polanco, a Dominican, at the same venue, on February 15, 1986, over 15 rounds, but knocked out Polanco in the 3rd round, in a return contest, again at Jakarta, on July 5. The I.B.F. champion then flattened Dong-Chung Lee in 10 rounds, also on his home ground, on December 3, before he forfeited his belt in order to make a challenge for the W.B.A. championship. This, as has been noticed, proved unsuccessful, when Kaosai Galaxy knocked him out.

At Pusan, South Korea, two native sons, Tae-Il Chang and Soon-Chun Kwan, boxed a close contest on May 17, 1987 to determine who would be the new I.B.F. champion to replace Pical. Chang won a split decision. He then tackled the former holder of the I.B.F. championship, Elly Pical, who won back his old title with a 13-round knockout on October 17. The Indonesian readily put his belt in jeopardy at Pontianak, versus Raul Diaz, of Colombia, on February 20, 1988, but he was very lucky to retain it. He was floored three times in an exciting fight before coming back with a couple of knockdowns himself to gain a close points victory.

Pical defended twice more successfully, outpointing Chang-Ki Kim of South Korea and Mike Phelps of U.S.A., although this last was only by a split decision after a rousing battle. The veteran lost his title on his next defence, however, when Juan Polo

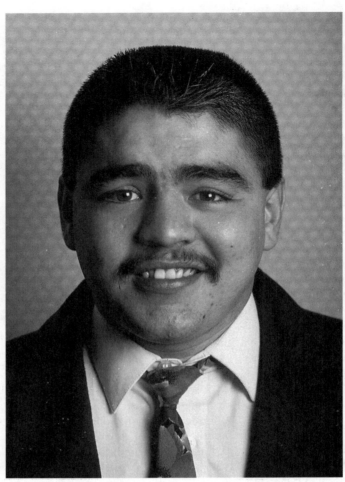

Perez won on points at Roanoke. The Colombian lost the title on his first defence to Robert Quiroga of the U.S.A., being outpointed in Sunderland, England. The all-action Quiroga settled down into a successful string of defences. He forced Vuyani Nene of South Africa to retire after three rounds at Benevento, outpointed an Italian, Vincenzo Belcrastro, at Capo d'Orlando, a Nigerian, Akeem Anifowashe, at San Antonio, a Colombian, Carlos Mercardo, at Salerno and a Puerto Rican, Jose Ruiz, at Las Vegas. On January 16, 1993, however, he surprisingly lost his unbeaten record and his title when stopped with 30 seconds of the fight remaining by Julio Cesar Borboa of Mexico, after a bloody fight in which both his eyes were cut and swollen. There was a demonstration in which beer cans were thrown into the ring by Quiroga's home supporters at San Antonio, but the losing champion had no complaints, and anyway he was behind on two of the cards.

Meanwhile the W.B.C. acquired a new champion when Jesus Rojas, in his second defence on April 8, 1988, was outpointed in Miami by Gilberto Roman, who embarked on a second spell as champion. Before the end of the year Roman had beaten three challengers: Yoshiyuki Uchida of Japan at Kawagoe (stopped, fifth), Kiyoshi Hatanaka of Japan at Nagoya (points) and Jesus Rojas, attempting to get the title back at Las Vegas (points). Two more defences in 1989 saw off Juan Carazo of Puerto Rico at Las Vegas (points) and the veteran former champion Santos Laciar, who was outpointed in Los Angeles. On November 7, 1989, however, Nana Yaw Konadu, of Ghana, outpointed him in Mexico City.

Konadu took the crown to Seoul less than two months later, and on January 2, 1990 dropped it on points to a South Korean, Sung-Il Moon. He proved to be another long-running champion in the division. Moon disposed of former champion Gilberto Roman in his first

Kaosai Galaxy who defended successfully nineteen times scores with a hard punch to the chin of Yong-Kang Kim in September 1990. Kim was knocked out in the sixth, one of a long line of unsuccessful challengers.

defence in Seoul, then won a technical decision over regular challenger Kenji Matsumara. In 1991 he stopped Nana Yaw Konadu in his return title match at Zaragoza, and then back in South Korea he knocked out Ernesto Ford of Panama and stopped Torsak Pongsupa of Thailand. Two more defences in Seoul in 1992 resulted in victories over Armando Muniz of Mexico and Greg Richardson of U.S.A. On February 27, 1993 Moon was challenged by the 33-year-old Hilario Zapata, the former light-flyweight and flyweight champion. The Panamanian was taking part in his 14th world title fight (18 wins), but he

had little defence against Moon's body attacks and was stopped in the first round.

The W.B.O. first recognised the division on April 29, 1989, when Jose Ruiz of Puerto Rico outpointed Jesus Rojas, the previous W.B.C. champion, at San Juan. Ruiz stopped his fellow-countrymen Juan Carazo, Angel Rosario and Wilfredo Vargas, and outpointed the Mexican Armando Velasco before he lost the title when outpointed by another Mexican, Jose Quirino, at Las Vegas on February 22, 1992.

Quirino lost the title on September 4, 1992 in Copenhagen, when the slim 24-

year-old Dane, Johnny Bredahl, comprehensively outpointed him. Bredahl's superb left jab won him a world title in only his 15th contest, and he and brother Jimmi (junior lightweight) created a record by becoming world champions on the same bill. Bredahl outpointed Rafael Caban, another Puerto Rican, on his first defence in March 1993.

THE FLYWEIGHTS

The first official flyweight champion was Jimmy Wilde. The class was created in England and the poundage at the time was 108 pounds. America followed suit the same year and accepted the group as a new division in boxing. The first championship bout was one that brought together Wilde and the Zulu Kid of America and Jimmy knocked out the American in the eleventh round in London on December 18, 1916, to gain top honors.

He held the title for a long time. With World War One on, Wilde competed in exhibitions and odd bouts in England until after the armistice was signed, after which he came to America and stirred up interest in the class. During a six months' stay, the Welshman was a busy campaigner, fighting such stars as Jack Sharkey, Mike Ertle, Babe Asher, Micky Russell, Frankie Mason, Zulu Kid, Battling Murray, Bobby Dyson, and Patsy Wallace. He then returned to his native country where on January 13, 1921, he was stopped by Pete Herman in a non-title bout in seventeen rounds.

For two years he remained idle until Tom O'Rourke, former manager of George Dixon and Joe Walcott, brought him to the United States to defend his title at the Polo Grounds.

Jimmy Wilde *(left)*, the "Mighty Atom," was a remarkable Welshman who held the world flyweight title. One of the greatest little fighting men of all time, he scored 75 knockouts during his career from 1911 to 1923. Pete Herman *(above)* of New Orleans proved too strong for Wilde in their bout on January 13, 1921. Although Herman had been boxing for seven years, this was his first bout on foreign soil.

Pancho Villa (above, left) posing with Johnny Buff before their clash for the American flyweight title in 1921, was the best ringman ever developed in the Philippine Islands. The referee, Patsy Haley, counted Buff out in the 11th round.

One year after winning the American title, Villa watched an aging Jimmy Wilde weigh in for their world championship match in New York. Among the many ring notables present was Philadelphia Jack O'Brien, seen standing directly behind Villa.

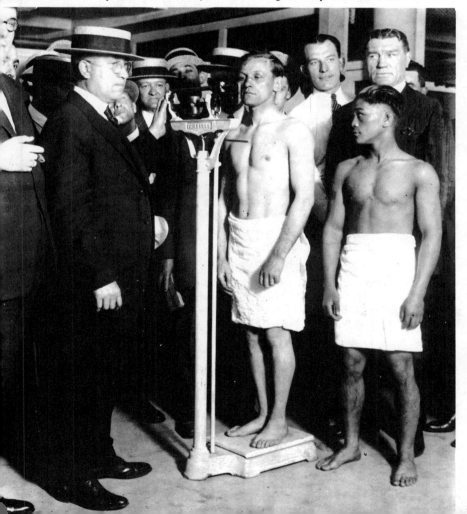

against Pancho Villa. In that affair, one of the most stirring bouts ever fought in the division, Pancho stopped "The Mighty Atom" in the seventh round. Villa was one of the classiest performers the division ever had. He was Jack Dempsey in miniature. A clever, tireless, relentless, hard-hitting flyweight, he was a colorful lad who drew the crowd at the gate. He had won the American flyweight title from Johnny Buff and lost it to Frankie Genaro and was now after the world crown.

The triumph of Villa came after 1.46 of fighting in the seventh round of a contest that will long be remembered. While it lasted, it was a battle royal. The crowd found itself rooting madly for the little Welshman could neither offset Villa's speed nor discount his volley of punches. Wild acclaim greeted the skill of the Filipino. Never since Battling Nelson was counted out on his feet in forty rounds by Ad Wolgast in 1910 in California did a champion pass more gloriously than did Wilde that night.

From the second round on, the pallid little Welshman didn't have a chance. Just as the bell sounded at the end of the second, Villa landed one flush on the jaw and down went the champion, flat. He was dragged to his corner and the rest of the fight was a test of endurance as well as one of the finest shows of the eternal fighting spirit that has ever been seen in a ring battle. Wilde's seconds called the punch that dropped him a foul, and most of the ringsiders agreed that it had been tossed after the bell rang. In England, such a blow would have brought about Pancho's disqualification.

In the third round, Wilde came out of his corner reeling and partially blinded, but he pressed into the Filipino like a panther. Villa was at him and shot rights and lefts into his face. Wilde reeled, but he would not give ground.

Wilde was rocked several times, but there was no letup in his attempt to keep going. Seldom was there such a display of endurance seen by a New York fight gathering since the time of

A great career came to a dramatic end as 31-year-old Jimmy Wilde, inactive since his defeat by Herman, came out of retirement to defend his flyweight laurels against the dynamic 22-year-old Villa. Although the tiny Welshman fought one of the most courageous battles ever seen in a championship bout, he was unable to hold off the relentless assaults of the younger, stronger, Villa. Wilde absorbed a terrific lacing, but fought back desperately, until eventually he collapsed in the seventh round *(right)*, and was counted out by referee Patsy Haley.

Nelson, the man they called the Durable Dane.

The sheer gameness of the Welsh mite convinced the spectators that he might still have a chance, frail and wobbly though he seemed. His remarkable reign as one of the greatest of world champions was about to come to a sickening end, but never did he fail to display the fighting qualities of a true title holder. His showing, and that of the mighty tyke of the Orient, placed that battle among the super-fistic contests of all time.

Wilde's finish was pathetic, for a brave little man went face down into the resin after taking a cruel beating. He had walked into the cannon's mouth, a sad, almost defiant smile on his face, made unsightly by the spiteful fists of the great little Filipino. A right hand blow put an end to the fight.

At the time, both of Wilde's eyes were swollen and closed until only a tiny slit gave him a sight of the slant-eyed terror in front of him. Age was horribly spiked and gaffed, youth was strutting from the fight unmarked, a vast crowd shrieking the praise of a

Villa's spectacular career ended tragically with this fight against Jimmy McLarnin in Oakland, California, on July 4, 1925. Pancho, suffering from infected teeth, insisted on going through with the bout. Villa *(left)* lost the decision, and the poison, spreading through his body, sent him to the hospital, where he died 10 days later.

strange little fellow from Manila who had just been crowned king.

Villa had a quick and tragic end. He fought Jimmy McLarnin on July 4, 1925, in Oakland, California, and died ten days later from blood poisoning from an infected tooth, the result of this contest.

After Fidel LaBarba had gained universal recognition as world flyweight king, he met Elky Clark, the British champion, who is seen lying flat on his face from a blow on the jaw in the first round. LaBarba received the verdict at the end of 12 rounds.

Confusion reigned in the flyweight division in 1933. Frankie Genaro (left) NBA title-holder and Midget Wolgast, New York champ, fought for the crown, but the verdict was a draw.

Fidel LaBarba started in 1924, when he won the amateur flyweight championship in the Olympics at Paris. After retiring in 1933, he completed his studies at Stanford University.

With Villa's passing, Frankie Genaro claimed the crown. He was outpointed on August 22, 1925, by Fidel LaBarba, born September 29, 1905, in New York City. LaBarba retired in 1927, and Corporal Izzy Schwartz of New York, born October 23, 1902, followed him to the throne after he whipped Newsboy Brown in New York City in fifteen rounds. Only New York accepted the Corporal as champion.

The N.B.A. refused to go along with that. Conditions in the class became greatly confused until an elimination was staged in 1929 in which Midget Wolgast outpointed Black Bill and the Midget got New York's support. Wolgast, born in Philadelphia, July 18, 1910, and Frankie Genaro then fought a draw of fifteen rounds in New York, and since Genaro was recognized by the N.B.A. as king of the class, two champions were in the field.

Genaro went to Paris, where he was knocked out in the second round on October 26, 1931, by Young Perez, born in Tunis, October 18, 1911. Perez claimed the world honors. A year later, Jackie Brown of England took over when he knocked out Perez in the thirteenth round to win European support.

The confusion continued as Small Montana, born in Negros, Philippines, February 24, 1913, outpointed Wol-

When La Barba retired temporarily in 1927, Corporal Izzy Schwartz whipped Newsboy Brown, and gained New York support.

Jackie Brown, a strong British flyweight, stopped Young Perez on October 31, 1932, in England, for the world crown.

Frankie Genaro, the American NBA champion, received a royal welcome in Paris upon his arrival for the flyweight contest with Young Perez. Genaro proved an easy opponent (below) for the French champion, who stopped him in two rounds. The French Federation of Boxing, as a result of this bout, declared Perez the world's flyweight champion.

One of the greatest flyweights in recent years, was a Scot, Benny Lynch, seen b with his hand raised in victory over the American champion, Small Montana. Ly triumph over Montana in Glasgow ended all confusion in the flyweight ranks.

gast for the U. S. crown and went abroad to seek a bout to decide world honors. In the meantime a great flyweight, Benny Lynch, born in Glasgow, Scotland, April 2, 1913, came forth to show his wares, and he took the measure of Jackie Brown at Manchester, stopping him in two rounds.

Lynch now was generally accepted as world champion, and when Montana challenged him, the Filipino was defeated in fifteen rounds, thus en-

Benny Lynch was officially shorn of his title on June 29, 1938, for failing to make weight for his bout in Paisley, Scotland, with Jackie Jurich of California. They were re-matched the same afternoon at catch-weights. Benny floored Jurich six times and knocked him out in the 12th round. Lynch died in Scotland in 1946, by then a physical wreck.

Rinty Monaghan, pride of Belfast, Ireland, who sang and danced after each bout, knocked out Paterson for the title.

Peter Kane, a sharp puncher from England, decisioned Jack Jurich in Liverpool, and claimed the vacant flyweight crown.

Jackie Paterson, Scotland's clever, hard-punching flyweight, won the title with a one-round knockout over Peter Kane.

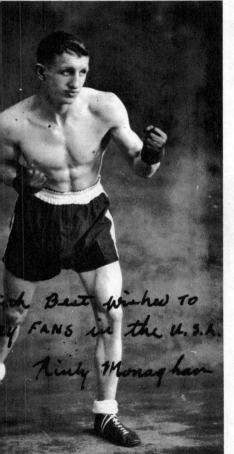

abling Lynch to end all confusion in the division.

When Lynch retired, Jackie Jurich of California and Peter Kane of England, the last two men to face Lynch in title bouts, fought on September 22, 1938, at Liverpool. Kane won, thus claiming world honors.

In most boxing circles Kane was recognized as world champion. During the war he was unable to defend his crown and temporarily vacated the throne, so that in 1941 and 1942 the championship was vacant. Then on June 19, 1943, Jackie Paterson of Scotland knocked out Kane in one round to gain international recognition, and on March 23, 1948, an Irish lad, Rinty Monaghan of Belfast, stopped Paterson in seven rounds to win the crown.

Rinty Monaghan, born August 21,

397

"Barrow Boy" Terry Allen, the first Englishman to win the flyweight championship in 37 years, has his hand raised by referee De Young, in token of victory over Honoré Pratesi, of France. The 15-round bout was held in London, on April 25, 1950.

Yoshio Shirai gave Japan a day to remember when on May 19, 1952, he won the world flyweight crown from Dado Marino in Tokyo. Shirai (above), the first to win a world title for his country, waves to his admirers before leaving the ring.

1920, in Belfast retired on April 25, 1950, and Terry Allen, born August 11, 1925, gained top ranking by defeating Honoré Pratesi of France in fifteen rounds in the Harringay Arena of London and became champion. He in turn was outpointed in fifteen rounds on August 1, 1950 in Hawaii by Dado Marino of Hawaii, born in Honolulu, August 26, 1916.

Then, for the first time in history, a world championship was won by a Japanese when Yoshio Shirai of Tokyo, born November 23, 1923, gained the verdict over Marino, May 19, 1952, at Tokyo in fifteen rounds. They fought again on November 15 of that year in

When Terry Allen, a world-traveller, journeyed to Honolulu to defend his title, he lost it to Salvador "Dado" Marino (right) in 15 rounds. Allen used a crouching position to good advantage, befuddling Marino in the early stages, but his style was later solved. Dado's left was effective as the bout neared its end. He piled up points and won a close but well-earned victory.

Pascual Perez, a vicious puncher from Argentina, lifted the crown from Yoshio Shirai, Japan's first world champion, in Tokyo on November 26, 1954. Referee Jack Sullivan raises Perez' hand (below) as new champion. Between them is manager Lozaro Koci. In return bout, Perez knocked out Shirai (above) in the fifth round. In a title bout on December 15, 1958, Perez retained his crown by winning a unanimous 15-round decision over Philippine flyweight champion Dommy Ursua in Manila.

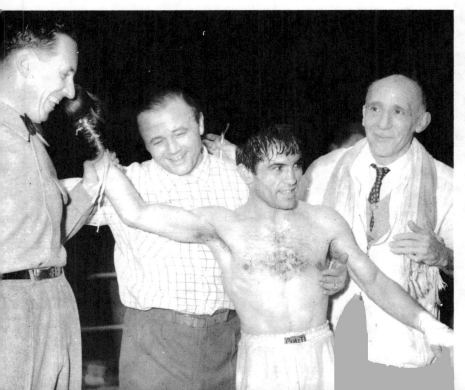

Tokyo, and Shirai won in fifteen rounds, to retain his crown. Tanny Campo of Manila tried to wrest it from him but also lost, as did Terry Allen as well as Leo Espinosa of the Philippines, all in fifteen round contests.

Then came a bout with Pascual Perez, a heavy-socking lad from Buenos Aires, who, after fighting a draw of ten rounds with Shirai in Perez's country, defeated Shirai in fifteen rounds in Tokyo on November 26, 1954, to win world honors. The Argentinian, born in Tupunagte, Mendoza, Argentina, March 4, 1926, became a fighting champion. He knocked out Shirai in five rounds; defeated Leo Espinosa in fifteen; halted Oscar Suarez in eleven; Ricardo Valdez in five; Dai Dower in the first; and Luis Angel Jimenez in ten—all championship fights.

Perez defended his title seventeen times from 1955 to 1959. On April 16, 1960, the thirty-four-year-old champ could not hold his own against a young aggressive opponent, Pone Kingpetch of Tailand, and lost the crown in a fifteen-round split decision, at Bangkok. In a return bout, September 22, at Los Angeles, Perez was knocked out in eight rounds.

Fighting Harada, ranked only tenth in the flyweight division, kayoed the Thai champion in the eleventh round October 10, 1962, at Tokyo in a vicious encounter.

Kingpetch became the first flyweight ever to regain the title. On January 12, 1963, at Bangkok, he reversed the pattern of his first fight with Harada, forcing the fight and keeping his foe on the defensive, thereby gaining a split decision.

Japan's Hiroyuki Ebihara, at twenty-three, had youth and strength to his advantage, while the twenty-

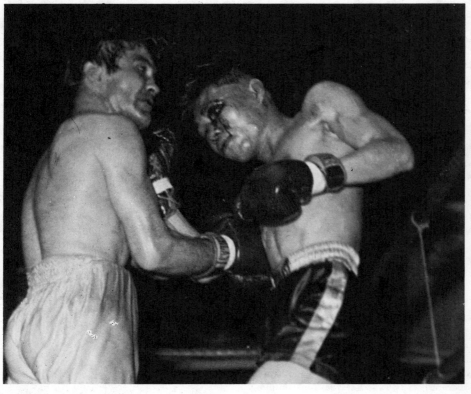

The veteran Perez, titleholder since 1954, finally met his match after 17 successful defenses, in Thailand's Pone Kingpetch, who dethroned the 34-year-old Argentinian on a split 15-round decision in Bangkok (*above*), despite suffering a deep cut over his eye. Kingpetch, his hand raised in victory (*right*), wears his new title belt.

Kingpetch, an idol in Thailand, lost the title to Japan's Fighting Harada on an 11-round knockout. However, in a return Kingpetch regained the crown on a 15-round verdict. Late *Ring* editor Nat Fleischer (*hand to forehead*) was one of the judges

seven-year-old champ had height and reach when they met at Tokyo, September 18, 1963. Ebihara overwhelmed Kingpetch, dropping him for a mandatory eight-count, then a volley of lefts and rights left Kingpetch prone and Ebihara the new champion in 2:07 of the first round.

Taking his training more seriously for his rematch with Ebihara, Kingpetch regained the title, for the second time, in fifteen action-packed rounds, on January 23, 1964 at Bangkok.

Salvatore Burruni of Italy, consistently beat defending champion King-

petch to the punch, hammering away with both hands to the face and body to gain a unanimous decision for the title, April 23, 1965 at Rome.

Scotsman Walter McGowan, British and Empire champion, became world champ when he decisioned Burruni at Tokyo, on June 14, 1966, by making

Kingpetch became an ex-champion for the second time when he ran into a Japanese buzzsaw named Hiroyuki Ebihara, who flattened the Thailander in the first round at Tokyo. *Above*, the second and final knockdown, and *right*, the new champion's happy handlers congratulate him while the dazed ex-titleholder receives assistance from his cornermen. It was a far different story four months later when Pone recaptured the flyweight crown for the second time by outpointing Ebihara in 15 rounds at Bangkok.

Kingpetch did not fight for more than a year. When he did, he lost his title to Italy's Salvatore Burruni in a 15-rounder.

the Italian run after him, then stepping in to deliver blows to Burruni's body.

Six months later, December 30, the title again changed hands when Chartchai Chionoi, of Thailand, kayoed McGowan at Bangkok. The attending physician, after examining a deep nose wound McGowan had received in the second round, halted the bout in round nine.

In his fifth defense in three years, Chionoi, at 110¾ pounds, lost the title to 111¾-pound Efren Torres at Mexico City, on February 23, 1969, when referee Arthur Mercante stopped the bout in the eighth round after the Thai's eye had swollen shut from Torres' constant jabbing.

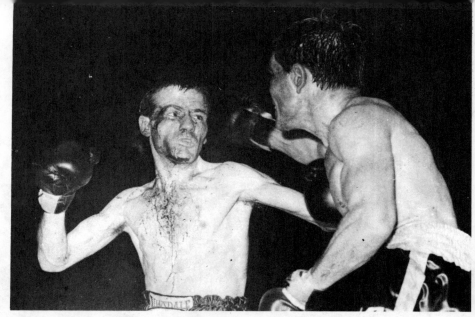

Walter McGowan became the first Briton to win the flyweight title in more than 15 years when he defeated Burruni at London in June, 1966, taking a 15-round decision.

Referee Sangvien Hiranyalekha raises hand of Chartchai Chionoi (*above, right*) after he was declared winner and new champion when McGowan (*above*) was unable to continue after 50 seconds of the ninth round due to a deep cut on his nose. (*Right*) *Ring* editor Nat Fleischer joins Chionoi in paying respects to the King of Thailand, who presents belt.

In a rematch, March 20, 1970, at Bangkok, Chionoi, using a classic left jab and lethal right hook, regained the flyweight crown, giving the Mexican champion very little room to do any damage with his powerful jabs.

Erbito Salvarria of the Philippines stopped Chionoi, on December 7, 1970, at Bangkok. The twenty-four-year-old Salvarria knocked down Chionoi, a few seconds into the second round with a staggering right hook,

then decked the Thai twice more before the fight was stopped.

The explosive Salvarria found himself in the unfamiliar position of defending against the Thailand southpaw, Venice Borkorsor, who threw jabs and left hooks at the outclassed Filipino. Borkorsor won a unanimous decision.

When Borkorsor gave up the flyweight title on July 10, 1973, to fight as a bantamweight, the World Boxing

Council selected Betulio Gonzales of Venezuela as their champion, while the World Boxing Association gave its title to Chionoi.

Gonzales lost his crown to Shoji Oguma of Japan, who won a fifteen-round split decision on October 1, 1974 in Tokyo, but Oguma lost a decision in his first defense against Miguel Canto of Mexico. Canto defended successfully twice in 1975, getting a decision against Gonzales at Monterey and stopping Jiro Takada of Japan in the eleventh at Merida.

Meanwhile Chionoi, after a defense against a Swiss challenger Fritz Chervet, who lost a decision, himself lost his W.B.A. title to Susumu Hanagata of Japan, who stopped Chionoi in the sixth at Yokohama. Hanagata then lost to previous champion Erbito Salvarria, who gained a decision at Toyama. Salvarria confirmed himself as W.B.A. champion on September 16, 1975, at Yokohama, by gaining a second decision over Hanagata in the return.

On February 27, 1976, Alfonso Lopez took over the title by stopping Salavarria in the final round at Manila, but after warding off a challenge from Shoji Oguma, who was outpointed at Tokyo on April 21, Lopez dropped his crown to Guty Espadas (Mexico) on a thirteen rounds stoppage at Los Angeles on October 2. Espadas caused Jiro Takada to retire in seven rounds at Tokyo on New Year's Day, 1977, and then stopped former champion, Alfonso Lopez in thirteen rounds in a return match at Merida on April 30. He next stopped Kimio Furesawa at Tokyo on January 2, 1978, but on August 13 at Maracay, was outpointed by Betulio Gonzalez (Venezuela). The new W.B.A. champion kept his crown against Martin Vargas, who was stopped in twelve rounds at Maracay on November 4. On January 29, 1979, however, he was held to a draw over fifteen rounds by Japanese challenger, Shoji Oguma at Hamatsu.

Miguel Canto (Mexico) maintained

Efren Torres *(above)* took the title from Chartchai Chionoi, stopping him in the eighth in 1969. The battlers bow to each other *(left)* before a rematch 13 months later, when Chionoi regained the crown on points.

403

his hold on the W.B.C. version of the flyweight title on December 15, 1975, by outpointing Ignacio Espinal at Merida, then went through the next three years without losing his championship as follows: 1976—May 15, Susumu Hanagata w.pts.15 Merida; October 3, Betulio Gonzalez w.pts.15 Caracas; November 19, Orlando Javierto w.pts.15 Los Angeles. 1977—April 24, Reyes Arnal w.pts.15 Caracas; June 15—Kimio Furesawa w.pts.15 Tokyo; September 17, Martin Vargas w.pts.15 Merida; November 30, Martin Vargas w.pts.15 Santiago. 1978—February 4 Shoji Oguma w.pts.15 Koriyama; April 18, Shoji Oguma w.pts.15 Tokyo; November 20, Tacomrom Viboochai w.pts.15 Houston.

On February 10, 1979, Canto outpointed challenger Antonio Avelar (Mexico) to give him a total of 14 successful defences. On March 18, however, the W.B.C. title changed hands when he lost on points to Chan Hee Park of Korea. In a return championship fight on September 9, he could only secure a draw. Chan Hee Park beat Tsutomu Igarashi (Japan) pts. 15 on May 20; Guty Espadas (Mexico) k.o. 2 on December 16; Arnel Allozal (Philippines) pts. 15 on February 9, 1980; Alberto Morales (Mexico) pts. 15 on April 12. Shoji Oguma (Japan) knocked out Chan Hee Park in nine rounds at Seoul on May 18, 1980 and kept his title by defeating Sung Jun Kim (Korea) on July 28 and Chan Hee Park (return title fight) on October 18, both being points wins over 15 rounds.

Back to the W.B.A. title. Betulio Gonzalez knocked out Ojuma in 12 rounds of a return fight on July 6, 1979, then lost his crown to Luis Ibarra (Panama) on a points decision at Maracay on November 17. On February 16, 1980 Ibarra was knocked out in two rounds by Tae Shik Kim (Korea) at Seoul, who outpointed Arnel Arrozal (Philippines) on his first defence on June 29, also at Seoul.

Tae Shik Kim was outpointed in turn by Peter Mathebula on December 13, 1980 at Los Angeles. Mathebula thus became the first black South African boxer to win a world title.

His reign, however, was restricted to 105 days when, before his own people at Soweto on March 28, 1981 he was knocked out in seven rounds by Santos Benigno Laciar (Argentina). The new champion was 22 and had been fighting professionally for four years. A class boxer, he was expected to reign for some time, yet at his first defence on June 6, he was outpointed by Luis Ibarra (Panama) at Buenos Aires after only 70 days as titleholder. On September 26 Juan Herrera (Mexico) took the title from Ibarra with a 15 rounds points win at Merida, then on December 19 he stopped Betulio Gonzalez (Venezuela), a former W.B.A. champion, in seven rounds also at Merida.

Laciar came back into the picture on May 1, 1982 by halting Herrera in 13 rounds at Merida, and he was to stay as champion for the next five years, with nine brilliant defences of his title against the pick of the world flyweights. After outpointing Antoine Montero on May 6, 1985 he relinquished his title in September to box as a super-flyweight and Hilario Zapata of Panama (former W.B.C. flyweight champion) outpointed Alonzo Gonzales over 15 rounds at Panama City to win the W.B.A. crown and become world champion for the third time.

Zapata continued a run of points victories with successful defences against Javier Lucas (Mexico) at Mexico City on January 31, 1986 and against Suichi Hozumi (Japan) at Nirasaki on April 7.

The W.B.A. champion won two further title contests in 1986, both on points in 15-rounders. On the first occasion he beat Dodie Penalosa at Manila, on July 5, and then travelled to Salvador, Brazil, where he licked Claudemir Dias on December 6. A couple of months later, when he went to Barranquilla, Colombia, to meet the challenge of Fidel Bassa on February 13, 1987, he was strongly favoured to win again. But the officials returned a unanimous verdict in favour of Bassa, after a hard battle, and a new champion was crowned.

In his first defence, the Colombian met Irishman Dave McAuley, on April 25, before a Belfast crowd. A thrilling contest ensued, with the champion on the verge of defeat more than once. But he proved too durable for his opponent and scored a knockout in the 13th round. A return contest between Fidel Bassa and Hilario Zapata took place on August 15, this time on the Panama boxer's home ground. The former champion dropped Bassa early on, and to the partisan crowd he appeared to have won the fight at the final bell. But the decision of a draw, with Bassa thus retaining the title, caused a riot in the arena.

The busy little Colombian finished the year's activity when he had no difficulty in completely outclassing the Dominican, Felix Marty, at Cartagena on December 18.

Bassa began 1988 by meeting Dave McAuley in a defence as hard as their previous contest, but without the knockdowns. Bassa proved a good points winner. He outpointed Raymond Medel and Julio Guidino but on September 30, 1989 at Barranquilla he was outpointed by the Venezuelan Jesus Rojas.

Charlie Magri of Great Britain (left) punching his way to the flyweight title by stopping champion Eleonceo Mercedes at Wembley in 1983.

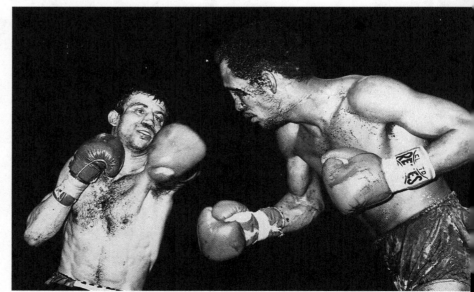

Meanwhile, the W.B.C. version of the championship had been just as active. Shoji Ogama repeated a points victory over Chan-Hee Park at Tokyo on February 3, 1981, but was knocked out in seven rounds by Antonio Avelar (Mexico) on May 12 at Mito, Japan. On August 30 he kept his crown with a two rounds knockout win over Tae-Shik Kim (Korea) at Seoul, but when he made his second defence on March 20, 1982, he was put away in 2 minutes 4 seconds by Prudencio Cardona (Colombia) at Tampico. Freddie Castillo (Mexico), who had been W.B.C. light-flyweight champion in 1978, won his second world crown on July 24 by outpointing Cardona over 15 rounds in his home-town of Merida, but he lost it on a points verdict to Eleoncio Mercedes (Dominica) at Los Angeles on November 6.

At Wembley Arena on March 15, 1983, Charlie Magri (Great Britain) retrieved the flyweight title for his country by stopping Mercedes (cut eye) in seven rounds, but the Londoner reigned for only six months, being halted by Frank Cedeno (Philippines) in six rounds on September 27, also at Wembley. On January 18, 1984 Kojo Kobayashi (Japan) took the title in two rounds from Cedeno in Tokyo, but suffered a like fate when making his first defence on April 9, also in the Japanese capital city, against Gabriel Bernal (Mexico). The new champion took the title to Nimes, France, on June 1, where he successfully defended it against Antoine Montero (France) with an 11th round stoppage, but when he ventured to Bangkok on October 8, he was outpointed over 12 rounds by Sot Chitalada (Thailand). Chitalada made two defences in 1985, stopping Charlie Magri in four rounds in London on February 20, but being held to a draw over 12 rounds by the former champ, Gabriel Bernal, on June 22 at Bangkok. On February 22, 1986, he outpointed Freddy Castillo (Mexico), another former champion, at Kuwait.

Chitalada made one more defence of the W.B.C. title in 1986, when he outpointed Gabriel Bernal over 12 rounds at Bangkok on December 10. It was not until September 6, 1987, also at Bangkok, that he appeared again, when he had no trouble in knocking out

Rae-Ki Ahn, of South Korea, in 4 rounds. He went on to stop Hideaki Kamishiro, of Japan, after 7 rounds at Osaka on January 31, 1988, when the challenger was badly cut about the eyes.

Chitalada lost the title when well outpointed by South Korea's Yong-Kang Kim at Pohang on July 23, 1988, when the long-reigning champion appeared weak at the weight. It was hinted he would return as a bantam, but after Kim had outpointed two challengers – Emil Romano of the Philippines and Yukhito Tamakuma of Japan – Chitalada returned as challenger and regained the crown by outpointing Kim at Trang on June 3, 1989.

Chitalada then added to his list of successful defences by outpointing Rik Siodoro of the Philippines and Carlos Salazar of Argentina, scoring a first-round knockout of Richard Clarke of Jamaica, and outpointing Jung-Koo Chang of South Korea, the former light-flyweight champion; but, in his first contest of 1991, on February 15, he was stopped in the sixth round by Muang-

Sot Chitalada (*left*), won the W.B.C. title in 1984 and reigned through 1988. This 1985 battle with former champ Gabriel Bernal was marked a draw.

chai Kitikasen, another former light-flyweight champion and a fellow Thai-lander, at Ayuthaya.

The I.B.F.'s involvement in the flyweight division commenced on December 24, 1983, when Soon-Chun Kwon was paired with René Busayon at Seoul. The Korean won by a 5-round knockout. He then went on to establish himself very well, defeating Roger Castillo, Ian Clyde, and Shinobu Kawashima, and boxing drawn bouts with Chong-Kwan Chung on two occasions, at Daejonn and Masan, South Korea. Then, on December 20, 1985 the two rivals met for a third time, and Chung stopped Kwon in 4 rounds. However, on April 27, 1986, the new champion was outpointed over 15 rounds by his name-sake, Bi-Won Chung. He, in turn, was beaten in the final round by Hi-Sup Shin, on August 2. Shin managed to make only one successful defence, versus Henry Brent, when their fight was stopped in the 13th round at Chunchon on November 22, before Dodie Penalosa knocked him out in 5 rounds on February 22, 1987, at Inchon. The Filipino defended his second world title against the South Korean, Chang-Ho Choi, at Manila on September 5, but his supporters saw him knocked out in 11 rounds, to suffer the second defeat of his career.

Choi's first defence was in Manila, and he was outpointed by the Filipino boxer Rolando Bohol over 15 rounds on May 6, 1988, but Bohol's hold on the title was as precarious, because he travelled to Wembley five months later and on October 5 was knocked out in the 11th round by Duke McKenzie from Croydon, a tall thin flyweight at 5ft 7in. The slick-boxing McKenzie stopped the American Tony de Luca on his first defence but then suffered his first defeat when Dave McAuley of Ireland, twice an unsuccessful challenger for the W.B.A. crown, proved too tough for McKenzie and scored a points win on June 7, 1989 at Wembley.

McAuley, who was also tall for a flyweight, and whose strengths lay in his ability to fight back after being

dropped, so that most of his contests were exciting, defended with gritty points wins over Dodie Penalosa of the Philippines at Wembley and then Louis Curtis, of the United States, Rodolfo Blanco of Colombia and Pedro Feliciano of Puerto Rico, followed by a tenth-round knockout of Jacob Matlala, these four all being at Belfast. But he lost his crown when he travelled to Bilbao, Spain, for a return with Blanco on June 11, 1992. Blanco and his connections had harboured a grudge since their first contest, when McAuley had taken the decision after being on the canvas four times, but this time it was McAuley's corner who set up the 'robbery' cry as McAuley recovered from a slow start to dominate the later rounds. However the judges had given all the early 'feeling-out' rounds to Blanco, and this was enough to gain a unanimous decision. Blanco's reign was short-lived, and McAuley was robbed of a 'rubber' match when Blanco took the belt to Thailand and was knocked out in the third round by the local Pichit Sitbangprachan in Bangkok on 29 November 1992.

Meanwhile the W.B.A. had found it difficult to find a long-running champion in the 1990s. Jesus Rojas dropped

the title when he went to Taejon for his first defence on March 10, 1990 and was outpointed by Yul-Woo Lee of South Korea. Lee dropped the crown on his first defence four months later on July 28, when he was stopped at Mito by Japan's Yukihito Tamakuma, who had challenged the previous year for the W.B.C. title. Tamakuma did manage a successful defence, but only by virtue of a draw with previous champion Jesus Rojas at Aomori. On his next outing, at Tokyo on March 14, 1991, he was outpointed by Elvis Alvarez of Colombia, the former W.B.O. champion. Alvarez was no more successful than his predecessors, losing on points at Seoul on June 1, 1991 to Yong-Kang Kim, the former W.B.C. champion and conqueror of Chitalada in 1989.

Kim brought some stability to the W.B.A. division, outpointing Luis Gamez of Venezuela at Inchon on October 5, 1991. This ended a run of six title fights which the champion had failed to win. Kim continued the good work with a further win against Jonathan Penalosa of the Philippines, but on September 26, 1992 the W.B.A. version reverted to its most erratic when Aquiles Guzman of Venezuela outpointed Kim, only to lose his first

Irishman Dave McAuley (left) took part in some of the most exciting contests, including this defence of his I.B.F. flyweight crown against Dodie Penalosa, a challenger from the Philippines. Many of McAuley's bouts saw both fighters on the canvas in turn.

McAuley (left) battles with a badly puffed eye and challenger Rodolfo Blanco of Columbia in Spain in 1992. Blanco won a hotly disputed decision.

defence on December 14, to David Griman, also of Venezuela, by unanimous decision in Mexico City.

The W.B.C. had more luck with their champions. Muangchai Kitikasem, who brought Chitalada's fine reign to an end, defended twice in 1991, first stopping Jung-Koo Chang in Seoul and then outpointing Alberto Jimenez of Mexico in Bangkok. On February 28, 1992 he stopped Sot Chitalada again, but his reign ended on June 23, 1992 when he was knocked out in the eighth round in Tokyo by Yuri Arbachakov of the C.I.S., who thus became the first world boxing champion from the break-up of the old Soviet Union. Arbachakov was backed by a Japanese syndicate and was professedly not too pleased with his experience of capitalist arrangements. However he proved himself with a points win in his first defence, in Tokyo in October when he dropped the previously unbeaten Korean Yun-Un Chin three times.

The first W.B.O. champion at the weight was Elvis Alvarez of Colombia who outpointed Miguel Mercedes of the Dominican Republic at Medellin on March 3, 1989. But Alvarez relinquished the title to try for one of the more prestigious versions. Isidro Perez of Mexico won the vacant title when, in the 12th round, he stopped Angel Rosario of Puerto Rico at Ponce on August 18, 1990. He then beat Alli Galvez of Chile, twice, but defending in Glasgow on March 18, 1992, he was outpointed by Scotland's Pat Clinton. Clinton made a successful defence in September against another Briton in Danny Porter, who was outpointed.

THE LIGHT-FLYWEIGHT CHAMPIONS

On April 4, 1975, the World Boxing Council set up a new division for boxers weighing no more than 108 pounds, when it recognized Franco Udella as champion, after he had won on a foul over Valentine Martinez (Mexico) in the 12th round at Milan. The Italian never defended the title which was won on September 13 by Luis Estaba (Venezuela) who knocked out Rafael Lovera (Paraguay) in four rounds at Caracas. The newcomer proved a most worthy champion, reigning for over two years during which he met and defeated eleven challengers, six of them inside the distance. On February 19, 1978 at Puerto La Cruz, however, he was stopped in 14 rounds by Freddie Castillo (Mexico), but on May 6 at Bangkok he was outpointed over 15 rounds by Netrnoi Son Vorasingh (Thailand). Estaba came back to try and regain his title on July 30, but was forced to retire in five rounds at Caracas.

Next champion was Sung-Yun Kim (Korea) who knocked out Vorasingh in three rounds at Seoul on September 30. He made three defences in 1979, being held to a draw by Hector Ray Melendez (Dominica) on March 31 and outpointing Siony Carupo (Philippines) on July 28 and Melendez on October 21. Shigeo Nakajima (Japan) outpointed Kim on January 3, 1980 at Tokyo, but he lasted only to March 24 when he lost on points to Hilario Zapata (Panama). Here was another outstanding champion, who reigned for two years during which he met and defeated eight challengers. Then he suffered a sensational defeat, being knocked out in two rounds by Mexico's Amado Ursua at Panama City, on February 6, 1982. Ursua kept the title only to April 13 when he lost a points verdict to Tadashi Tomori (Japan) at Tokyo.

Back into the limelight came the amazing Zapata. He outpointed Tomori at Kanazawa on July 20; did the same to Jung Koo Chang (South Korea) at Chonju on September 18 and stopped Tadashi Tomori in eight rounds at Tokyo on December 10. Chang got his own back with interest on March 26, 1983 when he stopped Zapata in three rounds at Seoul on March 26, 1983 and then proceeded to check the hopes of nine challengers, with two stoppages and the rest on points. In his contest with German Torres on April 17, 1985, there was a controversial incident in round seven when Chang dropped from what appeared to be a legitimate knockdown, and referee Arthur Mercante ruled it as a "slip". Under W.B.C. rules a knockdown scores an automatic two points

advantage, so the official's ruling made the difference between victory and defeat for the Mexican, who appealed unsuccessfully against the verdict.

In a return match at Kwanju on April 13, 1986, Chang kept his title with another points win over Torres.

The W.B.C. champion continued his winning ways. September 13 found him outpointing Francisco Montiel, at Seoul, and on December 14 he stopped Eduardo Tunon in 5 rounds at Inchon. Then, on April 19, 1987, he served Efren Pinto similarly in 6 rounds, and on June 28 he beat Augustin Garcia in 10, on both occasions at Seoul. He finished the year in fine style by easily outpointing his Mexican challenger, Isidro Peres.

Chang defended his title only once more and was again successful with an eighth-round stoppage of Hideyuki Ohashi of Japan in Tokyo. It was his 15th defence, and he then moved into the flyweight division, where he challenged Sot Chitalada.

Four months after the W.B.C.'s innovation, the W.B.A. followed suit by recognizing Jaime Rios (Panama) as its champion after he had outpointed Rigoberto Marcano (Venezuela) at Panama City on August 23, 1975. He outpointed Kazumori Tenryu (Japan) at Tokyo on January 3, 1976, but on July 1 at Santa Domingo he lost on a points verdict to Juan Guzman (Dominica). He had to give way to Yoko Gushiken (Japan) at Kotu on October 10. The new champion proved to be another long-reigning king, putting in no less than thirteen successful defences against the best at his weight in the four years he was head of the division, before he was stopped by Pedro Flores (Mexico) in 12 rounds at Okinawa. Flores made one defence, on March 8, 1981 when he lost to Hwan-Jin Kim (Korea), being halted in 13 rounds at Seoul. Kim outpointed Alfonso Lopez (Panama) on October 11, but dropped the title to Katsuo Tokashiki on points on December 16.

The Japanese boxer made five successful defences until July 10, 1983 when at Tokyo he was stopped in four rounds by Lupe Madera (Mexico). In a return title fight on October 23, Tokashiki was outpointed over 15 rounds. On May 28, 1984 Francesco

Quiroz (Dominica) knocked out Madera in nine rounds at Maracaibo, and on August 18 put paid to Victor Sierra (Panama) in two rounds. On May 29, 1985 at Miami, Joey Olivo (U.S.A.) took over from Quiroz with a points verdict, then made a points-winning defence against Mun-Jin Choi. But he lost his title to Yuh Myung-Woo (Korea) at Seoul on December 7, 1985.

The Korean defended successfully in 1986 against Jose de Jesus (Puerto Rico) with a points win at Suwan on March 9 and with a 12th round knockout of Tomohiro Kiuna (Japan) at Inchon.

Myung-Woo Yuh then placed his W.B.A. crown at stake versus Mario de Marco, at Seoul, and won on points over 15 rounds. His first fight the following year, also at Seoul, took place on March 1, when he was so far superior to his latest challenger, Eduardo Tunon, that the referee stopped the affair in the opening round. On June 7, at Pusan, the champion stopped Benedicto Murillo, from Panama, halfway through the 15th and final round, and he chalked up his seventh successful defence of his title when he outboxed Wilibardo Salazar, the Mexican, to win a unanimous points victory on February 7, 1988, at Seoul.

The outstanding champion continued with a points win over Jose de Jesus of Puerto Rico at Seoul, and two months later he knocked out in the sixth round Putt Ohyuthanakorn of Thailand in Pusan. Three months later and Bahar Udin of Indonesia was dealt the same fate, but a round later in Seoul, and three months after that, a Japanese, Katsumi Komiyama, was stopped in the tenth at Chungju. There was a four-month gap to the next defence, when an Argentinian, Mario de Marco, went the distance at Seoul. Three more months and another Japanese, Kenbun Taiho was counted out in the 11th round at Suanbo. Three months later, by now January 1990, and Hitashi Takashima, also of Japan, was stopped in the seventh at Seoul. Luis Gamez of Venezuela, the former mini-flyweight champion, was next to try, in Seoul, but was outpointed. He tried again seven months later in the same venue and with the same outcome. Kajkong Danphoothai of Thailand was stopped in the

tenth at Masan, and then on December 17, 1991 the unthinkable happened. The champion was outpointed by Hiroki Ioka of Japan at Osaka. Myung-Woo Yuh's reign had lasted for six years and he had made no fewer than 17 successful defences. Ioka was not going to relinquish the crown lightly after such a win and he defended successfully against Noel Tunacao and Bong-Jun Kim but then met Myung-Woo Yuh in a return at Osaka on November 18, 1992. Yuh reversed the previous decision and ended the year as champion once again.

The I.B.F. came into the act in 1983, when this new ruling body gave its blessing to a bout at Osaka between the Japanese Satoshi Shingaki and the Filipino Dodie Penalosa. The contest took place on December 10 and Penalosa defeated his opponent in 11 rounds. Thereafter the little champion made three impressive defences of the title, stopping Jae-Hong Kim, outpointing

Jum-Hwan Choi, and knocking out Yani Hagler. He then gave up the belt and title and entered the slightly heavier flyweight ranks, where he challenged Hilario Zapata, unsuccessfully as it happens, for his W.B.A. crown.

Pusan was the scene of the battle between Jum-Hwan Choi and Choo-Woon Park, two Koreans, to determine a new king. The former won a 15-rounder on December 7, 1986. He then outpointed Tacy Macalos on March 29, 1987, at Seoul, and on July 5 he faced Toshihiko Matsuda, the Japanese, once again at Seoul. The champion applied the finisher easily in the 4th round. He was back in action by August 9, at Jakarta, facing the challenge of Indonesia's Azadin Anhar. Choi outclassed his man and knocked him out in 3 rounds.

Choi's run ended on his next defence, when he was surprisingly outpointed by the Philippines' Tacy Macalos, fighting on home territory in Manila, on

Outstanding light-flyweight champion Myung-Woo Yuh (left) of South Korea outpointing Mario de Marco at Seoul in 1989.

November 5, 1988. Choi had outpointed Macalos 20 months earlier, and his loss broke a long-held grip of South Koreans on the light-flyweight title. In the tradition among the lighter weights of champions travelling to their opponent's territory, Macalos went to Bangkok to defend against Muangchai Kitikasem of Thailand, and was outpointed. Kitikasem stopped Macalos in a return, stopped Chung-Jae Lee of South Korea, and outpointed Abdy Pohan of Indonesia before he lost the title to an American, Michael Carbajal, at Phoenix on July 29, 1990.

Carbajal proved a very strong champion, accepting his challengers mainly from South and Central America. He knocked out Leon Salazar, of Panama, in the fourth at Scottsdale, knocked out

Macario Santos of Mexico in the second at Las Vegas, outpointed Javier Varquez of Mexico at Las Vegas, outpointed Hector Patri of Argentina at Davenport, outpointed Márcos Pancheco of Mexico at Phoenix and ended 1992 by stopping Robinson Cuesta of Panama in Phoenix.

Meanwhile, after Jung-Koo Chang relinquished the W.B.C. title, German Torres, a Mexican, won it by outpointing Soon-Jung Kang of South Korea at Seoul on December 11, 1988, but Yul-Woo Lee won it back for South Korea on March 19, 1989 at Taejon with a ninth-round knockout. Another Mexican, Humberto Gonzalez, took it off Lee with a points win at Seoul on June 25, 1989.

Gonzalez settled down to an impressive reign, beating off challengers from both sides of the world. He outpointed Jung-Koo Chang of South Korea at Seoul, knocked out Francisco Tejedor of Colombia at Mexico City, stopped a Cuban, Luis Monzote, and a South Korean, Jung-Keun Lim, both at Los Angeles, and knocked out a Mexican, Jorge Rivera, at Cancun. On December 19, 1990, however, he was shocked by Rolando Pascua of the Philippines, who knocked him out in the sixth round in Los Angeles. But Pascua lost to a Mexican, Melchor Cob Castro, who forced him to retire in the tenth round at Los Angeles on March 25, 1991, and less than three months later, on June 3, Gonzalez had the title back when he outpointed Castro at Las Vegas.

Gonzalez resumed his reign with the same success as before, outpointing Domingo Sosa, stopping the 1988 Olympic champion Kwang-Sun Kim of South Korea in Seoul, stopping Napa Kiabwanchai of Thailand and outpointing previous champion Melchor Cob Castro in their return.

On March 13, 1993 Gonzalez, as W.B.C. champion, met the I.B.F. champion, Michael Carbajal, at the Las Vegas Hilton to unify the two versions of the title. It was the richest fight ever held in the division. Gonzalez floored Carbajal for the first time in his career in the second round and again in the fifth, and was four points ahead on all the cards when the unbeaten Carbajal caught him with a classic left hook to the chin which knocked him out with one second of the seventh round remaining. It was Gonzalez's second career defeat.

The W.B.O. version of the title came into being on May 19, 1989, when Jose de Jesus of Puerto Rico stopped Fernando Martinez at San Juan. Successful defences followed against Isidro Perez, Alli Galvez and Abdy Pohan before he relinquished the title. On July 31, 199 a fellow Puerto Rican, Jose Camacho won the vacant title when he knocked out Mexico's Eddie Vallejo in the sixth round.

THE MINI-FLYWEIGHT OR STRAWWEIGHT CHAMPIONS

This division, with a weight limit of 105lb (7 stone 7lb), was instituted by the I.B.F. in 1987. The I.B.F., formed as a breakaway from the W.B.A. in 1983, had most support initially from Australia and Far Eastern countries, and has had most influence in the lighter weights. The I.B.F. called the division strawweight, a title followed by the W.B.C., but the W.B.A., on recognising the division, called it mini-flyweight. Most champions of all versions have come from South Korea, Japan, Thailand, the Philippines, Indonesia and Mexico.

The first I.B.F. champion was Kyung Yung Lee, of South Korea, who knocked out Masaharu Kawakami of Japan in the second round at Bujok on June 14, 1987. Lee relinquished the title, however, to challenge for the W.B.C. title, which was inaugurated four months later, on September 18 1987, at Osaka. The winner was Hirok Ioka of Japan, who outpointed Ma Thornburifarm. Ioka stopped Kyung Yung Lee, his first challenger, but los

Ohashi (left) of Japan successfully defending his W.B.C. strawweight title against Kiatwanchai.

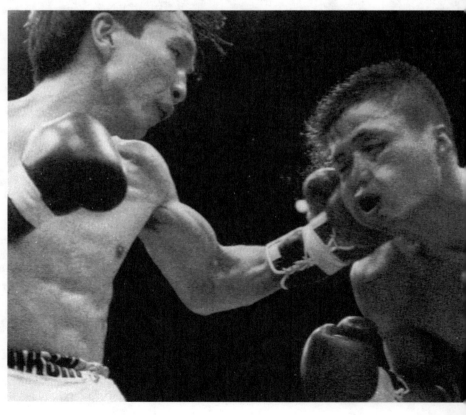

the title to Napa Kiatwanchai of Thailand, who drew with Ioka on his first challenge, in June 1988, but outpointed him in the return at Osaka on November 13, 1988, and stopped him in the 11th round in their third meeting in 1989, having outpointed John Arief of Indonesia in the meantime. Kiatwanchai failed to survive his next challenger, however, and was stopped in the 12th and the last round by South Korea's Jum-Hwan Choi at Seoul on November 12, 1989. Less than three months later, Choi copied his predecessor by taking the belt to the land of his challenger, and on February 7, 1990 he suffered the same fate of losing it. He was knocked out by Japan's Hideyuki Ohashi in the ninth round in Tokyo.

Ohashi made his two defences in Tokyo, first outpointing former champion Napa Kiatwanchai, but being stopped in the fifth round when a fiery Mexican, Ricardo Lopez, challenged on October 25, 1990. Lopez proved able to defend successfully at home or away and beat Kimio Hirano (Japan, stopped eighth, Shizuoka), Kyung-Yung Lee, the division's first champion (points, Inchon), Domingo Lucas, who had previously fought a draw for the I.B.F. version, (Philippines, points, Mexico City), Singprasert Kittikasem (Thailand, knockout fifth, Ciudad Madero), Rocky Lim (Thailand, knockout second, Tokyo) and Kwang-Soo Oh (South Korea, stopped ninth, Seoul). This last contest, on January 31, 1993, maintained an unbeaten record for Lopez which consisted of 32 victories.

The vacant I.B.F. title meanwhile was won by Samuth Sithnaruepol of Thailand, who outpointed In-Kyu Hwang of South Korea in Bangkok on August 29, 1988. Nico Thomas of Indonesia took the title from him at his second attempt, the first having been a draw. Both contests were at Jakarta, and that on June 17, 1989 Thomas won on points. Thomas, however, was knocked out in the fifth round on his first defence in Jakarta on September 21 by Eric Chavez of the Philippines, and Chavez continued the dismal record of I.B.F. champions by also losing on his first defence. He went to Bangkok on

February 22, 1990 and was stopped in the seventh round by Fahlan Lukmingkwan.

The Thailander at last gave this version of the title some stability, and made seven successful defences. These were: in 1990, Joe Constantino (Philippines, points), previous champion Eric Chavez in a return (points) and Domingo Lucas (Philippines, drew); in 1991, Abdy Pohan (Indonesia, points) and Andy Tabanas (Philippines, points); in 1992, Felix Naranjo (Colombia, knockout second) and Said Iskander (Indonesia, stopped eighth). All these contests were in Bangkok, as was that in which Lukmingkwan lost the title on September 6, 1992. He was outpointed by Manny Melchor of the Philippines, at which the I.B.F. crown reverted to type, for Melchor also defended in Bangkok, and on December 10 was himself outpointed by Rattanopol Sorvorapin, the title thus returning to Thailand.

The W.B.A. were third to recognise the division. The first champion was Luis Gamez of Venezuela, who on January 10, 1988 outpointed a South Korean, Bong-Jun Kim, at Pusan. But after stopping Kenji Yokozawa of Japan in the third round in Tokyo, Gamez relinquished the title to campaign as a light-flyweight. Bong-Jun Kim won the vacant crown by stopping Agustin Garcia of Colombia at Seoul on April 16, 1989. Kim outpointed fellow-Korean Sam-Jung Lee at Seoul, and at Inchon stopped in the ninth John Arief, an earlier W.B.C. challenger. In 1990 he stopped in the third Petchai Chuwatana of Thailand, won a fifth round technical decision over Silverio Barcenas of Panama and then outpointed him in a return, all at Seoul. He lost the title on February 2, 1991, when he was outpointed by another South Korean, Hi-Yon Choi, at Pujan. Choi made four successful defences. At Seoul, he outpointed Sugar Ray Mike of the Philippines, he outpointed Bong-Jun Kim in their title return and stopped Yuichi Hosono of Japan in the tenth round. At Inchon he knocked out Rommel Lawas of the Philippines in the third round. But on October 14, 1992, in Tokyo, he was challenged by the former W.B.C.

High jinks from Ricardo Lopez of Mexico in the Tokyo ring in which he took the W.B.C. strawweight title from Hideyuki Ohashi in 1990. Lopez remained unbeaten into 1993, having beaten off six challengers. The 105-lb division was introduced in 1987 and has been a lucrative source of titles for boxers from Mexico and the Far Eastern countries.

champion, Hideyuki Ohashi, and was outpointed.

Ohashi lost the W.B.A. version on his first defence, however, being clearly outpointed in Tokyo on February 10, 1993, by the aggressive Chana Porpaoin, of Thailand, although one judge made it a draw. Porpaoin was unbeaten in 27 contests.

The W.B.O. recognised Rafael Torres of Dominica as champion when he outpointed Tamil Carballo of Colombia at Santo Domingo on August 31, 1989. Torres outpointed Husni Ray of Indonesia in Jakarta on July 31, 1990, but relinquished the title, which was still vacant in 1993.

UPDATE FOR THE 1997 EDITION

HEAVYWEIGHTS

When Riddick Bowe outpointed Evander Holyfield to win the heavyweight title in 1992, he was widely hailed as the savior of the division, a dominant force that would make people forget the still-incarcerated Mike Tyson. But the combination of Bowe's lack of dedication and his manager Rock Newman's philosophy of making as much money as possible with as little risk as possible soon led to "Big Daddy's" downfall.

Bowe made his second defense of the W.B.A. and I.B.F. titles on May 22, 1993, in the champ's hometown of Washington, D. C. The challenger was lightly regarded journeyman Jesse Ferguson, who was quickly dispatched in the second round. The bout was poorly attended, and the public, tired of Bowe's propensity for defending the title against hopeless underdogs, demanded a competitive match. Therefore, on November 6, 1993, Bowe gave Holyfield a rematch in Las Vegas.

An inspired Holyfield, with a new trainer, Emanuel Steward, in his corner, regained the titles with a twelve-round decision over Bowe, who had grown soft on a diet of easy opponents. The bout was marked by one of the most bizarre incidents in boxing history. In the seventh round, a man flying a propeller-driven paraglider entered the outdoor arena at Caesars Palace and attempted to land in the ring. "Fan Man," however, became entangled in the ring ropes and fell backward into the crowd, where he was beaten by members of Bowe's camp before security guards arrived and arrested him. The fight was halted for almost thirty minutes while order was restored, and when action resumed, Holyfield alternately boxed and slugged his way to a close victory.

Lennox Lewis made his second defense of the W.B.C. title on October 1, 1993, in

A nonchalant-looking George Foreman watched as referee Joe Cortez counted out Michael Moorer in the tenth round of their 1994 heavyweight title bout. Trailing on points, Foreman floored Moorer with a booming right hand to regain the title he'd lost to Muhammad Ali twenty years earlier.

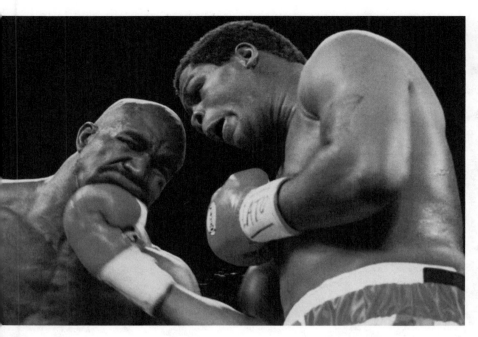

Riddick Bowe came off the deck to tally an eighth-round TKO of Evander Holyfield in the third of their thrilling three-fight series. No title was at stake in the 1995 bout, as Holyfield had lost the title to Michael Moorer the previous year.

Cardiff, Wales, against England's Frank Bruno, surviving a few rocky moments before recording a seventh-round technical knockout. The next opponent for Lewis was American Phil Jackson, who was stopped in the eighth round on May 6, 1994, in Atlantic City. A few weeks earlier, on April 22 in Las Vegas, Holyfield had lost the W.B.A. and I.B.F. titles to Michael Moorer in a twelve-round decision. It was a strangely lackluster performance by Holyfield, and a few days after the fight he announced his retirement, explaining that he'd been diagnosed as having a noncompliant left ventricle, a heart condition that only manifested itself during extreme physical exertion.

With both Holyfield and Tyson gone from the scene, Lewis was briefly considered the best heavyweight in the world. But that all changed on September 24, 1994, when Oliver McCall, Tyson's former sparring partner, traveled to London, England, where he knocked out Lewis in the second round to garner the W.B.C. crown.

The next stunning upset came on November 5, 1994, when former heavyweight champion George Foreman regained the title with a tenth-round, one-punch knockout of Moorer in Las Vegas.

Moorer, the first left-handed heavyweight champion in history, was way ahead on points when the forty-six-year-old Foreman connected with a right hand to the point of the chin that put Moorer down for a full count. Foreman's remarkable feat came twenty years after he'd lost the title to Muhammad Ali in "the Rumble in the Jungle."

Foreman's first defense of the I.B.F. title resulted in a controversial twelve-round decision over the lightly regarded German Axel Schulz on April 22, 1995. Most observers felt that Schulz had done enough to win, and the I.B.F. ordered a rematch. Foreman refused and was stripped of the title. He had already been stripped of the W.B.A. belt for not defending against the organization's top contender, Bruce Seldon.

On April 8, 1995, Seldon won the vacant W.B.A. title by stopping Tony Tucker in the seventh round. On December 9, 1995, South Africa's Frans Botha won a twelve-round decision over Schulz for the vacant I.B.F. crown. However, Botha tested positive for anabolic steriods after the match and was eventually stripped of the I.B.F. title for violating the organization's drug policy.

Tyson, who had been released from prison on March 25, 1995, began his comeback on August 19, 1995, at the MGM Grand in Las Vegas. Despite the fact that his opponent was the hopelessly outclassed Peter McNeeley, the bout attracted a capacity crowd of 16,736 and set a new pay-per-view record of $80 million.

McCall made one successful defense, a twelve-round decision over ex-champ Larry Holmes on April 8, 1995, but then

In his first bout since being released from prison, Mike Tyson had no trouble disposing of mismatched Peter McNeeley in the first round. After getting up from two knockdowns, McNeeley was disqualified when his trainer jumped into the ring in an effort to stop the fight.

Massive underdog Evander Holyfield became only the second man in boxing history to win the heavyweight title three times when he stopped Mike Tyson in the eleventh round of their 1996 bout in Las Vegas. Nevada bookies were hit almost as hard as Tyson when practically everybody bet on Holyfield.

lost the W.B.C. title to Bruno in a twelve-round decision on September 2, 1995, in London.

Following another tune-up fight—a third-round knockout of Buster Mathis Jr. on December 16, 1995—Tyson regained the W.B.C. title with a third-round knockout of Bruno on March 16, 1996, in Las Vegas. In three fights since coming out of prison, Tyson had grossed $65 million in purses.

On June 22, 1996, former champion Moorer won the vacant I.B.F. title by outpointing Schulz in Dortmund, Germany. Tyson then regained the W.B.A. title on September 7, 1996, by knocking out Seldon in the first round. The defending champion was so terrified he went down the first time from a punch that barely grazed the top of his head. The bout was stopped after Seldon was knocked down again.

After passing a battery of medical tests, Holyfield had meanwhile resumed his career on May 20, 1995, winning a ten-round decision over rugged Ray Mercer in Atlantic City. But when he lost a rubber match to Bowe in an eighth-round knockout on November 4, 1995, Holyfield was considered washed up. But the "Real Deal" persisted, and on November 9, 1996, following a fifth-round kayo of former light heavyweight and cruiserweight titleholder Bobby Czyz (on May 10, 1996), he challenged Tyson for the W.B.A. title.

Holyfield was a huge underdog, and most of the media predicted an easy victory for Tyson. But after surviving a booming right hand in the opening moments of the fight, Holyfield dominated. In the sixth round Tyson was knocked down for only the second time in his career when Holyfield connected with a left hook to the body. A vicious barrage of

punches staggered Tyson near the end of the tenth round, and when Holyfield hurt him again in the eleventh, referee Mitch Halpern stopped the fight. The startling upset victory allowed Holyfield to join Muhammad Ali as one of two men to win the heavyweight title three times.

Prior to the Holyfield-Tyson bout, Lennox Lewis had won a court battle with the W.B.C. that forced the Mexican-based organization to strip Tyson of the W.B.C. version of the title. On February 7, 1997, Lewis regained the W.B.C. belt by stopping previous conquerer McCall in the third round.

Tommy Morrison won the vacant W.B.O. title on June 7, 1993, with a twelve-round decision over Foreman, but lost it in his first defense when underdog Michael Bentt stopped him in the opening round on October 29, 1993. Bentt was no more successful, and also lost the

Mike Tyson bites into the ear of Evander Holyfield in the third round of their W.B.A. heavyweight match on Saturday, June 28, 1997, at the MGM Grand in Las Vegas.

belt in his first defense when England's Herbie Hide knocked him out in the seventh round, on March 19, 1994.

Hide was another short-term titleholder, losing the W.B.O. belt to Bowe in a sixth-round knockout on March 11, 1995, in Las Vegas. Bowe made one defense, stopping Cuban Jorge Gonzales in the sixth round on June 17, 1995, but relinquished the title shortly thereafter in order to pursue other options.

The vacancy was filled on June 29, 1996, when another Englishman, Henry Akinwande, stopped American Jeremy Williams in the sixth round. Akinwande stopped Russian immigrant Alexander Zolkins in his first defense on November 9, 1996, and outpointed Scott Welch on January 11, 1997, in his second defense.

Mike Tyson's attempt to regain the W.B.A. heavyweight title from Evander Holyfield ended in failure and disgrace on the evening of June 28, 1997, when he was disqualified in the third round for twice biting the defending champion on the ears.

Tyson's barbaric display, which resulted in the most bizarre ending in heavyweight championship history, led to the Nevada Boxing Commission's revocation of his license and a $3 million fine. He is allowed an annual appeal for reinstatement.

After being jarred by a right from Holyfield in the first, Tyson was cut over the right eye in the second by what referee Mills Lane ruled was an accidental head butt. The ex-champ got off to a good start in the third round, but appeared to become frustrated when his best punches failed to faze Holyfield.

Midway into the round, Tyson bit off a piece of Holyfield's right ear during a clinch. Lane called for a time-out and penalized Tyson two points, one for biting and one for pushing. Soon after action resumed, Tyson bit Holyfield on the left ear, and at the end of the round the referees disqualified him.

An enraged Tyson made several attempts to get at Holyfield after the fight was stopped, and also took a swing at police officers who were trying to restore order. Tyson, once the most popular boxer in the world, was booed out of the ring by the capacity crowd of 16,325, some of whom threw debris at him as he exited the MGM Grand Arena. The post fight melee spread to the casino lobby, where a number of people were crushed by panic-stricken patrons stampeding for the exit.

CRUISERWEIGHTS

The cruiserweights continued as boxing's most unpopular division, a no-man's-land between the light-heavyweight and heavyweight divisions. Except for Evander Holyfield, the 190-pound class has yet to produce a star-quality fighter.

I.B.F. champion Al Cole made five successful defenses and then relinquished the title to campaign as a heavyweight. American Alphonso Washington and German Tortsen May were matched for the vacant title on August 31, 1996, with Washington winning in a twelve-round decision.

Anaclet Wamba, the W.B.C. titleholder, made seven successful defenses, but when an injury kept him out of action for over a year, Marcelo Dominguez (of Argentina) knocked out Akim Tafer (of France) for the interim W.B.C. title on July 25, 1995. When Wamba stayed on the sidelines, however, Dominguez, an iron-jawed brawler, was made the full-fledged champion after his tenth-round knockout of Patrick Aoussi on July 5, 1996. On December 6, 1996, Dominguez retained the title with a seventh-round knockout of Jose Arimateia Da Silva in Buenos Aires, Argentina.

Bobby Czyz voluntarily relinquished the W.B.A. title in September 1993, and Orlin Norris (from the United States) knocked out Marcelo Figuero (of Argentina) in the sixth round to claim the vacant crown on November 6, 1993.

Norris made four successful defenses, but then lost the W.B.A. title to Philadelphian Nate Miller in an eighth-round knockout on July 22, 1995. Miller made four defenses, knocking out Reynaldo Giminez, Brian LaSpada, James Heath, and Alexander Gurov.

Argentina's Nestor Giovanni became the fourth W.B.O. cruiserweight champion when he won a twelve-round decision over Markus Bott in Germany on June 26, 1993. After beating Bott again in a rematch, Giovanni lost the title to German Dariusz Michalczewski with a tenth-round knockout on December 17, 199[ ] Michalczewski returned to the light-hea[vy]yweight division, where, prior to beati[ng] Giovanni, he'd campaigned without d[e]fending the title.

Germany's Ralf Rocchigiani and E[n]gland's Carl Thompson fought for t[he] vacant W.B.O. crown on June 10, 199[ ] with Rocchigiani scoring an eleven[th] round knockout. Rocchigiani successfu[lly] defended with decision wins over Ma[rk] Randazzo, Bashiru Ali, and Stephan A[l]ghern, and a knockout of Jay Snyder.

LIGHT HEAVYWEIGHTS

Virgil Hill, the left-handed W.B.[A.] light-heavyweight champion fro[m] Bismark, North Dakota, continued to tu[rn] back all challengers with his slick defe[n]sive style. On August 28, 1993, he talli[ed] the third defense of his second reig[n] winning a twelfth-round decision ov[er] Sergo Merani. Over the next three yea[rs] Hill racked up six more defenses, beati[ng] Saul Montana, Guy Waters, Frank Ta[te,] Crawford Ashley, Drake Thadzi, and L[ou] Del Valle. Montana was stopped in t[he] tenth-round, while all the others went t[he] twelve-round distance against the lig[ht] hitting champion.

As Hill was outsmarting one challeng[er] after another, I.B.F. champion Hen[ry] Maske was establishing himself as t[he] most popular German boxer since M[ax] Schmeling. After winning the belt fro[m] Prince Charles Williams, Maske made h[is] first defense on September 18, 1993, wi[n]ning a twelve-round decision over Ame[ri]can Anthony Hembrick in Dusseldorf.

Fighting exclusively in German[y,] Maske extended his unbeaten streak, su[c]cessfully defending the I.B.F. crown ni[ne] more times. He beat David Vedder, Ern[st] Magdaleno, Andrea Magi, Iran Barkle[y,] Egerton Marcus, Graciano Rocchigia[ni] (twice), Duran Williams, and John Scu[lly.]

Due to Maske's ability to draw hu[ge] crowds in his native land, his promot[er] was able to afford a purse large enough [to] lure W.B.A. champion Hill to Germa[ny] for a unification bout on November, 2[3,] 1996. Like Hill, Maske was a defensi[ve] specialist who relied on skillful boxi[ng] rather than punching power. As expecte[d,] the bout between the two safety-fir[st]

round knockout of Carl Jones on February 25, 1995, in London. In his next bout, the Jamaican veteran lost the title to Frenchman Fabrice Tiozzo on June 16, 1995.

Tiozzo made only one defense, winning a twelve-round decision over Canadian Eric Lucas on January 13, 1996. When Tiozzo failed to defend the title for more than a year, the W.B.C. matched former I.B.F. middleweight and super-middleweight champion Roy Jones with McCallum for the interim title. Jones won a twelve-round decision over the faded McCallum on November 22, 1996, and when Tiozzo decided he would fight as a cruiserweight, the W.B.C. made Jones the champion.

On March 21, 1997, in his first defense of the W.B.C. title, the previously undefeated Jones was disqualified for hitting challenger Montell Griffin while he was down. In the ninth round of a close fight, Jones dropped Griffin with a series of rights to the head. Then, with Griffin resting on one knee, Jones hit him with a right and a left. Griffin pitched forward, face first, and referee Tony Perez had no choice but to disqualify Jones and award the belt to Griffin.

Dariusz Michalczewski out-pointed American Leonzer Barber to win the W.B.O. cruiserweight title on September 9, 1994. The German held the title longer than any previous W.B.O. 175-pound titleholder, making successful defenses against Roberto Dominguez, Paul Carlo, Everado Armenta, Phillipe Michel, Asluddin Umarov, Christophe Girard (twice), and Graciano Rocchigiani.

SUPER-MIDDLEWEIGHTS

After winning the I.B.F. super-middleweight title, James Toney won five nontitle bouts before putting the title on the line against fellow American Tony Thornton on October 29, 1993. Thornton did well the first half of the bout, but Toney came on strong in the second half to retain the title in a twelve-round decision.

Toney, a volatile individual who had problems keeping his weight down, made two more successful defenses, knocking out Tim Littles and former I.B.F. light-heavyweight champion Prince Charles

Nate Miller upset Orlin Norris to win the W.B.A. curiserweight title in an eighth-round knockout in July 1995. Although somewhat mechanical in his approach, the Philadelphian's potent right hand made him perhaps the most dangerous cruiserweight since Evander Holyfield ruled the division in the 1980s.

technicians was far from thrilling, but after twelve close rounds, Hill was awarded a split decision, making him both the W.B.A. and I.B.F. 175-pound champion.

W.B.C. champ Jeff Harding lost the title in his third defense, when crafty Mike McCallum outpointed him over twelve rounds on July 23, 1994. McCallum, who had already held world titles at the junior-middleweight and middleweight levels, was past his prime when he beat Harding and only managed to make one successful defense, a seventh-

Williams. The savage twelfth-round knockout of Williams helped set up a much anticipated showdown between Toney and I.B.F. middleweight king Roy Jones. On November 18, 1994, they met in Las Vegas, with Jones winning a relatively easy, twelve-round decision. Toney, weakened by losing too much weight too quickly, was thoroughly outboxed, and was so distraught afterward, he threatened to shoot his manager, Jackie Kallen.

The multitalented Jones reigned as the I.B.F. 169-pound champion until moving up to the light-heavyweight division in November 1996. Prior to that, Jones recorded five successful defenses, defeating Antoine Byrd, Vinny Pazienza, Tony Thornton, Eric Lucas, and Bryant Brannon. It was lack of competition at super-middleweight, more than anything else, that prompted Jones to abandon the division.

W.B.A. champion Michael Nunn's fourth successful defense, a twelve-round decision over Merqui Sosa on December 18, 1993, was to be his last. He lost the title in his next bout, dropping a twelve-round split decision to lightly regarded Steve Little, a journeyman fighter from Allentown, Pennsylvania. Little, in turn, lost the W.B.A. belt in his first defense when another American, Frank Liles, outpointed him over twelve rounds on August 12, 1994.

Liles, a lanky, long-armed boxer with decent power, gave Nunn a crack at his old title on December 17, 1994, beating him in a twelve-round decision. Liles carried on to successfully defend the title with knockouts of Frederic Seillier, Tim Littles, and Segundo Mercado, and a twelve-round decision over Mauricio Amaral.

Due to his all-action style, W.B.C. titleholder Nigel Benn developed into one of England's most popular fighters. He made his third defense on June 26, 1993, stopping Lou Gent in the fourth round. That easy victory further whet the public's appetite for a showdown with Benn's W.B.O. counterpart, Chris Eubank, who had knocked out Benn in 1990. The rematch, held in Manchester on October 9, 1993, was fiercely contested, and after twelve give-and-take rounds the bout was ruled a draw, though the majority of observers thought Benn had held a slight advantage.

Benn strengthened his position in his fifth and sixth title defenses, scoring unanimous twelve-round decisions over rugged Juan Carlos Jimenez and hard-punching Henry Wharton. This set the stage for what was to be the most memorable battle of Benn's career.

American Gerald McClellan, the W.B.C. middleweight champion, was considered, pound-for-pound, perhaps the hardest puncher in boxing. When he announced he was moving up to super-middleweight to challenge Benn, the prevailing opinion was that McClellan would prove too powerful for the reckless Englishman. They met in front of a capacity crowd at the London Arena on February 25, 1995, and produced one of the most brutal fights in the history of the sport.

McClellan almost ended matters in the opening round when he knocked Benn through the ropes and onto the ring apron with a barrage of punches. Somehow Benn managed to jump back into the ring before the count of ten and survived the round. Then followed a see-saw slugging match that saw each man repeatedly connect with crushing blows to the head. Benn was knocked down again in the eighth, but beat the count and fought back with renewed intensity. After an accidental clash of heads stunned McClellan in the ninth, Benn took over. He landed a big right in the tenth, and McClellan sank to one knee. Shortly after he regained his feet, Benn jolted him with an uppercut, and McClellan went down for the full count.

Moments after the fight had been stopped, McClellan collapsed in his corner and was rushed to the hospital, where he underwent an emergency operation to remove a blood clot from his brain. The doctors were able to save McClellan's life, but he was so severely injured that he never fought again.

The grueling fight also took a lot out of Benn. He had enough left to make two more successful title defenses, knocking out Italian Vincenzo Mardiello and American Danny Perez, but was obviously not the same fighter he'd been before his punishing encounter with McClellan. On March 2, 1996, Benn lost the W.B.C. super-middleweight title to South African Sugarboy Malinga, who won a twelve-round split decision in a lackluster bout.

Malinga, a powder-puff puncher, lost the title to Nardiello in a twelve-round decision on July 2, 1996, in his first defense. Nardiello had no better luck hanging onto the title, and also lost the belt in his initial defense, when England's Robin Reid knocked him out in the seventh round on October 12, 1996, in Milan, Italy. Reid, a hard puncher with matinee-idol looks, broke the first-defense jinx on February 8, 1997, by knocking out South Africa's Giovanni Pretorious in the seventh round.

After drawing with Benn in an effort to add the W.B.C. super-middleweight title to the W.B.O. version he already held, Chris Eubank continued to rack up defenses of the W.B.O. title. The eccentric Englishman outpointed Graciano Rocchigiani, Ray Close, Mauricio Amaral, Dan Schommer, and Henry Warton, and stopped Sam Storey. His reign came to an end on September 9, 1995, when he lost a twelve-round decision to Ireland's Steve Collins.

Collins, who depended on conditioning to overcome more naturally gifted fighters, beat Eubank again in a rematch, and then outpointed Cornelius Carr on November 26, 1995, for his second defense. Next, he stopped Neville Brown in the eleventh round. Collins's fourth and fifth defenses came against Nigel Benn, and both bouts ended with Collins emerging victorious with fourth- and fifth-round technical knockouts.

In one of the most savage fights of all-time, England's Nigel Benn retained the W.B.C. super-middleweight title with a tenth-round knockout of American challenger Gerald McClellan in 1995. McClellan, who knocked Benn out of the ring in the first round, suffered serious brain injuries in the give-and-take bout and never fought again.

Challenger Joe Lipsey (right) missed with most of his big punches, but I.B.F. middleweight champion Bernard "the Executioner" Hopkins was on target with his in their 1996 title bout. Ignoring the managerial and promotional problems that plagued him, Hopkins retained the title with a vicious fourth-round knockout.

MIDDLEWEIGHTS

When I.B.F. middleweight champion James Toney relinquished the title to fight as a super-middleweight, a match between Roy Jones and Bernard Hopkins was held on May 22, 1993, in Washington, D.C., to fill the vacancy. Jones won a twelve-round decision, but only made one defense, a second-round knockout of Thomas Tate on May 27, 1994, before also moving up to the 168-pound class.

Again, Hopkins was involved in a bout to find a new I.B.F. champion. This time he was matched with Segundo Mercado, but the title remained vacant when Hopkins and Mercado battled to a twelve-round draw on December 17, 1994, in Segundo's homeland of Ecuador. On April 29, 1995, the pair fought again, and Hopkins emerged with the I.B.F. title after knocking out Mercado in the seventh round.

Hopkins, a no-nonsense workman with a telling punch, brought a measure of stability to the middleweight division. He made three defenses in 1996, knocking out Steve Frank, Joe Lipsey, and Bo James. On April 18, 1997, he made his fourth successful defense, knocking out former W.B.A. middleweight champion John David Jackson in the seventh round.

W.B.C. middleweight champion Gerald McClellan made two defenses of the belt he'd won from Julian Jackson, knocking out outclassed Jeffery Bell and Gilberto Baptist, both in the opening round. Then he made the fateful decision to move up to super-middleweight and challenge W.B.C. king Nigel Benn. It proved to be McClellan's last fight, for he suffered a career-ending brain injury during the bout, which he lost in a tenth-round knockout.

Ex-champ Julian Jackson, a native of the Virgin Islands, won the vacant W.B.C. title with a second-round knockout of Agostino Cardamone on March 17, 1995. Jackson was well past his prime, however, and on August 19, 1995, he lost the title to Texan Quincy Taylor in a sixth-round knockout in his first defense. The title changed hands again on March 16, 1996, when Keith Holmes, from Washington, D.C., stopped Taylor in the ninth round. Holmes survived his first defense, stopping England's Richie Woodall in the twelfth-round on October 19, 1996.

Reggie Johnson, the W.B.A. middleweight champion, lost the title to John David Jackson in an extremely close twelve-round decision on October 1, 1993, but the W.B.A. stripped Jackson of the title for participating in a nontitle bout without permission from the organization. Johnson was given an opportunity to regain the title when he was matched with Jorge Castro on August 12, 1994, but lost a twelve-round decision to the brawler from Argentina.

Castro held onto the W.B.A. title through four defenses, knocking out Alex Ramos, Anthony Andrews, and former champ John David Jackson. In his last successful defense, Castro won a twelve-round decision over another former titleholder, Reggie Johnson. Castro's reign ended, however, on December 19, 1995, when he lost a twelve-round decision to unbeaten Shinji Takehara in Tokyo, Japan.

Takehara turned out to be another short-term champion, and lost the W.B.A. crown to American William Joppy in a ninth-round knockout on June 24, 1996. In his first defense, Joppy retained the title with a sixth-round knockout of soft touch Ray McElroy.

Britain's Chris Pyatt won the vacant W.B.O. middleweight title on May 19, 1993, with a twelve-round decision over Sumbu Kalambay. Pyatt then made two successful defenses, knocking out Hugo Corti and Mark Cameron. In his third defense, Pyatt lost the belt to Steve Collins in a fifth-round technical knockout on May 11, 1994. Collins, however, immediately abandoned the title in order to move up to the super-middleweight division.

The W.B.O. vacancy at 160 pounds was filled on May 19, 1995, when New Yorker Lonnie Bradley stopped David Mendez in the twelfth round. Bradley knocked out Dario Galindez and Randy Smith in his first two defenses, and then won twelve round decisions over Lonny Beasley and former welterweight and junior-middleweight champion Simon Brown. In his fifth defense, on March 4, 1997, Bradley barely managed to keep the W.B.O. belt when Canada's Otis Grant held him to twelve-round draw in Las Vegas.

LIGHT-MIDDLEWEIGHTS

W.B.C. light-middleweight champion Terry Norris was considered practically unbeatable after knocking out challengers Troy Waters and Joe Gatti for his ninth and tenth successful defenses, but all that changed when he tackled former I.B.F. welterweight champion Simon Brown on December 18, 1993. Brown walked through Norris's best punches and won the title with a spectacular fourth-round knockout.

After defending the title with a twelve-round decision over Troy Waters, Brown gave Norris a rematch on May 7, 1994. Their second fight was of a very different character. Instead of trading punches with his dangerous opponent, Norris boxed cautiously from long range and regained the title with a twelve-round decision.

Next came Norris's weird three-bout series with club fighter Luis Santana, who had done little to earn a shot at the title and was considered a hopeless underdog. In the fifth round of their November 12, 1994, bout in Mexico City, Norris hit Santana in the back of the head while the challenger's back was turned. Santana fell to the floor and lay there for over five minutes as officials decided what to do. Eventually Santana, who was carried from the ring on a stretcher, was declared the new champion through the disqualification of Norris.

Many observers believed that Santana was faking, and when a rematch was held on April 8, 1995, in Las Vegas, Norris was highly favored to regain the W.B.C. title.

Nevertheless, controversy struck again when Norris hit Santana after the bell ended the third round, resulting in another disqualification win for Santana. Norris finally got it right in the third fight, on August 19, 1995, when he regained the title with a second-round knockout.

With the Santana nightmare behind him, Norris stopped David Gonzalez in the ninth round on September 16, 1995, and then won the I.B.F. version of the title with a twelve-round decision over Paul Vaden on December 16, 1995. Only the I.B.F. belt was at stake when Norris scored a second-round knockout of Jorge Luis Vado on January 27, 1996, but both the I.B.F. and W.B.C. titles were on the line when he knocked out Vincent Pettway in the eighth round a month later.

Norris further enhanced his standing as one of the finest fighters in the world by making two more defenses of the I.B.F. and W.B.C. titles, knocking out Alex Rios on September, 7, 1996, in the sixth round, and Nick Rupa in the tenth round on January 11, 1997.

Meanwhile, the I.B.F. title was switching hands so quickly it was hard to keep up with the changes. Italy's Gianfranco Rosi lost the title to American Vincent Pettway in a fourth-round knockout on September 17, 1994. Pettway was unable to keep it long, losing the belt in a fourteenth-round knockout to Paul Vaden on August 12, 1995. Vaden was another

short-reigning champ, losing the title to W.B.C. champion Terry Norris in his first defense with a unanimous twelve-round decision.

W.B.A. champion Julio Cesar Vasquez was far more successful than his I.B.F. counterparts. The bull-like brawler from Argentina made his third successful defense on July 11, 1993, winning a decision over Alejandro Ugueto. Vasquez continued to dominate his challengers, beating former W.B.A. welterweight champion Aaron Davis, Armand Picar, Ricardo Nunez, Ahmet Dottuev, Winky Wright, and Tony Marshall, but on March 4, 1995, Vasquez lost the title to W.B.C. welterweight champion Pernell Whitaker in a unanimous twelve-round decision in Atlantic City. The physically stronger Vasquez put Whitaker on the floor, but couldn't keep him there, and was outboxed the rest of the way.

Whitaker decided to drop back down to the 147-pound class and relinquished the W.B.A. belt without making a defense. Therefore, Americans Carl Daniels and Julio Cesar Green were matched on June 16, 1995 for the vacant crown, and Daniels took the title by decision. In his first defense, Daniels, leading on points, was knocked cold in the eleventh round with a single left hook thrown by none other but Julio Cesar Vasquez. It wasn't long, however, before Vasquez was an ex-champ again. On August 21, 1996, he traveled to France, where he was relieved of the title by local hero Laurent Boudouani, who stopped Vasquez in the fifth round. In his first defense, on March 29, 1997, Boudouani spoiled Daniels's bid to regain the title, winning a twelve-round decision in Las Vegas.

On October 30, 1993, after W.B.O. light-middleweight champion John David Jackson gave up the title to fight as a full-fledged middleweight, Verno Phillips knocked out fellow American Lupe Aquino in the seventh round to claim the

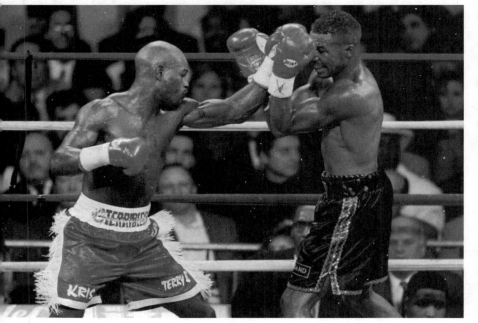

W.B.C. super-welterweight champion Terry Norris won the I.B.F. portion of the 154-pound title by outpointing Paul Vaden over twelve rounds in 1995. Vaden spent most of the bout on the defensive, resulting in a dull fight. At the time, however, the win made Norris the only reigning champ to hold more than one major title.

vacant title. Phillips held it until May 17, 1995, when he was outpointed by Italian Gianfranco Rosi, but the title was declared vacant again when Rosi failed his postfight drug test.

In order to find a new champion, Phillips was matched with England's Paul Jones on November 22, 1995, with Jones prevailing in a twelve-round decision. The title was soon vacant yet again when Jones refused to fight number-one contender Bronco McKart of the United States. The W.B.O. matched McKart with veteran Santos Cardona of Puerto Rico for the vacant crown on March 1, 1996, and McKart rallied from behind to stop Cardona in the ninth round.

McKart only kept the title until his first defense, when he lost a twelve-round decision to crafty left-hander Winky Wright on May 17, 1996. Wright's first defense was a twelve-round points win over Ensley Bingham, on November 9, 1996, in England.

idad of Puerto Rico, who knocked Blocker cold in the second round. Trinidad, a rangy boxer with a deadly punch, soon proved to be one of the era's finest fighters. By September 7, 1996, he'd recorded ten successful defenses, beating Luis Garcia, Anthony Stephens, Hector Camacho, Yori Boy Campas, Oba Carr, Roger Turner, Larry Barnes, Rodney Moore, Fred Pendleton, and Ray Lovato. Camacho was the only challenger who lasted the distance.

W.B.A. titleholder Crisanto Espana lost the title in his third defense to Ike Quartey, who stopped the Belfast-based Venezuelan in the eleventh-round on June 4, 1994. Quartey, a native of Ghana fighting out of France, was another of the outstanding 147-pounders of the time. His aggressive attitude and short, straight punches led to successful title defenses over Alberto Cortez, Jung Oh Park, An-

drew Murray, Vince Phillips, and Ol Carr. On April 12, 1997, he made his six defense with a fifth-round knockout Ralph Jones.

When W.B.O. champion Gert Jacobs declined to make a mandatory defense was stripped of the title, and on Octob 16, 1993, Ireland's Eamonn Loughran w pitted against American Lorenzo Smi for the vacant belt. Loughran won th decision and made five successful d fenses before he was dramatically knock out in the first round by Mexico's Jo Luis Lopez in a startling upset on April 1996.

The hard-hitting Lopez won his fi defense, knocking out Yori Boy Camp on October 6, 1996, but was stripped the title for failing his postfight drug te The vacant W.B.O. title was won by Ge many's Michael Loewe when he ou pointed Panama's Santiago Samaniego.

WELTERWEIGHTS

On the evening of September 10, 1993, the attention of the boxing world was focused on San Antonio, Texas, where Mexican icon and W.B.C. light-welterweight champion Julio Cesar Chavez was moving up in weight to challenge W.B.C. welterweight boss Pernell Whitaker. Chavez was considered the greatest Mexican fighter of all-time, but he was no match for the slick boxing and precision punching of Whitaker. Therefore, it came as a huge shock when, after twelve one-sided rounds, the decision was announced as a draw. Whitaker kept the title but was robbed of victory in perhaps the best performance of his distinguished career.

Whitaker continued his dominance of the 147-pound division, successfully defending the W.B.C. championship against Santos Cardona, Buddy McGirt, Gary Jacobs, Jake Rodriguez, Wilfredo Rivera (twice), and Diobelys Hurtado. But on April 12, 1997, he lost the title to Oscar De La Hoya in a close, controversial decision, despite the fact he'd scored the only knockdown in the bout.

Maurice Blocker's term as I.B.F. welterweight champion ended on June 19, 1993, at the explosive hands of Felix Trin-

The bizarre outfit he wore into the ring didn't help Hector Camacho when he challenged Felix Trinidad for the I.B.F. welterweight title in 1994. The younger, harder-hitting Trinidad dominated the fight and won a lopsided, twelve-round decision over the so-called Macho Man.

e Quartey won the W.B.A. welterweight belt in June 1994, knocking out Crisanto pana. The hard-hitting 147-pounder from Ghana moved his base of operation to rope in 1991, and also campaigned successfully in the United States.

IGHT-WELTERWEIGHTS

After Pernell Whitaker relinquished he I.B.F. 140-pound title to fight as a velterweight, on May 15, 1993, in Atlantic City, Charles Murray won a twelve-round lecision over Rodney Moore to claim the acant title. Murray made two successful

defenses and then lost the belt to Jake Rodriguez in a decision on February 13, 1994. Rodriguez's reign followed a similar pattern, and after two successful defenses, the left-handed Puerto Rican lost the championship in a sixth-round knockout to Kostya Tszyu on January 28, 1995.

Tszyu, a Russian based in Australia, soon proved to be one of the better

fighters the light-welterweight division has produced. A tireless worker with a powerful punch in both hands, Tszyu was popular in both Australia and the United States. He decisioned former champ Roger Mayweather in his first defense, then tallied three consecutive knockouts, stopping Hugo Pineda, Corey Johnson, and Jan Bergman. In his fifth defense, on January 18, 1997, the I.B.F. titleholder kept the belt under controversial circumstances. Tszyu knocked down outclassed challenger Leonardo Mas three times in the first round, but the final decking came a split second after the referee ordered the combatants to stop fighting. As Mas was unable to continue after the foul, the bout was declared a technical draw.

Although most observers considered Julio Cesar Chavez extremely lucky to receive a draw in his September 10, 1993, bout with W.B.C. welterweight champion Pernell Whitaker, the Mexican still had a massive following, especially among his countrymen and Mexican-Americans. It soon became clear, however, that Chavez was not the fighter he had been a few years earlier. After defending the W.B.C. light-welterweight crown with a fifth-round knockout of Andy Holligan on December 18, 1993, Chavez lost for the first time in his lengthy career, when the American Frankie "the Surgeon" Randall knocked him down and won a twelve-round decision on January 29, 1994. Chavez regained the title in his next fight, on May 7, 1994, but not without controversy. After a good start by Chavez, Randall appeared to be taking over the bout when an accidental clash of heads in the eighth round opened a deep gash on Chavez's forehead. The ringside doctor informed the referee that the cut was too severe to allow the fight to continue. According to W.B.C. rules, whoever was ahead on points at the time the fight was stopped would be the winner. To make matters even worse for Randall, he was penalized one point, even though the butt was ruled accidental. That point was the margin of difference which allowed Chavez to regain the title.

An aging Chavez made two more successful defenses of the W.B.C. title, then suffered the second loss of his career on June 7, 1996, when Oscar De La Hoya stopped him on cuts in the fourth round.

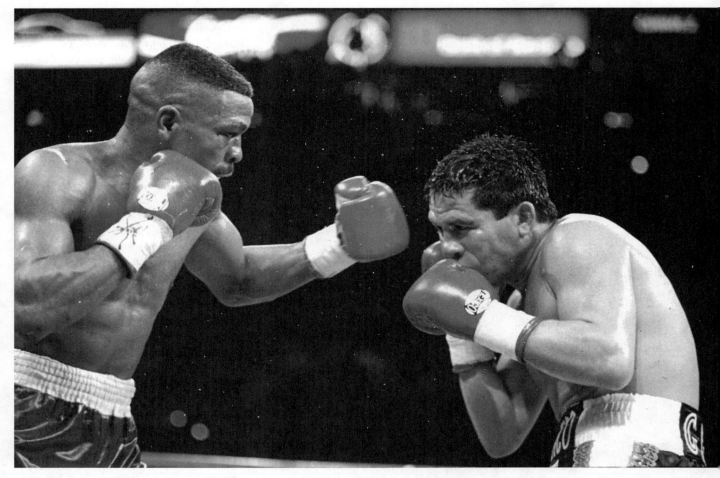

Underrated Frankie "the Surgeon" Randall became the first man to beat Mexican icon Julio Cesar Chavez when he won a twelve-round decision in 1994. The upset victory also earned Randall the W.B.C. super-lightweight title, which he lost back to Chavez in a controversial technical decision four months later.

De La Hoya successfully defended the title with a twelve-round decision over previously unbeaten Miguel Angel Gonzalez, the former W.B.C. lightweight champion, on January 18, 1997. De La Hoya then gave up the title to go after the W.B.C. 147-pound title, which he won.

W.B.A. light-welterweight champion Juan Coggi held the title until September 17, 1994, when he was outpointed by Frankie Randall in Las Vegas. Randall had sought in vain to obtain a third bout with Chavez, but had to settle for the W.B.A. belt when Chavez continued to duck him. Randall seemed jinxed. After two successful defenses he lost the belt back to Coggi in another controversial fight. In the fifth round of their January 13, 1996, rematch, Randall and Coggi bumped heads, and Coggi fell to the floor and claimed he was unable to continue. As the man from Argentina was slightly ahead on points at

the time, Randall once again lost a title on a technicality.

Randall garnered a third bout with Coggi on August 16, 1996, and regained the W.B.A. title with a twelve-round decision in Buenos Aires. Randall's third reign as 140-pound champion was brief, as he lost the title to Frenchman Khalid Rahilou in an eleventh-round knockout on January 11, 1997.

Carlos "Bolillo" Gonzalez lost the W.B.O. light-welterweight title to American Zack Padilla by decision on June 7, 1993. Padilla, a nonstop puncher, made four successful defenses and then retired. Puerto Rican Sammy Fuentes won the vacant title on February 10, 1995, knocking out Fidel Avedano in the second round. In his initial defense, Fuentes lost the W.B.O. belt to Giovanni Parisi, who stopped him in the eighth round on March 9, 1996, in Italy. Parisi gave ex-

champ Gonzalez a chance to regain the title on June 20, 1996, but managed to hold on to the belt with a twelve-round draw. Parisi's second defense of the W.B.O. belt came on October 10, 1996 when he stopped Sergio Rey in the fourth round.

LIGHTWEIGHTS

Mexico's Miguel Angel Gonzalez continued as W.B.C. lightweight champion defending the title a total of ten times. He found it increasingly difficult to make the 135-pound weight limit, however, and after a particularly taxing defense against American Lamar Murphy on August 19 1995, Gonzalez decided to relinquish the title and move up to the light-welterweight division.

On April 20, 1996, Murphy was matched with Frenchman Jean-Baptiste

Former Olympic gold medalist Oscar De La Hoya won the W.B.C. 140-pound belt with a bloody TKO of Julio Cesar Chavez in 1996. Chavez suffered a serious eye cut in the opening round and was unable to continue following the end of the fourth. Chavez later claimed he'd been cut in training.

fighter with a mediocre record, won the decision and the title on January 10, 1993. Fearless Freddie, as Pendleton was known, made just one successful defense, then lost the title to Calfornian Rafael Ruelas by decision on February 19, 1994.

Ruelas, a tireless pressure fighter, lost the I.B.F. title in his third defense when Oscar De La Hoya stopped him in the second round on May 6, 1995, in Las Vegas. De La Hoya, a glamorous boxer-puncher with a million-dollar smile, vacated the I.B.F. lightweight title without even bothering to make a single defense.

South Africa's Phillip Holiday won the vacant title by stopping Miguel Julio in the eleventh round on August 19, 1995. Holiday, a nonstop puncher who specialized in body blows, defended the I.B.F. title five times, beating Rocky Martinez, John Lark, Jeff Fenech, Joel Diaz, and Ivan Robinson. The give-and-take Robinson fight on December 21, 1996, was Holiday's first defense in the United States, and helped establish the champion as a television attraction in America.

Four months after his controversial decision over Dingaan Thobele, W.B.A. lightweight champion Tony "the Tiger" Lopez gave the South African another shot at the crown. Thobele, who many thought deserved to win the first fight, captured the belt in the rematch, winning a twelve-round decision on June 26, 1993. Thobele was unable to hang onto the title, however, and lost it to Orzubek Nazarov, who outpointed him on October 30, 1993, in Johannesburg.

Nazarov, a Japan-based Russian, was a powerful, technically skilled southpaw who proved to be a stable champion. He beat Thobele again in a rematch, then reeled off successful defenses against Joey Gamache, Won Park, Dino Canoy, and Adrian Taroreh.

W.B.O. 135-pound champion Giovanni Parisi beat Michael Ayers and Antonio Rivera in title defenses before giving up the title to fight as a light-welterweight. De La Hoya then won the vacant title by stopping former I.B.F. featherweight champion Jorge Paez in the second round on July 29, 1994. "The Golden Boy" breezed through six defenses, turning back the challenges of Carl Griffin, John Avila, John-John Molina, Rafael Ruelas, Genaro Hernandez, and James Leija.

Mendy for the vacant W.B.C. title in Levallois, France. Murphy got off to an aggressive start, but Mendy, a skillful, left-handed boxer, came on strong in the second half of the bout and won a decision. Mendy didn't keep the belt long, losing it to American Steve Johnston in a

twelve-round split decision on March 3, 1997.

After battling to a technical draw in their first bout, Americans Fred Pendleton and Tracy Spann were matched again in an effort to find a new I.B.F. lightweight champion. Pendleton, a good

Only Molina was tough enough to stand up to the champion's rapid-fire combination, and although the challenger lasted the distance, De La Hoya won the decision.

After De La Hoya gave up the W.B.O. title to fight as a light-welter, Arthur Grigorijan won the vacant title with a twelfth-round knockout of Antonio Rivera on April 13, 1996. Grigorijan, originally from Uzbekistan but based in Germany, knocked out American club fighter Gene Reed in his first defense, then won a twelve-round decision over defensive specialist Marty Jacubowski on November 16, 1996, for his second defense.

JUNIOR LIGHTWEIGHTS

When Azumah Nelson barely held onto the W.B.C. junior-lightweight title with a twelve-round draw against James Leija on September 10, 1993, it looked like his long career was beginning to catch up with the great African warrior. He'd been a pro since 1979, held world championships in two weight classes, and had competed in nineteen world title fights. It therefore came as no great surprise on May 7, 1994, when Leija took the title in their rematch via decision.

Leija, however, was unable to make even a single successful defense, and lost the title to Gabe Ruelas, brother of Rafael Ruelas, on September 17, 1994, by decision.

For a brief spell, it looked like Ruelas would be a dominant champion. He stopped Fred Liberatore in the second round in his first defense, then on May 6, 1995, he knocked out Colombian challenger Jimmy Garcia in the eleventh round. Garcia, brave but badly outclassed, took a terrible beating and died as a result of head injuries a few days after the fight.

Ruelas was distraught following the death of Garcia. He considered giving up boxing, but after a long layoff he returned to the ring on December 1, 1995, against former champion Nelson, who by that time was considered a relatively safe opponent. Nevertheless, Nelson proved far from washed up, and handed Ruelas a fierce beating that resulted in a fifth-round knockout victory for the man from Ghana.

Nelson took on old rival Leija in his first

Victory was sweet for Oscar De La Hoya when he won the I.B.F. lightweight champion ship with a second-round TKO of Rafael Ruelas in 1995. Referee Richard Steele w forced to intervene after "the Golden Boy" rendered Ruelas helpless with a blisteri series of punches.

Ghana's ageless Azumah Nelson is W.B.A. super-feather-weight champion again after scoring a fifth-round knockout of Gabriel Ruelas in 1995. During his lengthy career, Nelson has also beaten such outstanding fighters as Jeff Fenech, Wilfredo Gomez, and Jesse James Leija.

defense of his second reign as W.B.C. 130-pound titleholder. Nelson was thirty-seven at the time, and many experts thought the younger, fresher Leija would be able to beat the aging champion again. They were wrong. The Professor, as Nelson called himself, rolled back the calendar and kept the belt with a sixth-round knockout on June 1, 1996.

Nelson didn't defend again until March 22, 1997, when he returned to the United States to fight former W.B.A. junior-lightweight champion Genaro Hernandez, a lanky counterpuncher from California whose only loss had been to Oscar De La Hoya in a bid to win the lightweight title. Hernandez boxed circles around the rusty, slow-moving Nelson and won the title in a twelve-round split decision.

After Hernandez abandoned the W.B.A. crown to fight De La Hoya, South Korean Yong Soo Choi stopped Argentina's Victor Hugo Paz in the tenth round to claim the belt on October 21, 1995. Fighting exclusively in Asia, Choi went on to defend against Yamato Mitani (twice), Orlando Soto and Lakva Songnam.

After making seven successful defenses of the I.B.F. junior-lightweight title, John-John Molina also relinquished the belt and moved up in weight to try his luck against De La Hoya, but lost the decision in a rough-and-tumble contest.

American Ed Hopson won the title Molina had given up by knocking out Moises Pedroza on April 22, 1995. Hopson, a relatively inexperienced fighter, lost the belt on July 9, 1995, when Tracy Patterson, the adopted son of former heavyweight champion Floyd Patterson, knocked him out in the second round.

Patterson, who had previously held the W.B.C. light-featherweight title, was soon replaced by Arturo Gatti, who narrowly outpointed him on December 15, 1995. Gatti, a Canadian based in New Jersey, was an extremely hard puncher, especially with the left hook, but had a leaky defense and took unusual punishment, win or lose.

In his first defense, Gatti was forced to come off the floor to knock out Wilson Rodriguez in the sixth round of a thrilling slugging match. In his second defense, Gatti gave Patterson a chance to regain the title. For Gatti it proved a far easier fight the second time around, as he won a unanimous decision on February 22, 1997, in Atlantic City.

W.B.O. junior-lightweight champion Jimmi Bredahl was another fighter who had his dreams shattered by the flashing fists of De La Hoya. After making one defense of the title, Bredahl lost the belt when De La Hoya stopped him in the eleventh round on March 5, 1994.

De La Hoya moved up to lightweight after just one defense, a third-round knockout of Giorgio Campanella. He was replaced by Regilio Tuur, who won a twelve-round decision on September 24, 1994, over Eugene Speed to take the vacant title. The talented Tuur, a native of Suriname living in Holland, defended the W.B.O. 130-pound crown six times before retiring in 1996 to concentrate on his business interests.

FEATHERWEIGHTS

I.B.F. featherweight champion Tom Johnson, a versatile fighter equally adept at mixing it up on the inside as he was at boxing long-range, enjoyed a relatively long and distinguished reign, making eleven successful defenses of the title. Nevertheless, because he wasn't a knockout artist and failed to attract a large following in his native Detroit, Michigan, he was frequently forced to fight overseas in order to make a decent living. Besides making six defenses in the United States, he also defended the belt in France, Germany, England, and Ireland.

Johnson's appearances in Europe, where his skills were appreciated far more than they were back home, eventually led to a million-dollar showdown with W.B.O. champion Naseem Hamed, who was at the time the most popular fighter in the United Kingdom. They met in London on February 8, 1997, and Hamed won the I.B.F. title with an eighth-round knockout in a brilliant, up-from-the-floor performance.

Gregorio "Goyo" Vargas lost the W.B.C. 126-pound crown in his first defense when American Kevin Kelley outpointed him on December 4, 1993. Kelley, known as the Flushing Flash because of his all-action fighting style and outgoing personality, looked like he was settling in for a long reign after outpointing Jesse Benavides and stopping Jose Ramos in his first two defenses, but on January 7, 1995, he was stopped in the eleventh round, due to badly swollen eyes, by Mexican challenger Alejandro Gonzalez.

Gonzalez did only marginally better than his predecessor, making three defenses before losing the W.B.C. belt via decision on September 23, 1995, in Sacramento, California, to fellow Mexican and former champion Manuel Medina. Medina, a savvy but light-punching veteran, soon became an ex-champ again, losing the title to Filipino Luisito Espinoza on December 11, 1995, in Tokyo, Japan.

Espinoza, the former W.B.A. bantamweight champion, found new life at 126 pounds and defended against Alejandro Gonzalez on March 1, 1996, scoring a fourth-round knockout in Gonzalez's hometown of Guadalajara. He then decisioned Cesar Soto in front of a crowd of over one hundred thousand fans in Manila on July 6, 1996 (the fight was sponsored by the Filipino government and admission was free). In his third defense of the W.B.C. belt, Espinoza knocked out Nobutoshi Hiranaka in Fukuoka, Japan, on November 2, 1996, in the eighth round.

South Korean Yung-Kyul Park's reign as W.B.A. featherweight champion came to an end on December 4, 1993, when Venezuela's Eloy Rojas won a twelve-round decision. Rojas, an excellent boxer with a stiff if not devastating punch, made his first defense on March 19, 1994, stopping Japan's Seiji Asakawa in the fifth round of a bout held in Kobe, Japan. Rojas went on to record a total of six successful defenses, but lost the W.B.A. crown to Wilfredo Vazquez on May 18, 1996, in a sizeable upset.

Puerto Rico's Vazquez, who had previously held W.B.A. bantamweight and light-featherweight titles, was considered past his prime and unlikely to unseat the well-regarded Rojas. But when they met on May 18, 1996, in Las Vegas, the thirty-five-year-old Vazquez walked through Rojas's best punches to tally an eleventh-round knockout in a rousing contest.

The hard-punching Vazquez proved his win over Rojas was no fluke, defending the title against Bernardo Mendoza on December 7, 1996, and Yuri Watanabe on March 30, 1997. Both challengers were knocked out in the fifth round.

Wales's Steve Robinson made seven

Challenger Wilfredo Vazquez finally caught up to defending W.B.A. featherweight champion Eloy Rojas in the late rounds of their 1996 title bout to register an eleventh-round TKO. The crafty, hard-hitting Vazquez had previously won world titles in the bantamweight and junior-featherweight divisions.

successful defenses of the W.B.O. feather-weight title, turning back the challenges of Sean Murphy, Colin McMillan, Paul Hodkinson, Freddy Cruz, Duke McKenzie, Domingo Damigella, and Pedro Ferradas. But in his eighth defense he was totally outclassed by Naseem Hamed, who knocked out the Welshman in the eighth round to win the W.B.O. belt.

Hamed, an extroverted character with a wildly unorthodox style, was a huge draw-ing card in Britain. His antics and unde-niable fighting prowess led to four defenses of the W.B.O. title before he added the I.B.F. version to his collection by stopping Tom Johnson. In his first defense of both belts, Hamed knocked out Billy Hardy in the first round on May 3, 1997, in Manchester.

LIGHT-FEATHERWEIGHTS

Kennedy McKinney hung onto the I.B.F. light-featherweight title through five successful defenses. In the last of these, on April 16, 1994, he gave Welcome Ncita, the South African he'd won the title from, a chance to regain the crown. Again, it was a close fight with Ncita having early success, but the American finished the stronger of the two, winning a unanimous twelve-round decision.

In his next defense, McKinney re-turned to South Africa, where he had beaten Jose Rincones the previous year, to defend against Vuyani Bungu. Bungu, a quick, crafty boxer, took the I.B.F. title away from McKinney by decision on Au-gust 20, 1994.

Bungu, from the impoverished Mdantsane township, had been raised in a two-room house without running water, and knew what it meant to go hungry. In his first defense he decisioned Felix Camacho on November 19, 1994, in Pre-toria, South Africa.

Bungu continued to beat back chal-lengers on a regular basis. In his eighth defense, on April 5, 1997, he gave McKin-ney an opportunity to win back the title. Bungu built a big early lead, withstood a late rally from McKinney, and retained the belt with a twelve-round majority decision.

W.B.C. light-featherweight champion Tracy Harris Patterson unexpectedly lost the title to Hector Acero-Sanchez in a twelve-round decision on August 26, 1994. Acero-Sanchez, a native of the Dominican

Republic, was a feather-fisted defensive specialist who used his height and reach to good advantage, but in his first defense he barely held onto the title in a twelve-round draw. His opponent, Mexican veteran Daniel Zaragoza, scored the bouts only knockdown, and many observers thought he should have won.

The W.B.C. ordered Acero-Sanchez to give Zaragoza another shot, and on November 6, 1995, the title changed hands again when Zaragoza won a twelve-round decision. Zaragoza, who had previously reigned as both W.B.C. bantamweight and light-featherweight champion, was almost thirty-six when he beat Acero-Sanchez, but still a remarkable performer. Despite a tendency to suffer facial cuts in practically every bout, Zaragoza, using a combination of skill, durability, and courage, continued to fool the experts who figured he was past due for retirement.

Zaragoza made the first two defenses of his second reign as W.B.C. 122-pound champion in Japan, knocking out Joichiro Tatsuyoshi in the eleventh round and Tsuyoshi Hadara in the seventh. In his third defense on January 11, 1997, Zaragoza traveled to Boston, where he turned in one of the finest performances of his long career, outpointing previously unbeaten Irishman Wayne McCullough, who had given up the W.B.C. bantamweight title to fight for Zaragoza's title. For his fourth defense, the ageless Mexican returned to Japan, where he fought Tatsuyoshi again, keeping the title with a twelve-round victory on April 14, 1997.

W.B.A. light-featherweight champion Wilfredo Vazquez made a total of nine successful defenses, the last of which, on January 7, 1995, came against longtime bantamweight champion Orlando Canizales, who was moving up in weight. Although the gifted Canizales was favored to win, Vazquez abandoned his usual attacking style and boxed his way to a twelve-round split decision. It looked like age and a long career had finally caught up with the Puerto Rican when Antonio Cermeno, a speedy, mobile boxer from Venezuela, outpointed Vazquez and took the title on May 13, 1995.

Though far from spectacular, the agile, fast-punching Cermeno proved to be a highly competent champion. He decisioned rugged Jesus Salud for his first

defense, then proceeded to beat Yober Ortega, Yuchi Kasai, and Angel Chacon by decision, and Eddie Saez via knockout. Chacon, who Cermeno fought on May 5, 1997, in Coconut Grove, Florida, was unbeaten going in but couldn't quite keep up with Cermeno's busy pace and accurate punching.

England's Duke McKenzie lost the W.B.O. light-featherweight title in his first defense, dropping a twelve-round decision to Daniel Jiminez on June 9, 1993. Jiminez, from Camuy, Puerto Rico, did somewhat better, keeping the belt through four defenses before losing it on points to Mexico's Marco Antonio Barrera on March 31, 1995.

Barrera, who many thought was destined to be Mexico's newest superstar, was undefeated in thirty-five fights when he won the title from Jiminez. A brutal body puncher, he ripped through his first four challengers with ease, but in his fifth defense, on February 3, 1996, chinks in his armor began to appear. His opponent, Kennedy McKinney, nailed him repeatedly with flush rights during a spectacular slugging match. Both men were down and rocked repeatedly before Barrera finally prevailed in a twelfth-round TKO in one of the best fights of the year.

It was back to relatively tame defenses after the McKinney thriller, and Barrera stopped Jesse Benavides, Orlando Fernandez, and Jesse Magana in his next three title fights. Then, on November 22, 1996, Barrera defended against former W.B.A. bantamweight champion Junior Jones in Tampa, Florida. Like McKinney, Jones had no trouble finding Barrera's head with right hands. In the fifth round, Jones floored the defending champion with a right that also opened a cut over Barrera's eye. Barrera beat the count but was soon pinned on the ropes, where he took further punishment. Just as Barrera began to sag to the floor, his trainer jumped into the ring, forcing the referee to disqualify the Mexican.

Jones, from Brooklyn, New York, gave Barrera a rematch on April 18, 1997, in Las Vegas. For the first half of the bout, Barrera turned boxer in an effort to stay away from Jones's dangerous right. This tactic worked to a degree, but Jones usually stayed a punch or two ahead, and Barrera switched back to his old, aggres-

sive style for the last few rounds. The Mexican's body shots had Jones hanging on down the stretch, but after twelve close rounds, the American kept the title with a unanimous decision.

BANTAMWEIGHT

I.B.F. bantamweight champion Orlando Canizales's long reign extended through sixteen consecutive defenses, breaking a division record that was set by Manuel Ortiz in 1946. Despite his many accomplishments, Canizales was never able to earn the sort of money his talent deserved. By the start of 1995 he had pretty much run out of viable 118-pound challengers, and he decided to put on a few pounds to challenge W.B.A. light-featherweight champion Wilfredo Vazquez. They met on January 7, 1995, and after twelve close rounds, Vazquez retained the title by decision. It was Canizales's first loss since 1986, and although he continued to fight successfully, his best days were behind him.

The I.B.F. title Canizales had abandoned in order to fight Vazquez was won by South Africa's Mbulelo Botile, who knocked out Colombian southpaw Harold Mestre on April 29, 1995, to claim the belt. Botile, a conservative boxer with a dangerous right hand, made his first defense on July 4, 1995, winning a twelve-round decision over Sam Stewart in Johannesburg. He finished a highly successful year by knocking out Reynaldo Hurtado in the second round. In 1996 Botile tallied three more defenses, knocking out Ancee Gedeon and Bong Arlos, and outpointing Aristead Clayton.

Victor Rabanales's run as W.B.C. bantamweight champion came to an end on March 28, 1993, when South Korean Jung Il Byun outpointed him to take the belt. Byun made just one successful defense and then lost the title to Japan's Yasuei Yakushiji via decision on December 23, 1993. Yakushiji did a little better, hanging onto the W.B.C. belt for four defenses before losing the title to Ireland's Wayne McCullough on July 30, 1995.

McCullough, who had won a silver medal at the 1992 Olympics, had relocated to Las Vegas at the start of his pro career to work with venerable trainer Eddie

Futch. His hard-fought twelve-round decision over Yakushiji in Japan was celebrated by fans in both Ireland and the United States, where he had become a popular TV attraction before winning the title. The Pocket Rocket, as McCullough was known, went home to Belfast for his first defense, knocking out Johnny Bredahl in the eighth round on December 2, 1995.

McCullough struggled to make weight for his second defense, and although he retained the title with a twelve-round decision over Jose Luis Bueno in Dublin, he took a lot of punishment in the process. Realizing he was draining himself making 118 pounds, McCullough moved up to the light-featherweight division, where he challenged W.B.C. champion Daniel Zaragoza on January 11, 1997. Unfortunately for McCullough, the cagey Mexican veteran proved too smart and too tough, and despite a strong finish in the last two rounds, McCullough lost the decision in a rousing fight.

Thailand's Sirimongkol Singmansuk succeeded McCullough as W.B.C. bantamweight champion, first knocking out Bueno to become interim champion, then gaining full recognition by winning a twelve-round decision over Jesus Sarabia in Bangkok on February 15, 1997. In his next fight on April 26, 1997, Sirimongkol stopped Javier Campanrio in the fourth round.

Jorge Eliecer Julio lost the W.B.A. bantamweight title to American Junior Jones by decision on October 23, 1993. Jones made one successful defense, a twelve-round decision over Elvis Alvarez on January 8, 1994. At the time Jones was considered a budding star, but on April 22, 1994, he was knocked out in the eleventh round by Texan John Michael Johnson in a stunning upset. Johnson, in turn, lost the belt in his first defense, when Daorung MP Petroleum stopped him in the first on July 16, 1994, in Uttaradit, Thailand.

The W.B.A. bantamweight title continued to bounce from hand to hand like a used car with a bad transmission. Petroleum was outpointed by fellow Thai Veeraphol Sahaprom on September 17, 1995. Then, on January 29, 1996, Sahaprom was knocked out in the second round by South African Nana Konadu,

who had previously held the W.B.C. version of the 118-pound crown. Konadu was soon an ex-champion again when MP Petroleum, by then fighting under the name Daorung C. Siriwat, won a ten-round technical decision on October 27, 1996.

Puerto Rico's Rafael Del Vale made two successful defenses of the W.B.O. bantamweight title, knocking out Wilfredo Vargas and outpointing Miguel Lora. Both defenses were held in Puerto Rico, but when Del Vale traveled to England to defend against Ghana's Alfred Kotey, he lost the title by decision on July 30, 1994. Kotey, a gifted but lazy boxer, didn't keep it long, losing to Daniel Jiminez by decision on October 21, 1995. Once again, the title changed hands quickly when Wales's Robbie Regan outpointed Jiminez on April 26, 1996.

LIGHT-BANTAMWEIGHTS

Hard-hitting Julio Borboa made five successful defenses of the I.B.F. light-bantamweight title, stopping Carlos Mercado, Rolando Pascua, Jose Roman, and Jaji Sibali, and outpointing Joel Luna. Nevertheless, on August 29, 1994, he lost the belt to Colombia's Harold Grey in a twelve-round decision. In his first two defenses, Grey outpointed Vincenzo Belcastro in Italy, and then decisioned Orlando Tobon in Colombia. Next, Grey gave ex-champ Borboa a rematch on March 18, 1995. Once again Grey proved slightly superior and won a twelve-round decision to retain the title.

In his next defense, Grey was outpointed by Argentina's Carlos Salazar on October 7, 1995. Salazar made one defense, a sixth-round technical knockout of Antonello Melis, and then lost the I.B.F. 115-pound crown back to Grey in a decision on April 27, 1996.

Grey's second stint as champion only lasted until his first defense, when he was viciously knocked out in the second round by Danny Romero on August 24, 1996, in Romero's hometown of Albuquerque, New Mexico. Romero, the former I.B.F. flyweight champion, was a devastating puncher with movie-star looks. In his first defense, Romero overcame a cut eye to

hammer brave but outgunned Polo Saucedo into a twelfth-round technical knockout. Romero continued his rampage in his next defense, knocking out Jaji Sibali in the sixth round on March 8, 1997.

W.B.C. light-bantamweight champ Sung Kil Moon lost the title to Mexico's Jose Luis Bueno by decision on January 13, 1993, in Pohang, South Korea. However, Bueno was quickly relieved of the title when Japan's Hiroshi Kawashima outpointed him on May 4, 1994. Fighting exclusively in Japan, Kawashima, a speedy southpaw with a long reach, made six successful defenses, but on February 20, 1997, he lost the belt to Filipino Gerry Penalosa in a narrow, twelve-round split decision.

South Korea's Hyung Chul Lee stopped Katsuya Onizuka in the ninth round on September 18, 1994, to take the W.B.A. light-bantamweight title. Lee only managed one successful defense, a twelfth-round stoppage of Tomonori Tamura, before losing the title to Alimi Goitia in a fourth-round knockout on July 22, 1995. Goitia, a left-hander from Venezuela, made three successful defenses, including another win over Lee, before losing the belt to Thailand's Yokthai Sithoar in an eighth-round knockout on August 24, 1996.

Sithoar, powerful but relatively inexperienced when he won the title, made his first defense on November 10, 1996, stopping Jack Siahaya in the second round. In his next two defenses, Sithoar outpointed Aquiles Guzman and drew with Satoshi Iida.

Denmark's Johnny Bredahl relinquished the W.B.O. 115-pound title after three defenses in order to fight at a heavier weight. The vacant title was won by American Johnny Tapia, who stopped Henry Martinez in the eleventh round on October 12, 1994, before a large and wildly enthusiastic crowd in the new champ's hometown of Albuquerque, New Mexico.

Tapia, a passionate performer and a recovering cocaine addict, turned out to be one of the W.B.O.'s most talented and popular champions. Through March 8, 1997, when he stopped Jorge Barrera in three rounds, Tapia racked up ten successful defenses.

FLYWEIGHTS

After winning the I.B.F. flyweight title from Rodolfo Blanco, Phichit Sithbangprachan made five successful title defenses, but after the fifth, a twelve-round decision over Jose Zepeda on May 8, 1994, he relinquished it. The vacant title was won by American power-puncher Danny Romero, who took a twelve-round decision over Francisco Tejedor on April 22, 1995, in Las Vegas.

Romero, a handsome, charismatic slugger, defended the title by stopping Miguel Martinez in the sixth round on August 29, 1995. In his next fight, a non-title bout with journeyman Willy Salazar, Romero's career almost came to a premature end. Salazar landed a searing right in the opening round that fractured the orbital bone behind Romero's left eye. Romero gamely fought on, but was eventually forced to withdraw at the end of the seventh round on the advice of the ringside doctor.

A few days after the first loss of his career, Romero underwent surgery to repair his damaged eye. During his recovery period, he gave up the I.B.F. 112-pound belt because he was having difficulty making the weight. When he returned to action it was at light-bantamweight, where he soon won his second world title.

Danny Romero, a native of Albuquerque, New Mexico, won the I.B.F. flyweight title in 1995 and the I.B.F. junior bantamweight crown the following year. His all-action style and boyish good looks made him a popular TV attraction.

The vacant I.B.F. crown was won by Mark "Too Sharp" Johnson on May 4, 1996, when the Washington, D.C., native knocked out Francisco Tejedor with one punch in the opening round. Johnson, the first African American to win the flyweight championship, was a highly skilled boxer with an excellent punch. He stopped Raul Perez in his first defense, then decisioned Alejandro Montiel on February 10, 1997, in his second defense. Montiel tried every dirty trick in the book, but Johnson withstood the assault to win convincingly.

W.B.A. flyweight champion David Griman proved to be still another short-term titleholder. After successful defenses over Hiroki Ioka and Alvarado Mercado, he

Francisco Tejedor struggles in vain to get to his feet after being nailed with a deadly left hand from Mark Johnson in the first round of their 1996 bout for the vacant I.B.F. flyweight title.

431

lost the belt to Saen Sow Ploenchit with a twelve-round decision on February 13, 1994.

Thailand's Ploenchit, a savvy but light-punching boxer, enjoyed a much longer run as champion, making a total of nine successful defenses. Except for an October 1995 decision over Hiroki Ioka in Japan, all of Ploenchit's fights were in Thailand, where he attracted large crowds. Nevertheless, on November 24, 1996, he suffered the first defeat of his career, losing a twelve-round decision and the W.B.A. flyweight belt to Venezuela's Jose Bonilla. In his initial defense, Bonilla, a quick counterpuncher, stopped Ioka in the seventh round of a bout held in Osaka, Japan.

Yuri Arbachakov, another Japan-based Russian, was an aggressive fighter with a potent right-hand punch. He made three defenses of the W.B.C. flyweight title in 1993, outpointing Isaias Zumudio and Nam Hoon Cha, and stopping Muangchai Kittikasem. Arbachakov's reign continued at a steady pace as he made two successful defenses in 1994, two more in 1995, and another pair in 1996. After his ninth defense, a ninth-round knockout of Takato Toguchi on August 26, 1996, Arbachakov took time off to have hand surgery.

Pat Clinton lost the W.B.O. flyweight title to South Africa's Jacob "Baby Jake" Matlala in an eighth-round knockout on May 15, 1993. Matlala, a veteran who had finally won a version of the world title in his thirteenth season as a pro, made three successful defenses before being stopped in the eighth round by Alberto Jimenez on February 11, 1995.

Mexico's Jimenez stopped Wales's Robbie Regan in his first defense, and went on to hold the belt through four more defenses before Argentina's Carlos Salazar, who had briefly reigned as I.B.F. bantamweight champion, stopped him in the tenth round on December 13, 1996, to annex the title.

LIGHT-FLYWEIGHTS

The first Michael Carbajal–Humberto "Chiquita" Gonzalez match had been such a sensation the pair were matched again on February 19, 1994, with both the I.B.F. and W.B.C. versions of the light-flyweight title on the line. Instead of slugging it out with Carbajal as he had in their first bout, Gonzalez turned boxer. The change in strategy puzzled the defending champion, and Gonzalez regained the belts with a twelve-round decision.

After Gonzalez defended the titles with

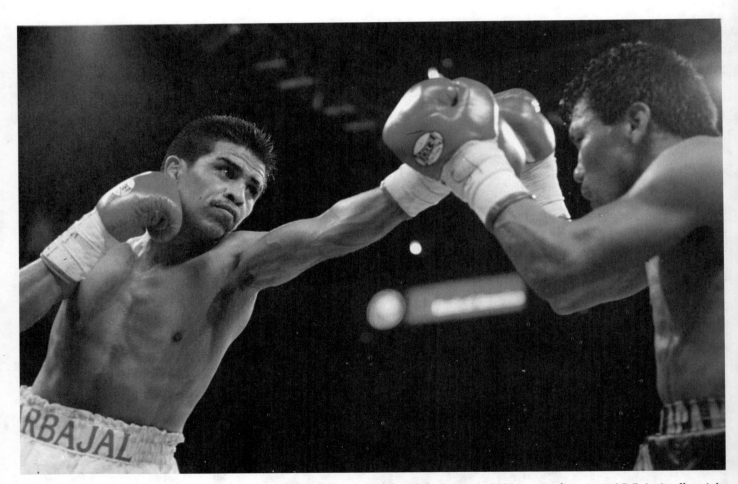

Michael Carbajal won a hard-fought twelve-round decision over Melchor-Cob Castro in 1996 to win the vacant I.B.F. junior-flyweight title. It was the start of Carbajal's second reign as 108-pound champion. It had taken him two years to bounce back from his two losses to Chiquita Gonzalez.

a seventh-round knockout of Juan Cordoba, he fought a rubber match with Carbajal, once more boxing his way to a decision win on November 12, 1994. Having finally established his superiority over Carbajal, Gonzalez knocked out Jesus Zuniga in the fifth round on March 31, 1995.

Gonzalez's third reign as light-flyweight champion ended on July 15, 1995, when he was stopped by Thailand's Saman Sorjaturong in the seventh round of another give-and-take brawl. Gonzalez retired from the ring after losing the titles, and Sorjaturong proved to be a worthy successor.

After stopping Yuichi Hosono in his first defense, the deadly punching Sorjaturong was stripped of the I.B.F. title, but continued to enjoy a successful reign as W.B.C. titleholder. By April 13, 1997, he

had made seven defenses, six inside the distance, and established himself as one of Thailand's most popular fighters of all-time.

After the I.B.F. took the title away from Sorjaturong, Carbajal and Mexico's Melchor Cob Castro were matched for the vacant title, with Carbajal winning a twelve-round decision on March 16, 1996. It looked like Carbajal was settling in for a lengthy reign when he was upset by Mauricio Pastrana, who took the title by decision on January 18, 1997.

After beating Hiroki Ioka to win the W.B.A. light-flyweight title, Myung Woo Yuh made one successful defense, outpointing Yuichi Honsono on July 25, 1993, and then he retired. The vacant title was won by Leo Gamez, who stopped Shiro Yahiro in the ninth round on October 21, 1993.

Gamez, from Venezuela, made three defenses before losing the W.B.A. belt to Hi Yong Choi via decision on February 4, 1995. Choi, from South Korea, managed one successful defense, then passed the title on to Panama's Carlos Murillo in a twelve-round decision on January 13, 1996. On May 21, 1996, there was another new champion after Japan's Keiji Yamaguchi outpointed Murillo over twelve rounds.

The seemingly endless changes at the top of the W.B.A. light-flyweight pile continued when Yamaguchi lost the title to Phichitnoi C. Siriwat, who stopped the Japanese boxer in the second round on December 3, 1996.

Michael Carbajal won the W.B.O. portion of the light-flyweight title by outpointing Josue Camacho on July 15, 1994, but soon gave up the title in order to

W.B.C. strawweight champion Ricardo Lopez showed why he's never been beaten when he blasted out Ala Villamor in the eighth round of their 1996 bout in Las Vegas. The Mexican is a master technician with knockout power in both fists, but at only 105 pounds, you've got to be outstanding just to get noticed.

challenge I.B.F. and W.B.C. champion Humberto Gonzalez. The vacancy was filled by Jacob Matlala, who won a five-round technical decision over Paul Weir on November 8, 1995. Matlala, the South African who had previously held the W.B.O. flyweight crown, stopped Weir in the tenth round of his first defense on April 13, 1996.

MINI-FLYWEIGHTS OR STRAWWEIGHTS

Mexico's Ricardo Lopez gradually emerged as the most prominent 105-pound fighter in the world. Despite chronic hand problems that stalled his career from time to time, the W.B.C. strawweight champion's prestige grew as he tallied one successful defense after another. He was a master boxer whose economical movement and textbook combinations reminded connoisseurs of the great champions of a bygone era, and despite his diminutive size, Lopez's knockout percentage was among the best in the sport.

By the end of 1996, Lopez had recorded eighteen successful title defenses and was undefeated in forty-four pro bouts, scoring thirty-four victories via knockout. Among his title-fight victims

was Saman Sorjaturong, who went on to be an outstanding light-flyweight champion after being stopped by Lopez on July 3, 1993. Despite a promotional boost from Don King, Lopez suffered from a field of challengers that even the most hardcore boxing fans had never heard of. Although a unification bout with one of the other organization's champions might have partially solved the problem, Lopez's close ties to W.B.C. president Jose Sulaiman made such a solution politically untenable.

I.B.F. mini-flyweight champion Ratanapol Sor Vorapin was an aggressive southpaw who knew the benefit of working on his opponent's body. After winning the title from Manny Melchor, he made four defenses in each of the next three years, but on March 16, 1996, he was stripped of the title for failure to make the weight for a defense against Lee Castillo. The fight went on as scheduled, but even though Sor Vorapin stopped Castillo in the eleventh round, he no longer held the belt. In his next fight, however, on May 18, 1996, Sor Vorapin won the vacant title with a twelve-round decision over Jun Arlos.

After regaining the title he never lost in the ring, Sor Vorapin knocked out Joseph Orgaleza in the third round on July 13, 1996, Oscar Andrade in the third round on September 28, 1996, and Gustavo Vera

on November 24, 1996, bringing his total number of title defenses to fourteen.

Chana Porpaoin, another of Thailand's many top-notch fighters, defended the W.B.A. 105-pound crown eight times. He beat Carlos Murillo (twice), Ronnie Magrano, Keun Young Kang, Manuel Herrera, and Jin Ho Kim on points, and stopped Rafael Torres and Ernesto Rubillar. On December 2, 1995, however, Porpaoin was outpointed by Rosendo Alvarez of Nicaragua.

Alvarez, a dangerous combination puncher, made his first defense on March 30, 1996, stopping Kermin Guardia in the champion's hometown of Managua. In his second defense, Alvarez journeyed to Japan, where he stopped Takashi Shiohama in the eighth round on October 1, 1996.

Alex Sanchez was crowned the new W.B.O. strawweight champion on December 22, 1993, by stopping Orlando Malone in the first round of a bout held in Sanchez's native Puerto Rico. Sanchez made three defenses in 1994, beating Alex Garcia, Carlos Rodriguez, and Oscar Andrade—all inside the distance. Although Sanchez continued to fight on a regular basis, only two of his next seven fights were title bouts. He decisioned Rafael Orozco on January 28, 1995, and Tomas Rivera on July 29, 1995.

AS WE GO TO PRESS

At publication time there is no question that Evander Holyfield is the premiere heavyweight of the 1990s, underscored by his two victories over Tyson. His popularity was also enhanced by the stoic demeanor he displayed during the infamous ear-biting incident in the second fight. Rather than rest on his laurels, Holyfield, already a millionaire many times over, decided to consolidate his heavyweight title. As we go to press, he is scheduled to meet the I.B.F. champion, Michael Moorer, who had outpointed him in a unification bout in 1994.

Waiting in the wings are bouts involving Lennox Lewis and George Foreman. The latter's career has inspired another aging ex-champ, Larry Holmes, to return to continue his career.

Among the welterweights, Oscar De La Hoya, anxious to prove his worth by fighting as many marquee names as possible, has found an attractive new challenger in Hector "Macho" Camacho. Although Camacho hasn't held a major title since vacating the W.B.O. junior welterweight title in 1992, he revitalized his career by knocking out Sugar Ray Leonard in the fifth round on March 1, 1997 in Atlantic City, spoiling Leonard's comeback. The De La Hoya-Camacho bout is scheduled for the new Thomas and Mack Center in Las Vegas. The bout is dubbed "Opposites Attack" by promoter Bob Arum.

Middleweight champion Sugar Ray Robinson poses for the camera in a publicity still. Robinson was one of the most popular fighters of his era winning the middleweight crown on five separate occasions, and defeating such legendary boxers as Jake "the Bronx Bull" La Motta, Carmen Basilio, and Gene Fullmer.

436

Joe Louis, the "Brown Bomber," held the heavyweight championship title from 1937 to 1949, the longest streak in boxing history, outdistancing even the great John L. Sullivan who held the title from 1882 to 1892 and the renowned Jack Dempsey who held the crown from 1919 to 1926.

"Iron Mike" Tyson, whose off-the-canvas antics got him a jail term for rape and whose on-the-canvas antics got him a suspension and a three million dollar fine for twice biting the ear of Evander Holyfield.

INDEX

Aba, Johnny, 354
Abrams, George, 235
Aaron, Barney, 291
Acaries, Louis, 258
Aceves, Mauricio, 289, 329
Adams, Clarence, 388
Adigue, Pedro, 286, 287
Aguilar, Rodolfo, 285, 328
Ahumada, Jorge, 207, 208
Aidala, Artie, 171, 245, 352
Akai, Hidekazu, 288
Akins, Virgil, 277, 278
Albarrado, Oscar, 257
Ali, Bash, 185, 187
Ali, Kamel Boru, 332, 335
Ali, Muhammad, 160–166, 168, 170–171, 173–78, 182, 184, 207, 251, 281 See also Clay, Cassius
Allen, Marcellus, 212
Allen, Terry, 398, 399
Allen, Tom, 50–54, 293
Alli, Terence, 290, 327
Allozal, Arnel, 404
Altamarino, Javier, 329
Alvarado, Jorge, 331
Alvarez, Elvis, 406, 407
Alvarez, Francisco, 387, 388
Amaya, Antonio, 331
Ambers, Lou, 269, 272, 291, 292, 313–318
Amundsen, Ron, 260
Anaya, Romeo, 383, 384
Anderson, Ray, 207
Andries, Dennis, 210, 211, 212
Andujar, Dio, 388
Angol, Derek, 187
Angott, Sammie, 318, 319, 350
Angulo, Ruffino, 211, 212
Anhar, Azadin, 409
Anifowashe, Akeem, 390
Anthony, Tony, 204
Antuofermo, Vito, 252
Apostoli, Fred, 232–234
Aquino, Lupe, 258, 260
Aranada, Pascual, 361
Arbachakov, Yuri, 407
Arcari, Bruno, 287
Arcel, Ray, 133
Archibald, Joey, 349
Arguello, Alexis, 326, 332, 358
Arief, John, 411
Armstrong, Henry, 262, 270–273, 291, 314–316, 348, 349
Arnal, Reyes, 404
Arredondo, Rene, 286
Arredondo, Ricardo, 331, 332
Arroyo, Harry, 329
Arrozal, Arnel, 404
Arter, Joko, 361
Asakawa, Seiji, 362
Asher, Babe, 392
Ashley, Crawford, 213
Asprilla, Aquilino, 260
Attell, Abe, 336, 342–345
Attell, Monte, 342
Avelar, Antonio, 386, 404, 405
Avila, Diego, 387
Ayala, Mike, 359, 363, 364
Azevedo, Joe, 291

Backus, Billy, 279, 281
Badenhorst, Franie, 365
Badilla, Benito, 364
Bae, Sok-Chul, 389
Baek, In-Chul, 212, 258
Baer, Buddy, 132, 134, 137, 142
Baer, Max, 119, 122–25, 129
Baez, Pablo, 281
Baines, Tom, 78
Bainge, Bill, 42
Baker, Mike, 257
Baker, Sammy, 310

Baker, Snowy, 85
Baldwin, Matty, 291, 343
Ball, Hughes, 261
Ballarino, Mike, 331
Ballas, Gustavo, 389
Baltazar, Tony, 290
Banke, Paul, 365, 366
Bannon, George, 352
Barbello, Rocco, 236
Barber, Leonzer, 212
Barbour, Warren, 98
Barcenas, Silvero, 411
Barkley, Iran, 211, 213, 254, 256
Barnes, Harold, 117, 277
Barrett, Pat, 285
Barrientos, Ireneo 'Rene', 331, 332
Barrios, Faustino, 333
Barrone, Nick, 143
Barrow, Mun, 127
Barry, Dave, 110, 112–13
Barry, Jimmy, 336, 367, 369
Bartolo, Sal, 350, 351
Basilio, Carmen, 215, 245–248, 275–277
Bass, Benny, 312, 331, 346
Bassa, Fidel, 404
Bassett, Percy, 353
Bassey, Hogan, 353, 354
Batista, Danito, 385
Batoto, Socrates, 384
Battalino, Bat, 347, 348
Beard, Jackie, 334
Beasley, Tom, 39
Becerra, Joe, 381
Beecher, Henry Ward, 59
Bejines, Francisco, 386
Bejines, Oscar, 329
Belbouli, Taoufik, 186, 187
Belcastro, Vincenzo, 365, 390
Belcher, Jem, 22–25, 28
Belcher, John, 16
Beleno, Ever, 362
Bell, Tommy, 273, 274
Belloise, Mike, 317, 349
Beltran, Fernando, 387
Benavides, Jesse, 366
Bendigo, 35–36
Benes, Marijan, 258
Benichou, Fabrice, 361, 362, 365, 366
Benitez, Wilfredo, 253, 257, 281, 287
Benjamin, Joe, 291
Benn, Nigel, 214, 254, 255
Bennett, Lonnie, 208
Benton, Bernard, 185
Benvenuti, Nino, 251, 256
Berbick, Trevor, 178, 180, 181
Berg, Jackie "Kid", 286, 291
Berger, Sam, 88
Berks, Joe, 25
Berl, Al, 245
Berlenbach, Paul, 188, 194, 195
Berna, Bobby, 363, 364
Bernal, Gabriel, 405
Bernasconi, Dom, 377
Bernstein, Jack, 331
Bernstein, Joe, 342
Berrios, Miguel, 353
Bertini, Silvano, 257
Berumen, Ramon, 280
Beshore, Freddie, 142, 146
Bester, Bush, 258
Bethelmi, Idelfonso, 332
Bettino, Melio, 199–201
Bey, David, 179
Beya, Mwehu, 212
Biggs, Tyrell, 182
Bimstein, Whitey, 135, 238, 314, 377
Birkie, Hans, 128
Bi-Won Chung, 405
Bizzaro, Lou, 326
Black, Julian, 128, 133
Blackburn, Jack, 129, 133
Blake, George, 118, 119
Blake, Robin, 329
Blanca, Ari, 389
Blanco, Rodolfo, 406, 407
Blocker, Maurice, 259, 260, 283, 284, 285
Bloom, Phil, 291
Bodzianowski, Craig, 187
Bogan, Freddie, 336
Bogs, Tom, 251

Bohol, Rolando, 405
Bonaglia, Michele, 115
Bong-Jun Kim, 409, 411
Bonner, Jack, 218
Booze, Tyrone, 187
Borboa, Julio Cesar, 390
Borkorsor, Venice, 384, 403
Bossi, Carmelio, 256
Bott, Marcos, 187
Bottiglieri, Salvatore, 334
Boulware, Vince, 212, 213
Bouttier, Jean-Claude, 251
Bowdry, Jess, 205
Bowe, Riddick, 184
Bowen, Andy, 296–298
Bowker, Joe, 372
Bowler, James, 50
Boyle, Crockey, 342
Boza-Edwards, Cornelius, 327, 332
Braddock, James, J., 122, 124–26, 129–30, 142, 196
Brady, Bill, 71, 82
Brain, Benjamin, 16–17, 19
Bramble, Livingstone, 328
Bratton, Johnny, 273, 274
Braxton, David, 258
Braxton, Dwight, 209 See also Oawi, Dwight Muhammad
Brazier, Harold, 289
Bredahl, Jimmi, 335, 391
Bredahl, Johnny, 335, 391
Breland, Mark, 283, 284
Brennan, Bill, 96, 100
Brent, Henry, 406
Brescia, Jorge, 129
Brettle, Bob, 43, 48
Brighton, Bill, 337
Brisbane, Arthur, 56, 117
Briscoe, Benny, 251, 252
Britt, Jimmy, 220, 299–302
Britt, Willus, 220
Britten, Fred, A., 266
Britton, Jack, 262, 264–266, 306
Broad, Kid, 342
Broadus, "Doc", 172
Bronson, Ray, 264
Broome, Harry, 36–37, 291
Broughton, Jack, 8, 10–13
Brouilard, Lou, 231, 232, 268
Brown, Al, 336, 367
Brown, Bobby Jo, 285
Brown, Charlie, 329
Brown, George, K. O., 223
Brown, Glenwood, 285
Brown, Jackie, 395, 396
Brown, Joe, 321–323
Brown, K. O., 344
Brown, Natie, 128, 130
Brown, Newsboy, 395
Brown, Simon, 285
Brown, William, 196
Brunette, Brian, 287
Bruno, Frank, 181, 183
Buchanan, Ken, 325
Buelow, Arthur, 132
Buff, Johnny, 336, 367, 374, 393
Bugner, Joe, 173, 176
Bumphus, Johnny, 283, 287
Burge, Dick, 291, 298
Burke, Jack, 296, 297
Burke, James, 34, 40
Burman, Joe, 367, 374
Burman, Red, 132
Burn, Ben, 31
Burn, Bob, 31
Burnett, Jesse, 185, 208
Burns, Frankie, 336, 367, 373, 374
Burns, Jack, 59
Burns, Tommy, 84–85, 87–89, 159, 348
Burows, Jack, 27
Burruni, Salvatore, 401, 402
Busayon, René, 394
Busceme, James, 326
Busso, Johnny, 326
Byrd, Antoine, 213
Byrne, Simon, 33–34
Byron, Lord, 17, 20, 24–25

Caba, Jose, 350, 359, 360
Caban, Rafael, 391
Cabanela, Fernando, 384, 385
Cabrera, Danilo, 332, 360

Caicedo, Fernando, 335
Calderwood, Chic, 206
Caldwell, Johnny, 382, 384
Callahan, Frankie, 291
Callahan, Jack, 258
Callahan, Mushy, 156, 286
Cellajas, Victor, 361
Callura, Jackie, 350
Camacho, Hector, 290, 327, 332
Camacho, Jose, 410
Camara, Martin, 260
Camel, Marvin, 185, 186
Campanino, Miguel, 281
Campi, Eddie, 367
Campo, Luis Alberto, 388
Campo, Tanny 399
Canete, Carlos, 331
Canizales, Gaby, 385, 387
Canizales, Orlando, 387, 388
Cannon, Tom, 32
Canto, Miguel, 403, 404
Canzoneri, Tony, 269, 286, 291, 292, 312–314, 346, 367, 376
Cappai, Fabrizio, 362
Caramanolis, Richard, 212
Carazo, Juan, 390, 391
Carbajal, Michael, 409, 410
Carballo, Tamil, 411
Cardiff, Patsy, 61
Cardona, Prudencio, 405
Cardona, Ricardo, 364
Carlin, Ray, 133
Carmona, Chango, 326
Carmona, Changuito, 387
Carnera, Primo, 122–23, 125, 129, 196
Carney, Jim, 291, 295, 296
Carpentier, Georges, 95–96, 100–102, 106, 188, 189, 190, 192, 225
Carrasco, Pedro, 326
Carrasquilla, Hector, 359, 364
Carroll, Hal, 207
Carruthers, Jimmy, 379–381
Carter, Frank, 234
Carter, Jack, 26–27, 31, 33
Carter, Jimmy, 320–322
Carter, Johnny, 385
Carupo, Siony, 408
Casey, Doc, 126
Casicas Rudy, 364
Castanon, Roberto, 359
Castellano, Tony, 174
Castellini, Miguel Angel, 257
Castillejos, Francisco Javier, 260
Castillo, Chucho, 833, 384
Castillo, Freddie, 405, 408
Castillo, Roger, 405
Castillo, Ruben, 332, 359
Castro, Alberto, 389
Castro, Amancio, 329
Castro, Amando, 389, 390
Castro, Jorge, 259
Castro, Melchor Cob, 410
Catari, Omar, 335
Caunt, Ben, 35–36
Cavanagh, Billy, 317
Cavicchi, Franco, 158
Cayton, Bill, 183
Cedeno, Frank, 389, 405
Celestine, Jerry, 209
Cepeda, Ricardo, 361
Cerdan, Marcel, 216, 240
Cervantes, Antonio, 286, 287
Cervantes, Jose, 363
Chacon, Bobby, 328, 332, 358, 359
Chae-Keun Lim, 257
Chambers, Arthur, 293
Chan Hee Park, 404, 405
Chan-Mok Park, 361
Chan-Yung Park, 365, 385
Chandler, Jeff, 385
Chandler, Tom, 57, 216
Chaney, George, K. O., 331, 367
Chang-Ho Choi, 389, 406
Chang-Ki Kim, 390
Chang-Kyun Oh, 388
Chapman, Red, 346
Charles, Ezzard, 128, 142–44, 149, 158, 203
Chavez, Celso, 389
Chavez, Eric, 411
Chavez, Julio Cesar, 285, 289, 290, 327, 328, 332

Chavez, Guerrero, 287
Chervet, Fritz, 403
Chil-Sung Chun, 329
Chionoi, Chartchai, 402, 403
Chip, George, 216, 223, 225, 226, 313
Chitalada, Sot, 405, 407, 408
Chocolate, Kid, 331, 347
Chong-Kwan Chung, 405
Chong-Pal Park, 212
Choo-Woon Park, 409
Choynski, Joe, 67, 71–72, 79
Christoforidas, Anton, 200, 201
Chul-Ho Kim, 388, 389
Chung-Byong Kwan, 389
Chung-Ill Choi, 332
Chung-Jae Lee, 409
Churchill, Frank, 367
Chuvalo, George, 162, 166, 169
Chuwatana, Petchai, 411
Ciminez, Jose, 287
Clabby, Jimmy, 216, 223, 225, 264
Clark, Elky, 384
Clark, Johnny, 293
Clark, Scott, 281
Claudio, Victor, 212
Clay, Cassius, 158, 159, 160, 281 See also Ali, Muhammad
Clayton Zack, 174, 175, 176, 326
Cleary, Mike, 63–64
Clemente, Fel, 359
Clinton, Pat, 407
Clyde, Ian, 405
Cobb, Randall (Tex), 178
Coburn, Joe, 45, 49–53
Cochran, Freddie, 272, 273
Cockell, Don, 149, 151
Coetzee, Gerry, 180
Coffee, Jerome, 386
Coggi, Juan Martin, 287, 289
Cohen, Max, 251
Cohen, Robert, 380
Cokes, Curtis, 279, 280
Cole, Al, 187
Coleman, Clarence, 290
Colima, Bert, 228
Collins, Lion, 365
Collins, Mike, 286
Collins, Ron, 255
Collins, Steve, 254, 255
Collins, Tom, 212
Commey, Percy, 363
Condori, Ruben, 389
Conn, Billy, 132, 135–40, 158, 188, 200, 201
Conn, Mark, 207
Constantino, Joe, 411
Conteh, John, 208, 209
Contreras, Israel, 387, 389
Cook, Eddie, 387
Cooney, Gerry, 178, 179, 181, 182
Cooper, Arthur, 78
Cooper, Bert, 184, 185
Cooper, Gypsy, 261, 291
Cooper, Henry, 137
Cooper, Henry, 162, 163
Coopman, Jean-Pierre, 177
Corbett, Harry, 82
Corbett, James J., 56, 61, 66, 68–69, 71–72, 74, 76–77, 80, 82–83, 88, 90, 114, 128–129, 151, 158, 188, 196
Corbett, Young (III) 268, 342
Corcoran, Peter, 14–16
Cordoba, Victor, 212, 213, 214
Corletti, Eduardo, 167
Coronado, Francisco, 359
Corri, Eugene, 229
Cortes, Alberto, 289
Costa, Carmelo, 353
Costa, Elmer, 168
Costa, Everaldo, 281
Costello, Bill, 288
Costello, Tom, 63, 65
Coulon, Johnny, 336, 367, 373
Covington, Hayden C., 165
Cowdell, Pat, 359, 360
Cowler, Tom, 88
Crawford, Jim, 78
Crawley, Peter, 33, 37
Crawley, Tyrone, 328
Creedon, Dan, 79
Cribb, Tom, 25–29
Criqui, Eugene, 345

Croot, Walter, 369
Crossley, Fred, 59
Crous, Piet, 186
Crowley, Jim, 117
Cruz, Antonio Reyes, 288
Cruz, Freddy, 366
Cruz, Leonardo, 363, 364
Cruz, Roberto, 286
Cruz, Ramon, 365
Cruz, Steve, 360, 361
Cruz, Teo, 324, 328
Cuello, Miguel, 208
Cuevas, Jose, 281
Cumberland, Duke of, 10–11, 13
Curcetti, Salvatore, 334
Curley, Jack, 84, 190
Curry, Bruce, 287
Curry, Don, 254, 258, 259, 282
Curtis, Dick, 291
Curtis, Louis, 406
Curto, Vinni, 212
Curvis, Brian, 279
Cusick, James, 45
Czyz, Bobby, 187, 210, 211, 212

Dade, Harold, 378
D'Agata Mario, 380
Dagge, Exkhard, 257
Daggert, Charles, 144
Daho, Najib, 333
Daigle, Kevin, 259
Dale, Roy, 251
Daley, Bill, 277
Daley, Jim, 80
Dal Rovere, Sidnei, 334
Dalton, James, 59
Dalton, Tom, 15
D'Amato, Cus, 183, 206
Damiani, Francesco, 185
Daniels, Carl, 259
Daniels, Robert, 187
Daniels, Terry, 171
Danphoothai, Kajkong, 408
Darcy, Les, 216, 223, 225
Darts, Jack, 14, 16
Davila, Alberto, 384, 385, 386
Davis, Aaron, 285
Davis, Anthony, 185
Davis, Bill, 52
Davis, Eddie, 209, 211
Davis, Howard, 289, 312, 326
Davis, Joe, 15
Davis, Johnny, 209
Davis, Tom, 27
Davison, Dwight, 253
Davison, John, 362
Dean, Bill, 261
Decima, Pedro, 366
DeCoursey, Billy, 372
DeJesus, Esteban, 325–327
DeJesus, Francisco, 258
DeJesus, Jose, 408, 410
De la Cruz, Francisco Tomas, 333
Delaney Billy, 82
Delaney, Jack, 188, 194, 195, 196
De la Puz, Loves, 386
De la Rosa, Johnny, 333, 359
Dele, Gilbert, 260
De Leon, Carlos, 185, 186, 187
De Leva, Ciro, 385
Delgado, Freddie, 212
Dell'Aquila, Francisco, 254
De Luca, Tony, 406
Del Valle, Rafael, 387
De Marco, Mario, 408, 409
De Marco, Paddy, 321
De Marco, Tony, 277–279
Dempsey, Jack ("Nonpareil"), 78–79, 215, 219, 220, 261
Dempsey, Jack, 57, 85, 93, 95–107, 110–15, 128, 142, 151, 153, 157, 158, 192, 393
Denning, Jack, 119
De Oliveira, Joao Cardosa, 366
De Oliveira, Miguel, 257
De Paula, Jose, 359
Descamps, François, 100, 190, 192
Develos, William, 390
De Villa, Diego, 390
De Vorse, Paul, 360
De Witt, Doug, 254
De Young, Moss, 398

Dias, Claudemir, 404
Diaz, Elio, 282
Diaz, Jorge Urbina, 365
Diaz, Policarpo, 329, 330
Diaz, Raul, 390
Dillon, Jack, 188, 190, 216, 223, 225
Dineen, Jim, 218
Dipley, Walter, 224
Dixie, Kid, 263
Dixon, George, 67, 299, 336, 338, 339–342, 367, 368, 392
Dobovan, Matt, 257
Dokes, Michael, 180, 184
Donaldson, John, 57–59
Dong-Chung Lee, 390
Dong-Hoon Lee, 389
Dong Kyun Yun, 363
Donovan, Arthur, 132, 135, 272, 309, 316, 317
Donovan, Professor Mike, 50, 57–58, 65, 216, 219
Dorazio, Gus, 132
Dorsey, Troy, 361, 362
Douglas, James, 181, 183, 184
Doux, Scott, 178
Dower, Dai, 399
Downes, Terry, 208, 248, 249
Downes, Tyrone, 361
Downey, Bryan, 227
Downey, Jack, 248
Drayton, Buster, 258
Driscoll, Jem, 305, 344
Driscoll, Tim, 362
Duane, Carl, 363
Duarte, Frankie, 365, 385
Duffy, Paddy, 261
Duk-Koo Kim, 328
Dundee, Angelo, 160, 164, 170
Dundee, Joe, 266, 267
Dundee, Johnny, 291, 306, 308, 313, 331, 345, 367
Dundee, Vince, 216, 231, 232, 276
Dunn, Jere, 53, 67
Dunn, Jim, 50
Dunn, Richard, 177
Dupas, Ralph, 256, 322
Duplessis, John, 290
Du Plooy, Johnny, 185
Duran, Jose, 257
Duran, Massimilliano, 187
Duran, Richard, 365
Duran, Roberto, 213, 252, 253, 254, 255, 258, 281, 325, 326, 327
Duran, Samuel, 388
Durelle, Yvon, 204
Durham, Yank, 171, 172
Dwyer, Dan, 56
Dwyer, John, 52
Dyson, Bobby, 392

Earp, Wyatt, 79
East, Morris, 289
Eastwood, Barney, 285
Ebihara, Hiroyuki, 400, 401
Echeverria, Orlando, 322
Echegaray, Victor, 331
Edison, Thomas, A., 73
Edison, Jay, 174
Edwards, Billy, 293
Edwards, Willie, 210
Egula, Esteban, 360
Elizondo, Roberto, 326
Elliott, Carlos, 260
Elliott, Jim, 51–52, 67
Ellis, Dick, 78
Ellis, Jimmy, 166–67, 168, 169–70
Ellis, Lester, 333
Elorde, Flash, 331
Elvilea, Gilles, 282
Emanuel, Armand, 194
Emebe, Jean-Marie, 211
Erne, Frank, 291, 296, 297, 341, 342
Ertle, Harry, 101, 193
Ertle, Johnny, 373, 374
Ertle, Mike, 392
Escalera, Alfredo, 332
Escobar, Sixto, 377, 378
Espada, Angel, 281
Espadas, Gustave, 389, 403, 404
Espana, Crisanto, 285
Espana, Ernesto, 327, 328

Esparragoza, Antonio, 361
Espinal, Eusebio, 389
Espinal, Ignacio, 404
Espinosa, Leo, 399
Espinosa, Louie, 361, 364, 386, 387
Essett, Ronnie, 212, 214
Estaba, Luis, 407, 408
Estrada, Jesus, 359
Estrada, Juan J., 364
Ettore, Al, 129
Eubank, Chris, 213, 214, 255
Evangelista, Alfreda, 177, 178

Famechon, Johnny, 356, 357
Farley, James A., 106, 228
Farr, Tommy, 122, 126, 130, 151
Fearns, Duggan, 16
Featherstone, Willie, 211
Feldman, Lou, 347
Feliciano, Pedro, 406
Felix, Barney, 160
Fenech, Jeff, 334, 335, 361, 363, 364, 365, 386
Fernandez, Orlando, 366
Fernandez, Perico, 287
Fernandez, Rocky, 334
Fernandez, Vilomar, 326, 327
Fernando, Mark, 333
Ferns, Clarence (Kid), 264
Ferns, Rube, 263
Fewterell, William, See Futrell, William
Fields, Jackie, 266–268
Figg, James, 7–10, 13
Finighty, Simon, 368
Finnegan, Chris, 207
Firpo, Luis, 96, 103–6, 157
Fitzpatrick, John, 63, 65
Fitzpatrick, Bob, 71, 75–83, 128, 158, 163, 188, 189, 190, 215, 218, 219, 261
Fitzsimmons, Floyd, 106
Flaherty, Martin, 299
Fleischer, Nat, 161, 169, 271, 277, 400, 401
Fletcher, Frank, 253
Flood, John, 58–59
Flores, Elino, 331
Flores, José Maria, 183
Flowers, Tiger, 227
Flynn, Jim, 90
Folley, Zora, 164, 165, 166
Forbes, Eddie, 113
Forbes, Frank, 140
Forbes, Harry, 343, 344, 367
Force, Harry, 217
Ford, Al, 286
Ford, Ernesto, 389, 391
Ford, Patrick, 359, 360
Foreman, George, 171–176, 184
Foster, Bob, 207, 208
Foster, Pop, 268
Fourie, Pierre, 207, 208
Fox, Billy, 200
Fox, Richard K., 59, 63, 70
Fox, Tiger, Jack, 199
Francis, Kid, 375
Frank, Scott, 179
Franklin, Matt, 209. See also Muhammad, Matthew Saad
Fratto, Rocky, 258
Frazee, Harry, 90
Frazier, Alfonso, 286
Frazier, Joe, 166, 172–174, 176–179, 207
Frazier, Marvis, 179
Frazier, Tyrone, 211
Freeman, Charles, 36
Freeman, Tommy, 268
Frias, Arturo, 328
Fuentes, Moises, 365
Fuentes, Sammy, 289
Fujii, Paul, 286
Fullam, Frank, 141, 320
Fuller, William, 40
Fulljames, George, 216, 219, 261
Fullmer, Gene, 244, 248, 249
Fulton, Fred, 88, 96–97
Furesawa, Kimio, 403, 404
Furlano, Nicky, 288
Furuyama, Lion, 287
Fusari, Charley, 237
Futch, Eddie, 176

Futrell, William, 23–24

Gainer, Al, 124, 199
Galaxy, Kaokar, 385, 386
Galaxy, Kaosai, 386, 389, 390, 391
Galento, Tony, 124, 132, 135, 142
Galexi, Sak, 333
Galindez, Victor, 208, 209
Gallagher, Charley, 52
Gallardo, Jesus, 212
Galloway, Manning, 285
Galvano. Mauro, 214
Galvez, Alli. 407, 410
Gamache, Joey, 329, 335
Gamez, Luis, 406, 408, 411
Ganigan, Andy, 326
Gans, Joe, 264, 291, 292, 299, 300, 301, 342
Gant, Johnny, 281
Garcia, Augustin, 408
Garcia, Ceferino, 233, 235, 270, 272
Garcia, Cleo, 364, 385
Garcia, Danny, 285
Garcia, Jorge, 359
Garcia, Lorenzo, 287
Garcia, Luis, 285
Gardiner, Dai, 362
Gardner, Carl, 158
Gardner, George, 80, 188, 189
Gardner, Oscar, 342
Gardner, Tony, 257
Garza, Jaime, 363
Garza, Loreto, 289
Gault, Henry, 379
Gavilan, Kid, 262, 273, 275
Gaymon, Dorcey, 186
Gazo, Eddie, 257, 258
Genaro, Frankie, 313, 367, 395, 396
Gervacio, Julio, 364, 366
Giambra, Joey, 256
Giardello, Joey, 249, 250
Gibbons, Mike, 216, 224, 225, 262, 263, 264
Gibbons, Tom, 103, 106, 113, 188, 264
Gibbs, Harry, 163, 385
Gilmore, Harry, 291, 336
Giminez, Carlos, 214, 287
Giordana, Ralph, 268
Giovanni, Nestor, 212
Glick, Joe, 310
Glickman, Bernie, 277
Glover, Mike, 264
Godfrey, George, 67
Godoy, Arturo, 132–33
Goldman, Charley, 145
Goldman, Sam, 313
Goldstein, Abe, 367, 374, 375
Goldstein, Ruby, 140, 147, 154–55, 157, 238, 242, 279, 280, 310
Gomez, Antonio, 358
Gomez, Harold, 331
Gomez, Wilfredo, 332, 359, 360, 363, 364, 385, 386
Gonzales, Alonzo, 404
Gonzales, Betulio, 403, 404
Gonzales, Miguel Angel, 329, 330
Gonzales, Paul, 388
Gonzales, Carlos, 290
Gonzalez, Gerrardo. See Galivan, Kid
Gonzalez, Humberto, 410
Gonzalez, Manuel, 258, 279, 283
Gonzalez, Ranolfo, 328
Gonzalez, Rodolfo, 287, 289, 326
Goodrich, Jimmy, 311
Goodwin, Nat, 59
Gordon, Jack, 174
Gordon, S. T., 185
Goss, Joe, 49–51, 54–55, 58
Goss, Woody, 168
Graham, Billy, 275
Graham, Bushy, 375
Graham, Herol, 254, 255
Graney, Ed, 81
Grant, Bunny, 286
Grant, Uriah, 187
Graves, Kid, 264
Gray, Clyde, 281

Graziano, Rocky, 215, 235–239, 273
Greb, Harry, 109, 113, 122, 188, 191, 192, 193, 194, 216, 224, 227, 228
Green, Dave, 281
Greer, Michael, 185, 186, 187
Gregorio, Videl, 376
Gregory, Eddie, 208. See also Muhammad, Eddie Mustapha
Gregory, Steve, 258
Gregson, Bob, 21–22
Griffen, Corn, 124–125
Griffen, Johnny, 338
Griffith, Emile, 250, 251, 278–280
Griffiths, Tuffy, 194
Griffo, Young, 291, 296, 336
Griman, David, 389, 407
Grossman, Lee, 167
Grove, Calvin, 335, 361
Guest, Milton, 282
Guiden, Gary, 258
Guidino, Julio, 404
Guiseppe, Fitzroy, 287
Gully, John, 21–22, 28
Gumbs, Roy, 212
Gunguluza, Jackie, 335
Gushiken Yoko, 408
Gutierrez, Lupe, 334, 361
Gutierrez, Mauro, 361
Guzman, Aquiles, 406
Guzman, Juan, 408

Hagler, Marvin, 210, 251–253, 254
Hagler, Yani, 409
Hague, Ian, 87
Haley, Leroy, 287, 288
Haley, Patsy, 291, 309, 310, 393, 394
Halimi, Alphonse, 380–382
Hall, Jem, 78–79
Hamada, Tsuyoshi, 288
Hamas, Steve, 120, 197
Hammie, Cherif, 353
Hamilton, Duke of, 16
Hammer, Ever, 308
Hamsho, Mustafa, 252, 253
Hamza, Al, 285
Hanagata, Susumu, 403, 404
Harada, Masahiko "Fighting" 383, 384, 400
Harding, Jeff, 211, 212
Hardy, Billy, 288
Hargrave, Earl, 258
Harrington, Stan, 256
Harris, Harry, 367, 369, 371
Harris, Ronnie, 252
Harris, Roy, 156
Harris, Sam, 342, 370
Hart, Marvin, 10, 84
Harvey, Len, 230
Hassan, Ramzi, 211, 212
Hatanaka, Kiyoshi, 366, 390
Hatcher, Gene, 283, 287
Haugen, Greg, 290, 329
Havnaa, Magne, 187
Hawkins, Dal, 336
Hayles, Percy, 286
Hayward, Stan, 256
Healey, Bill, 137
Hearns, Thomas, 211, 214, 253, 254, 257, 258, 281, 282
Heenan, John C., 41–49, 52, 54
Heeney, Tom, 113–14, 195
Hembrick, Anthony, 212
Hemple, Jack, 93
Henneberry, Bill, 379
Henrique, Joao, 287
Herman, Kid, 343
Herman, Pete, 336, 367, 373, 374, 392
Hernandez, Angel, 260, 290
Hernandez, Carlos, 286
Hernandez, Emilio, 385
Hernandez, Genaro, 335
Hernandez, Jose, 256
Hernandez, Leonel, 331, 358
Herrera, Carlos, 257
Herrera, Ernesto, 249, 359
Herrera, Isaac, 326
Herrera, Juan, 404
Herrera, Rafael, 383, 384
Hicken, Abe, 293
Hickman, Tom, 30–31

Hicks, Tommy, 207
Hill, Virgil, 211
Hilton, Matthew, 254, 258, 259
Hines, Robert, 259
Hinton, Gary, 288
Hiranaka, Akinobu, 289
Hirano, Kimio, 411
Hiranyelekha, Sangvien, 402
Hi-Sup Shin, 405
Hi-Yon Choi, 411
Hodkinson, Paul, 361, 362
Hoffman, George, 194
Hogan, Ben, 52
Holland, Fritz, 223
Hollands, Hammer, 31
Hollywood, Dick, 337
Holmes, Larry, 178, 179, 180, 182, 184, 186, 210
Holmes, Lindell, 212, 213, 214
Holyfield, Evander, 183, 184, 186
Honeyghan, Lloyd, 282, 283, 284, 285
Hooper, Courtney, 289
Hooper, William, 19–20
Hope, Maurice, 257
Hosono, Yuichi, 411
Hostack, Al, 233, 234
Houseman, Lou, 188
Hozumi, Suichi, 404
Huat, Eugene, 376
Hudkins, Ace, 228, 229, 267
Hudson, Joshua, 31–32
Huh Chun, 366
Humez, Charles, 243, 274, 275
Humphries, Joe, 225, 312
Humphries, Richard, 18–20
Hunt, Babe, 124
Hurley, Jack, 310
Hurst, Sam, 48
Hutchins, Fred, 257
Hutchins, Len, 208
Hwan-Jin, Kim, 408
Hwan-Kil Yuh, 333
Hyer, Jacob, 39
Hyer, Tom, 38–41, 53, 55, 88

Ibanez, Luis, 389
Ibarra, Luis, 404
Igarashi, Tsutomu, 404
Ihetu, Richard. See Tiger, Dick
Ilueca, Gilberto, 384
Impellettiere, Ray, 196
Ingleston, George, 23
Ingraham, Judge Joe, 165
In-Kyu Hwang, 410
Ioka, Hiroki, 409, 410, 411
Iriarte, Miguel, 385
Isaacs, Harry, 20
Ishii, Koki, 389
Ishimatsu, Guts, 326
Iskander, Said, 411
Isogami, Shuichi, 385
Iwata, Kenji, 331

Jack, Beau, 291, 292, 318, 319
Jackson, Hurricane, 151, 154–55
Jackson, John, 23–25
Jackson, John David, 260
Jackson, Julian, 255, 258, 260
Jackson, Peter, 72
Jackson, Tyrone, 333, 361
Jackson, Willie, 291, 308, 367
Jacob, Thierry, 365, 366, 386
Jacobs, Jack, 20
Jacobs, Jim, 183
Jacobs, Joe, 117, 121, 135, 193
Jacobs, Joey, 335
Jacobs, Mike, 120, 125–26, 128–29, 137, 142, 232, 273, 314, 348, 378
Jacobsen, Gert Bo, 285, 286, 329
Jacobson, Gus, 158
Jacquot, Rene, 259
Jadick, Johnny, 286
Jae Do Park, 257
Jae-Hong Kim, 409
Jae-Suk Park, 389
Jamieson, Capt. Tom, 65
Jarvis, John, 213, 214
Javierto, Orlando, 404
Jeannette, Joe, 86
Jeby, Ben, 231, 232
Jeffra, Harry, 349, 378

Jeffries, James J., 77–78, 80–84, 87–88, 93, 158
Jenkins, Lou, 317, 318
Jensen, Willie, 388, 389
Jerome, Frankie, 367, 376
Jiminez, Alberto, 407
Jiminez, Louis, 399
Jiminez, Nestor, 384
Jin-Shik Choi, 333
Ji-Won Kim, 364
Jockgham, Noree, 366
Jofre, Eder, 358, 381, 382, 384
Johansson, Ingemar, 157–58, 174
Johnson, Charley, 352
Johnson, Harold, 204, 205, 206, 247
Johnson, Jack, 81, 84–88, 90–92, 139, 159, 221, 222, 263
Johnson, Jim, 90
Johnson, Marvin, 208, 209, 210, 211
Johnson, Phil, 205, 206
Johnson, Reggie, 254, 255
Johnson, Tom, 16–17, 20
Johnson, Tom 'Boom Boom', 362
Johnson, Vonzell, 209
Johnson, Jimmy, 134, 345
Jones, Anthony, 329
Jones, Colin, 282
Jones, Doug, 100
Jones, Gorilla, 231
Jones, Harry ("the Sailor Boy"), 261
Jones, Jersey, 249
Jones, Leroy, 178
Jones, Paddington, 261
Jong-Il Byon, 388
Joo-Do Chun, 390
Joo-Ho, 258
Jordan, Ben, 340
Jordan, Don, 277, 309
Jorgensen, Phil, 331
Joseph, Eddie, 132, 136–37, 273
Josselin, Jean, 279, 280
Joyce, Willie, 286
Juchau, Tom, 14
Julio, Jorge Eliecer, 387
Jum-Hwan Choi, 409, 411
Jun-Suk Hwang, 260, 282
Jung-Keun Lim, 410
Jung Koo Chang, 405, 407, 408, 410
Jurich, Jackie, 397

Kacar, Slobodan, 208
Kahut, Joe, 198
Kalambay, Sumbu, 254
Kalule, Ayub, 258
Kamishiro, Hideaki, 404, 405
Kamiyama, Hitoshi, 260
Kane, Peter, 207, 397
Kansas, Rocky, 291, 308, 311
Kaplan, Hymie, 317
Kaplan, Louis, 345, 346
Kassahara, Yu, 364
Kasugai, Ken, 390
Katsuma, Katsuo, 389
Kaufman, Al, 86
Kawakami, Masaharu, 410
Kawashima, Shinobu, 405
Kearns, Jack, 90–97, 99, 202, 230
Kearns, Soldier, 89
Keating, Johnny, 337
Kelly, Brian, 207
Kelly, Honest John, 77
Kelly, Hugo, 220
Kelly, Tommy, 367, 368
Kendall, Andy, 205
Kenrick, Jim, 373
Kenty, Hilmer, 327
Kessler, Harry, 150, 164
Ketchel, Stanley, 86, 215, 216, 220–224, 230, 236, 264
Ketchell, Steve, 129
Khumalo, Nika, 285
Kiabwanchai, Napa, 410
Kiatkriengkrai, Thanomjit, 362
Kiatvayupak, Tomgta, 287
Kiatwanchai, Napa, 410, 411
Ki-Jun Lee, 365
Kilbane, Johnny, 336, 343–345
Kilpatrick, John Reed, 142

Kilrain, Jake, 60–61, 63–67, 72
Kim, Ki-Soo, 256
Kim Sa Wang, 359
Kinchen, James, 211, 212, 214
King, Don, 176, 180, 183
King, Tom, 46, 48–50, 52
Kingpetch, Pone, 400–402
Kitakasen, Muangchai, 405, 406, 409
Kittikasem, Singprasert, 411
Kiuna, Tomohiro, 408
Ki-Yung Chung, 361
Klaus, Frankie, 216, 224–226
Klick, Frankie, 331
Kline, Patsy, 343
Knight, Harold, 333
Kobayashi, Chaiki, 386
Kobayashi, Hiroshi, 331
Kobayashi, Kojo, 405
Kobayashi, Royal, 358, 359, 363
Komiyama, Katsuma, 408
Konadu, Nana Yaw, 390, 391
Koopman, Rudi, 209
Kotei, David, 359
Kpalogo, Mensah, 385
Krause, Harry, 159, 162
Kreiger, Solly, 233
Kudo, Masashi, 258
Kwang-Gu Park, 3
Kwang-Min Kim, 287
Kwang-Soo Oh, 411
Kwang-Sum Kim, 410
Kyung-Duk Ahn, 290
Kyung-Yung Lee, 410, 411

La Barba, Fidel, 367, 395
La Blanche, George, 219
Laciar, Santos Benigno, 389, 390, 404
Laguna, Ismael, 323–326
Lally, Brett, 259
Lalonde, Don, 187, 211, 214
La Motta, Jake, 223, 240, 241
Lampkin, Jeff, 187
Lampkin, Kelvin, 361
Lampkin, Ray, 325
Lane, Kenny, 286, 322
Langan, Jack, 30–32
Langford, Sam, 87, 262, 264
Langham, Nat, 43, 215
Laporte, Juan, 333, 334, 359, 360
Larkin, Tippy, 286
La Rocca, Nino, 282
Lasisi, Joe, 211
La Starza, Roland, 146–49
Lastra, Cecilio, 359
Latka, George, 355
Latzo, Pete, 264, 265
Lavigne, George, 291, 293, 296, 297
Lawal, Racheed, 285
Lawlor, Pat, 260
Lawas, Rommel, 411
Layne, Alfredo, 332, 334
Layne, Rex, 146
Lazer, Roy, 128
Lazzaro San, 267
Le Doux, Scott, 178
Lee, William "Caveman", 252
Legra, José, 357, 358
Leslie, Jock, 351
Leon, Caspar, 336, 367, 369
Leon, Genaro, 285
Leonard, Benny, 291, 292, 305–309, 311, 312
Leonard, Sugar Ray, 211, 212, 214, 253, 254, 258, 259, 260, 281–283
Lesnevich, Gus, 142, 200, 201, 202
Levinsky, Battling, 113, 190, 192
Levinsky, King, 129, 229
Lewis, Hedgemon, 280–282
Lewis, Lennox, 184, 285, 290
Lewis, John Henry, 132
Lewis, Ted Kid, 262, 264, 265
Lewis, Willie, 224
Licata, Tony, 251
Liotta, Leonardo. See De Marco, Tony
Lim, Rocky, 411
Limon, Rafael, 332
Lindstrom, Danny, 212
Lira, Johnny, 327

Liston, Sonny, 158, 159–62, 164
Little, Freddie, 256
Little, Steve, 260
Loayza, Stanislaus, 310, 311
Lockridge, Rocky, 332, 333, 359, 360
Logart, Isaac, 277
Logist, Bob, 187
Loi, Duilio, 286
Lomas, Joey, 167
Lomski, Leo, 124, 194, 196, 197
Londas, Daniel, 334, 335
London, Brian, 163
London, Jack, 87
Lonsdale, Lord, 286
Lopez, Alfonso, 403, 408
Lopez, Alvaro, 185, 208, 209
Lopez, Danny, 359
Lopez, Ernie, 279
Lopez, Gerardo, 365
Lopez, Hector, 330
Lopez, Jose Mario, 361
Lopez, Lucio, 386
Lopez, Ricardo, 411
Lopez, Tony, 329, 333, 334
Lopopolo, Sandro, 286
Lora, Miguel, 386, 387
Loubet, Nat, 163, 207
Lovera, Rafael, 408
Lovitt, Bill, 160
Lucas, Domingo, 411
Lucas, Javier, 404
Lujan, Jorge, 360, 364, 384, 385, 386
Lukmingkwan, Fahlan, 411
Lumumba, Patrick, 187
Lupino, Maurizio, 387
Lynch, Benny, 336, 396, 397
Lynch, Charley, 367
Lynch, Joe, 336, 363, 367, 374, 375
Lyons, Tom, 14–15
Lyons, Wild Bill, 230

MacDonald, Bill, 160
MacDonald, Jack, 44
MacDonald, Jim, 210
MacDonald, Rod, 186
Mace, Jem, 48–51, 54, 78
Machon, Max, 121, 132
Macias, Paul, 380
Mack, Marvin, 212
Mackay, Big, 344
Macone, Harry, 34
Madden, Bartley, 113
Madden, Billy, 58–59
Maddox, George, 26, 28
Madera, Lupe, 408
Mafuz, Eddie, 277
Magallano, Elmer, 386
Magri, Charlie, 404, 405
Maher, Peter, 75–79
Makhatini, Patrick, 187
Maldonado, Orlando, 389
Malcolm, Jeff, 285
Malinga, Thulani, 213, 214
Malitz, Mike, 166
Maloney, Jim, 195, 229
Mamby, Saoul, 287, 288
Manca, Fortunato, 256
Mancini, Ray, 290, 326, 328
Mandell, Sammy, 291, 292, 311, 312
Mandot, Joe, 291
Manfredo, Al, 272
Manley, Joe, 288
Manning, Mal, 276
Mannion, Sean, 258
Mansfield, Judge Walter E., 165, 166
Mantell, Frank, 224, 225
Marcano, Alfredo, 331, 358
Marcano, Rigoberto, 408
Marcel, Ernesto, 358
Marciano, Rocky, 128, 142–52, 179, 180, 204

Marek, Max, 128
Marino, Dado, 398
Marino, Tony, 375
Marmolejo, Jose, 361
Marques, Felix, 390
Marquez, Javier, 361
Marrero, Adriano, 287
Marsh, Terry, 288
Marshall, Justice Thurgood, 166
Marshall, Marty, 159
Martelli, Mauro, 284, 285
Martin, Bob, 191
Martin, Eddie, 367, 374, 375
Martin, Jack, 215
Martin, Jerry, 209
Martin, Leotis, 166–67
Martin, Vincent, 331
Martinez, Emilio, 199
Martinez, Fernando, 410
Martinez, Gerardo, 385
Martinez, Mario, 329, 333, 334
Martinez, Rodolfo, 384
Martinez, Valentin, 407
Martinez, Vince, 277
Marty, Felix, 393
Maruyama, Jackai, 389
Maske, Henry, 212
Mason, Frankie, 374, 392
Mason, Harry, 291
Massera, Charley, 128
Massey, Lew, 331
Mastrodonato, Michele, 260
Matteoni, Dario, 214
Mathebula, Peter, 404
Mathis, Buster, 168, 169
Mathison, Harold, 117
Matlala, Jacob, 406
Matsuda, Toshihiko, 409
Matsumura, Kenji, 389, 390, 391
Matsumoto, Koji, 362
Matthews, Harry, 146–47
Matthews, Matty, 263
Mattioli, Rocky, 257
Maturana, Miguel, 386
Muriello, Tammy, 139–40, 200, 201
Maurullo, Tony, 194
Maxim, Joey, 143, 153, 202, 243
Maynard, Andrew, 187
Mayor, Angel, 360, 361
Maysonet, Jorge, 285
Mayweather, Roger, 288, 289, 290, 331, 332
Mazzinghi, Sandro, 256
McAllister, Jimmy, 351
McAuley, Dave, 404, 406, 407
McAuliffe, Jack, 67, 290–296
McCallum, Mike, 254, 255, 256, 258
McCarney, Billy, 89
McCarthy, Billy, 78
McCarthy, Cal, 338, 368
McCarthy, Luther, 88–89
McClellan, Gerald, 255, 256
McCluskey, Country, 40
McCoole, Mike, 49, 51, 53–54
McCormick, Macon, 58
McCoy, Al (heavyweight), 132
McCoy, Al (middleweight), 226, 313
McCoy, Kid, 77, 93, 188, 189, 215, 223, 262, 263
McCrory, Glenn, 187
McCrory, Milton, 258, 282
McCrory, Steve, 386
McDonald, Duncan, 61
McDonald, Jim, 209, 210
McDonnel, Jim, 334
McDonough, Frank, 161
McFadden, George, 291, 344
McFarland, Packy, 262, 265, 314
McGirt, James, 285, 288, 289
McGoorty, Eddie, 216, 223, 225
McGovern, Hugh, 341
McGovern, Terry, 336, 340–342, 369–371
McGowan, Walter, 401, 402
McGraw, Phil, 310
McGuigan, Barry, 360
McKay, Sandy, 34
McKenzie, Duke, 366, 387, 388, 406
McKinney, Kennedy, 365

McLaglen, Victor, 86
McLarnin, Jimmy, 262, 268–270, 310–312, 367, 394
McMahon, Bearcat, 91
McMillan, Colin, 362, 363
McNeeley, Tom, 158
McPartland, Kid, 191, 291, 298
McTigue, Mike, 190, 193, 194, 197
McVey, Connie, 77
McVey, Sam, 86
Meade, Eddie, 316
Medal, Mark, 257, 258
Medel, Raymond, 404
Medina, Hector, 326
Medina, Manuel, 362
Meekins, John, 289
Meggs, George, 13
Melchor, Manny, 411
Melendez, Hector Ray, 408
Mellish, Col. Harry, 21
Mellody, Honey, 264
Melo, Mario, 212
Mendez, Ramon, 251
Mendoza, Daniel, 16, 18–21, 23
Mendoza, Luis, 364, 366
Menken, Adah Isaacs, 41
Merani, Sergio, 212
Mercado, Carlos, 390
Mercante, Arthur, 158, 171, 172, 402, 408
Mercedes, Eleonceo, 404, 405
Mercedes, Miguel, 407
Mercer, Kay, 185
Meyers, Dutch, 228
Meyran, Octavio, 183
Meza, Juan "Kid", 363, 364
Miceli, Joe, 276
Michael, Barry, 333
Mihara, Tadischi, 258
Mike, Sugar Ray, 411
Mildenberger, Karl, 163–64, 166, 167
Miller, Freddie, 348, 349, 352
Miller, Ray, 203, 351
Milligan, Tommy, 229
Mills, Freddie, 200, 201, 202, 209
Milson, Baker, 14
Milton, Dennis, 255
Minami, Hisao, 256
Minchillo, Luiji, 258
Min-Keun Oh, 361
Minter, Alan, 251, 252
Minus, Ray, 386, 387, 388
Miranda, Mario, 359
Misako, Masahiro, 257
Miske, Billy, 100
Mitchell, Brian, 332, 334, 335
Mitchell, Charlie, 60–63, 65, 74–75, 296
Mitchell, Frankie, 290, 334
Mitchell, Irving, 359, 361
Mitchell, Kenny, 366
Mitchell, Myron, 286
Mitchell, Richie, 286, 291, 307
Mitchen, Jimmy, 293
Mohammed, Prince, 210
Molina, Juan, 333, 334, 335
Molinares, Tomas, 284
Molineaux, Tom, 26–28, 30–40
Monaghan, Rinty, 397
Monahan, Walter, 100
Monroe, Marty, 137–140
Monserrat, Edgar, 386–389
Montana, Small, 395, 396
Montano, Tony, 256
Montero, Antoine, 389, 404, 405
Montgomery, Bob, 291, 319, 320
Montiel, Francisco, 408
Montilla, Miguel, 287
Montoya, Eduardo, 361
Montreal, Young, 367
Monzon, Carlos, 251, 252, 279, 290
Monzote, Luis, 410
Moore, Archie, 150–51, 155, 202–205
Moore, Davey, 257, 258
Moore, Davy, 354, 355
Moore, Memphis Pal, 367
Moorer, Michael, 185, 212
Morales, Alberto, 404
Morales, Fernie, 388
Morales, Ulises, 364
Moran, Azael, 385

Moran, Frank, 89–90, 93
Moran, Owen, 343, 372
Moran, Pal, 284, 344
Moreno, Ricardo, 353
Morgan, Danny, 212, 213
Morgan, Tod, 331
Morris, Carl, 88–89, 96
Morris, Wayne, 255
Morrison, Tommy, 185
Morrissey, John, 40–42, 50, 54
Moukhine, L., 156
Moyer, Denny, 251, 256
Muangroi-Et, Vichit, 364
Muangsurin, Prayoonsak, 364, 365, 390
Muangsurin, Saesak, 287
Mugabi, John, 253, 256, 258, 259, 260
Mugurama, Takuya, 364, 385
Muhammad, Eddie Mustapha, 209 See also Gregory, Eddie
Muhammad, Matthew Saad, 209 See also Franklin, Matt
Muldoon, William, 58, 64–65, 70, 103
Mun-Jin Choi, 408
Mundine, Tony, 251
Muniz, Armando, 280–282, 391
Miniz, Oscar, 385
Munro, Jack, 84
Murata, Eijiro, 385
Murillo, Benedicto, 408
Murphy, Billy, 336, 338
Murphy, Bob, 203
Murphy, Dan, 64
Murphy, Frank, 336, 338
Murphy, Jack, 78
Murphy, Jim, 368
Murphy, Johnny, 65
Murphy, Kid, 373
Murphy, Lee Roy, 186
Murphy, Tommy, 304, 344
Murray, Battling, 392
Musto, Tony, 132
Mutti, Chisanda, 186
Mwale, Lottee, 209
Myer, Billy, 291, 292
Myung-Woo Yuh, 408, 409

Nakajima, Schunichi, 389
Makajima, Shigeo, 408
Nakayama, Waruinge, 363
Napoles, José, 251, 279–282
Nardiello, Dr. Vincent, 352
Naranjo, Felix, 411
Nardiello, Vincenzo, 213
Nash, Charlie, 326
Nati, Valerio, 365, 366
Navarrete, Rolando, 332
Navarro, George, 361
Navarro, Jimmy, 388
Navarro, Ruben, 332
Nazario, Juan, 328, 329
Neale, Ned, 32
Neate, Bill, 30–32
Needham, Danny, 261, 262
Negron, Ismael, 255
Neil, Frankie, 343, 372
Nelson, Azumah, 329, 333, 334, 335, 359, 360, 361
Nelson, Battling, 291, 292, 300, 304, 343, 393, 394
Nelson, Johnny, 187
Nemoto, Shig, 359
Nene, Vuyani, 390
Netto, Daniel, 185, 187
N'Gobeni, Jerry, 335
Nieves, Giovanni, 362
Noel, Claude, 327, 328
Nolasco, Livio, 363
Nolasco, Pedro, 361
Noon, Anthony, 337
Norris, James D., 142
Norris, Orlin, 260
Norris, Terry, 258, 259, 260, 284, 285
Norton, Ken, 173, 174, 177, 178
Nova, Lou, 124, 132–33, 137
Numata, Hisami, 384
Numata, Yoshiaki, 331, 332
Nunn, Michael, 213, 214, 254, 256

O'Baldwin, Ned, 50

Obed, Elisha, 257
Obelmejias, Fulgencio, 212, 252
O'Brien, Philadelphia Jack, 81, 86, 188, 189, 221, 222, 393
Ocasio, Osvaldo, 178, 186
O'Connell, Larry, 187
O'Connel, Paddy, 34
Odhiambo, John, 186
O'Dowd, Mike, 226, 227
O'Grady, Sean, 326, 327
Oguma, Shoji, 389, 403, 404, 405
Ohashi, Hideyuki, 408, 410, 411
Ohyuthanakorn, Putt, 408
Okun, Yale, 124
Olajide, Michael, 214, 253, 254
Olin, Bob, 198, 199
Oliva, Patrizio, 285, 287
Olivares, Ruben, 358, 359, 383, 384
Olivo, Joey, 408
Olson, Bobo, 204, 243, 275
Oma, Lee, 143, 200
Onizuka, Katsuya, 390
Ordonez, Juvenal, 360
Orme, Harry, 215
Orono, Rafael, 388, 389
O'Rourke, Tom, 338, 339, 368, 392
Orozco, Felipe, 360, 363
Ortega, Gaspar, 277
Ortega, Rafael, 359
Ortiz, Carlos, 286, 323, 324
Ortiz, Manuel, 367, 378
Ortiz, Rafael, 290
O'Sullivan, Jack, 110
Otti, Emanuel, 212
Overlin, Ken, 233, 235
Owen, Johnny, 362, 384, 385
Owens, Tom, 21
Ozaki, Jujio, 284

Pace, George, 378
Paddock, Tom, 35–37, 43, 48
Padilla, Carlos, 176
Paez, Jorge, 329, 334, 361, 362
Page, Greg, 179, 180
Painter, Ned, 31
Palacios, Jose, 281
Palacio, Ruben, 362, 363, 364, 366
Palma, Sergio, 364
Palmer, Pedlar, 342, 369–371
Palomino, Carlos, 281, 282
Palzer, Al, 89
Pancheco, Marcos, 410
Papke, Billy, 216, 220, 221, 222, 224, 225, 226
Paret, Benny (Kid), 278–280
Parisi, Giovanni, 329
Park, Chong-Pal, 212
Parke, Ivan, 102
Parkey, Rickey, 186
Parkinson, Jack, 50
Parks, Lamar, 255
Parlov, Mate, 185, 208, 209
Pascua, Rolando, 410
Pasieron, Polly, 212
Pastor, Bob, 130, 132, 134–135
Pastrano, Willie, 206
Paterson, Jackie, 313, 397
Patri, Hector, 416
Patterson, Floyd, 10, 151, 153–159, 162, 163, 166, 167, 174, 176, 204, 366
Patterson, Tracy Harris, 366
Paul, Jimmy, 290, 328, 329
Paul, Melvin, 211
Paul, Tommy, 347, 348
Payakarun, Kongtorance, 389
Payakarun, Samart, 363
Paycheck, Johnny, 132, 134
Pazienza, Vinny, 260, 289, 290, 329
Peak, Mike, 211
Pearce, Henry, 21–22, 25
Pedroza, Eusabio, 359, 360, 384
Pedroza, Rafael, 389
Pelkey, Arthur, 88–89
Penalosa, Dodie, 404, 406, 409
Penalosa, Jonathon, 406
Pender, Paul, 248, 249
Pendleton, Freddie, 329, 330

Pep, Willie, 336, 350–353
Percy, Earl (Duke of Northumberland), 26
Peres, Isidro, 407, 408, 410
Perez, Irleis, 329
Perez, Juan Polo, 390
Perez, Pascual, 399, 400
Perez, Raul, 335, 366, 386, 387
Perez, Tony, 170, 174
Perez, Young, 377, 395, 396
Pergaud, Louis, 209
Perkins, Eddie, 286
Perrins, Isaac, 16–17
Perroni, Patsy, 128, 194
Perry, William, 36–37, 43
Peters, Sam, 16
Petit, Monsieur, 14
Petrolle, Billy, 291, 310, 311
Petronelli, Toni, 287
Phelan, Gen. John, 271
Phelps, Mike, 390
Pian, Charles, 277
Piaskpwy, Gerhard, 256
Pical, Elly, 389, 390
Pimental, Jesus, 384
Pinango, Bernardo, 364, 385
Pinango, Carlos, 360
Pinder, Enrique, 383, 384
Pineda, Rafael, 284, 289, 290
Pinto, Efren, 408
Pintor, Lupe, 363, 364, 384, 385, 386
Pitalua, Alfredo, 326
Pladner, Emil, 313, 377
Pohan, Abdy, 409, 410, 411
Polanco, Cesar, 390
Poll, Jesus, 364
Pompey, Yolande, 204
Poontarat, Payao, 389
Porpaoin, Chana, 411
Porter, Danny, 407
Pratchett, Dwight, 333
Pratesi, Honoré, 398
Prescott, Johnny, 167
Primera, Luis, 278
Pruitt, Adolph, 286
Pryor, Aaron, 287, 288, 326
Pultz, Boone, 187
Purdy, Jack, 195
Puryea, Earl, 367
Pyatt, Chris, 260

Qawi, Dwight Muhammad, 186, 187, 209, 210
Quarry, Jerry, 165, 166, 167, 168
Quarry, Mike, 207
Quintana, Indian, 377
Quirino, Jose, 391
Quiroga, Robert, 390
Quiroz, Francesco, 408

Rabanales, Victor, 388
Rademacher, Pete, 155–156
Rae-Ki Ahn, 404, 405
Ramirez, Roberto, 389
Ramirez, José Luis, 289, 326, 327, 328, 329
Ramos, Fernando, 362, 366
Ramos, Mando, 325, 326
Ramos, Sugar, 354, 355
Randall, Jack, 215
Randolph, Charlie, 278
Randolph, Leo, 364
Rangel, Alfred, 362
Rangel, Eddie, 388
Ranzany, Pete, 281
Ratliff, Alfonso, 185
Ray, Husni, 411
Reagan, Johnny, 217
Reagan, Johnny (bantamweight), 372
Recht, Bill, 171, 245
Reeson, Sam, 187
Reid, Chris, 213
Reilly, Pete, 196
Rengifo, Jovita, 386, 388
Reyes, Armando, 362
Reynard, Jean-Mare, 361
Riasco, Rigoberto, 358, 363
Rice, Major Cushman, 93
Richardson, Dick, 158
Richardson, Greg, 364, 387, 388, 391
Richardson, Bill, 26–27, 29, 39

Rickard, Tex, 87, 96–97, 101, 105–107, 110, 113–115, 292, 301, 367
Rimmer, Joe, 27
Rios, Jaime, 408
Risco, Babe, 232, 233
Risko, Johnny, 113, 115, 195, 229
Ritchie, Willie, 303–305
Rivadeneyra, Oscar, 209
Rivas, Vicente, 286
Rivera, Antonio, 329, 335, 361
Rivera, Joe, 289
Rivera, Jorge, 410
Rivera, José, 334
Rivers, Joe, 280, 291, 303–305
Robertson, Floyd, 356
Robinson, Sea, 257
Robinson, Steve, 362
Robinson, Sugar Ray, 143, 203, 215, 216, 220, 240–248, 262, 276, 277
Robles, Rudy, 251
Rocap, Jimmy, 373
Rocchigiani, Graziano, 213
Rocchigiani, Ralf, 187
Rocha, Miguel, 329, 330
Rodel, Boer, 89
Roderick, Ernie, 272
Rodriguez, Eduardo, 282
Rodriguez, Juan, 385
Rodriguez, Luis, 279, 283
Rojas, Alvaro, 322
Rojas, Eloy, 362
Rojas, Jesus, 365, 389, 390, 391, 404, 406
Rojas, Raul, 332, 356
Rojas, Refugio, 333
Roldan, Juan, 253, 254
Rollo, Piero, 382
Roman, Edgar, 385
Roman, Gilberto, 389, 390
Roman, José "King," 174
Romano, Emil, 405
Romero, Orlando, 328
Romero, Pedro, 389
Rondeau, Johnny, 174
Rondon, Vincent, 207
Rooke, George, 57–58, 216
Rooney, Kevin, 183
Root, Jack, 84, 188, 189
Rosales, Fino, 356
Rosario, Angel, 391, 407
Rosario, Edwin, 289, 326, 327, 328
Rose, Lionel, 332, 383, 384
Rosenberg, Charley Phil, 367, 375
Rosenbloom, Maxie, 124, 198, 199, 230
Rosenohn, William, 157
Rosi, Gianfranco, 258, 259, 260
Ross, Barney, 269–272, 286, 291, 292, 313, 314
Rossito, Mario, 286
Rossman, Mike, 208, 209
Roth, Al, 313
Roth, Senator William, 255
Rothschild, Baron, 61–62
Rothwell, William. See Corbett, Young
Rottoli, Angelo, 183
Rouse, Roger, 205
Routis, André, 346, 347
Rowlandson, Thomas, 261
Roxborough, John, 128
Ruan, Clyde, 360
Rubaldino, Roberto, 384, 385
Ruddock, Razor, 183, 184, 285
Ruelas, Gabriel, 335
Ruggirello, Salvatore, 230
Ruhlin, Gus, 80–83
Ruiz, Jose, 390, 391
Russell, Mickey, 392
Ryan, Paddy, 54–55, 59
Ryan, Tommy, 82, 212, 215, 223, 262, 263

Sacco, Ubaldo, 287
Saddler, Sandy, 331, 351–353
Sadler, Dick, 172, 173, 174, 178
Salas, Lauro, 321, 331
Salazar, Carlos, 405
Salazar, Leon, 409
Salazar, Wilibardo, 408

442

Saldanho, Horacio, 280
Saldivar, Vincente, 326, 355–358
Salica, Lou, 370
Salud, Jesus, 364, 365, 366
Salvarria, Erbito, 403
Sam, Doug, 209
Sam, Dutch, 261, 291
Sam, Young Dutch, 261, 291
Sam-Jung Lee, 411
Sanabria, José, 365
Sanchez, Clemente, 357, 358
Sanchez, Eloy, 382, 384
Sanchez, Enrique, 386
Sanchez, Salvador, 359
Sandoval, Ricardo, 385
Sangaree, Moussa, 362
Sangchili, Baltazar, 376, 377
Sang-Ho Lee, 289
Sang-Hyun Kim, 287
Sangor, Joey, 376
Sanstol, Pete, 376
Santana, Luis, 285
Santana, Miguel, 329
Santos, Carlos, 257, 258
Santos, Macario, 410
Santry, Eddie, 340, 342
Sarron, Petey, 272, 348, 353
Savage, Richard, 361
Savino, Jackie, 232
Savold, Lee, 146
Saxton, Johnny, 277, 278
Sayers, Tom, 36–37, 41, 43–48, 215
Scalzo, Petey, 349, 350
Schaaf, Ernie, 123–124
Schiff, Dr. Alexander, 316
Schmeling, Max, 115–122, 125–126, 128–132, 142, 158, 159, 194, 230
Schwartz, Izzy, 395, 396
Scott, Frasier, 250
Scott, Lester, 126
Scott, Phil, 116, 119
Scozza, Lou, 124, 198
Scypion, Wilfred, 253
Seabrooks, Kelvin, 386, 387, 388
Sears, David, 209, 210
Sedillo, Mike, 212
Seelig, Eric, 230, 231
Segawa, Yukio, 364
Segura, Francisco, 335
Sekgapane, Norman, 287
Seki, Mitsunori, 348
Sekorski, Rick, 183
Sellers, Henry, 15–16
Sequenan, Red, 333
Serrano, Sam, 331
Servo, Marty, 237, 273
Seung-Hoon Lee, 284, 364, 365, 386, 388
Seung-In Suh, 357
Sharkey, Jack (Boston), 96, 110, 113, 115–119, 122, 129, 194–197, 229, 230
Sharkey, Little Jack, 331, 367, 392
Sharkey, Tom, 77, 79, 80, 82–84
Shaughnessey, Mike, 262
Shavers, Earnie, 177, 178
Shaw, Battling, 281
Shelton, Tom, 27
Sherry, Don, 255
Shibata, Kenji, 257
Shibata, Kuniaki, 331, 332, 357, 358
Shields, Randy, 281
Shields, Ronnie, 288
Shingaki, Satoshi, 386, 409
Shirai, Yoshio, 398, 399
Shucco, Tony, 124
Sibaca, Bashew, 360
Sibson, Tony, 210, 252, 253, 254
Sierra, Victor, 408
Sierro, Humberto, 351
Siki, Battling, 192, 193, 194
Sikora, Frank, 155
Siler, George, 371
Siler, Tom, 84
Silvers, Pal, 309
Simms, Eddie, 129
Simon, Abe, 132, 134, 137
Sims, Robbie, 254
Singer, Al, 291, 292, 312, 313
Singletary, Ernie, 212

Siodoro, Rik, 405
Sitbangprachan, Pichit, 406
Sitbobay, Thalerngsak, 387, 390
Sithnarvepol, Samuth, 411
Skog, Harald, 206
Skosana, Simon, 366, 385
Skouma, Said, 258
Slack, Jack, 11, 13–14, 16, 24–25
Slack, Slasher, 48
Slade, Herbert A., 61, 78
Slade, Jimmy, 155
Slattery, Jimmy, 188, 194, 195, 196, 198
Slavin, Frank, 67
Slayton, Bill, 174
Smiler, Bob, 15
Smith, Ed, 89
Smith, Eddie, 301, 302
Smith, George, 163
Smith, Gunboat, 88, 91, 119
Smith, James "Bonecrusher," 179, 181
Smith, Jeff, 216, 223, 225
Smith, Jem, 63
Smith, John, 12
Smith, Kosie, 208
Smith, Lonnie, 288, 290
Smith, Midget, 367
Smith, Mysterious Billy, 261–263, 298
Smith, Solly, 339
Smith, Wallace Bud, 321, 322
Snead, Hurley, 387
Snipes, Renaldo, 178
Sok-Chul Bae, 389
Soleno, Julio Soto, 389
Solis, Enrique, 359
Solis, Julian, 377
Solis, Rafael, 332
Solomons, Jack, 381
Someli, Louie, 329
Songktrat, Chamrern, 379, 380
Soo-Hwan Hong, 364, 380, 381
Soon-Chun Kwan, 389, 390, 405
Soon-Kyun Chung, 364
Soose, Billy, 216, 233, 235
Soria, Ramon, 388
Sormachi, Ryu, 259, 281
Sorvorapin, Rattanapol, 411
Sosa, Diego, 331
Sosa, Domingo, 410
Soto, Cesar, 387
Spann, Tracy, 330
Spencer, Thad, 166, 167
Spinks, Leon, 177, 178, 180, 186, 209, 210
Spinks, Michael, 180, 181, 182, 183, 209, 210
Spring, Tom, 28, 30–32
Sproul, André, 90
Squires, Bill, 159
Stable, José, 279
Stafford, Roger, 282
Stand, Bert, 228
Stander, Ron, 171
Stanley, Digger, 372
Starling, Marlon, 254, 282, 283, 284
Stecca, Loris, 364
Stecca, Maurizio, 361, 362
Steele, Freddie, 232, 233
Steele, Richard, 289
Stephens, Randy, 186
Stevens, Bill, 13, 15
Stevenson, George, 11
Stewart, Alex, 183
Stewart, Leslie, 210, 211, 212
Stewart, Walker, 126
Stolz, Allie, 318
Stracey, John H., 280, 281
Straus, Nathan, 309
Stretch, Gary, 255
Stribling, Billy ("Young"), 115, 118–119, 188, 193–195
Stringer, Jack, 31
Suarez, Lupe, 334
Suarez, Justo, 311
Suarez, Oscar, 399
Sugiyama, Mitsuru, 361
Sukhotai, Thanoujit, 384
Sullivan, Carl, 213
Sullivan, Dave, 336, 339, 340
Sullivan, Jack, 399
Sullivan, Jack (Twin), 216, 220, 264
Sullivan, Jim, 224

Sullivan, John L., 48, 53–71, 88, 90, 93, 95, 127, 129, 144, 151
Sullivan, Mike (Twin), 220, 264
Sullivan, Steve, "Kid," 331
Sullivan, Tommy, 343
Sullivan, Yankee, 39–41, 55
Sung-Il Moon, 386, 390, 391
Sung Jun Kim, 404, 408
Sutherland, Murray, 209, 212
Sweeney, Dan, 81
Swift, Owen, 337
Swindell, Frankie, 212

Tabanos, Andy, 411
Tae-Il Chang, 389, 390
Tae-Jin Moon, 332
Tae Shik Kim, 404, 405
Taiho, Kenbun, 408
Takada, Jiro, 403
Takahashi, Yoshinori, 286
Takashima, Hitashi, 408
Takayama, Masataka, 325
Takeda, Masuaki, 335, 362
Talmage, Thomas De Witte, 59
Tamakuma, Yukhito, 405, 406
Tate, Frank, 211, 213, 253, 254
Tate, John, 180
Tate, Thomas, 255
Tatsuyoshi, Joichiro, 388
Taylor, Arnold, 384
Taylor, Bernard, 360
Taylor, Bud, 367, 376
Taylor, George, 8
Taylor, Meldrick, 259, 284, 285, 289
Taylor, Myron, 361
Tejedor, Francisco, 410
Tendler, Lew, 291, 307, 308, 367
Tenryu, Kazumori, 408
Terranova, Phil, 350, 351
Terrell, Ernie, 162, 164, 166, 167
Teru, Hurricane, 386
Tessman, Mark, 207
Thackeray, William, 46
Thil, Marcel, 228, 229
Thomas, Duane, 258
Thomas, Joe, 220, 224
Thomas, John, 325
Thomas, Nico, 411
Thomas, Pinklon, 179, 180, 181, 184
Thompson, Cyclone, 224
Thompson, George, 41
Thompson, Jeff, 212
Thompson, Young Jack, 266–268
Thornton, Tony, 214
Thornton, Wayne, 206
Thorpe, Bill, 48
Tiberi, Dave, 255, 256
Tiberia, Domenico, 257
Tiger, Dick, 206, 207, 208, 249, 250
Tillis, James, 180
Tillman, Henry, 183, 186
Tiozzo, Christophe, 212
Tiozzo, Fabrice, 211
Tokashiki, Katsuo, 408
Toles, Roscoe, 128
Tomonari, Hikaru, 331
Tomori, Tadashi, 408
Toney, James, 213, 214, 254, 255, 256
Tonna, Gratien, 251
Toro, Pete, 283
Torres, Battling, 286
Torres, Efren, 402, 403
Torres, German, 408, 410
Torres, Jose, 359
Torres, José "Chegui," 206
Torres, Rafael, 411
Toweel, Vic, 367, 378, 379
Tracy, Bill, 293
Traversaro, Aldo, 209, 210
Tremaine, Carl, 367
Trice, Tyrone, 259, 260, 285
Troy, Willie, 155
Trujillo, Carlos, 282
Tsujimoto, Shoji, 281
Tubbs, Tony, 180, 181, 182
Tucker, Tony, 181, 182, 184, 185, 290
Tunacao, Noel, 409
Tunney, Gene, 85, 96,

106–114, 151, 188, 191, 193
Tunon, Eduardo, 408
Turner, Bill, 15
Turner, Gil, 277
Turner, J.T., 137
Turpin, Randy, 143, 216, 241–243
Tyson, Darryl, 329, 330
Tyson, Mike, 181–186

Uchida, Yoshiyuki, 390
Udella, Franco, 407
Udin, Bahar, 408
Uehara, Yasatsune, 331
Ulloa, Cardenio, 385, 387
Upham, Arthur, 78
Ursua, Dommy, 399
Ursua, Amado, 408
Utagawa, Zensuke, 358
Uzcudun, Paulino, 115, 120, 122, 129, 196, 229
Uziga, Jose, 386

Vaca, Jorge, 283, 284, 285
Valasquez, Miguel, 287
Valdes, Raul, 389
Valdes, Reuben, 364
Valdes, Rodrigo, 251, 252
Valdez, Jose, 387
Valdez, Ricardo, 399
Valentino, Pat, 142
Vallardares, Jaime, 331
Vallejo, Eddie, 410
Valoy, Tommy, 364
Van Horn, Darrin, 213, 259
Van Ostrand, Steve, 40
Vargas, Gregorio, 362
Vargas, Martin, 403, 404
Vargas, Wilfredo, 387, 388, 391
Varquez, Javier, 410
Vasquez, Julio Cesar, 259
Vasquez, Robert, 326
Vasquez, Wilfredo, 366, 385, 386
Vedder, David, 187, 211, 212
Velasco, Armando, 391
Viboochai, Tacomron, 404
Vidella, Pedro, 282
Vilchez, Manuel, 364
Villa, Emiliano, 258, 287
Villa, Pancho, 268, 336, 367, 374, 393, 394
Villablanca, Benedicto, 331
Vilaflor, Ben, 331
Villasana, Marcos, 361, 362
Villegas, Pedro, 335
Viruet, Edwin, 326
Volbrecht, Harold, 281, 283
Vorasingh, Netrnoi Son, 408

Wajima, Koichi, 257
Walcott, Jersey Joe, 139, 140–145, 147–149, 158, 161, 205, 206
Walcott, Joe (Barbados), 218, 262–264, 298, 392
Walker, Mickey, 119, 196, 198, 228–230, 261, 265–267, 321
Walker, Nicky, 213
Walker, Dr. William, 133, 271
Wallace, Nunc, 368
Wallace, Patsy, 392
Walsh, Jimmy, 343, 372
Waltham, Ted, 164, 202
Wamba, Anaclet, 187
Ward, Jack, 342
Ward, Jem, 32–34, 36
Ward, Nick, 36
Warr, Bill, 16, 18
Warren, Frankie, 288
Warring, James, 187
Waruinge, Philip, 385
Wasajja, Mustapha, 209
Washington, Adolpho, 211
Watanabe, Jiro, 389
Watanabe, Yuji, 335
Waters, Guy, 212
Waters, Troy, 259
Watson, Michael, 213, 214, 254, 255
Watson, Professor, 71
Watt, Jim, 326, 327
Waxman, Max, 267
Weaver, Mike, 178, 180
Webb, Jimmy, 164

Weill, Al, 152, 314, 316
Weir, Charlie, 258
Weir, Ike, 336, 338
Welch, Jack, 92, 303, 304
Wells, Matt, 291, 344
Welsh, Freddie, 291, 304, 305
Wepner, Chuck, 176
West, Tommy, 218
Weston, Harold, 281
Whitaker, Pernell, 285, 289, 290, 327, 329, 330
White, Charley, 77, 291, 307
White, Johnny, 342
White, Sailor, 89
White, Slugger, 319
White, Tommy, 342
Whitfield, Ted, 279
Whittaker, Paul, 212
Wilde, Jimmy, 336, 367, 374, 393, 394
Wilkes, George, 41
Wallard, Jess, 89–93, 96–99, 106
Williams, Carl, 179, 180, 183
Williams, Charley, 153
Williams, Cleveland "Big Cat," 164
Williams, Ernie, 322
Williams, Ike, 291, 292, 319–321
Williams, Kid, 336, 367, 373, 374
Williams, "Prince" Charles, 211
Williams, Robbie, 186
Williamson, J.B., 210
Willis, John, 40
Willis, Harry, 106, 110
Wilson, Jackie, 349, 350
Wilson, Johnny, 226–228
Wingfield, Donnell, 187
Winstone, Howard, 356, 357
Winters, Thomas. See Spring, Tom
Witherspoon, Tim, 178, 179, 181
Wolfe, Glenn, 255, 260
Wolfe, Jack "Kid," 363
Wolgast, Ad, 291, 301–304, 393
Wolgast, Midget, 395
Wood, Ike, 26
Wood, Will, 16, 19
Woods, Cockey, 57
Wormwald, Joe, 50
Wright, Chalky, 349–351

Yajima, Yoshiaki, 212
Yamabe, Buzzsaw, 324
Yarosz, Teddy, 232, 266
Yokai, Masahiro, 287
Yokozawa, Kenji, 411
Yong-Hoon Lee, 388
Yong-Man Chun, 387
Yong-Kang Kim 389, 391, 405, 406
Yong Oh Ho, 327
Young, Billy, 89
Young, Jimmy, 177
Young, Paddy, 243
Yuh Myung-Woo, 408, 409
Yul-Woo Lee, 406, 410
Yung-Kil Chung, 284
Yung-Kyun Park, 361, 362
Yun Sok Hwan, 389
Yun-Un Chin, 407

Zamora, Alfonso, 384, 385
Zanon, Lorenzo, 178
Zale, Tony, 137, 215, 231, 233–236, 238, 239, 240
Zapata, Hilario, 391, 404, 408, 409
Zaragoza, Daniel, 365, 366, 386
Zarate, Carlos, 364, 365, 384, 385
Zecca, Mike, 153
Zivic, Eddie, 272
Zivic, Fritzie, 272, 273
Zivic, Jack, 272
Zivic, Joe, 272
Zivic, Pete, 272
Zulu, Kid, 374, 392
Zulueta, Orlando, 322, 331
Zuniga, Rafael, 361
Zurita, Juan, 319, 321

INDEX TO
1997 UPDATE

Acero-Sanchez, Hector, 428–29
Akinwande, Henry, 416
Ali, Bashiru, 416
Alvarez, Elvis, 430
Alvarez, Rosendo, 434
Amaral, Mauricio, 418, 419
Andrade, Oscar, 434
Andrews, Anthony, 420
Anghern, Stephan, 416
Aoussi, Patrick, 416
Arbachakov, Yuri, 432
Arlos, Bong, 429
Arlos, Jun, 434
Armenta, Everado, 417
Asakawa, Seiji, 427
Ashley, Crawford, 416
Avedano, Fidel, 424
Avila, John, 425
Ayers, Michael, 425

Baptist, Gilberto, 420
Barber, Leonzer, 417
Barkley, Iran, 416
Barnes, Larry, 422
Barrera, Jorge, 430
Barrera, Marco Antonio, 429
Began, Robbie, 432
Belcastro, Vincenzo, 430
Bell, Jeffery, 420
Benavides, Jesse, 427, 429
Benn, Nigel, 418–20
Bentt, Michael, 414
Bergman, Jan, 423
Bingham, Ensley, 422
Blanco, Rodolfo, 431
Blocker, Maurice, 422
Bonilla, Jose, 432
Borboa, Julio, 430
Botha, Frans, 413
Botile, Mbuelo, 429
Bott, Markus, 416
Boudouani, Laurent, 421
Bowe, Riddick, 412–14, 416
Bradley, Lonnie, 420
Brannon, Bryant, 418
Bredahl, Jimmi, 427
Bredahl, Johnny, 430
Brown, Neville, 419
Brown, Simon, 420, 421
Bruno, Frank, 413
Bueno, Jose Luis, 430
Bungu, Vuyani, 428
Byrd, Antoine, 418
Byun, Jung Il, 429

Camacho, Felix, 428
Camacho, Hector, 422
Camacho, Josue, 433
Cameron, Mark, 420
Campanella, Giorgio, 427
Campanrio, Javier, 430
Campas, Yori Boy, 422
Canizales, Orlando, 429
Canoy, Dino, 425
Carbajal, Michael, 432, 433
Cardamone, Agostino, 420
Cardona, Santos, 422
Carlo, Paul, 417
Carr, Oba, 422
Castillo, Lee, 434
Castro, Jorge, 420
Castro, Melchor Cob, 432, 433
Cermeno, Antonio, 429
Cha, Nam Hoon, 432
Chacon, Angel, 429
Chavez, Julio Cesar, 422–25
Choi, Hi Yong, 433
Choi, Yong Soo, 427
Clayton, Aristead, 429
Clinton, Pat, 432
Close, Ray, 419
Coggi, Juan, 424
Cole, Al, 416
Collins, Steve, 419, 420
Cordoba, Juan, 433
Cortez, Alberto, 422
Cortez, Joe, 412
Corti, Hugo, 420
Cruz, Freddy, 428
Czyz, Bobby, 414, 416

Damigella, Domingo, 428
Daniels, Carl, 421
Da Silva, Jose Arimateia, 416
Davis, Aaron, 421
De La Hoya, Oscar, 422–27
Del Vale, Rafael, 430
Del Valle, Lou, 416
Diaz, Joel, 425
Dominguez, Marcelo, 416
Dominguez, Roberto, 417
Dottuev, Ahmet, 421

Eliecer, Jorge, 430
Espana, Crisanto, 422, 423
Espinoza, Luisito, 427
Eubank, Chris, 419
Eubanks, Chris, 418

Fenech, Jeff, 425, 426
Ferguson, Jesse, 412
Fernandez, Orlando, 429
Ferradas, Pedro, 428
Figuero, Marcelo, 416
Foreman, George, 412, 413
Frank, Steve, 420
Fuentes, Sammy, 424
Futch, Eddie, 429–30

Galindez, Dario, 420
Gamache, Joey, 425
Gamez, Leo, 433
Garcia, Alex, 434
Garcia, Jimmy, 426
Garcia, Luis, 422
Gath, Arturo, 427
Gatti, Joe, 421
Gedeon, Ancee, 429
Gent, Lou, 418
Giminez, Reynaldo, 416
Giovanni, Nestor, 416
Girard, Christophe, 417
Goitia, Alimi, 430
Gomez, Wilfredo, 426
Gonzales, Jorge, 416
Gonzalez, Alejandro, 427
Gonzalez, Carlos "Bolillo," 424
Gonzalez, David, 421
Gonzalez, Humberto
   "Chiquita," 432, 434
Gonzalez, Miguel Angel, 424
Grant, Otis, 420
Green, Julio Cesar, 421
Grey, Harold, 430
Griffin, Carl, 425
Griffin, Montell, 417
Grigorijan, Arthur, 426
Griman, David, 431–32
Guardia, Kermin, 434
Gurov, Alexander, 416
Guzman, Aquiles, 430

Hamed, Naseem, 427, 428
Harding, Jeff, 417
Hardy, Billy, 428
Heath, James, 416
Hembrick, Anthony, 416
Hernandez, Genaro, 425, 427
Herrera, Manuel, 434
Hide, Herbie, 416
Hill, Virgil, 416
Hiranaka, Nobutoshi, 427
Hodkinson, Paul, 428
Holiday, Phillip, 425
Holligan, Andy, 423
Holmes, Keith, 420
Holmes, Larry, 413
Holyfield, Evander, 412–16
Honsono, Yuichi, 433
Hopkins, Bernard "the
   Executioner," 420
Hopson, Ed, 427
Hosono, Yuichi, 433
Hurtado, Diobelys, 422
Hurtado, Reynaldo, 429

Iida, Satoshi, 430
Ioka, Hiroki, 431–433

Jackson, John David, 420, 421
Jackson, Julian, 420
Jackson, Phil, 413
Jacobs, Gary, 422
Jacobsen, Gert, 422
Jacubowski, Marty, 426
James, Bo, 420
Jimenez, Alberto, 432
Jimenez, Juan Carlos, 418
Jiminez, Daniel, 429, 430

Johnson, Corey, 423
Johnson, John Michael, 430
Johnson, Mark "Too Sharp," 431
Johnson, Reggie, 429
Johnson, Tom, 427, 428
Johnston, Steve, 425
Jones, Carl, 417
Jones, Junior, 429, 430
Jones, Paul, 422
Jones, Ralph, 422
Jones, Roy, 417–18, 420
Joppy, William, 420
Julio, Miguel, 425

Kalambay, Sumbu, 420
Kang, Keun Young, 434
Kasai, Yuchi, 429
Kawashima, Hiroshi, 430
Kelley, Kevin, 427
Kim, Jin Ho, 434
Kithkasem, Muangchai, 432
Konadu, Nana, 430
Kotey, Alfred, 430

Lark, John, 425
LaSpada, Brian, 416
Lee, Hyung Chul, 430
Leija, Jesse James, 425–26
Lewis, Lennox, 412–14
Liberatore, Fred, 426
Liles, Frank, 418
Lipsey, Joe, 429
Little, Steve, 418
Littles, Tim, 417, 418
Loewe, Michael, 422
Lopez, Jose Luis, 422
Lopez, Ricardo, 433, 434
Lopez, Tony "the Tiger," 425
Lora, Miguel, 430
Loughran, Eamonn, 422
Lovato, Ray, 422
Lucas, Eric, 417, 418
Luna, Joel, 430

McCall, Oliver, 413, 414
McCallum, Mike, 417
McClellan, Gerald, 418–20
McCullough, Wayne, 429–30
McElroy, Ray, 420
McGirt, Buddy, 422
McKart, Bronco, 422
McKenzie, Duke, 428, 429
McKinney, Kennedy, 428, 429
McMillan, Colin, 428
McNeeley, Peter, 413
Magana, Jesse, 429
Magdaleno, Ernie, 416
Magi, Andrea, 416
Magrano, Ronnie, 434
Malinga, Sugarboy, 419
Malone, Orlando, 434
Marcus, Egerton, 416
Mardiello, Vincenzo, 419
Marshall, Tony, 421
Martinez, Henry, 430
Martinez, Miguel, 431
Martinez, Rocky, 425
Mas, Leonardo, 423
Maske, Henry, 416
Mathis, Buster, Jr., 414
Matlala, Jacob "Baby Jake," 432,
   434
May, Tortsen, 416
Mayweather, Roger, 423
Medina, Manuel, 427
Melchor, Manny, 434
Melis, Antonello, 430
Mendez, David, 420
Mendoza, Bernardo, 427
Mendy, Jean-Baptiste, 424–25
Merani, Sergo, 416
Mercado, Alvarado, 431
Mercado, Carlos, 430
Mercado, Segundo, 418, 420
Mercer, Ray, 414
Mestre, Harold, 429
Michalczewski, Dariusz, 416–17
Michel, Phillipe, 417
Miller, Nate, 416, 417
Mitani, Yamato, 427
Molina, John-John, 425–27
Montana, Saul, 416
Montiel, Alejandro, 431
Moon, Sung Kil, 430
Moore, Rodney, 422, 423
Moorer, Michael, 412–14
Morrison, Tommy, 414
Murillo, Carlos, 433, 434

Murphy, Lamar, 424–25
Murphy, Sean, 428
Murray, Andrew, 422
Murray, Charles, 423

Nazarov, Orzubek, 425
Ncita, Welcome, 428
Nelson, Azumah, 426–27
Norris, Orlin, 416–17
Norris, Terry, 420–21
Nunez, Ricardo, 421
Nunn, Michael, 418

Onizuka, Katsuya, 430
Orgaleza, Joseph, 434
Orozco, Rafael, 434
Ortega, Yober, 429

Padilla, Zack, 424
Paez, Jorge, 425
Parisi, Giovanni, 424, 425
Park, Jung Oh, 422
Park, Won, 425
Park, Yung-Kyul, 427
Pascua, Rolando, 430
Pastrana, Mauricio, 433
Patterson, Tracy Harris, 427,
   428
Paz, Victor Hugo, 427
Pazienza, Vinny, 418
Pedroza, Moises, 427
Penalosa, Gerry, 430
Pendleton, Fred, 422, 425
Perez, Danny, 419
Perez, Raul, 431
Petroleum, Daorung MP, 430
Pettway, Vincent, 421
Phillips, Verno, 421–22
Phillips, Vince, 422
Picar, Armand, 421
Pineda, Hugo, 423
Ploenchit, Saen Sow, 432
Porpaoin, Chana, 434
Pretorious, Giovanni, 419
Pyatt, Chris, 420

Quartey, Ike, 422, 423

Rabanales, Victor, 429
Rahilou, Khalid, 424
Ramos, Alex, 420
Ramos, Jose, 427
Randall, Frankie "the Surgeon,"
   423, 424
Randazzo, Marc, 416
Reed, Gene, 426
Regan, Robbie, 430
Reid, Robin, 419
Rey, Sergio, 424
Rincones, Jose, 428
Rios, Alex, 421
Rivera, Antonio, 425, 426
Rivera, Tomas, 434
Rivera, Wilfredo, 422
Robinson, Ivan, 425
Robinson, Steve, 427–28
Rocchigiani, Graciano, 416, 417,
   419
Rocchigiani, Ralf, 416
Rodriguez, Carlos, 434
Rodriguez, Jake, 422, 423
Rodriguez, Wilson, 427
Rojas, Eloy, 427–28
Roman, Jose, 430
Romero, Danny, 430–31
Rosi, Gianfranco, 421–22
Rubillar, Ernesto, 434
Ruelas, Gabriel, 426
Ruelas, Rafael, 425, 426
Rupa, Nick, 421

Saez, Eddie, 429
Sahaprom, Veeraphol, 430
Salazar, Carlos, 430, 432
Salazar, Willy, 431
Salud, Jesus, 429
Samaniego, Santiago, 422
Sanchez, Alex, 434
Santana, Luis, 421
Sarabia, Jesus, 430
Saucedo, Polo, 430
Schmeling, Max, 416
Schommer, Dan, 419
Schulz, Axel, 413, 414
Scully, John, 416
Seillier, Frederic, 418
Seldon, Bruce, 413, 414
Shiohama, Takashi, 434

Sibali, Jaji, 430
Singmansuk, Sirimongkol, 430
Siriwat, Daorung C., 430
Siriwat, Phichitnoi C., 433
Sithbangprachan, Phichit, 431
Sithoar, Yokthai, 430
Smith, Lorenzo, 428
Smith, Randy, 420
Snyder, Jay, 416
Songnam, Lakva, 427
Sorjaturong, Saman, 433, 434
Sor Vorapin, Ratanapol, 434
Sosa, Merqui, 418
Soto, Cesar, 427
Soto, Orlando, 427
Spann, Tracy, 425
Speed, Eugene, 427
Stephens, Anthony, 422
Stewart, Sam, 429
Storey, Sam, 419
Sulaiman, Jose, 434

Tafer, Akim, 416
Takehara, Shinji, 420
Tamura, Tomonori, 430
Tapia, Johnny, 430
Taroreh, Adrian, 425
Tate, Frank, 416
Tate, Thomas, 420
Tatsuyoshi, Joichiro, 429
Taylor, Quincy, 420
Tejedor, Francisco, 431
Thadzi, Drake, 416
Thobele, Dingaan, 425
Thompson, Carl, 416
Thornton, Tony, 417, 418
Tiozzo, Fabrice, 417
Tobon, Orlando, 430
Toguchi, Takato, 432
Toney, James, 417, 418, 420
Torres, Rafael, 434
Trinidad, Felix, 422
Tszyu, Kostya, 423
Tucker, Tony, 413
Turner, Roger, 422
Tuur, Regilio, 427
Tyson, Mike, 412–16

Ugueto, Alejandro, 421
Umarov, Asfuddin, 417

Vaden, Paul, 421
Vado, Jorge Luis, 421
Vargas, Gregorio "Goyo," 427
Vargas, Wilfredo, 430
Vasquez, Julio Cesar, 421
Vazquez, Wilfredo, 427–29
Vedder, David, 416
Vela, Gustavo, 434
Villamor, Ala, 433

Wamba, Anaclet, 416
Warton, Henry, 419
Washington, Alphonso, 416
Watanabe, Yuri, 427
Waters, Guy, 416
Waters, Troy, 421
Weir, Paul, 434
Welch, Scott, 416
Wharton, Henry, 418
Whitaker, Pernell, 421–23
Williams, Duran, 416
Williams, Jeremy, 416
Williams, Prince Charles, 416,
   417–18
Woodall, Richie, 420
Wright, Winky, 421, 422

Yahiro, Shiro, 433
Yakushiji, Yasuei, 429, 430
Yamaguchi, Keiji, 433
Yuh, Myung Woo, 433

Zaragoza, Daniel, 429, 430
Zepeda, Jose, 431
Zolkins, Alexander, 416
Zumudio, Isaias, 432
Zuniga, Jesus, 433